Kenya

Northern Kenya p268
Masai Mara & Western Kenya p110
Central Highlands & Laikipia p146
Southern Rift Valley p87
Nairobi p54
Lamu & the North Coast p236
Southeastern Kenya p181
Mombasa & the South Coast p202

THIS EDITION WRITTEN AND RESEARCHED BY

Anthony Ham, Stuart Butler, Kate Thomas

PLAN YOUR TRIP

JOHN BRADLEY / LONELY PLANET ©

ZEBRAS, NANYUKI P155

ERIC LAFFORGUE / LONELY PLANET ©

DHOW, LAMU P254

ON THE ROAD

Contents

UNDERSTAND

SURVIVAL GUIDE

SPECIAL FEATURES

Welcome to Kenya

Vast savannahs peppered with immense herds of wildlife. Snow-capped mountains on the equator. Traditional peoples who bring soul and colour to the earth. Welcome to Kenya.

Stirring Landscapes

When you think of Africa, you're probably thinking of Kenya. It's the lone acacia silhouetted against a horizon stretching into eternity. It's the snow-capped mountain almost on the equator and within sight of harsh deserts. It's the lush, palm-fringed coastline of the Indian Ocean, it's the Great Rift Valley that once threatened to tear the continent asunder, and it's the dense forests reminiscent of the continent's heart. In short, Kenya is a country of epic landforms that stir our deepest longings for this very special continent.

Proud Peoples

Peopling that landscape, adding depth and resonance to Kenya's age-old story, are some of Africa's best-known peoples. The Maasai, the Samburu, the Turkana, Swahili, the Kikuyu: these are the peoples whose histories and daily struggles tell the story of a country and of a continent – the struggle to maintain traditions as the modern world crowds in, the daily fight for survival in some of the harshest environments on earth, the ancient tension between those who farm and those who roam. Drawing near to these cultures, even coming to understand them a little better through your presence among them, could just be a highlight of your visit.

Abundant Wildlife

This is the land of the Masai Mara, of wildebeest and zebras migrating in their millions with the great predators of Africa following in their wake. But Kenya is also home to the red elephants of Tsavo, to Amboseli elephant families in the shadow of Mt Kilimanjaro and to the massed millions of pink flamingos stepping daintily through lake shallows. Africa is the last great wilderness where these creatures survive. And Kenya is the perfect place to answer Africa's call of the wild.

Conservation's Home

The survival and abundance of Kenya's wildlife owes everything to one of Africa's most innovative and successful conservation communities. Through some pretty tough love – Kenya pioneered the use of armed rangers to protect rhinos and elephants – Kenya stopped the emptying of its wilderness, bringing its wildlife back from the brink after the poaching holocaust of the 1970s and 1980s. More than that, in places like Laikipia and the Masai Mara, private and community conservancies bring tourism together with community development and wildlife conservation in a near-perfect marriage. In other words, if you want your visit to make a difference, you've come to the right place.

Why I Love Kenya

By Anthony Ham, Author

Kenya is where my love affair with Africa took hold and promised never to let go. Wildlife (big cats especially) and wilderness rank among the grand passions of my life and it was here that I saw my first lion on the march (in Amboseli), my first cheetah on the hunt (Tsavo East), my first leopard on a kill (Tsavo West) and where I came so close to elephants (Taita Hills) and black rhinos (Lewa) that I could have reached out to touch them. This is the home of Maasai and Samburu friends who give me hope that the old ways can survive.

For more about our authors, see page 416.

Above: Elephants at a watering hole

Kenya

0 100 km
0 60 miles
ELEVATION
3000m
2000m
1000m
500m
250m
0
Lake Turkana
Remote, beautiful and tribally rich (p287)
Samburu National Reserve
One of Kenya's best parks (p274)
Kakamega Forest
Kenya's richest tropical rainforest (p136)
Laikipia
Kenyan conservation's true home (p153)
Mt Kenya
Soaring summit and Rift Valley views (p165)
Meru National Park
Wildlife without the crowds (p176)
SOUTH SUDAN
ETHIOPIA
UGANDA
SOMALIA
Ilemi Triangle (disputed)
Not always open; check with authorities
Lokichoggio
Lake Chew Bahir
Fort Banya
Ileret
Sibiloi NP
Central Island NP
Lake Turkana
Ferguson's Gulf
Kalokol
Lodwar
Eliye Springs
Loima Hills
Lorukumu
Turkwel River
Moroto
Lokichar
Mega
Moyale
Malka Mari NP
Mandera
Takaba
El Wak
Buna
Dida Galgalu Desert
Ngaso Plain
Sigiso Plain
Huri Hills
Kalacha
North Horr
Maikona
Chalbi Desert
South Island NP
Loyangalani
Mt Kulal (2293m)
Lake Logipi
Marsabit NR
Marsabit
Marsabit NP
Woyamdero Plain
Tarbaj
Wajir
South Horr
Kaisut Desert
Baragoi
Losai NR
Laisamis
Mattews Range
Maralal NS
Maralal
Wamba
Samburu NR
Shaba NR
Buffalo
Archer's Post
Ewaso Ngiro River
Habaswein
Lorian
Mado Gashi
Soroti
Mbale
Tororo
Malaba
Mt Elgon (4321m)
Suam
Mt Elgon NP
Kitale
Webuye
Bungoma
Kapenguria
Marun River
Marich Pass
Marich
Sigor
Wei-wei
Nasolot NR
South Turkana NR
Lokori
Kerio
Cherangani Hills
Saiwa Swamp NP
Soy
Tot
Kerio Valley/ Kamnarok NR
Kapedo
Iten
Loruk
Lake Baringo
Rumuruti
Valley
River

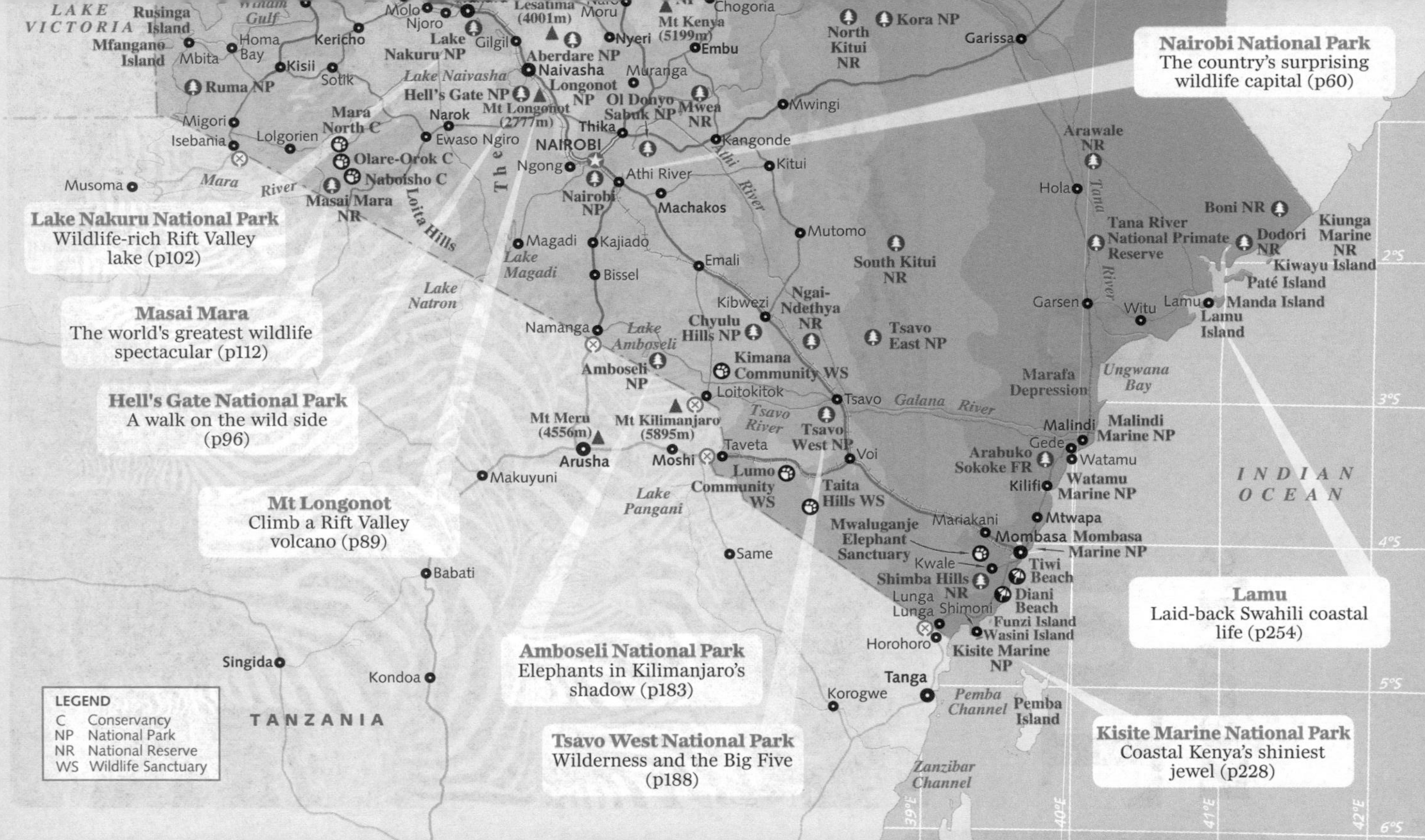

Nairobi National Park
The country's surprising wildlife capital (p60)
Lake Nakuru National Park
Wildlife-rich Rift Valley lake (p102)
Masai Mara
The world's greatest wildlife spectacular (p112)
Hell's Gate National Park
A walk on the wild side (p96)
Mt Longonot
Climb a Rift Valley volcano (p89)
Amboseli National Park
Elephants in Kilimanjaro's shadow (p183)
Tsavo West National Park
Wilderness and the Big Five (p188)
Lamu
Laid-back Swahili coastal life (p254)
Kisite Marine National Park
Coastal Kenya's shiniest jewel (p228)
LEGEND
C Conservancy
NP National Park
NR National Reserve
WS Wildlife Sanctuary
LAKE VICTORIA
Rusinga Island
Mfangano Island
Mbita
Homa Bay
Kisii
Kericho
Sotik
Ruma NP
Migori
Isebania
Lolgorien
Mara North C
Olare-Orok C
Naboisho C
Masai Mara NR
Mara River
Musoma
Molo
Njoro
Lake Nakuru NP
Gilgil
Lesatima (4001m)
Moru
Aberdare NP
Naivasha
Lake Naivasha
Hell's Gate NP
Mt Longonot (2777m)
Longonot NP
Narok
Ewaso Ngiro
Loita Hills
Nyeri
Mt Kenya (5199m)
Chogoria
Embu
Muranga
Ol Donyo Sabuk NP
Mwea NR
Thika
NAIROBI
Ngong
Athi River
Nairobi NP
Machakos
Kangonde
Kitui
Mwingi
Athi River
Magadi
Lake Magadi
Kajiado
Bissel
Emali
Lake Natron
Namanga
Lake Amboseli
Amboseli NP
Chyulu Hills NP
Kimana Community WS
Kibwezi
Ngai-Ndethya NR
Loitokitok
Mt Meru (4556m)
Mt Kilimanjaro (5895m)
Arusha
Moshi
Taveta
Tsavo River
Tsavo West NP
Tsavo
Voi
Lumo Community WS
Taita Hills WS
Lake Pangani
Makuyuni
Same
Babati
Singida
Kondoa
TANZANIA
Korogwe
Tanga
Mutomo
North Kitui NR
Kora NP
South Kitui NR
Tsavo East NP
Garissa
Galana River
Arawale NR
Hola
Tana River
Tana River National Primate Reserve
Garsen
Witu
Boni NR
Dodori NR
Kiunga Marine NR
Kiwayu Island
Paté Island
Lamu
Manda Island
Lamu Island
Ungwana Bay
Marafa Depression
Malindi
Malindi Marine NP
Gede
Watamu
Watamu Marine NP
Arabuko Sokoke FR
Kilifi
Mtwapa
Mariakani
Mombasa
Mombasa Marine NP
Mwaluganje Elephant Sanctuary
Kwale
Tiwi Beach
Diani Beach
Shimba Hills NR
Lunga Lunga
Shimoni
Funzi Island
Wasini Island
Horohoro
Kisite Marine NP
Pemba Channel
Pemba Island
Zanzibar Channel
INDIAN OCEAN
2°S
3°S
4°S
5°S
6°S
39°E
40°E
41°E
42°E

Kenya's Top 18

1

Masai Mara

1 Its rolling savannah studded with flat-top acacia trees, the Masai Mara, which encompasses both the Masai Mara National Reserve (p112) and the private conservancies that surround it, is an iconic East African landscape that's home to some of the highest concentrations of wildlife on the planet. It's fantastic at any time but from July to October, the Mara's plains are flooded with hundreds of thousands of wildebeest on their great migration, along with herds of zebras, elephants and giraffes. Trailing this walking buffet are prides of lions, lurking leopards, solitary cheetahs and packs of hyenas. If you only visit one place in Kenya, make it the Mara.

Amboseli National Park

2 There's possibly no better place in the world to watch elephants than Amboseli National Park (p183) in the country's south. A big part of the appeal is the setting – Africa's highest mountain, the snow-capped Mt Kilimanjaro, is the backdrop for seemingly every picture you'll take here. Just as significant, Amboseli was spared the worst of Kenya's poaching crisis and these elephants are remarkably tolerant of humans (allowing you to get *really* close). And their tusks are among the biggest in Kenya.

ANUP SHAH / GETTY IMAGES ©

2

CHARLES BOWMAN / GETTY IMAGES ©

Hiking Mt Kenya

3 Occupying the heart of the country and a special place in the hearts of the Kikuyu people, Mt Kenya (p165), the country's highest peak and the second highest on the continent, is not a mountain to be admired from afar. With four days, some determination and several layers of warm clothing, you could find yourself standing on the frozen summit of Point Lenana, mere minutes from the equator, but a whole world away from the other African experiences. Trail between Tooth Col and Austrian Hut

Tsavo West National Park

4 Tsavo West National Park (p189) is a wilderness experience par excellenc a vast and dramatic landscape where wilc life lurks in the undergrowth. All of Africa's charismatic megafauna are present here, including rhinos, but it's the cats – leopards, lions and cheetahs – who bring this ecosystem to life. Against a backdrop of r soils, volcanic outcrops and sweeping savannah plains, these lions of legend (it wa here that the legendary maneaters of Tsav once roamed) laze about in the shade, wa ing for the right moment to pounce.

OHN WARBURTON-LEE / GETTY IMAGES ©

JOHN WARBURTON-LEE / GETTY IMAGES ©

amburu National Reserve

5 Samburu (p274) might not enjoy the me of other Kenyan arks, but that's just the ay we like it. This stunng arid landscape of enya's soulful north is ven life by the Ewaso giro River, its palminged banks as beautiful s any waterways in inland enya. Wildlife, too, is rawn to the river and its nterland, the rugged errain swarming with ephants, lions and leoprds, but also some sigature northern species, mong them the bluegged Somali ostrich and he endangered Grevy's ebra.

Laikipia

6 In the shadow of Mt Kenya, this plateau (p153) hosts a network of conservancies and private wildlife reserves – it is both beautiful and one of the most exciting stories in African conservation. At the forefront of efforts to save endangered species such as lions, African wild dogs, Grevy's zebras and black rhinos, the plateau's ranches offer an enticing combination of high-end lodge accommodation, big horizons and charismatic megafauna. Best of all, this is a more intimate experience than your average national park, with scarcely another vehicle in sight. Lewa Wildlife Conservancy (p162)

Mt Longonot

7 Mt Longonot (p89) not only has the near-perfect shape we imagine all volcanoes to have, it's also the most accessible of Kenya's Rift Valley climbs. Unlike the more famous Mt Kenya ascent, the climb to the crater rim is more of a strenuous 90-minute hike than a serious expedition; even the climb, circumnavigation and descent can be accomplished in four hours. The rewards are glorious Rift Valley views (including overlooking Hell's Gate National Park) and a bird's-eye view down to the lost forests of the crater floor.

9

ʀemote Lake ᴛurkana

ʒ Amid the deserts and horizonless tracts ıat characterise so much ᶠ Kenya's north, Lake ᴜrkana (p283) glitters ᴋe a jade and turquoise ıirage. Rising from its ᴀaters is Teleki, one of ıe world's most perfectly ıaped volcanic cones, ʰhile the shores are dot- ᵉd with dusty and utterly ıtriguing villages that are ome to the beguiling mix ᶠ traditional peoples – ᴜrkana, Samburu, abbra, El Molo – who all this isolated corner ᶠ Africa home. And there ʳe crocodiles here. Lots ᶠ them.

Kakamega Forest

9 Paths lace the Kakamega Forest (p136) and offer a rare opportunity to ditch the safari 4WD and stretch your legs. This ancient forest is home to an astounding 330 bird species, 400 butterfly species and seven different primate species. Like all rainforests, though, the trees themselves are the chief attraction here, and in the forest gloom you'll stumble upon the botanical equivalent of beauty and the beast: delicate orchids and parasitic figs that strangle their hosts as they climb towards the light.

Wandering Lamu Backstreets

10 Lamu (p254) is surely the most evocative destination on the Kenyan coast. With no cars around, the best way to get to know this graceful town is by wandering its backstreets, admiring the grand old Swahili doors, peeking into hidden courtyards bursting with unexpected colours, slipping into an easy chair and sipping on a fruit juice, and accepting all invitations to stop and shoot the breeze. Do all this and the backstreets of Lamu will become a place you'll dream of forever.

Lake Nakuru National Park

11 Another of Kenya's world-class parks, this park (p102) is dominated by one of the Rift Valley's most beautiful lakes. The waters are lined on one side by an abrupt escarpment and the shoreline is at times given colour and texture by massed birdlife (that may or may not include flamingos). But Lake Nakuru is also a wildlife haven for land-borne mammals, home as it is to tree-climbing lions, leopards, the highly endangered Rothschild's giraffes, zebras, buffaloes, various primate species and some of Kenya's most easily spotted rhinos.

Kisite Marine National Park

12 Hiding away like a secret jewel is the laid-back isle of Wasini, close to the border of Tanzania. You can sail to it from Diani Beach or Shimoni like an Omani sultan in a magnificent dhow, and dive overboard to snorkel with fish big and small in the stunning Kisite Marine National Park (p228), which fringes the island. Or you can come under your own steam and walk the footpaths to the near-forgotten village of Mkwiro – the perfect spot to be engulfed by Swahili culture.

Hell's Gate National Park

13 It's one thing to watch Africa's megafauna from the safety of your vehicle, quite another to do so on foot or on a bicycle. Hell's Gate National Park (p96) – a dramatic volcanic landscape of red cliffs, otherworldly rocky outcrops and deep canyons in Kenya's Rift Valley – may lack predators, but experiencing the African wild at close quarters certainly gives most people frisson. By placing you in the landscape, Hell's Gate heightens the senses, bringing alive the African wild like no other national park in Kenya. Fischer's Tower (p98)

Nairobi National Park

14 No other city in the world can boast a national park (home to four of the Big Five) within sight of city skyscrapers. The park (p60) may have its detractions, and as one of Africa's smallest parks, it's almost completely encircled by human settlements, but this is an important refuge for the endangered black rhino (more than 50), all three big cats and abundant birdlife. There's also an elephant orphanage, a nearby breeding centre for the Rothschild giraffe and numerous opportunities to forget you're in Nairobi at all. David Sheldrick Wildlife Trust (p63)

15

DAVID ELSE / GETTY IMAGES ©

16

Mt Elgon

15 Far enough away from well-trammelled tourist trails to feel like an adventure, Mt Elgon (p142), with its summit of Koitoboss at 4187m, encompasses an astonishing range of landscapes. Hiking trails climb through rainforest to bamboo jungles before traversing alpine moorland with all the weird-and-wonderful flora that brings. Rich birdlife, the odd primate species (black-and-white colobus, as well as blue and de Brazza's monkeys), the opportunity to look out over two countries and the chance to climb without a guide are other selling points.

Aberdares

16 Rising up from the eastern edge of the Rift Valley like the spine of central Kenya, the verdant Aberdares (p147) don't feel like Kenya at all. Yes, there's wildlife, and some of it's pretty unusual, from high-altitude elephants and rhinos to rare mountain bongos and black leopards. But this is a place of sprawling farms, dense forests and walking trails that pass among flora that has no right residing this close to the equator. For mountain-trekking, it's a fine alternative to the busier trails of nearby Mt Kenya.

Watamu

17 Kenya's Indian Ocean coast is one of Africa's prettiest shores and Watamu (p241) is one of its prettiest beaches. Sitting roughly halfway between Mombasa and Lamu, it's a fine base for exploring the Kenyan coast with its long stretches of white sand, translucent waters and coves sheltered by palm trees. Plenty of water sports (from fishing to windsurfing), traces of the coast's African heritage and a healthy dose of *hakuna matata* add up to one of those places you'll never want to leave.

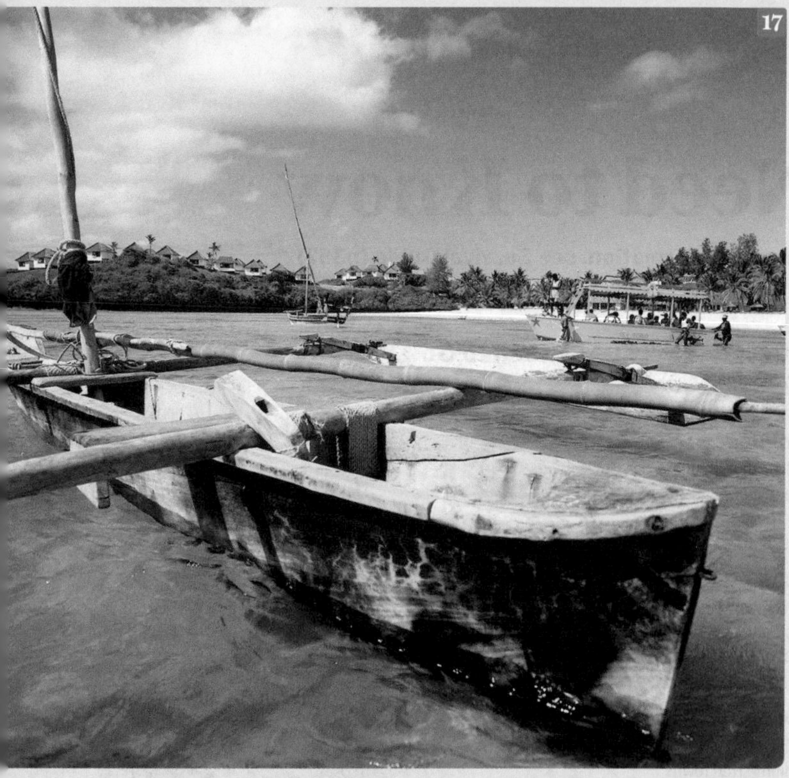

17

⁄leru National ⁄ark

18 One of Kenya's most underrated ⁄arks, Meru (p176) is ⁄ beguiling mix of iconic ⁄frican landscapes (fer- ⁄le hills, river forests, ⁄aobabs and doum palms) ⁄nd a fine range of fauna ⁄ncluding black and white ⁄hinos, elephants, lions ⁄nd zebras). Meru is also ⁄here the lion legends of ⁄eorge Adamson's *Born* ⁄*ree* came into being. But ⁄bove all else, Meru is the ⁄afari as it used to be, with ⁄nusually quiet trails and ⁄e thrill of stumbling upon ⁄ildlife when you least ⁄xpect it.

NIGEL PAVITT / GETTY IMAGES ©

18

Need to Know

For more information, see Survival Guide (p367)

Currency
Kenyan shilling (KSh)

Language
English and Swahili; other tribal languages also spoken.

Visas
Issued on arrival for most nationalities and valid for three months.

Money
ATMs in large- to medium-sized towns only. All banks change US dollars, euros and UK pounds. Credit cards accepted in most midrange and top-end hotels, restaurants and shops.

Mobile Phones
Local SIM cards widely available and can be used in most international mobile phones. Mobile coverage extensive but patchy in wilderness areas and parks.

Time
East Africa Time (GMT/UTC plus three hours).

When to Go

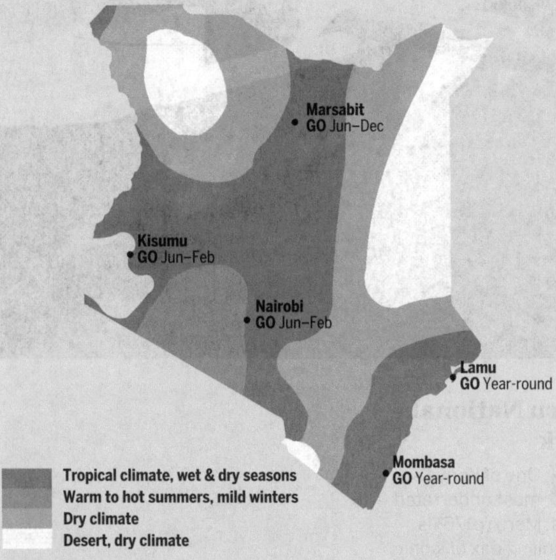

High Season
(Jul–Oct, Jan & Feb)

- Wildebeest in the Mara from mid-July to October.
- January and February offer hot, dry weather good for wildlife watching.
- Sky-high lodge prices, especially July to October. Book coastal accommodation in advance.

Shoulder
(Nov & Dec)

- Short rains fall in October and November, but travel is still possible.
- Prices at most lodges and parks drop on 1 November, but advance reservations are still required.

Low Season
(Mar–May)

- Long rains mean accommodation is much quieter and prices are low.
- Wildlife is harder to spot, some tracks are impassable and mosquitoes are rife.

Useful Websites

Eco Tourism Kenya (www.ecotourismkenya.org) Excellent resource for gauging the sustainability of Kenyan tourism.

Kenya Association of Tour Operators (www.katokenya.org) Full list of KATO-approved member companies.

Kenya Wildlife Service (www.kws.org) Conservation news and information on national parks and reserves.

Lonely Planet (www.lonelyplanet.com/kenya) Destination information, hotel bookings, traveller forums and more.

Safari Bookings (www.asafribookings.com) Invaluable resource for choosing safari operators and destinations.

Important Numbers

Regional area codes must be dialled in full, followed by the number, if calling from within Kenya; the code's '0' is dropped if calling from overseas.

International access code	☎000
Kenya country code	☎254
Directory enquiries	☎991
Police, ambulance & fire	☎999
Tourist helpline (24 hour)	☎020-604767

Exchange Rates

Australia	A$1	KSh74
Canada	C$1	KSh74
Europe	€1	KSh105
Japan	¥100	KSh77
NZ	NZ$1	KSh69
UK	UK£1	KSh138
US	US$1	KSh91

For current exchange rates see www.xe.com

Daily Costs

Budget: Less than US$75

- Cheap hotels (US$8–20) and camping (from US$20)
- Eat in local restaurants (meals US$2–5)
- Stock up in supermarkets; carry own camping equipment
- Travel by matatu (minibus)
- Share wildlife drives with other travellers

Midrange: US$75–225

- Double room in midrange hotels: US$50–200
- Independent safaris with car rental: US$75–100 per day
- Full board in lodges

Top End: More than US$225

- Double room in top hotels: US$200 and up
- No-expenses-spared safaris in luxury tented camps

Opening Hours

Banks 9am to 3pm Monday to Friday, 9am to 11am Saturday

Post Offices 8.30am to 5pm Monday to Friday, 9am to noon Saturday

Restaurants 11am to 2pm and 5pm to 9pm: some remain open between lunch and dinner

Shops 9am to 3pm Monday to Friday, 9am to 11am Saturday

Supermarkets 8.30am to 8.30pm Monday to Saturday, 10am to 8pm Saturday

Arriving in Kenya

Jomo Kenyatta International Airport, Nairobi (p382) Taxis cost KSh1500 to KSh2000. They take 30 minutes to one hour to the city centre, depending on traffic; book at the 'information' desk in the arrivals hall. There's a danger of theft on city bus 34 (one way KSh40) so it's best avoided. Taxis are the only option at night.

Moi International Airport, Mombasa (p382) There is no public transport. Taxis cost KSh1200 and take 20 to 30 minutes into the city.

Getting Around

Transport in Kenya varies greatly, from hang-on-for-your-life matatus to comfortable internal flights. Consider renting a 4WD (with or without driver) to really make the most of your trip.

Air Quite extensive domestic network, from commercial jets between cities to small-plane charters and scheduled services into national park airstrips.

Car Renting your own 4WD is the best way to explore wild Kenya on your own: if you're not experienced in African conditions, most rentals include a driver for not much more.

Bus and Minibus Buses and matatus provide intercity public transport but standards vary. As a general rule, the more you pay, the more comfortable and safer you'll be, especially on popular routes such as Nairobi–Mombasa and Nairobi–Nakuru.

For much more on **getting around**, see p382

If You Like...

Big Cats

The sight of prowling predators is guaranteed to produce a frisson of excitement, and it's the big cats – lions, leopards and cheetahs – that most visitors come to see.

Masai Mara National Reserve The best place to spot all three cats, often on a kill from July to October. (p112)

Tsavo East National Park Another good spot for relatively easy sightings of lions and cheetahs. (p196)

Tsavo West National Park Big cats are elusive here but tracking them down is half the fun. (p189)

Amboseli National Park Good for lions and cheetahs in the dry season (May to October and January to March). (p183)

Ol Pejeta Conservancy Go lion-tracking after dark. (p160)

Lewa Wildlife Conservancy Good for all three big cats without the crowds. (p162)

Meru National Park Lions regularly sighted. (p176)

Lake Nakuru National Park Resident leopards and lions. (p102)

Nairobi National Park All three present within sight of the capital. (p60)

Elephants or Rhinos

The African elephant and the rhinoceros (black and white) are enduring icons of a continent. Both are in peril, but both are also relatively easy to track down in Kenya.

Lewa Wildlife Conservancy Get up close and personal with elephants and more than 100 rhinos. (p162)

Tsavo West National Park An important sanctuary for black rhinos; also 'red' elephants. (p189)

Aberdare National Park Elephants and black rhinos on the Central Highlands' forested slopes. (p150)

Ol Pejeta Conservancy East Africa's largest refuge for the endangered black rhino. (p160)

Lake Nakuru National Park One of the best places in Kenya to see the highly endangered black rhino. (p102)

Nairobi National Park Rhinos in abundance with skyscrapers nearby. (p60)

Amboseli National Park As close as you'll ever get to a big-tusked elephant with Mt Kilimanjaro in the background. (p183)

Samburu National Reserve Elephants set against one of Kenya's most beautiful regions. (p274)

Tsavo East National Park Kenya's largest elephant population, with more than 11,000. (p196)

Marsabit National Park Kenya's northernmost elephants. (p281)

Birdwatching

Kenya is one of Africa's premier destinations for twitchers, with around 1100 bird species recorded. Northern migrant species escaping Europe's winter begin arriving in November.

Lake Nakuru National Park Flamingos (maybe), pelicans and 400 other species. (p102)

Amboseli National Park More than 370 bird species, including raptors and the grey-crowned crane. (p183)

Lake Bogoria National Reserve Another flamingo spectacular when conditions are right, with internationally recognised wetlands. (p107)

Kakamega Forest Reserve Rainforest habitat and more than 330 recorded species. (p137)

Tsavo West National Park The Ngulia Hills are an important flyway for migratory species. (p189)

p: Cheetahs, Masai Mara National Reserve (p112)
ttom: Roan antelope, Ruma National Park (p129)

Saiwa Swamp National Park Over 370 bird species in just over 15 sq km. (p145)

Arabuko Sokoke Forest Reserve Prolific birdlife in a wonderful stand of indigenous forest. (p244)

Lake Baringo Over one-third of Kenya's species have been recorded here. (p108)

Hiking

They may not let you get out of your vehicle in national parks, but Kenya is a fabulous hiking destination whether you're keen to climb a mountain or stay within sight of your lodge.

Mt Kenya Climb Africa's second-highest mountain and gaze out upon Kenya in all its glory. (p165)

Mt Elgon Uncrowded trails lead to the top of this stirring mountain on the cusp of Uganda. (p144)

Mt Longonot Accessible Rift Valley volcano with views down into the crater's lost world. (p89)

Hell's Gate National Park One of few national parks where you're encouraged to explore on foot. (p96)

Aberdare National Park Unusual alpine flora and fauna and quiet walking trails. (p150)

Around Amboseli Walk into the Chyulu Hills or out onto the plains with Maasai guides and gun bearers. (p186)

Mbulia Conservancy Hike through thick woodland to viewpoints out over the immensity of Tsavo. (p195)

Matthews Range Trek these spectacular highlands in the heart of Samburu country. (p278)

Beaches

Kenya's coastline is utterly gorgeous, home to some heaving resorts but many more quiet and idyllic beaches – the places you'll always remember as your own slice of paradise.

Shela Beach With 12km of white sand and one of Lamu's most beautiful beaches. (p262)

Watamu Enjoy 7km of unspoiled beach with a lovely fishing village nearby. (p241)

Manda Island The land time forgot, with sand dunes, mangroves and quiet beaches. (p264)

Tiwi Beach The alter ego to Diani Beach and its equal in beauty. (p219)

Diani Beach A crowded but still stunning beach. (p220)

Dhow Trips

Travelling the East African coast in a dhow (ancient Arab sailing vessel) carries echoes of ancient civilisations and trade winds past. Their slow rhythm is perfectly suited to this tropical coast.

Mkwiro There's no other way to reach this quieter-than-quiet village. (p229)

Matondoni Watch dhows being built, then sail around the Lamu archipelago for a day. (p263)

Lamu Find yourself a good captain and sail between Lamu and Manda Island for the day. (p254)

Takwa The pick of the Lamu archipelago trips. (p264)

Diving & Snorkelling

Reefs proliferate all along Kenya's coastline and the diving and snorkelling here rank among the best in East Africa. There are top-notch dive schools, or snorkel off the back of a dhow.

Malindi Marine National Park Excellent diving from July to February. (p246)

Manda Toto Island The snorkelling here is highly favoured among devotees of the Lamu archipelago. (p264)

Kisite Marine National Park Snorkel with the dolphins, with diving also possible. (p228)

Watamu Marine National Park Fabulous reefs, fish and sea turtles. (p241)

Diani Beach Professional dive schools and even a purpose-sunk shipwreck. (p220)

Luxury Lodges

Kenya does luxury extremely well, and nothing quite beats the experience of returning from a day's safari to be pampered with luxury accommodation, spa and massage packages and impeccable standards of personal service.

Ol Donyo, Around Amboseli The sort of lodge and location that safari dreams are made of. (p186)

Segera Retreat, Segera Ranch, Laikipia Peerless cottages that take you back to *Out of Africa*. (p159)

Giraffe Manor, Nairobi Top-end luxury wedded to world-class service, and a Rothschild's giraffe looking in your window. (p72)

Sasaab Lodge, Samburu Northern Kenya's finest with river views near Samburu National Reserve. (p277)

Cottar's 1920s Camp, Masai Mara Safari nostalgia in overdrive with peerless levels of comfort. (p123)

Campi ya Kanzi, Around Amboseli Supremely comfortable tents, gorgeous setting and Kili views. (p187)

Finch Hatton's Safari Camp, Tsavo West National Park Dress for dinner and eat from bone china deep in the African wilds. (p194)

Mara Plains, Masai Mara Palatial tents with details no one else has thought of. (p123)

Tortilis Camp, Amboseli National Park Fine Kilimanjaro views from this ecolodge; the family rooms are simply extraordinary. (p184)

Elsa's Kopje, Meru National Park Stunning lodge and a real sense of oneness with the African wilderness. (p177)

Escaping the Crowds

The wildebeest migration is not the only mass migration in Kenya from July to October – visitors also arrive in the millions. Avoiding them is easier than you think.

Meru National Park A match for the more famous parks of Kenya's south, but without the crowds. (p176)

Segera Ranch One of Laikipia's premier properties with excellent wildlife viewing for an elite few. (p159)

Il Ngwesi Group Ranch Immerse yourself in the Maasai wilderness close to Lewa and Laikipia. (p164)

Campi ya Kanzi (p187)

Ruma National Park You'll have wild Africa all to yourself, with rhinos and fascinating antelope species. (p129)

Loyangalani The essence of remote northern Kenya, with fascinating cultures and Lake Turkana. (p288)

Paté Island Leave the modern world behind on this enchanted island in the Lamu archipelago. (p265)

Olare-Orok Conservancy The Mara's high concentrations of predators, but just one tent for every 700 acres. (p123)

Mfangano Island Blissfully quiet Lake Victoria islands with rock paintings. (p131)

Culture & Wildlife Immersion

Community-run projects now run hand in hand with conservation and can offer travellers opportunities that will live long in the memory.

Lewa Wildlife Conservancy Visit local schools and Maasai communities as part of the new conservation model. (p162)

Ewangan Catch a glimpse of Maasai life on relatively equal terms. (p118)

Campi ya Kanzi Explore Maasailand with the Maasai then visit a Maasai village. (p187)

Ol Pejeta Conservancy Track lions, pat a blind rhino and draw near to critically endangered wildlife. (p160)

David Sheldrick Wildlife Trust Encounter orphaned elephants en route to freedom. (p63)

Month by Month

TOP EVENTS

Annual Wildebeest Migration, from July

Migratory Birds, peaking in November

Maulid Festival, December

Lake Turkana Festival, June

International Camel Derby, August

January

One of the most popular months for visiting Kenya. Animals congregate around waterholes and bird migration is well and truly under way. Days are usually warm and dry.

Dry-Season Gatherings

It can depend on the October/November rains, but perennial water sources have dried up, drawing predators and prey alike to the last remaining waterholes. Wildlife watching at this time can be tense, exhilarating and intensely rewarding.

Birds in Abundance

Migratory bird species have by now arrived in their millions, giving Kenya close to its full complement of more than 1100 bird species. Rift Valley lakes and other wetlands are, in most years, a birdwatcher's paradise.

February

High season in Kenya. Days are hot and dry, accommodation is often full, there's excellent wildlife watching around waterholes, and countless bird species on show.

March

Kenya's big annual rains begin, flooding much of the country and making wildlife viewing difficult. But if the rains are late, it may be worth visiting now: prices are rock-bottom.

Late-Rains Safari

The cheapest time to visit Kenya – roads can be impassable, mosquitoes are everywhere and wildlife disperses. But if the rains are late, conditions couldn't be better, with wildlife desperate for a drink and most birds still around.

April

The inundation continues to batter the country. Getting around (and spotting wildlife) is difficult. Unless the rains have failed entirely, avoid visiting now.

May

The rains usually continue well into May. By late May, the rains may have subsided; when they stop and you can see the horizon, the country is wonderfully green, although wildlife can still be tough to spot.

June

Kenya emerges from the rains somewhat sodden but ready to make up for lost time. The annual migration of wildebeest and zebras in their millions sometimes begins midmonth, but doesn't really take hold until July.

Rhino Charge

This charity cross-country rally in aid of Rhino Ark and other worthy conservation causes challenges mad motorists to reach the finish line in the straightest line possible, whatever the crazy obstacles. The location changes annually. (p356)

Lake Turkana Festival

One of the country's biggest cultural events, this fascinating festival focuses on the numerous tribal groups that inhabit Northern Kenya, among them the El Molo, Samburu, Pokot and the Turkana. (p290)

Run with Lions

In late June or early July, Lewa Wildlife Conservancy hosts one of the world's more unusual marathons, with a winning combination of watching wildlife and serious fundraising. (p163)

July

The wildebeest and zebra migration is in full swing. So too is the annual migration of two-legged visitors who converge on the Mara. Weather is fine and warm, with steaming conditions on the coast.

Annual Wildebeest Migration

Following the rains, wildebeest begin arriving in the Masai Mara National Reserve (the Mara) anywhere between mid-June and mid-July and stay around until October, with predators following in their wake. It's the greatest wildlife show on earth.

Return to Amboseli

When the rains begin in March the herbivores of Amboseli (elephants, antelope, zebras…), followed by the predators, leave for grasslands outside the park. By July, they're on their way back within park confines.

August

The mid-year high season continues; the Mara is still the focus, but other parks are also rewarding. Europeans on holiday flock to Kenya; prices go up, room availability goes down.

Kenya Music Festival

The country's longest-running music festival is held over 10 days in Nairobi, drawing worthy international acts along with its predominantly African cast of stars. (p68)

International Camel Derby

Maralal's International Camel Derby, in early August, offers serious camel racing and a chance to join the fun. A huge event. (p283)

September

Crowds drop off ever so slightly, but the weather remains fine and the Mara is still filled to bursting with wildlife, so prices and visitor numbers remain high.

October

A great time to visit; the wildebeest are usually around until mid-October, and migratory birds begin arriving. The best season for diving and snorkelling begins just as visitor numbers start to fall.

Here Come the Rains

Unlike the main rainy season from March to May, the short rains that usually begin in October and continue into November cause only minor disruptions to safaris. Rains are generally localised and heavy, but only last for an hour or two each day.

Tusker Safari Sevens

Nairobi hosts this highly regarded international rugby tournament. Drawing world-class rugby-union players, the tournament spills over into November. (p68)

November

In normal years, the short rains appear almost daily throughout this month, but disruptions are minimal. Some animals range beyond the parks, birds arrive in great numbers and prices fall.

Migratory Birds

Birdwatchers couldn't hope for a better time to visit, as millions of birds and hundreds of species arrive for their wintering grounds while Europe shivers.

December

A reasonable time to visit, with lower prices and fine weather, plenty of migratory birds in residence and much of the country swathed in green.

East African Safari Rally

This classic-car rally in late November or early December is more than 50 years old. The rally traverses Kenya, Tanzania and Uganda and is open to pre-1971 vehicles only.

Maulid Festival

This annual celebration (22 Dec 2015 and 11 December 2016) of the Prophet Mohammed's birthday rouses Lamu from its slumber. Muslims from up and down the coast converge on the town. Everyone is welcome (p255) .

Itineraries

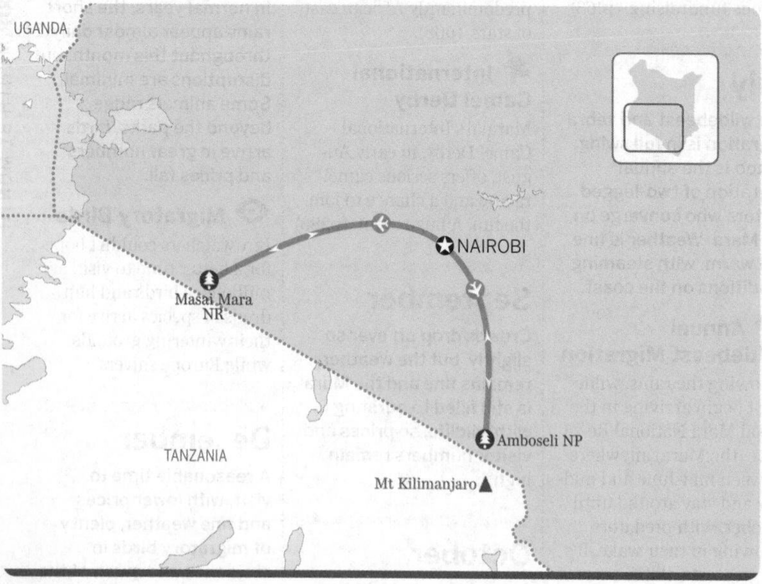

Safari Njema

Ideal for those with limited time, this classic safari route brings you face to face with the continent's most charismatic creatures. To do it in a week, you'll need to fly between the three destinations. *Safari njema* – have a good trip!

Begin in **Nairobi**. Kenya's (in)famous capital is not without charm – track down endangered giraffes, orphaned elephants and the Big Five set against a backdrop of not-so-distant skyscrapers. Plan on one full day, then fly from the capital's Wilson Airport to the **Masai Mara National Reserve**. Between July and October, the Mara hosts the annual wildebeest migration, one of the greatest wildlife concentrations on earth, but the Mara is worth visiting any time. Three days is a minimum, but spend four if you can.

Staying in Maasailand, fly, possibly via Nairobi, to **Amboseli National Park**, where you can get closer to elephants than almost anywhere else in Africa. From here, the views of Mt Kilimanjaro, Africa's highest peak, are without rival in Africa. After two nights, you'll fly back to Nairobi, wondering why you're not staying longer.

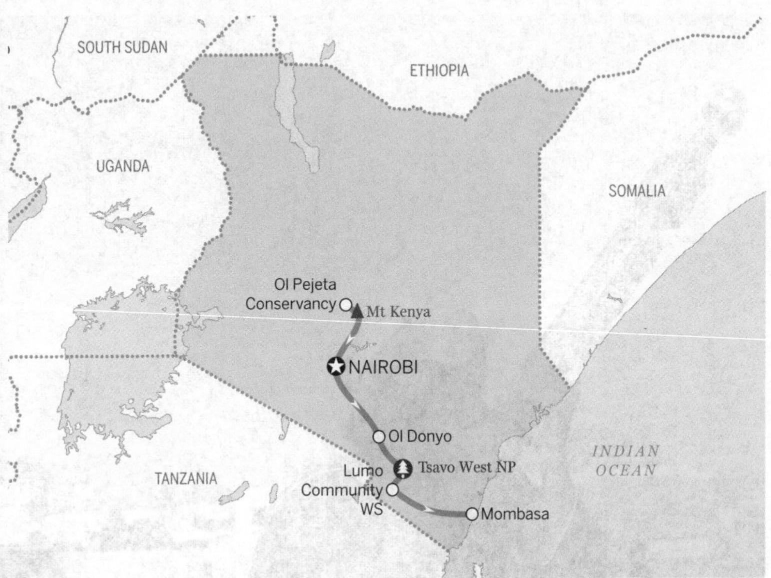

Big Five & Big Mountains

Seeing the Big Five (elephant, lion, leopard, rhino and buffalo) has become a mantra for African wildlife watchers – the term was coined by white hunters for those species deemed most dangerous to hunt. With three weeks to cover all this territory, you could easily get around in your own rented vehicle.

Ol Pejeta Conservancy, up on the Laikipia Plateau, is the closest place to Nairobi where you can see the Big Five. One of few Laikipia conservancies you can visit without checking in to a luxury lodge, Ol Pejeta has plenty of organised activities to get you lion-tracking, cycling within sight of rhinos or simply walking out into the wild. Stay for at least three days to make the most of it.

Before leaving Kenya's Central Highlands, allocate a week for one of East Africa's most rewarding adventures – the trek to the summit of **Mt Kenya**, Africa's second-highest peak, will leave you gasping for both air and superlatives.

Travelling via Nairobi, consider a two-night detour to **Ol Donyo**, a supremely luxurious lodge in the Amboseli ecosystem and on the foothills of the Chyulu Hills. Although rhinos are elusive, it's a rare chance to see the Big Five without the crowds.

From Ol Donyo, it's a straightforward drive to wildlife-rich **Tsavo West National Park**, which offers a real taste of the African wilderness and has the advantage of being home to all the Big Five – see them all in one day and you've hit the safari jackpot. Close to the southern fringes of Tsavo West, the **Lumo Community Wildlife Sanctuary** is also good for the Big Five.

From here you can head down the highway to the ancient Swahili port of **Mombasa**, where you can either fly straight home, or start a whole new journey exploring the Kenyan coast.

NIGEL PAVITT / GETTY IMAGES ©

Top: Swahili man playing a *siwa*, Lamu (p254)

Bottom: Passengers going to Funzi Island (p227)

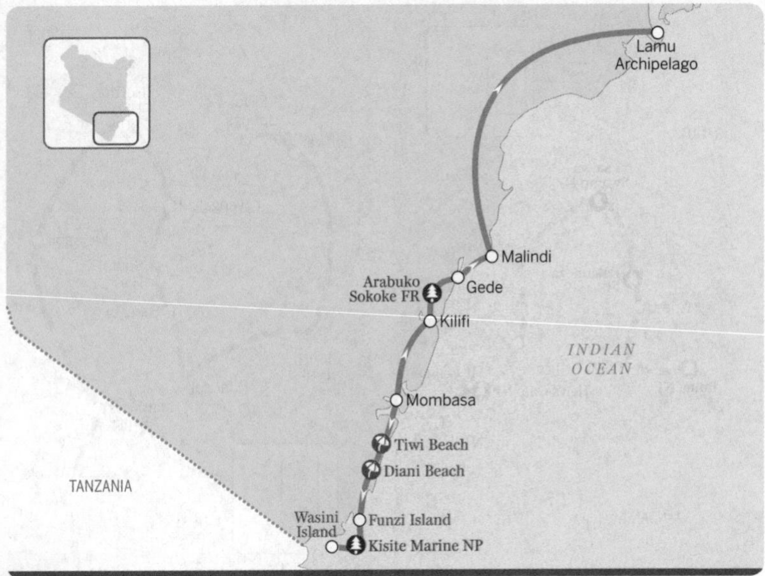

Sun, Surf & Swahili

Whether you're interested in exploring the remaining vestiges of Swahili culture or simply kicking back on the beach for days on end, don't miss the chance to explore Kenya's sun-drenched coast. Three weeks is a minimum to make this journey, which can be made on public transport, but you could take far longer if you find a beach you never want to leave. Check the security situation before setting out.

First explore the coastal gateway of **Mombasa**, one of the truly great port cities on earth and the essence of East Africa. It gets steaming hot here, so after a few days your first stop heading south should be **Tiwi Beach**, a tranquil white-sand paradise popular with independent travellers. Just down the road, you can head on to the package-holiday destination of **Diani Beach** for a taste of the full-on resort experience with plenty of water sports thrown in.

Near the Tanzanian border, **Funzi** and **Wasini** islands provide a dose of unspoilt coastal life; on the latter Mkwiro is somewhere close to paradise. These islands also afford easy access to the excellent **Kisite Marine National Park**. Whether you spot crocodiles along the banks of mangrove-lined rivers or dolphins crashing through the surf, a visit to the marine park is a wonderful complement to Kenya's terrestrial wildlife destinations. Offshore, humpback whales are a possibility from August to October. A trip in a traditional dhow is also a must. Allow at least a week in this area.

Heading north back on the coastal trail, make a quick stop in the charming town of **Kilifi** before pressing on to **Arabuko Sokoke Forest Reserve**, one of the largest remaining tracts of indigenous coastal forest in East Africa, with prolific birdlife, forest elephants and the golden-rumped elephant shrew.

Further north are the **Gede** ruins, an ancient Swahili city dating back to the 13th century. Another historic destination along the Swahili coast is **Malindi**, a 14th-century trading post that's now one of the country's leading beach destinations for Italian holiday-makers. It has bucketloads of charm once you get beyond the beach. This itinerary ends at the wonderful **Lamu Archipelago**, a veritable tropical paradise and Swahili heritage gem.

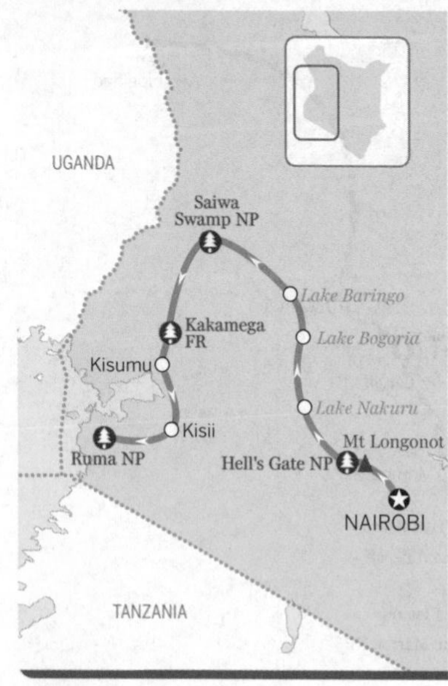

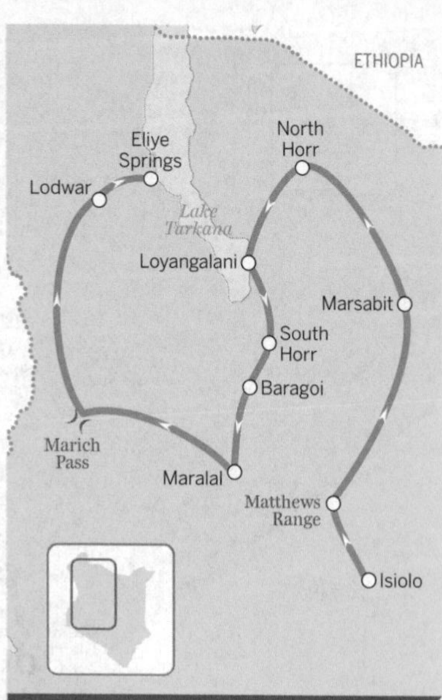

Rift Valley & Wetlands

Kenya's Rift Valley ranks among Africa's defining geological marvels. To complete this itinerary in two weeks, you'll need your own set of wheels.

Begin near **Nairobi** at the Olepolos Country Club, contemplating the Rift's glory while nursing a Tusker. Drive north to, and then climb **Mt Longonot**, one of the Rift's prettiest vantage points, and walk amid the dramatic rock forms of **Hell's Gate National Park**. Allow a couple of days around here. Then it's an easy hop to lakes **Nakuru**, **Bogoria** and **Baringo**.

Take the loop through the Cherangani Hills to the lovely **Saiwa Swamp National Park**, a real wetland treat.

Heading south, explore the lush **Kakamega Forest Reserve**, then pass through **Kisumu** on your way to busy **Kisii**, which is a handy hub for Lake Victoria's small islands, and tiny **Ruma National Park**, a rarely visited gem.

Desert Frontiers

This adventurous trail winds through the barren but beguiling landscape around Lake Turkana. You could take forever if you try to explore the area by public transport – rent a 4WD with a driver to get around.

The eastern gateway to this region is **Isiolo**. As you make your way north, the **Matthews Range** is great for walkers. Back on the road, **Marsabit** is a dusty tribal centre, home to a fine national park, and is a quintessentially northern Kenyan outpost.

Take the western loop to Turkana via **North Horr**, heading for the tiny lakeside settlement of **Loyangalani**, a base for trips into even more remote parts. From here the trail leads south again, passing all kinds of scenic zones and the stopover towns of **South Horr** and **Baragoi**. It's worth stopping for a couple of days in **Maralal**, to replenish supplies and sample the joys of camel trekking.

If the remote north has you under its spell, head up to the other side of Turkana, passing through the lush western area around **Marich Pass** to reach sweltering **Lodwar** and the lovely lakeshore at **Eliye Springs**.

Plan Your Trip
Safaris

Safari has to be one of the most evocative words ever to infiltrate the English language. In Kiswahili, safari quite literally means 'journey', though to eager visitors flocking to the Kenyan national parks, it means so much more. From inspiring visions of wildebeests fording raging rivers and lions stalking their prey through the savannah grass, to iridescent flamingos lining a salty shore at sunset, a safari into the wild is untamed Africa at its finest.

Planning a Safari

Booking

Many travellers prefer to get all the hard work done before arriving in Kenya by booking from home, either through travel agents or directly with safari companies. This ensures that you'll be able to secure a spot at the more famous lodges, especially during peak seasons when places start filling up months in advance. However, while most safari operators will take internet bookings, making arrangements with anyone other than a well-established midrange or top-end operator can be a risky business. If you're going for a budget option, you should certainly wait and do your research on the ground when you arrive.

If you want to book a safari once in Kenya, allow at least a day to shop around, don't rush into any deals and steer clear of any attempts of intimidation by touts or dodgy operators. The best way to ensure you get what you pay for is to decide exactly what you want, then visit the various companies in person and talk through the kind of package you're looking for. Budget travellers should also check out the various backpackers' accommodation choices around Nairobi, as most also organise safaris.

Need to Know

Best Wildlife Experience

Annual wildebeest migration at Masai Mara National Reserve (p112) from July to October.

Best Times to Avoid

The rainy season (late March to May).

Best Safari Planning Resources

Try www.safaribookings.com, www.ecotourismkenya.org or www.responsibletravel.com.

Best Safari Circuits

The Mara Circuit (p34) and the Southern Circuit (p34).

Best Specialist Safaris

For birdwatching, Ben's Ecological Safaris (p38); for camel safaris, Wild Frontiers (p286); for cultural insight, IntoAfrica (p38); for cycling, Bike Treks (p38); for DIY, Adventure Upgrade Safaris (p389).

Costs

Compared to other countries on the continent, Kenya is not always the cheapest destination for safaris. That said, most safari operator quotes include just about everything, such as park entrance fees, the costs of accommodation or tent rental, transport costs from the starting base to the park, and the costs of fuel plus a driver/guide for wildlife drives. However, this varies enough that it's essential to clarify before paying. Drinks (whether alcoholic or not) are generally excluded, and budget camping safari prices usually exclude sleeping-bag hire. Prices quoted by agencies or operators usually assume shared (double) room/tent occupancy, with supplements for single occupancy ranging from an additional 20% to 50% of the shared-occupancy rate.

If you're dealing directly with lodges and tented camps rather than going through a safari operator, you may be quoted 'all-inclusive' prices. In addition to accommodation, full board and sometimes park fees, these usually include two 'activities' (usually wildlife drives, or sometimes one wildlife drive and one walk) per day, each lasting about two to three hours. They generally exclude transport costs to the park. Whenever accommodation-and-full-board-only prices apply, and unless you have your own vehicle, you'll need to pay extra to actually go out looking for wildlife, and costs can be considerable.

Budget Safaris

Most safaris at the lower end of the price range are camping safaris. In order to keep costs to a minimum, groups often camp outside national park areas (thereby saving camping fees) or stay in budget guesthouses outside the park. Budget operators also save costs by working with larger groups to minimise per-person transport costs, and by keeping to a no-frills set-up with basic meals and a minimum number of staff. For most safaris at the budget level, as well as for many midrange safaris, daily kilometre limits are placed on the vehicles.

For any budget safari, the bare minimum cost for a registered company is about US$75 to US$100 per person per day, which should include transport, food (three meals per day), park entry and camping fees, tents and cooking equipment. Sleeping-bag hire will cost you an additional US$10 to US$15 for the duration of the trip.

Midrange Safaris

Most midrange safaris use lodges, where you'll have a comfortable room and eat in a restaurant. Overall, safaris in this category are reliable and reasonably good value. A disadvantage is that they may have somewhat of a packaged-tour or production-line feel. This can be minimised by selecting a safari company and accommodation carefully, by giving attention to who and how many other people you travel with, and by

BEATING SAFARI SCAMS

Every year we get emails from readers complaining about bad experiences on safari, such as dodging park fees and ignoring client requests, to pure rip-offs and outright criminal behaviour. For the most part, these incidents are perpetrated by Nairobi's budget companies, which shave every possible corner to keep their costs down.

A persistent feature of Kenya's safari scene are the street touts, who will approach you almost as soon as you step out of your hotel in the streets of Nairobi and Mombasa. They're not all bad guys, and the safari you end up with may be fine, but you'll pay a mark-up to cover their commission.

We can't stress enough how important it is to take your time with your booking. Talk to travellers, do as much research as possible, insist on setting out every detail of your trip in advance, don't be pressured into anything and don't pay any substantial amounts of cash up front. If in doubt, think seriously about stretching your budget to use a reputable midrange firm. And even though we recommend some operators, satisfaction is by no means guaranteed whoever you go with.

Of course, we receive plenty of positive feedback as well, so don't let potential problems put you off. Indeed, wildlife safaris can be utterly unforgettable experiences for all the right reasons, so it's certainly worth making the effort to book one – just keep your wits about you.

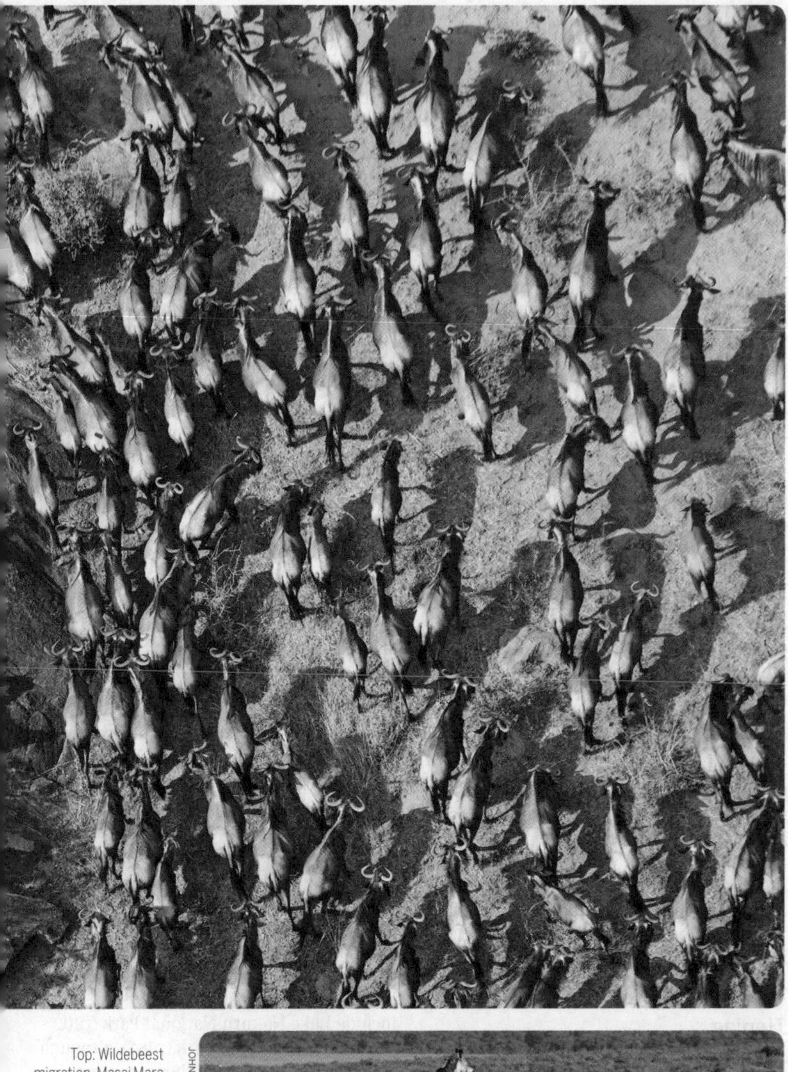

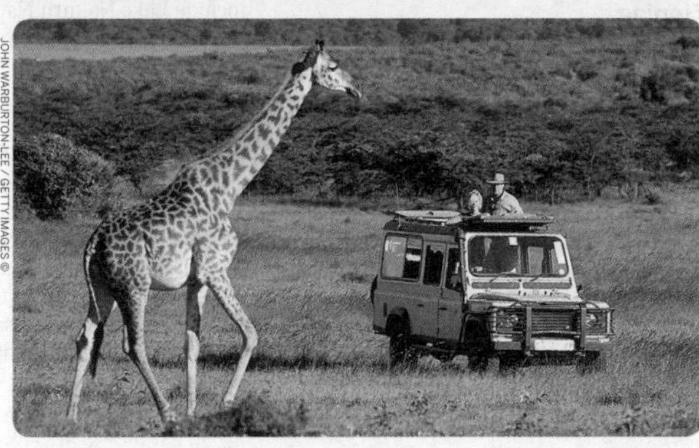

Top: Wildebeest migration, Masai Mara National Reserve (p112)

Bottom: Giraffe, Masai Mara (p112)

JOHN WARBURTON-LEE / GETTY IMAGES ©

DON'T HURRY

When planning your safari, don't be tempted to try to fit too much in to your itinerary. Distances in Kenya are long, and hopping too quickly from park to park is likely to end with you tired, unsatisfied and feeling that you haven't even scratched the surface. Try instead to plan longer periods at just one or two parks – exploring in depth what each has to offer, and taking advantage of cultural and walking opportunities in park border areas.

avoiding the large, popular lodges during peak season.

In high season you're looking at US$150 to US$200 per person per night (usually full board) for staying in lodges or tented camps, though these prices do drop a bit in the low season.

Top-End Safaris

Private lodges, luxury tented camps and even private fly-in camps are used in top-end safaris, all with the aim of providing guests with as 'authentic' and personal a bush experience as possible without forgoing the creature comforts. For the price you pay (from US$220 up to US$600 or more per person per day), expect a full range of amenities, as well as top-quality guiding. Even in remote settings without running water you will be able to enjoy hot, bush-style showers, comfortable beds and fine dining. Also expect a high level of personalised attention and an intimate atmosphere – many places at this level have fewer than 20 beds.

Tipping

Assuming service has been satisfactory, tipping is an important part of the safari experience, especially to the drivers/guides, cooks and others whose livelihoods depend on tips. Many operators have tipping guidelines, although in general you can expect to tip about US$3 to US$5 per staff member per day from each traveller. This value should increase substantially if you're on a top-end safari, part of a large group or if an especially good job has been done.

When to Go

Wildlife can be seen at all times of year, but the migration patterns of the big herbivores (which in turn attract the big predators) are likely to be a major factor in deciding when to go. From July to October, huge herds of wildebeest and zebras cross from the Serengeti in Tanzania to the Masai Mara. This is probably prime viewing time as the land is parched, the vegetation has died back and the animals are obliged to come to drink at the ever-shrinking waterholes. Not surprisingly, most safari companies increase their rates at this time.

Birdwatching is especially good from October to March.

The long rains (from March to May) transform the national parks into a lush carpet of greenery. It's very scenic, but it does provide much more cover for the wildlife to hide behind, and the rain can turn the tracks into impassable mush. Safaris may be impossible in the lowland parks during this time. Such problems are also possible during the short rains (from October to November), although getting around is rarely a problem.

Itineraries

Most itineraries offered by safari companies fall into one of three loosely defined 'circuits', which can all be combined for longer trips. Treks up Mt Kenya are a fourth option, sold separately or as an add-on.

The Mara Circuit

The standard safari itinerary centres on the Masai Mara (p112). The shorter versions generally involve two nights in the park and two half-days travelling. Possible add-ons include Lake Nakuru National Park (p102) or Amboseli National Park (p183), although consider flying between them to maximise your time.

The Southern Circuit

Offered as the main alternative to the Mara, southern itineraries make a beeline for Amboseli National Park (p183) and its famous Kilimanjaro backdrop. Anything longer than a three-day trip here should allow you to also visit Tsavo West (p189) for a couple of nights, with a couple more days required to add on Tsavo East (p196) as well. Most companies will give you the

Top: Olive baboons, Lake Nakuru National Park (p102)

Bottom: Safari accommodation, Ol Donyo, Chyulu Hills National Park (p188) option of being dropped in Mombasa at the end of this route rather than heading back to Nairobi.

The Northern Circuit

The focal point of any northern safari is Samburu National Reserve (p274), which you could also combine with one or more of the conservancies around Laikipia (p153). For Lake Turkana (p283), you'll need at least a week to visit due to the long distances involved.

Types of Safaris

Birdwatching Safaris

Many safari companies offer some kind of birdwatching safari, though the quality is not always up to par for serious birders – if you are one, quiz any prospective companies at length before making a booking. Origins Safaris (p38) is one reliable specialist.

Camel Safaris

A camel safari is a superb way of getting right off the beaten track and into areas where vehicle safaris don't or can't go. Most camel safaris go to the Samburu and Turkana tribal areas between Isiolo and Lake Turkana, where you'll experience nomadic life and mingle with tribal people. Wildlife may also be plentiful, although it's the journey itself that is the main attraction.

You have the choice of riding the camels or walking alongside them. Most caravans are led by experienced Samburu *moran* (warriors), and accompanied by English-speaking tribal guides who are well versed in bush lore, botany, ornithology and local customs. Most travelling is done as early as possible in the cool of the day, and a campsite established around noon. Afternoons are time for relaxing, guided walks and showers before drinks and dinner around the campfire.

All companies provide a full range of camping equipment (generally including two-person tents) and ablution facilities. The typical distance covered each day is 15km to 18km so you don't have to be superfit to survive this style of safari.

The following companies offer camel safaris of varying lengths:

- ➡ Treefrog Cottage/Bobong Camp (p155)
- ➡ Desert Rose (p288)
- ➡ Wild Frontiers (p286)
- ➡ Yare Camel Club & Camp (p284)

Camping Safaris

Few things can match the thrill of waking up in the middle of the African bush with nothing between you and the animals except a sheet of canvas and the dying embers of last night's fire.

Camping safaris cater for budget travellers, the young (or young at heart) and those who are prepared to put up with a little discomfort to get the authentic bush experience. At the bottom of the price range, you'll have to forgo luxuries such as flush toilets, running water and cold drinks, and you'll have to chip in with chores such as putting up the tents and helping prepare dinner. Showers are provided at some but not all campsites, although there's usually a tap where you can scrub down with cold water. The price of your safari will include three meals a day cooked by the camp cook(s), although food will be of the plain-but-plenty variety.

There are more comfortable camping options, where there are extra staff to do all the work, but they cost more. A number of companies have also set up permanent campsites where you can just drop into bed at the end of a dusty day's drive.

Cultural Safaris

With ecofriendly lodges now springing up all over Kenya, remote population groups are becoming increasingly involved with tourism. There is also a growing number of companies offering cultural safaris, allowing you to interact with locals in a far more personal way than the rushed souvenir stops that the mainstream tours make at Maasai villages. The best of these combine volunteer work with more conventional

BUDGET SAFARIS

In addition to the larger safari companies, numerous budget accommodation options in Nairobi organise camping safaris for budget travellers. These include the following:

- ➡ Milimani Backpackers & Safari Centre (p71)
- ➡ Wildebeest Eco Camp (p72)

tour activities, and provide accommodation in tents, ecolodges and village houses.

One company that receives consistently good reviews for its cultural safaris is IntoAfrica (p38).

Flying Safaris

These safaris essentially cater for the well-off who want to fly between remote airstrips in the various national parks and stay in luxury tented camps. If money is no object, you can get around by a mixture of charter and scheduled flights and stay in some of the finest camps in Kenya – arrangements can be made with any of the lodge and tented-camp safari operators.

Lodge & Tented-Camp Safaris

Safari lodges make up the bulk of most safari experiences, ranging from five-star luxury to more simple affairs. In the lodges you can expect rooms with bathrooms or cottages with air-conditioning, international cuisine, a terrace bar beneath a huge *makuti* (palm-thatched) canopy with wonderful views, a swimming pool, wildlife videos and other entertainments, and plenty of staff on hand to cater for all your requirements. Almost all lodges have a waterhole and some have a hidden viewing tunnel that leads right to the waterside.

If you can't do without luxuries, there's a whole world of luxurious lodges with swimming pools and bars overlooking waterholes, and remote tented camps that re-create the way wealthy hunters travelled around Kenya a century ago. Some of the lodges are beautifully conceived and the locations are to die for, perched high above huge sweeps of savannah or waterholes teeming with African wildlife. Most are set deep within the national parks, so the safari drives offer maximum wildlife-viewing time.

The luxury-tented camps tend to offer semipermanent tents with fitted bathrooms (hot showers are standard), beds with mosquito nets, proper furniture, fans and gourmet meals served alfresco in the bush. The really exclusive ones are even more luxurious than the lodges and tend to be *very* expensive.

Motorcycle Safaris

Operating out of Diani Beach, **Fredlink Tours** (Map p220; ☎040-3300253; www.motorbike-safari.com; Diani Plaza) runs motorcycle safaris to the Taita Hills, Rift Valley, Tsavo West and the Kilimanjaro foothills.

GUIDE ACCREDITATION

A good indicator of any guide's level of expertise and experience is the accreditation system run by the Kenya **Professional Safari Guides Association** (www.safariguides.org). It isn't perfect, but all applicants must sit for an exam to progress to the next level and it remains a fairly effective system. A full (although not always updated) list of accredited guides can be found on the website.

- Bronze: basic knowledge of guiding and wildlife
- Silver: advanced knowledge of guiding and wildlife, and at least three years' experience
- Gold: the elite, with (at last count) just 21 in the whole country

Walking & Cycling Safaris

For the keen walker or cyclist, and those who don't want to spend all their time in a safari minibus, there are a number of options, from short rides to multiday expeditions.

Booking a Safari

The service provided by even the best safari companies can vary, depending on the driver, the itinerary, the behaviour of the wildlife, flat tyres and breakdowns and, of course, the attitude of the passengers themselves. We try to recommend some of the better companies, but this shouldn't take the place of your own hands-on research.

Useful Resources

Ecotourism Society of Kenya (ESOK; ☎0726366080, Nairobi 020-2574059; www.ecotourismkenya.org) Maintains a list of member companies and lodges who subscribe to its code of conduct for responsible, sustainable safaris. Click on 'Members' under the Directory Listing heading on the homepage.

Kenyan Association of Tour Operators (KATO; ☎0722434845, Nairobi 020-713348;

www.katokenya.org) It may not be the most powerful regulatory body in the world, but most reputable safari companies subscribe, and going with a KATO member will give you *some* recourse in case of conflict.

Kenya Professional Safari Guides Association (KPSGA; ☎Nairobi 020-2342426; www.safariguides.org) Your guide's accreditation by this body is a good indicator of quality and experience.

ResponsibleTravel.com (www.responsibletravel.com) A good place to start planning a culturally and environmentally responsible safari.

Safari Bookings (www.safaribookings.com) Fabulous online resource for comparing safari operators and destinations.

Uniglobe Let's Go Travel (www.uniglobeletsgotravel.com) A searchable database of lodges and other forms of accommodation as well as a useful safari finder.

Safari Companies

The following list of safari companies is by no means exhaustive. We've chosen these places either because of first-hand experience, consistently positive reports from travellers, and/or the fact that they've been around for a while. Most are members of the Kenyan Association of Tour Operators (p37). More recommended companies are found elsewhere in this chapter, as well as in the Outdoor Activities chapter (p40) and the Overland Tours section of the Transport chapter (p384).

Abercrombie & Kent (Map p60; ☎Nairobi 020-6950000; www.abercrombiekent.com; Abercrombie & Kent House, Mombasa Rd, Nairobi; top end) Luxury travel company with excellent safaris to match.

Basecamp Explorer (☎0733333709; www.basecampkenya.com; Nairobi Head office, Gold Rock Bldg, off Mombasa Rd; top end) Scandinavian-owned ecotourism operator offering comprehensive and often luxurious camping itineraries with an environmentally sustainable focus.

Ben's Ecological Safaris (☎0722861072, Nairobi 020-2431591; www.bensecologicalsafaris.com; 4th fl Aqua Plaza, Muranga'a Rd, Nairobi; midrange to top end) Birdwatching specialists but good for just about any natural history or cultural safaris, across East Africa.

Bike Treks (☎Nairobi 020-2141757; www.angelfire.com/sk/biketreks; Kabete Gardens, Westlands, Nairobi; midrange) Bike Treks offers specialised trips with everything from quick three-day jaunts to full-on expeditions; they might even have you cycling through the Masai Mara…

Bushbuck Adventures (☎0722356838, Nairobi 020-7121505; www.bushbuckadventures.com; Peponi Rd, Westlands, Nairobi; top end) Small company specialising in personalised (including walking) safaris. It has a private, semipermanent camp in the Masai Mara.

Eastern & Southern Safaris (Map p66; ☎Nairobi 020-2242828; www.essafari.co.ke; 6th fl, Finance House, Loita St, Nairobi; midrange to top end) Classy and reliable outfit aiming at the midrange and upper end of the market, with standards to match. They do all the classic Kenyan trips.

Eco-Resorts (☎0733618183; www.eco-resorts.com; top end) US-based company with a variety of activity-based volunteer and cultural packages and customised safaris around Kenya. A proportion of profits go to community and conservation projects.

Gametrackers (Map p60; ☎Nairobi 020-200255; www.gametrackersafaris.com; Seminary Rd, off Magadi Rd, Karen, Nairobi; midrange to top end) Long-established and reliable company with a full range of camping and lodge safaris around Kenya; one of the best operators for Lake Turkana and the north.

IntoAfrica (☎UK 0114-2555610; www.intoafrica.co.uk; 40 Huntingdon Cres, Sheffield, UK; midrange to top end) One of the most highly praised safari companies in East Africa, IntoAfrica specialises in 'fair-trade' trips providing insights into African life and directly supporting local communities. Combining culture *and* wildlife viewing is a speciality.

Natural Tours & Safaris (Map p66; ☎Mombasa 041-2226715, Nairobi 0720894288; www.naturaltoursandsafaris.com; 1st fl, Gilfillan House, Kenyatta Ave, Nairobi; midrange to top end) Well-organised safaris visiting all the major parks.

Origins Safaris (Map p66; ☎Nairobi 020-3312137; www.originsafaris.info; EcoBank Towers, Standard St, Nairobi; top end) A natural history and cultural focus, with everything from expert birdwatching to Samburu circumcision ceremonies, as well as other more mainstream safaris.

Pal-Davis Adventures (Map p56; ☎Nairobi 020-2522611, 0733919613; www.pal-davisadventures.com; 1st fl, Bhavesh Business Centre, Ngara Rd, Nairobi; midrange to top end) Small Kenyan company that gets excellent reports from travellers for their wide range of personalised safaris.

Pollman's Tours & Safaris (Map p60; ☎Nairobi 020-3337234; www.pollmans.com; Pollman's House, Mombasa Rd, Nairobi; midrange to top end) Kenyan-based operator that covers all the main national parks, with coastal and Tanzanian trips as well.

Private Safaris (Map p60; ☎Mombasa 0722203780, Nairobi 020-3607000; www.privatesafaris.co.ke; 2nd fl, Mobil Plaza, Muthaiga, Nairobi; top end) Another safari agent offering trips that can be highly customised, Private can book trips all throughout sub-Saharan Africa.

Safari Icon Travel (Map p66; ☎0724112227, Nairobi 020-2242818; www.safariicon.com; 4th fl, Nacico Chambers, cnr Kenyatta & Moi Aves; midrange) Well-regarded local company that covers a wide range of safari options in Kenya, Tanzania and Uganda.

Safe Ride Tours & Safaris (Map p66; ☎Nairobi 020-2101162; www.saferidesafaris.com; 2nd fl, Avenue House, Kenyatta Ave, Nairobi; budget) A relatively new budget operator recommended for camping excursions around the country.

Samburu Trails Trekking Safaris (☎Nairobi 020-2631594; www.samburutrails.com; budget to top end) Small British specialist outfit offering a range of foot excursions in some less-visited parts of the Rift Valley.

Savage Wilderness Safaris (Map p70; ☎Nairobi 020-7121590; www.savagewilderness.org; Sarit Centre, Westlands, Nairobi) Offers organised and customised walking, climbing and mountaineering trips, including climbs up Mt Kenya.

Somak Travel (Map p60; ☎Nairobi 020-4971000; www.somak-nairobi.com; Somak House, Mombasa Rd, Nairobi; midrange to top end) Kenyan-based operator with more than 30 years of experience on the safari circuit. Somak is a home-grown favourite.

Southern Cross Safaris (Map p60; ☎Nairobi 020-2434600; www.southerncrosssafaris.com; Symbion House, Karen Rd, Nairobi; midrange to top end) Professional Kenyan company Southern Cross is a good choice for individually designed safaris.

Do-It-Yourself Safaris

A DIY safari is a viable and enticing proposition in Kenya. Doing it yourself has several advantages over organised safaris, primarily total flexibility, independence and being able to choose your travelling companions. However, as far as costs go, it's generally true to say that organising your own safari will cost at least as much, and usually more, than going on an organised safari to the same areas. And you will, of course, need to book your own accommodation well in advance (if you're staying in lodges or tented camps) or carry your own camping equipment.

DIY Safari Companies

We recommend all of the following local companies. Most are focused on renting vehicles, but they may be able to make some arrangements on your behalf and/or provide camping equipment for an additonal cost.

- Adventure Upgrade Safaris (p389)
- Central Rent-a-Car (p389)
- Market Car Hire (p389)
- Pal-Davis Adventures (p38)
- Tough Trucks Kenya (☎Nairobi 020-2228725; www.toughtruckskenya.com)

Private Drivers

Choosing a driver can almost be as important as choosing a safari company – they will, after all, be your constant companion throughout your trip – and there are some travellers who base their visit around the availability of certain drivers. In most cases, the drivers will make the necessary vehicle arrangments, and some drivers double as guides, fixers and interpreters. Drivers we recommend include:

Duncan Waikwa (☎0722305206; waikwabull@gmail.com)

John Chege (☎0787422845; chege.john@gmail.com)

Peter Chomba (☎0727739769; peddcho@yahoo.com)

Peter Ndirangu (☎0721922594; peterwamae1@gmail.com)

Camping Equipment

Some companies offer camping equipment for rent. Expect to pay from KSh250 per day for a sleeping bag with liner, KSh550 for a two-person dome tent and KSh150 per day for a gas stove (gas canisters are extra). On most items there is a deposit of KSh2000 to KSh3000. It's also possible to hire a vehicle and camping equipment as one package. Adventure Upgrade Safaris (p389) is one such operator.

Companies in Nairobi that rent out camping equipment include Atul's (p80) and X-treme Outdoors (p80).

Plan Your Trip

Outdoor Activities

Kenya is not just about seeing – there's also so much to do here, from walking up some of Africa's highest peaks to drifting out over the Masai Mara in a balloon, from snorkelling the Indian Ocean to cycling within sight of wild rhinos. So get down from your vehicle and explore.

Top Activities

Best Ballooning

Head to the Masai Mara National Reserve (p112) in Western Kenya – the best season is July to October.

Best Mountaineering

Scale the heights in Mt Kenya National Park (p165) in the Central Highlands from June to October.

Best Diving & Snorkelling

The Lamu archipelago's Manda Toto Island (p264) is the best option, from October to March.

Best Mountain Trekking

Head for Mt Elgon (p144) in Western Kenya or the Rift Valley's Mt Longonot (p89). Best time to go is June to February.

Best Cultural Trekking

Hike with Maasai Trails (p120) in Loita Hills in the Masai Mara. The best time is from June to February.

Best Windsurfing

Try Lamu (p254) & Manda Island (p264), from December to March.

Best for Water Sports

Diani Beach (p220), south of Mombasa, is great year-round.

Planning Your Trip

When to Go

Kenya is a fantastic year-round activities destination, with one important exception: we generally recommend that you avoid the long rains which run from sometime in March (or later) through to May. At this time trails (and access roads) can be impassable, and underwater visibility is generally poorer. The shorter rains in October and November tend to be more localised and heavy downpours rarely last longer than an hour or two. These 'short rains' (as they're known locally) will rarely disrupt your plans to get active.

What to Take

There are few requirements for most activities. Operators who organise whitewater rafting and other similar sports will provide the necessary equipment; bicycles and mountain bikes can be rented in Kenya, but serious cyclists and bikers may want to bring their own. Most hikers head out onto the trail under their own steam (good boots are a must), but even those who plan on joining an organised hike with a guide will usually need to bring their own equipment.

Airborne Activities

Ballooning

A balloon trip in and around the Masai Mara is a superb way of seeing the savannah and its animals. The almost ghostly experience of floating silently above the plains with a 360-degree view of everything beneath you is incomparable, and it's definitely worth the considerable outlay; prices start at around US$500 per person.

The flights typically set off at dawn and go for about 1½ hours, after which you put down for a champagne breakfast. You will then be taken on a wildlife drive in a support vehicle and returned to your lodge.

Governors' Balloon Safaris (☎0733268888, Nairobi 020-2734000; www.governorscamp.com; per person US$500) This extremely professional company operates out of Little Governors' Camp in the Mara.

Transworld Balloon Safaris (☎Nairobi 020-4451620; www.transworldsafaris.com/ballooning.php) Dawn departures from the Sarova Mara Lodge, Mara Safari Lodge and Mara Serena Lodge.

Flying

Flying lessons are easily arranged in Nairobi and are much more affordable than in Europe, the USA and Australasia. Scenic flights include trips on the plane that appeared in *Out of Africa* at Segera Retreat (p159), and flying safaris at Lewa Wildlife Conservancy (p162).

Aero Club of East Africa (Map p60; ☎0733832488, Nairobi 020-6000479; www.aeroclubea.com; Wilson Airport, Nairobi) Flying club with a long and distinguished history.

Ninety-Nines Flying Club (Map p60; ☎0728606479, Nairobi 020-6006935; www.99flying.com; Wilson Airport, Nairobi) Respected flying school.

Land Activities

Climbing & Mountaineering

Kenya isn't particularly well-known for its rock-climbing, but that's more to do with a lack of infrastructure rather than a lack of suitable places.

One useful resource is the Mountain Club of Kenya (p65) in Nairobi. Members have a huge pool of technical knowledge about climbing in Kenya. Savage Wilderness Safaris (p45) offers organised and customised walking, climbing and mountaineering trips, including climbs up Mt Kenya.

Where to Climb

- ➡ Mt Kenya (p165)
- ➡ Tsavo West National Park (p189)
- ➡ Ndoto Mountains (p278)
- ➡ Hell's Gate National Park (p96)

Cycling & Mountain-Biking

If you're just after a trundle rather than some serious cycling, many local companies and accommodation places around the country (particularly campgrounds) can arrange bicycle hire. Prices generally start at KSh600 to KSh1000 per day, but always check the quality of the bike as standards vary wildly. The only national park where you're allowed to cycle is Hell's Gate National Park.

An increasing number of companies offer more serious cycling trips in Kenya. Expect to pay around US$120 per day.

Bike Treks (☎Nairobi 020-2141757; www.angelfire.com/sk/biketreks; Kabete Gardens, Westlands, Nairobi; midrange) Bike Treks offers specialised trips with everything from quick three-day jaunts to full-on expeditions; they might even have you cycling through the Masai Mara...

Rift Valley Adventures (☎0712426999, 0707734776; www.riftvalleyadventures.com; half-/full-day cycling per person from US$70/120) This highly recommended operator runs cycling tours through Ol Pejeta Conservancy or mountain-biking on Mt Kenya.

Where to Cycle or Mountain Bike

- ➡ Masai Mara National Reserve (p112)
- ➡ Ol Pejeta Conservancy (p160)
- ➡ Hell's Gate National Park (p96)
- ➡ Mt Kenya (p165)
- ➡ Solio Game Reserve (p153)

Trekking

Kenya has some of the best trekking trails in East Africa, ranging from strenuous mountain ascents to rolling hill country and forests. It is, of course, always worth checking out the prevailing security situation in the area you wish to trek, not to mention the prevalence of any wild animals you might encounter along the trail. In some instances, it may be advisable to take a local guide, either from the Kenyan Wildlife Service (KWS) if they operate in the area, or a local village guide.

Where to Trek

The following places are all good for proper mountain trekking in varying degrees of difficulty:

- Mt Kenya (p165)
- Mt Elgon National Park (p144)
- Mt Longonot (p89)
- Cherangani Hills (p142)

RESPONSIBLE TREKKING & CLIMBING

Rubbish

- Carry out all your rubbish.
- Never bury rubbish: digging disturbs soil and ground cover and encourages erosion. Buried rubbish will likely be dug up by animals, which may be injured or poisoned by it.
- Minimise waste by taking minimal packaging and no more food than you will need. Take reusable containers or stuff sacks.
- Sanitary napkins, tampons, condoms and toilet paper should be carried out despite the inconvenience. They burn and decompose poorly.

Human Waste Disposal

- Where there is a toilet, please use it. Where there is none, bury your waste. Dig a small hole 15cm deep and at least 100m from any watercourse. Cover the waste with soil and a rock.

Washing

- Don't use detergents or toothpaste in or near watercourses, even if they are biodegradable.
- For personal washing, use biodegradable soap and a water container at least 50m away from the watercourse. Disperse the waste water widely to allow the soil to filter it fully.
- Wash cooking utensils 50m from watercourses using a scourer, sand or snow instead of detergent.

Erosion

- Stick to existing tracks and avoid short cuts.
- If a well-used track passes through a mud patch, walk through the mud so as not to increase the size of the patch.

Fires & Low-Impact Cooking

- Don't depend on open fires for cooking. Cook on a lightweight kerosene, alcohol or shellite (white gas) stove and avoid those powered by disposable butane gas canisters.
- Ensure that you fully extinguish a fire after use.

Wildlife Conservation

- Place gear out of reach and tie packs to rafters or trees.
- Do not feed the wildlife as this can lead to animals becoming dependent on handouts.

- Loita Hills (p119)
- Aberdare Natoinal Park (p150)
- Ndoto Mountains (p278)

For forest hiking, we especially like the following:

- Kakamega Forest Reserve (p137)
- Matthews Range (p278)
- Arabuko Sokoke Forest Reserve (p244)

Useful Trekking Resources

For more trekking information, get hold of a copy of Lonely Planet's *Trekking in East Africa;* it may be out of print but remains the definitive guide to trekking the region.

Among the operators we recommend, consider Savage Wilderness Safaris (p45), which offers trekking around the country, and Maasai Trails (p40), which runs cultural trekking in the Masai Mara's Loita Hills.

Mountain Club of Kenya (MCK; www.mck.or.ke) The Mountain Club of Kenya in Nairobi organises frequent trekking weekends around the country. They have also published a couple of guides, including *Guide to Mount Kenya and Kilimanjaro* (by Iain Allan) and the invaluable *Mountains of Kenya* (by Paul Clarke).

PERSONAL TREKKING EQUIPMENT CHECKLIST

- Sturdy hiking boots.
- A good-quality sleeping bag – at high altitude (such as Mt Kenya), nights can be bitterly cold and the weather can turn nasty at short notice.
- Warm clothing, including a jacket, jersey (sweater) or anorak (windbreaker) that can be added or removed.
- A sleeping sheet, a warm, but lightweight sleeping bag.
- A sturdy but lightweight tent.
- Mosquito repellent.
- A lightweight stove.
- Trousers for walking, preferably made from breathing, waterproof (and windproof) material such as Gore-Tex.
- Air-filled sleeping pad.
- Swiss Army knife.
- Torch (flashlight) or headlamp with extra batteries.

Water Activities

A whole world of water activities awaits in Kenya. Snorkelling is popular and can easily be arranged locally and inexpensively. Some of the larger resorts have water-sports centres giving visitors the opportunity to try out everything from jet skis and banana boats to bodyboarding and surfing.

Diani Beach, south of Mombasa, is the best place to go if you want to try any (or all) of these activities. Malindi (p246) can also be good.

Diving & Snorkelling

The Kenyan coast promises some of the best diving and snorkelling in Africa beyond the Red Sea. There are a number of professional dive centres, and in addition to myriad fish species and colourful coral, charismatic marine mammals – including dolphins, sea turtles, whale sharks and humpback whales (August to October) – also frequent these waters.

If you aren't certified to dive, almost every hotel and resort on the coast can arrange an open-water diving course. They're not much cheaper (if at all) than anywhere else in the world – a five-day PADI certification course starts at around US$470. Trips for certified divers including two dives go for around US$100.

When to Dive & Snorkel

There are distinct seasons for diving in Kenya. October to March is the best time.

From June to August it's often impossible to dive due to the poor visibility caused by the heavy silt flow from some rivers. That said, some divers have taken the plunge in July and found visibility to be a very respectable 7m to 10m, although 4m is more common.

Where to Dive & Snorkel

There is a string of marine national parks spread out along the coast between Shimoni and Malindi. As a general rule, these are the best places to dive and snorkel, and the better marine parks are those further away from Mombasa.

JAMES WARWICK / GETTY IMAGES ©

Top: Cycling, Mt Kenya (p165)

Bottom: Ballooining, Masai Mara National Reserve (p112)

- Malindi Marine National Park (p246)
- Manda Toto Island (p264)
- Kisite Marine National Park (p228)
- Diani Beach (p220)
- Wasini Island (p228)
- Malindi Marine National Park (p246)
- Watamu Marine National Park (p241)

Fishing

For freshwater fishing, there are huge Nile perch as big as a person in Lake Victoria(p124) and Lake Turkana (p283). Some of the trout fishing around Mt Kenya (p165) and the Aberdares (p150) is exceptional.

The deep-sea fishing on the coast is some of the best in the world, and various private companies and resorts in the following places can arrange fishing trips. Boats cost from US$250 to US$500 and can usually fit four or five anglers. The season runs from August to April.

- Diani Beach (p220)
- Watamu (p241)
- Malindi (p246)
- Shimoni (p228)
- Mtwapa (p235)

Sailing

Kilifi (p238), Mtwapa (p235) and Mombasa (p204) all have sailing clubs, and smaller freshwater clubs can also be found at Lake Naivasha (p92) and Lake Victoria (p124), which both have excellent windsurfing and sailing. If you're experienced, you may pick up some crewing at the yacht clubs; you'll need to become a temporary member.

While rarely hands-on, a traditional dhow trip out of Lamu is an unforgettable sailing experience.

Water Sports

Windsurfing & Kitesurfing

Conditions on Kenya's coast are ideal for windsurfing – the country's offshore reefs protect the waters, and the winds are usually reasonably strong and constant. Most resort hotels south and north of Mombasa have sailboards for hire. Further north, the sheltered channel between Lamu and Manda Islands is one of the best places for windsurfing on the coast.

Kitesurfing is also possible at Diani Beach and Malindi.

Where to Windsurf

- Lamu (p254) and Manda Island (p264)
- Watamu (p241)
- Malindi (p246)
- Diani Beach (p220)

White-Water Rafting

The most exciting times for a white-water rafting trip are from late October to mid-January and from early April to late July, when water levels are highest.

Savage Wilderness Safaris (☎Nairobi 020-7121590; savagewilderness.org) Savage Wilderness Safaris, run by the charismatic Mark Savage, is easily Kenya's most experienced operator for white-water rafting, with trips on the Tana, Athi and Mathioya rivers. Depending on water levels, rafting trips start from four to five hours, but longer trips (450km, three weeks' duration) are also possible; most trips last one to four days and cover up to 80km.

Where to Go Rafting

The Athi/Galana River (p196) has substantial rapids, chutes and waterfalls and there are also possibilities on the Tana River (p252) and Ewaso Ngiro River near Isiolo (p269).

Plan Your Trip

Travel with Children

Kenya is a wonderful destination in which to travel as a family. Yes, there are vaccinations to worry about and Africa can seem like a daunting place to take the kids, but just about any kind of trip is possible. You're more likely to have a hassle-free time if you're prepared to spend a little extra and take comfort over adventure for the core of the trip. And it's worth remembering: loads of families simply cast their worries aside and have the holiday of a lifetime.

Best Regions for Kids

Masai Mara & Western Kenya

A safari in the Masai Mara, particularly during the extraordinary spectacle of the massed wildebeest migration (July to October), is surely one of the most memorable experiences your child will ever have in nature. If you take your kids to one wildlife reserve, make it the Masai Mara.

Southern Rift Valley

Shorter distances, better roads, scenic variety, child-friendly parks and great big lakes make the Rift Valley the best overall part of inland Kenya for little people.

Lamu & the North Coast

You could go anywhere along Kenya's coast and find your family's own little slice of paradise. But there's something about the languid pace of life in and around Lamu that seems perfectly suited to a family holiday, (but check the security situation first). On the south coast Diani Beach has loads to offer younger travellers.

Kenya for Kids

Beach Holidays

Beach holidays are a sure-fire way to keep the kids happy, and factoring in some beach time to go with the safari can be a good idea. Kenya's beaches alone should be sufficient, but some of the water sports on offer, such as snorkelling, may be suitable for children, depending on their age. And packing a picnic lunch and sailing out to sea on a dhow (a traditional old sailing boat) is a fine way to spend some fun family time.

Safaris

The safari could have been custom-built for children. Driving up almost to within touching distance of elephants, watching lion cubs gambolling across the plains or holding their breath as a cheetah accelerates across the plains – these are experiences that will stay with your kids for a lifetime.

Culture

Children find it so much easier to break down the barriers of language and culture than do adults, and watching your child play in the dust with a Maasai boy or girl of their own age is an unforgettable experience for children and parents alike. Learning a little of the language and getting to know how children from different cultures spend their days will grab the attention of most children. Better still, their interactions may even help the adults among you to find your entry point into conversations that you'd never dream of starting on your own.

Children's Highlights

National Parks & Reserves

- **Masai Mara National Reserve** Africa's charismatic megafauna in abundance. (p112)
- **Lake Nakuru National Park** Lions, leopards and playful monkeys with easy access. (p102)
- **Nairobi National Park** A kid-sized park with no time for interest levels to flag. (p60)
- **Shimba Hills National Reserve** A quick half-day safari from the coast with good roads all the way. (p218)
- **Hell's Gate National Park** Walk and cycle with megafauna. (p96)

Activities

- **Ballooning** Ride high over the Masai Mara in a balloon. (p115)
- **Dolphin watching** Swim with the dolphins at Kisite Marine National Park. (p228).
- **Snorkelling** Snorkel at Manda Toto Island to discover a whole new underwater world. (p264)
- **Sailing** Take a dhow trip from Lamu for a picnic lunch on the beach. (p262)
- **Elephant feeding** Feed the elephants at Nairobi's David Sheldrick Wildlife Trust. (p63)

Beaches

- **Diani Beach** Plenty of child-friendly facilities. (p220)
- **Malindi** Ditto. (p246)
- **Shela** White sand and plenty of space close to Lamu. (p262)
- **Watamu** Another quiet but fabulous beach close to a fishing village. (p241)
- **Manda Island** Show the kids what East Africa's beaches used to be like. (p264)
- **Kipungani** A Lamu favourite largely devoid of hassle. (p263)

Planning

Local attitudes towards children vary in Kenya just as they do in the West, but kids will generally be welcomed anywhere that's not an exclusively male preserve, especially by women with families of their own.

Accommodation

Safari lodges can handle most practicalities with aplomb, whether it's an extra bed or cot, or buffet meals that will have something even the fussiest of eaters will try. Some lodges have children's playgrounds, and almost all have swimming pools. In non-lodge accommodation, your chances of finding what you need (such as cots) increase the more you're willing to pay.

Budget hotels are probably best avoided for hygiene reasons. Most midrange accommodation should be acceptable, though it's usually only top-end places that cater specifically for families. Camping can be exciting for the little ones, but you'll need to be extra careful that your kids aren't able to wander off unsupervised into the bush.

WHAT TO PACK

While supplies of the following are available in most large supermarkets, they can be expensive. Bring as much as possible from home:

- canned baby foods
- child-friendly insect repellent (not available in Kenya)
- child seat if you're hiring a car or going on safari
- disposable nappies
- powdered milk

TOP KENYA BOOKS FOR KIDS

Aimed at children learning about the diverse peoples of the region, the Heritage Library of African Peoples: East Africa is an excellent series. Otherwise, here are some of our favourites:

➡ *Mama Panya's Pancakes: A Village Tale from Kenya* by Joyce Cooper Arkhurst (suitable 4 to 8 years)

➡ *Maasai & I* by Virginia Kroll

➡ *Kenya (Discover Countries)* by Chris Ward

➡ *Kenya: Letters from Around the World* by Ali Brownlie Bojang

➡ *For You Are a Kenyan Child* by Kelly Cunnane

➡ *Jambo Means Hello* by Muriel L Feelings

Most hotels will not charge for children under two years of age. Children between two and 12 years who share their parents' room are usually charged 50% of the adult rate; you'll also get a cot thrown in for this price. Large family rooms are sometimes available, and some places also have adjoining rooms with connecting doors. Be warned that some exclusive lodges impose a minimum age limit for children. Others, though, are more welcoming and lay on child-friendly activities.

Some of the very top-end safari camps operate 'Warrior Training' programs where your little'un's learn how to track elephants, lions and buffalo, light fires without matches, use a bow and arrow and other such things you don't really want them knowing how to do!

Eating

Kenyans are family friendly, and dining out with children is no problem. Hotel restaurants occasionally have high chairs, and while special children's meals aren't common, it's easy enough to find items that are suitable for young diners. Supermarkets stock boxes of fresh juice, and fresh fruit (tangerines, bananas and more) are widely available.

Health

Consult your doctor well in advance of travel as some vaccinations or medications (including some for preventing malaria) are not suitable for children under 12.

Transport

Safari vehicles are usually child-friendly, but travelling between towns in Kenya on public transport is not always easy with children. Car sickness is one problem, and young children tend to be seen as wriggling luggage, so you'll often have them on your lap. Functional seatbelts are rare even in taxis, and accidents are common – a child seat brought from home is a good idea if you're hiring a car or going on safari. You might also want to consider flying some parts of the journey in order to avoid long road journeys.

Top: Dhow, Diani Beach (p220)

Bottom: Masai Mara National Reserve (p112)

Regions at a Glance

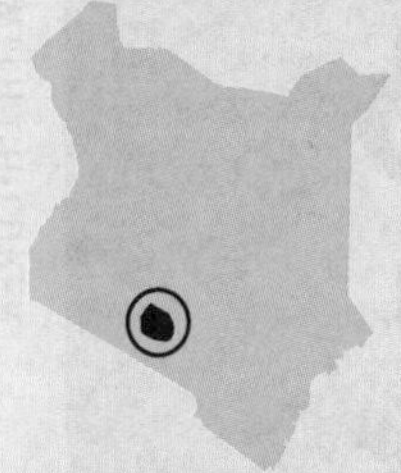

Nairobi

Wildlife
Museums & Slums
Food

City-Fringe Wildlife

Track down the Big Five against an unlikely backdrop of not-so-distant skyscrapers in Nairobi National Park. With a centre for orphaned elephants and a nearby giraffe-breeding centre, Nairobi ranks among Kenya's most surprising wildlife-watching experiences.

Past & Present

Kenya's National Museum is one of Africa's best, an august colonial-era institution that tells Kenya's story exceptionally well, while the Karen Blixen Museum returns you to the realm *Out of Africa* nostalgia. For something completely different, tour Kibera, Nairobi's pulsating heart.

Kenya's Table

Nairobi's culinary variety far surpasses anything you'll find elsewhere in the country. Here there's everything from fast and furious local places to upmarket options that evoke Nairobi's colonial past. And then there's Carnivore, one of Africa's most celebrated restaurants.

p54

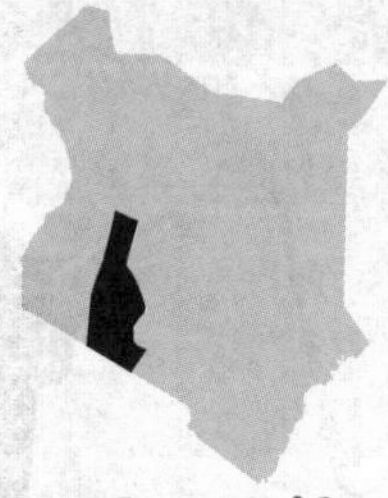

Southern Rift Valley

Landscape
Wildlife
Activities

The Rift Fracture

The drama of Kenya's Rift Valley is one of natural Africa's grand epics, with astonishing rock formations and expansive lakes that are the aesthetic antidote to the horizonless world of the Masai Mara savannah.

Flamingo & Rhino

The Rift Valley lakes are such rare natural phenomena that strange bed fellows are drawn here to cohabit. Delicate flamingos (when the mood takes them) and prehistoric rhinos are the headline acts among many, with fantastic birdlife (over one-third of Kenya's species) guaranteed.

Hike the Rift

While Mts Kenya and Kilimanjaro get all the attention, discerning hikers look to the relatively untrampled summits of Mt Longonot and Mt Susua. And there's nothing like a foot safari through Hell's Gate National Park for heightening the senses.

p87

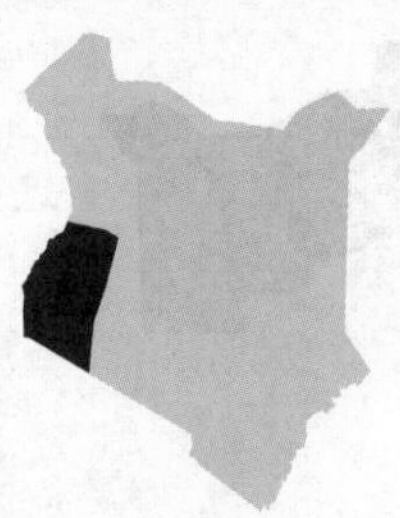

Masai Mara & Western Kenya

Wildlife
Landscape
Birdwatching

Great Migrations

Western Kenya's Masai Mara, together with the Tanzania's Serengeti, is home to the greatest wildlife show on earth. The great predators – lions, leopards, cheetahs – share the plains with the vast congregations of zebras and wildebeest, while elephants and giraffes look on.

Africa in Microcosm

The vast savannah plains of the Masai Mara may grab the headlines, but Western Kenya also boasts Lake Victoria, one of Kenya's most underrated natural wonders, as well as soaring mountains and forests that evoke the endless stands of green in Central Africa.

Birds in Paradise

From graceful secretary birds on the plains of the Mara, to bumbling bright turacos in the jungles of Kakamega, the west flutters with birdlife. Other top spots include Saiwa Swamp and the islands of Lake Victoria.

p110

Central Highlands & Laikipia

Wildlife
Activities
Landscape

Wildlife Plateau

With not a national park to be seen, Laikipia is nonetheless one of the best places in Kenya to see wildlife, from lions and African wild dogs to black and white rhinos. The focus for all this abundance are the cattle-ranches-turned-conservancies which are home to much cutting-edge conservation.

Climbing Mt Kenya

Walk or climb Mt Kenya, Africa's second-highest peak and you'll never forget the incongruity of snows this close to the equator or the sweeping views that extend out across the continent.

The Aberdares

Africa's highest-dwelling elephant herd and all manner of weird and wonderful plants and animal inhabits this forested realm that's utterly unlike the Africa of popular imagination.

p146

Southeastern Kenya

Wildlife
Landscape & Culture
Activities

Pick of the Parks

From the elephant-and-Kili views of Amboseli to the vast, rugged beauty of the Tsavo parks with their history of man-eating lions and rescued rhinos, southeastern Kenya is the scene of some of Kenya's most soulful wildlife experiences.

The Maasai Heartland

The Maasai presence here lends personality to a thinly populated landscape of sweeping savannah plains, volcanic cinder cones and jagged peaks. The ranches around Amboseli and the western foothills of the Chyulu Hills in particular are where the two come together most memorably.

Caves & Climbing

Spelunkers will relish the prospect of the world's longest lava tube in the Chyulu Hills National Park. Climbing is also possible in Tsavo West, as is hiking along the western fringe of the Chyulu Hills.

p181

Mombasa & the South Coast

Beaches
Wildlife
Culture

Sun, Sand & Sea

Despite the occasional rash of package-tourism development, some of East Africa's finest beaches are found on Kenya's south coast. Away from sands that sparkle like crystals, there are islands galore and world-class diving.

Beach & Safari

From elephants, buffaloes and giraffes in the inland reserves to whale sharks and dolphins by the dozen in the oceans, there's a lot of wildlife to be tracked down around here, but it's the profusion of birds that really stands out.

Cultural, Coastal Vibes

Choose from the big-city attractions of Mombasa, with its ancient fort, twisting streets and bubbling contemporary character, or the quiet life found in fishing villages up and down the coast – getting wrapped up in the coast's Swahili culture couldn't be easier.

p202

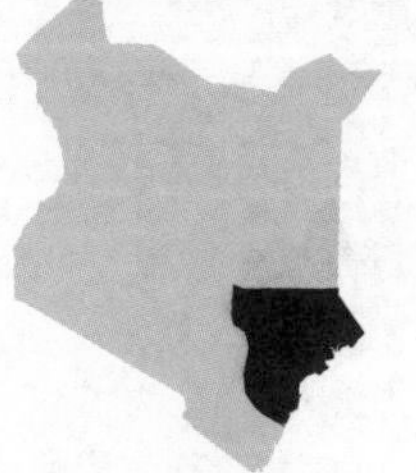

Lamu & the North Coast

Beaches
Wildlife
Culture

Beach Safari

If the security situation allows, pack a bucket and spade and struggle to choose between the lively beach at Malindi, the mellow vibes of Watamu or, maybe best of all, an island-hopping trip by dhow around the sublime sands of the Lamu archipelago.

Butterflies & Elephant Shrews

For most wildlife-watchers the north coast is all about the birds. Everywhere you go around here you'll be accompanied by the sing-song notes of hundreds of different birds, but look a bit harder and you'll find elephant shrews, thousands of butterflies and fish in a plethora of colours.

Live Like a Swahili

Put simply, Lamu is the ultimate immersion in all things Swahili. This gorgeous town of narrow streets and *bui-bui*-clad women is the oldest in Kenya and the most complete Swahili settlement in existence.

p236

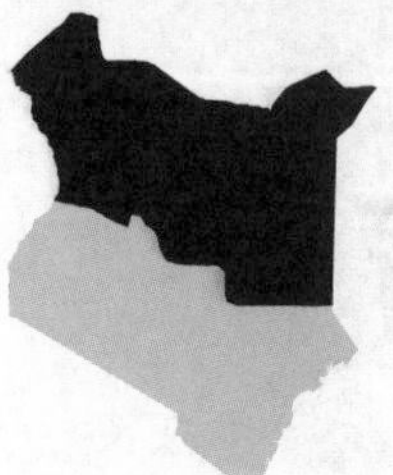

Northern Kenya

Adventure
Wildlife
Culture

The Road Less Travelled

These remote frontier lands where Kenya, Ethiopia, South Sudan and Somalia collide are only just starting to register with foreign tourists, thus giving wannabe explorers a genuine opportunity to go where few have trodden before. You're almost guaranteed, too, to stumble upon large mammals outside of protected areas.

Wild Lands

Deserts where the horizons never seem to end and one of Africa's most beautiful lakes, Lake Turkana, more than compensate for the long days in the saddle on rough tracks you'll need to get here.

A Tribal Heartland

From butterfly-bright Samburu warriors, to the dramatically pierced Turkana women and the elegant Gabbra peoples who wander the burning deserts with their camels, northern Kenya is arguably the tribal heartland of Kenya.

p268

On the Road

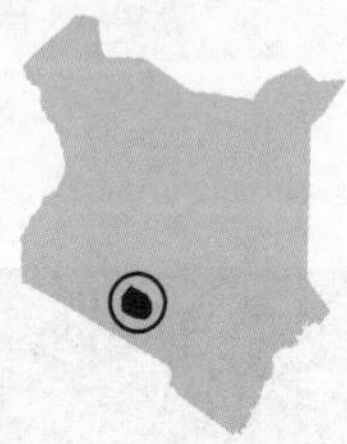

Nairobi

POP 3.363 MILLION / ELEVATION 1661M

Includes ➡

Best of Nature

- Nairobi National Park (p60)
- David Sheldrick Wildlife Trust (p63)
- Giraffe Centre (p63)
- Acacia Camp (p86)

Best of Culture

- Bomas of Kenya (p65)
- National Museum (p57)
- African Heritage House (p65)
- Karen Blixen's House & Museum (p64)

Why Go?

Telling people that you like Nairobi is like voicing a guilty secret. Yes, Nairobi's reputation precedes it. And yes, it's a city where it pays to keep your wits about you. But there are many people who don't just like Nairobi but who wouldn't want to live anywhere else. For those who call it home, the city's muscular, cosmopolitan charms include a vibrant cultural life, fabulous places to eat and exciting nightlife. If you're just passing through, this melting pot of people and attractions has the intriguing National Museum, an unlikely national park (black rhinos and all), an irresistible elephant orphanage, the ground zero for the Rothschild's giraffe, Karen Blixen's former home and so much more. Welcome to one of Africa's most dynamic cities, a place you'll almost certainly pass through and one that you could just learn to like if you give it half a chance.

When to Go

Nairobi

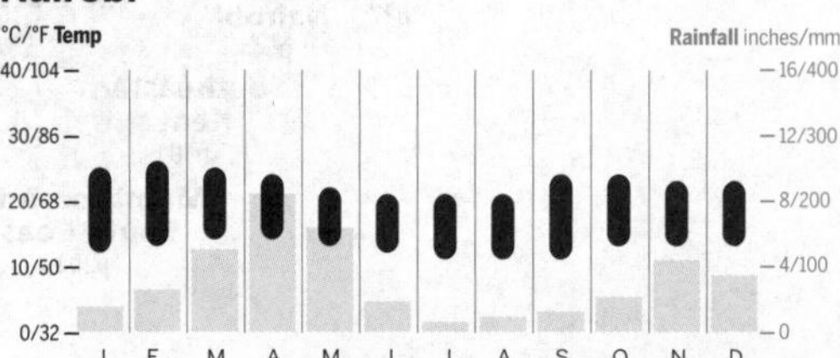

Jan & Feb, Jun–Sep The driest months; Nairobi National Park is at its best

Oct & Nov The rain cools things off without causing more than the usual traffic jams

Mar–May You don't want to be here when it rains, and rains, and rains...

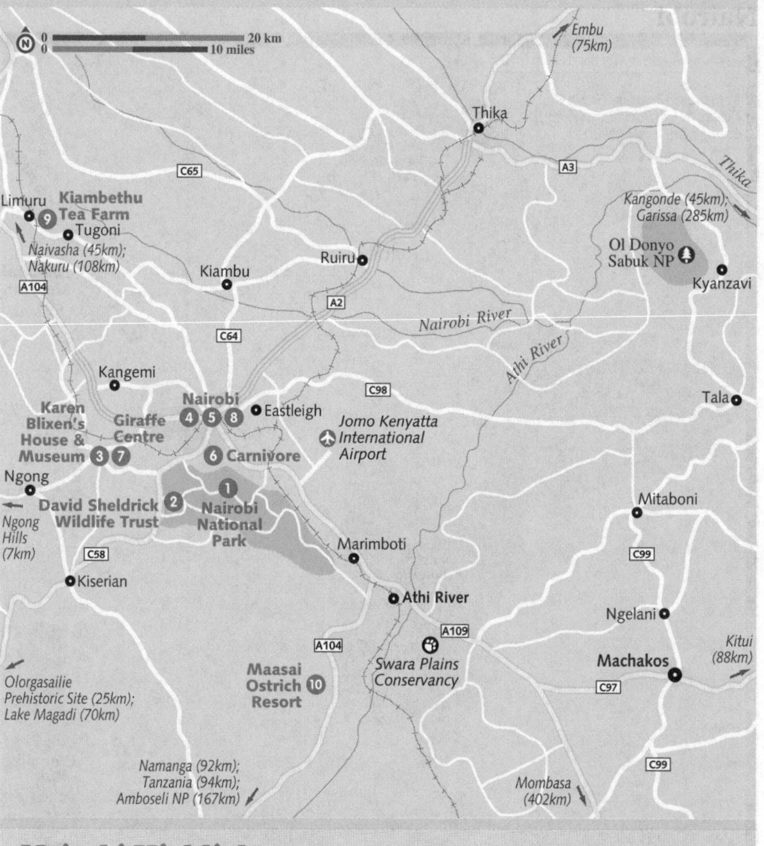

Nairobi Highlights

1. Searching for wildlife in the most incongruous of places at **Nairobi National Park** (p60)
2. Bottle-feeding a gleeful group of baby elephants at the **David Sheldrick Wildlife Trust** (p63)
3. Indulging your inner Meryl Streep at the Railway Museum and **Karen Blixen's House & Museum** (p64)
4. Deepening your understanding of all things Kenyan at the **National Museum** (p57)
5. Learning how much of Nairobi lives by taking a tour of **Kibera** (p73)
6. Making the essential foodie pilgrimage to **Carnivore** (p75)
7. Tangling tongues with an endangered Rothschild's giraffe at Langata's **Giraffe Centre** (p63)
8. Listening for the echoes of tall tales told by colonial types at **Lord Delamere Terrace & Bar** (p77)
9. Taking to the hills to learn about tea at **Kiambethu Tea Farm** (p86)
10. Trying to take a selfie while riding an ostrich at the **Maasai Ostrich Resort** (p86)

History

Nairobi is a completely modern creation, and everything here has been built in the last 115 years. As the tracks of the East African Railway were laid down between Mombasa and Kampala, a depot was established at a small stream known to the Maasai as *uaso nairobi* (cold water). The Maasai were quickly removed from the land, as the British East Africa protectorate had ambitious plans to open up the interior to white colonial settlement.

Nairobi

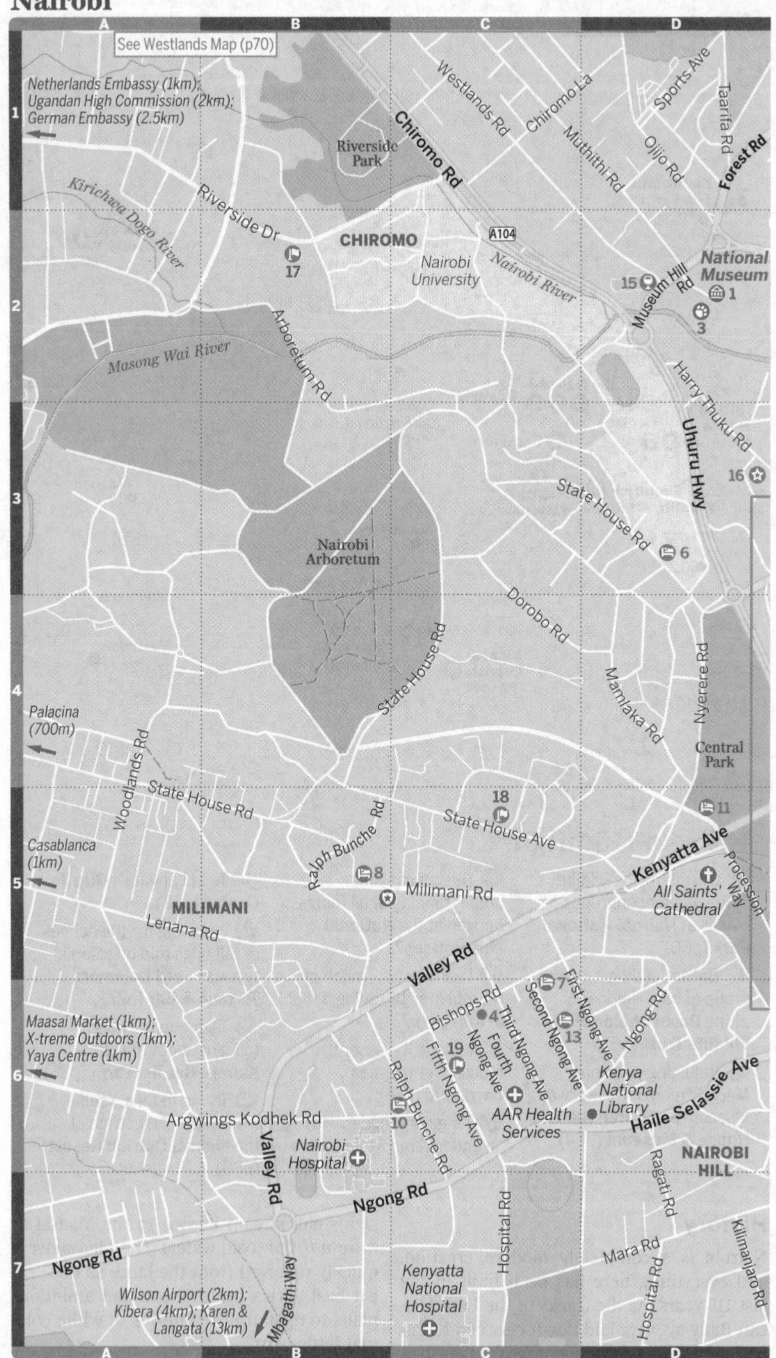

See Westlands Map (p70)
Netherlands Embassy (1km); Ugandan High Commission (2km); German Embassy (2.5km)
Riverside Park
Chiromo Rd
Westlands Rd
Chiromo La
Muthithi Rd
Sports Ave
Ojijo Rd
Taarifa Rd
Forest Rd
Kirichwa Dogo River
Riverside Dr
CHIROMO
A104
Nairobi University
Nairobi River
17
15
Museum Hill Rd
National Museum
1
3
Masong Wai River
Arboretum Rd
Harry Thuku Rd
Uhuru Hwy
16
State House Rd
Nairobi Arboretum
6
Dorobo Rd
State House Rd
Mamlaka Rd
Nyerere Rd
Palacina (700m)
Central Park
Woodlands Rd
State House Rd
18
11
State House Ave
Ralph Bunche Rd
Kenyatta Ave
Casablanca (1km)
8
Milimani Rd
All Saints' Cathedral
Processional Way
MILIMANI
Lenana Rd
Valley Rd
7
First Ngong Ave
Second Ngong Ave
Bishops Rd
4
Third Ngong Ave
13
Ngong Rd
Maasai Market (1km); X-treme Outdoors (1km); Yaya Centre (1km)
19
Fourth Ngong Ave
Fifth Ngong Ave
Kenya National Library
Haile Selassie Ave
Ralph Bunche Rd
AAR Health Services
Argwings Kodhek Rd
10
Valley Rd
Nairobi Hospital
NAIROBI HILL
Ragati Rd
Ngong Rd
Hospital Rd
Mara Rd
Kilimanjaro Rd
Ngong Rd
Wilson Airport (2km); Kibera (4km); Karen & Langata (13km)
Mbagathi Way
Kenyatta National Hospital
Hospital Rd

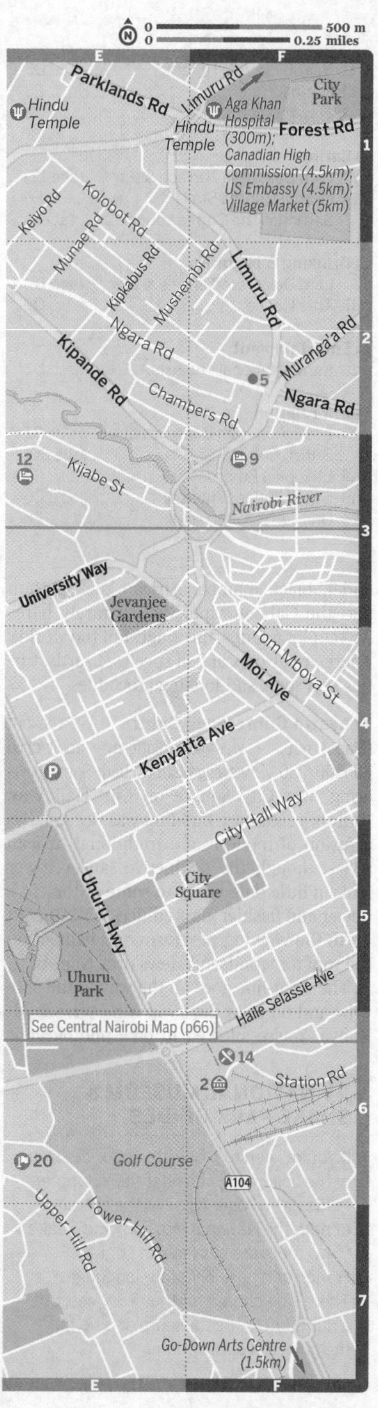

In addition to its strategic position between the coast and British holdings in Uganda, Nairobi benefited from its hospitable environment – water was abundant and the high elevation enjoyed cooler temperatures than the coast. Although Nairobi was blighted by frequent fires and an outbreak of the plague, by 1907 the booming commercial centre had replaced Mombasa as the capital of British East Africa.

Quite early on, the colonial government built some grand hotels to accommodate the first tourists to Kenya – big-game hunters, lured by the attraction of shooting the country's almost naively tame wildlife. In 1946, Nairobi National Park was established as the first national park in East Africa.

After achieving independence in 1963, Nairobi grew too rapidly, putting a great deal of pressure on the city's infrastructure. Enormous shanty towns of tin-roofed settlements appeared on the outskirts of the capital. In the name of modernisation, almost all of the colonial-era buildings were replaced by concrete office buildings, which today characterise much of the modern city.

As Kenya's and East Africa's largest city, Nairobi continues to face enormous challenges. Terrorist attacks on the US embassy in 1998 killed more than 200 people, while in December 2007 the shanty towns of Nairobi were set ablaze as riots broke out following the disputed presidential election. And in recent years, the Somali Islamist group has claimed responsibility for a spate of bombings on transport around Nairobi's Eastleigh suburb, as well as for the devastating attack on the exclusive Westgate Shopping Mall on 21 September 2013; 67 people died in the latter assault.

Sights

City Centre

★National Museum MUSEUM
(Map p56; ☎Nairobi 020-8164134; www.museums.or.ke; Museum Hill Rd; adult/child KSh1200/600, combined ticket with Snake Park KSh1500/1000; ⏲8.30am-5.30pm) Kenya's wonderful National Museum, housed in an imposing building amid lush, leafy grounds just outside the centre, has a good range of cultural and natural history exhibits. Aside from the exhibits, check out the life-sized fibreglass model of pachyderm celebrity Ahmed, the massive elephant who became a symbol of Kenya at

Nairobi

Top Sights
1 National Museum....D2

Sights
2 Railway Museum....F6
3 Snake Park....D2

Activities, Courses & Tours
4 ACK Language & Orientation School....C6
Kenya Youth Voluntary Development Projects....(see 10)
Nature Kenya....(see 1)
5 Pal-Davis Adventures....F2

Sleeping
6 Central YMCA....D3
7 Fairview Hotel....C6
8 Heron Hotel....B5
9 Kahama Hotel....F3
10 Nairobi International Youth Hostel....C6
11 Nairobi Serena Hotel....D5
12 Norfolk Hotel....E3
13 Town Lodge....C6

Eating
Lord Delamere Terrace & Bar....(see 12)
14 Nyama Choma Stalls....F6
Savanna: The Coffee Lounge....(see 1)

Drinking & Nightlife
Lord Delamere Terrace & Bar....(see 12)
15 Tree House....D2

Entertainment
16 Kenya National Theatre....D3

Information
17 Australian High Commission....B2
British Council....(see 20)
18 Ethiopian Embassy....C5
19 South Sudan Embassy....C6
20 UK High Commission....E6

the height of the 1980s poaching crisis, and who was placed under 24-hour guard by Jomo Kenyatta; he's in the inner courtyard next to the shop.

The museum's permanent collection is entered via the **Hall of Kenya**, with some ethnological exhibits, but this is a mere prelude. In a room off this hall is the **Birds of East Africa** exhibit, a huge gallery of at least 900 stuffed specimens. In an adjacent room is the **Great Hall of Mammals**, with dozens of stuffed mammals. Off the mammals room is the **Cradle of Humankind** exhibition, the highlight of which is the **Hominid Skull Room** – an extraordinary collection of skulls that describes itself as 'the single most important collection of early human fossils in the world'.

Upstairs, the **Historia Ya Kenya** display is an engaging journey through Kenyan and East African history. It's well-presented, well-documented and offers a refreshingly Kenyan counterpoint to colonial historiographies. Also on the 1st floor, the **Cycles of Life** room is rich in ethnological artefacts from Kenya's various tribes and ethnic groups.

Snake Park ZOO

(Map p56; www.museums.or.ke; Museum Hill Rd; adult/child KSh1200/600, combined ticket with National Museum KSh1500/1000; 8.30am-5.30pm) In the grounds of the National Museum, the zoo-like Snake Park has some impressive snake species, including the puff adder, black mamba, African rock python and the Gaboon viper (which rarely bares its 4cm-long fangs, the longest in the world). There are also local fish species, lizards, turtles and some sad-looking crocodiles.

Kenyatta Conference Centre LOOKOUT

(Map p66; viewing platform adult/child KSh500/250; viewing platform 9am-6pm) Towering over City Square on City Hall Way, Nairobi's signature building was designed as a fusion of modern and traditional African styles, though the distinctive saucer tower looks a little dated next to some of the city's newer and flashier glass edifices. Take the lift up to the **viewing platform** and helipad on the roof for wonderful views over Nairobi.

The sight-line goes all the way to the suburbs and on clear days you can even see Mt Kenya. You're allowed to take photographs

NATIONAL MUSEUM & SNAKE PARK GUIDES

If you're keen to really get under the skin of the collection, consider the volunteer guides who linger close to the entrance of both the National Museum and Snake Park. Tours are available in English, French and possibly other languages. There's no charge for their services, but a donation to the museum or a tip for the guides is appropriate.

from the viewing level but not elsewhere in the building.

Railway Museum MUSEUM

(Map p56; Station Rd; adult/child KSh500/100; ⌚8am-5pm) The main collection here is housed in an old railway building and consists of relics from the East African Railway. There are train and ship models, photographs, tableware, and oddities from the history of the railway, such as the engine seat that allowed visiting dignitaries like Theodore Roosevelt to take potshots at unsuspecting wildlife from the front of the train.

In the grounds are dozens of fading locomotives in various states of disrepair, dating from the steam days to independence. You can walk around the carriages at your leisure. At the back of the compound is the steam train used in the movie *Out of Africa*. It's a fascinating introduction to this important piece of colonial history.

The museum is reached by a long lane beside the train station.

National Archives ARCHIVES

(Map p66; ☎Nairobi 020-749341; Moi Ave; ⌚8.30am-5pm Mon-Fri, 8.30am-1pm Sat) FREE Right in the bustling heart of Nairobi is the distinctive National Archives, the 'Memory of the Nation', a vast collection of documents and reference materials. It's mainly used by students and researchers, but the ground-floor atrium and gallery display an eclectic selection of contemporary art, historical photos of Nairobi, cultural artefacts, furniture and tribal objects.

Uhuru Park PARK

(Map p66) FREE An expanse of manicured green on the fringe of the CBD, this attractive city park is a popular respite from all the downtown noise and bustle. It owes its existence to Wangari Maathai, a Kenyan Nobel Peace Prize winner. In the late 1980s, she fought to save the park from the bulldozers of the former Moi government. Upon her death in late 2011, her funeral was held in the park and attended by thousands of mourners.

During the day, the park attracts picnicking families, businessmen stepping out of the office and just about anyone in need of a little green. It's not safe after dark.

Parliament House NOTABLE BUILDING

(Map p66; www.parliament.go.ke; Parliament Rd) If you fancy a look at how democracy works (or doesn't) in Kenya, it's possible to obtain a free permit for a seat in the public gallery at Parliament House when the parliament is in session; visit the gate office to obtain a visitor permit and remember that applause is strictly forbidden... If parliament is out of session, you can tour the buildings by arrangement with the sergeant-at-arms,

NAIROBI IN...

Two Days

Start by getting up close and personal with wildlife at the **Giraffe Centre** (p63) and the **David Sheldrick Wildlife Trust** (p63). A visit to **Karen Blixen's House & Museum** (p64) is recommended for *Out of Africa* fans, then go shopping at the **Kazuri Beads & Pottery Centre** (p64) and **Utamaduni** (p79). In the evening, dine at **Carnivore** (p75) and dance at the **Simba Saloon** (p79).

On day two, head downtown to visit the **National Museum** (p57), view the city from the **Kenyatta Conference Centre** (p58), and step back in colonial time at the **Railway Museum** (p59); for lunch, join the scrum at the nearby **Nyama Choma Stalls** (p74). Have a drink at the legendary **Thorn Tree** (p75) or **Lord Delamere Terrace & Bar** (p77). In the evening, eat posh at **Tamarind Restaurant** (p75) and have a whole lot of fun at **Simmers** (p77).

Four Days

Spend the best part of your third day in **Nairobi National Park** (p60). For dinner, eat at the **Karen Blixen Coffee Garden** (p76).

For your final 24 hours, take a tour of **Kibera shanty town** (p73), do a bit of shopping in the **curio markets** (p80), eat at **Haandi** (p75), Kenya's best Indian restaurant, then drink the night away at **Gypsy's Bar** (p77).

although agree to any fee before you begin. Start at KSh100 and see where it gets you.

American Embassy Memorial Garden GARDENS

(Map p66; Moi Ave; admission KSh100; ⊙8am-6pm) This well-tended walled garden occupies the former site of the American embassy, which was destroyed by terrorist bombings in 1998. It's a lovely spot, despite being right between busy Moi and Haile Selassie Aves. The entrance fee pays for maintenance, and keeps numbers down.

Nairobi National Park

★Nairobi National Park PARK

(Map p60; ☎Nairobi 020-2423423; www.kws.org/parks/parks_reserves/NANP.html; adult/child US$50/25) Welcome to Kenya's most accessible yet incongruous safari experience. Set on the city's southern outskirts, Nairobi National Park (at 117 sq km, it's one of Africa's smallest) has abundant wildlife which can, in places, be viewed against a backdrop of city skyscrapers and airliners coming in to land – it's the only national park on earth that borders a capital city. Remarkably, the animals seem utterly unperturbed by it all.

Nairobi National Park

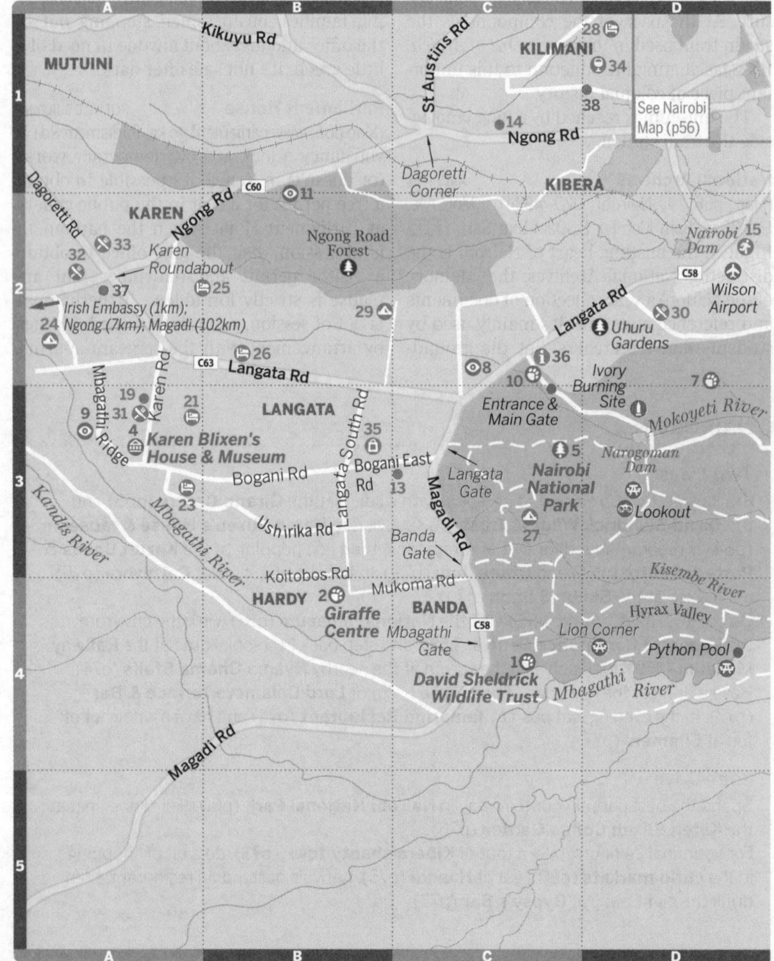

➡ **Wildlife**

Nairobi National Park has acquired the nickname 'Kifaru Ark', a testament to its success as a rhinoceros (*kifaru* in Kiswahili) sanctuary. The park is home to the world's densest concentration of black rhinoceros (over 50). But even proximity to Kenya's largest city couldn't prevent poachers from killing one of the park's rhinos in August 2013. It was the first such attack in six years.

Lions and hyenas are also commonly sighted within the park; park rangers at the entrance usually have updates on lion movements. You'll need a bit of patience and a lot of luck to spot the park's resident cheetahs and leopards. Other regularly spotted species include gazelle, warthog, zebra, giraffe, ostrich and buffalo.

The park's wetland areas also sustain approximately 400 bird species, which is more than in the whole of the UK.

➡ **Ivory Burning Monument**

Not far inside the park's main Langata Road gate, the Ivory Burning Monument marks the spot where, in 1989, Kenyan President Daniel arap Moi burnt 12 tons of ivory at a site near the main gate. This dramatic event improved Kenya's conservation image

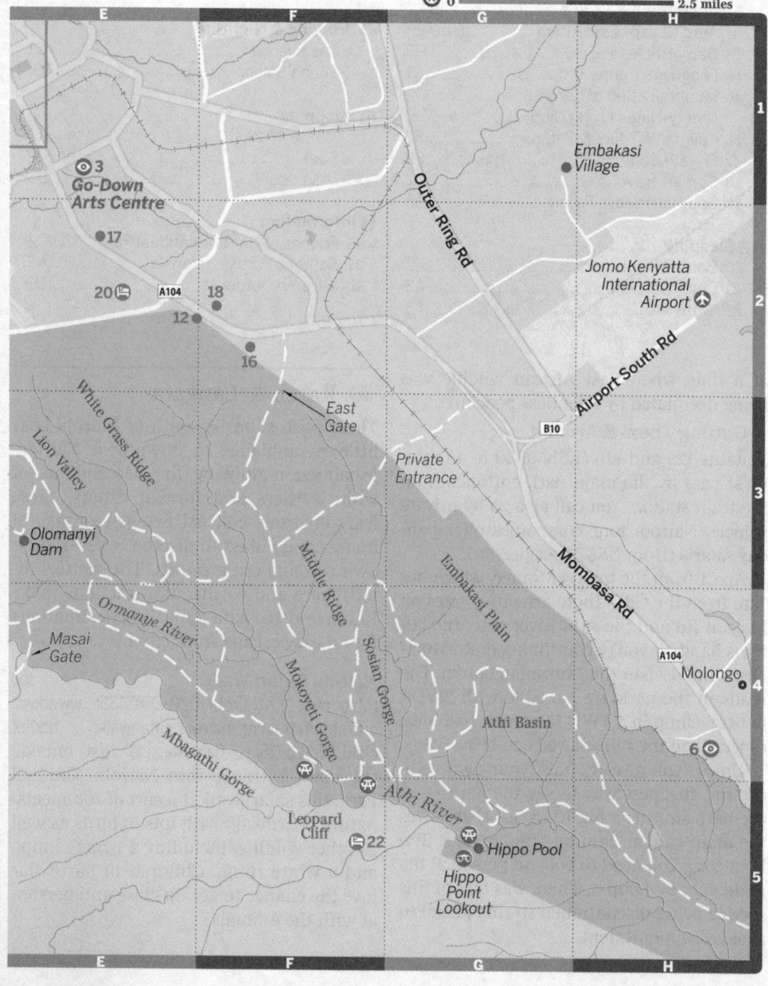

Nairobi National Park

Top Sights

1	David Sheldrick Wildlife Trust	C4
2	Giraffe Centre	B4
3	Go-Down Arts Centre	E1
4	Karen Blixen's House & Museum	A3
5	Nairobi National Park	C3

Sights

6	African Heritage House	H4
7	Animal Orphanage	D2
8	Bomas of Kenya	C2
9	Kazuri Beads & Pottery Centre	A3
10	Nairobi Safari Walk	C2
11	Ngong Hills Racecourse	B2

Activities, Courses & Tours

12	Abercrombie & Kent	E2
	Aero Club of East Africa	(see 15)
13	Gametrackers	C3
14	Language Center Ltd	C1
15	Mountain Club of Kenya	D2
	Ninety-Nines Flying Club	(see 15)
16	Pollman's Tours & Safaris	F2
17	Private Safaris	E2
18	Somak Travel	F2
19	Southern Cross Safaris	A3

Sleeping

20	Boma Nairobi	E2
21	Dea's Gardens	A3
22	Emakoko	F5
	Giraffe Manor	(see 2)
23	House of Waine	A3
	Karen Blixen Cottages	(see 31)
24	Karen Camp	A2
25	Margarita House	B2
26	Milimani Backpackers & Safari Centre	B2
27	Nairobi Tented Camp	C3
28	Palacina	D1
29	Wildebeest Eco Camp	B2

Eating

30	Carnivore	D2
31	Karen Blixen Coffee Garden	A3
32	Talisman	A2
33	Tin Roof Cafe	A2

Drinking & Nightlife

34	Casablanca	D1
	Simba Saloon	(see 30)

Shopping

	Maasai Market	(see 38)
	Souk	(see 33)
35	Utamaduni	B3

Information

36	Friends of Nairobi National Park	C2
37	Southern Cross Safaris	A2
38	X-treme Outdoors	D1

at a time when East African wildlife was being decimated by relentless poaching.

➡ **Getting There & Around**

Matatus 125 and 126 (KSh50, 30 to 45 minutes) pass by the main park entrance from the train station. You can also go by private vehicle. Nairobi tour companies offer half-day safaris (from US$75 per person).

Apart from the main entrance, which lies 7km from the CBD, there are other gates on Magadi Rd and the Athi River gate; the latter is handy if you're continuing on to Mombasa, Amboseli or the Tanzanian border. The roads in the park are passable with 2WDs, but travelling in a 4WD is never a bad idea, especially if the rains have been heavy.

Unless you already have your own vehicle, the cheapest way to see the park is on the park shuttle, a big KWS bus that leaves the main gate at 2pm on Sunday for a 2½-hour tour. You need to book in person at the main gate by 1.30pm. There was talk of this service being discontinued so ring ahead to avoid disappointment.

Karen & Langata

These posh suburbs south of Nairobi bear little resemblance to downtown Nairobi. Inhabited mainly by the descendants of white settlers and foreign expats, these leafy environs conceal extensive ranks of houses and villas, all discreetly set in their own colonial-era grounds. The genteel atmosphere and wealth of attractions make Karen and Langata appealing destinations for an easy escape from city life.

Nairobi Safari Walk ZOO

(Map p60; ☎Nairobi 020-2587435; www.kws.org/about/training/nairobi_safariwalk; adult/child US$25/15; ⏲6am-sunset) Just outside the main entrance into Nairobi National Park, this safari walk is a sort of zoo-meets-nature boardwalk with lots of birds as well as other wildlife, including a pygmy hippo and a white rhino. Children in particular love the chance to get up close and personal with the animals.

Animal Orphanage ZOO
(Map p60; ☎Nairobi 020-2587411; www.kws.org/parks/education/animal_orphanage; adult/child US$25/15; ⌚8.30am-5.30pm) Just inside the main gate to Nairobi National Park, this animal orphanage houses formerly wild animals that have been recovered by park rangers. Although the conditions the animals are kept in are less than inspiring, the orphanage does protect animals that would have died without human intervention. It also serves as a valuable education centre for locals and school children who might not otherwise have the chance to interact with wildlife.

★**Giraffe Centre** WILDLIFE RESERVE
(Map p60; ☎Nairobi 020-8070804; www.giraffecenter.org; Koitobos Rd; adult/child KSh1000/500; ⌚9am-5pm) This centre, which protects the highly endangered Rothschild's giraffe, combines serious conservation with enjoyable activities. You can observe, hand-feed or even kiss one of the giraffes from a raised wooden structure, which is quite an experience. You may also spot warthogs snuffling about in the mud, and there's an interesting self-guided forest walk through the adjacent **Gogo River Bird Sanctuary**.

This is one of Kenya's good-news conservation stories. In 1979 Jock Leslie-Melville (the Kenyan grandson of a Scottish earl) and his wife Betty began raising a baby giraffe in their Langata home. At the time, when their African Fund for Endangered Wildlife (AFEW) was just getting off the ground, there were no more than 120 Rothschild's giraffes (which differ from other giraffe subspecies in that there is no patterning below the knee) in the wild. Unlike the more common reticulated and Masai giraffes, the Rothschild's giraffe had been pushed to the brink of extinction by severe habitat loss in western Kenya.

Today, the population numbers more than 300, and the centre has successfully released these charismatic creatures into Lake Nakuru National Park (home to around 45 giraffes), Mwea National Reserve, Ruma National Park and Nasalot National Reserve.

To get here from central Nairobi by public transport, take matatu 24 via Kenyatta Ave to the Hardy shops, and walk from there. Alternatively, take matatu 26 to Magadi Rd, and walk through from Mukoma Rd. A taxi should cost around KSh1000 from the city centre.

★**David Sheldrick Wildlife Trust** WILDLIFE RESERVE
(Map p60; ☎Nairobi 020-2301396; www.sheldrickwildlifetrust.org) Occupying a plot within Nairobi National Park, this nonprofit trust was established in 1977, shortly after the death of David Sheldrick, who served as the anti-poaching warden of Tsavo National Park. Together with his wife Daphne, David pioneered techniques for raising orphaned black rhinos and elephants and reintroducing them back into the wild, and the trust retains close links

THE TROUBLE WITH NAIROBI NATIONAL PARK

There's one very good reason why Nairobi has its own national park: cities and wildlife don't mix. As Nairobi boomed in the early 20th century, conflicts between humans and animals were rampant. Early residents of the capital were forced to carry guns at night to protect themselves from lions and rhinos, while herd animals routinely raided country farms. As a result, the colonial government of British East Africa set about confining the game animals to the Athi plains to the west and south of Nairobi. In 1946, Nairobi National Park became the first national park in British East Africa, although the event was not without controversy, as the Maasai pastoralists were forcibly removed from the parklands.

The conflict between human and wildlife continues in the park today. The park is fenced in parts to keep the wildlife out of the city, although it's not a closed system and is instead kept open to allow animals to migrate along a narrow wildlife corridor to southern Kenya or the Masai Mara. With human settlements almost completely encircling the park, however, such corridors are almost completely closed and the migrations will soon be a thing of the past. What that means for animals that survive by following the rains or for the ecosystems within the park is a topic of great concern for conservationists.

For more information about efforts to save the park, contact **Friends of Nairobi National Park** (Map p60; ☎Nairobi 020-500622; www.fonnap.wordpress.com; Kenya Wildlife Service Headquarters, Langata Rd). The group aims to protect migration corridors connecting in with other Kenyan regions as well as raising awareness about the park.

with Tsavo for these and other projects. The centre is one of Nairobi's most popular attractions, and deservedly so.

After entering at 11am, visitors are escorted to a small viewing area centred on a muddy watering hole. A few moments later, much like a sports team marching out onto the field, the animal handlers come in alongside a dozen or so baby elephants. For the first part of the viewing, the handlers bottle-feed the baby elephants – a strangely heartwarming sight.

Once the little guys have drunk their fill, they proceed to romp around like big babies. The elephants seem to take joy in misbehaving in front of their masters, so don't be surprised if a few break rank and start rubbing up against your leg! The baby elephants also use this designated timeslot for their daily mud bath, which makes for some great photos; keep your guard up as they've been known to spray a tourist or two with a trunkful of mud.

While the elephants gambol around, the keepers talk about the individual orphans and their stories. Explanations are also given about the the broader picture of the orphans project and some of the other projects the David Sheldrick Wildlife Trust is involved in. There's also the opportunity to 'adopt' one of the elephants.

The Trust is also home to a number of orphaned rhinos, many of which, like the baby elephants, mingle with wild herds in Nairobi National Park during the day. One exception is Maxwell, a blind rhino who lives in a large stockade for his protection.

To get here by bus or matatu, take 125 or 126 from Moi Ave and ask to be dropped off at the KWS central workshop on Magadi Rd (KSh60, 50 minutes). It's about 1km from the workshop gate to the Sheldrick centre – it's signposted and KWS staff can give you directions. Be advised that at this point you'll be walking in the national park, which does contain predators, so stick to the paths. A taxi should cost between KSh1500 and KSh2000 from the city centre.

★Karen Blixen's House & Museum HISTORIC BUILDING

(Map p60; www.museums.or.ke; Karen Rd; adult/child KSh1200/600; ⏲9.30am-6pm) If you loved *Out of Africa*, you'll love this place. This museum is the farmhouse where author Karen Blixen lived between 1914 and 1931. She left after a series of personal tragedies, but the lovely colonial house has been preserved as a museum. The museum is set in expansive gardens, and is an interesting place to wander around. That said, the movie was actually shot at a nearby location, so don't be surprised if things don't look entirely right!

Guides (non-mandatory, but useful) are included in the admission fee, but they do expect a tip.

The museum is about 2km from Langata Rd. The easiest way to get here by public transport is by matatu 24 via Kenyatta Ave, which passes right by the entrance. A taxi should cost between KSh1500 and KSh2000 from the city centre.

Kazuri Beads & Pottery Centre CRAFT CENTRE

(Map p60; ☎Nairobi 020-2328905; www.kazuri.com; Mbagathi Ridge; ⏲shop 8.30am-6pm Mon-Sat, 9am-5pm Sun, factory 8am-4.30pm Mon-Fri, 8am-1pm Sat) An interesting diversion in Karen, this craft centre was started up by an

KAREN BLIXEN

The suburb of Karen takes its name from Karen Blixen, aka Isak Dinesen, a Danish coffee planter and aristocrat who went on to become one of Europe's most famous writers on Africa. Although she lived a life of genteel luxury on the edge of the Ngong Hills, her personal life was full of heartbreak. After her first marriage broke down, she began a love affair with the British playboy Denys Finch Hatton, who subsequently died in a plane crash during one of his frequent flying visits to Tsavo National Park (see page 85 for more information). After the farm came close to bankruptcy, Blixen returned to Denmark, where she began her famous memoir *Out of Africa*. The book is one of the definitive tales of European endeavour in Africa, but Blixen was passed over for the 1954 Nobel Prize for Literature in favour of Ernest Hemingway. She died from malnutrition at her family estate in Denmark in 1962.

Out of Africa was made into a movie in 1985, starring Meryl Streep, Robert Redford and one of the retired trains from Nairobi's Railway Museum. The final production was terrific from a Hollywood perspective, but leaves out enough of the colonial history to irk historians and Kenyan nationalists alike.

English expat in 1975 as a place where single mothers could learn a marketable skill and achieve self-sufficiency. From humble beginnings, the workforce has burgeoned to over 100. A free tour takes you into the various factory buildings, where you can observe the process from the moulding of raw clay to the glazing of the finished products. There's also a gift shop with fixed prices.

Bomas of Kenya CULTURAL CENTRE
(Map p60; ☎Nairobi 020-8068400; www.bomasofkenya.co.ke; Langata Rd; adult/child KSh800/400; ⏲performances 2.30-4pm Mon-Fri, 3.30-5.15pm Sat & Sun, 'villages' 10am-6pm Sat & Sun) The talented resident artists at this cultural centre perform traditional dances and songs taken from the country's various tribal groups, including Arabic-influenced Swahili *taarab* music, Kalenjin warrior dances, Embu drumming and Kikuyu circumcision ceremonies. It's touristy, of course, but still a spectacular afternoon out. The complex consists of a number of bomas or villages, each constructed in the architectural style of Kenya's major ethnic groups.

The centre is at Langata, near Nairobi National Park's main gate. Bus or matatu 125 or 126 runs here from Nairobi train station (KSh50, 30 minutes). Get off at Magadi Rd, from where it's about a 1km walk, clearly signposted on the right-hand side of the road. A taxi should set you back between KSh1500 and KSh2000.

African Heritage House BUILDING
(Map p60; ☎0721518389; www.africanheritagebook.com; off Mombasa Rd) FREE Designed by Alan Donovan, an African-heritage expert and gallery owner, this stunning exhibition house overlooking Nairobi National Park can be visited by prior arrangement only. The mud architecture combines a range of traditional styles from across Africa, and the interior is furnished exclusively with tribal artefacts and artworks. For those with a bit of money to burn, it's possible to negotiate overnight stays, formal meals and luxurious transfers by steam train or helicopter.

Watch this space, however, as the government's plans for a new railway line between Nairobi and Mombasa has placed the house in serious danger of being demolished.

Activities

Nature Kenya BIRDWATCHING
(Map p56; ☎0771343138, Nairobi 020-3537568; www.naturekenya.org; temporary membership per person KSh200) Organises a variety of outings, including half-day bird walks that depart from the National Museum. Annual membership costs US$40. Contact them for more information.

Mountain Club of Kenya CLIMBING
(MCK; Map p60; www.mck.or.ke; Wilson Airport) The club meets at 8pm every Tuesday at the clubhouse behind Langata Shopping Centre. Members organise frequent climbing and trekking weekends around the country and have a huge pool of technical knowledge about climbing in Kenya.

Tours

★Explore Kibera TOUR
(www.explorekibera.com; per person US$29; ⏲9am & 2pm daily) Running since 2009, these three-hour tours take you deep into Kibera from the famous railway track to markets and local beadmakers and other artisans.

★Kibera Tours TOUR
(☎0721391630, 0723669218; kiberatours.com; per person KSh2500) This well-regarded tour by two Kibera residents takes you to Toi Market,

WHERE TO RELIVE *OUT OF AFRICA* IN KENYA

It was the film that made an entire generation long for East Africa. If you ever dreamed of following in the footsteps of Meryl Streep and Robert Redford, this list may just guide your path around Kenya.

Karen Blixen's House & Museum, Nairobi Where the real-life Karen Blixen actually lived (if not where the film was shot…).

Railway Museum, Nairobi (p59) Board the steam train used in the movie.

Grave of Denys Finch Hatton, Ngong Hills (p85) Disappointingly unkempt for the last resting place of Blixen's celebrated lover.

Segera Retreat, Laikipia (p159) See (and perhaps even go for a ride in) the very plane in which Meryl Streep and Robert Redford flew out across the savannah.

Shaba National Reserve, Northern Kenya (p274) Many of the outdoor scenes were filmed here; northeast of Isiolo.

Central Nairobi

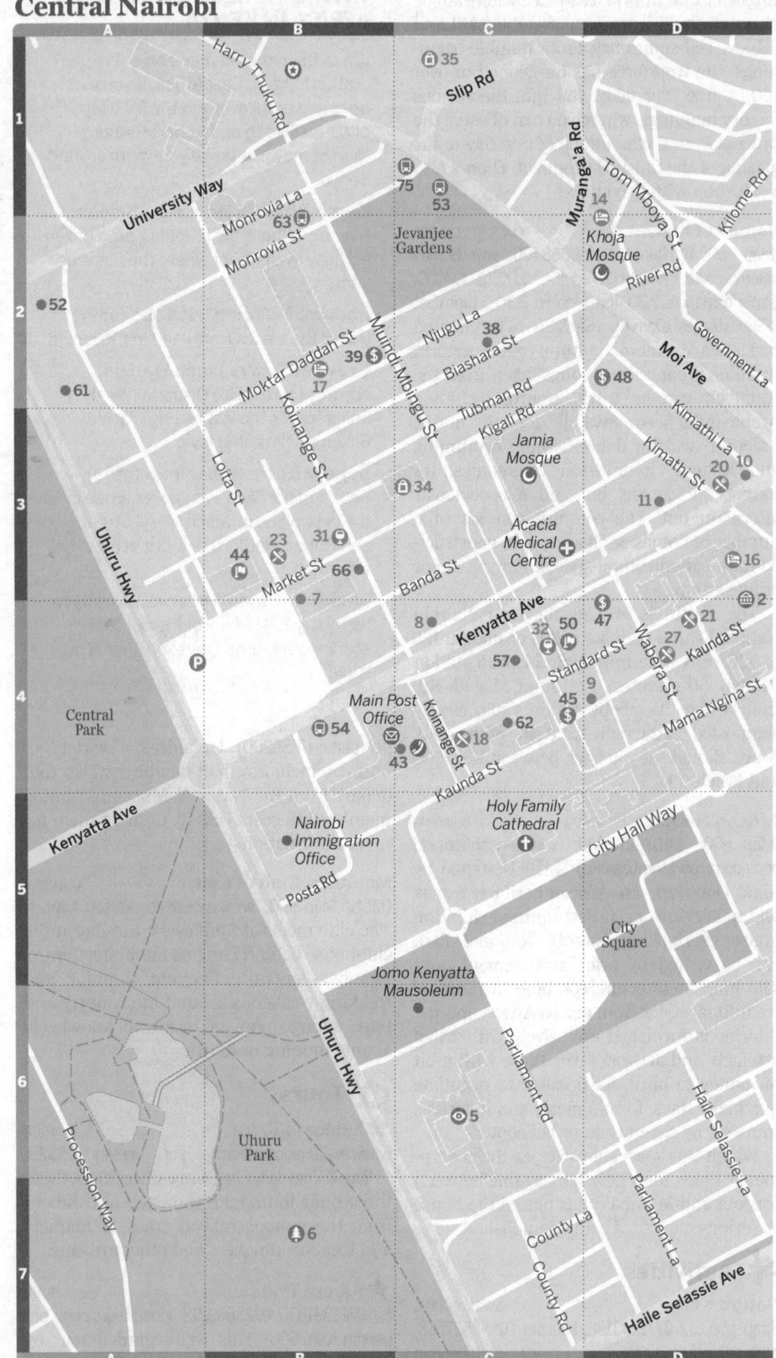

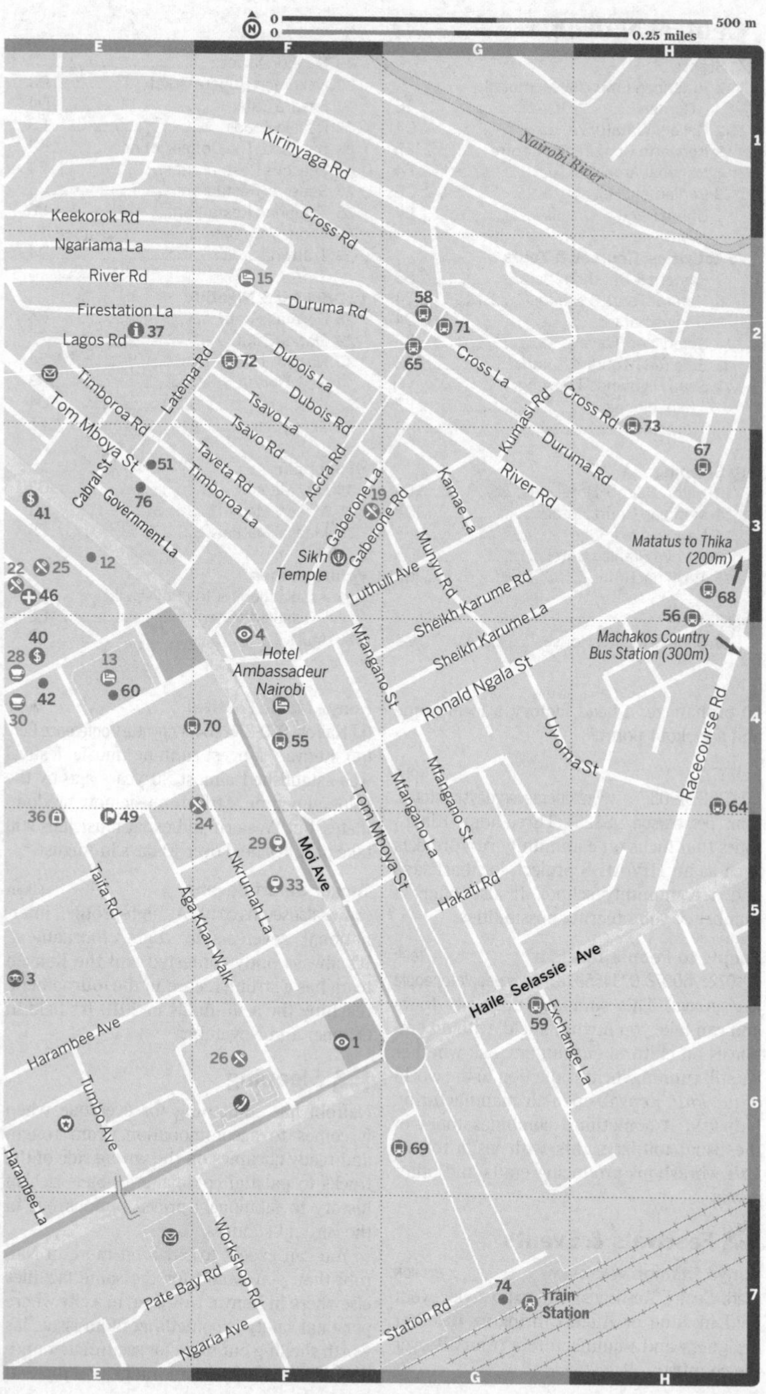

0
500 m
0
0.25 miles
E
F
G
H
1
2
3
4
5
6
7
Nairobi River
Kirinyaga Rd
Cross Rd
Keekorok Rd
Ngariama La
River Rd
15
Firestation La
Lagos Rd
37
Duruma Rd
58
71
65
72
Latema Rd
Dubois La
Dubois Rd
Tsavo La
Tsavo Rd
Timboroa Rd
Tom Mboya St
Cross La
Kumasi Rd
Cross Rd
73
Duruma Rd
67
River Rd
51
76
Taveta Rd
Timboroa La
Accra Rd
Cabral St
Government La
41
Gaberone La
19
Gaberone Rd
Kamae La
Munyu Rd
Matatus to Thika (200m)
12
22
25
46
Sikh Temple
Luthuli Ave
68
Sheikh Karume Rd
56
Sheikh Karume La
4
Machakos Country Bus Station (300m)
40
28
13
Hotel Ambassadeur Nairobi
Mfangano St
Ronald Ngala St
42
60
30
70
55
Uyoma St
Racecourse Rd
Mfangano St
Mfangano La
Tom Mboya St
36
49
24
64
29
Moi Ave
33
Nkrumah La
Hakati Rd
Taifa Rd
Aga Khan Walk
Haile Selassie Ave
3
59
Exchange La
Harambee Ave
1
26
Tumbo Ave
69
Harambee La
Workshop Rd
Pate Bay Rd
74
Train Station
Station Rd
Ngaria Ave

Central Nairobi

Sights
1 American Embassy Memorial Garden F6
2 Gallery Watatu D4
3 Kenyatta Conference Centre E5
4 National Archives F4
5 Parliament House C6
6 Uhuru Park B7

Activities, Courses & Tours
7 Eastern & Southern Safaris B3
8 Natural Tours & Safaris C4
9 Origins Safaris D4
10 Safari Icon Travel D3
11 Safe Ride Tours & Safaris D3
12 Sana Highlands Trekking Expeditions E3
Tropical Winds (see 44)

Sleeping
13 Hilton Nairobi Hotel E4
14 Meridian Court Hotel D2
15 New Kenya Lodge F2
16 Sarova Stanley Hotel D3
17 Terminal Hotel B2

Eating
18 Beneve Coffee House C4
19 Malindi Dishes F3
20 Nakumatt Supermarket D3
21 Pasara Café D4
22 Ranalo Foods E3
23 Savanna: The Coffee Lounge B3
24 Seasons Restaurant F4
25 Seasons Restaurant E3
26 Tamarind Restaurant F6
Thorn Tree Café (see 16)
27 Trattoria D4

Drinking & Nightlife
28 Dormans Café E4
29 Florida 2000 F5
30 Nairobi Java House E4
31 New Florida B3
32 Simmers C4
33 Zanze Bar F5

Shopping
34 City Market C3
35 Maasai Market C1
36 Maasai Market E5

Information
37 Association for the Physically Disabled of Kenya E2
38 Atul's C2

an orphanage, a bead factory, a local home and a lookout point.

KUFET TOUR
(☎0721751905; www.kiberaeverydayslumtours.com; per person US$25) Three-hour Kibera tours that focus on community-run projects such as an HIV/AIDS project, local artisans and a community school. It also offers a number of volunteering possibilities.

People to People Tourism TOUR
(☎0722750073, 0734559710; www.peopletopeopletourism.com) This company does city tours and can take you further afield, with an emphasis on cultural encounters. Ask whether it's still running its introduction to the world of *jua kali*, Kenya's open-air manufacturing industry; it sometimes combines tours of the usual tourist sights with visits to *jua kali* workshops producing crafts and other goods.

Festivals & Events

Kenya Fashion Week FASHION
(Sarit Centre, Westlands) An expo-style event held in June or August, bringing together designers and manufacturers from all over the country.

Kenya Music Festival MUSIC
(☎Nairobi 020-2712964; Kenyatta Conference Centre) Kenya's longest-running music festival was established almost 80 years ago by the colonial regime. African music now predominates, but Western and expat musicians still take part. It's held over 10 days in August.

Tusker Safari Sevens RUGBY
(www.safarisevens.com) A high-profile, international seven-a-side rugby tournament. It's always hotly contested and the Kenyan team has a strong record in the tournament, reaching the semi-finals in 2011. It's held in October and November.

Sleeping

Nairobi has something for everyone when it comes to accommodation, from rough-and-ready cheapies on the wrong side of the tracks to palatial colonial-era hotels rich in history to fabulously priced options out in the verdant suburbs.

You can expect to pay a bit more in Nairobi than you would for the same facilities elsewhere in Kenya. However, in a city where personal safety is something of an issue, it's worth shelling out more for secure surroundings. The majority of midrange and top-end

39	Barclays Bank	B2
40	Barclays Bank	E4
41	Barclays Bank	E3
42	DHL	E4
43	EMS Office	C4
44	French Embassy	B3
45	Goldfield Forex	C4
46	KAM Pharmacy	E3
	Link Forex	(see 50)
47	Postbank	D4
48	Standard Chartered Bank	D2
49	Tanzanian Embassy	E5
50	Uganda High Commission (Consular Section)	C4

Transport

51	Adventure Upgrade Safaris	E3
	Airport Bus Departure Point	(see 70)
52	Avis	A2
	Budget	(see 52)
53	Bus & Matatu Stop	C1
54	Bus & Matatu Stop (for Hurlingham & Milimani)	B4
55	Bus Stop (for Langata, Karen & Airport)	F4
	Bus Stop (for Westlands)	(see 53)
56	Buses to Kisii & Migori	H3
57	Central Rent-a-Car	C4
58	Dream Line	G2
59	Easy Coach	G6
60	Egypt Air	E4
61	Emirates	A2
62	Ethiopian Airlines	C4
63	KBS Booking Office	B2
64	KBS Bus Station	H4
	Kenya Airways	(see 44)
	KLM	(see 44)
65	Main Bus & Matatu Area	G2
66	Market Car Hire	B3
	Matatus to Eldoret	(see 59)
67	Matatus to Kericho & Kisumu	H3
	Matatus to Kibera	(see 55)
68	Matatus to Naivasha, Nakuru, Nyahururu & Namanga	H3
69	Matatus to Wilson Airport, Nairobi National Park, Langata & Karen	G6
70	Metro Shuttle Bus Stand	E4
71	Modern Coast Express	G2
72	Mololine Prestige Shuttle	F2
73	Narok Line	H2
74	Railway Booking Office	G7
75	Riverside Shuttle	C1
76	Tough Trucks Kenya	E3

places also tend to throw in a hearty buffet breakfast.

City Centre

Central YMCA HOTEL $

(Map p56; Nairobi 020-2724116; State House Rd; dm/s/d from KSh1000/1400/2100; P) While it might not inspire the Village People to dedicate a song to it, this central spot has a decent range of passable rooms. Note that you don't need to be a man or a Christian to stay at the YMCA, though you'll certainly be in the majority here if you're either. Breakfast is available for KSh500, and other meals for KSh750.

Terminal Hotel HOTEL $

(Map p66; Nairobi 020-2228817; Moktar Daddah St; s/d/tr KSh2000/2500/2800) Although it's lacking in quality compared to other midrange offerings, the Terminal Hotel is preferable to the rock-bottom budget crash pads in the city centre. The emphasis here is on doing the basics well, with no overblown attempts at tourist frills, and the clean and adequate rooms speak for themselves.

New Kenya Lodge HOTEL $

(Map p66; Nairobi 020-2222202; www.nksafari.com; River Rd; dm/s/d with shared bathroom KSh750/1000/1500) This classic, long-standing shoestringer's haunt has seen better decades (some of the beds sag prodigiously), though it's got an aged charm if you're not too fussy about things like, well, cleanliness. Budget safaris are possible, the staff here is friendly, and there's hot water in the evening (or so they claim).

★ **Kahama Hotel** HOTEL $$

(Map p56; Nairobi 020-3742210; www.kahamahotels.co.ke; Murang'a Rd; s/d from US$50/60; P) Almost equidistant between the city centre and the National Museum, this place is a terrific choice. Its catchcry is 'Economy with Style' and it pretty much lives up to it, with pleasant rooms, comfy beds and free wifi. The only downside? The new highway passes by the front door – ask for a room at the back.

★ **Sarova Stanley Hotel** HOTEL $$

(Map p66; Nairobi 020-2757000; www.sarovahotels.com/stanley; cnr Kimathi St & Kenyatta Ave; s/d from US$104/128; P) A Nairobi classic. The original Stanley Hotel was established in 1902 – past guests include Ernest Hemingway, Clark Gable, Ava Gardner and Gregory Peck – and the hotel makes a cameo appearance in some of Hemingway's works.

Westlands

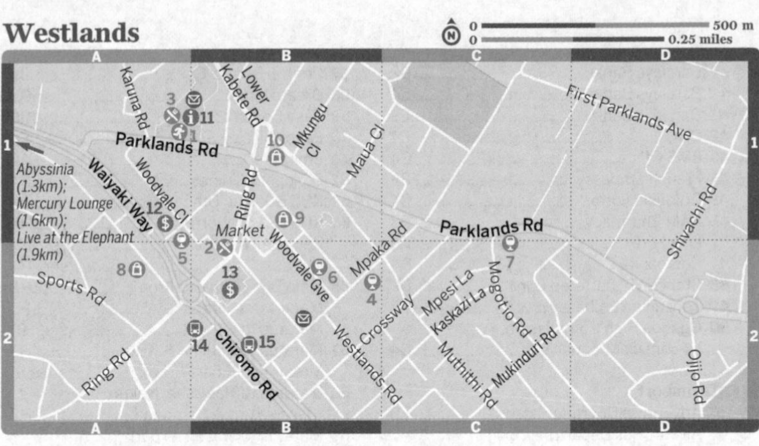

Westlands

Activities, Courses & Tours
1 Savage Wilderness Safaris.................... A1

Eating
2 Open House.................... B2
3 Uchumi.................... A1

Drinking & Nightlife
4 Black Diamond.................... B2
5 Gypsy's Bar.................... A1
6 Havana Bar.................... B2
7 K1 Klub House.................... C2

Shopping
8 Spinners Web.................... A2
9 Undugu Craft Shop.................... B1
10 Westland Curio Market.................... B1

Information
11 Automobile Association of Kenya.................... A1
12 Barclays Bank.................... A1
13 Travellers Forex Bureau.................... B2

Transport
14 Bus & Matatu Stands.................... B2
15 Bus & Matatu Stands.................... B2

The latest version boasts large and luxurious rooms, and colonial decor prevails inside, with lashings of green leather, opulent chandeliers and old-fashioned fans.

The real highlight (at least from our perspective!) is the Thorn Tree Café (p75), which inspired Lonely Planet's online community. Rates vary considerably with the seasons and availability, and are generally cheaper on weekends.

Meridian Court Hotel HOTEL **$$**
(Map p66; Nairobi 020-2220006; www.meridianhotelkenya.com; Muranga'a Rd; s/d from KSh8650/9850; P @) The elaborate lobby is rather more prepossessing than the rooms, but it's hardly worth complaining when you're essentially getting a suite for the price of a standard room. There's no great luxury involved and some of the furnishings have seen better days, but the pool, bar and restaurants make it terrific value in this price range. The superior rooms are rarely worth the extra.

Hilton Nairobi Hotel HOTEL **$$$**
(Map p66; Nairobi 020-2250000; www.hilton.com; Mama Ngina St; r from US$185; P @) A distinct Nairobi landmark, the Hilton dominates the centre of town with its somewhat dated round tower, occupying virtually an entire block with rooms, restaurants, shops and a whole slew of business facilities. Although it isn't as atmospheric as some of Nairobi's more seasoned top-end hotels, the Hilton remains one of the best deals in town for upmarket travellers.

Nairobi Serena Hotel HOTEL **$$$**
(Map p56; Nairobi 020-2822000; www.serenahotels.com; Procession Way, Central Park; r from US$210; P @) Consolidating its reputation as one of the best top-flight chains in East Africa, this entry in the Serena canon has a fine sense of individuality, with its international-class facilities displaying a touch of safari style. Of particular note is the onsite Maisha health spa. Opt for one of the amazing

garden suites, where you can take advantage of your own private patio, complete with mini-pergola.

As the hotel is right opposite Uhuru Park, avoid walking anywhere from here at night.

Norfolk Hotel HOTEL $$$
(Map p56; ☎Nairobi 020-2265000; www.fairmont.com/norfolkhotel; Harry Thuku Rd; r from US$289; P ❄ 📶 🏊) Built in 1904 but overhauled many times since, Nairobi's oldest hotel was *the* place to stay during colonial days. The hotel remains the traditional starting point for elite safaris, and the Lord Delamere Terrace is still Nairobi's most famous meeting place. Thanks to the leafy grounds, it has an almost rustic feel, although the recently renovated rooms have lost a little of that classic Norfolk look.

Milimani & Upper Hill

Milimani Backpackers & Safari Centre BACKPACKERS $
(Map p60; ☎0722347616, 0718919020; www.milimanibackpackers.com; Karen St, St Helens Lane, off Langata Rd, Milimani; camping KSh700, dm KSh1000, cabins s/d KSh2200/2500; @ 📶) This terrific place is one of the friendliest accommodation options in town, and whether you camp out back, cosy up in the dorms or splurge on your own cabin, you'll end up huddled around the fire at night, swapping travel stories and dining on home-cooked meals (from KSh500) with fellow travellers. The friendly staff can also help you book a safari, organise onward travel or simply get your bearings.

Nairobi International Youth Hostel HOSTEL $
(Map p56; ☎Nairobi 020-2738046; www.yhak.org; Ralph Bunche Rd, Milimani; dm KSh750-1000, d KSh3000; P @) This well-looked-after budget option isn't as atmospheric as Milimani Backpackers, but Kenya's HI instalment is still a comfortable and relaxed spot to meet other travellers. It offers the usual range of hosteller-catered amenities including an activity centre, booking desk, cybercafe, bar-restaurant and a communal lounge. Any matatu or bus going down either Valley or Ngong Rds will get you here; always take a taxi when returning at night.

Town Lodge HOTEL $$
(Map p56; ☎Nairobi 020-2881600; www.clhg.com; Second Ngong Ave, Milimani; s/d from KSh11,700/16,100; P @ 📶) The focus here is on affordable comfort for business travellers, with attractive if somewhat sterile rooms. It's one of the best-value midrange options in Nairobi – there's a small gym, excellent breakfasts and you can take advantage of the bars and restaurants at the Fairview next door.

Heron Hotel HOTEL $$
(Map p56; ☎Nairobi 020-2720740; www.heronhotel.com; Milimani Rd, Milimani; s/d from US$111/134; P 📶 🏊) It's hard to see why anyone would pay top-end prices when places like the Heron are around. Rooms are modern, extremely comfortable and well-appointed, while the staff is attentive and professional. The location is quiet and there's not even the merest trace of Buffalo Bill's, a notorious brothel that once occupied the site. Highly recommended.

WHERE TO STAY IN NAIROBI?

The heart and soul of Nairobi is the city centre, so if you want to go to bed and wake up in the centre of it all, look no further. The main budget area is between Tom Mboya St and River Rd, where you'll find dozens of small hotels and guesthouses. Staying in this area is something of a budget-travellers' tradition, but remember that these are some of Nairobi's meanest streets. The area west of Moi Ave is generally fine, and has a range of options, although it empties after dark and on weekends.

The eastern districts of Nairobi Hill and Milimani host a clutch of reliable business hotels and upmarket lodges, as well as some backpacker spots, all pleasantly removed from the congestion of the city centre. If you want to be a bit further out, there's expat-friendly Westlands and Parklands.

For a decidedly different take on Nairobi, consider heading right out into Karen, Langata and Nairobi National Park. For the most part, accommodation out here is at the top end, though the charm exuded by many of these properties is worth every shilling. If that's out of your price range, however, there are a couple of campsites worth checking out.

Fairview Hotel HOTEL $$$
(Map p56; ☎Nairobi 020-2711321; www.fairviewkenya.com; Bishops Rd, Milimani; s/d/ste from KSh16,300/18,700/26,000; ❄📶🏊) An excellent top-end choice that puts many of the more prestigious and pricier places in town to shame. The Fairview is nicely removed from the central hubbub and defined by its winding paths and green-filled grounds. It all creates a refined atmosphere, especially around the charming courtyard restaurant.

Palacina BOUTIQUE HOTEL $$$
(Map p60; ☎Nairobi 020-2715517; www.palacina.com; Kitale Lane; ste 1-/2-person US$330/498, penthouse US$830, 1-/2-bedroom apt per month US$2995/4150; P📶🏊) The fabulous collection of stylish suites – at what was one of the first genuine boutique hotels in Kenya – is perfect for well-heeled sophisticates who still like the personal touch. Intimate rooms are awash with calming tones, boldly accented by rich teak woods, lavish furniture and private Jacuzzis.

Mombasa Rd

Boma Nairobi HOTEL $$$
(Map p60; ☎Nairobi 020-3904000, 0719050000; www.theboma.co.ke; r from US$245; P❄@📶) Owned by the Red Cross, this smart hotel is popular with NGOs and business people alike for its quiet location that's equally handy for the centre, Nairobi National Park and the airport, its excellent and well-equipped rooms and professional service.

Nairobi National Park

★**Emakoko** LODGE $$$
(Map p60; ☎0787331632, 0771238218; www.emakoko.com; Uhuru Gardens; s/d US$525/860; P@📶🏊) This stunning, artfully designed lodge inhabits a rise overlooking Nairobi National Park and the Mbagathi River. It's a wonderful way to begin or end your Kenyan safari by bypassing the hassles of Nairobi altogether, and the rooms and public areas are exquisite. Ask for one of the rooms that look out over the park.

Nairobi Tented Camp TENTED CAMP $$$
(Map p60; ☎0733884298, 0774136523; www.nairobitentedcamp.com; Nairobi National Park; s/d full board US$193/260; P) 🍃 Staying here inside Nairobi National Park helps you forget that one of Africa's largest cities is just a few kilometres away. This luxury tented camp offers the full-on safari experience. The eight tents are like those you'll find in Kenya's better-known parks, and there's a real (and somewhat incongruous) sense of solitude. Park entrance fees are not included.

Karen & Langata

★**Wildebeest Eco Camp** TENTED CAMP $
(Map p60; ☎0734770733; wildebeestecocamp.com; 151 Mokoyeti Road West, Langata; garden tent s/d from KSh4500/5500, deluxe garden tents s/d US$113/138) This fabulous place in Langata is arguably Nairobi's outstanding budget option. The atmosphere is relaxed yet switched on, and the accommodation is spotless and great value however much you're paying. The deluxe garden tents are as good as many exclusive such places out on safari – for a fraction of the price. A great Nairobi base.

Karen Camp CAMPGROUND $
(Map p60; ☎Nairobi 020-8833475, 0723314053; www.karencamp.com; Marula Lane, Karen; camping US$7, dm/s/d US$15/35/50, tw with shared bathroom US$40; P) You wouldn't expect to find a backpacker-friendly option out here in affluent Karen, which is why we like this friendly little spot so much. The quiet location and smart facilities are reason enough to make the trek out to the shady campsites, spick-and-span dorms and simple rooms (with mosquito nets).

Dea's Gardens GUESTHOUSE $$
(Map p60; ☎0733747443, 0734453761; www.deasgardens.com; Kwarara Road, off Ndege Rd; per person KSh7700) Following a similar formula to its sister property in Naivasha, Dea's Gardens Nairobi has simple yet light-filled and attractive rooms ranged across two floors of a large Karen home. The garden is green and lovely and Lisa is a gracious host.

Margarita House GUESTHOUSE $$
(Map p60; ☎Nairobi 020-2018421; www.themargaritahouse.com; Lower Plains Rd, Karen; s/d from US$85/119; P📶🏊) Tucked away on a quiet street on Karen's north side, this tranquil guesthouse is one of the few midrange options in the area, and thankfully it's a good one. Rooms are large and comfortable, contemporary artworks adorn the walls, and Elizabeth and Joel are welcoming hosts. The roads can be a little confusing around here – print out the detailed directions from its website.

★**Giraffe Manor** HISTORIC HOTEL $$$
(Map p60; ☎Nairobi 020-8891078; www.thesafaricollection.com; Mukoma Rd, Karen; s/d full board

from US$772/1124; P) Built in 1932 in typical English style, this elegant manor is situated on 56 hectares, much of which is given over to the adjacent Giraffe Centre (p63). As a result, you may find a Rothschild's giraffe peering through your bedroom window first thing in the morning. And yet, the real appeal of the Giraffe Manor is that you're treated as a personal guest by the owners.

Here you can use their chauffeur, sample their wines and dine in lavish excess. Literary buffs should ask for the Karen Blixen room, decked out with furniture the famous author gave the owners when she left Africa for the last time.

★ **House of Waine** BOUTIQUE HOTEL $$$
(Map p60; ☎0734699973, Nairobi 020-2601455; www.houseofwaine.com; Maasai Lane, off Bogani Rd, Karen; s/d from US$330/500; P❄@📶🏊) Sophistication and style are the hallmarks of this stunning boutique offering out in Karen. Every room is different according to its theme – we love the slate-grey colour

KIBERA

Kibera (which is derived from a Nubian word *kibra*, meaning forest) is a sprawling urban jungle of shanty-town housing. Home to as many as one million residents, Kibera is the world's second-largest shanty town (after Soweto in Johannesburg, South Africa). Although it covers 2.5 sq km in area, it's home to somewhere between a quarter and a third of Nairobi's population, and has a density of an estimated 300,000 people per sq km. The neighbourhood was thrust into the Western imagination when it featured prominently in the Fernando Meirelles film *The Constant Gardener,* which is based on the book of the same name by John le Carré. With the area heavily polluted by open sewers, and lacking even the most basic infrastructure, residents of Kibera suffer from poor nutrition and disease, not to mention violent crime.

Although it's virtually impossible to collect accurate statistics on shanty towns, with the demographics changing almost daily, the rough estimates for Kibera are shocking enough. According to local aid workers, Kibera is home to one pit toilet for every 100 people; its inhabitants suffer from an HIV/AIDS infection rate of more than 20%; and four out of every five people living here are unemployed.

History

The British established Kibera in 1918 for Nubian soldiers as a reward for service in WWI. However, following Kenyan independence in 1963, housing in Kibera was rendered illegal by the government. But this new legislation inadvertently allowed the Nubians to rent out their property to a greater number of tenants than legally permitted and, for poorer tenants, Kibera was perceived as affordable despite the questionable legalities. Since the mid-1970s, though, control of Kibera has been firmly in Kikuyu hands, who now comprise the bulk of the population.

Orientation

Kibera is located southwest of the CBD. The railway line heading to Kisumu intersects Kibera, though the shanty town doesn't actually have a station. However, this railway line does serve as the main thoroughfare through Kibera, and you'll find shops selling basic provisions along the tracks.

Visiting the Shanty Town

A visit to Kibera is one way to look behind the headlines and touch on, albeit briefly, the daily struggles and triumphs of life in the town; there's nothing quite like the enjoyment of playing a bit of footy with street children aspiring to be the next Didier Drogba. Although you could visit on your own, security is an issue, and such visits aren't always appreciated by residents. The best way to visit is on a tour. Three companies we recommend are Explore Kibera (p65), Kibera Tours (p65) and KUFET (p68).

Getting There & Away

You can get to Kibera by taking bus 32 or matatu 32c from the Kencom building along Moi Ave. Be advised that this route is notorious for petty theft, so be extremely vigilant and pay attention to your surroundings.

scheme in the Tembo room – and the atmosphere is one of soothing and perfectly conceived spaces. The garden is a real Nairobi oasis and it's little wonder that it has fast become Nairobi's premier address.

Karen Blixen Cottages BOUTIQUE HOTEL $$$
(Map p60; ☎Nairobi 020-882138, 0733616206; www.karenblixencoffeegarden.com; 336 Karen Rd, Karen; s/d US$330/515; P 📶 🏊) Located near Karen Blixen's House & Museum (p64), this gorgeous clutch of spacious cottages is centred on a formal garden, and adjacent to a small coffee plantation and a country restaurant. It's sophisticated, supremely comfortable and if you're keen on having an *Out of Africa* experience, then look no further.

Eating

Cheap canteens and fast-food eateries fuel a good number of Nairobi's office workers in the CBD, though there are several upmarket places that can set the scene for that crucial business lunch. If you're planning on having dinner anywhere in the city centre, be sure to take a taxi back to your accommodation as the streets empty out once the sun goes down.

For dinner it's worth heading out to the suburbs, where there are dozens of choices of cuisine from all over the world. Karen has the best range, though there are some good choices elsewhere.

City Centre

★ **Savanna: The Coffee Lounge** CAFE $
(Map p56; Museum Hill Rd; snacks from KSh200, mains KSh500-700; ⏰7am-8pm Mon-Sat, 9am-6pm Sun) This classy little chain has outposts across Nairobi, including another **branch** (Map p66; Loita St; snacks from KSh200, mains KSh500-700; ⏰7am-8pm Mon-Sat, 9am-6pm Sun) in the town centre, but we particularly like the tranquillity of this branch inside the grounds of the National Museum. Decor is safari chic without being overdone, service is friendly and unobtrusive, and dishes include pies, wraps, samosas, sandwiches, burgers, pasta, soups and salads.

★ **Beneve Coffee House** CAFE $
(Map p66; ☎Nairobi 020-217959; cnr Standard & Koinange Sts; mains KSh150-350; ⏰7am-4pm Mon-Fri) This small self-service cafe has locals queuing outside in the mornings waiting for it to open. Food ranges from African- and Indian-influenced stews to curries, fish and chips, samosas, pasties and a host of other choices, all at low, low prices.

Nyama Choma Stalls KENYAN $
(Map p56; Haile Selassie Ave; mains around KSh500) At these backstreet stalls near the Railway Museum, behind the Shell petrol station, foreigners are a rare sight, but you'll be warmly welcomed and encouraged to sample Kenyan dishes such as *matoke* (cooked mashed plantains) and wonderful barbecued meat.

Pasara Café INTERNATIONAL $
(Map p66; ground fl, Lonrho Bldg, Standard St; dishes KSh275-395; ⏰7am-midnight Mon-Sat) At the forefront of Nairobi's burgeoning cafe culture, this stylish, modern bar-brasserie has a nifty selection of snacks, sandwiches, grills and breakfasts, always offering something that bit more ambitious than the usual cafeteria fare; try the chicken tikka burger and a milkshake for example.

Malindi Dishes KENYAN $
(Map p66; Gaberone Rd; mains KSh150-400; ⏰noon-8pm Sat-Thu, 3-8pm Fri) This small Swahili canteen serves great food from the coast, including pilau (curried rice with meat), birianis (spicy rice casseroles) and coconut fish, with side dishes such as *ugali* (maize- or cassava-based staple), naan and rice. You'll get a grand halal feed here, but true to its Muslim roots, it's closed for prayer at lunchtime on Friday.

Ranalo Foods AFRICAN $
(Map p66; ☎0770785897; Kimathi St; ⏰8am-11pm) There's nothing all that special going on here, but that is partly the point. It's all about good honest local cooking with dishes such as fried tilapia – fish is the speciality here, true to the restaurant's Luo roots in western Kenya.

Seasons Restaurant KENYAN $
(Map p66; Mutual Bldg, Kimathi St; mains KSh450-600, buffets KSh600; ⏰24hr) The cafeteria vats here always brim with cheap Kenyan and Western favourites, which is probably why this local chain has a strong following. The buffet is small but (unusually for those who've been staying in safari lodges) entirely African in orientation. It claims to be open 24 hours, but we didn't pass by at 4am to check.

The Nairobi Cinema **outlet** (Map p66; Uchumi House, Aga Khan Walk, Nairobi Cinema; mains KSh390-500, buffets KSh500; ⏰24hr) has a popular bar and beer garden where you can bring your own alcoholic beverage and pay a small corkage fee.

★Thorn Tree Café INTERNATIONAL **$$**
(Map p66; ☎Nairobi 020-228030; Sarova Stanley Hotel, cnr Kimathi St & Kenyatta Ave; mains KSh1000-2100; ⏰11am-10pm) The Stanley's legendary cafe still serves as a popular meeting place for travellers of all persuasions, and caters to most tastes with a good mix of food. The original thorn-tree noticeboard in the courtyard gave rise to the general expression, and inspired Lonely Planet's own online Thorn Tree Travel Forum. The menu ranges from grilled giant prawns to Kenyan-style chicken stew.

While the cafe is now on its third acacia, and the noticeboard's not quite the paperfest it once was, a little nostalgia is de rigueur, even if only to pause and recognise an original landmark on the Cape to Cairo overland trail.

Trattoria ITALIAN **$$**
(Map p66; ☎Nairobi 020-340855; www.trattoria.co.ke; cnr Wabera & Kaunda Sts; mains KSh900-1450; ⏰7am-midnight) Some things just don't change and thank God for that! This popular and classy downtown Italian restaurant, swathed in trellises and plants, offers excellent pizzas, homemade pasta, risottos, varied mains and a whole page of desserts. The atmosphere and food are excellent. It's packed every night, especially the upstairs balcony section.

★Tamarind Restaurant SEAFOOD **$$$**
(Map p66; ☎Nairobi 020-2251811; www.tamarind.co.ke; off Harambee Ave; mains KSh1100-2800; ⏰lunch & dinner Mon-Sat) Kenya's most prestigious restaurant chain runs Nairobi's best seafood restaurant, located in the monumental National Bank Building. The splendid menu offers all manner of exotic flavours, and the lavish dining room is laid out in a sumptuous modern Arabic-Moorish style. Starters range from Hibiscus-flamed seafood to an exquisite seafood platter.

Smart dress is expected, and you'll need to budget at least KSh2500 for the full works – much more if you want wine or cocktails and lobster – though seafood gourmands agree that it's money well spent. There's another outpost at Karen Blixen Coffee Garden (p76).

WORTH A TRIP

FOR THE LOVE OF MEAT

Love it or hate it, **Carnivore** (Map p60; ☎0733611608, Nairobi 020-605933; www.tamarind.co.ke/carnivore/; off Langata Rd, Karen; buffet from KSh3000; ⏰noon-3pm & 6.30-11pm; Ⓟ) is hands down the most famous *nyama choma* (barbecued meat) in Kenya, an icon among tourists, expats and wealthier locals for the past 25 years. At the entrance is a huge barbecue pit laden with real swords of beef, pork, lamb, chicken and farmed game meats.

Carnivore was voted by UK magazine *Restaurant* to be among the 50 best restaurants in the world in 2002 and 2003. This honour was largely in recognition of the fact that you could dine here on exotic game meats. In recent years, however, strict new laws mean that zebra, hartebeest, kudu and the like are now off the menu, and you have to be content with camel, ostrich and crocodile, in addition to more standard offerings. You also get soup, salads and sauces to go with the meats.

As long as the paper flag on your table is flying, waiters will keep bringing the meat, which is carved right at the table; if you're in need of a breather, you can tip the flag over temporarily. Note that dessert and coffee (but not other drinks) are included in the set price.

This meat-fest does have its critics – prices are high and the waiters, hats and all, can seem like the ringmasters of a circus with their enthusiastic bonhomie. But if you take it for what it is, you'll leave satisfied.

At lunchtime, you can get to Carnivore by matatu 126 from the city centre – the turn-off is signposted just past Wilson Airport, from where it's a 1km walk. At night, it's best to hire a taxi, which should run to about KSh800 each way depending on your bargaining skills.

At night you may wish to stay on for an all-night dance-athon at the adjacent Simba Saloon (p79).

Westlands

Haandi Restaurant INDIAN **$$**
(☎Nairobi 020-4448294; The Mall Shopping Centre, Ring Rd, Westlands; mains KSh750-1700; ⏰noon-2.30pm & 6.30-10.30pm; ❄) Widely regarded as the best Indian restaurant in Kenya, Haandi rises above its nondescript shopping-mall location. The expansive menu includes wonderful Mughlai (North Indian) spreads, tandoori dishes and plenty of vegetarian curries. Most dishes are served with Haandi's signature stacks of naan and piles of basmati rice. It has sister restaurants in

WORTH A TRIP

NYAMA CHOMA AT THE RIFT

If you've your own wheels and a taste for barbecued meat, take the road southwest out of Nairobi, past Kiserian on the road to Lake Magadi to Corner Baridi where this fine, simple little place, **Olepolos Country Club** (☎0714032122; Corner Baridi, C58; meals from KSh750; ⏰10am-5.30pm Mon-Thu, 10am-8pm Fri, 9am-midnight Sat & Sun), serves up roasted meat and roast chicken. Wash it down with cold Tuskers as you look out over the Rift Valley, and we reckon you're somewhere close to heaven.

It's around 34km southwest of downtown Nairobi near the town of Kisamis. If you don't have your own wheels, take matatu 126 as far as Kiserian and then hire a taxi.

Kampala and London, and even sells its own souvenir T-shirts.

Abyssinia ETHIOPIAN $$
(☎0725151515; Brookside Grove, Westlands; mains KSh500-900; ⏰11am-11pm) Consistently good reviews from expats, locals and travellers alike make this an excellent choice for high-quality Ethiopian cooking. Aside from the rich tastes of the varied main dishes, the *injere* (Ethiopian crepe-like bread) is perfectly light, just as it should be. It's worth coming here just for the coffee ceremony.

Open House INDIAN $$
(Mapp70; ☎0727726345; www.openhouserestaurant.co.ke; Ring Rd, Westlands; mains KSh500-950) Ask any long-term resident of Nairobi for their favourite Indian restaurant and a fair few of them will plump for Open House. The service is friendly, but the food is outstanding, from the signature chilli paneer or butter chicken to divine ginger mushrooms. The number of Indians eating here seals it for us.

Karen

★Talisman INTERNATIONAL $$
(Map p60; ☎0705999997; www.thetalismanrestaurant.com; 320 Ngong Rd, Karen; mains KSh1200-2200; ⏰8am-10pm Tue-Sat, 9am-10pm Sun) This classy cafe-bar-restaurant remains fashionable with the Karen in-crowd, and rivals any of Kenya's top eateries for imaginative international food. The comfortable lounge-like rooms mix modern African and European styles, the courtyard provides some welcome air, and specials such as pan-seared ostrich fillet perk up the palate no end.

Tin Roof Cafe CAFE, INTERNATIONAL $$
(Map p60; ☎0706348215; www.facebook.com/TinRoofCafe; Dagoretti Rd, Karen; mains from Ksh500; ⏰8.30am-5.30pm; 📶) This place has all the necessary ingredients to be a Nairobi favourite – a quiet garden setting in Karen, great coffee, the city's best salad bar and a commitment to healthy eating. Our only complaint? It doesn't open for dinner. Due to popular demand, it began to open on Sundays not long after our visit. Souk (p79), a fabulous shopping experience, is on the same property.

Karen Blixen Coffee Garden INTERNATIONAL $$$
(Map p60; ☎0719346349; www.tamarind.co.ke; Karen Rd, Karen; mains KSh820-2390; ⏰7am-10pm) This upmarket option, run by the ubiquitous Tamarind group, offers diners and snackers five different areas in which to enjoy a varied menu, including the plush L'Amour dining room, the historic 1901 Swedo House and the main section, which is a smart restaurant set in a veritable English country garden. Its Sunday lunch buffet (KSh1650) is popular, and excellent value.

It's just down the road from Karen Blixen's House & Museum (p64).

Self-Catering

Nakumatt Supermarket SUPERMARKET $
(Map p66; www.nakumatt.net; Kenyatta Ave; ⏰8.30am-8pm) The principal supermarket chain in Nairobi and Kenya as a whole, Nakumatt has a huge selection of Kenyan and Western foods and other products. There are other branches, including at **Village Market** (Limuru Rd, Gigiri).

Uchumi SUPERMARKET $
(Map p70; Sarit Centre, Parklands Rd, Westlands; ⏰8am-8pm) Once the main supermarket chain in town, Uchumi has a good range of items.

Drinking & Nightlife

Western cafe culture has hit Nairobi, and been seized upon enthusiastically by local expats and residents pining for a decent cup of Kenyan coffee. Nairobi is the best place in the country for *real* coffee. All of the cafes reviewed here offer at least some form of food, whether it's a few cakes or a full menu, but none serve alcohol.

There are plenty of cheap but very rough-and-ready bars around Latema Rd and River Rd, although these places aren't recommended for female travellers; even male drinkers should watch themselves. There are some safer watering holes around Tom Mboya St and Moi Ave, and some restaurants and hotels are fine places for a drink.

Out in Westlands and Karen, the drinking scene brings in a lot more expats. Everywhere, foreign women without a man in tow will draw attention. Due to the high number of female prostitutes, men will generally get the bulk of the hassle. Dress casual but nice at these places.

City Centre

★Nairobi Java House CAFE

(Map p66; ☎ Nairobi 020-313565; www.nairobijavahouse.com; Mama Ngina St; coffee KSh150-350; ⏰ 6.30am-10pm Mon-Fri, 7am- 9pm Sat, 8am-8pm Sun) This fantastic coffeehouse is rapidly turning itself into a major brand, and you may see its logo on T-shirts as far afield as London and beyond. Aficionados say the coffee's some of the best in Kenya, and there are plenty of cakes and other sweet and savoury treats (even New York cheesecake).

Dormans Café CAFE

(Map p66; www.dorman.co.ke; Mama Ngina St; coffee KSh125-375; ⏰ 6.30am-8.30pm Mon-Sat, 9am-7.30pm Sun) Established in the 1960s, this venerable firm has only recently branched out into the cafe business, but has certainly made an aggressive Starbucks-style start, opening a shiny pine outlet right opposite its main rival, Nairobi Java. The coffee's good (everything from cappuccino to iced coffee and hazelnut mocha) and the selection of teas is impressive.

★Lord Delamere Terrace & Bar BAR

(Map p56; www.fairmont.com/NorfolkHotel; Norfolk Hotel, Harry Thuku Rd; ⏰ 6.30am-10.30pm) Once one of Africa's classic bars, the Lord Delamere Terrace was the starting point for so many epic colonial safaris, and the scene of tall tales told by men such as Ernest Hemingway and the Great White Hunters of the early 20th century. Not much of the old atmosphere remains, but come here as a pilgrimage to the Africa of old.

★Simmers BAR

(Map p66; ☎ Nairobi 020-217659; cnr Kenyatta Ave & Muindi Mbingu St; ⏰ 8am-1am) If you're tired of having your butt pinched to the strains of limp R&B in darkened discos, Simmers could be your place. The atmosphere at this open-air bar-restaurant is amazing, with enthusiastic crowds turning out to wind and grind the night away to parades of bands playing anything from Congolese rumba to Kenyan *benga* (contemporary dance).

The women here are more likely to be locals out for a giggle rather than working girls out for business, so being hassled is relatively rare. With free-flowing Tusker, a separate shots bar and plenty of *nyama choma* (barbecued meat) to keep the lion from the door, it's no wonder the place always feels like a party.

Florida 2000 CLUB

(Map p66; ☎ 0706577009; www.floridaclubskenya.com; Moi Ave; men/women KSh300/200; ⏰ 9pm-6am) This big dancing den, known by everyone as F2, is near City Hall Way. It works to a fairly uncomplicated formula of booze, beats and tightly packed bodies. As is typical in Nairobi, every night is a little different: Thursday is techno trance, Friday is rumba, Saturday could be soul and so on.

New Florida CLUB

(Map p66; ☎ Nairobi 020-2215014; www.floridaclubskenya.com; Koinange St; men/women KSh300/200) The 'Madhouse' (or 'Maddi' to its friends) is a big, rowdy club housed in a bizarre, blacked-out saucer building above a petrol station. The music ranges from jazz to the customary weekend mish-mash of Western pop. Whatever night you choose, it's usually mayhem, crammed with bruisers, cruisers, hookers, hustlers and curious tourists, but it's great fun if you're in the right mood (or just very drunk).

Zanze Bar BAR

(Map p66; Kenya Cinema Plaza, Moi Ave; ⏰ 6pm-late) A lively and friendly top-floor bar with pool tables, a dance floor, cheap beer and reasonable food. During the week things are relatively quiet, but from Friday to Sunday it rocks until the early hours, with a much more relaxed vibe than the big clubs.

Westlands & Parklands

★Gypsy's Bar BAR

(Map p70; Woodvale Grove; ⏰ 11am-4am) This is one of the most popular bars in Westlands, pulling in a large, mixed crowd of Kenyans, expats and prostitutes. Snacks are available, and there's decent Western and African music, with parties taking over the pavement in summer.

K1 Klub House BAR

(Map p70; ☎Nairobi 020-749870, 0714579265; www.klubhouse.co.ke; Parklands Rd; ⏲24hr) At the western end of Westlands, the Klub House is another old favourite. The spacious bar has plenty of pool tables and excellent DJs spinning reggae, dancehall, hip-hop and R&B until late. Watch for live bands on Saturday nights, Tuesday night is jazz, while Wednesday is Ladies' night.

Tree House NIGHTCLUB

(Map p56; ☎0721447241; www.treehousenairobi.wordpress.com; Westlands Rd; ⏲6pm-6am Tue-Sun) About halfway between the CBD and Westlands, close to the National Museum, this stalwart draws massive crowds for the top-notch DJs, excellent live music and overwhelming sound system. Tuesday is hip-hop and R&B night, and it all cranks up from there. The crowd is mixed local and expat and the decor eclectic, with a tree right in the middle and handmade furnishings.

Havana Bar BAR

(Map p70; ☎Nairobi 020-4450653, 0723265941; www.havana.co.ke; Woodvale Grove, Westlands; ⏲noon-3am) Thursday nights at the Havana Bar are one of Nairobi's hottest tickets, drawing a broad cross-section of Nairobi night owls, prostitutes among them. Latin tunes that often stray into techno provide a varied soundtrack, and you can lubricate the night with anything from Kenyan coffee, South African wines and middle shelf international spirits to a rather fine mojito. Ask for the menu of Cuban cigars.

Mercury Lounge COCKTAIL BAR

(www.mercurylounge.co.ke; ABC Place, Westlands; ⏲4pm-1am Sun-Thu, 4pm-3am Fri & Sat) This sophisticated cocktail bar is smooth as silk, with vaguely retro curves in the decor and a fine list of cocktails to keep the well-to-do crowd happy. It kicks off the week in suitably sedate fashion with Monday Blues, then Tuesday is 'Wine & Jazz', Thursday is all about salsa and Friday is all about nostalgia.

Black Diamond NIGHTCLUB

(Map p70; 1st fl, Bishan Plaza, Mpaka Rd, Westlands; ⏲6pm-6am) When all is said and done for the night, there's always Black Diamond – as one aficionado assured us, it's 'good for late-night drunkeness'. The music is mostly African, the crowd's a great mix (including a few working girls…) and it's difficult not to feel that all's right with the world on their open-air terrace under Nairobi's stars.

Think techno, house, occasional live music and DJs you can dance to. Tuesday is karaoke night.

Milimani

Casablanca BAR, LOUNGE

(Map p60; ☎Nairobi 020-2723173; Lenana Rd, Hurlingham; ⏲6pm-2am Mon-Thu, 6pm-6am Fri & Sat) Lounge-style chillout venues are all the rage in Nairobi but this Moroccan-style lounge bar was doing it long before the trend took hold. It continues to be a hit with Nairobi's fastidious expat community, and you don't have to spend much time here to become a convert. Shisha pipes, wines and cocktails conspire to ease you into what's bound to end up a late night.

YOU KNOW YOU'RE IN NAIROBI WHEN…

- The main topic of conversation is the terrible traffic, followed by an experience/discussion/argument on/with/against a Ma-3 (matatu – because *tatu* means 3 in Swahili…)
- You hear people talking in sheng, a street slang that mixes English with Swahili
- Ghetto FM (sheng radio station) or Radio Jambo with Mbusi ('Goat' – a popular presenter) is playing on the radio
- Your plans for the weekend are plans for 'Sato' (Saturday)
- You spot the marabou storks near Nyayo Stadium Roundabout
- You see a Maasai warrior walking down the road chatting on a cellphone
- You find yourself caught in rush-hour traffic going *out* of the city at 9am on Friday morning
- Did we mention the traffic?

Karen

Simba Saloon CLUB
(Map p60; Nairobi 020-501706; www.tamarind.co.ke/simba-saloon; off Langata Rd; admission KSh250-400; 5pm-late Wed-Sun; minibus 126, taxi) Next door to Carnivore out on the road to Karen, this large open-air bar and nightclub pulls in a huge crowd. There are video screens, several bars, a bonfire, and unashamedly Western music on the dance floor, although you might get the occasional African superstar playing live. It's usually crammed with wealthy Kenyans, expat teenagers, travellers and NGO workers, plus a fair sprinkling of sex workers.

☆ Entertainment

★ **Live at the Elephant** LIVE MUSIC
(0721946710; Gate 3, Kanjata Rd; from 8pm Fri) This could just be our favourite live music venue in town. It draws a trendy, upmarket crowd with its fair share of Nairobi hipsters for the regular program of up-and-coming artists (mostly Kenyan with some from further afield in Africa). It's in the Lavington area. Check out the Facebook page (www.facebook.com/LiveAtTheElephant) to see what's coming up.

To get here from central Nairobi, take Waiyaki Way through Westlands, turn left at James Gichuru Rd – Kanjata Rd is the first street on the left.

★ **Blankets & Wine** LIVE MUSIC
(0720801333, 0736801333; blanketsandwine.com; tickets KSh1500-2500; 1st Sun of month) This monthly picnic-concert is one of the best-loved features on Nairobi's live music circuit. Musicians vary but the underlying principle is to support local and other East African acts, from acoustic and singer-songwriter to rock and roots. Families are welcome and the venue changes each month – next door to Simba Saloon is one of the popular locations.

Kenya National Theatre THEATRE
(Map p56; Nairobi 020-2225174; Harry Thuku Rd; tickets from KSh300) This is the major theatre venue in Nairobi. As well as contemporary and classic plays, there are special events such as beauty pageants, which are less highbrow but still culturally interesting. Check out the *Daily Nation* to see what's on. It's opposite the Norfolk Hotel.

FIND YOUR WAY AROUND THE NAIROBI NIGHT

For information on entertainment in Nairobi and for big music venues in the rest of the country, get hold of the *Saturday Nation*, which lists everything from cinema releases to live-music venues. There are also plenty of suggestions in the magazine *Going Out*. Nightclubs usually open from 9pm until 6am, although they may close earlier if things are quiet.

One cool way to tap into what's happening is to rummage around on **Kenya Nights Events** (www.facebook.com/KenyaNights), where you'll find everything from hipster hangouts to the hottest electronica venues, from DJ events to entry points into Nairobi's thriving underground music scene.

Shopping

★ **Souk** ARTS & CRAFTS
(Map p60; 0706348215; www.souk-kenya.com; Dagoretti Rd; 9.30am-5.30pm Mon-Sat) Some of Kenya's more creative artists, photographers, leatherworkers and other high-quality artisans and artists have come together under one roof and the result is some of Kenya's most discerning shopping experiences. It shares premises with the equally excellent Tin Roof Cafe (p76).

★ **Utamaduni** HANDICRAFTS
(Map p60; www.utamaduni.com; Bogani East Rd, Karen; 9am-6pm) Utamaduni is a large crafts emporium, with more than a dozen separate rooms selling all kinds of excellent African artworks and souvenirs. Prices start relatively high, but there's *none* of the hard sell you'd get in town. A portion of all proceeds goes to the Kenya Wildlife Foundation. There's an on-site restaurant and playground. It's close to the Giraffe Centre.

Banana Box HANDICRAFTS
(www.bananabox.co.ke; Sarit Centre, Westlands; 9.30am-6pm Mon-Sat, 10am-2pm Sun) Amid the rather less-altruistic commercialism of the Sarit Centre, Banana Box works in conjunction with community projects and refugee groups and offers modern uses for traditional objects. It's one of the better handicrafts stores around town, with an upmarket feel but reasonable prices.

NAIROBI ART GALLERIES

The **Go-Down Arts Centre** (Map p60; ☎0726992200; www.thegodownartscentre.com; Dunga Rd; admission free; ⏲9am-5pm Mon-Fri), a converted warehouse in the Industrial Area, contains 10 separate art studios and is rapidly becoming a hub for Nairobi's burgeoning arts scene, bringing together visual and performing arts with regular exhibitions, shows, workshops and open cultural nights.

One of Nairobi's longest-established galleries, the central **Gallery Watatu** (Map p66; ☎Nairobi 020-2024857; Lonhro House, Standard St), has regular exhibitions of paintings, photography and some sculpture, and many of the items are for sale; be prepared to part with upwards of KSh20,000. It also has a good permanent display.

Spinners Web HANDICRAFTS
(Map p70; ☎Nairobi 020-2072629, 0731168996; www.spinnerswebkenya.com; Getathuru Gardens, off Peponi Rd, Spring Valley; ⏲9.30am-6.30pm Mon-Fri, 9.30am-5.30pm Sat & Sun) This place works with workshops and self-help groups around the country. It's a bit like a handicrafts version of Ikea, with goods displayed the way they might look in a Western living room. There are some appealing items, including carpets, wall-hangings, ceramics, wooden bowls, baskets and clothing.

Undugu Craft Shop HANDICRAFTS
(Map p70; www.undugukenya.org; Woodvale Grove, Westlands; ⏲8.30am-5.30pm Mon-Fri, 9am-2pm Sat) This nonprofit organisation supports community projects in Nairobi and has crafts including wood and soapstone carvings, basketwork and fair-trade food products.

City Market MARKET
(Map p66; Muindi Mbingu St; ⏲9am-5pm Mon-Fri, 9am-noon Sat) The city's main souvenir business is concentrated in this covered market, which has dozens of stalls selling wood carvings, drums, spears, shields, soapstone, Maasai jewellery and clothing. It's a hectic place and you'll have to bargain hard (and we mean *hard*), but there's plenty of good stuff on offer. It's an interesting place to wander around in its own right, though you generally need to be shopping to make the constant hassle worth the bother.

Westland Curio Market MARKET
(Map p70; Parklands Rd, Westlands; ⏲9am-5pm Mon-Sat) This complex of stalls, located at a road junction, has the usual tourist kitsch as well some genuine tribal objects, such as Turkana wrist-knives and wooden headrests. Like at the City Market, you're going to need to bargain hard here, though the sales pressure is a bit softer. It's near the Sarit Centre in Westlands.

Maasai Market MARKET
(Map p66; off Slip Road; ⏲Tue) Busy, popular Maasai Market is held every Tuesday on the waste ground near Slip Rd in town. Souvenirs on offer include beaded jewellery, gourds, baskets and other Maasai crafts, but you'll have to bargain hard. The market is open from early morning to late afternoon. Other locations include Friday behind the **Village Market shopping complex** (Village Market, Limuru Rd), **downtown** (Map p66; opposite Reinsurance Plaza, Taita Rd) on Saturday, and on Sunday next to the **Yaya Centre** (Map p60; Argwings Kodhek).

Information

CAMPING EQUIPMENT

Atul's (Map p66; ☎Nairobi 020-2225935; Biashara St; ⏲9am-1pm & 2-5pm Mon-Fri, 9am-4pm Sat) Hires out everything from sleeping bags to folding toilet seats.

X-treme Outdoors (Map p60; ☎0736411527; www.xtremeoutdoors.co.ke; Yaya Centre, Hurlingham; ⏲9am-5pm Mon-Fri, 9am-4pm Sat) All manner of camping equipment and other useful outdoor equipment.

DANGERS & ANNOYANCES

First-time visitors to Nairobi are understandably daunted by the city's unenviable reputation. 'Nairobbery', as it has been nicknamed by jaded residents and expats, is often regarded as the most dangerous city in Africa, beating stiff competition from Johannesburg, Abidjan and Lagos. Read the local newspapers and you'll quickly discover that carjacking, robbery and violence are daily occurrences, and the social ills behind them are unlikely to disappear in the near future.

The most likely annoyance for travellers is petty theft, which is most likely to occur at budget hotels and campsites. As a general rule, you should take advantage of your hotel's safe and never leave your valuables out in the open. While you're walking around town, don't bring anything with you that you wouldn't want to lose. As an extra safety precaution, it's best to only carry money in your wallet, and hide your credit cards and bank cards elsewhere.

In the event that you are mugged, never, ever resist – simply give up your valuables and, more often than not, your assailant will flee the scene rapidly. Remember that a petty thief and a violent aggressor are very different kinds of people, so don't give your assailant any reason to do something rash.

While it's important to understand the potential dangers and annoyances that are present, you shouldn't let fear exile you to your hotel room – remember that the majority of foreign visitors in Nairobi never experience any kind of problem. Exude confidence, practise street smarts, don't wear anything too flashy and you should encounter nothing worse than a few persistent safari touts and the odd con artist. Who knows? You may actually end up really enjoying your time in Nairobi.

Potential Trouble Spots

Compared to Johannesburg and Lagos – where armed guards, razor-wired compounds and patrol vehicles are the norm – Nairobi's Central Business District (CBD, bound by Kenyatta Ave, Moi Ave, Haile Selassie Ave and Uhuru Hwy) is quite relaxed and hassle-free. Walking around this area by day is rarely a problem. There are also plenty of *askaris* (security guards) about in case you need assistance.

Once the shops in the CBD have shut, the streets empty rapidly and the whole city centre takes on a deserted and slightly sinister air. After sunset, mugging is a risk anywhere on the streets, and you should always take a taxi, even if you're only going a few blocks. This will also keep you safe from the attentions of Nairobi's street prostitutes, who flood into town in force after dark. Uhuru Park is a very pleasant place during daylight hours, but it accumulates all kinds of dodgy characters at night.

There are a few other places where you do need to employ a slightly stronger self-preservation instinct. Potential danger zones include the area around Latema and River Rds (east of Moi Ave), which is a hot spot for petty theft. This area is home to the city's bus terminals, so keep an eye on your bags and personal belongings at all times if passing through here.

Scams

Nairobi's handful of active confidence tricksters seem to have relied on the same old stories for years, and it's generally easy to spot the spiels once you've heard them a couple of times.

As a general rule, always exercise caution while talking to anyone on the streets of Nairobi. While there are genuinely good people out there, the reality is that foreign tourists are an easy target for scamming.

Safari Touts

It is almost a certainty that at some point during your time in Nairobi you will be approached on the street by safari touts. Most of these persistent guys are hoping to drag you into an operator's office, where they can expect to receive a small commission. A small minority are hoping to distract you with their glossy brochures while they deftly lift your wallet.

This is not to say that safari touts are bad people – a good number of them really do want to help you make a booking. With that said, it's better to err on the side of caution and work directly with a reliable operator.

Nairobi Bump

Apart from the regular safari rip-offs, you should be careful of something known as the 'Nairobi bump'. The usual tactic is for a scammer to bump into you in the street, and then try to strike up a small conversation. If this happens, keep walking, as it's probably the most effective way of preventing your wallet or backpack from being stolen.

Old Friends?

You should also be wary of anyone who says they work at your hostel/hotel/campsite, even if they actually know the names of the staff there. We have received countless letters from travellers who have been duped into handing over money on the street for seemingly valid reasons, such as buying groceries for the evening's dinner. If someone claiming to be from your accommodation asks for money, be sceptical and just walk away.

Hard-luck Stories

One classic Nairobi con trick that you'll likely be subjected to is the refugee story, commonly combined with the equally well-worn university scam. In this gambit, it turns out that your interlocutor has coincidentally just won a scholarship to a university in your country (the amount of research they do is quite astounding), and would just love to sit down and have a chat with you about life there.

Then at some point you'll get the confidential lowering of the voice as the story kicks in with 'You know, I am not from here...', leading into an epic tale of woe that involves them having walked barefoot all the way from Juba or Darfur to flee the war. While once restricted to stories with a Sudanese focus, they could include stories from Zimbabwe, Somalia or just about any troubled African nation.

Of course, once you've shown due sympathy they'll come to the crux of the matter: they have to get to Mombasa or Dar es Salaam or elsewhere to confirm their scholarship and fly out for their studies, and all they need is a few thousand shilling – not that they could ask you, their new friend, for that much money, though anything you could spare to help them out would be greatly appreciated (you get the idea).

There are variations on the theme. One traveller wrote telling us how, after refusing to give anything, he was approached by two 'policemen' who promptly arrested the scammer and warned the traveller that he was in trouble for conspiring with an illegal immigrant. If this happens to you, ask to see police ID and try to enlist the help of people around you.

Terrorism

International terrorism first reared its head in modern Nairobi in August 1998 when al-Qaeda operatives bombed the US embassy, killing more than 200 people. Since 2011, Kenya's high-profile military presence in neighbouring Somalia has increased the risk of terrorist reprisals. The most serious attack was on the Westgate Shopping Mall on 21 September 2013, with 67 people killed, while bombings on buses and matatus, primarily in the Eastleigh area of the capital, have also claimed a number of lives.

Be vigilant. Avoid Eastleigh. Otherwise, go about your daily business and remember that while terrorism can happen anywhere, your chances of being caught up in such an incident are extremely low.

EMERGENCY

Emergency services (☎999) The national emergency number to call for fire, police and ambulance assistance. A word of warning, though – don't rely on prompt arrival.

Police (☎Nairobi 020-240000) Phone for less-urgent police business.

St John's Ambulance (☎2210000)

Tourist Helpline (☎Nairobi 020-604767; ⏲24hr)

INTERNET ACCESS

Your hotel is probably your best bet. Otherwise, there are hundreds of internet cafes in downtown Nairobi, most of them tucked away in anonymous office buildings in the town centre and few of which seem designed to last the distance. Connection speed is decent assuming you're not streaming YouTube, though machine quality varies wildly. It can be difficult to find any cyber cafe open in the downtown area on Sunday.

MEDICAL SERVICES

Nairobi has plenty of health-care facilities that are used to dealing with travellers and expats, which is a good thing as you're going to want to avoid the Kenyatta National Hospital – although it's free, stretched resources mean you may come out with something worse than you had when you went in.

AAR Health Services (Map p56; ☎0731191 070, 0725225225; www.aarhealth.com/aar_ke/; Williamson House, Fourth Ngong Ave; ⏲7.30am-8pm Mon-Fri, 8am-6pm Sat, 9am-5pm Sun) Probably the best of a number of private ambulance and emergency air-evacuation companies. It also runs private clinics at various locations around Nairobi, including in Westlands.

Acacia Medical Centre (Map p66; ☎Nairobi 020-2212200; info@acaciamed.co.ke; ICEA Bldg, Kenyatta Ave; ⏲7am-7pm Mon-Fri, 7am-5pm Sat, 8am-5pm Sun) Privately run clinic in the city centre.

Aga Khan Hospital (☎Nairobi 020-3662020; Third Parklands Ave; ⏲24hr) A reliable hospital with 24-hour emergency services.

KAM Pharmacy (Map p66; ☎Nairobi 020-2227195; www.kampharmacy.com; Executive Tower, IPS Bldg, Kimathi St; ⏲8.30am-6pm Mon-Fri, 8.30am-2pm Sat) A one-stop shop for medical treatment, with a pharmacy, doctor's surgery and laboratory.

Nairobi Hospital (Map p56; ☎Nairobi 020-2846000; www.nairobihospital.org; off Argwings Kodhek Rd; ⏲24hr) One of the city's largest hospitals.

MONEY

Jomo Kenyatta International Airport has several exchange counters in the baggage reclaim area and a **Barclays Bank** (⏲24hr) with an ATM outside in the arrivals hall. There are Barclays branches with guarded ATMs throughout the city centre and further afield – some of these are shown on the map. The other big bank is Standard Chartered Bank, which has numerous downtown branches. Foreign-exchange bureaus offer slightly better rates for cash than the banks. There are dozens of options in the town centre, so it's worth strolling around to see who is currently offering the best deal.

POST

Main Post Office (Map p66; ☎Nairobi 020-243434; Kenyatta Ave; ⏲8am-6pm Mon-Fri, 9am-noon Sat) The vast main post office is a well-organised edifice close to Uhuru Park. Around the back of the main building is the **EMS office** (Map p66; ⏲8am-8pm Mon-Fri, 9am-12.30pm Sat), for courier deliveries, and there's a Telkom Kenya office upstairs. Other post office locations are shown on the map.

TELEPHONE

Telkom Kenya (Map p66; ☎Nairobi 020-232000; Haile Selassie Ave; ⏲8am-6pm Mon-Fri, 9am-noon Sat) Telkom Kenya has dozens of payphones and you can buy phonecards. Many stands downtown sell Telkom Kenya phonecards and top-up cards for prepaid mobiles. Alternatively, there are numerous private agencies in the centre of town offering international telephone services.

MAJOR MATATU ROUTES

TO	FARE	DURATION	DEPARTURE POINT
Eldoret	KSh800	6 hr	Easy Coach Terminal
Kericho	KSh750	3 hr	Cross Rd
Kisumu	KSh700-1000	4 hr	Cross Rd
Meru	KSh750	3 hr	Main Bus & Matatu Area
Naivasha	KSh350	1½ hr	cnr River Rd & Ronald Ngala St
Nakuru	KSh500	3 hr	cnr River Rd & Ronald Ngala St
Namanga	KSh500	2 hr	cnr River Rd & Ronald Ngala St
Nanyuki	KSh500	3 hr	Main Bus & Matatu Area
Narok	KSh500	3 hr	Cross Rd
Nyahururu	KSh500	3½ hr	cnr River Rd & Ronald Ngala St
Nyeri	KSh500	2½ hr	Latema Rd

TOILETS

It may come as a shock to regular travellers to Africa, but Nairobi now has a handful of staffed public toilets around the downtown area offering flush toilets with a basic level of cleanliness. Signs will indicate if you need to pay (about KSh10). Some central shopping centres, such as Kenya Cinema Plaza, have free public conveniences.

TOURIST INFORMATION

Despite the many safari companies with signs saying 'Tourist Information', there is still no official tourist office in Nairobi. For events and other listings you'll have to check the local newspapers or glean what you can from a handful of magazines, which take a bit of effort to hunt down.

The vast noticeboards found at the Sarit Centre and Yaya Centre are good places to look for local information. All sorts of things are advertised here, including language courses, vehicles for sale and houses for rent.

TRAVEL AGENCIES

Bunson Travel (☎ Nairobi 020-3685990; www.bunsontravel.com; 2nd fl, Park Place, Limuru Rd) A good upmarket operator (part of the Carlson Wagonlit stable) selling air tickets and upmarket safaris.

ℹ Getting There & Away

AIR

Nairobi is the main arrival and departure point for international flights, although some touch down in Mombasa as well.

Nairobi has two airports:

Jomo Kenyatta International Airport (NBO; Map p60; ☎ 0722205061, Nairobi 020-822111; www.kaa.go.ke) Most international flights to and from Nairobi arrive at this airport, 15km southeast of the city. There are two international terminals and a smaller domestic terminal; you can walk easily between the terminals.

Wilson Airport (WIL; Map p60; ☎ 07242 55343, 0724256837; www.kaa.go.ke) Located 6km south of Nairobi's city centre on Langata Rd; with some flights between Nairobi and Kilimanjaro International Airport or Mwanza in Tanzania, as well as scheduled and charter domestic flights.

BUS

Bus Stations

In Nairobi, most long-distance bus company offices are in the River Rd area, clustered around Accra Rd and the surrounding streets, although some also have offices on Monrovia St for their international services. You should always make your reservation up to 24 hours in advance and check (then double check) the departure point from where the bus leaves.

Machakos Country Bus Station (Landhies Rd) The Machakos Country Bus Station is a hectic, disorganised place with buses heading all over the country; it serves companies without their own departure point. However, if you can avoid coming here, do so as theft is rampant.

DEPARTURE TIMES

Most long-distance bus services (to Mombasa or Kisumu, for example), leave in the early morning or late evening. If you have a choice, choose the former as travelling after dark on Kenya's roads increases the chances of being involved in an accident.

BUSES FROM NAIROBI

TO	FARE	DURATION	COMPANY
Eldoret	KSh1250	7-8 hr	Easy Coach
Kakamega	KSh1450	7½ hr	Easy Coach
Kisumu	KSh1400	7 hr	Easy Coach, Modern Coast (Oxygen)
Malaba	KSh1250	9-12 hr	Easy Coach
Malindi	KSh1100-1800	10-13 hr	Modern Coast (Oxygen), Dream Line
Mombasa	KSh500-1800	6-10hr	Modern Coast (Oxygen), Dream Line

Bus Companies

Dream Line (Map p66; ☎0731777799) A reliable company connecting Nairobi to Mombasa and Malindi.

Easy Coach (Map p66; ☎0726354301, 0738200301; www.easycoach.co.ke; Haile Selassie Ave, Nairobi) Long-standing company serving western Kenyan destinations as well as running some international buses to Uganda.

Modern Coast Express (Oxygen; Map p66; ☎0726778852, 0713202255; www.moderncoastexpress.com; cnr Cross Lane & Accra Rd) Safer, more reliable and slightly more expensive buses to Mombasa, Malindi and Kisumu, with Mombasa–Dar es-Salaam amd Nairobi–Kampala services.

Riverside Shuttle (Map p66; ☎0722220176; www.riverside-shuttle.com; Monrovia St) Mostly international services to Arusha, Moshi and Kilimanjaro International Airport (Tanzania).

MATATU

Most matatus leave from the chaotic Latema, Accra, River and Cross Rds and fares are similar to the buses. Most companies are pretty much the same, although there are some that aim for higher standards than others. Mololine Prestige Shuttle, which operates along the Nairobi–Naivasha–Nakuru–Eldoret route, is one such company, with others set to follow their example on other routes.

PEUGEOT (SHARED TAXI)

As with matatus, most of the companies offering Peugeot shared taxis have their offices around the Accra, River and Cross Rds area. Departures vary on demand, but you can usually find cars heading to Eldoret, Isiolo, Kabarnet, Kericho, Kisumu, Kitale, Meru, Malaba and Nakuru. Fares are about 20% higher than the same journeys by matatu. Most services depart in the morning.

TRAIN

Until the new Nairobi–Mombasa railway line comes into existence, a few (perhaps many) years from now, the existing railway is slow, old and unreliable but still something of an African epic. Do it because you love trains and aren't in a hurry, not for reasons of comfort or speed.

Scheduled departure times from Nairobi are at 6.30pm on Monday, Wednesday and Friday. All going well, you should arrive in Mombasa at 9.45am the following morning. Tickets cost US$75/55 per adult/child for 1st class (two-bed berths) and US$65/45 for 2nd class (four-bed berths) including bed and breakfast (you get dinner with 1st class). Book as far in advance as possible.

Railway Booking Office (Map p66; Station Rd; ⌚9am-noon & 2-6.30pm) Nairobi train station has a small booking office. You need to come in person to book tickets a few days in advance of your intended departure. On the day of departure, arrive early.

ℹ Getting Around

TO/FROM JOMO KENYATTA INTERNATIONAL AIRPORT

Kenya's main international airport (p83) is 15km out of town, off the road to Mombasa.

Taxi We recommend that you take a taxi (KSh1500 to KSh2000, but you'll need to bargain hard) to get to/from the airport, especially after dark. If you book at one of the 'information' desks at the airport, you'll still end up in a public taxi, but it isn't any more expensive.

Bus A far cheaper way to get into town is by city bus 34 (KSh40), but a lot of travellers get robbed on the bus or when they get off. Always hold onto valuables and have small change ready for the fare. Buses run from 5.45am to 9.30pm weekdays, 6.20am to 9.30pm Saturdays and 7.15am to 9.30pm Sundays, though the last few evening services may not operate. Heading to the airport, the main departure point is along Moi Ave, right outside the Hotel Ambassadeur Nairobi. Thereafter, buses travel west along Kenyatta Ave.

TO/FROM WILSON AIRPORT

To get to Wilson Airport (p83), the cheapest option is to take bus or matatu 15, 31, 34, 125 or 126 from Moi Ave (KSh35, 15 to 45 minutes depending on traffic). A taxi from the centre of town will cost at least KSh1000, depending on the driver. In the other direction, you'll have to fight the driver down from KSh1500. The entrance to the airport is easy to miss – it's just before the large petrol station.

CAR

If you are driving, beware of wheel-clampers: parking in the centre is by permit only (KSH200), available from the parking attendants who roam the streets in bright yellow jackets. If you park overnight in the street in front of your hotel, the guard will often keep an eye on your vehicle for a small consideration.

MATATU

Nairobi's horde of matatus follows the same routes as buses and display the same route numbers. For Westlands, you can pick up 23 on Moi Ave or Latema Rd. Matatu 46 to the Yaya Centre stops in front of the main post office, and 125 and 126 to Langata leave from in front of the train station. As usual, you should keep an eye on your valuables while on all matatus.

There are plans to phase out matatus and replace them with larger (and fewer) minibuses to reduce traffic congestion. No new matatu licences were being issued at the time of research, but don't expect to notice any difference in the short term.

TAXI

As people are compelled to use them due to Nairobi's endemic street crime, taxis here are overpriced and under-maintained, but you've little choice, particularly at night. Taxis don't cruise for passengers, but you can find them parked on every other street corner in the city centre – at night they're outside restaurants, bars and nightclubs.

Fares around town are negotiable but end up pretty standard. Any journey within the downtown area costs KSh500, from downtown to Milimani Rd costs KSh600, and for longer journeys such as Westlands or the Yaya Centre, fares range from KSh750 to KS900. From the city centre to Karen and Langata is around KSh1200 one way.

> **DOMESTIC BAGGAGE**
>
> Note that the check-in time for domestic flights is one to two hours before departure. Also be aware that the baggage allowance is only 15kg, as there isn't much space on the small turboprop aircraft.

AROUND NAIROBI

Ngong Hills

The green and fertile Ngong Hills were where many white settlers set up farms in the early colonial days. It's still something of an expat enclave, and here and there in the hills are perfect reproductions of English farmhouses with country gardens full of flowering trees – only the acacias remind you that you aren't rambling around the home counties of England.

The hills provide some excellent walking, but robbery has been a risk in the past; ask locals for the latest information. If you're worried, take an organised tour or an escort from the Ngong police station or KWS office.

Sights

Grave of Denys Finch Hatton HISTORIC SITE

(☎0723758639) Close to Pt Lamwia, the summit of the range, is the grave of Denys Finch Hatton, the famous playboy and lover of Karen Blixen. The site is now almost completely overgrown and is difficult to find 4km up the hill from Kiserian; ask someone to show you the way from Kiserian, and expect to pay a KSh250 tip.

A large obelisk marks his grave, inscribed with a line from 'The Rime of the Ancient Mariner', one of his favourite poems. The inscription reads 'He prayeth well, who loveth well/Both man and bird and beast'. There are legends about a lion and lioness standing guard at Finch Hatton's graveside, but these days they'd have trouble getting past the padlocked gate. Call ahead to make sure the custodian of the key is nearby.

Ngong Hills Racecourse STADIUM

(Map p60; ☎Nairobi 020-573923; Ngong Rd) Several Sundays a month, hundreds of Nairobi residents flee the noise and bustle of the city for the much more genteel surroundings of the Ngong Hills Racecourse, just east of Karen. The public enclosure is free to enter; entry to the grandstand is KSh150. There are usually three races every month during the season, which runs from October to July. You can get here on the Metro Shuttle bus (KSh60, 30 minutes) and matatus 24 or 111 (KSh30), all from Haile Selassie Ave.

In the past, races had to be cancelled because of rogue rhinos on the track, but the

WORTH A TRIP

ACACIA CAMP

Just 36km from central Nairobi, off the busy Nairobi–Mombasa Rd, **Acacia Camp** (☎Nairobi 020-2529500; www.swaraplains.com; s/d full board US$105/195; P 🛜), located within the Swara Plains Conservancy, is a wonderful escape from city life. The camp is extremely comfortable without being over the top, with well-appointed bungalows, good food and lovely gardens in the shade of acacias.

The ranch itself is spread out over 81 sq km and is home to giraffes, zebras, wildebeest, warthogs, a host of gazelles and antelopes and more than 270 bird species (but not cheetahs as advertised on its website); the only predator is a resident hyena. For additional charges, there are game drives.

biggest danger these days is stray balls from the golf course in the middle!

Sleeping

Maasai Ostrich Resort LODGE $$
(☎1-888-790-5264, 050-2502128; www.maasaiostrich.com; off A104; s/d from US$80/125; P 🏊) Combining an ostrich farm and a hotel is a fairly unusual idea, but, then again, why not? Certainly the simple but comfortable farmhouse accommodation and gardens provide a nice setting, and there's a range of activities (including ostrich riding!) to keep you busy in an otherwise unpromising area.

To get out here, take the road towards Namanga (A104) and turn left at the sign. Southbound public transport can get you to the turn-off, but it's another 7km to the farm itself.

Kiambethu Tea Farm

A visit to the **Kiambethu Tea Farm** (☎0733769976, Nairobi 020-2012542; www.kiambethu farm.co.ke; guided tour & lunch per person KSh2600) is a wonderful chance to get an insight into Kenya's tea plantations (Kenya is the world's largest exporter of black tea), as well as being an immensely enjoyable excursion from the city. The guided tour takes you through the history of Kenyan tea-growing, visits the lovely colonial-era farmhouse and can also encompass a nearby stand of primary forest.

Advance bookings are essential and some Nairobi tour companies can make the necessary arrangements, including transport. If you're coming in your own vehicle, print out the detailed directions from its website. The farm is around 25km northwest of central Nairobi.

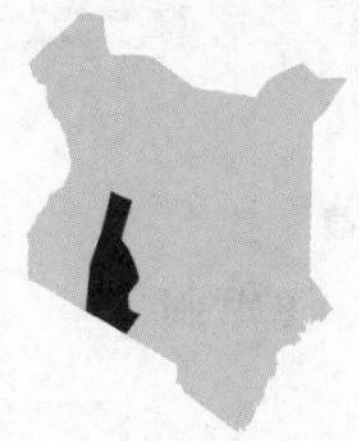

Southern Rift Valley

Best of Nature

- ➡ Lake Nakuru National Park (p102)
- ➡ Lake Baringo (p108)
- ➡ Lake Bogoria National Reserve (p107)
- ➡ Longonot National Park (p89)
- ➡ Hell's Gate National Park (p96)

Best of Culture

- ➡ Egerton Castle (p106)
- ➡ Elsamere (p93)

Why Go?

It's hard to believe that the geological force that almost broke Africa in two instead created such serene landscapes. But this southern slice of Africa's Great Rift Valley is cool and calm, swathed in forest and watered by moody mineral lakes that blanch and blush with the movements of pelicans and flamingos. There's no gold in these valleys and hills; it's green all the way, from pretty Lake Naivasha to Elmenteita's forest halo.

The altitude peaks and dips all the way from Nairobi to Nakuru, ensuring pleasant weather almost year-round. Only Lake Baringo, further north, feels the heat, although the hippos, crocodiles and fish eagles don't seem to mind.

Come for the green and the peace but don't miss the peaks that push skywards; Mt Longonot and, to a lesser degree, the Menengai Crater, offer some of the most exciting views around. Perhaps that's why this region is a birdwatcher's dream. And at Lake Nakuru National Park, the lions seem to agree; they've taken to climbing the trees. The Southern Rift Valley may be serene, but there's plenty to talk about around the campfire.

When to Go

Nakuru

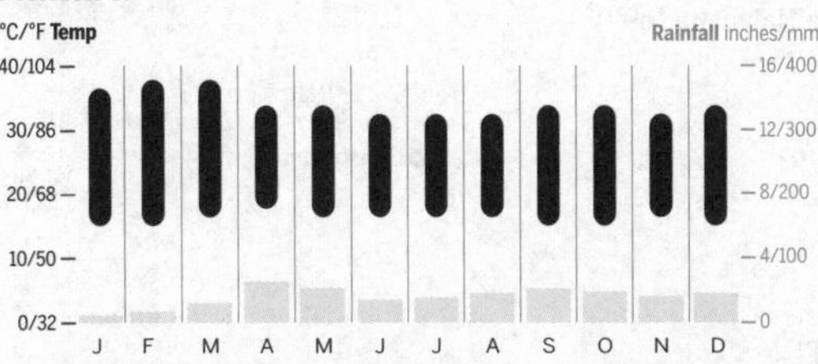

Nov–Mar Migratory bird species abound; weather is clear, dry and hot after November rains.

Jun–Oct Generally fine weather, no rains until October; good for climbing Mt Longonot.

Apr & May Avoid as rains drench the valley, mosquitoes proliferate and some roads are impassable.

Rift Valley Highlights

1. Viewing the slinky silhouettes of tree-climbing lions, as well as black and white rhinos at **Lake Nakuru National Park** (p102)
2. Watching self-conscious hippos shuffle into the spume, and then drifting off to their baritone song, at wild **Lake Baringo** (p108)
3. Trying to out-sprint a buffalo against the red-cliffed gorges of **Hell's Gate National Park** (p96)
4. Spotting pea-green chameleons beneath a disco ball sky at **Kembu Farm** (p106) in Njoro
5. Scaling the volcanic rim of **Mt Longonot** (p89) for a kestrel's-eye view of the great Rift Valley
6. Feeling pure, plutonic water soften your skin at the natural pedicure pools of **Lake Elmenteita** (p98)
7. Visiting the former home of Joy Adamson (of *Born Free* fame) then taking a boat out onto **Lake Naivasha** (p92)

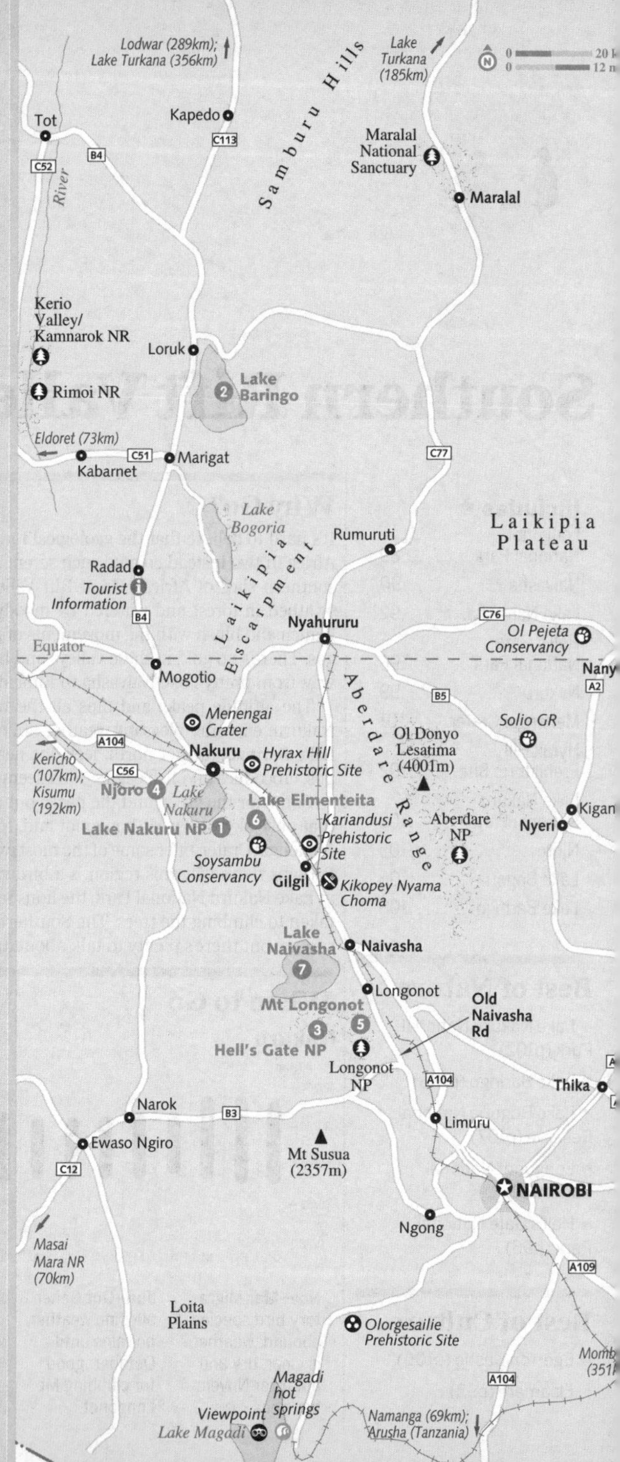

Lake Magadi & Around

The most mineral-rich of the Rift Valley's soda lakes is Lake Magadi, south of Nairobi. It is almost entirely covered by a thick encrustation of soda that supports small colonies of flamingos and gives the landscape a bizarre lunar appearance. It makes an interesting day trip from Nairobi, especially if you have your own transport and enough time to spot wildlife en route.

The lake's thick soda crust is formed when the mineral-rich water, pumped up from hot springs deep underground, evaporates rapidly in the 38°C temperature to leave a mineral layer. A soda-extraction factory 'harvests' this layer and extracts sodium chloride (common salt) and sodium carbonate (soda), which are then put straight onto trains to Mombasa. Not surprisingly, Magadi is purely a company town, run by the unimaginatively named Magadi Soda Co, for factory staff and their families.

To travel beyond the southern end of town, a checkpoint charges KSh300. It's worth it, for the causeway leads across the most visually dramatic part of this strange landscape to a **viewpoint** on the western shore; you'll need a 4WD. Otherwise you can head to the **hot springs** further south. The springs aren't particularly dramatic, but you can take a dip in the deeper pools and there are large numbers of fish that have adapted to the hot water. You may run into local Maasai, who will offer to show you the way and 'demonstrate' everything for you for a small fee.

Sights

Olorgasailie Prehistoric Site ARCHAEOLOGICAL SITE
(adult/child KSh500/250; sunrise-sunset) Travelling between Lake Magadi and Nairobi, take the turn-off for the famous Olorgasailie Prehistoric Site. Several important archaeological finds were made by the Leakeys in the 1940s at this site, 40km north of Magadi, including hundreds of hand axes and stone tools thought to have been made by Homo erectus about half a million years ago. Fossils have also been discovered and some are still there, protected from the elements by shade roofs. Supposedly free guided tours are compulsory, although a tip is expected.

Sleeping

Olorgasailie Campsite CAMPGROUND $
(Hwy C58; camping KSh250, new/old bandas KSh800/500) This campsite, at the gate of the Olorgasailie Prehistoric Site, is your only option out here. It's fairly basic (you'll need to bring your own food, bedding and drinking water), but you'll feel like you're properly in the bush.

Getting There & Away

Magadi is 105km southwest of Nairobi. The C58 road from Nairobi sees little traffic, but potholes are a constant problem. There's usually one matatu a day to Nairobi (KSh300), leaving in the morning and returning to Magadi in the evening.

Longonot National Park

One of the shapeliest peaks in all the Rift Valley, Mt Longonot (2776m) and its serrated crater rim offer fabulous views. The dormant volcano rises 1000m above the baking-hot valley floor and was formed 400,000 years ago; it last erupted in the 1860s. The **park** (050-50255; www.kws.org; adult/child US$20/10) itself covers only 52 sq km, and was set up to protect the volcano's ecosystem and little else. The name 'Longonot' comes from the Maasai name Olo Nongot, which means 'Mountain of Many Summits'.

The trail is clear and easy to follow and taking along a ranger is not necessary, although a good one will certainly enhance your trek; rangers can be arranged at the main gate as you enter.

WILDLIFE OF THE RIFT VALLEY

Kenya's Rift Valley is one of the country's premier birdwatching regions, with an astonishing congregation of species year-round, but especially during the November to March migration period. Flamingos are generally present year-round, but can move from lake to lake.

Lake Nakuru National Park (p102) is one of Kenya's finest parks, with both black and white rhinos in residence, as well as lions, leopards, reintroduced Rothschild's giraffes, zebras, buffaloes, olive baboons and black-and-white colobus monkeys.

WORTH A TRIP

MT SUSUA

Less frequented than Longonot but with a crater that's even more of a lost world, this unique volcano is well worth the considerable effort of visiting. The steep outer crater protects a second inner crater, whose rim peaks at 2357m and begs to be trekked. There's also a network of unexplored caves on the east side of the mountain, some of which are home to baboons.

There's no designated route and all land is owned by local Maasai, so you'll have to find someone from the nearby villages that dot the B3 Nairobi–Narok road to guide you. It's a 90-minute drive from Nairobi to the point where you leave the tarmac road, whereafter it's a further 2½ hours to the crater's outer rim. It takes about eight hours to circumnavigate the outer crater, meaning that you'll need to camp overnight (and be completely self-sufficient in food and water). Is it worth it? Absolutely, not least because you and the Maasai will have it all to yourselves.

Activities

The one- to 1½-hour hike from the park gate up to the crater rim (2545m) is strenuous but, without question, worth the considerable effort. There are two steep stretches that will challenge those not used to hiking. Your reward is to emerge at the lip of the crater rim for superb views of the 2km- to 3km-wide crater – a little lost world hosting an entirely different forest ecosystem.

It takes between 1½ and 2½ hours to circumnavigate the crater; watch for occasional steam vents rising from the crater floor. A guide to the crater rim and back is KSh1500 (KSh2500 including the summit).

Sleeping

Most people stay in Lake Naivasha, a 30-minute drive away.

Oloongonot Campsite CAMPGROUND $
(camping US$25) This campsite sits just beyond the gate on the way up to the Mt Longonot crater. There's space to pitch a tent and a toilet and shower block but no firewood; you'll need to bring all your own food and cooking supplies.

Getting There & Away

If you're driving, Mt Longonot is 75km northwest of Nairobi on the Old Naivasha Rd. If you're without a vehicle, take a matatu from Naivasha to Longonot village, from where there's a path (ask locals) to the park's access road.

Naivasha

POP 182,000

The gateway to the lake, this small country town knows a thing or two about hard work. Migrants come from all over Kenya, basing themselves in Naivasha to work at the flower farms that dot the lake's shoreline. Meet them in the brightly painted cafes all over town, plastered with cheery names and cheesy slogans.

While Naivasha makes an interesting coffee break, there isn't much to keep you here. The lake, with its much better sleeping options, is a mere 18km away. Still, if you need a bed, a snack or an ATM, your best bet is Moi Ave.

Sleeping

La Belle Inn HOTEL $
(Map p91; ☎050-3510404, 0722683218; Moi Ave; s/d KSh3000/4000; 📶) This shabby but charming colonial hotel was built in 1922 and is a delight. Rooms are set around an inner courtyard; they are comfortable but elderly, infused with a certain grandmotherly charm. Anyone can take tea (or meals) on the verandah, complete with 1970s-era table numbers, bow-tied waiters and old-fashioned tablecloths.

Wanibuku Hotel HOTEL $
(Map p91; ☎050-2030287; Moi Ave; s/d KSh1000/2000) Although it looks like an overpopulated block of inner city flats, this hotel has clean rooms in a central location. Windows overlook the courtyard and the noise carries, especially on weekend nights. The doubles and twins are decidedly nicer than the singles, and have televisions.

Silver Lodge HOTEL $
(Map p91; ☎0717465226; Kenyatta Ave; s/d KSh600/1000) Well, they've gone to the trouble of cheering up the concrete yard, splashing it in baby blue and pink, so that counts for something. The rooms here are fine if you're stuck for cheap digs in Naivasha, but

would be depressing for anything longer than a night. In a reasonably secure back courtyard, with a restaurant attached.

Eating & Drinking

Delamere Indian Restaurant RESTAURANT $
(Map p92; Naivasha–Nakuru Highway; mains from KSh400; ⏲8am-10pm; 🅿✍) A peaceful garden restaurant bang on the Naivasha–Nakuru highway? Indeed there is. Delamere serves good, fast Indian food to a loyal crowd and is popular with everyone from local families to tourists heading north. Grab one of the shaded picnic tables in the garden and enjoy views out over the fields.

Jolly Cafe CAFE $
(Map p91; Kenyatta Ave; meals from KSh300; ⏲6am-10pm) Jolly by name, and by nature too. This colourful, old-fashioned caff offers cheery service and greasy plates of fried chicken, masala chips and breakfast dishes, served with a side of local gossip and loaded with spirit.

Smiles Café KENYAN $
(Map p91; Kariuki Chotara Rd; meals KSh100-150; ⏲breakfast, lunch & dinner) As cheap and cheerful as the name suggests, this little green-and-white treasure offers cholesterol-filled fried breakfasts and hearty stews. It's always busy and conversations come easy.

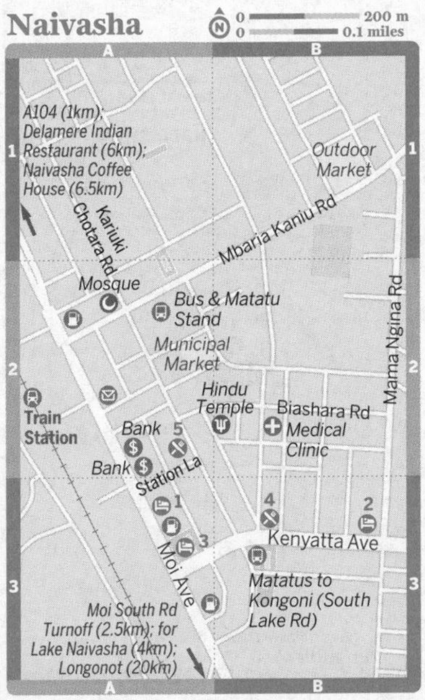

Cool Breeze CAFE $
(Map p91; Kenyatta Ave; dishes from KSh80) Marry a greasy spoon with an American diner and this is what you'll get: a low-slung cafe with buckets of charm and a clear sense of humour (there's no breeze whatsoever). This is a good meeting spot, and it does slightly more adventurous things like local yoghurt shakes and fresh mango juice, alongside the usual local favourites.

Drinking & Nightlife

Naivasha Coffee House CAFE
(Map p92; Naivasha-Nakuru Highway; ⏲6am-9pm) This sleek hole-in-the-wall coffee stop serves herbal teas, hot chocolate, frappucinos and caramel concoctions, as well as – obviously – decent coffee. Find it opposite the petrol station at the Delamere Service Station. Next door, there's a fruit shop selling freshly squeezed passionfruit and beetroot juices, among others.

Thrills Place CLUB
(Map p91; Moi Ave; ⏲5pm-dawn Wed-Sat) FREE The least seedy of Naivasha's clubs, you'll find local DJs, a disco ball and dancing till dawn at this popular place. We'll let you decide if the name rings true.

Getting There & Away

The main **bus and matatu station** (Map p91; off Mbaria Kaniu Rd) is close to the municipal market. Frequent buses and matatus leave for Nakuru (KSh200, 1¼ hours) and Nairobi (KSh350, two hours).

Frequent matatus run around the south side of the lake to Kongoni (KSh100) and Fisherman's Camp area (KSh100, 45 minutes). They depart from the bus station and from Kenyatta Ave.

Naivasha

Sleeping
1 La Belle Inn A3
2 Silver Lodge B3
3 Wanibuku Hotel A3

Eating
4 Cool Breeze B3
Jolly Cafe .... (see 2)
5 Smiles Café A2

Drinking & Nightlife
Thrills Place .... (see 1)

Lake Naivasha

A short drive from Nairobi and a world away from the capital's choked arteries is Lake Naivasha, the highest of the Rift Valley lakes (at 1884m above sea level). Hugged by grassy banks and shingled with cacti and sand olive trees, the lake extends like a vast, sunlit sea. Stand on one side of it and you won't see the other; only clouds of water birds and the pinkened ears of hippos, peeking like submarine periscopes above the surface. Superb starlings, their eyes shiny like sequins, flit between the acacia trees and later, take on the night sky: you don't see stars like this in Nairobi.

But there's more to this spot than the lovely blue lake. Translucent tents of flower farms line Moi South Lake Rd, and rose growers board buses on their way to work. By nightfall, the flowers they grow will be in Europe. Gospel song drifts from roadside churches while down by the shoreline, campfires are lit by happy campers. You can ride among giraffes and zebras, sip on a glass of Rift Valley red, and relax in the garden at Elsamere, the former home of late *Born Free* personality Joy Adamson.

Most of the lake is ringed by an electric fence, so hippo attacks are rare. A greater threat is the traffic, which loops around the road at speed: take care when out walking.

History

A vast range of plains animals and a plethora of birdlife have long called the verdant shoreline home, as have the Maasai, who considered it prime grazing land. Unfortunately for the Maasai, the splendour of the surroundings wasn't lost on early settlers, and it was one of the first areas settled, eventually becoming the favourite haunt of Lord Delamere and the decadent Happy Valley set of the 1930s.

Lake Naivasha

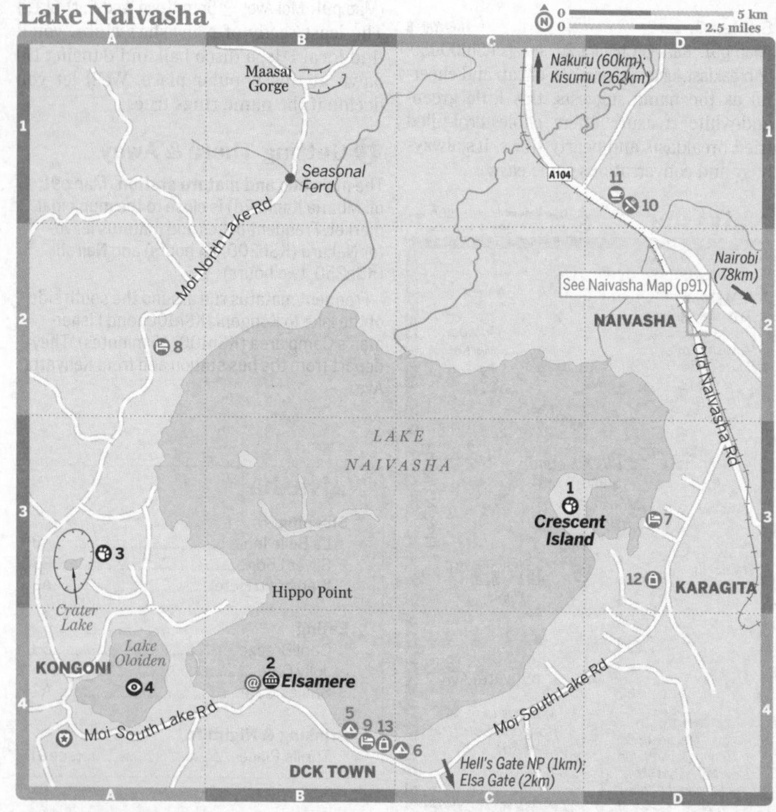

Amazingly, between 1937 and 1950, the lake was Kenya's main airport, with British Overseas Airways Corporation's Empire and Solent flying-boats landing here after their four-day journey from Southampton.

Sights & Activities

★Elsamere
MUSEUM

(Map p92; ☎Nairobi 020-2050964, 0722648123; www.elsamere.com; admission KSh1050; ⊙8am-6.30pm; P) Stippled with sisal, yellow fever trees and candelabra euphorbia, this is the former home of the late Joy Adamson of *Born Free* fame. She bought the house in 1967 with her husband George, and did much of her painting, writing and conservation work here until her murder in 1980. Guests can attend regular screenings of a flickering 1970s film about Joy's life and her myriad love affairs, notably with Elsa the lioness.

There's also a fascinating museum housed in the couple's former master bedroom, brimming with cloth-bound animal behaviour manuals, dusty typewriters, photographs and Joy's art. In the yard, the vehicle in which George was shot dead, sits empty.

Entry includes high tea (with cakes) on the peaceful lawn, and front-row seats to study the resident black and white colobus monkeys. You can also visit the conservation centre in the grounds, or even stay here in one of the lovely garden rooms (p94).

Crater Lake Game Sanctuary
WILDLIFE RESERVE

(Map p92; per person US$25, plus car KSh200) Surrounding a beautiful volcanic crater lake fringed with acacias, this small sanctuary has many trails, including one for hikers along the steep but diminutive crater rim. The jade-green crater lake is held in high regard by the local Maasai, who believe its alkaline waters help soothe ailing cattle. As well as the impressive 150 bird species recorded here, giraffes, zebras and other plains wildlife are also regular residents on the more open plains surrounding the crater.

Leopards, servals, caracals and aardvarks have also been spotted; the lone hippo who once lived here has moved on. While walking, remember that buffaloes lurk in the woods. There are also night safaris and guided nature walks for those staying at the sanctuary's camp (p95).

Lake Oloiden
LAKE

(Map p92; boat safaris per 30/60min KSh2000/4000) Lake Naivasha may be a freshwater lake, but the alkaline waters of its near neighbour Lake Oloiden draw small but impressive flocks of flamingos. Boat safaris are available. Apart from anything else, the real appeal here is that it's one of the few stretches of public land in the area where you can walk near to the lakeshore.

★Crescent Island
WILDLIFE RESERVE

(Map p92; admission US$30; ⊙8am-6pm) This private island sanctuary can be reached by boat, or by driving across the narrow, swampy causeway from Sanctuary Farm. It's one of the few places in the Rift Valley where you can walk among giraffes, zebras, waterbucks, impalas and countless bird species. Lucky visitors might even spot a leopard. Island walks, led by a guide, last between 90 minutes and three hours. It's also a good spot for a picnic lunch.

Boat Safaris

Most of the camps and lodges along Lake Naivasha's southern shore rent out boats (per boat per hour from KSh3000); most

Lake Naivasha

Top Sights

1	Crescent Island	C3
2	Elsamere	B4

Sights

3	Crater Lake Game Sanctuary	A3
4	Lake Oloiden	A4

Sleeping

5	Camp Carnelley's	B4
	Crater Lake Camp	(see 3)
6	Crayfish Camp	C4
	Crescent Camp	(see 6)
	Elsamere Lodge	(see 2)
7	Enashipai	D3
	Fisherman's Camp	(see 5)
8	Olerai House	A2
9	Sanctuary Farm	B4

Eating

	Club House	(see 9)
10	Delamere Indian Restaurant	D1
	Lake Naivasha Country Club	(see 6)
	Lazybones	(see 5)
	Tamu Tamu	(see 5)

Drinking & Nightlife

11	Naivasha Coffee House	D1

Shopping

12	Elmenteita Weavers	D3
13	Fired Earth	B4
	Lake Naivasha Farm Shop	(see 13)

ROSES ARE RED...

Depending on who you talk to, Lake Naivasha's blooming flower industry is either a blessing or a curse. The lake's fresh water bestows it with a unique ecosystem (many other Rift Valley lakes are highly alkaline) which means it can also be used for irrigation purposes.

Roses are the main export, and astoundingly, flowers picked here in the early morning can be at Europe's flower auctions the same day. The industry attracts migrant workers from all over Kenya, and although it has been regulated in recent years, working conditions inside the flower farms aren't easy. Visitors to Lake Naivasha may spot tired factory workers snoozing by the road as they wait for shuttle buses to carry them home.

Many flower farms are improving conditions for workers, and some of the better factories offer tours for visitors. Ask at your guesthouse or campsite for information.

boats have seven seats and come with pilot and lifejackets. Places where nonguests can organise a boat rental include Fisherman's Camp and Elsamere.

Sleeping

Moi South Lake Road

★Camp Carnelley's CAMPGROUND, BANDAS $
(Map p92; ☎050-50004, 0722260749; www.campcarnelleys.com; Moi South Lake Rd; r from KSh2500, bandas Ksh6000-12,000, dm Ksh800, camping Ksh600-800; P) Right on the shoreline, this lovely, quiet spot has chic *bandas* (thatched huts), simple twin rooms with woolly blankets and camping pitches within earshot of the hippos. Head down to the wooden-beamed bar with its hip couches, roaring fireplace and creative menu. Boats are on standby for lake safaris.

Fisherman's Camp CAMPGROUND, BANDAS $
(Map p92; ☎Nairobi 020-2139922, 0718880634, 0726870590; www.fishermanscamp.com; bandas per person KSh1000-2000, camping KSh600, tent hire KSh500; P) Scruffier and more sociable than its next-door neighbour Carnelley's, Fisherman's Camp attracts a young, backpacker crowd keen to eat and drink in the restaurant and hang out at the volleyball court. It's set in nice lake-shore gardens, shaded by dappled fever trees. The rooms are simple but comfortable (prices rise on weekends). Also plays host to the **Rift Valley Music Festival** each August.

Crayfish Camp CAMPGROUND $
(Map p92; ☎0720226829; www.crayfishcamp.co.ke; camping KSh700, s/d KSh4750/7500, fantasy r per person KSh2200; P) Fancy sleeping in a converted boat with leopard print curtains? How about a romantic night crammed into a broken-down bus or a toy-sized 4WD? There are 82 rooms ranging from vanilla doubles to fantasy options, plus a theme pub, a kids' play area and a restaurant serving milkshakes. Still, it does feel a bit like a 1980s holiday camp.

The disco gets going every night.

★Sanctuary Farm BOUTIQUE HOTEL $$
(Map p92; www.sanctuaryfarmkenya.com; s/d KSh15,000/20,000, camping KSh6000; P) Within a private 400-acre conservancy and dairy farm, this beautiful place makes the perfect weekend escape from Nairobi. The rooms are stylish, high-quality and elegant, and there's access to a cosy wi-fi lounge/library. You can also go riding among giraffes and zebras. Lovely breakfasts, good wines and delicious, healthy mains are on offer at the farm-to-table restaurant. Book online.

★Dea's Gardens GUESTHOUSE $$
(☎0734453761, 0733747433; www.deasgardens.com; Moi South Lake Rd; half-board KSh9350) This charming guesthouse is run by the warm and elegant Dea. The main house (with two rooms) is a gorgeous chalet of Swiss inspiration, while the two cottages in the lush grounds are large and comfortable. Meals are served in the main house with Dea as your host. Warmly recommended.

★Elsamere Lodge HOTEL $$
(Map p92; ☎050-2021055; www.elsamere.com; s/d KSh9500/15,000; P) The conservation centre at the very lovely former home of Joy Adamson (p93) also doubles as a lodge with high novelty value. You can stay here, in pleasant bungalows dotted through the pretty garden where wild colobus monkeys roam, and enjoy high tea in the Adamson's dining room.

Crescent Camp TENTED CAMP $$
(Map p92; ☎0715286001; s/d KSh12,000/16,000; P) There are 19 luxury tents set in

landscaped surrounds here, plus a simple restaurant and a cute jungle-themed bar. Three of the tents are wheelchair-accessible.

Enashipai HOTEL $$$

(Map p92; ☎051-2130000, 0713254035; www.enashipai.com; s/d US$350/485; P@🛜🏊) By far the sleekest of the resorts along the lake shore, Enashipai comes from the Maasai name meaning 'state of happiness', and it's no misnomer. If you like your resorts polished and luxurious, with a private, gated-community feel, you're at the right place. Warm staff, a good restaurant and an ultra-chic spa make it easy to unwind here.

Moi North Lake Road

The north side of the lake is wilder than the south, with fewer villages and flower farms. Hippos often wander into the road at night, so take care when driving after dark.

Olerai House GUESTHOUSE $$$

(Map p92; ☎Nairobi 020-8048602; www.olerai.com; s/d full board US$495/800) Hidden under a blanket of tropical flowers, this beautiful house is like something from a fairy tale, where petals dust the beds and floors, zebras and vervet monkeys hang out with pet dogs, and the rooms are a delight. Perhaps best of all, the camp is owned by renowned elephant conservationists Iain and Oria Douglas-Hamilton – if they're at home, there are few more fascinating hosts in Kenya.

Crater Lake Camp LUXURY CAMP $$$

(Map p92; ☎050-2020613; www.craterlakecamp.com; r from US$166) This tented camp, inside the private Crater Lake Game Sanctuary (p93), nestles among trees and overlooks the tiny jade-green crater lake. The tents aren't exactly luxurious, but they are extremely comfortable, and the honeymoon tent contains a whirlpool bath and other romantic essentials. Nature walks and night safaris are included in the price.

Eating

Almost all of the campsites and guesthouses have their own restaurants, so there is little in the way of independent dining.

Tamu Tamu CAFE $

(Map p92; Moi South Lake Rd, DCK Village; mains KSh90-250; ⏰lunch & dinner Mon-Sat) This local joint has bright-blue walls and long, communal benches. It serves beef dishes, beans, *gari* (cassava) and chapati, with sides of village gossip and Nollywood films. On South Lake Rd, between Carnelley's Camp and Crayfish Camp.

★Lazybones RESTAURANT $$

(Map p92; Camp Carnelley's, Moi South Lake Rd; mains from KSh450) Camp Carnelley's hip restaurant is popular with NGO workers and other Nairobians at weekends. Grab one of the gorgeous low-slung sofas, or pull up a chair around the roaring fireplace. Co-owner Chrisi's creative menu includes Indian fusion dishes, great salads, fresh fish and even breakfast smoothies. There's also a selection of wines, beers and spirits. Out back, you'll find a pool table.

★Club House RESTAURANT $$

(Map p92; ☎0722761940; Sanctuary Farm; lunch KSh2000, dinner KSh2500) Farm-to-table sustainable cuisine is more exciting when there are giraffes and hippos to spy on in the distance. The signature eatery at Sanctuary Farm is relaxed but stylish, with tables strewn over a wooden verandah. Inside, there are framed black-and-white posters and Rift Valley wines. Expect dishes such as beetroot salad, red pepper chicken, home-baked focaccia and baklava with pineapple sorbet. Reservations only.

Lake Naivasha Country Club BUFFET $$

(Map p92; ☎0703048200; Moi South Lake Rd; buffet KSh2000; 🛜) The country club is a bit of an institution in these parts, and is *the* place to be seen having lunch. The daily

DON'T MISS

KIKOPEY NYAMA CHOMA CENTRE

It's not often we give a cluster of restaurants their own coverage, but this agglomeration of roadside barbecued-meat stalls 31km north of Naivasha is famous throughout Kenya. Kikopey is a major truck stop, and it's no surprise why. These places don't survive long if their meat isn't perfectly cooked. The restaurants closest to the road hassle new arrivals, and try to draw you in. We tried Acacia Restaurant, a little back from the main road on a side road, and found it outstanding, but they're all good. You'll pay around KSh400 per kilo of meat.

buffet here is very good, served inside the somewhat stiff dining room or outside on the lush green lawn. There's everything from a salad bar to a chicken grill, and a very tempting dessert counter. The plush hotel wing is adjacent.

Shopping

There are three artisanal shops at Lake Naivasha, all within 500m of another. If you don't have your own transport, bank on a 10-minute walk towards the lake, from the small junction with Moi South Lake Rd.

Elmenteita Weavers CRAFTS
(Map p92; off Moi South Lake Rd; 8am-5pm) This tiny cooperative turns out beautiful rugs, throws and bags, and does a nice line in wooden souvenirs – including cute salt and pepper pots. Most things in the store are handmade by the two friendly weavers on the loom in the back.

Lake Naivasha Farm Shop FOOD
(Map p92; 0733237813; off Moi South Lake Rd; 9.30am-5pm) This is the place to come for Rift Valley wines and other local delights, including artisanal sweet-chilli pickle, lime marmalade and honey from the foot of Mt Longonot. If you're self-catering, browse the upmarket essentials, such as veggies, eggs, milk and spices.

Fired Earth ARTS & CRAFTS
(Map p92; off Moi South Lake Rd; 8am-5pm) You'll be welcomed by three male potters at this simple, friendly workshop. Watch the spinning kiln and browse the small store, where there's a range of lamps, bowls, cups and mosaic coasters for sale.

Getting There & Away

Frequent matatus (KSh100, one hour) run along Moi South Lake Rd between Naivasha town and Kongoni on the lake's western side, passing the turn-offs to Hell's Gate National Park and Fisherman's Camp (KSh70). Taxis charge upwards of KSh2000 for the hop from Naivasha.

Bora Bora Backpacker Bus (0722504655; www.boraborabackpackerbus.com; KSh1500) Bora Bora backpacker bus was in the process of launching at the time of research, offering easy shuttle runs from Nairobi to Lake Naivasha and beyond.

Nickson Gatimu (0726797750) Nickson Gatimu does taxi pick-ups in both direction, and also acts as an informal guide to Naivasha and the lake.

Getting Around

Most lodges and camps hire mountain bikes if you're heading for Hell's Gate National Park; costs start from KSh700 per day. Check the bikes carefully before paying.

Matatu hops around the lake shore cost upwards of KSh50, depending on distance. The drivers know most of the lodges and campsites and can drop you close by.

Hell's Gate National Park

Dry and dusty but infinitely peaceful, **Hell's Gate** (0726610508, Nairobi 020-2379467; www.kws.org; adult/child US$30/20, bike hire KSh600, car entry KSh350, camping US$35; P) is that rare thing: an adventurous Kenyan park with large animals, safe to explore by bicycle or on foot.

Large carnivores are very rare, so you can cycle to your heart's content past grazing zebras, giraffes, impalas and buffaloes, spot rock hyraxes as they clamber up inclines and chase dust clouds as they swirl in the wind. And if the pedalling isn't enough exercise, hike the gorge or climb Fischer's Tower.

In the early morning the park is all aglow; its rich ochre soils and savannah grasses squeezed between looming cliffs of rusty columnar basalt. The hushing wind passing between the rock formations gives it an otherworldly feel. Outside of the midday heat, the park is a good place for quiet meditation, and there are lots of great picnic spots, too.

Sights

Hell's Gate Gorge CANYON
The gorge that runs through the heart of the park is a wide, deep valley hemmed in by sheer, rusty-hued rock walls. Marking its eastern entrance is Fischer's Tower, a 25m-high volcanic column named after Gustav Fischer, a German explorer who reached the gorge in 1882. Commissioned to find a route from Mombasa to Lake Victoria, Fischer was stopped by territorial Maasai, who slaughtered almost his entire party.

All through this valley you'll come across zebras, the occasional giraffe, warthogs and various antelope species, while birds of prey circle overhead. Sadly, extensive geothermal excavation is now taking place close to the gorge, prompting complaints from visitors and concerns for the health of some animals. The road towards the gorge is now tarmacked, and you may spot industrial pipes.

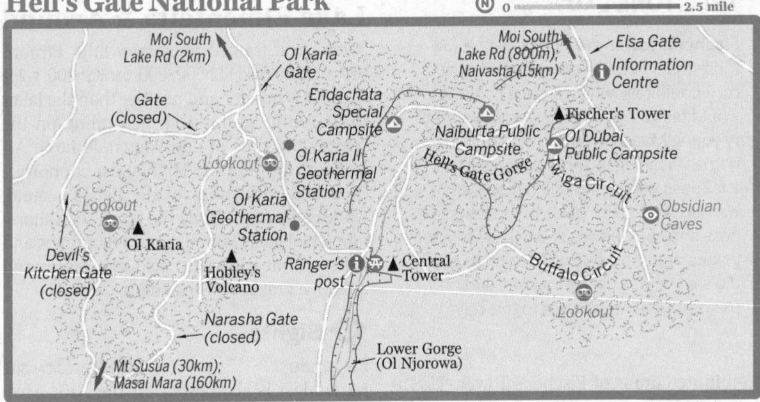

Lower Gorge CANYON

(Ol Njorowa; guide per hr KSh500) Rising from the main gorge's southern end is the large Central Tower, an unusual volcanic plug. A picnic site and ranger's post are close by, from where a walk descends into the Lower Gorge (Ol Njorowa). In some places the riverbed is dry, in others you'll find yourself scrambling down a steep and slippery descent. Some steps have been cut into the rock, and some parts may be perilous. We recommend taking a guide.

Buffalo Circuit PARK

A well-signposted track loops away to the south from close to the main Elsa gate, climbing up and over the hills before rejoining the main valley after 14km. En route, you'll have some outstanding views of Mt Longonot, and there's generally more wildlife here, including giraffes, various antelope species and the odd buffalo or two. The Buffalo Circuit would be a fairly strenuous walk or cycle, but it's accessible by 2WD vehicle, except after heavy rain.

Close to the Elsa gate end of the trail, a side track leads for 2km to the **Obsidian Cave**, where you'll find moderately interesting examples of the glassy black rock so characteristic of Rift Valley lava flows.

Activities

Cycling

Cycling is our favourite way to explore the park, and the main Hell's Gate Gorge is relatively flat; the distance from Elsa gate to the Lower Gorge is around 7km. Bicycles are available at Lake Naivasha junction for Ksh500 per hour and at Elsa gate.

Elsa Gate Bike Hire BICYCLE RENTAL

(per day KSh600) Mountain bikes can be rented at Elsa gate, but test them out rigorously before handing over the money – dodgy brakes and gears are common problems, although rangers are on hand to assist.

Walking

Hiking through the park and its wildlife is incredibly rewarding and relatively leisurely. Allow a full day and take plenty of supplies.

Rock Climbing

The sheer rock walls of Hell's Gate are just made for climbing and, thankfully, the park has two resident safety-conscious climbers.

Simon Kiane & James Maina ROCK CLIMBING

(0727039388, 0720909718) Simon and James work as climbing instructors and guides on weekends; they also have some basic equipment. They offer relatively easy 10- to

HELL'S GATE NATIONAL PARK

Why Go Dramatic volcanic scenery; a chance to walk or cycle through wildlife areas.

When to Go June to March.

Practicalities There's an Information Centre at Elsa gate.

Budget Tips Get any matatu circling the Lake Naivasha to drop you at the junction to Elsa gate, where you can hire a bike for the 2km to the gate itself. Bike rental here runs cheaper than at the Information Centre.

THE STONE LADY

Fischer's Tower may look like nothing more than a needle of rock, but if that rock could talk, which it once could, it would tell you how it was actually a pretty young Maasai woman, sent from her home village against her wishes to marry a fearless warrior. As she left she was warned not to turn back, but in her sadness she couldn't resist one last longing glance at her old home. As soon as she did so, she was cast into stone and remains rooted to the spot to this day.

15-minute climbs of Fischer's Tower (US$10 to US$20) and more challenging routes on the gorge's sheer red walls (US$100). If they're not in their usual place at the base of Fischer's Tower, give them a call or check at the park gate before you enter.

Sleeping

Most visitors stay at one of Lake Naivasha's many lodges and camps, but the park has three gorgeous, if rudimentary, campgrounds.

Naiburta Public Campsite CAMPGROUND $
(camping US$35) Naiburta, sitting on a gentle rise on the northern side of the Hell's Gate Gorge and commanding fine views west past Fischer's Tower, is the most scenic site in the area, and has basic toilets, an open *banda* for cooking and freshwater taps.

Ol Dubai Public Campsite CAMPGROUND $
(camping US$35) Resting on Hell's Gate Gorge's southern side and accessible from the Buffalo Circuit track, Ol Dubai has basic toilets, a cooking *banda* and fresh water. It offers views west to the orange bluffs, and the puffs of steam from the geothermal power station at the far end of the park.

Endachata Special Campsite CAMPGROUND $
(camping US$40) This 'special' campsite has no services, and besides absolute solitude, offers no more ambience than the cheaper public sites.

Getting There & Around

The usual access point to the park is through the main Elsa gate, 2km from Moi South Lake Rd. With the two gates on the northwest corner of the park closed, the only other gate is Ol Karia.

Lake Elmenteita & Around

Serene and framed by shaggy hills, **Elmenteita** (adult/child KSh500/200, car KSh200, guide KSh300) is quieter and prettier than the lakes to its south. Squint and, depending on the season and time of day, you could be in Arizona or the Scottish Highlands; euphorbia, cacti and rocks stipple the higher ground, while cattle graze along the green soda shoreline. The lake is famous for its flamingos and pelicans, but you might also spot zebras and antelope grazing on the edges.

Sights

Kariandusi ARCHAEOLOGICAL SITE
Kariandusi is signposted off the A104 Hwy near Lake Elmenteita. It was here in the 1920s that the Leakeys (a family of renowned archaeologists) discovered numerous obsidian and lava tools made by early humans between 1.4 million and 200,000 years ago. Two excavation sites are preserved and two galleries display a brief history of early human life.

Volcanic Pools SPRING
FREE This series of tiny volcanic pools on the western side of Lake Elmenteita is used by Maasai women and local communities. You can reach them in about 30 minutes, starting from Oasis Eco Camp and following the shoreline clockwise, dipping back behind the hill. Barely big enough to soak both feet, the pools are perfect for improvised pedicures: you'll emerge with baby-soft skin. Be sure to exercise patience and respect if you find the pools already in use.

Soysambu Conservancy WILDLIFE CONSERVANCY
(0711235039; www.soysambuconservancy.org; adult/child US$47/24) This private conservancy offers quite extensive wildlife viewing, and camping. It is home to colobus monkeys, Rothschild's giraffes and about 450 species of birdlife.

Sleeping

Oasis Eco Camp ECO LODGE $$
(0729940165, 0729910410; www.oasis.co.ke; Lake Elmenteita; full-board bandas from KSh6000, camping Ksh500, tent hire Ksh1000; P) Homely and peaceful, Oasis is nestled at the foot of the lake. The *bandas* combine hip duplex balconies with simple, grandmotherly decor, and the food is freshly prepared. Breakfast is served picnic-style, right by the lake.

★ **Sunbird Lodge** LODGE $$$
(☎0733555777, 0715555777; www.sunbirdkenya.com; off Naivasha-Nakuru highway, Lake Elmenteita; d with full board from US$320; P 🛜 ≋) With a gorgeous view of the lake and beautiful rooms tumbling down the cliffside, Sunbird really gets it right. The rooms are stylish but not pretentious, the decor is lovely with attention to detail, there's a curved pool, hyraxes hopping between rocks and lots of sundowner nooks. Even if you're not staying here, stop by for lunch and enjoy the warm welcome. Rates may be more favourable if you book via an agent.

Sleeping Warrior LODGE $$$
(☎0727067418, 0735408698; www.sleepingwarriorkenya.com; Soysambu Conservancy, Lake Elmenteita; per person full-board US$175-440; ❄ 🛜 ≋) Inside the private Soysambu Conservancy and named for the shape of the mountain formation that cradles it, the Sleeping Warrior is exquisitely remote. So much so that it took us 90 minutes to reach it from the main road. Still, you'll be richly rewarded for doing so; its stark beauty is softened by luxurious, arty lodges with sleek balconies and plunge pools.

Firefinches flit through the trees and buffaloes and giraffes graze down below. The restaurant, although a little stiff, serves fine food and wine. The adjacent tented camp often has more favourable rates. You'll need a 4WD to reach the lodge (pickups can be arranged).

Elmentaita Country Lodge LODGE $$$
(☎Nairobi 020-2220572; www.seasonshotelskenya.com; s/d with full board from US$131/213, cottages US$191/294; P 🛜 ≋) Opened in 2010, this fine, expansive property on a rise overlooking the lake is still popular despite the new kids on the block. Most rooms are well-sized, all look towards the lake, and the decor, though a little dated, has some character.

Nakuru

POP 300,000

Speed through Nakuru on your way to the lakes, and you might wonder why anyone would choose to stay here. At first glance, Kenya's fourth largest city is grim and provincial, without much to offer besides a convenient refuel. But stick around longer and we bet you'll start to like it: Nakuru is changing fast, gentrifying around the edges and adopting some of the better aspects of Nairobi – minus the traffic, the stress and the crime.

If you don't want to fork out to overnight at Lake Nakuru, the city makes a good base for exploring the park and surrounds.

Tours

Pega Tours SAFARIS
(Map p100; ☎0722776094, 0722743440; www.pegatours.co.ke; Utalii Arcade, Kenyatta Ave) Good budget tour company that organises reasonably priced trips to Lake Nakuru and beyond, with knowledgeable guides. Homestays can also be arranged (from KSh1500).

Sleeping

★ **Milimani Guest House** GUESTHOUSE $$
(☎Nairobi 020-2441366, 0788619990; Maragoli Ave; s/d KSh4000/6000; P 🛜) Just outside of town at the foot of the crater, this well-run, stylish place looks like a modern country pile. Rooms wrap around a living room furnished with sofas and a fireplace, and breakfast is served in the pretty garden. The rooms are bright and clean with hip touches, although noise carries at night.

Merica Hotel HOTEL $$
(Map p100; ☎051-2214232, 0706676557; www.mericagrouphotels.com; Kenyatta Ave; s/d US$120/185; ❄ 🛜 ≋) A longtime favourite with tour groups and business travellers, the Merica is starting to show its age. Nevertheless, it has good, well-equipped rooms housed in a whitewashed tower that wraps around a sunlit atrium. Very centrally located.

Midland Hotel HOTEL $$
(Map p100; ☎051-221212, 0738900380; www.midlandhotel.co.ke; Geoffrey Kamau Way; r KSh4100-12,000; P 🛜) A Nakuru institution, the Midland first opened in 1906 as an upmarket hotel for first-class rail travellers. More than a century later, it's still going strong. The architecture won't excite you but the renovated rooms are modern, and there's a downstairs restaurant. Those not travelling first class will be glad to learn of the budget rooms out back.

Kivu Resort HOTEL $$
(☎0726026894; Lake Naivasha Rd; r from US$45; P 🛜 ≋) This simple, U-shaped little resort sits 1.5km from Lake Naivasha's main gate. Rooms come without fanfare or pretension, and are basic for the price. Still, you can't beat the location. Residents' rates are far

Nakuru

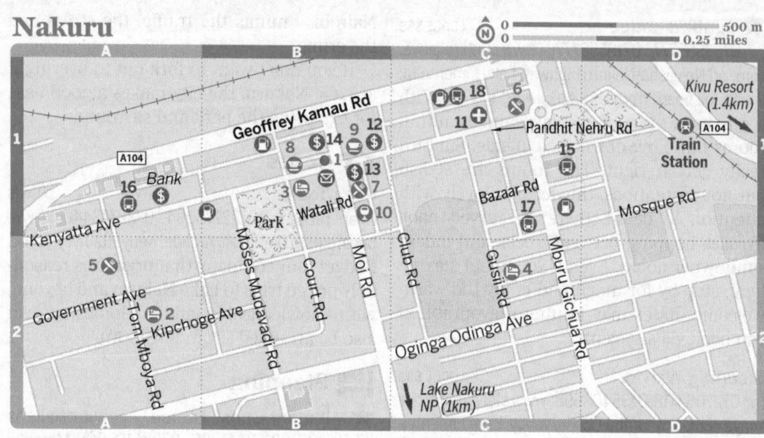

Nakuru

Activities, Courses & Tours
1 Pega Tours B1

Sleeping
2 Bontana Hotel A2
3 Merica Hotel B1
4 Midland Hotel C2

Eating
5 Hygienic Butchery A2
6 Java House C1
Nakumatt .... (see 6)
7 Planet Fries B1

Drinking & Nightlife
8 Moca Loca B1
9 Nakuru Coffee House B1
10 Whistles Guava B1

Information
11 Aga Khan University Hospital C1
12 Barclays Bank B1
13 Kenya Commercial Bank B1
14 Standard Chartered Bank B1

Transport
15 Bus & Matatu Station C1
16 Easy Coach A1
17 Matatus to Kampi ya Samaki & Marigat C1
18 Molo Line C1

cheaper, if you fancy bargaining. There's a tuk-tuk stage 100m away.

Bontana Hotel HOTEL $$
(Map p100; ☎051-2210134; www.bontanahotel-nakuru.com; Tom Mboya Rd; s/d from US$120/180; P❄☎) The statue of the buffalo seems to promise great things, but the lower rooms in this large hotel complex are a little dated. Still, you're away from the noise of traffic and there are the usual mod cons, including a reasonable restaurant and individual balconies. The better rooms are on the top floor.

Eating

Planet Fries CAFE $
(Map p100; Watali Rd; mains from KSh500; ⊙breakfast, lunch & dinner) This quaint old diner does the usual chicken and *nyama choma* (barbecued meats) plates, plus Indian variations. Outside on the pavement terrace, you'll sit on shabby blue parlour chairs, pushed up against checked tablecloths. The sizzling steak has a cult following.

Hygienic Butchery KENYAN $
(Map p100; Tom Mboya Rd; mains KSh180-250; ⊙lunch & dinner) Great name, great place. The Kenyan tradition of *nyama choma* is alive and well here. Sidle up to the counter, try a piece of tender mutton or beef and order half a kilo (per person) of whichever takes your fancy, along with chapatis or *ugali* (maize- or cassava-based staple). The meat will then be brought to your table, carved up, and you dig in with your hands. Bliss! It also serves stews, barbecued chicken and other dishes.

Nakumatt SUPERMARKET $
(Map p100; Westside Mall) The best-stocked supermarket in Nakuru.

Java House CAFE $$
(Map p100; www.nairobijavahouse.com; Westside Mall; mains from KSh400; ⊙breakfast, lunch & dinner; ❄☎) Kenya's answer to Starbucks has

come to town, and Nakuru couldn't be happier about it. Located on the ground-floor terrace of Westside Mall, the Nakuru branch has the same range of hot drinks, sandwiches, quesadillas, salads and other delights as Java House Nairobi. The cakes are imported from the capital, but everything else is made on site.

 Drinking & Nightlife

Moca Loca CAFE
(Map p100; ☎0708084839; Kenyatta Ave) Nakuru loves its coffee and Moca Loca is the new caffeinated kid in town. Located on the 2nd floor of a corner building, it's a stylish spot for people-watching; Parisian-style window boxes frame the booths. Besides coffee, there are pancake breakfasts, sandwiches, salads and burgers.

Nakuru Coffee House CAFE
(Map p100; Kenyatta Ave; coffee cup/mug KSh50/120) This '50s-style cafe was around way before the newest coffee chains and contenders. If you like your coffee simple and honest, served with a dollop of Nakuru chat, this is your spot.

Whistles Guava BAR
(Map p100; cnr Moi & Watali Rds; wi-fi) Formerly Guava cafe, this sleek bar now has a confusing double-barelled name, but inside it's rather sophisticated. Expect flat-screen televisions, DJ nights, a well-stocked bar and tables as tall as high heels. There's wi-fi, too, and bar dishes to sate late-night hunger pangs.

Information

Changing cash in Nakuru is easy, with numerous banks and foreign-exchange bureaus. Barclays ATMs are the most reliable. Kenya Commercial Bank (KCB) ATMs are renowned for swallowing cards in this area.

Aga Khan University Hospital (Nakuru Medical Centre; Map p100; Kenyatta Ave) Various lab services including malaria tests.

Getting There & Away

BUS

Easy Coach (Map p100; Kenyatta Ave) Easy Coach is one of several bus companies offering services to Nairobi (KSh500, three hours), Eldoret (KSh650, 2¾ hours) and Kisumu (KSh750, 3½ hours).

MATATUS

Ordinary matatus leave from the chaotic stands along Mburu Gichua Rd. Services include Naivasha (KSh150 to KSh200, 1¼ hours), Eldoret (KSh300, 2¾ hours), Nairobi (KSh400, three hours) and Kisumu (KSh500 to KSh600, 3½ hours).

Matatus for Lake Baringo (Kampi ya Samaki; KSh250, 2½ hours) or Marigat (for Lake Bogoria; KSh150, two hours) leave from the southern end of Pandhit Nehru Rd.

Molo Line (Map p100; Geoffrey Kamau Way; tickets KSh500) Molo Line, the most reputable of the matatu companies, runs services to Nairobi, leaving when full from opposite the old Odeon cinema. There are 10 seats, usually with belts, and drivers tend to stick to the speed limit.

PARKING

Street parking in central Nakuru requires a ticket from the nearest warden; ask at your hotel for help.

Menengai Crater

With transport and 15 minutes to play with, you can be out of the grimy streets of Nakuru and standing on the rim of the **Menengai Crater** (adult/child KSh600/200, guides KSh1000; ⏲7am-5pm), a 485m-high natural cauldron and local beauty spot. Outside of weekends, it's a peaceful place that affords striking views down below onto a cushion of lush vegetation. The crater was formed over one million years ago, and the last eruption was about 350 years ago.

Geothermal excavation is now taking place on the crater floor, so it's hard to tell if those plumes of steam rising from the bottom are indeed the souls – as the story goes – of defeated Maasai warriors, or swirling clouds of dust.

On the crater's western side is the **Mau Mau Cave**, where guerrillas hid from British colonial forces during the Mau Mau uprising.

You can, at least in theory, camp atop the crater for KSh650 per person. There's a small group of *dukas* (shops) at the main viewpoint selling drinks and trinkets.

A motorbike taxi from town to the top of the crater should cost around KSh800.

Tours

James Maina HIKING
(☎0723031150; jamesmaina11@yahoo.com) If you want to take on the Menengai Crater on foot, James Maina, a good local guide, can take you down into the crater and back up again (a four-hour roundtrip) or to the Mau Mau Cave. It's an isolated 6km walk from the main gate; hikers should never make the climb alone.

Hyrax Hill Prehistoric Site

This **archaeological site** (adult/child KSh500/250; ⊙9am-6pm), 4km outside Nakuru, is a great spot for a peaceful amble away from the rhinos and tourists. It contains a museum and the remains of three settlements excavated between 1937 and the late 1980s, the oldest being possibly 3000 years old, the most recent 200 to 300 years old. You're free to wander the site, but it's rather cryptic and a guide is useful – a tip of KSh150 is plenty.

The **North-East Village**, which is believed to be about 400 years old, sits closest to the museum and once housed 13 enclosures. Only the 1965 excavation of **Pit D** remains open. It was here that a great number of pottery fragments were found, some of which have been pieced together into complete jars and are displayed in the museum.

From Pit D the trail climbs to the scant remains of the stone-walled **hill-fort** near the top of Hyrax Hill itself. You can continue to the peak, from where there's a fine view of Lake Nakuru in the distance. Looking down the other side of the hill, you'll see two 'C'-shaped Iron Age stone **hut foundations** at the base. Just north of the foundations, a series of Iron Age **burial pits** containing 19 skeletons was found. The majority were male and lots of them had been decapitated, so a number of colourful explanations have been offered.

Nearby, two Neolithic **burial mounds** and several other Iron Age **burial pits** were also discovered. The large collection of items found in these pits included a real puzzle – six Indian coins, one of them 500 years old, and two others dating from 1918 and 1919.

On a more lively note, there's a *bao* (traditional game that's played throughout East Africa) board carved into a rock outcrop between the Iron Age settlements and the museum.

Local matatus to Naivasha or Nairobi will take you past the turn-off (about 1km from the site), just south of Nakuru.

Lake Nakuru National Park

Just two hours' drive from Nairobi, **Lake Nakuru** (☎0726610508, 0726610509; www.kws.co.ke; adult/child $80/40; ⊙6.30am-6.30pm) is among Kenya's finest national parks. Flanked by rocky escarpments, pockets of forest and at least one waterfall, the park is pretty year-round. Rising water levels in 2014 forced the park's famous flamingos to flee, but water levels are prone to fluctuation and depending on the time of your visit, they may be back in residence. You can also expect to see both black and white rhinos; look past the hordes of horny baboons and you'll see hippos, or perhaps a lucky leopard or two. There are also about 50 rare tree-climbing lions in the park, spotted several times per week. The usual zebras, buffaloes and Rothschild's giraffes seal the deal.

The forested area below **Flamingo Hill** is a favourite lion-spotting point. It's here that you should look up, not down as you are used to in other parks – lionesses love to sleep in these trees. Leopards frequent the same area, and are also seen around **Makolia camp**.

The caves beneath **Lion Hill** in the park's northeast once served as a de facto lion cub nursery. These days, they are more commonly frequented by snakes. Pythons lurk in the cool, forested areas early in the mornings.

⊙ Sights

Lake Circuit PARK

The park's relatively small size (180 sq km, depending on the reach of the lake) makes it easy to get around in a day. The forests anywhere in the park are good for leopards and rare tree-climbing lions imported from eastern Kenya. The park's black and white rhinos (around 60 altogether) tend to stick fairly close to the lake shore and sightings are common.

The health of the white rhinos in particular is monitored carefully by the rangers; coloured patches on the skin are likely to reflect recent medical treatment. Warthogs are common all over the park, as are beautiful waterbucks, zebras and buffaloes, while Thomson's gazelles, impalas and reedbucks can be seen further into the bush. Around the cliffs you may catch sight of hyraxes and birds of prey amid the countless baboons; the latter by no means shy about enthusiastically reproducing in public. Black-and-white colobus monkeys are present in small numbers in the forests near the eastern shore of the lake. A small herd of hippos generally frequents the lake's northern shore. Even if the flamingos aren't in residence, the thousands of preening pelicans still put on a show. The once spectacular

Lake Nakuru National Park

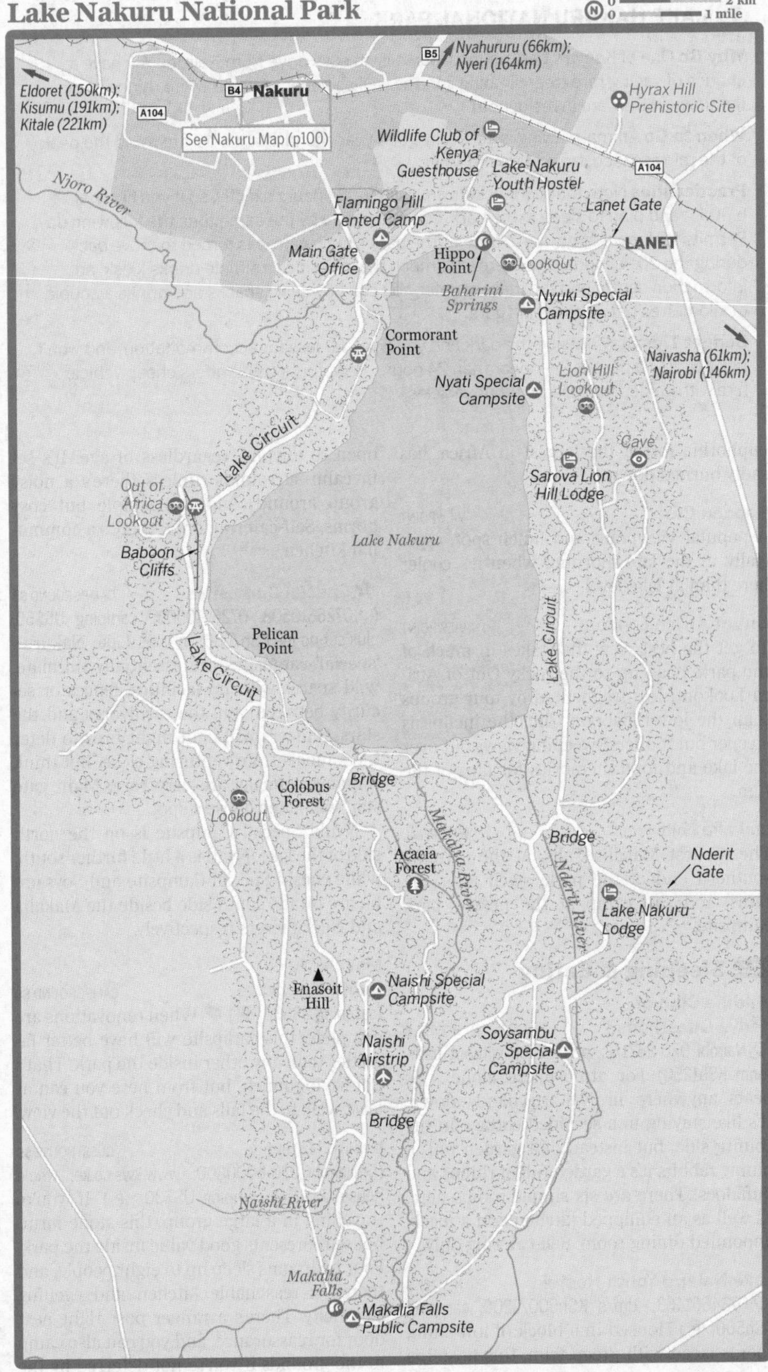

LAKE NAKURU NATIONAL PARK

Why Go One of Kenya's best national parks is an easy drive from Nairobi. You have a chance of seeing rare tree-climbing lions as well as both black and white rhinos (plus flamingos if they are in residence).

When to Go Animal viewing is generally good year-round, but it's best to avoid the peak of the rainy season, from March to May.

Practicalities Note that park tickets are valid for 24 hours exactly, so if you enter at 6.30am and plan to sleep in the park, you must leave by the same time the following day. Permits for longer stays are available. The park's main gate was forced to move back during the 2014 floods, and there isn't much there besides a simple drinks kiosk, an information centre and the main counter. You can buy basic snacks and drinks a couple of kilometres before the main gate.

Budget Tips Stay outside the park and you'll pay far less for accommodation, and won't risk needing a permit for longer than 24 hours. Pega Tours (p99) offers cheap vehicle hire with guides for those without vehicles.

euphorbia forest, the largest in Africa, has sadly burned down.

Baboon Cliffs VIEWPOINT

A popular viewpoint and lunch spot, especially in the late morning when it's cooler here than at lake level.

Out of Africa Lookout VIEWPOINT

To get the best view that takes in much of the park, head up to the rocky Out of Africa Lookout; less frequented by tour groups than the lower Baboon Cliff, the incline is steeper but it offers sweeping views out over the lake and fond memories for fans of the film.

Makalia Falls WATERFALL

The modest Makalia Falls, at the extreme southern end of the park, swell after the rains. You can camp at the nearby park campsite.

Sleeping & Eating

Wildlife Club of Kenya Guesthouse HOSTEL $

(Nairobi 020-267172; per person without bathroom KSh1250) For atmosphere alone, this beats anywhere in Nakuru hands down. It's like staying in a secluded cottage in the countryside, but instead of a garden full of bunny rabbits it's a garden full of rhinos and buffaloes! There are six simple rooms here, as well as an equipped kitchen and a nicely appointed dining room. Self-catering only.

Lake Nakuru Youth Hostel HOSTEL $

(0734661463; dm/s KSh500/1200, camping KSh500; P) Housed in a block of low-slung rooms laced with green trim, this hostel is open to anyone, regardless of age. It's set in calm surrounds (unless there's a noisy group around) and has simple but cosy dorms. Self-catering only; there's a communal kitchen.

★**Special Campsites** CAMPGROUND $$

(0726610508, 0726610509; camping US$50, plus set-up fee KSh7500; P) Lake Nakuru's 'special' campsites are essentially intimate, wild spaces with no facilities, fences or security between you, the carnivores and the stars. Rangers will light night fires to deter the animals from venturing close. But think romance; attacks are very rare. Main gate staff will help choose a spot.

Nyuki Special Campsite is on the north side of the lake, Nyati is a little further south, while Naishi Special Campsite and Soysambu are on the south side beside the Makalia and Nderit rivers respectively.

Makalia Falls Public Campsite CAMPGROUND $$

(camping US$30; P) When renovations are complete, this campsite will have better facilities than any other inside the park. That's not saying much, but from here you can at least walk to the falls and check out the view.

Naishi House GUESTHOUSE $$

(Nairobi 020-6000800; www.kws.co.ke; whole house US$250, camping US$30; P) If you're travelling in a large group, this stone farmhouse represents good value inside the park. Four bedrooms sleep up to eight people, and there's a reasonable kitchen and evening electricity. There's a ranger post right next door for reassurance, and you can also camp in the grounds if you're not deterred by the cheeky baboons. Rangers will lead the way from the main gate.

Sarova Lion Hill Lodge LODGE $$$
(☎ Nairobi 020-2315139, 0703327774; www.sarovahotels.com; s/d full board US$366/486; P 📶 🏊) Sitting high up the lake's eastern slopes, this lodge offers first-class service and comfort. The views from the open-air restaurant-bar and from most rooms are great. Rooms are understated but pretty, while the flashy suites are large and absolutely stunning. It's certainly one of the friendlier top-end places, and on quiet days you may even get the residents' rate, which is less than half that quoted here.

Lake Nakuru Lodge LODGE $$$
(☎ 0720404480, Nairobi 020-2687056; www.lakenakurulodge.com; s/d full board US$300/400; P @ 📶 🏊) The big draw here is the view, stretching from the rustic wooden bar and pool into the park. It's a great dawn-to-dusk wildlife viewing spot. The lodge itself has pleasant, garden rooms with wall-to-ceiling balcony windows, and there's a decent buffet restaurant and a helpful staff. Even if you're not staying here, this is *the* place for lunch.

Flamingo Hill Tented Camp TENTED CAMP $$$
(☎ 0702884482; www.flamingohillcamp.com; per person from US$195; P 📶 🏊) 🍃 Flamingo Hill strikes a nice balance between chic and wild. The safari bar might be a little over-styled, but the 30 luxury tents are lovely, with all mod cons. There's free wi-fi, a fire pit, a decent restaurant and very helpful staff. The camp is close to the main gate, so if your permit requires you to leave early, you'll have more time in bed.

ℹ Getting There & Away

KWS has somewhat Disney-fied the road from Nakuru to Lake Nakuru National Park, with flamingo street lights and bizarre faux zebras stuffed into glass tanks. The park is accessible in a 2WD. If you don't have your own wheels, Pega Tours (p99) in Nakuru is a good bet. Their daily hire rates include a pop-top minibus and a knowledgeable driver/guide, from KSh2500 per person (based on four guests).

Njoro

POP 57,000

Karen Blixen once described dusty little Njoro as one of her favourite places. 'Few places are more lovely than Njoro,' she said. And we think she might have been right; there's the climate, for starters, plus acres and acres of fertile farmland and a history worthy of novels.

In a fertile strip up above the lip of Lake Nakuru, Njoro was once slated as the potential capital of British East Africa by the influential British settler Lord Delamere. Delamere's close friend Beryl Markham, the first woman to fly westbound solo across the Atlantic, grew up nearby. Markham's dreams may have come to fruition, but Njoro's did not. The large railway station never saw the traffic planned for it; the wide town square never saw the herds of oxen envisaged and the American grid system was never the envy of the international visitors imagined.

But like all places that once harboured big dreams, Njoro retains a dose of magic. It also makes a good base for exploring Lake Nakuru to the south, and Bogoria and Baringo to the north.

CROSSING THE EQUATOR

'You are now in the northern hemisphere,' proclaims the sign, 38km north of Nakuru at the curve of the equator. And things do look different, although that has more to do with the drop in altitude than the mathematics of the planet. You'll feel the breeze dry out, spot sisal plantations where there were flower farms, watch Fresian cows give way to giant tortoises and feel Nakuru's soft chocolatey soil harden and crack. Unzip your jacket and slap on the sunscreen, because you're entering a whole new climatic zone.

If you're following the main Nakuru–Baringo road north, there's a tourist information centre at the equator, marked by a spherical metal monument. The centre is sparse but has clean-ish washrooms; the enthusiastic staff can advise on exploring Lake Baringo and the surrounding area, including hiking the 150km Trans-Rift Trail.

Further north, the small town of **Radad** is famous for its artisanal honey, renowned for its antiseptic qualities and reputed to be among the purest and sweetest in Kenya. You'll see the beehives high up in the acacia trees – they look like fat, wooden logs. The honey is for sale in glass bottles and jars at stalls along the roadside. From Marigat to Baringo, the road is rough and unsealed, but still negotiable without a 4WD.

DON'T MISS

EGERTON CASTLE

If you want to muse on lost love and where it goes, visit **Egerton Castle** (Njoro; non-resident US$12), on the outskirts of Njoro. A replica of Tatton Hall in England, the castle was constructed between 1938 and 1954 by Lord Maurice Egerton – who also set up the agricultural training college that would later become Egerton University.

With cared-for gardens and a small petting zoo that includes llamas and tortoises, it makes a pleasant afternoon picnic spot.

After falling for a wealthy woman in England, Egerton set about persuading her to come and live with him in Kenya. She refused, stating that only a castle would be fit for her needs. And so Egerton constructed one, taking his time over a period of 16 years (well, there was a war going on) and importing everything from statement bath taps to a self-playing organ for the grand ballroom. But alas, as Egerton soon found out, timing is everything: by the time the castle was complete, Egerton's love had fallen for another. Broken and bitter, he lived out his days on the 32 acre estate until he died in 1958, threatening any woman who came close with gunfire.

Although much of the furniture was looted after Egerton's death, the castle has been lovingly restored – in keeping with local taste – by a group of university students and is now the closest thing to a British National Trust property in Kenya's Rift Valley. If you're not put off by Egerton's sorry tale, you can, ironically, get married here.

Sights

Kenana Knitters ARTS & CRAFTS

(0715262303; Kenana Farm; 8.30am-5pm Mon-Fri) FREE What began as a hobby for three ladies knitting under a tree now employs more than 1200 local people and exports all over the world. The knitters use plant and flower dyes – including beetroot and dahlia – and sustainable wool and cotton in their cute, quirky designs. You can tour the innovative natural workshop, hear the story of how this became one of the most impressive nonprofit initiatives in the region, and make a stop in the lovely shop.

Sleeping

★ **Kembu Farm** COTTAGES $$

(0722361102, 0722355705; www.kembufarm.com; off C56 road; r KSh4500-15,400, camping Ksh550; P) Green and peaceful, Kembu Farm has nine cosy cottages set in beautiful gardens on the edge of Njoro. Each cottage tells a story; you can sleep in the restored childhood home of aviator Beryl Markham, in a vintage 1920s railway carriage, or in a hip treehouse. The food is home-cooked and delicious, the welcome is warm and there's real attention to detail, including working fireplaces.

The farm is home to wild chameleons, as well as working Fresian dairy cows – kids can get muddy and stuck in. It's also a popular stop among overlanders.

Ziwa Bush Lodge LODGE $$$

(0707698822; www.ziwalodge.com; r from KSh12,000; P) With fresh, sleek rooms set in spacious, manicured grounds, this small resort marries safari chic with the peace and quiet of the Njoro countryside. It's owned by an Australian family and visits to a nearby supported orphanage can be arranged. It's near the Rift Valley Institute of Science & Technology.

Drinking & Nightlife

Njoro Country Club SPORTS BAR

(Golf Course) It's worth stopping by to see who's propping up the bar at this old-fashioned country club. There's an ancient pool table, a piano, television, outdoor tables and a golf course. Simple meals are on offer.

Lake Bogoria

Designated a wetland of international importance, Lake Bogoria is rather tempestuous. On a good day it appears sleek and pretty but is punctuated by hot springs bursting forth from the veneer of calm. There's even more going on beneath the surface: in recent years, rising water levels have sent the lake's famous flamingos flying and tempered the strength of the springs. Still, birdwatchers will be sated whatever the season: the rare and impressive greater kudu lurks in the undergrowth.

Sights & Activities

Lake Bogoria National Reserve PARK
(☎Nairobi 020-6000800; www.kws.org; adult/child US$25/15) Lake Bogoria is backed by the bleak Siracho Escarpment, and moss-green waves roll down its rocky, barren shores. A road that becomes a rough track (and then peters out entirely) runs along the lake's western shore, which is where flamingos gather. About halfway along the lake, **hot springs and geysers** spew boiling fluids from the earth's insides. If you're here early in the morning, you may have the place to yourself.

While the isolated wooded area at the lake's southern end is home to leopards, klipspringers, gazelles, caracals and buffaloes, an increase in human activity means that the greater kudu is increasingly elusive. You can explore on foot or bicycle. If you'd like a guide, enquire at Loboi gate.

Kesubo Swamp BIRDWATCHING
Just outside Lake Bogoria National Reserve's northern boundary and on the road in from the main B4 road north, Kesubo Swamp is a birdwatcher's paradise: more than 200 species have been recorded and one lucky person spotted 96 species in one hour – a Kenyan record. You'll need to park your car close to Lake Bogoria Spa Resort and walk around the perimeter.

Sleeping & Eating

The pretty Fig Tree Camp, basic Riverside Camp and equipped Acacia Camp make up the trio of camping options within the reserve, although you won't find them open if the lake is flooded. If they are operating, all three charge KSh500 per person. Check in with KWS before travelling, or at Emsos gate upon arrival.

The nearby town of Marigat is a good place to buy local produce or to have a meal.

Lake Bogoria Spa Resort HOTEL $$
(☎Nairobi 020-2249055, 0710445627; www.lakebogoria-hotel.com; s/d from KSh9000/10,000, camping KSh1200; P ≋) Set in lovely grounds, the biggest draw here is the pool, which is fed by a nearby hot spring. Otherwise, the rooms don't quite live up to expectation, but they are perfectly comfortable and will do fine for a night or two. Discounts are available for students.

RIFT VALLEY LAKES IN PERIL

Kenya's Rift Valley lakes may seem pristine, but their ecosystems are facing serious threats to their wellbeing.

Despite being listed as Kenya's fourth Ramsar site in January 2002, Lake Baringo faces numerous threats, among them droughts, falling water levels, severe siltation due to soil erosion around the seasonal *luggas* (dry river beds) and overfishing. In 2014, the lake rose dramatically, wiping out half of Roberts' Camp. At the time of research, the water was only just beginning to recede. The same fate befell Lake Bogoria, sending flamingos fleeing to lakes with a higher green algae content.

In the case of Lake Naivasha, tourism and the wealth generated by the flower farms has spawned massive development. In addition, pesticides and fertilisers are seeping into the lake. Irrigation has further destabilised erratic water levels; the lake is currently receding and now only spreads over 139 sq km, which is, according to the World Wide Fund for Nature, around half of its original size. The lake's ecology has also been interfered with on a number of other occasions, notably with the introduction of foreign fish (for sports and commercial fisheries), crayfish, the South American coypu (an aquatic rodent that initially escaped from a fur farm) and various aquatic plants, including the dreaded water hyacinth.

For these reasons Naivasha has been the focus of conservation efforts and in 1995, after years of lobbying from the Lake Naivasha Riparian Association (LNRA), the lake was designated a Ramsar site, officially recognising it as a wetland of international importance. Besides educating the locals dependent on the lake about the environmental issues involved, the LNRA, **Elsamere Conservation Centre** (www.elsamere.com) and other organisations work to establish a code of conduct among the local growers that will maintain the lake's biodiversity. Among the positive outcomes is that since 2007, all local businesses have been required to submit environmental-impact statements. But much remains to be done.

Lake Baringo & Lake Bogoria National Reserve

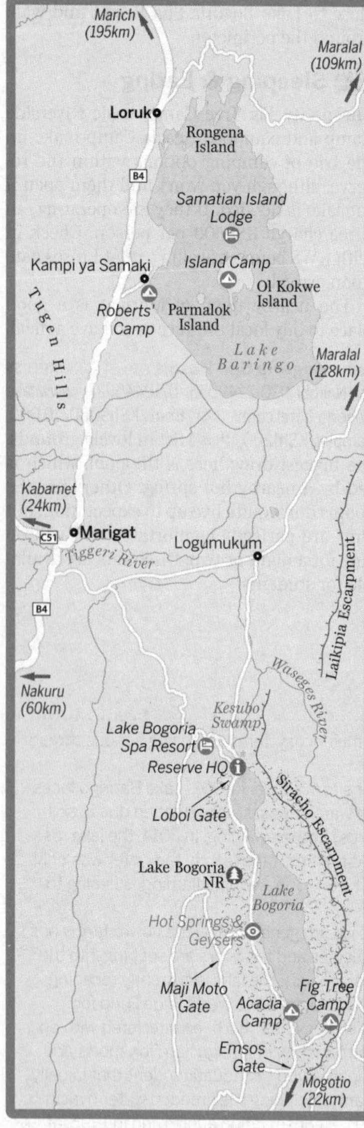

Getting There & Away

Entrances are at Loboi (north), Emsos (south) and Maji Moto (west); only Loboi is accessible by 2WD vehicle. The nearest petrol is in Marigat.

Matatus run to Loboi gate from Marigat (KSh100, 30 minutes). Regular matatus serve Marigat from Nakuru (KSh250, two hours) and Kabarnet (KSh165, 1¼ hours).

Lake Baringo

Wild and beautiful, Lake Baringo is the most remote of the Rift Valley lakes. Steeped in stories, its harsh climate and rocky islets give it a faraway feel; on a hot day, this freshwater lake has more in common with northern Kenya than the rest of the Rift Valley.

This is the turf of adventurers; Baringo isn't fenced, so there's a high chance of hippos emerging, with the timing of vampires, from the shoreline. The murky waters hold crocodiles too, so best keep your swimsuit in your bag. Up above, the skies are filled with over 460 species including owls, nightjars and rare Hemprich's hornbills. Birdwatching in Kenya rarely gets better than this.

The small village of **Kampi ya Samaki**, on Lake Baringo's shore, is the gateway to the lake. Lake Baringo is not a fee-paying park, but the community charges a toll (KSh200) to access the lake; keep your receipt.

Activities

Boat Rides

A boat ride, naturally, is by far the best way to experience the lake. A speciality is a trip to see fish eagles feeding; the birds dive for fish at a whistle.

Trips generally cost around KSh3000 per hour and the most reliable ones are organised by **Lake Baringo Boats Excursions** (0721548657; boatexcursions@lake-baringo.com; Kampi ya Samaki; per boat per hr KSh3000), from Island Camp and Roberts' Camp.

Bird & Nature Walks

Even the most cynical are easily won over by Baringo's birdlife, and it can be hard to resist setting off on a dawn walk – this is when the birds are most active and twitchers will be in their element. Roberts' Camp leads excellent one- to three-hour walks for between KSh400 and KSh500 per person; night-time bird walks can also be arranged.

Tours

Roberts' Camp and Island Camp both offer tours (KSh1200 per person) to Pokot and Njemps villages close to the lake, where you can eat at a *manyatta* (traditional homestead) and feel seriously drab in comparison in the style stakes.

Trips to visit bush clinics – where snake bites are treated using natural remedies – can also be arranged from Robert's Camp (from KSh300 per person).

Sleeping

★Roberts' Camp CAMPGROUND $
(0717176656; Kampi ya Samaki; bandas KSh2500-4500, tents KSh2000-4000, camping KSh500; P) A legend in its own right, this atmospheric camp sits right on the lake shore. The *bandas* are nicely decorated, with eco loos, and there's ample space for camping, plus the Thirsty Goat bar-restaurant. The helpful staff can organise boat rides and scorpion-spotting nature walks. After dark, keep your eyes peeled for hippos, fireflies and the ghosts of old adventurers.

Sadly part of the camp was destroyed by high water levels in 2014; at the time of research renovation work was planned.

★Island Camp TENTED CAMP $$
(0735919878, 0728478638; www.islandcamp.com; Lake Baringo; full-board incl boat transfers from US$300;) Stylish but relaxed, this gorgeous tented camp covers the tip of an island in the middle of Lake Baringo. The superior tents have private plunge pools and Kenyan art. There's an atmospheric bar, community initiatives, wild gardens made for birdwatching, and a spa tent. Day visitors are welcomed for lunch.

Staff can arrange activities including bird walks, excursions to the hot springs and sundowners atop a nearby island.

Samatian Island Lodge LUXURY VILLA $$$
(Nairobi 020-2115453, 0712579999; Lake Baringo; island from US$1000;) Set on a private island, this intimate luxury spot can only be rented in its entirety. There's room for 12 in beautiful thatched *bandas*, and plenty going on in terms of nature and activities, including jetski hire. The food is good, healthy and served by candlelight.

Eating

Self-caterers should note that while some food – notably fresh fish – may be available at Baringo, fresh vegetables and fruit are generally in short supply in these arid parts. Bring much of what you need – Marigat usually has a simple selection.

Thirsty Goat INTERNATIONAL $$
(Roberts' Camp, Kampi ya Samaki; mains KSh450-650; breakfast, lunch & dinner) Even if you're not staying at Roberts' Camp, the Thirsty Goat is an institution worth visiting. Sip sundowners, listen to snorting hippos, grab a book from the small library or prop up the bar with your travel banter. The menu includes homemade fishcakes, meat from the grill and vegetarian dishes.

★Island Camp Restaurant BUFFET $$$
(0728478638, 0724874661; www.islandcamp.com; Island Camp, Lake Baringo; buffet KSh2000; lunch;) A popular weekend activity, if you can call it that, is to charter a boat and hop across to Island Camp's sleek restaurant for lunch. The buffet includes a mix of cold dishes such as gazpacho, Indian mains, salads and lovely desserts, served overlooking the lapping water. Make sure you call ahead to secure a table.

Getting There & Away

Lake access is easiest from Kampi ya Samaki on the lake's western shore, some 15km north of Marigat on a rough road.

A 25-seater bus leaves for Nakuru each morning (KSh350) between 6.30am and 9.30am (it departs when full).

Slightly more regular pick-up trucks head to Marigat (KSh100, 30 minutes) and you can catch more frequent matatus from there to Nakuru (KSh300, two hours) or Kabarnet (KSh200, 1¼ hours).

At the time of research, there were plans for scheduled biweekly plane services from Nairobi with Fly540.

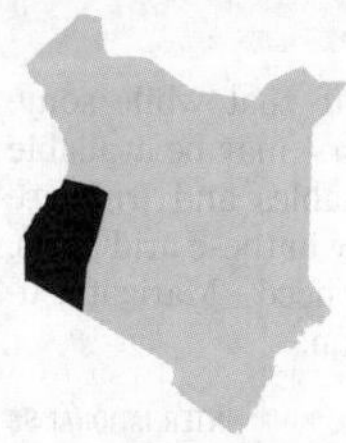

Masai Mara & Western Kenya

Includes ➡

Best of Nature

- ➡ Conservancies surrounding the Masai Mara (p120)
- ➡ Masai Mara National Reserve (p112)
- ➡ Kakamega Forest Reserve (p136)
- ➡ Saiwa Swamp National Park (p145)
- ➡ Mt Elgon National Park (p142)

Best of Culture

- ➡ Learning about Maasai culture at Maji Moto Group Ranch (p120)
- ➡ Bullfighting near Kakamega (p122)

Why Go?

For most people, the magic of western Kenya is summed up in two poetic words: Masai Mara. Few places on Earth support such high concentrations of animals, and the Mara's wildebeest-spotted savannahs are undeniably the region's star attraction. Drama unfolds here on a daily basis, be it a stealthy trap coordinated by a pride of lions, the infectious panic of 1000 wildebeest crossing a river, or the playful pounce of a cheetah kitten on its sibling.

But there's much more to western Kenya than these plains of herbivores and carnivores. The dense forests of Kakamega are buzzing with weird and wonderful creatures, the rain-soaked hills of Kericho and their verdant tea gardens bring new meaning to the word 'green', and amid the boat-speckled waters of Lake Victoria lies a smattering of seldom-visited islands crying out for exploration.

When to Go

Kisumu

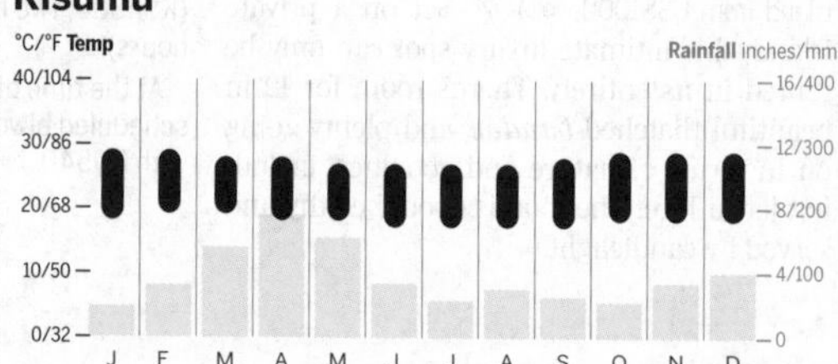

Mar–May The 'heavy rains' fall at this time, particularly in the cooler Western Highlands.

Jul–Oct With the arrival of the wildebeest migration, the Masai Mara groans with herbivores.

Nov–Dec The 'lesser rains' appear briefly before things really dry out in January.

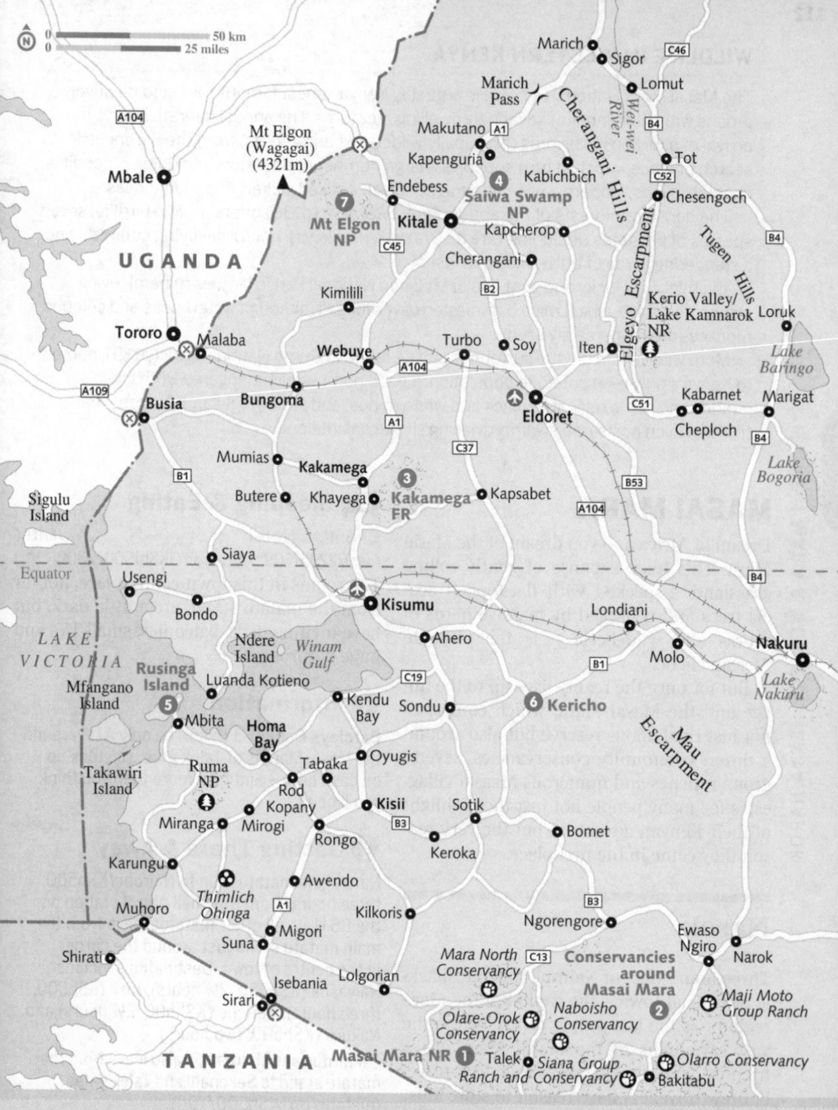

Western Kenya Highlights

1. Getting caught up in the swirling wildebeest traffic jams of the **Masai Mara National Reserve** (p112), the greatest animal show on Earth

2. Having the world's finest safari experience – and benefiting the locals – in one of the **conservancies** (p120) surrounding the Masai Mara

3. Scouring leaf litter for creepy-crawlies and searching for thumbless colobus in **Kakamega Forest Reserve** (p136)

4. Wading through the backwaters of **Saiwa Swamp National Park** (p145) in a hunt for paddling antelope

5. Throwing away your watch and making plans to stay forever on Lake Victoria's idyllic islands, including **Rusinga Island** (p130)

6. Brewing a proper cuppa in **Kericho** (p133), the tea capital of Africa

7. Searching for salt-loving elephants in the caves of **Mt Elgon National Park** (p142)

WILDLIFE IN WESTERN KENYA

The Masai Mara National Reserve is arguably Kenya's most famous park and positively groans with all manner of savannah-dwelling creatures. The annual migration sees the arrival of a million herbivores (principally wildebeest and zebras) from the Serengeti in search of grass, which in turn supports a large number of predators, including crocodiles, cheetahs, lions, leopards, hyenas, caracals, black-backed jackals and mongooses.

The dense rainforests of Kakamega Forest Reserve (p136) offers prolific birdlife, seven species of primates (including rare de Brazza's monkeys), nocturnal flying squirrels and a staggering array of butterflies and insects.

You might get lucky and spot one of Mt Elgon National Park's famous mineral-loving elephants (p142), which mine bat-infested caves for salt, although waterbucks and colobus monkeys are more readily seen.

More wildlife and unique surrounds can be found at Ruma National Park (p129), home to Kenya's only roan antelope population, a good number of endangered Rothschild's giraffes and some relocated black and white rhinos; and at Saiwa Swamp National Park (p145), which hosts rare swamp-dwelling sitatunga antelope.

MASAI MARA

Dream of Africa and you dream of the Masai Mara. This huge expanse of gently rolling grassland – specked with flat-topped acacia trees and trampled by massive herds of zebras and wildebeest – is the ultimate African cliché.

But for once the reality lives up to the image and the Masai Mara, which comprises not just the famous reserve but also around a dozen community conservancies, several group ranches and numerous Maasai villages, is for many people not just the highlight of their Kenyan adventure but the very reason they came in the first place.

Narok

POP 24,000

Three hours west of Nairobi, this ramshackle provincial town – the capital of the Mara region – is the last proper centre before the vast savannahs of the Masai Mara. It's a friendly and surprisingly hassle-free place, but few travellers have reason to stop. Most people roll on in, browse the curio shops while their driver refuels, then roll on out again.

Sights

Narok Museum MUSEUM
(B3 Hwy; adult/child KSh500/250; 9am-6pm)
The town's only official attraction is the small Narok Museum and its displays on traditional and contemporary Maasai culture, as well as that of other Maa-speaking people.

Sleeping & Eating

Chambai Hotel HOTEL $
(0722957609; s/d from KSh1500/2300; P)
The rooms in this town-centre place, not far from the matatu stand, are a little dark, but have inviting beds, balconies, small TVs and huge bathrooms.

Information

Barclays Bank (B3 Hwy) The only ATM around the Masai Mara is at Talek gate, so stock up on cash here – and take more than you think you'll need.

Getting There & Away

Narok Line matatus run to Nairobi (KSh500, three hours) from the Shell petrol station on the B6 Hwy. All other matatus leave from the main matatu stand just around the corner in the centre of town. Destinations include Naivasha (KSh350, 2½ hours), Kisii (KSh500, three hours), Kericho (KSh500, 2½ hours) and Nakuru (KSh500, two hours).

Matatus and share taxis also leave from the matatu stand to Sekenani and Talek gates (matatu/taxi KSh500/700).

It's much cheaper to fill up with petrol here than in the reserve.

Masai Mara National Reserve

The world-renowned **Masai Mara National Reserve** (adult/child US$80/45, subsequent days if staying inside the reserve US$70/40; 6am-7pm) is a huge expanse of tawny, sunburnt grasslands pocked with acacia trees and heaving with animals big and small. Impressive at any time of year, it's at its best between July and October when around a million migrating wildebeest and thousands of topis, zebras and other animals pour into the reserve from Tanzania in search of the fresh grass generated by the rains. It is, arguably, the most spectacular wildlife show on the planet and the one thing that no visitor to Kenya should even consider missing.

The Masai Mara (or Mara, as locals affectionately refer to it) is the northern extension of Tanzania's equally famous Serengeti Plains and is jointly managed by the Narok County Council and the Mara Conservancy (on behalf of Trans-Mara County Council).

Reliable rains and plentiful vegetation underpin this extraordinary ecosystem and the millions of herbivores it supports. Wildebeest, zebras, impalas, elands, reedbucks, waterbucks, black rhinos, elephants, Masai giraffes and several species of gazelle all call the short-grass plains and acacia woodlands of the Mara home. This vast concentration of wildlife accounts for high numbers of predators, including cheetahs, leopards, spotted hyenas, black-backed jackals, bat-eared foxes, caracals and the highest lion densities in the world.

Sights

Central Plains

The southeast area of the park, bordered by the Mara and Sand Rivers, is characterised by rolling grasslands and low, isolated hills. With the arrival of the migration, enormous herds of wildebeest and zebras, as well as other plains wildlife, graze here. The riverine forests that border the Mara and Talek Rivers are great places to spot elephants, buffaloes and bushbucks. Leopards are sometimes seen near the Talek and Sand Rivers and around the Keekorok valleys.

Rhino Ridge & Paradise Plains

Rhino Ridge is a good area to see black-backed jackals, as they're known to use the old termitaria here for den sites. Lookout Hill is worth a detour as it offers phenomenal views over the seasonal Olpunyaia Swamp. You may also get lucky and spot one of the few black rhinos that inhabit the reserve anywhere between Lookout Hill and Rhino Ridge and in the vicinity of Roan Hill.

For lions, the Marsh Pride near Musiara Swamp and the Ridge Pride near Rhino Ridge both starred in the BBC's *Big Cat Diary* and are fairly easy to find.

Cheetahs are far more elusive, but are sometimes found hunting gazelles on the Paradise Plains.

Mara River

Pods of hippos can be found in any of the major rivers, with the largest and most permanent concentrations occurring in the Mara River. The river is also home to huge Nile crocodiles and is the scene where wildebeest make their fateful crossings during the migration. The New Mara Bridge in the south is the only all-weather crossing point and another great place to see hippos.

Pods of hippos can be found in any of the major rivers, with the largest and most

MASAI MARA NATIONAL RESERVE

Why Go The 1510 sq km of open rolling grassland that makes up the Mara offers the quintessential African safari experience, with lion sightings virtually guaranteed.

When to Go The Mara is superb at any time, but is at its best during the annual wildebeest migration from July to October.

Practicalities The Masai Mara's fame means that it can get very busy (and very pricey) during the annual migration. Bring a windbreaker jacket for early morning wildlife drives and don't forget a good pair of binoculars. Gates are open from 6am to 6.30pm.

Budget Tips It is possible to visit the Masai Mara on a budget. Many of the cheaper places to stay just outside the reserve allow camping and self-catering. To share costs on safaris, join a group safari in Nairobi, scour the noticeboards at Nairobi backpackers, or go to www.lonelyplanet.com/thorntree in search of travel companions. Be aware that the much-peddled three-day Nairobi–Mara safaris mean a large proportion of your time will be spent travelling to and from the Mara. It makes sense to add in at least one extra day.

Masai Mara National Reserve

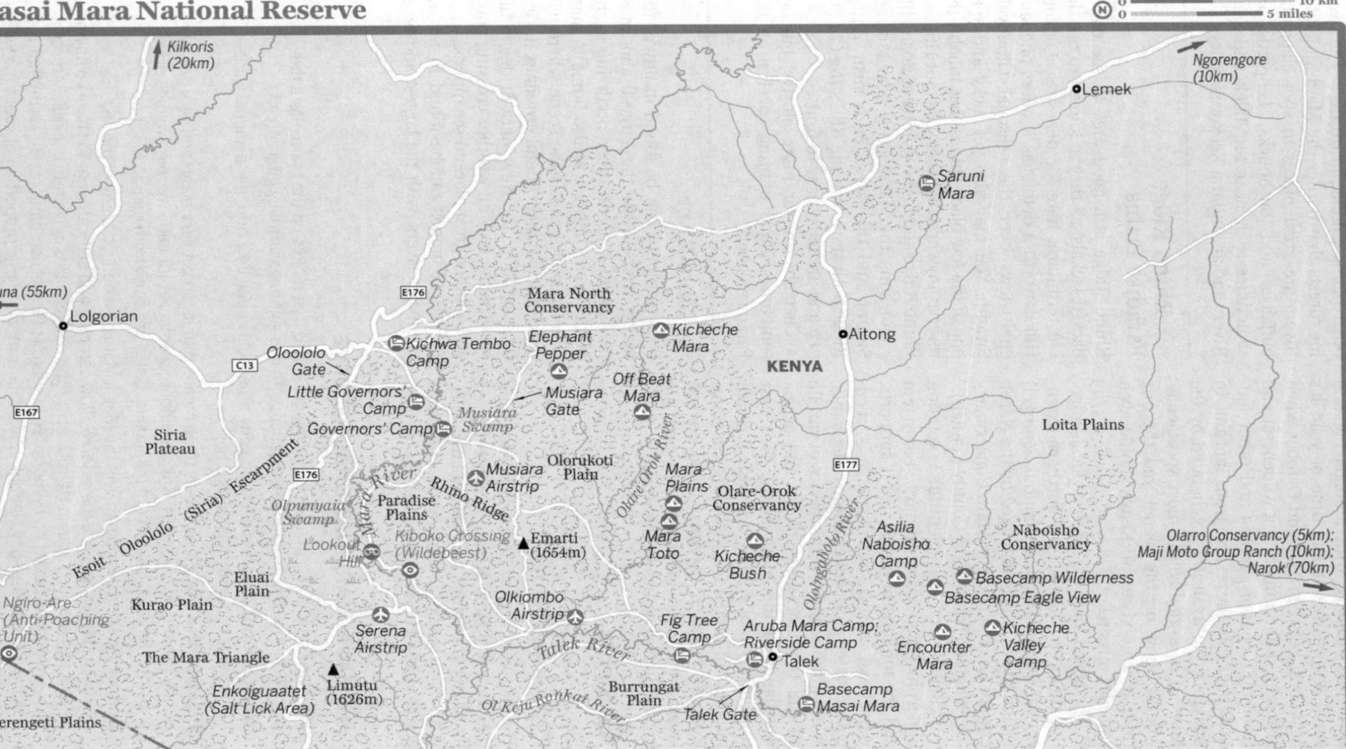

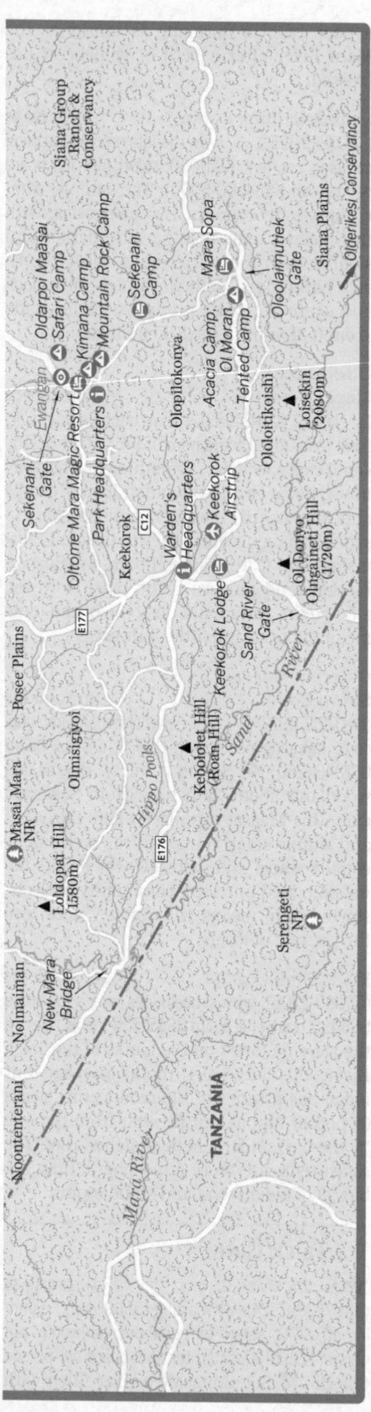

permanent concentrations occurring in the Mara River. The river is also home to huge Nile crocodiles, and is the place where wildebeest make their fateful crossings during the migration. The New Mara Bridge in the south is the only all-weather crossing point and another great place to see hippos.

The Mara Triangle & Esoit Oloololo (Siria) Escarpment

Unlike the rest of the park, which is under the control of the Narok County Council, the northwest sector of the reserve is managed by the nonprofit Mara Conservancy. The only way to reach this part of the park is from either the Oloololo gate or via the New Mara Bridge. Consequently, this area is less visited than elsewhere, despite having high concentrations of wildlife.

The Oloololo Escarpment, which forms the northwest boundary of the park, was once wooded, but fire and elephant damage mean that it's now mostly grasslands. Rock hyraxes and klipspringers can be readily seen here.

Activities

Wildlife Drives

Whether you're bouncing over the plains in pursuit of elusive elephant silhouettes or parked next to a pride of lions, listening to their bellowed breaths, wildlife drives are the highlight of a trip to the Mara.

Virtually all places to stay organise safaris. At some (cheaper places) it will be in a battered old Land Rover or similar, with the camp manager or other staff member driving you. With luck you'll be on your own, or at least in a very small group. In the more expensive places that cater more to package tourists, safaris will be conducted in 'pop-top' minivans and there can be up to a dozen other guests. The super-exclusive lodges will use state-of-the-art customised vehicles with open sides. It's common (but not certain) that your party will have a vehicle and expert tracker to yourself. Self-drive safaris in your own vehicle are also perfectly possible.

During the busy Christmas and migration seasons, it can seem there are as many minivans as animals.

Balloon Safaris

Several companies operate dawn balloon safaris and there's no better way to start your day than soaring majestically over the rolling grasslands. Flights (per person

US$450 to US$500) can be booked at most of the lodges or campsites and include a 'champagne' (it's very rarely real champagne) breakfast, wildlife drive and transport to and from the launch point.

Guided Nature Walks

One of the best ways to experience the African bush is on foot. You'll learn all about the medicinal properties of various plants, see the telltale signs of passing animals and have some thrilling encounters with wildlife. Many lodges and camps can arrange a guided walk. Rates vary between lodges and camps, but generally average US$20 per person.

As it's forbidden to walk within the reserve, guided walks generally take place in the company of a Maasai *moran* (warrior) outside the park.

Maasai Manyatta Visits

The Maasai are synonymous with the Masai Mara, and their slender frames, blood-red cloaks, ochre hairstyles and beaded jewellery make them instantly recognisable. Despite their reputation as fearsome warriors with somewhat lofty dispositions, some Maasai *manyattas* (villages) now welcome visitors (around US$20 per person).

Village visits can be organised through any lodge or camp or, if travelling under your own steam, you can just turn up at any of the villages (look for the signs saying something along the lines of 'cultural village' – don't just stroll into a proper Maasai *manyatta* unannounced!).

Sleeping & Eating

Make no mistake about it, accommodation in the Masai Mara can be very expensive. Remember, though, that in most cases all meals are included and in many of the top-end places, drinks and safari activities are also part of the deal. It's possible to keep prices right down by camping and self-catering. This also adds to the excitement, with just a thin sheet of canvas between you and the great outdoors – and all its toothy creatures.

Sekenani Gate

Kimana Camp TENTED CAMP $$
(0734599955; full board per person KSh5500;) This fairly large (34 tents), but otherwise tranquil, camp set in a shady patch of forest is unusually good value. Tents have three beds and hot-water bathrooms. There's also a pool, but it's normally as murky as the Mara River after a herd of wildebeest has crossed.

Mountain Rock Camp TENTED CAMP $$
(0722511252; www.mountainrockkenya.com; camping per tent KSh1000, safari tent full board per person KSh4500-5000) The simple safari tents here come in two categories, with the cheaper tents being a little darker and smaller than the pricier ones. All have private bathrooms, cloth wardrobes, firm beds and share the same pretty woodland glade around 3km from the Sekenani gate.

Oltome Mara Magic Resort TENTED CAMP $$
(Nairobi 020-2498512; www.oltomemaramagic.com; tent s/d full board from US$75/150; P) This small camp, which is something of a halfway house between the top-notch luxury camps and the nearby cheaper options, has 13 semipermanent tents. They're tastefully furnished and feature stone floors, wooden verandahs and modern bathrooms. However, a few tears and mould on some of the tents mean the price is a little optimistic.

Oldarpoi Maasai Safari Camp TENTED CAMP $$$
(0721731927; www.oldarpoimaracamp.com; camping per person US$20, s/d full board US$140/260) Set on a hill of dry acacia woodland about 3km back from Sekenani gate, this Maasai-run place offers fairly hot and simple safari tents, but the welcome is equally warm and, with 40% of profits being ploughed into local community projects, staying here means your money goes into the pockets of locals.

Mara Simba Lodge LODGE $$$
(050-22051; www.simbalodges.com; s full board US$495, d & tw full board US$575; P) Set in the riverine forest on the banks of the Talek River, this large (84 room) package-tour lodge has a series of interconnecting decks (a pod of hippos can be seen from the one by the bar) under a huge thatched roof. The safari tents are more atmospheric than the blocks of older wood-and-stone rooms.

Talek Gate

★ **Aruba Mara Camp** TENTED CAMP $$
(0723997524; www.aruba-safaris.com; camping KSh700, safari tent without bathroom per person KSh3000, safari tent full board per person €85-115) Set alongside a river filled with

TROUBLE IN EDEN

In many ways the Masai Mara National Reserve is the epitome of the African dream. Its golden, bleached savannah is covered with unparalleled densities of animals, great and small, and the vast majority of it is untouched by the destructive hand of man. Visitors can't help but be bowled over by its natural riches.

The reality is that not everyone is happy with this wildlife haven. Many local Maasai living in the immediate vicinity of the reserve feel they gain nothing from its presence, despite the sacrifices and hardships they face because of it. The issues they raise are:

- Not being allowed to graze their cattle inside the reserve, which many of them consider to be 'their' land.
- Insufficient and poorly organised compensation when animals kill their cattle outside of the reserve.
- Neglected needs of the Maasai communities. Many communities don't have sufficient access to clean, safe water sources and education and health facilities. Many lodges and camps in and around the reserve advertise their community development projects, but many Maasai dispute that all of this money actually goes to such projects.

Ironically another problem the reserve faces comes from safari tourism itself. Sightings of big cats tend to attract large numbers of vehicles, and when the lion, cheetah or leopard eventually moves away, many guides (aware their clients want to see such animals up close) break park rules by following the animals off the designated tracks.

Such constant attention has led some animals to change their patterns of behavior – for instance, cheetahs now frequently attempt to hunt under the midday sun, when most tourists are having lunch in their camp (unfortunately, it's also a time when the chance of a successful kill is radically reduced). Reports are now showing that many animals are spending less time in the reserve itself, choosing to roam in the surrounding conservancies where there are fewer safari vehicles (and, incidentally, where local communities also gain more from tourism).

toothy crocs, this is arguably the Mara's best-value camp. There are nine wonderfully plush 'tents' with good self-contained bathrooms as well as several small but comfortable tents (meals not included) that share bathrooms. The nearby campsite is decent, with a kitchen area and reliable hot water in the shower block.

Add €30 to the prices and it'll give you a package that includes two daily safari drives.

Riverside Camp HOTEL, CAMPGROUND $$
(☎0717697358; www.riversidecampmara.com; camping US$10, s/d full board US$115/200) Occupying a prime bend on the Talek River, these basic, self-contained chipboard rooms are currently rather uninspiring but they're just a stone's throw from the river and, with patience, you could well spot the hippos and baboons that live along its banks.

It's recently been taken over by a British guy who is busy renovating the place and has big plans for the future.

★ **Basecamp Masai Mara** LODGE $$$
(☎0733333909; www.basecampexplorer.com; tent s/d full board US$400/720;) 'Eco' is a much-abused word in the tourism industry, but to see what an ecofriendly hotel really looks like, come to this upmarket lodge where everything is based around sustainabilty and recycling.

If all this green scheming makes you think the accommodation might be rustic, fear not. Tents fall squarely into the luxury bracket with open-air showers and stylish furnishings.

Fig Tree Camp TENTED CAMP, LODGE $$$
(☎Nairobi 020-605328; www.madahotels.com; s/d full board from US$435/580;) Vegetate on your tent's verandah, watching the Talek River gently flow past this sumptuous camp with a colonial-days feel. The gardens are about the most luxurious you'll ever see, and the bathrooms about the biggest and most inviting you'll find under canvas.

Oloolaimutiek Gate

Acacia Camp TENTED CAMP $
(☎0713751532; camping KSh600, tent per person US$22, full board per person US$80) Thatched roofs shelter closely spaced, spartan,

DON'T MISS

EWANGAN MAASAI VILLAGE HOMESTAY

Some years ago a young Maasai man, James Ole Lesaloi, from the Sekenani area got fed up with the lack of development and opportunities for the Maasai living around the reserve and set up **Semadep** (Sekenani Maasai Development Project; ☎0721817757; www.semadepngo.com; Sekenani), with the aim to change the lives of the local Maasai. Fast forward a few years and the project, with little publicity or outside help, has been remarkably successful and includes a school, clinic, water projects, orphans projects and a media centre to its list of credits. But for tourists what is perhaps most interesting is the opportunity it offers to stay in a genuine Maasai *manyatta* (village) and get a real understanding of Maasai life and culture – and the issues they face.

It's hoped that as the idea gets more popular other *manyattas* under Semadep guidance will also allow homestays (though to really work, no *manyatta* could host more than one small group at a time). For the few people who've stayed so far, almost all come away saying it was the highlight of their Kenyan travels.

A traditional Maasai *manyatta* 2km north of Sekenani gate, **Ewangan** (☎0721817757; www.maasaimaravillage.com; per person full board US$70, children free) offers a homestay with the Maasai. A number of families, and a whole load of cows and goats, live in the *manyatta* and during your stay you're likely to help with daily chores such as milking the cows and goats and making jewellery. You'll also be encouraged to visit various Semadep projects.

Accommodation is basic – a hut with no electricity or running water – but it's all very cosy and the food is excellent. It's a particularly fun experience for children (we've stayed there with a four year old and an 18 month old and they much preferred this to the fancy lodges and wildlife drives).

semipermanent tents in this quaint campground. There are numerous cooking areas, a bar and a campfire. The communal bathrooms are clean and hot water flows in the evening. The only downside for campers is the lack of shade.

Mara Sopa LODGE $$$
(☎Nairobi 020-25161660; www.sopalodges.com; s/d full board US$214/248;) With over 100 rooms, this is one of the largest lodges in the Masai Mara and at busy times it can feel like a real package-tour production line. That said, the landscaped grounds are pleasant, there's a big pool complex and the rooms are very presentable, if a little dated. Technically the lodge is just inside the Siana Group Ranch and Conservancy, but seeing as guests are taken on safari in the adjacent national reserve, we have included it here.

Ol Moran Tented Camp TENTED CAMP $$$
(☎Nairobi 020-882923; www.olmorantentedcamp.com; tent s/d/tr full board from US$195/254/371; P) The safari tents here come in two flavours: the 'superior' are large with a wooden deck and a smart bathroom, while the 14 'standard' tents are smaller and simpler, but entirely presentable. Walk-in rates are frequently considerably lower then the official rates.

Musiara & Oloololo Gates

There's only top-end accommodation in this part of the park.

Kichwa Tembo Camp TENTED CAMP $$$
(☎Nairobi 020-3688620; www.andbeyond.com; s/d full board US$782/1030;) Just outside the northern boundary of the reserve, Kichwa has been recently renovated and has permanent tents with grass-mat floors, stone bathrooms and tasteful furnishings. Hop in a hammock and take in spectacular savannah views. The camp has an excellent reputation for its food and is well positioned for the migration river-crossing points.

Governors' Camp TENTED CAMP $$$
(☎0733616204, Nairobi 020-2734000; www.governorscamp.com; tent s/d full board US$718/1150;) This camp, and Little Governors' Camp, is widely regarded as the most magisterial camp in the reserve itself and offers great service, a pleasing riverside location and activities aplenty.

The camp is surprisingly large (32 tents), which means it lacks the intimacy of many of the similarly priced places in the neighbouring conservancies.

Little Governors' Camp TENTED CAMP **$$$**
(☎0733616204, Nairobi 020-2734000; tent s/d full board US$826/1320;) Surrounding a waterhole, the 17 tents here are crammed with memories of colonial times and offer some of the reserve's most memorable nights under canvas.

Inside the Reserve

It's only possible to camp within the reserve in its Mara Triangle sector, in either the **public campsite** (per person US$20) or **special campsite** (per person US$30) – private campsites that can be reserved. You will need to be totally self-sufficient, to the point of bringing your own firewood (using the dead wood within the park is prohibited).

★ **Mara Toto** TENTED CAMP **$$$**
(☎Nairobi 020-6000457; www.greatplainsconservation.com; s/d full board US$1343/1790;) A tiny camp that's so well hidden under the riverside trees it's impossible to see until you're pretty much in it. The five tents are the epitome of refined-safari style with leather armchairs, old travellers' trunks and brass bucket showers. As decadent as the camp is, this isn't a place for those scared of the bush. After dark the camp echoes to the sounds of lions roaring and hippos splashing around the river.

Mara Serena Safari Lodge LODGE **$$$**
(☎0732123333; www.serenahotels.com; s/d full board US$424/638;) This large, resort-style lodge, which has a pool complex and even a gym, would be a better fit in a city rather than a supposed wilderness. Of all the park lodges, however, it has the best view. Built on a small hill, most rooms have commanding views over not one, but two, migration crossing points.

Information

Although the main reserve is managed by the Narok County Council, and the **Mara Triangle** (www.maratriangle.org) is managed by the Mara Conservancy, both charge the same, and an admission ticket bought at one is valid at the other. Keep hold of this ticket, as you will be asked to present it when travelling between the

OFF THE BEATEN TRACK

THE LOITA HILLS

To the northeast of the Masai Mara National Reserve are the little-known and spellbindingly beautiful Loita Hills. When accessing them from the Mara area, the hills start out dry and unimpressive, but if you bounce along for enough hours (and we mean hours and hours – the roads here are some of the worst in Kenya), things start to change. The vegetation becomes greener and much more luxuriant, eventually becoming a virtual tangled jungle. The mountains also grow ever bigger, peaking at a respectable 2150m.

This is the most traditional corner of Maasai land and change, though it's coming, is way behind many other parts of the country. Despite the number of Maasai living here, it's also an area of unexpected wildlife – colobus monkeys swing through the trees, turacos light the skies with colour, and huge numbers of buffaloes, forest pigs and bushbucks move through the shadows. What makes this area so extraordinary is that it's not covered by any official protection and yet the forests remain fairly untouched. The reason is that there are many places in the forests sacred to the Maasai and the elders tightly control the felling of trees and grazing of cattle. It's a brilliant example of how traditional cultures can thrive alongside wildlife without outside aid.

The best way to explore this area is on foot. Maasai Trails, based out of the beautiful and low-key **Jan's Camp** (☎0718139359; www.maasaitrails.com; s/d full board US$250/400) – about the only accommodation option in the hills bar a few basic boardings and lodgings in some villages – are the people to help you with this. They organise everything from four-night stays, with two nights at Jan's Camp and two nights bush camping in forest glades where forest pigs frequently snort their way past your tent at night, to much longer hikes of up to 12 days.

The longer options take you completely across and over the Loita Hills and down into the Rift Valley near Lake Magadi. Should you prefer something less strenuous, Jan's Camp can just be used as a base for day hikes – it would also work as a good base for birdwatchers. Prices for walks depend on the number of people and the length of hike.

Stays at Jan's Camp are normally included in the walking package rates.

reserve's Narok and Transmara sections and on your eventual exit.

All vehicles seem to get charged KSh1000 at the gates instead of the KSh400 fee for vehicles with less than six seats – be insistent but polite and all will be well.

The only ATM in the area is a KCB one in Talek village (and note that KCB ATMs can be a little temperamental with foreign cards!), so come prepared with more cash than you think you'll need.

For more on the Masai Mara and surrounding conservancies see the independent website www.maasaimara.com.

Getting There & Away

AIR

Airkenya (Nairobi 020-3916000; www.airkenya.com), **Mombasa Air Safari** (0734400400; www.mombasaairsafari.com), **Safarilink** (Nairobi 020-600777; www.flysafarilink.com) and **Fly540** (0710540540; www.fly540.com) – flying under the name of SAX – each have daily flights to any of the eight airstrips in and around the Masai Mara. Flights start at US$250 return.

MATATU, CAR & 4WD

Although it's possible to arrange wildlife drives independently, keep in mind that there are few savings in coming here without transport or pre-arranged wildlife drives. That said, it is possible to access Talek and Sekenani gates from Narok by matatu (KSh500), and from Kisii a matatu will get you as far as Kilkoris or Suna on the main A1 Hwy, after which you will have problems.

For those who drive, the first 52km west of Narok on the B3 and C12 are smooth enough, but after the bitumen runs out you'll find there's just as much rattle as there is roll and you'll soon come to dread this road. The C13, which connects Oloololo gate with Lolgorian out in the west, is very rough and rocky, and it's poorly signposted – a highway it's not.

Petrol is available (although expensive) at Mara Sarova, Mara Serena and Keekorok Lodges, as well as in Talek village.

Getting Around

If you do arrive by matatu, you can organise wildlife drives with most of the big lodges in and around the reserve (although you cannot do this with lodges inside the private conservancies) and even some of the cheaper camps. Typically they charge around KSh12,000 to KSh15,000 for a full day's vehicle and driver hire, which can be split between as many people as can be comfortably squeezed into the vehicle. There's no public transport within the park.

Maji Moto Group Ranch

Closer to Narok town than the reserve itself, Maji Moto (which translates as hot water and, true enough, there are some hot springs here) is a blissfully tourist-free, 600-sq-km group ranch. Its distance from the main Mara ecosystem, and the abundance of Maasai communities in the area, mean that wildlife numbers are far lower than in other conservancies, but this is a different type of conservancy, where the emphasis is as much on enjoying and learning about Maasai culture as it is animals. If you want a totally different kind of 'safari' experience, this could be the place.

THE MASAI MARA AREA CONSERVANCIES

Changing the face of conservation and tourism in Kenya are the private and community conservancies, many of which now border the Masai Mara National Reserve. Each conservancy operates in a slightly different manner, but the general idea is to make tourism, conservation and the rights of local peoples work hand in hand to the mutual benefit of all. Most conservancies involve the local Maasai landowners leasing their communal lands for an average of 15 years at a time to several high-end lodges. The Maasai are still allowed to graze their cattle in the conservancies and receive a guaranteed income from each camp. In addition, all camps have to contribute to community-development projects.

In return the wildlife is allowed to live in peace and the lodges can offer their clients a very exclusive kind of safari with minimal other visitors, as those not staying in the conservancies are not allowed to enter. Visitors also get the opportunity to partake in activities not allowed in the reserve itself, such as walking safaris and bush breakfasts.

Entry fees to the conservancies are covered in the nightly cost of accommodation. The costs and the necessity of keeping things quiet and exclusive preclude the availability of budget accommodation. However, prices include all meals, drinks, safaris, guides and other activities – things not always included with top-end places in the reserve proper.

Sleeping

★ Maji Moto Eco-Camp TENTED CAMP **$$**
(716430722, 041-2006479; www.majimotocamp.com; per person full board US$80) Set on a hillside among granite rocks contorted into fantastical plasticine shapes, Maji Moto is around 60km north of the reserve proper. The camp is a fairly simple but beautifully conceived creation where guests sleep in large dome tents with mattresses on the floor.

It's a brilliant camp for families, with warrior training, dances, village visits, bush walks, full-day safaris to the Mara and soaks in the hot springs all on offer. Multiday walking safaris to the Masai Mara can be organised and your stay genuinely helps the locals.

Mara North Conservancy

Established in 2009, the 30,000-hectare **Mara North Conservancy** (www.maranorth.com), which abuts the northwestern edge of the Masai Mara National Reserve, is one of the better known, more popular and more successful (in terms of benefits to both the local community and the local wildlife) of the Mara-area conservancies.

The countryside here is an absolute cliché of what East Africa is supposed to look like: the flat-topped acacias, the long golden grass and animals everywhere. Leopard sightings are common and there are lots of very large lions, as well as some cheetahs and masses of plains wildlife. In fact, during the migration the horizon can be utterly covered in the black dots of wildebeest and seeing lions on a kill is very common.

Sleeping

★ Elephant Pepper TENTED CAMP **$$$**
(0730127000; www.elephantpeppercamp.com; s/d full board US$952/1588;) This intimate camp has eight tents that are luxurious without being over the top and food that is of a genuinely high standard. But what really makes Elephant Pepper stand out is its setting, under a dense thicket of trees with views over rolling grasslands that, at times, can be a seething mass of grunting, growling and trumpeting megafauna.

In fact, so much wildlife can sometimes be found right outside the (unfenced) camp that lying in your tent at night, listening to the sounds of the African night, might leave you feeling like a part of the food chain! For most people it's wonderfully exhilarating, but for those with a nervous disposition, it may all prove a bit much.

★ Saruni Mara TENTED CAMP **$$$**
(0735950903, Nairobi 020-2180497; www.saruni.com; s/d full board US$910/1520;) Way to the north of any of the other camps, and virtually on the border of the conservancy, this breathtaking camp has around a dozen tents dusted with antique furnishings and colonial bric-a-brac. Some even have open log fires inside! The setting, in animal-packed, forested hills, is very different to most other camps

There are quite a few Maasai *manyattas* on the plains just below Saruni Mara, and this human presence does mean that wildlife can be scarcer and you may have to drive up to 45 minutes to really get into the heart of the conservancy. On the plus side, there are lots of opportunities for bush walks and cultural encounters.

It also runs a family-friendly 'warrior for a week' programme where children can learn the art of lighting fires without matches and other such skills you don't really want them learning!

Off Beat Mara TENTED CAMP **$$$**
(0704909355; www.offbeatsafaris.com; s/d all-inclusive US$740/1480;) With just six tents, this is one of the smallest and most personable of the Mara North camps with bush-chic tents filled with heavy wooden furnishings that exude an authentic old-African-safari feel. Wildlife abounds around the camp and there's even a resident lion pride whose nightly growls may seep into your dreams.

The camp has a charming young staff and excellent guides, including a specialist walking guide who takes guests on long bush walks through valleys filled with wildlife

Kicheche Mara TENTED CAMP **$$$**
(Nairobi 020-2493569; www.kicheche.com; s/d full board $US835/1400;) Stunningly sited in a lush green vale rammed with zebras, impalas and, in the river that passes close to camp, a hippo or two. It has a handful of giant, seriously luxurious tents stretched along nearly 1km of hillside. If all that wasn't enough, there's an often-seen leopard resident in the area.

Naboisho Conservancy

Created in 2011, the Naboisho Conservancy is flourishing. There's plenty of wildlife here, including cheetahs, elephants and a fair few lions, as well as all the plains wildlife, and the landscape is a classic mix of open grasslands and light acacia woodlands.

Sleeping

★Basecamp Wilderness TENTED CAMP **$$$**
(☎0733333909; www.basecampkenya.com; Naboisho; s/d full board US$400/720) Of all the camps in the Mara conservancies, Wilderness is probably the most authentically safari. There are five simple but very comfortable tents with hot bucket showers and good beds set in a hidden valley that's home to a resident leopard and lots of other animals. Guests are encouraged to walk here from sister camp, Basecamp Eagle View. If you want to get even closer to nature, 'fly camping' trips are offered out of here.

Staying here isn't just a wild experience, it's also great value and affordable to mere mortals.

Asilia Naboisho Camp TENTED CAMP **$$$**
(☎Nairobi 020-2324904; www.asiliaafrica.com; s/d all-inclusive US$1230/1930) So what if the tents here, with their huge beds and indoor and outdoor showers, are the most extravagant around. What people really stay here for is the opportunity to walk for kilometres over animal-crammed savannah with an expert South African guide. If that wasn't enough, the wildlife viewing right outside the tents is superb, with big cats frequently passing right through the camp.

Encounter Mara TENTED CAMP **$$$**
(☎Nairobi 020-2034197; www.encountermara.com; s/d full board US$783/1250) This very welcoming camp, which has some of the most impressive tents in Naboisho, is buried away among a patch of woodland but with views over a salt lick and waterhole. A big plus is the hide down by the waterhole, where happy hours can be spent birding and getting seriously close to the animals.

Basecamp Eagle View TENTED CAMP **$$$**
(☎0733333909; www.basecampkenya.com; s/d full board US$530/980;) The most upmarket of the three Basecamp offerings around the Mara. The six tents here are stretched along a ridge with mind-boggling views over a salt lick and miles of savannah. Despite the undisputed luxury, Eagle View still follows the company ethos of uncompromising sustainability. Excellent walking safaris are a highlight of a stay here.

Kicheche Valley Camp TENTED CAMP **$$$**
(☎Nairobi 020-2493569; www.kicheche.com; s/d full board US$925/1580) Six fabulously attractive tents spaced around a waterhole that draws wildlife right up to (and into) the edge of camp. The tents, all of which have wooden terraces facing the setting sun, feel very open, which gives guests a real sensation of being immersed in the bush.

All the tents have electric sockets and the safari jeeps are designed with photographers in mind, thanks to the addition of bean bags. Such touches shouldn't be a surprise though, since one of the owners is renowned wildlife photographer Paul Goldstein.

WESTERN BULLFIGHTING

Bullfighting (between two bulls) is one of the more popular 'sports' in western Kenya, and Khayega (6km south of Kakamega) has Saturday morning showdowns at the **bullfighting grounds**. They start at 7am (the whole thing wraps up at around 8am) with a whole lot of horn blowing, drumming, chanting and stick waving.

The purpose-bred bulls are fed on molasses-spiked grass and, to help them conserve their energy, isolated from heifers, making them understandably tetchy. Then the bulls are fed secret concoctions guaranteed to make them even more aggressive.

When the bulls meet, they'll lock horns and fight until one submits and turns tail. Besides a bruised ego or two, no bulls are injured during the show of strength (cattle are valued too highly for owners to put them at risk). There are no safety barriers, so spectators should keep their distance and be prepared to run or climb a tree should a bull break away. The winning bull (and all of the crowd) then race to the next venue, usually about 1km to 2km away, where they meet up with a similar winner and the whole performance is repeated.

Bullfighting is practised mostly by the Isukha and Idako peoples.

Olare-Orok Conservancy

Established in 2006 (as Olare Motorogi), this is now one of the longest established and most successful of the conservancies. It also has one of the highest concentrations of animals, including loads of predators, and the lowest densities of tourists – just one tent for every 280 hectares.

Sleeping

★Mara Plains TENTED CAMP $$$
(www.greatplainsconservation.com; s/d all-inclusive US$1150/2300;) This utterly captivating camp has a dozen tents – sorry, palaces – in which the beds and showers are carved from old wooden railway sleepers and quality rugs laze across the floors. The highlight for most, though, are the big, free-standing brass bathtubs overlooking a river of wallowing hippos.

The food is some of the best of any of the camps and the manager-hosts are charmers. As an added bonus, each tent is supplied with a box of high-quality Canon camera equipment and binoculars to borrow.

Kicheche Bush TENTED CAMP $$$
(Nairobi 020-2493569; www.kicheche.com; s/d full board US$925/1580) Run with the kind of casual efficiency that brings guests back again and again, Kicheche Bush has six well-spaced, enormous tents set within a light fringe of trees, beyond which stretches some of the most reliably impressive wildlife countryside in the whole Mara region.

Olarro Conservancy

The private Olarro Conservancy has been around for a while, but never really worked in the past. Today, with new management and investment the conservancy is quickly coming into its own, with lots of wildlife now present.

Sleeping

Olarro Lodge LODGE $$$
(Dubai +971-43253322, lodge 0737463731; www.olarrokenya.com; s/d all-inclusive US$490/840;) The only accommodation option within the conservancy is this sublime lodge halfway up a lightly forested hill. This is one of the most luxurious places to stay in all the region, with highlights including the interconnecting pools, the giant fire pit surrounded by cushions, the superb food and a terrace with views that go for kilometres.

Its other unique feature is the night safaris using high-tech night-vision binoculars – you'll never step foot outside of your tent in the dark again after using these!

Olderikesi Conservancy

In the far southeast of the Mara region, on the border of Tanzania and the famous Serengeti, the Olderikesi Conservancy covers around 8000 hectares. Though it's been in existence for many years, the conservancy's managers will openly say that it's only since 2011 that everything has clicked into place and the conservancy has started functioning as they hoped it would.

One of the most exclusive of the Mara conservancies, it's also one of the richest in wildlife, including large numbers of lions.

Sleeping

★Cottar's 1920s Camp TENTED CAMP $$$
(0733773378; www.cottars.com; s/d full board US$1184/1974;) One of the most remote camps in the greater Mara region, Cottar's, owned by a legendary safari family, induces a misty-eyed sense of longing from those lucky enough to have visited. As the name suggests, the enormous tents are dressed up like a well-to-do 1920s gentleman, with all manner of colonial and safari memorabilia.

But there's more to Cottar's than just elegant style. There's some of the best food of any camp, a beautiful pool, fantastic guides and a host of activities for children.

Siana Group Ranch and Conservancy

This vast conservancy contains a huge array of habitats, including heavily forested mountain slopes, gunky swamps and open grasslands, which means there's plenty of wildlife to be found. The conservancy managers are still going through the fine print with the local Maasai so the way the conservancy functions may change.

Sleeping

Sekenani Camp TENTED CAMP $$$
(Nairobi 020-891169; www.sekenani-camp.com; s/d all inclusive US$288/462;) Set within a jungly tangle of trees and waterways

in a beautiful bird-filled valley, this discreet and memorable camp has a unique raised treetop walkway leading from the pool and bar-restaurant area to the tents, which are large and comfy without being over the top. The camp supports a solid community-help programme.

LAKE VICTORIA

Spread over 68,000 sq km, yet never more than 80m deep, Lake Victoria, one of the key water sources of the White Nile, might well be East Africa's most important geographical feature, but is seen by surprisingly few visitors. This is a shame, as its humid shores hide some of the most beautiful and rewarding parts of western Kenya – from untouched national parks to lively cities and tranquil islands.

Kisumu

POP 322,700

Set on the sloping shore of Lake Victoria's Winam Gulf, Kisumu might be the third-largest town in Kenya, but its relaxed atmosphere is a world away from that of Nairobi and Mombasa.

Until 1977 the port was one of the busiest in Kenya, but decline set in with the collapse of the East African Community (the EAC was originally established by Kenya, Tanzania and Uganda to promote a common market within the region) in that same year due to political squabbling, and the port sat virtually idle for two decades.

Recently increased cooperation and the revival of the EAC (which now also includes Rwanda and Burundi) in 2000 has helped establish Kisumu as an international shipment point for petroleum products. Surprisingly the lake plays no part (raw fuel for processing is piped in from Mombasa and the end products are shipped out by truck) so, while the lake may have been the lifeblood for Kisumu's inception, the city sits with its back to the water. Nonetheless, with Kisumu's fortunes again rising, and the water hyacinth's impact reduced (see box below), it's hoped Lake Victoria will once more start contributing to the local economy.

Sights & Activities

Kisumu Museum MUSEUM
(Nairobi Rd; admission KSh500; 8am-6pm) Southwest of the town centre, this museum has three main sections. The first covers western Kenya's three principal linguistic groups: Luo, Bantu and Kalenjin. The second attraction is a traditional Luo homestead depicting the fictitious life of Onyango as he undergoes the rite of passage to establish his own family compound. The last section is a small aquarium displaying the nearby lake's aquatic assets and a reptile house holding examples of all the local snakes you don't want to meet.

Impala Sanctuary WILDLIFE RESERVE
(www.kws.go.ke; adult/child US$25/15; 6am-6pm) On the road to Dunga, this 1-sq-km sanctuary is home to a small impala herd and provides important grazing grounds for local hippos. In addition to the impalas, there are cages of other Kenyan antelope and monkeys, but frankly it's an awful lot of money to pay for what is essentially a small zoo!

VICTORIA'S UNWELCOME GUESTS

Lake Victoria's 'evolving' ecosystem has proved to be both a boon and a bane for those living along its shores. For starters, its waters are a haven for mosquitoes and snails, making malaria and bilharzia (schistosomiasis) all too common here. Then there are the Nile perch, introduced 50 years ago to combat mosquitoes, but which eventually thrived, growing to over 200kg in weight and becoming every fishing-boat captain's dream. The ravenous perch have wiped out more than 300 species of smaller tropical fish unique to the lake.

Last but not least is the ornamental water hyacinth. First reported in 1986, this exotic pond plant had no natural predators here and quickly reached plague proportions, even managing to shut down much of the lake's shipping industry. Millions of dollars have been ploughed into solving the problem, with controversial programmes such as mechanical removal and the introduction of weed-eating weevils. The investment seems to be paying off, with the most recent satellite photos showing hyacinth cover dramatically reduced from the 17,230 hectares it once covered.

Kisumu

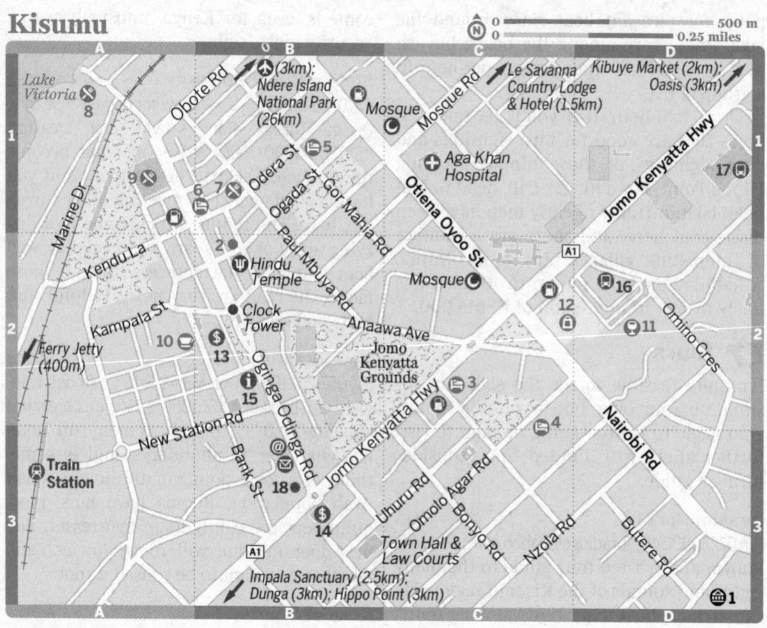

Kisumu

Sights
1 Kisumu Museum ... D3

Activities, Courses & Tours
Ibrahim Nandi ... (see 5)
Integri Tours ... (see 3)
2 Zaira Tours & Travel ... B2

Sleeping
3 Duke of Breeze ... C2
4 New East View Hotel ... C2
5 New Victoria Hotel ... B1
6 Sooper Guest House ... B1

Eating
7 Green Garden Restaurant ... B1
8 Railway Beach Restaurants ... A1
9 The Laughing Buddha ... A1

Drinking & Nightlife
10 Juiz Parlour ... A2
11 Social Centre ... D2

Shopping
12 Main Market ... C2

Information
13 Barclays Bank ... B2
14 Kenya Commercial Bank ... B3
15 Shiva Travels ... B2

Transport
16 Bus & Matatu Station ... D2
17 Easy Coach ... D1
18 Kenya Airways ... B3

Ndere Island National Park PARK
(www.kws.go.ke; adult/child US$25/15; 6am-6pm) Gazetted as a national park in 1986, this 4.2-sq-km island has never seen tourism take off. It is forested and very beautiful, housing a variety of bird species, plus occasionally sighted hippos, impalas (introduced) and spotted crocodiles, a lesser-known cousin of the larger Nile crocodiles.

There's nowhere to stay and, although twice-daily matatus reach the shore just opposite the island, your only reliable option to get to Ndere is with chartered boats. Expect to pay around KSh15,000 to KSh17,000 for a half-day trip. Chartered boat trips can be arranged with any of the boat captains offering sightseeing trips from Hippo Point.

Hippo Point Boat Trips BOAT TOUR
Hippo Point, sticking into Lake Victoria at Dunga, about 3km south of town, is a beautiful spot at which you're highly unlikely to see any hippos. It is, though, the launch

point for pleasant boat rides around the lake. Prices vary among the boats, but expect to pay KSh500 per person, per hour in a group of five.

On a two-hour trip you'll be taken to areas that are good for bird sightings and even sightings of those hippos avoiding Hippo Point. For a longer trip, head to Maboko Island. Traces of early man have been discovered here, and there are a number of interesting villages plus good birding. A half-day package for up to 10 people is likely to cost in the region of KSh15,000.

Tours

It's quite feasible to see the sights of Kisumu on your own, but if you don't know your eagle from your egret, or want to visit further afield with limited time, consider hiring a guide.

Ibrahim Nandi TOURS
(0723083045; ibradingo@yahoo.com) A well-known and trusted tour guide to the many sights and sounds of the Kisumu region. He can arrange boat trips, birdwatching tours, nature walks and excursions to Ndere Island National Park. He can be contacted through the New Victoria Hotel.

Integri Tours TOURS
(0700517969; www.integritour.com; Duke of Breeze, off Jomo Kenyatta Hwy) Professional operator with some excellent day-trip itineraries.

Zaira Tours & Travel SAFARIS
(0722788879; Ogada St) The best safari operator in town, with pop-top minivans and 4WDs.

Sleeping

Some of the cheaper Kisumu hotels are known for poor security, so consider using your own padlock to secure your room, or deposit valuable items with reception. If you're finding the humidity hard to deal with, you'll be pleased to know that most rooms in Kisumu are equipped with fans.

★**New East View Hotel** HOTEL $
(0711183017; Omolo Agar Rd; s KSh1700-2300, d KSh2300-2800; P) The town's stand-out cheapie is one of many family homes in the area that have been converted into hotels. Splashed in bright colours, it retains just enough furniture and decoration to give the rooms a homely, pre-loved feel and the welcome is, even for Kenya, unusually warm. Security is also tight.

Sooper Guest House BACKPACKERS $
(0725281733; www.sooperguesthse.com; Oginga Odinga Rd; s/tw/d excl breakfast KSh1200/1500/1600;) Sooper has become the de facto backpackers in town and you have a good chance of meeting other travellers here. The rooms, which come in a dizzying array of styles, are immaculately well kept and have hot showers, though those facing the road are very noisy. Helpful staff and good security.

New Victoria Hotel HOTEL $
(057-2021067; Gor Mahia Rd; s without bathroom excl breakfast KSh1050, s/d/tr excl breakfast KSh1650/2450/3500) This Yemeni-run hotel has character in abundance and is something of a focal point for the town's small Arab population. Rooms have fans, mosquito nets and comfy foam mattresses. The next-door mosque will rouse you at 5am, whether you want to be roused or not.

Duke of Breeze HOTEL $
(0717105444; off Jomo Kenyatta Hwy; s KSh2200-3000, d KSh2900-3800, tr KSh4000;) Popular with Peace Corp volunteers, the Duke has large rooms that have seen better days. The real attractions are the roof-top restaurant, the cinema-sized TV showing big sporting matches and the relaxed, chilled vibe.

Le Savanna Country Lodge & Hotel HOTEL $$
(057-2021159, 0714995510; www.lesavannacountrylodge.com; Dewchurch Dr, Ondiek Hwy; s/d KSh5750/6750; P) This delightfully calm place is where everyone who's anyone likes to stay when in town. The large, well-dressed rooms have good bathrooms, fast in-room wi-fi and no exterior noise or disturbance. There's also a reasonable in-house restaurant and a quiet garden bar. It's around 2km north of town and a KSh100 *boda-boda* (motorcycle taxi) ride.

Eating

The fact that Kisumu sits on Lake Victoria certainly isn't lost on restaurants here, and fish is abundant on menus. If you want an authentic local fish fry, there are no better places than the dozens of smoky tin-shack **restaurants** (Railway Beach; Fish & ugali around KSh500; Roughly 8.30am-8.30pm) sitting on the lake's shore at Railway Beach at the end of Oginga Odinga Rd. A midsized fish served with *ugali* (maize- or cassava-based staple) or rice is sufficient for two people.

Green Garden Restaurant INTERNATIONAL $
(Odera St; mains KSh380-500; ⌚8am-11pm) Surrounded by colourful murals and potted palms, the Green Garden is an oasis of culinary delight set in an Italian-themed courtyard. As you would expect, it's an expat hotspot and the word is that the tilapia (fish) in a spinach and coconut sauce is the way to go. Be prepared to wait a long time for your meal.

The Laughing Buddha INTERNATIONAL $
(Swan Centre, Accra St; mains KSh350-500; ⌚10.30am-11pm Tue-Sun; ✎) The Laughing Buddha has a limited menu (made even more so by the fact that half the items probably won't be available) of pastas, pizzas and chips in dozens of different flavours, which will likely come as a surprise to anyone who grew up thinking chips were just chips! The streetside tables earn it big points.

Drinking & Nightlife

Kisumu's nightlife has a reputation for being even livelier than Nairobi's. Check flyers and ask locals who are plugged into the scene. Be careful when leaving venues as muggings and worse have occurred. Solo women should take a chaperone. Clubs are liveliest on Friday and Saturday night, although folks don't get bumping and grinding until after 10pm.

Juiz Parlour CAFE
(off Station Rd; juice from KSh70; ⌚7.30am-8pm) You name it and they'll stick it in a blender and pulverise the bejesus out of it. The pumpkin-and-beetroot juice looked foul so we shared a very special moment with a mango-and-pineapple combo instead.

Oasis LIVE MUSIC
(Kondele, Jomo Kenyatta Hwy; admission KSh150-200) With live music most nights, this is the place to see Lingala music performed by Congolese bands. Be prepared for a fair bit of shaking and sweating.

Social Centre DANCE
(off Omino Cres; admission around KSh100) Tucked behind the main matatu stage, this club is big on *ohangla* (Luo traditional music) with the odd Kiswahali hip-hop tune thrown in for good measure.

WORTH A TRIP

SIMBI LAKE

The pint-sized lakeside village of Kendu Bay, 80km from Kisumu, has little to offer apart from the strange volcanic Simbi Lake a couple of kilometres from town. The circular lake, sunk into the earth like a bomb crater, has a footpath around it and is an excellent twitching spot. The town itself, which is a charming place that feels exactly as you imagine remote Africa would feel, sees very few tourists and the reception is staggeringly warm.

Shopping

Main Market MARKET
(off Jomo Kenyatta Hwy; ⌚from 7am) Kisumu's main market is one of Kenya's most animated markets and certainly one of its largest – it now spills out onto the surrounding roads. If you're curious, or just looking for essentials such as suits or wigs, it's worth a stroll around. Runs until around mid-afternoon.

Kibuye Market MARKET
(Jomo Kenyatta Hwy; ⌚Sun) Come past the huge Kibuye Market on any quiet weekday and you'll find it as empty as a hyena's heart, but visit on a Sunday and it transforms into a blossoming spring flower of colour and scents.

Information

Aga Khan Hospital (☎057-2020005; Otiena Oyoo St) A large hospital with modern facilities and 24-hour emergency room.

Barclays Bank (Kampala St) With ATM.

Kenya Commercial Bank (Jomo Kenyatta Hwy) With ATM (Visa only).

Moscom Cyber (Mega Plaza, Oginga Odinga Rd; per hr KSh60; ⌚8am-7pm Mon-Sat) One of many internet cafes around town.

Post Office (Oginga Odinga Rd)

Shiva Travels (☎0733635200; Oginga Odinga Rd) Airline ticketing and hotel reservations.

Getting There & Away

AIR

Fly540 (www.fly540.com), **Jambo Jet** (☎Nairobi 020 3274545; www.jambojet.com) and **Kenya Airways** (☎0711022090; www.kenya-airways.com; Alpha House, Oginga Odinga Rd) offer daily flights to Nairobi (from KSh5500, 50 minutes).

MATATUS FROM KISUMU

TO	FARE	DURATION
Busia	KSh300-370	2 hr
Eldoret	KSh450-500	2½ hr
Homa Bay	KSh350-400	3 hr
Isebania	KSh700	4 hr
Kakamega	KSh200	1¾ hr
Kericho	KSh350	2 hr
Kisii	KSh350	2 hr
Kitale	KSh500	4 hr
Nairobi	KSh1000-1200	5½ hr
Narok	KSh800	5 hr
Nakuru	KSh800	3½ hr

BOAT

Despite the reduced hyacinth in the Winam Gulf, ferry services to Tanzania and Uganda haven't resumed. That said, there are always plans in the works, so ask around.

BUS & MATATU

Buses, matatus and Peugeots (shared taxis) to numerous destinations within Kenya battle it out at the large bus and matatu station just north of the main market. Peugeots cost about 25% more than matatus.

Easy Coach (www.emanamba.com; Jomo Kenyatta Hwy) offers the smartest buses out of town. Its booking office and departure point are in the car park just behind (and accessed through) Tusky's Shopping Centre. It has daily buses to Nairobi (KSh1400, seven hours, every couple of hours), Nakuru (KSh800, 4½ hours, every couple of hours) and Kampala (KSh1500, seven hours, 1.30pm and 10pm).

TRAIN

Despite having a beautiful old train station, Kisumu's station hasn't seen a locomotive pull in for years. There's constant talk of rekindling the service, but don't hold your breath.

Getting Around

BODA-BODA & TUK-TUK

Both *boda-bodas* and tuk-tuks (motorised minitaxis) have proliferated and they are a great way to get around Kisumu. A trip to Hippo Point should be no more than KSh50/150 for a *boda-boda*/tuk-tuk.

MATATU

Matatus 7 and 9, which travel along Oginga Odinga Rd and Jomo Kenyatta Hwy, are handy to reach the main matatu station, main market and Kibuye Market – just wave and hop on anywhere you see one.

TAXI

A taxi around town costs between KSh100 and KSh200, while trips to Dunga range from KSh250 to KSh400, with heavy bargaining.

Homa Bay

POP 32,174

Homa Bay has a slow, tropical, almost central African vibe, and the near-total absence of other tourists means it's extraordinarily and genuinely friendly. There is little to do other than trudge up and down the dusty, music-filled streets or wander down to the lake edge to watch the **marabou storks** pick through the trash as they wait for the fishermen and their morning catch.

Alternatively, the energetic may like to climb some of the cartoon-like hills that surround the town. The easiest summit to bag is the unmistakable conical mound of **Asego Hill**, which is just beyond the town and takes about an hour to clamber up.

The town also makes a great base from which to visit Ruma National Park and Thimlich Ohinga.

Sleeping & Eating

Twin Towers Hotel HOTEL $
(☎0775612195; s/d from KSh2500/3000) The Twin Towers (slightly unfortunate name, that) is a solid choice if all you require is a comfy bed and a bathroom that doesn't require a biohazard suit to enter. It can suffer quite badly from street noise, though. The restaurant here offers decent, if unimaginative, mains for around KSh300. It's right in the town centre near the banks, mosque and park.

Homa Bay Tourist Hotel HOTEL $$
(☎0727112615; s/d from KSh2850/4350; P 📶) This lakeside 'resort' is the town's original hotel and though the rooms are rather faded they also have character and are a pleasure to sleep in. The expansive lawns, running down to the water's edge, are home to many a colourful songbird and there's an outdoor bar with live music on Saturdays (so avoid rooms at the front).

It's a short way from the town centre, down by the lake.

Hippo Buck HOTEL $$
(☎0723262000; www.hippobuck.com; s US$35-70, d US$40-100; P ❄ 📶) There's much that's right about this smart place at the town's edge. The cheapest standard rooms are sparkling-clean, white-tiled cubes and from there on the more you pay the fancier the rooms become. So what's wrong with this hotel? The non-resident rates, which make it very overpriced. Fortunately, they'll almost certainly give you the resident rates (s/d from KSh2000/2500), which makes it a bargain. It's located a short way east of the town centre, at the top of the hill on the road from Kisii.

Information

Barclays Bank (Moi Hwy) With ATM.

KWS Warden's Office In the district commissioner's compound, it's the place for information on Ruma Naional Park.

Getting There & Away

The Easy Coach office is just down the hill from the bus station, in the Total petrol station compound. It has buses to Nairobi (KSh1000, nine hours) at 8.30am and 8pm. Several other companies and matatus (operating from the bus station) ply the routes to Mbita (KSh250, 1½ hours), Kisii (KSh200, 1½ hours) and Kisumu (KSh300, three hours).

Ruma National Park

Bordered by the dramatic **Kanyamaa Escarpment** and home to Kenya's only population of roans (one of Africa's rarest and largest antelope) is the seldom visited, 120-sq-km **Ruma National Park** (☎0723097573; www.kws.go.ke; adult/child US$20/10, vehicle from KSh300; ⏰6am-6pm). Besides roans, other rarities such as Bohor's reedbucks, Jackson's hartebeests, the tiny oribi antelope and Kenya's largest concentration of endangered Rothschild's giraffes can also be seen here. The most treasured residents are 28 (very hard to see) rhinos, both black and white, that have been translocated from other parks.

Birdlife is also prolific, with 145 different species present, including the migratory blue swallow that arrives between June and August.

Sights & Activities

Although dense bush in large parts of the park makes seeing animals difficult, you'll have more success in the open savannah areas – many visitors are surprised by just how much wildlife is visible in Ruma. In just a short visit you can expect to see masses of giraffes as well as impalas, waterbucks and zebras. The area around the airstrip is particularly rewarding.

Sleeping & Eating

There are two simple **campsites** (public/special camping US$20/30) near the main gate. The Nyati special campsite is the more scenic. In either case you need to be totally self-sufficient with food and water.

Oribi Guesthouse COTTAGES $$
(☎0723097573; www.kws.go.ke; cottage excl breakfast KSh9000; P) This KWS-run guesthouse, near the park headquarters, is extortionate if there are only two of you, but quite good value for groups. It has dramatic views over the Lambwe Valley and is well equipped with solar power, hot showers

RUMA NATIONAL PARK

Why Go Few people visit this small and scenic park, but those who do are often surprised by the quantity of wildlife, which includes rhinos, roans and Rothschild's giraffes.

When to Go Best in the dry season of June to February. During the rains, tracks can become impassable.

Practicalities Easily accessible from Homa Bay, but to be there at dawn when animals are most visible, stay in the park.

Budget Tips The park is set up for those with vehicles, but if you don't have your own wheels, contact the KWS rangers in Homa Bay, who may be able to arrange a jeep for you.

WORTH A TRIP

THIMLICH OHINGA

South of Ruma National Park, **Thimlich Ohinga Archaeological Site** (admission KSh1000) is one of East Africa's most important archaeological sites. It holds the remains of a dry-stone enclosure, 150m in diameter and containing another five smaller enclosures, thought to date back as far as the 15th century.

Getting to Thimlich is a problem without your own transport, though not completely impossible (with patience). Head 12km down the Homa Bay–Rongo road then turn right at Rod Kopany village, heading southwest through Mirogi to the village of Miranga. The site is signposted from there.

If you don't have wheels, take a matatu from Kisii towards Isebania on the Tanzania border and hop out at Suna. Take another matatu from here towards Karunga and ask to be let out at the junction for Thimlich Ohinga or Miranga (you might find a matatu going directly from Suna to here). From the junction, hunt about for any kind of transport to the entrance of Thimlich Ohinga.

and a fully functioning kitchen, but bring your own food.

Getting There & Away

With your own vehicle, head a couple of kilometres south from Homa Bay and turn right onto the Mbita road. After about 12km you'll come to the main access road, which is signed just as Kenya Wildlife Services (coming from Homa Bay, you might not see the sign as it faces the other way), and from there it's another 11km to the park entrance. The park's roads are in decent shape, but require a mega-4WD in the rainy season.

Mbita & Rusinga Island

POP 28,000

Mbita and Rusinga Island (connected by a causeway) are delightful. Tiny, languid and rarely visited, they offer a glimpse of an older Africa – an Africa that moves to the gentle sway of the seasons rather than the ticking of a clock. This is the sort of place where schoolchildren abandon their classes to watch you pass by and old women burst into song at your arrival.

Sights & Activities

Tom Mboya's Mausoleum HISTORIC SITE

A child of Rusinga and a former sanitary inspector in Nairobi, Mboya was one of the few Luo people to achieve any kind of political success. He held a huge amount of influence as Jomo Kenyatta's right-hand man and was widely tipped to become Kenya's second president before he was assassinated in 1969. His tomb and a small museum dedicated to his life are on the island's north side.

To get there from the causeway and Rusinga town, take the right-hand road at the junction and, after around 12km, take the road off to the right with the sign pointing to Kolunga Beach. Turn right again about 50m later, continue straight for around 700m and, at the junction with the small sign to the museum, go right. It's the bullet-shaped building (which symbolises the bullet that killed him) in front of you. Entry is by donation – KSh200 should be enough. There are no set opening hours but the caretaker will quickly turn up to show you around.

Mbasa Island WILDLIFE RESERVE

Also known as Bird Island, Mbasa is home to a wide variety of wetland birds, including long-tailed cormorants (which have a breeding colony here), fish eagles, marsh harriers and little white egrets. Bird concentrations are thickest at sunset, when peripatetic birds return to roost. To get here you'll need to arrange a boat with a local fisherman or ask at the Wayando Beach Club Eco Lodge; expect to pay between KSh4000 and KSh7000 per boat.

Sleeping & Eating

Rusinga Guesthouse GUESTHOUSE $

(☎0705146134; rusingaguesthouse@yahoo.com; Rusinga; s KSh1200-1500, d/tw KSh1500/1700; P, wi-fi) Far enough from the bars to offer a quiet night's sleep, this guesthouse sets a bar of its own in terms of value for money. The rooms are pristine and the mosquito nets are yet to acquire holes. The staff are endearingly shy and the restaurant can sort you out with the standard chicken or fish options (mains KSh210 to KSh300).

Elk Guesthouse HOTEL **$**
(Mbita; r KSh400-700) Next to the matatu stand in the centre of Mbita town, this inviting little place has bright and clean rooms set around a plant-stuffed courtyard. Cheaper rooms share bathrooms. The restaurant out front fries up some great fish dishes (around KSh400).

★ **Wayando Beach Club Eco Lodge** BANDA, CAMPGROUND **$$**
(☎0723773571, 0708593513; www.wayandobeachclub.com; Rusinga; camping KSh950, camping incl breakfast & using lodge tents KSh1500, s/d banda incl breakfast KSh3500/7000; Ⓟ) Four kilometres from the causeway (turn right at the junction) is this large American-owned grassy compound with easy lake access, loads of birds in the gardens, campsites under the acacia trees and a couple of very comfortable and colourful stone *bandas*. There's also a cool bar-restaurant (dinner KSh850).

It can sort out good guides and arrange boat hire. The owner is involved in all manner of eco-projects on the island.

Getting There & Away

The best way of getting from Mbita to Kisumu is to take the ferry (foot passenger KSh150, vehicle from KSh800, one hour) to Luanda Kotieno on the northern shore of the narrow Winam Gulf and catch a connecting matatu (KSh300, two hours). Boats leave Mbita at 7am, 10am, 2pm and 5pm. Coming from the other direction, boats depart Luanda Kotieno at 8am, 10am, noon, 3pm and 5.30pm.

The road between Mbita and Homa Bay has been upgraded and is now surfaced for all but a small section. Matatus (KSh250, 1½ hours) frequently pass between the two, or there are a few normal buses (KSh200) as well as a daily bus to Kisumu (KSh500). To get around the island, you might find a taxi in Mbita for a half-day loop, stopping at sites of interest for around KSh1000, or a *boda-boda* (known as a *piki-piki* here) will do the same for about half that price.

Mfangano Island

POP 17,000

If you want to fall totally off the radar then Mfangano Island, sitting out in the placid lake waters, is an idyllic place to get lost. Home to many a monitor lizard, inquisitive locals, intriguing rock paintings and the imposing but assailable Mt Kwitutu (1694m), Mfangano Island is well worth a day or two.

Sights & Activities

Rock Paintings ARCHEOLOGICAL SITE
(admission KSh500) These rock paintings, often featuring sun motifs, are both revered and feared by locals (which has hindered vandalism) and are thought to be the handiwork of the island's earliest inhabitants, Bantu Pygmies from Uganda. The entry fee is used to help fund some very needy children at the local orphanage. The orphanage and the rock paintings are found near the settlement of Kakiimba, a 3km (KSh150) *boda-boda* ride from Sena, the island's 'capital'.

Tours

George Ooko Oyuko TOURS
(☎0716537317; per day KSh500) Local George Ooko Oyuko can act as a guide to the rock paintings and other sites, as well as help

WHERE BOYS BECOME MEN

The Bungoma/Trans-Nzoia district goes wild in August with the sights and sounds of the Bukusu Circumcision Festival, an annual jamboree dedicated to the initiation of local boys into manhood. The tradition was apparently passed to the Bukusu by the Sabaot tribe in the 19th century, when a young hunter cut the head off a troublesome serpent to earn the coveted operation.

The evening before the ceremony is devoted to substance abuse and sex. In the morning the youngsters are trimmed with a traditional knife in front of their entire village.

Unsurprisingly, this practice has attracted a certain amount of controversy in recent years. Health concerns are prevalent, as the same knife can be used for up to 10 boys, posing a risk of HIV/AIDS and other infections. The associated debauchery also brings a seasonal rush of underage pregnancies and family rifts that seriously affect local communities.

Education and experience now mean that fewer boys undergo the old method, preferring to take the safe option at local hospitals. However, those wielding the knife are less likely to let go of their heritage. To quote one prominent circumciser: 'Every year at this time it's like a fever grips me, and I can't rest until I've cut a boy.'

organise ascents of Mt Kwitutu. He can also arrange homestays (KSh400), though be prepared for some extremely basic conditions, a humbling experience and a warm reception.

Sleeping & Eating

Joyland Hotel HOTEL $
(Sena; s/tw with shared bathroom excl breakfast KSh400/800) Although the basic rooms are essentially clean, those with delicate sensibilities might find the shared toilets a bit grim. Food is available in the attached (and only) restaurant in Sena.

Mfangano Island Camp RESORT $$$
(Nairobi 020-2734000; www.governorscamp.com; s/d full board US$609/970; closed Apr & May;) Nestled into the banks of beautifully maintained gardens alive with monitor lizards and birdlife, these stone-and-thatch cottages, 6km north of Sena, are the smartest digs on Lake Victoria. The camp was formerly a fishing resort, and now offers a number of other water sports, all of which are included in the tariff.

Getting There & Away

Boats ply the lake waves between Mbita and Mfangano Island daily (foot passenger KSh200, car KSh800, 1½ hours). In theory they leave at 10am and 5pm, returning at 8am and 2pm. In practice they go only when full and dangerously overloaded. Usually they call at Takawiri Island en route, stop at Mfangano's 'capital', Sena, and then carry on around the island, stopping at most villages on the way.

Private boats can be arranged through Wayando Beach Club Eco Lodge (p131) for between KSh8000 and KSh15,000, depending on boat type, for a full-day trip from Rusinga.

WESTERN HIGHLANDS

Despite media impressions depicting a land of undulating savannah stretching to the horizon, the real heart and soul of Kenya, and the area where most of the people live, is the luminous green highlands. Benefiting from reliable rainfall and fertile soil, the Western Highlands are the agricultural powerhouse of the country – the south is cash-crop country, with vast patchworks of tea plantations covering the region around Kisii and Kericho; while further north, near Kitale and Eldoret, dense cultivation takes over.

The settlements here are predominantly agricultural service towns, with little of interest unless you need a chainsaw or water barrel. For visitors the real attractions lie outside these places – the rolling tea fields around Kericho, the tropical beauty of Kakamega Forest, trekking on Mt Elgon, the prolific birdlife in Saiwa Swamp National Park and exploring the dramatic Cherangani Hills.

Kisii

POP 97,000

Let's cut straight to the chase. Kisii is a noisy, polluted and congested mess, and most people (quite sensibly) roll right on through without even stopping. However, it's an important transport point and there's a good chance you'll pass through at some point in your explorations of western Kenya.

While the feted Kisii soapstone obviously comes from this area, it's not on sale here. Quarrying and carving take place in the Gusii village of **Tabaka**, 23km northwest of Kisii. Soapstone is relatively soft and pliable (as far as rocks go) and with simple hand tools and scraps of sandpaper the sculptors carve

WEST TO UGANDA

There are two main border crossing points into Uganda: **Malaba** and **Busia**. Both are generally pain free as Ugandan (or Kenyan) visas are available on arrival. Both towns have a couple of banks where you can exchange cash, but unless you're a fan of bureaucracy it's easier to use one of the numerous moneychangers prowling around. Just make sure you know the exchange rate beforehand (but don't expect them to match it) and count your money carefully. The Kenyan border is open 24 hours, but we've heard the Ugandan one runs to a more 'flexible' timetable, so try to arrive in daylight hours. It's also prudent to keep an eye on your bus. Nothing irritates the drivers more than someone who hasn't the sense to take note of where they park.

If you get stuck in either town for the night, you'll find a couple of ropy places to put your head down for the night. Thankfully, onward matatus are fairly easy to come by on both sides of the border.

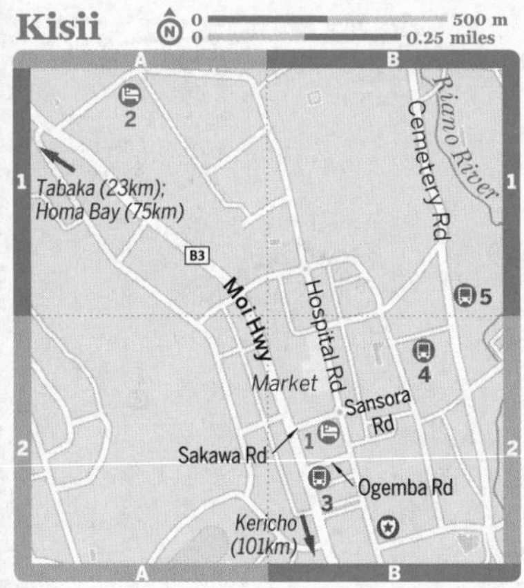

Kisii

Sleeping

1 Nile Restaurant, Fast Food & Guesthouse B2
2 St Vincent Guesthouse A1

Transport

3 Easy Coach B2
4 Matatus B2
5 Matatus to Tabaka B1

chess sets, bowls, animals and the unmistakable abstract figures of embracing couples. Each artisan specialises in one design before passing it on to someone else to be smoothed with wet sandpaper and polished with wax. Most pieces are destined for the curio shops of Nairobi and Mombasa and trade-aid shops around the world. As you would expect, prices are cheaper here than elsewhere. If you're undaunted by adding a few heavy rocks to your backpack, you can save a packet.

Sleeping & Eating

St Vincent Guesthouse GUESTHOUSE $

(0733650702; s/d/tw KSh1500/2000/2400; P) This Catholic-run guesthouse off the Moi Hwy isn't the place for a party, but it's hands down the best place to stay in Kisii. Rooms are very clean and cosy, it's quiet and security is good. No alcohol allowed.

Nile Restaurant, Fast Food & Guesthouse HOTEL $

(0786706089; Hospital Rd; excl breakfast s & d KSh1000-1500, tw KSh2000) Clean, cheap rooms and a central location make the Nile the best deal in the town centre. The icing on the cake is that the 2nd-floor restaurant (mains KSh200 to KSh300) has a commanding view of the chaos below.

Getting There & Away

The congested matatu terminal in the centre of town is a chaos of loud, and often somewhat drunk, people trying to bundle you onto the nearest matatau, whether or not you want to go where it's going. If you do manage to pick your own matatu, you'll find regular departures to Homa Bay (KSh200, 1½ hours), Kisumu (KSh300, 2½ hours), Kericho (KSh500, two hours) and Isebania (KSh300, 1¾ hours) on the Tanzanian border.

Tabaka matatus (KSh100, 45 minutes) leave from Cemetery Rd. Returning, it is sometimes easier to catch a boda-boda (KSh70 to KSh100) to the 'Tabaka junction' and pick up a Kisii-bound matatu there.

Easy Coach has twice-daily departures to Nairobi (KSh900, eight hours, 10am and 9.30pm). It also has a bus to Narok (KSh550, four hours, 1pm), which is handy for the Mara.

Kericho

POP 150,000

Kericho is a haven of tranquillity. Its surrounds are blanketed by a thick patchwork of manicured tea plantations, each seemingly hemmed in by distant stands of evergreens, and even the town centre seems as orderly as the tea gardens. With a pleasant climate and a number of things to see and do, Kericho makes for a very calming couple of days.

Sights & Activities

Tea Plantations FARM

Kericho is the centre of Africa's most important tea gardens and the countryside surrounding the town is one of interlocking tea estates mixed with patches of forest. You might expect tea-plantation tours to be touted left, right and centre, but they are surprisingly few and far between. If you just want to take a stroll in the fields, the easiest plantations to get to are those behind the Tea Hotel.

If you want something more organised, **Harman Kirui** (0721843980; kmtharman@yahoo.com; per person KSh200) organises fun and informative tea-estate and factory tours. Most tours involve walking around the fields and watching the picking (note that the pickers don't work on Sunday). If you want to actually see the process through

Kericho

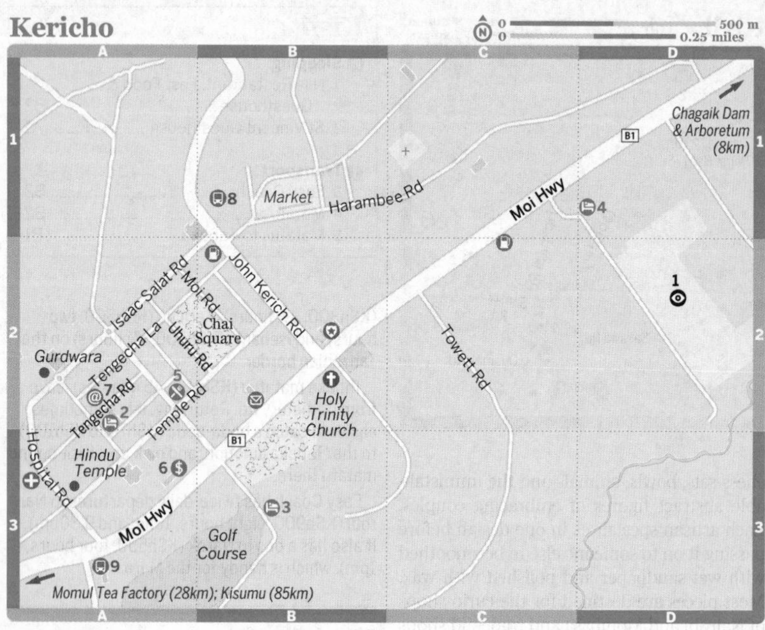

Kericho

Sights
1 Tea Plantations ... D2

Sleeping
2 New Sunshine Hotel ... A2
3 Sunshine Upper Hill Hotel ... B3
4 Tea Hotel ... D1

Eating
5 Litny's Restaurant ... A2

Information
6 Barclays Bank ... A3
7 Mynet Cyber ... A2

Transport
8 Bus & Matatu Stand ... B1
9 Buses to Kisumu, Kisii & Homa Bay ... A3

to the end by visiting a factory, you should book at least four days in advance through the Tea Hotel or by emailing Harman directly. The factory most often visited is the **Momul Tea Factory** (admission KSh500; Mon-Sat), which is 28km from Kericho (for those without transport, Harman can arrange a car for KSh3000). The factory has 64 collection sites servicing the area's small-scale farmers and processes a staggering 15 million kilograms of green leaf a year. Note no processing takes place on Monday.

Arboretum GARDENS
(B4 Hwy; closed when raining) Eight kilometres east of town, this tropical park is popular with weekend picnickers and colobus, vervet and red-tailed monkeys (best seen in the early morning). The main attraction is the shade afforded by the tropical trees planted by estate owner Tom Grumbley in the 1940s. The nearby Chagaik Dam is responsible for the lovely lily-covered pond.

Sleeping & Eating

Being a stronghold of the Kipsigis people, this is good place to try *kimyet* (maize-meal served with vegetables and beef) or *mursik* (soured milk). Naturally, tea is extremely popular and drunk from dawn to supper and every opportunity in between.

New Sunshine Hotel HOTEL $
(052-2030037, 0725146601; Tengecha Rd; s/d/tr KSh2000/2700/3000;) Without doubt, the best budget hotel in town (not that the competition is especially stiff). The rooms, while not large, are spotless and the showers are actually hot rather than lukewarm. The attached restaurant (meals KSh320 to KSh550) does a roaring trade.

Sunshine Upper Hill Hotel HOTEL $$
(☎0721700358; www.sunshinehotel.co.ke; s KSh4000-5000, d KSh5000-6000; P 📶) This large hotel block, consisting of modern new rooms overlooking the town park, is where biusness types settle in to do important stuff in Kericho. The rooms have comfortable beds, vast bathrooms and in-room wi-fi.

Tea Hotel HOTEL $$
(☎0714510824; Moi Hwy; camping KSh700, s/d US$70/95; P 📶 🏊) This grand property was built in the 1950s by the Brooke Bond company and still has a lot of (very faded) period charm. The hotel's most notable features are the vast hallways and dining rooms full of mounted animal heads, and its beautiful gardens with their tea-bush backdrops. Many of the rooms, though, are literally falling to pieces.

Litny's Restaurant KENYAN $
(Temple Rd; mains KSh250-400; ⏱5.30am-8pm) Along with New Sunshine Hotel, this is regarded as one of the better restaurants in town, though in truth the fried chicken and chips here was no different to the fried chicken and chips we ate elsewhere.

Information

Barclays Bank (Moi Hwy) With ATM that accepts Visa and occasionally Mastercard.

Mynet Cyber (off Tengecha Rd; per hr KSh45; ⏱8am-8pm) Down a little covered alley, this is one of several internet places in town.

Post Office (Moi Hwy)

Getting There & Away

Most buses and matatus operate from the main stand in the town's northwest corner, while those heading south and west (such as to Kisii and Kisumu) leave from the Total petrol station on Moi Hwy.

Matatus to Kisumu (KSh300, 1½ hours), Kisii (KSh300, two hours), Eldoret (KSh400 to KSh500, 3½ hours) and Nakuru (KSh300, two hours) are frequent. The odd Peugeot also serves these destinations, but costs about 25% more.

Easy Coach offers the best buses, but its office, and departure point, is inconveniently located out of town, opposite the Tea Hotel and inside the Libya petrol station. It has buses to Nairobi (KSh1100) throughout the day, as well as frequent buses to Nakuru (KSh550) and Kisumu (KSh500).

ANYONE FOR TEA?

Kenya is one of the world's largest tea exporters, along with the likes of India and Sri Lanka, with tea accounting for 28% of the country's export income. It's unique in that up to 80% of its tea is produced by small landholders.

Tea picking is a great source of employment around Kericho, with mature bushes picked every 17 days and the same worker continually picking the same patch. Good pickers collect their own body weight in tea each day!

Despite Kericho producing some of the planet's best black tea, you will have trouble finding a cup of the finest blends here – most of it's exported.

Kakamega

POP 100,000

There is no real reason to stay in this agricultural town, but if you arrive late in the day it can be convenient to sleep over and stock up with supplies before heading to nearby Kakamega Forest Reserve.

KEEP

The Kakamega Environmental Education Programme, **KEEP** (☎0704851701), is a local initiative that aims to educate the local community and visitors to the wonders of the Kakamega Forest and the threats it's under. The organisation runs various community and conservation programmes and has been credited with much of the sucess in slowing the pace of destruction of the forest. In recognition of its work it was awarded 2013 Ecotourism Enterprise of the Year by Eco Tourism Kenya. The group has an office by the KEEP *bandas* (thatched huts; p138) and will be happy to answer any questions on the forest.

KEEP also offers guided forest walks (though many of its guides are interchangeable with those of the Kakamega Rainforest Tour Guides Association). A two-hour walk costs KSh500 and a half-day walk, KSh1000.

Sights

Crying Stone of Ilesi LANDMARK

The Crying Stone of Ilesi is a local curiosity perched on a ridge 3km south of town. The formation, looking like a solemn head resting on weary shoulders, consists of a large boulder balanced atop a huge column of rock, down which 'tears' flow.

Market MARKET

It's worth poking your nose into the town's municipal market. It operates every day but is at its loudest on Saturday and Wednesday mornings when, as if by magic, people appear from all over the surrounding countryside.

Sleeping & Eating

While there are lots of local eateries, there are few to get excited about. Seemingly without exception, they serve chicken, fish or beef, fried or 'wet fried' (which means it comes with gravy).

Friends Hotel HOTEL $

(☎0721917541; Mumias Rd; s/d excl breakfast KSh1500/1800) Friends has comfortable rooms that are unusually clean, pleasing to the eye and come with 24-hour hot water. Downstairs is a well-regarded restaurant (mains KSh300 to KSh400). It's the best deal in town.

Information

Barclays Bank (A1 Hwy) With ATM.

KWS Area Headquarters Kakamega Forest information, located 1.5km from the town centre.

Post Office (A1 Hwy)

Getting There & Away

Easy Coach (off Mumias Rd) has buses to Nairobi (KSh1450) via Nakuru (KSh950) at 8am and 8pm. Matatus, which leave from behind the market, will whizz you to Kitale (KSh300, three hours) and Eldoret (KSh300, two hours).

To get to Kakamega Forest Reserve, take a matatu to Khayega (KSh50, 30 minutes), followed by a *boda-boda* to the reserve (KSh200, 45 minutes).

Matatus for Kisumu (KSh200, 1¾ hours) can be caught near the Total petrol station on the northern edge of town.

Kakamega Forest

Not so long ago, much of western Kenya was hidden under a dark veil of jungle and formed a part of the mighty Guineo-Congolian forest ecosystem. However, the British soon did their best to turn all that lovely virgin forest into tea estates. Now all that's left is this slab of tropical rainforest surrounding Kakamega.

Though seriously degraded, this forest is unique in Kenya and contains plants, animals and birds that occur nowhere else in the country. It's especially good for birders, with turacos, which are like flying turkeys that have been given a box of face paints, being a favourite with everyone. Other standout birds include flocks of African grey parrots and noisy hornbills that sound like helicopters when they fly overhead. If you prefer your animals furrier, Kakamega is home to several primates, including graceful colobus monkeys, black-cheeked-white-nosed monkeys and Sykes monkeys.

Sights & Activities

The best way – indeed the only real way – to appreciate the forest is to walk. While guides are not compulsory, they are well worth the extra expense. Not only do they prevent you from getting lost, but most are walking encyclopedias and will reel off both the Latin and common names of almost any plant or insect you care to point out, along with any of its medicinal properties.

There are two main patches of forest. The northern Kakamega Forest National Reserve (also known as the Buyangu area) has a variety of habitats, but is generally very dense with considerable areas of primary forest and regenerating secondary forest. The forest here is managed by the Kenyan Wildlife Service (KWS). There's a total ban on grazing, wood collection and cultivation in this zone. The southern section (known as Isecheno) forms the Kakamega Forest Reserve. Predominantly forested, this region supports several communities and is under considerable pressure from both farming and illegal logging, but entry fees are lower and it has better accommodation.

Kakamega Forest National Reserve PARK

(www.kws.go.ke; adult/child US$25/15, vehicles KSh300) Rangers state that trails here vary in length from 1km to 7km. Of the longer walks, Isiukhu Trail, which connects Isecheno to the small Isiukhu Falls, is one of the most popular and takes a minimum of half a day. The 4km drive or walk to Buyangu Hill allows for uninterrupted views east to the Nandi Escarpment.

Kakamega Forest

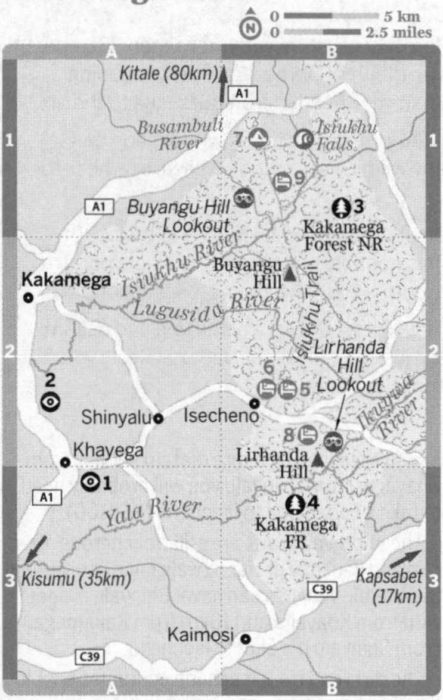

Kakamega Forest

Sights

1. Bullfighting Grounds ... A3
2. Crying Stone of Ilesi ... A2
3. Kakamega Forest National Reserve ... B1
4. Kakamega Forest Reserve ... B3

Activities, Courses & Tours

Kakamega Rainforest Tour Guides ... (see 6)

Sleeping

5. Forest Rest House ... B2
   Isikuti Guesthouse ... (see 9)
6. KEEP Bandas ... B2
7. New De Brazza's Campsite ... B1
8. Rondo Retreat ... B2
9. Udo's Bandas & Campsite ... B1

Guides, from a local association called **Kafkogoa** (☎0724143064), cost KSh2000 for up to three hours and can be arranged at the park gates.

Kakamega Forest Reserve PARK
(adult/child KSh600/150) Kakamega Forest Reserve is the more degraded area of the forest, yet it's the more popular area with tourists. The five-hour return hike to Lirhanda Hill for sunrise or sunset is highly recommended. An interesting short walk (2.6km) to a 35m-high watchtower affords views over the forest canopy and small grassland.

Next to the forest reserve office is the **Kakamega Rainforest Tour Guides** (☎0706158556; per person short/long walk KSh500/800) office, which supplies knowledgeable guides to the forest for a variety of walks, including recommended night walks (KSh1500 per person) and sunrise/sunset walks (KSh1000 per person).

Sleeping & Eating

Kakamega Forest National Reserve

If staying in the Kakamega Forest National Reserve, you'll have to pay park entry fees for each night you're here.

Udo's Bandas & Campsite BANDA $
(☎Nairobi 020-2654658; www.kws.go.ke; camping adult/child US$20/15, bandas per person US$40) Named after Udo Savalli, a well-known ornithologist, this lovely KWS site is tidy, well maintained and has seven simple thatched *bandas* (huts). Nets are provided, but you will need your own sleeping bag and other supplies. There are long-drop toilets, bucket showers and a communal cooking and dining shelter.

New De Brazza's Campsite CAMPGROUND $
(☎0706486786; camping KSh1000, bandas per person KSh1250) Just before the park gates and hidden down a squiggle of squelchy, muddy lanes (ask for directions at the park gate), this simple campsite is as basic as basic gets. There's no electricity and the toilets are the kind where the long-drops aren't long enough. The setting, though, is top notch.

Isikuti Guesthouse GUESTHOUSE $$
(☎Nairobi 020-2654658; www.kws.go.ke; cottage US$60) Hidden in a pretty forest glade close to Udo's is the KWS Isikuti cottage, which has equipped kitchen and bathroom and an idyllic setting. It can sleep up to four people.

Kakamega Forest Reserve

Forest Rest House GUESTHOUSE $
(camping KSh650, r per person KSh500) The four rooms of this wooden house, perched on stilts 2m above the ground and with views straight onto a mass of jungle, might be very basic (no electricity, no bedding and cold-water baths that look like they'd crash

KAKAMEGA FOREST

Why Go For a rare chance to see a unique rainforest ecosystem with more than 330 species of birds, 400 species of butterflies and seven different primate species, including the rare de Brazza's monkey. During darkness, hammer-headed fruit bats take to the air.

When to Go The best viewing months are June, August and October, when many migrant bird species arrive. October also sees many wildflowers bloom, while December to March are the driest months.

Practicalities As the northern section of the forest is managed by KWS and the southern section by the Kenyan Forest Department, it is not possible to visit the whole park without paying both sets of admission charges. Both areas have their pros and cons.

Budget Tips Entry fees to the southern Kakamega Forest Reserve are lower, and accommodation generally cheaper, than in the northern Kakamega Forest National Reserve, so it makes sense for budget travellers to base themselves here.

through the floorboards if you used one), but they'll bring out the inner Tarzan in even the most obstinate city slicker.

KEEP Bandas BANDA $
(☎0704851701; camping in safari tent per person KSh650, banda per person with shared bathroom KSh900) The *bandas* here are almost swallowed up by jungle, but even though all you get is a small hut with no electricity and communal cold-water showers, it's very atmospheric. Meals (KSh350 to KSh500) can be arranged with the caretaker if you don't wish to self-cater in the basic kitchen.

★ Rondo Retreat GUESTHOUSE $$$
(☎0733299149, 056-2030268; www.rondoretreat.com; s/d full board KSh17,600/22,000; P) To arrive at Rondo Retreat is to be whisked back to 1922 and the height of British rule. Consisting of a series of wooden bungalows filled with a family's clutter, this gorgeous and eccentric place is a wonderful retreat from modern Kenya. The gardens are absolutely stunning and worth visiting even if you're not staying.

Make sure you're around for the afternoon tea and cake on the verandah. Dinner is a fairly formal affair: you should dress smart (no shorts). Profits go to a Christian charity.

Getting There & Away

KAKAMEGA FOREST NATIONAL RESERVE

Matatus heading north towards Kitale can drop you at the access road, about 18km north of Kakamega town (KSh80). It's a well-signposted 2km walk from there to the park office and Udo's.

KAKAMEGA FOREST RESERVE

Regular matatus link Kakamega with Shinyalu (KSh70), but few go on to Isecheno. Shinyalu is also accessed by a rare matatu service from Khayega. From Shinyalu you will probably need to take a *boda-boda* to Isecheno (KSh100).

The improved roads are still treacherous after rain and you may prefer to walk once you've seen the trouble vehicles can have. Shinyalu is about 7km from Khayega and 10km from Kakamega. From Shinyalu it's 5km to Isecheno.

The dirt road from Isecheno continues east to Kapsabet, but transport is rare.

Eldoret

POP 289,000

The Maasai originally referred to this area as *eldore* (stony river) after the nearby Sosiani River, but this proved too linguistically challenging for the South African Voortrekkers who settled here in 1910 and they named their settlement Eldoret instead.

In 2008 Eldoret achieved notoriety when 35 people (mostly Kikuyus) were burnt alive in a church on the outskirts of town. This incident was the largest single loss of life during the 2007 post-election violence.

Today, Eldoret is a thriving service town straddling the Kenya–Uganda highway. It's the principal economic hub of western Kenya, but for the traveller there is little to see and even less to do. The highlight is a visit to the **Doinyo Lessos Creameries Cheese Factory** (Kenyatta St; ⏲8am-6pm) to stock up on any one of 20 different varieties of cheese.

Sleeping

White Highlands Inn HOTEL $
(☎0734818955; Elgeyo St; s/d KSh2000/2500; P) In a quiet corner on the edge of town, this place offers good value. Its spacious rooms were so spotless that we actually lay in the bathtub as opposed to just looking at it wist-

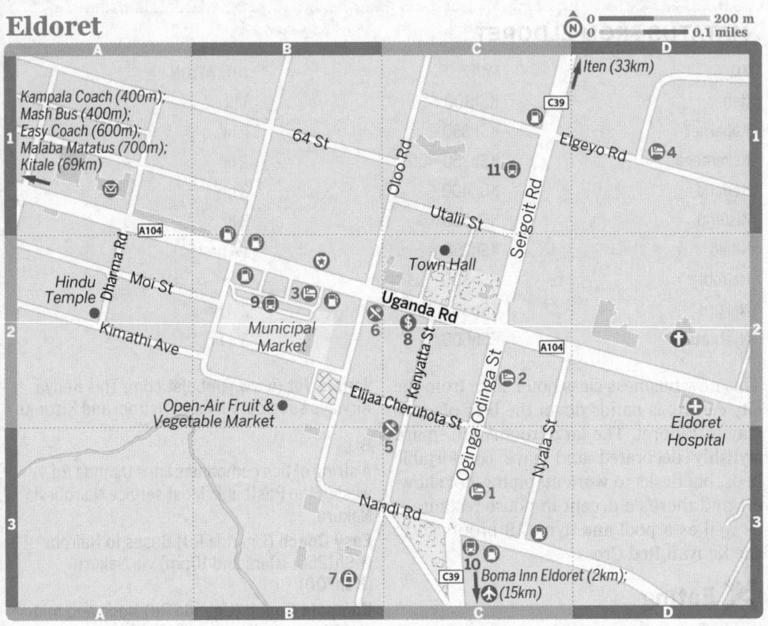

fully. The whole complex is a bit rambling, but retains a certain old-fashioned charm and has a popular bar and less-popular restaurant.

White Castle Motel HOTEL $
(053-2033095; Uganda Rd; s/d/tw KSh1500/2150/3000;) While it has little in the way of frills or personality, and suffers dreadfully from noise from the matatu stand next door, the White Castle is still a sound choice. It's centrally located, comparatively clean, the security is top-notch and the staff delightful.

The street-level restaurant is similarly reliable and, surprisingly, most things on its menu are actually available. Its basement disco only opens on weekends, when it becomes, as the publicity says, 'The best place to shake a leg in the north Rift Valley'.

Aya Inn HOTEL $
(0708046117; Oginga Odinga St; r KSh1000-2000) Cheap and, if you ignore the less-than-appealing entrance, surprisingly decent rooms set around a fairly quiet courtyard. Even so, it's best to opt for one of the quieter, secluded rooms with hot water.

Klique Hotel HOTEL $
(0732060903; www.kliquehotel.com; Oginga Odinga St; r excl breakfast from KSh2500;) This well-run and secure place is somewhat down at heel, but everything is kept clean and tidy and the rooms have bathtubs you might actually choose to use. One of the better-value city-centre options.

Eldoret

Sleeping
1 Aya Inn C3
2 Klique Hotel C2
3 White Castle Motel B2
4 White Highlands Inn D1

Eating
5 Sunjeel Palace C3
6 Will's Pub & Restaurant B2

Shopping
7 Doinyo Lessos Creameries Cheese Factory B3

Information
8 Barclays Bank C2

Transport
9 Bus & Matatu Stand B2
10 Local Matatus C3
11 Matatus to Iten & Kabarnet C1

★ **Boma Inn Eldoret** HOTEL $$$
(0719025000; www.bomahotels.com; Elgon View, off Elgon Rd; r from KSh12,650; P)

MATATUS FROM ELDORET

TO	FARE	DURATION
Iten	KSh100	1 hr
Kabarnet	KSh350	2 hr
Kakamega	KSh350-400	2 hr
Kericho	KSh400	3 hr
Kisumu	KSh500	3 hr
Kitale	KSh250	1¼ hr
Nairobi	KSh800	6 hr
Nakuru	KSh300	2¾ hr
Nyahururu	KSh600	3½ hr

This new business-class hotel, 2km from the city centre, is hands down the best place to stay in Eldoret. The large rooms are smart, stylishly decorated and have comfortable beds, big desks to work at, piping-hot showers and there's a decent in-house restaurant as well as a pool and gym. All profits go to the Kenyan Red Cross.

Eating

Will's Pub & Restaurant INTERNATIONAL **$**
(Uganda Rd; mains KSh100-450; ⏲9am-midnight) Looks and feels like an English pub, with similarly heavyweight food – steak and fried breakfasts – but it also produces a few African dishes of the *ugali* and beef-stew ilk. The big-screen TV makes it a great place for a cold beer, and the low-key vibe makes it a safe spot for solo female travellers.

★ **Sunjeel Palace** INDIAN **$$**
(Kenyatta St; mains KSh450-600; ⏲11am-11pm; 📝) This formal, dark and spicy Indian restaurant serves superb, real-deal curries. Portion sizes are decent and if you mop up all the gravy with a freshly baked butter naan, you'll be as rotund as Ganesh himself.

Information

Barclays Bank (Uganda Rd) With ATM.
Eldoret Hospital (☎053-2062000; www.eldorethospital.com; Makasembo Rd) One of Kenya's best hospitals, with a 24-hour emergency unit. It's off Uganda Rd.
Post Office (Uganda Rd)

Getting There & Away

AIR

Fly540 (☎053-2030814; www.fly540.com; Eldoret international airport) Frequent flights between Eldoret and Nairobi, and less frequently to Lodwar and Juba (South Sudan).

Jambo Jet (www.jambojet.com) This Kenya Airways subsidary flies to Nairobi and Kisumu.

BUS

A string of bus companies lines Uganda Rd west of the Postbank. Most service Nairobi via Nakuru.

Easy Coach (Uganda Rd) Buses to Nairobi (KSh1250, 10am and 10pm) via Nakuru (KSh700).

Kampala Coach (Uganda Rd) Noon and midnight buses to Kampala (KSh2000, six hours).

Mash Bus (Uganda Rd) Direct bus to Mombasa (KSh2000, 12 hours, 5pm).

MATATU

The main matatu stand is in the centre of town by the municipal market, though some local matatus and more Kericho services leave from Nandi Rd. Irregular matatus to Iten and Kabarnet leave from Sergoit Rd. Further west on Uganda Rd, matatus leave for Malaba on the Uganda border.

Getting Around

A matatu to or from the international airport costs KSh80, and a taxi will cost around KSh1000 to KSh1500. *Boda-bodas* (especially the motorised variety) can be found on most street corners.

Kitale

POP 106,100

Agricultural Kitale is a friendly market town with a couple of interesting museums and a bustling market. It makes an ideal base for explorations of Mt Elgon and Saiwa Swamp National Parks. It also serves as the take-off point for a trip up to the western side of Lake Turkana.

Kitale

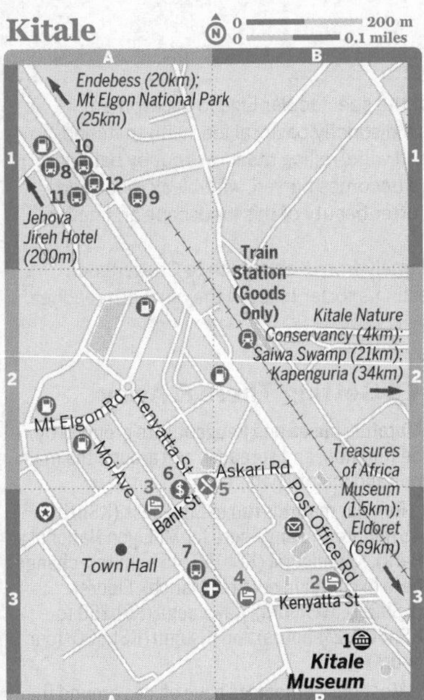

Kitale

Top Sights

1 Kitale Museum B3

Sleeping

2 Alakara Hotel B3
3 Bongo Lodge A3
4 Iroko Twigs Hotel B3

Eating

5 Iroko Boulevard Restaurant A2

Information

6 Barclays Bank A3

Transport

7 Easy Coach A3
8 Main Bus & Matatu Park A1
9 Matatus to Eldoret & Nairobi A1
10 Matatus to Kapenguria A1
11 Matatus to Kisumu & Kakamega A1
12 Matatus to Marich Pass A1

Sights & Activities

★Kitale Museum MUSEUM

(A1 Hwy; adult/child KSh500/250; 9.30am-6pm) Founded on the collection of butterflies, birds and ethnographic memorabilia left to the nation in 1967 by the late Lieutenant Colonel Stoneham, this museum has an interesting range of ethnographic displays of the Pokot, Akamba, Marakwet and Turkana peoples. There are also any number of stuffed dead things shot by various colonial types, including a hedgehog and a cheetah with a lop-sided face.

The outdoor exhibits include some traditional tribal homesteads and a collection of snakes, tortoises and crocodiles, plus an interesting 'Hutchinson Biogas Unit'.

If big cats with funny heads don't do it for you, the small nature trail that leads through some not-quite-virgin rainforest at the back of the museum will surely please you. It's a good place for birdwatching and their are lots of colobus monkeys.

Kitale Nature Conservancy ZOO

(Ndura; 0720309108; A1 Hwy; admission US$10; 8am-7pm) This place looks as if it was designed by Frankenstein after he converted to Christianity and dropped acid. Though you could come here for the picnic tables or play parks, the butterfly spotting or the birdwatching, or maybe even for the incredibly kitsch portrayal of biblical scenes, you'll probably do as most do and immediatley follow the 'Deformed Animals' signs. And deformed (and rather distressed looking) animals is exactly what you'll find.

Treasures of Africa Museum MUSEUM

(A1 Hwy; admission KSh500; 9am-12.30pm & 2-5pm Mon-Sat) This private museum is the personal collection of Mr Wilson, a former colonial officer in Uganda and quite a character. Based mainly on his experiences with the Karamojong people of northern Uganda, Mr Wilson's small museum illustrates his theory that a universal worldwide agricultural culture existed as far back as the last ice age.

It's a little hard to find. Take the road next to the petrol station at the south end of town (opposite the Kitale Club), then first left and left again over the grass with the wheel trails on it. It's a good idea to call ahead to check it's open.

Sleeping

Jehova Jireh Hotel HOTEL $

(0716805512; s/d from KSh1500/2800) A solid choice that boasts spacious, quiet and clean rooms with exceptionally helpful management. It's not quite as God-fearing as it sounds. There's an excellent downstairs restaurant that serves food later than most.

WORTH A TRIP

CHERANGANI HILLS

Northeast of Kitale, forming the western wall of the spectacular Elgeyo Escarpment, are the Cherangani Hills. This high plateau has a distinctly pastoral feel, with thatched huts, patchwork *shambas* (small farm plots) and wide, rolling meadows cut by babbling brooks. Right up on the summits the landscape becomes barren, with bleak moorlands. You could easily spend weeks absorbed in the utter beauty of this landscape and never come across another tourist.

There are a couple of great five-day treks, namely from Kabichbich to Chesengoch and from Kapcherop to Sigor, and some interesting shorter hikes in the northern reaches of the hills.

Iroko Twigs Hotel HOTEL $
(☎0773475884; Kenyatta St; s/d KSh3000/3500; wi-fi) If you can overlook a few missing bathroom tiles and a little wear and tear, this is far and away the smartest hotel in town. The rooms (doubles more than singles) are pleasingly decorated with polished wood and art and there are coffee- and tea-making facilities and even dressing gowns in the wardrobes. Cosy cafe downstairs.

Alakara Hotel HOTEL $
(☎072280023; Kenyatta St; s/d without bathroom KSh1100/1200, s/d KSh1500/2000; P) The most inviting super cheapie in town is safe, friendly, clean and has comfortable beds and reliable(ish) hot water. It also has a good bar, restaurant and TV room.

Bongo Lodge HOTEL $
(Moi Ave; s/d excl breakfast KSh1000/1200) One reader commented that this place 'looks like the scene of a murder'. If you're the kind of backpacker afraid of sleeping in murder scenes, you're going to be disappointed to hear that the Bongo still has some of the better budget beds in town.

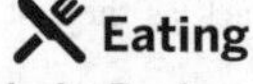

Eating

Iroko Boulevard Restaurant KENYAN $
(Askari Rd; mains KSh150-280; 6.30am-6.30pm) It's got style, it's got glamour, it's got big-city aspirations and it's totally unexpected in Kitale. With cheap dishes and an old Morris car hanging from the ceiling, this is the most popular place to eat in town. There are two other places in town with very similar names and menus – all are good.

Information

Barclays Bank (Bank St) With ATM. Other banks are next door.
Post Office (Post Office Rd)

Getting There & Away

Matatus, buses and Peugeots are grouped by destination, and spread in and around the main bus and matatu park.

Regular matatus run to Endebess (KSh100, 45 minutes, change here for Mt Elgon National Park), Kapenguria (KSh150, 45 minutes, change here to continue north to Marich), Eldoret (KSh250, 1¼ hours), Kakamega (KSh250 to KSh300, 2½ hours) and Kisumu (KSh500, four hours).

Most bus companies have offices around the bus station and serve Eldoret (KSh200, one hour), Nakuru (KSh700, 3½ hours), Nairobi (KSh900, seven hours) and Lodwar (KSh1500, 8½ hours) each day.

Easy Coach (Moi Ave) runs to Nairobi (KSh1350, seven hours) via Nakuru (KSh850, 3½ hours) at 8am and 8pm.

Mt Elgon National Park

Straddling the Ugandan border and peaking with Koitoboss (4187m), Kenya's third-highest peak, and Uganda's Wagagai (4321m), the slopes of Mt Elgon are a sight indeed, or at least they would be if they weren't buried under a blanket of mist and drizzle most of the time.

With rainforest at the base, the vegetation ascends through bamboo jungle to alpine moorland featuring the giant groundsel and giant lobelia plants.

Common animals include buffaloes, bushbucks (both of which are usually grazing on the airstrip near Cholim gate), olive baboons, giant forest hogs and duikers. The lower forests are the habitat of the black-and-white colobus monkeys and blue and de Brazza's monkeys.

There are more than 240 species of birds here, including red-fronted parrots, Ross's turacos and casqued hornbills. On the peaks

Mt Elgon National Park

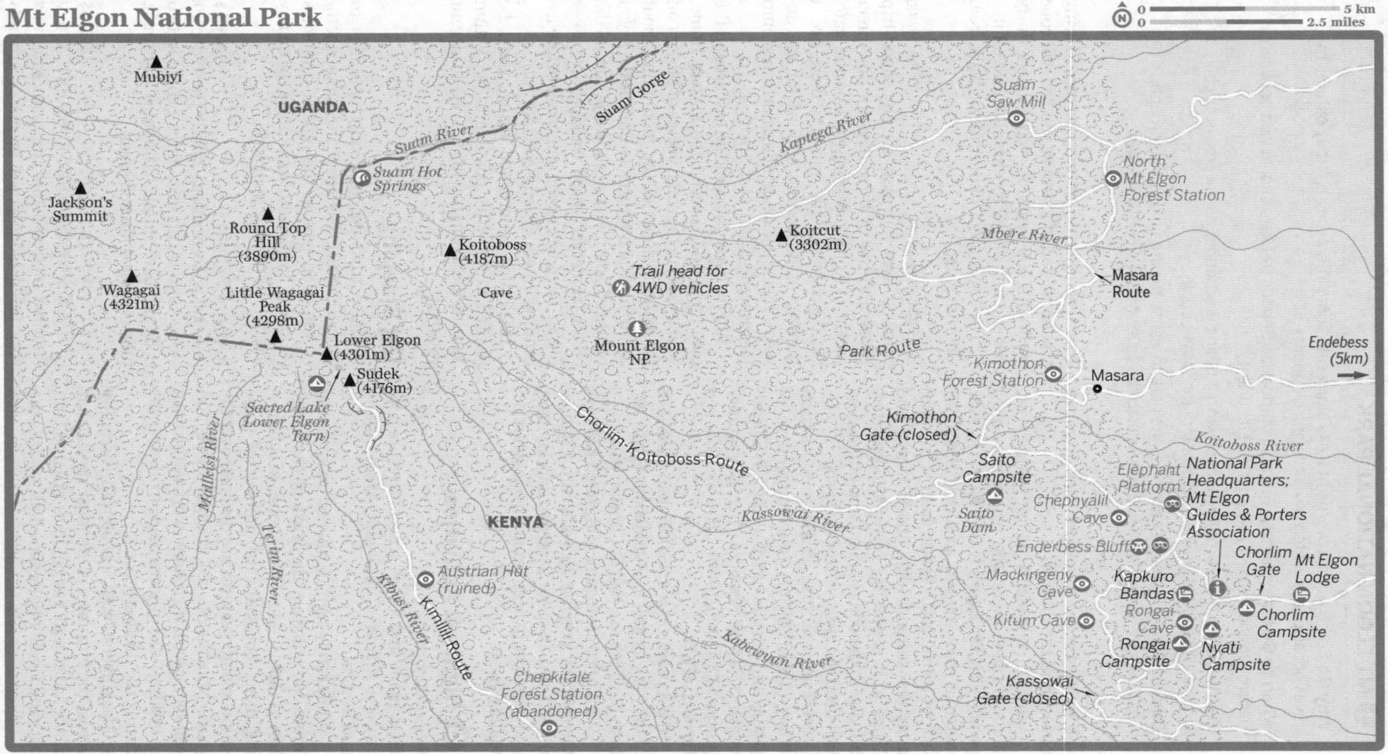

0 — 5 km
0 — 2.5 miles

Mubiyi
UGANDA
Suam Gorge
Suam River
Suam Saw Mill
Kaptega River
Suam Hot Springs
North Mt Elgon Forest Station
Jackson's Summit
Round Top Hill (3890m)
Koitoboss (4187m)
Koitcut (3302m)
Mbere River
Masara Route
Wagagai (4321m)
Little Wagagai Peak (4298m)
Cave
Trail head for 4WD vehicles
Mount Elgon NP
Park Route
Endebess (5km)
Lower Elgon (4301m)
Sudek (4176m)
Kimothon Forest Station
Masara
Sacred Lake (Lower Elgon Tarn)
Chorlim-Koitoboss Route
Kimothon Gate (closed)
Koitoboss River
Saito Campsite
Elephant Platform
National Park Headquarters; Mt Elgon Guides & Porters Association
Malkisi River
Terim River
KENYA
Saito Dam
Chepnyalil Cave
Kassowai River
Enderbess Bluff
Chorlim Gate
Mt Elgon Lodge
Austrian Hut (ruined)
Mackingeny Cave
Kapkuro Bandas
Kibusi River
Kimilili Route
Rongai Cave
Chorlim Campsite
Kitum Cave
Rongai Campsite
Nyati Campsite
Kabewyan River
Chepkitale Forest Station (abandoned)
Kassowai Gate (closed)

MT ELGON NATIONAL PARK

Why Go Some superb overnight treks along with some interesting half-day options to caves occasionally visited by salt-loving elephants.

When to Go It's extremely wet most of the year. Serious trekkers should visit between December and February when it is at its driest.

Practicalities Waterproof gear and warm clothing is essential, as the area is as chilly as it is wet. Altitude may also be a problem for some people.

Budget Tips The easiest section of the park to visit is the area accessed through Chorlim gate, from where you can walk to the caves and surrounding forest.

you may even see a lammergeier dropping bones from the thin air.

While there's plenty of interesting wildlife and plants here, the real reason most people visit **Mt Elgon National Park** (www.kws.go.ke; park entrance adult/child US$30/20, vehicles from KSh350; ⏲6am-6pm) is to stand atop the summit high above Kenya and Uganda. It is possible to walk unescorted, but due to the odd elephant and buffalo you will need to sign a waiver to do so.

Mt Elgon Guides & Porters Association (☎0733919347) is a cooperative of guides and porters based at the KWS headquarters. Their services (per day guide/porter KSh3000/1000) can be booked through KWS.

KWS produces a 1:35,000 map (KSh450) of the park as well as a guidebook (KSh750), both of which are sold at Chorlim gate.

With prior arrangement through KWS it's theoritically possible to walk into Uganda, though this is quite a recent development and we're yet to hear from anyone who's actually done it.

Sights & Activities

Elkony Caves CAVE

Four main lava tubes (caves) are open to visitors: **Kitum**, **Chepnyalil**, **Mackingeny** and **Rongai**.

While rarely seen, elephants are known to 'mine' for salt from the walls of the caves. Kitum holds your best hope of glimpsing them, but sadly the number of these saline-loving creatures has declined over the years. Nonetheless, a torchlight inspection will soon reveal their handiwork in the form of tusking – the grooves made by their tusks during the digging process.

Mackingeny, with a waterfall cascading across the entrance, is the most spectacular of the caves and has colonies of large fruit bats and smaller horseshoe bats towards the rear. If you plan on entering, be sure to bring whatever kind of footwear you feel will cope well with 100 years of accumulated, dusty bat shit and all the roaches that feed off it.

The caves are a 6km drive or walk from Chorlim gate.

Koitoboss Trek HIKING

Allow at least four days for any round-trip hikes, and two or three days for any direct ascent of Koitoboss from the Chorlim gate. Once you reach the summit, there are a number of interesting options for the descent, including descending northwest into the crater to **Suam Hot Springs**.

Alternatively you could go east around the crater rim and descend the Masara Route, which leads to the small village of Masara on the eastern slopes of the mountain (about 25km) and then returns to Endebess. Or you can head southwest around the rim of the crater (some very hard walking) to **Lower Elgon Tarn**, where you can camp before ascending **Lower Elgon Peak** (4301m).

If all this sounds too tiring, you'll be pleased to know it's possible to get within 4km of the summit with a 4WD in decent weather.

Sleeping

If you're trekking, your only option is to camp (US$20). The fee is the same whether you drop tent in the official campsites (Chorlim, Nyati, Saito and Rongai) or on any old flat spot during your trek.

Kapkuro Bandas BANDA $

(www.kws.go.ke; per banda US$50) These decent stone *bandas* can sleep three people in two beds and have simple bathrooms and small, fully equipped kitchen areas.

Mt Elgon Lodge LODGE $$

(☎0722875768; s/d/tr US$40/65/100) A few hundred metres before the main gate, this very faded lodge is set in grassy grounds with views down to the lowlands. Rooms are plain but clean and meals are available.

Getting There & Away

From Kitale, catch an Endebess-bound matatu to the park junction (KSh100, 45 minutes), from where it's a 15-minute motorbike taxi ride (KSh100 to KSh150) to the park gate. Be sure to grab your driver's phone number so you can contact him for a ride back to Endebess.

Saiwa Swamp National Park

North of Kitale, the small, rarely visited **Saiwa Swamp National Park** (www.kws.go.ke; adult/child US$25/15; 6am-6pm) is a real treat. Originally set up to preserve the habitat of Kenya's only population of sitatunga antelope, the 15.5-sq-km reserve is also home to blue, vervet and de Brazza's monkeys and some 370 species of birds. The fluffy black-and-white colobus and the impressive crowned crane are both present, and you may see Cape clawless and spot-throated otters (watchtower 4 is the best place from which to look for these).

The park is only accessible on foot and walking trails skirt the swamp. Duckboards go right across it, and there are some rickety observation towers.

Guides are not compulsory, though your experience will be greatly enhanced by taking one.

SAIWA SWAMP NATIONAL PARK

Why Go Kenya's smallest national park has great appeal to ornithologists, thanks to profuse birdlife. It's also the most reliable place to see the semi-aquatic sitatunga antelope.

When to Go The park can be visited at any time, though access roads become very slippery after rain.

Practicalities This is an easy and cheap park for independent travellers to visit, but a knowledgeable guide is useful.

Budget Tips Stay in Kitale and catch a matatu to the junction for the park. Walk to the gates and explore the park without the aid of a guide.

Tours

Maurice Sinyereri TOURS
(0728272339; ornithological day tour KSh2400) Expert bird guide Maurice has been involved with Saiwa since its earliest days and is a highly regarded guide to the park. Ask him about his bird-collecting past.

Sleeping

Public Campsite CAMPGROUND $
(www.kws.go.ke; camping US$20; P) A lovely site with flush toilets, showers, two covered cooking *bandas* and colobus in the trees above.

Sitatunga Treetop House HUT $
(www.kws.go.ke; tree house US$50; P) Perched on stilts overlooking the Saiwa swamp, this KWS tree house can sleep three in a double and single bed. It has electricity, bedding and mosquito nets. There are no cooking facilities, but you can use those at the campsite next door.

Sirikwa Safaris GUESTHOUSE $$
(Barnley's Guesthouse; 0723917953; www.sirikwasafaris.com; camping KSh500, tents excl breakfast s/d KSh1500/2500, s/d with shared bathroom excl breakfast KSh4500/6000) Owned and run by the family that started Saiwa, this beautiful old farmhouse is 11km from the swamp. You can chose between camping in the grounds, sleeping in a well-appointed safari tent or, best of all, opting for one of the two bedrooms full of *National Geographic* magazines, old ornaments and antique sinks.

The mother and son who run it will entertain you for hours with stories from their more than 70 years in Kenya. Traditional English meat-and-two-veg-style meals are available (dinner KSh1500) and they can organise superb excursions, including ornithological tours of the Cherangani Hills and Saiwa Swamp.

It's 5km north of the park turn-off road on the Kitale–Lodwar road.

Getting There & Away

The park is 18km northeast of Kitale. Take a matatu towards Kapenguria and get out at the second signposted turn-off (KSh80, 15 minutes), from where it's a 5km walk or KSh100 *moto-taxi* ride.

Central Highlands & Laikipia

Includes ➡

Best of Nature

- ➡ Meru National Park (p176)
- ➡ Ol Pejeta Conservancy (p160)
- ➡ Lewa Wildlife Conservancy (p162)
- ➡ Mt Kenya National Park (p165)
- ➡ Aberdare National Park (p150)

Best Luxury Lodges

- ➡ Segera Retreat (p159)
- ➡ Sanctuary at Ol-Lentille (p161)
- ➡ Mount Kenya Safari Club (p157)
- ➡ Lewa Safari Camp (p163)
- ➡ Elsa's Kopje (p177)

Why Go?

The Central Highlands are the green-girt, red-dirt spiritual heartland of Kenya's largest tribe, the Kikuyu. This is the land the Mau Mau (p304) fought for, the land the colonists coveted and the land whose natural, cyclical patterns define the lives of the country's largest rural population. These highlands form one of the most evocative sections of Africa's Great Rift Valley. It is here that Mt Kenya, Africa's second-highest mountain, rises into the clouds – climbing it is one of the great rites of passage of African travel. In its shadow lie two of Kenya's most intriguing national parks: rhino- and lion-rich Meru National Park; and Aberdare National Park, home to some of the oldest mountains on the continent. And then there's Laikipia, fount of so much that's good about modern conservation. It's also the scene for some of the best wildlife-watching anywhere in Kenya.

When to Go

Nanyuki

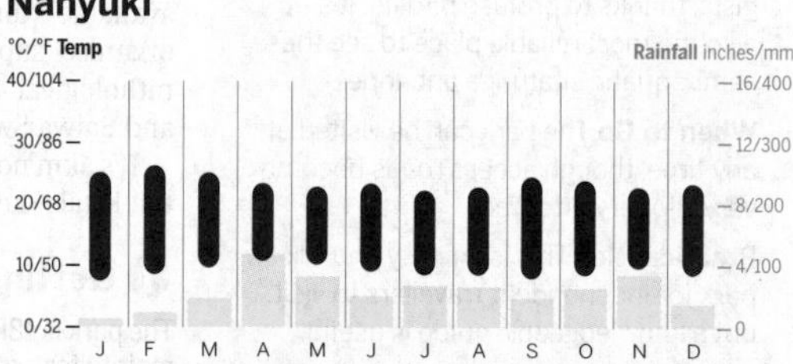

Mid-Jan–Feb & mid-Jul–Aug Your best chance of favourable weather to bag Mt Kenya.

Mar–early Jun The long rains fall everywhere.

Oct & Nov The short rains make a brief appearance.

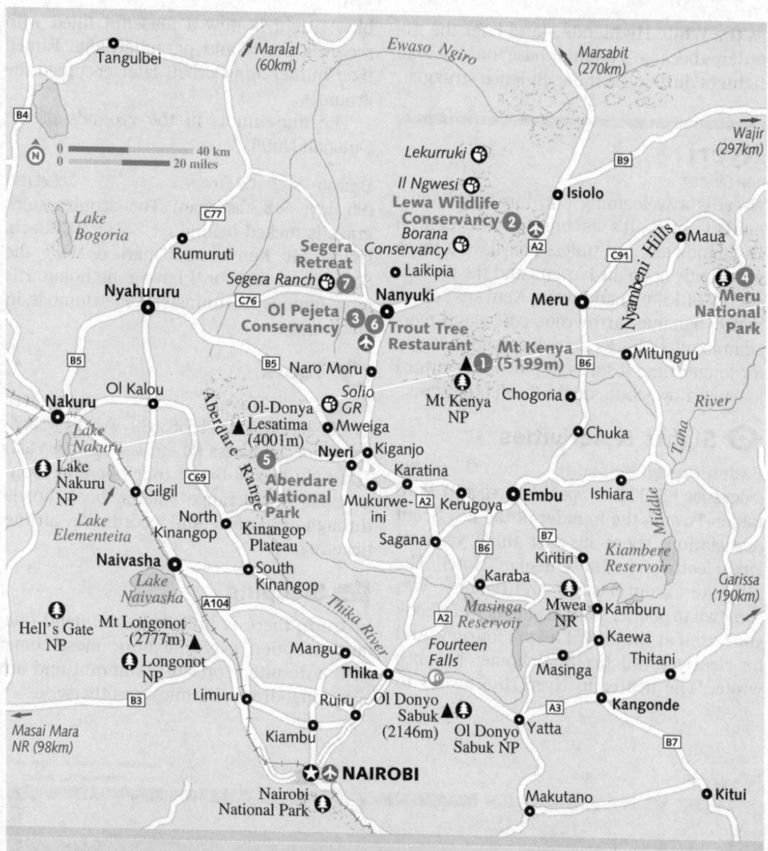

Central Highlands Highlights

1. Holding a frozen Kenyan flag in your frozen hands atop the frozen summit of Point Lenana, 16km from the equator on **Mt Kenya** (p165)
2. Doing a David Attenborough with an orphaned rhino then getting up close and personal with its wild cousins at **Lewa Wildlife Conservancy** (p162)
3. Spending an evening learning how to track lions at **Ol Pejeta Conservancy** (p160)
4. Communing with the ancestors of some of Africa's most famous lions on safari in **Meru National Park** (p176)
5. Trekking through the otherworldly forests where elephants and bongo antelopes lurk in **Aberdare National Park** (p150)
6. Fishing for your supper then climbing a tree at one of Kenya's most original restaurants, **Trout Tree Restaurant** (p173)
7. Indulging in *Out of Africa* nostalgia alongside contemporary art at the sublime **Segera Retreat** (p159)

ABERDARES

The cloud-kissed contours of the brown-and-grey slopes of the Aberdare Range, dubbed Nyandarua (Drying Hide) by the Kikuyu, stretch 160km from South Kinangop, east of Naivasha, up to the Laikipia Escarpment northwest of Nyahururu. In doing so, they form the solid spine of western Central Province.

But there's more to this soulful range of mountains than its geography, and the Aberdares still evoke strong feelings. In colonial times, this was a bastion of white settlement – the area was often referred to as the White Highlands – and later the Aberdares became a popular base for Mau Mau fighters during the independence struggle.

Nyeri

POP 125,357

Nyeri is a welcoming and bustling Kikuyu market town. It's as busy as the Central Highlands get, but unless you have a thing for chaotic open-air bazaars and the restless energy of Kikuyu and white Kenyans selling maize, bananas, arrowroot, coffee and macadamia nuts, there's no real reason to linger for longer than it takes to plot your onward journey. Boy Scouts might think otherwise.

Sights & Activities

Baden-Powell Museum MUSEUM

(admission KSh300; opened on request) Lord Baden-Powell, the founder of the Boy Scout Association, spent his last three years at Paxtu cottage in the Outspan Hotel. The ultimate scoutmaster's retirement was somewhat poetic: to 'outspan' is to unhook your oxen at the end of a long journey. And he clearly loved his final home: he once wrote, 'The nearer to Nyeri, the nearer to bliss'. Paxtu is now a museum filled with scouting scarfs and paraphernalia. Famed tiger-hunter Jim Corbett later occupied the grounds.

The museum is in the grounds of the Outspan Hotel.

Baden-Powell's Grave CEMETERY

(B5 Hwy; 8.30am-5pm) The scoutmaster's grave is tucked behind **St Peter's Church**, facing Mt Kenya and marked with the Scouts trail sign for 'I have gone home'. His more famous Westminster Abbey tomb is, in fact, empty.

Tours

Bongo Asili Travel TOUR

(061-2030884, 0725556358; www.bongoasili-travel.com; off Kanisa Rd; 9am-5pm Mon-Sat) The only locally based tour operator, Bongo Asili can arrange safaris, book hotels throughout Kenya and coordinate airline ticketing.

Sleeping

In truth, there is little to recommend one budget option over the next; most come with a desultory on-site restaurant and an occasional drunk, harmless or otherwise.

Nyeri

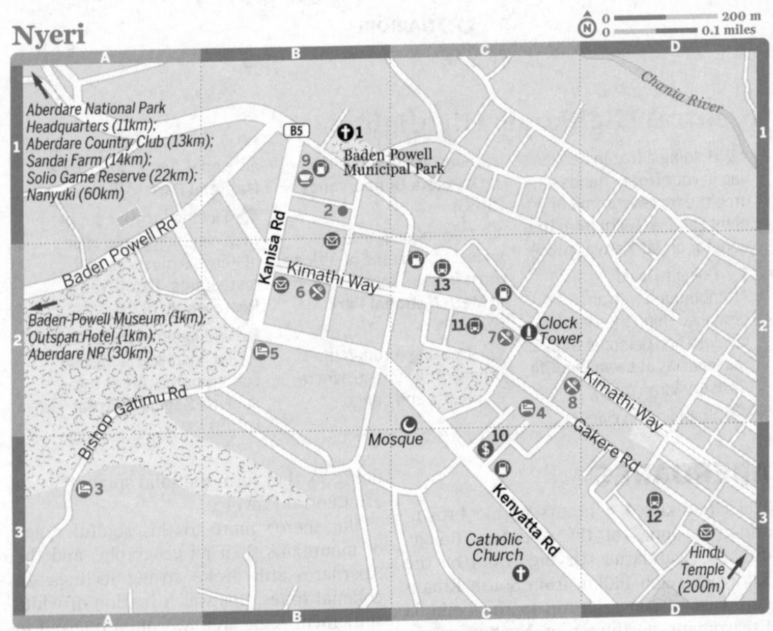

WILDLIFE IN THE CENTRAL HIGHLANDS

Much of the Central Highlands' best wildlife viewing can be found in the conservancies and privately owned reserves on the Laikipia Plateau. Rhinos are best seen at Meru National Park (p176), Ol Pejeta Conservancy (p160) and Lewa Wildlife Conservancy (p162). Meru National Park is also particularly good for lions. The jungle of Aberdare National Park (p150) supports rare bongo antelope, elephants and black rhinos, although the thick cover makes sightings infrequent. Like Mt Kenya National Park, the real stars here are the flora.

Nyama Choma Village Accommodation HOTEL $
(☎0788174384; Gakere Rd; r excl breakfast KSh1200) With its light-blue walls and blue-linoleum showers, Nyama Choma is as colourful as it is cheap. And as you'd expect with a name like Nyama Choma meat-eaters will love this place.

Green Hills Hotel HOTEL $$
(☎061-2030604, 0716431988; www.greenhills.co.ke; Bishop Gatimu Rd; s/d from KSh500/7700, s/d ste KSh23,000/28,000; P 📶 🏊) The best deal in town is actually a little way out of Nyeri. The small drive is worth it for the palm-lined, poolside ambience and general sense of serenity. A few questionable style choices notwithstanding, the rooms are nicely turned out and comfortable.

White Rhino Hotel HOTEL $$
(☎061-2030944, 0726967315; www.whiterhinohotel.com; Kanisa Rd; s/d/tw KSh6000/7000/7500; P @ 📶) Since its remodelling in 2011, the hotel now boasts smart rooms that are polished to an inch of their lives, and swanky, tiled bathrooms. With three bars and two restaurants, this is the top hotel in the city centre.

★ **Sandai Farm** GUESTHOUSE $$$
(☎0721656699; www.africanfootprints.de; camping KSh500, s/d full board US$145/250, cottages from US$80; P @) Fourteen kilometres northwest of town (ask locals for directions), Sandai is run by the effervescent Petra Allmendinger, whose enthusiasm and warm welcome make this a great weekend escape from Nairobi's bustle or for those looking for something a little more personal than what's on offer elsewhere.

Accommodation is either in the extremely cosy lodge, where you will feel like part of the family, or in self-contained cottages that can accommodate up to six. Both are pleasantly eccentric. Horse riding, nature walks (the farm's guide, Sammy, is an excellent birdwatcher) and wildlife drives can all be organised here. It's also a good base for Solio Game Reserve.

Aberdare Country Club HOTEL $$$
(☎Nairobi 0737799990; www.aberdarecountryclub.com; s/d/tr full board US$195/260/370, day entry adult/child KSh500/300; P 🏊) This stately stone club acts as the staging post for those going to the Ark in Aberdare National Park. Rooms are enjoyably old world, with wooden furnishings, parquetry floors and even fireplaces in some rooms.

Nyeri

Sights
Baden-Powell's Grave .... (see 1)
1 St Peter's Church B1

Activities, Courses & Tours
2 Bongo Asili Travel B1

Sleeping
3 Green Hills Hotel A3
4 Nyama Choma Village Accommodation C2
5 White Rhino Hotel B2

Eating
Green Hills Hotel .... (see 3)
6 Raybells B2
7 Rayjo's Café C2
8 Samrat Supermarket C2

Drinking & Nightlife
9 Julie's Coffee Shop B1

Information
10 Barclays Bank C3

Transport
11 Local Matatus C2
12 Lower Bus Stand D3
13 Upper Bus Stand C2

HIGHLANDS HISTORY

The first *wazungu* (white) settlers arrived in the Central Highlands in the 19th century. At the height of white settlement as many as 10,000 white settlers lived here; many were granted 999-year leases over the land. It mattered little to the colonial authorities, of course, that Africans, especially the Kikuyu, were here before them: from as early as the 1880s, the authorities displaced the Kikuyu from their homes to make way for white agriculture and the Mombasa–Uganda railway.

It was perhaps no surprise that, having borne the brunt of colonialism's abuses, the Kikuyu shouldered much of the burden of nationalism's struggle and formed the core of the Mau Mau rebellion in the 1950s. That struggle was largely fought in highland valleys, and the abuses of the anti-insurgency campaign were largely felt by highland civilians. The movement, combined with the general dismantling of the British Empire, forced colonial authorities to reassess their position and eventually abandon Kenya.

It was a Kikuyu, Jomo Kenyatta, who assumed presidency of the new country, and the Kikuyu who assumed control over the nation's economy. They also reclaimed their rich fields in the Central Highlands, although many *wazungu* farmers remain, and their huge plots can be seen stretching all along the highways between Timau, Meru and Nanyuki.

Outspan Hotel HOTEL $$$
(☎061-2032424, Nairobi 020-4452095; www.aberdaresafarihotels.com; s/d from US$179/276; P 📶 ≋) This atmospheric lodge was last decorated in the 1950s, when wood panelling was the height of interior design, and some of the plumbing seems to date from then as well… Nineteen of the 34 standard rooms have cosy fireplaces, and all have a whiff of history that won't necessarily be to everyone's taste.

The dining room is a cross between the Hogwarts School hall (from the Harry Potter films) and a colonial retreat. A Kikuya cultural group performs here daily at 1.45pm (nonguests adult/child US$15/10).

Eating & Drinking

The Outspan and White Rhino Hotels have lively bars.

Green Hills Hotel INTERNATIONAL $$
(Bishop Gatimu Rd; mains/buffets KSh750/800; ⏲7am-10pm) The full buffet here (when numbers permit) is an impressive piece of work, with some tasty mixed-grill options done up in a satisfyingly fancy fashion. Steaks are tender and come sizzling on a platter with a good mix of vegies.

Rayjo's Café KENYAN $
(Kimathi Way; meals KSh100-200; ⏲noon-9pm) This tiny canteen is usually packed with customers, including bus and matatu (minibus transport) drivers, notoriously good judges of cheap places to eat.

Raybells INTERNATIONAL $
(Kimathi Way; mains KSh150-500; ⏲6am-8pm) Pretty much anything you want to eat (well, anything Kenyan or Western), from pizza to *nyama choma* (barbecued meat), is available and cooked passably well here. You may want to avoid the fresh juice as it has tap water added to it.

Julie's Coffee Shop CAFE
(Kanisa Rd; ⏲7am-3pm; 📶) The best place in town for genuine espresso coffee and free wi-fi. Snacks cost KSh50 to KSh150.

Getting There & Away

The Upper Bus Stand deals with sporadic buses and a plethora of matatus to destinations north and west of Nyeri including Nanyuki (KSh250, one hour), Nyahururu (KSh350, 1¼ hours) and Nakuru (KSh550, 2½ hours). From the Lower Bus Stand, matatus head in all directions south and east including Thika (KSh300, two hours) and Nairobi (KSh500, 2½ hours).

Aberdare National Park

While there's plenty of reason to wax rhapsodic over herds of wildlife thundering over an open African horizon, there's also something to be said for the soil-your-pants shock of seeing an elephant thunder out of bush that was, minutes before, just plants. And that's why people love **Aberdare National Park** (☎0774160327, Nairobi 020-2046271; www.kws.org; adult/child US$60/30; ⏲6am-6pm). Camera reflexes are tested as the abundant wildlife pops unexpectedly out of bushes, including elephants, buffaloes, black rhinos, spotted hyenas, bongo antelopes, bush pigs, black servals and rare black leopards.

The elephants are something of an anomaly. This is the highest-altitude resident elephant herd in Africa and it once migrated between the Aberdares and Mt Kenya, but human settlements and fences now block the route between these two upland habitats and the herd is effectively confined to the Aberdares.

The tallest regions of this range can claim some of Kenya's most dramatic up-country scenery, packed with 300m waterfalls, dense forests and serious trekking potential. The park has two major environments: an eastern hedge of thick rainforest and waterfall-studded hills known as the **Salient**, and the **Kinangop plateau**, an open tableland of coarse moors that huddles under cold mountain breezes.

A 400km-long electric fence completely encircles the park. Powered by solar panels, the fence is designed to reduce human-animal conflict by keeping would-be poachers and cattle on one side and marauding wildlife on the other.

Sights & Activities

To trek within the park requires advance permission from the warden at park headquarters, who may (depending on where you plan to walk) insist on providing an armed ranger to guide and protect you against inquisitive wildlife (KSh2000/4000 per half-/full day).

The **Northern Moorland** and its four main peaks (all 3500m to 4000m) are excellent trekking spots; the tallest mountain in the park is **Ol Donyo Lesatima** (4000m), a popular bag for those on the East African mountain circuit. Between Honi Campsite and Elephant Ridge is the site of the **hideout** of Mau Mau leader Dedan Kimathi, who used these mountains as a base; many of his companions learned the ropes of jungle warfare in Burma in WWII.

On the **Kinangop Plateau**, from the dirt track that connects the Ruhuruini and Mutubio West gates, it is possible to walk to the top of **Karura Falls** and watch Karura Stream slide over the rocky lip into the 272m abyss. Weather permitting, you may be able to make out the misty veil of Kenya's tallest cascade, the **Gura Falls** (305m), in the distance. Unfortunately there are no tracks to Gura Falls or the base of Karura Falls. You can, however, visit the far smaller **Chania Falls** further north.

Sleeping

Public Campsite CAMPGROUND $
(0774160327; www.kws.go.ke; camping per adult/child US$20/15) Basic sites with minimal facilities – some have water.

Sapper Hut BANDA $
(0774160327; www.kws.go.ke; bandas US$45) A simple *banda* (thatched-roof hut) with an open fire, two beds and a hot-water boiler, overlooking a lovely waterfall on the Upper Magura River. It's best to bring your own gear.

Kiandongoro Fishing Lodge CABIN $$
(0774160327; www.kws.go.ke; cottages US$210) Two large stone houses sleep seven people each and command a good view of the moors that sweep into the Gura River. There are two bathrooms in each house. All utensils and linens are provided, along with gas-powered kitchens, paraffin cookers and fireplaces.

Tusk Camp CABIN $$
(0774160327; www.kws.go.ke; cottages US$120) This dark and cosy alpine cottage located near Ruhuruini gate sleeps six people. The lounge area is comfy, with great views (if the fog hasn't rolled in), and plenty of rhinos around if you're lucky. Hot water,

ABERDARE NATIONAL PARK

Why Go Two interesting ecosystems to explore: a dense rainforest and high, Afro-alpine moorlands with great trekking possibilities and some spectacular waterfalls.

When to Go The park receives plenty of rain year-round. The driest months are January to February and June to September.

Practicalities During the rains, roads are impassable, and the numbered navigation posts in the Salient are often difficult to follow. The most straightforward visit is to drive between the Ruhuruini and Mutubio West gates.

Budget Tips Camp at public campsites or organise a day trip with other travellers from Nyeri.

Aberdare National Park

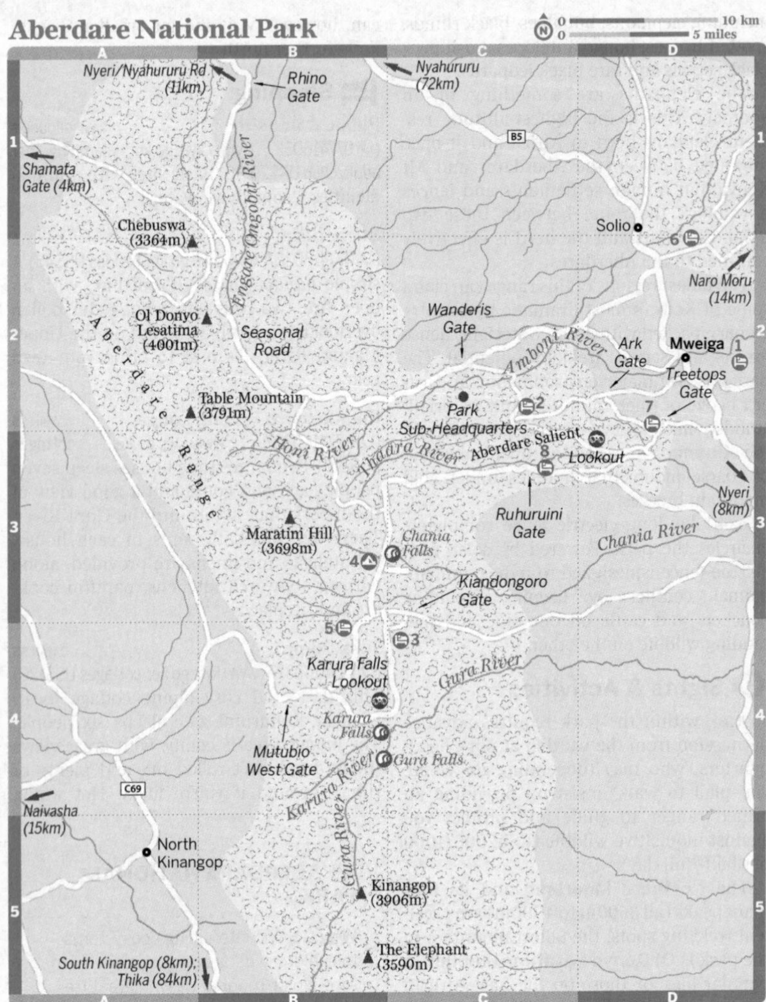

blankets, kerosene lamps, a gas cooker and some utensils are provided.

Aberdare National Park

Sleeping

1 Aberdare Country Club........................D2
2 Ark..C2
3 Kiandongoro Fishing Lodge C4
4 Public Campsite....................................B3
5 Sapper Hut..B4
6 Solio Game Reserve Lodge D2
7 Treetops...D2
8 Tusk Camp...C3

★ Treetops HISTORIC HOTEL $$$

(☎061-2032425; www.aberdaresafarihotels.com; s/d US$229/352, s/d ste US$279/402; P @) Treetops is sold as part of a package with the Outspan Hotel (p150) in Nyeri. Guests are given lunch at the Outspan, transported to Treetops, where they dine and sleep before being returned to the Outspan the following morning for breakfast. Rooms are small and the 2012 renovations have done wonders for this place with dark-wood floors, ochre feature walls and attractive prints. There's also excellent wildlife viewing.

RIGHT ROYAL CONNECTIONS

Trivia for royalphiles: Treetops isn't actually the spot where Princess Elizabeth became Queen Elizabeth II. Yes, Liz was sleeping in Treetops when George VI died in 1952, but in 1954 Mau Mau guerrillas blew the original lodge to twigs. Three years later, a much larger rendition was built on the opposite side of the waterhole. 'Every time like the first time', goes the Treetops slogan, and we agree: sleeping here feels like travelling back to the day that the 25-year-old Elizabeth went to bed a princess and awoke a queen.

Fifty-eight years later, another young lady, this time a commoner, answered 'yes' to a question that will eventually see her crowned the queen of the Commonwealth. On the verandah of a small log cabin, high on the flanks of Mt Kenya, Prince William asked Kate Middleton to be his wife. Under the guise of fishing on Lake Alice, William and Kate travelled to the remote Rutundu cabins, where he popped the big question. And so it is that while the fishing trip was a complete failure, Prince William still managed quite the catch.

The suites are better value than the standard rooms and high rollers can splurge for the Queen Elizabeth 'suite', which has a picture of the monarch and – wait for it – a double bed!

Ark HOTEL **$$$**
(☎ 0737-799990; www.thearkkenya.com; s/d/tr US$180/305/434) The Ark dates from the 1960s, has large rooms and has a lounge that overlooks a waterhole. Watch buffaloes as you sip wine in a moulded chair lifted from *Austin Powers* and you'll have an idea of the ambience. An excellent walkway leads over a particularly dense stretch of the Salient, and from here and the waterhole lounge you can spot elephants, rhinos, buffaloes and hyenas. Sold as an overnight excursion from the Aberdare Country Club (p149) in Nyeri.

ℹ Information

Unusually for Kenya, excellent 1:25,000 maps are available at the gates.

ℹ Getting There & Away

Access roads from the B5 Hwy to the Ark, Treetops and Ruhuruini gates are in decent shape. Keep in mind that it takes a few hours to get from the Salient to the moorlands and vice versa.

LAIKIPIA

Set against the backdrop of Mt Kenya, the Laikipia Plateau extends over 9500 sq km (roughly the size of Wales) of semiarid plains, dramatic gouges and acacia-thicket-covered hills. This patchwork of privately owned ranches, wildlife conservancies and small-scale farms has become one of the most important areas for biodiversity in the country. It boasts wildlife densities second only to those found in the Masai Mara, is the last refuge of Kenya's African wild dogs and it's here that some of the most effective conservation work in the country is being done. Indeed, these vast plains are home to some of Kenya's highest populations of endangered species, including half of the country's black rhinos and half of the world's Grevy's zebras. For more information on the region's ecosystems and wildlife, contact the **Laikipia Wildlife Forum** (☎ 0726500260; www.laikipia.org) and pick up a copy of *Laikipia – A Natural History Guide*, which is sold at many lodge gift shops across the region.

Solio Game Reserve

The family-run, private, 77-sq-km (19,000 acre) **Solio Game Reserve** (☎ 061-2055271; B5 Hwy; admission US$70), and part of the larger Solio Ranch, is Kenya's oldest rhino sanctuary and an important breeding centre for black rhinos; many of the horned beasts you see wandering national parks were actually born here. The physical contours of the park, which run between clumps of yellow-fever acacia, wide skies and wild marsh, are lovely in and of themselves and in addition to rhinos you'll see oryxes, gazelles, hartebeests, giraffes, lions, hyenas and buffaloes. Self-drive safaris are permitted but you will need to be accompanied by a Solio guide (KSh750). Poaching is a particular problem here with a number of rhinos lost in the battle.

The reserve is 22km north of Nyeri.

Solio Game Reserve Lodge LODGE **$$$**
(☎ Nairobi 020-5020888; www.thesafaricollection.com; s/d ste full board US$1015/1684; P 📶) Built

in 2010, this upmarket lodge forsakes the classic look of so much safari accommodation and goes instead for a refreshing contemporary look – slick curves, whitewashed walls and colourful prints. The suites are enormous and utterly gorgeous. Horse riding, mountain biking and helicopter trips are part of the mix.

Nyahururu (Thomson's Falls)

POP 36,450 / ELEV 2360M

This unexpectedly attractive town leaps out of the northwest corner of the highlands and makes a decent base for exploring the western edge of the Aberdares. Its former namesake, Thomson's Falls, are beautiful in their own right with great trekking potential, but they're largely off limits due a series of serious assaults in the area, with women a particular target.

Sights & Activities

Thomson's Falls WATERFALL
(adult/child KSh250/150) At the time of writing, the falls were not safe to visit. Set back in an evergreen river valley and studded with sharp rocks and screaming baboons, the white cataracts plummet over 72m. The dramatic sight of looking up at the falls as baboons pad over the surrounding cliffs is worth the drenching you get from the fall's spray.

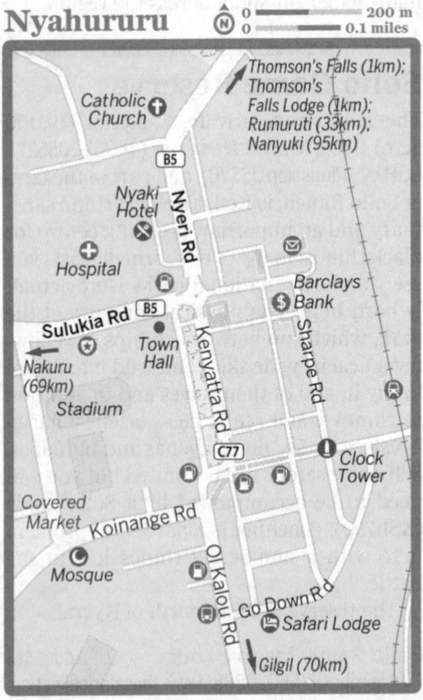

Sleeping & Eating

It's best to eat early in Nyahururu; for reasons we couldn't fathom, most eateries were shutting shop by 7pm.

Safari Lodge HOTEL $
(065-2022334; Go Down Rd; s/d excl breakfast KSh750/1500; P) Clean toilets with *seats;* big, soft beds with couches in the rooms; a nice balcony; TV and a place to charge your phone – what did we do to deserve this luxury? Especially at this price, which makes Safari one of the best budget deals around.

Thomson's Falls Lodge HOTEL $$
(065-2022006; www.thomsonsfallslodge.org; off B5 Hwy; camping KSh750, s/d/tr KSh5000/6000/9000; P) The undisputed nicest splurge in the area sits right above the falls and does a great job of instilling that good old 'I'm a colonial aristocrat on a hill-country holiday' vibe. Rooms are spacious but cosy, with parquetry floors, thanks in no small part to the log fireplaces.

Nyaki Hotel KENYAN $
(mains from KSh350; 6.30am-7pm) Serves standard Kenyan fare in a standard Kenyan setting: bare bones, smiling service and about 100 watts away from being well lit. Off Nyeri Rd.

Thomson's Falls Lodge BUFFET $$
(065-2022006; breakfast/lunch/dinner buffets KSh550/1000/1250; 7am-7pm) This is the best (and only) place in town to go for a fancy feast. There's a set buffet for each of the day's three meals, and while they're pricey for this area, you'll walk away well stuffed and satisfied. It's located off the B5 Hwy.

Getting There & Away

There are numerous matatus that run to Nakuru (KSh220, 1¼ hours) and Nyeri (KSh350, 1¾ hours) until late afternoon. Less plentiful are services to Naivasha (KSh400, two hours), Nanyuki (KSh420, three hours) and Nairobi (KSh500, 3½ hours). The occasional morning matatu reaches Maralal (KSh600, four hours).

Several early-morning buses also serve Nairobi (KsH450, three hours).

THE NINE-MONTH COUP

During the colonial period, the appointed leaders of tribal Africa were headmen and, by and large, men they were (and, usually, remain). But there's one exception from the history books.

These are the facts as we know them: Wangu wa Makeri was a Kikuyu, born in the second half of the 19th century. In 1901 she was appointed head'man' of Weithaga, thereby becoming the only female ruler in colonial Kenya. Wangu made a point of literally using men as furniture, discarding traditional Kikuyu stools for the backs of Kikuyu males. Perhaps unsurprisingly, stories suggest her rule was warmly approved of by Kikuyu women.

And so the wily (and, more pertinently, fertile) men of the Kikuyu tribe hatched one of the most unique coup plots in history (disclaimer: we are now leaving the realm of history and entering the space of tribal folklore). They all did their husbandly duty and impregnated their wives, including Wangu, more or less simultaneously. This ensured that in nine months, the chief and her supporters were either in labour, nursing or too heavily pregnant to prevent the reascendancy of male Kikuyu-dom.

North to Maralal

The 130km drive from Nyahururu to Maralal along the C77 is bumpy but straightforward, despite the tarmac running out at Rumuruti (we do hope you said goodbye, because you won't see it again any time soon). Punctures on this route are common and don't be at all surprised to see large groups of elephants, giraffes and zebras racing your vehicle along the edge of the road.

Sights

Mugie Ranch RANCH

(062-2031235; www.mugieranch.com; wildlife drives adult/child US$30/15) At the very western edge of the Laikipia plateau, the Mugie Ranch is a 200-sq-km working ranch and private game reserve, and is crawling with heavyweight animals – almost half of the ranch is given over to the 89-sq-km Mugie Sanctuary with big cats, elephants, Grevy's zebras and endangered Jackson's hartebeests. Sadly there are no longer any rhinos – poaching forced the ranch to move the remaining 25 rhinos in 2012 to other sites around the country.

There is also a golf course with six holes, each of which is played from three different tees to make up a full round of 18.

Sleeping

Mugie Lodge LODGE $$$

(062-2031235; www.mugieranch.com; s/d full board US$470/860;) Mugie Lodge, high on an escarpment overlooking Mugie Ranch, has six attractive cottages, each with big glass windows to take advantage of the views.

Treefrog Cottage CAMPGROUND, BANDA $

(0735243075; olmaisor@africaonline.co.ke; camping per person KSh500, 4-bed bandas KSh5000) Perched on a hill with grand views of the plains below, the Kenyan-/English-run Bobong Camp and Treefrog Cottage offers basic (and overpriced) *bandas* that will house a family of four, but you need to be fully self-sufficient. Camping is also possible. It also offers some of the cheapest camel treks (per day including guide KSh2500) in the north. You must provide all your own camping equipment and food.

Treefrog Cottage is in Rumuruti, 42km northwest of Nyahururu.

Nanyuki

POP 36,142

This small but bustling mountain town makes a living off sales, be it of treks to climbers, curios to soldiers of the British Army (which has a training facility nearby) or drinks to pilots of the Kenyan Air Force (this is the site of its main airbase). For all that mercantilism, it's laid-back for a market town. Nanyuki also serves as a gateway to the Laikipia Plateau, one of Africa's most important wildlife conservation areas.

Sights & Activities

Nanyuki is a popular base for launching expeditions to climb Mt Kenya's Sirimon or Burguret Routes. One local group worth contacting for information and excellent trekking programs is Montana Trek & Information Centre (p167). There's also the possibility of camel safaris at Nanyuki River Camel Camp (p156).

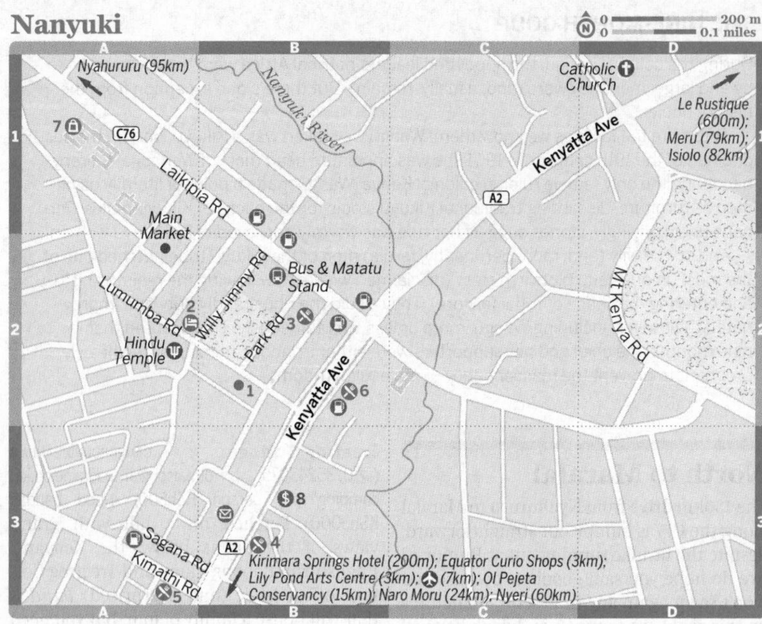

Nanyuki

Activities, Courses & Tours
1 Montana Trek & Information Centre B2

Sleeping
2 Ibis Hotel A2

Eating
3 Kungu Maitu Hotel & Butchery B2
4 Marina Grill & Restaurant B3
5 Nakumart Supermarket A3
6 Walkers Kikwetu B2

Shopping
7 Nanyuki Spinners & Weavers A1

Information
8 Barclays Bank B3
Boma Holidays .... (see 5)

Otherwise, you should stroll 3km south to the **equator** (there's a sign) and get a lesson from the men who make a living giving demonstrations of the Coriolis force (see p158).

Mt Kenya Wildlife Conservancy Animal Orphanage ZOO
(☎062-2032406; www.animalorphanagekenya.org; Mount Kenya Safari Club; per person KSh1500; ⏰8am-12.30pm & 1.30-5.30pm) It may come off a little zoolike at first but this orphanage is one of the few places in the world to have successfully bred the rare mountain bongo. Its success is such that there are now plans to release some of the captivate-bred antelope into the Mt Kenya forests to bolster the current population of around 70. Children, and anyone who wants to have a baby monkey scramble over their head, will love this place.

Lily Pond Arts Centre ART GALLERY
(☎0702006501; www.lilypondartscentre.com; off Nairobi–Nanyuki Rd; ⏰8am-7.30pm Sun-Thu, to 11pm Fri & Sat) This fascinating centre has many strings to its bow, among them some fascinating examples of contemporary African art. It's 3km south of town and signposted off the main highway.

Sleeping

Nanyuki River Camel Camp HUT $
(☎0722-361642; www.fieldoutdoor.com; camping KSh1250, huts without bathroom half/full board KSh5000) The most innovative sleep in town (well, 4km outside of it, off the C76 Hwy) is this ecocamp, set in a dry swab of scrub. The camp offers lodging in genuine Somali grass-and-camel-skin huts imported from Mandera; they have been relocated to sit close to the Nanyuki River.

The camp is best known for its camel treks; it's a good idea to give it at least 48 hours advance notice as the camels are often grazed many kilometres away. Somali food such as *nyiri nyiri* (fried camel jerky with cardamom) is a house speciality but also requires advance notice.

Kirimara Springs Hotel HOTEL $
(0726370191; www.kirimaraspringshotel.com; Kenyatta Ave; s/d/tw KSh2300/3000/3500; P) While Kirimara isn't going to win any architecture awards, and its website's claim that the rooms are comfortable and luxuriously furnished is plainly absurd, the friendly staff and spacious and bright rooms were cleaner and cheaper than others in this price bracket. The rooms on the western side of the building catch less traffic noise, while those on the east get glimpses of Mt Kenya.

Ibis Hotel HOTEL $
(0714420888; nanyuki@ibishotels.co.ke; Willy Jimmy Rd; s/d/tw excl breakfast KSh1300/1600/2300;) The Ibis (which bears no resemblance to the international chain) is a little smarter than most other nearby cheapies; the few extra shillings buy you a little more cheer and a slightly larger bathroom. This multilevel building encloses a covered courtyard restaurant that is better than most. Angle for a room with Mt Kenya views.

★**Kongoni Camp** BANDA $$
(0702868888, 062-2031225; www.kongonicamp.com; s US$56-95, d or rondavels US$100-175; P@) Founded by a friendly local-turned-Londoner-turned-local-again, Kongoni has five, concrete circular *bandas* as well as some newer rooms that are simple but designed with a touch of safari flair. It's one of the few genuinely midrange options around town and there's a large barnlike restaurant-cum-bar.

★**Mount Kenya Safari Club** HOTEL $$$
(Nairobi 020-2265555; www.fairmont.com; d from US$533; P@) For our money this is *the* top-end resort in the Central Highlands – it's the kind of place that makes you want to grow a moustache, kick back and smoke a pipe. The rooms have a luxurious, classic look to them and are decorated to a sumptuous standard, all with their own open fires and exquisite bathrooms. The whole shebang overlooks the Mt Kenya Wildlife Conservancy.

There are more facilities here than you can shake a Maasai throwing stick at (including a heated pool, clay tennis court, topiary maze, wedding chapel and art gallery). Keep an eye on its website as special rates are sometimes promoted there.

Eating

★**Kungu Maitu Hotel & Butchery** KENYAN $
(off Laikipia Rd; meals KSh200; 8am-10pm) Friendly and utterly local, this simple place serves up Nanyuki's best barbecued meats. Choose your cuts of meat on the way, order a chapati or samosa to go with it and wait for it all to appear at your table. We found the toilets (upstairs) to be bearable only if you hold your breath and close your eyes – if you can wait, do so.

Walkers Kikwetu BUFFET $
(Kenyatta Ave; mains KSh200-450; 7am-11pm Mon-Sat) *Kikwetu* means 'ours' in Kikuyu and provides the inspiration behind the menu. Several African dishes from various tribes are brought together and served buffet-style (but charged according to the dishes you select). If you haven't tried *matoke* (cooked plantains), pilau (Swahili curried rice) or *mukimo* (mashed beans and vegetables), here's your chance.

Marina Grill & Restaurant INTERNATIONAL $
(Kenyatta Ave; mains KSh150-500; 8am-10.30pm) Popular with trekking groups, British soldiers and Kenyan Air Force officers (the odd cross-section that is Nanyuki), this place does good burgers and pizza and has a nice rooftop eating area for those needing fresh air.

★**Lily Pond Arts Centre** CAFE $$
(0702006501, 0726734493; www.lilypondartscentre.com; off Nairobi–Nanyuki Rd; 2-/3-course menus KSh950/1150; 8am-7.30pm Sun-Thu, to 11pm Fri & Sat) Fabulous home-cooked meals to be enjoyed while looking out over a lily pond right on the equator (you enter the restaurant from the southern hemisphere, but eat in the north...) make for a winning combination here. You choose from a selection of dishes that might include soup or a Kenyan beef curry.

It's part of the impressive Lily Pond Arts Centre around 3km south of town (or 220m south of the turn-off to Ol Pejeta Conservancy).

LOCAL KNOWLEDGE

PETER MUTUNGA: PROFESSOR OF THE CORIOLIS FORCE

'Hello sir. Welcome to the equator! Would you like a demonstration of the Coriolis force?'

'Hello. Sure.'

'Now we are at the centre. On either side is the northern [gestures north] and southern [gestures south] hemisphere. If I pour water from this pitcher into this bowl with a hole inside it [holds up bowl] 20m to the north, it will drain clockwise. Observe!'

He does so, dropping a stick in the water to demonstrate its draining direction.

'Wow.'

'Now, if we go 20m to the south, it will go out in an anticlockwise direction.' He repeats the procedure.

'OK.'

'This whole effect is known as the Coriolis force. It was described by Gaspard de Coriolis in 1835 and is based off Newton's second law of motion. Now, here at zero degrees, when I pour out the water, it will drain out in a straight line. Watch!' (The water drains out in a straight line.)

'Wow! That's pretty impressive, Peter.'

'Thank you. I am the professor of the Coriolis force. I am also an entrepreneur. Would you like to give me a tip?'

Author's note: while the demonstration seems to work, scientists say the Coriolis force doesn't actually cause water to drain in the manner Mutunga depicted.

Cape Chestnut INTERNATIONAL $$
(☎0705250650; www.capechestnut.com; mains from KSh600; ⏲8.30am-6pm Sat-Thu, to 11.30pm Fri; 📶) This coffee garden is a terrific place to come to eat, a little removed from the Nanyuki scrum. The food is excellent with dishes like rack of Timau lamb or rainbow trout with fresh greens, and the atmosphere is relaxed and popular with local expats. Friday night is tapas night. It's off Kenyatta Ave, 1km south of town.

Le Rustique INTERNATIONAL $$
(☎0721609601; www.lerustique.co.ke; off Kenyatta Ave; mains KSh1000-2200; ⏲noon-3pm & 6-11pm) This one-time Nairobi favourite has upped sticks and headed north to Nanyuki. The food, overseen to every last detail by owner Maike Potgeiter, is excellent with pizzas, crêpes and an excellent wine list. But the atmosphere is as much of a drawcard, with an open fireplace for those cold Laikipia evenings or the quiet garden when things are warmer.

★ **Tusks Restaurant** INTERNATIONAL, BUFFET $$$
(Mount Kenya Safari Club; lunch buffets KSh5000, dinner 4-course set menus KSh6000; ⏲12.30-2.30pm & 6.30-9.30pm) If you are looking to splurge then this place at the Mount Kenya Safari Club is the place to do it. Sink back into a sofa in the drawing room or saunter over to the pool and take in the vista. The buffet lunch is varied and outstanding, while the dinner set menu is equally memorable. Cocktails in the adjacent Zebar include a gemstone martini (with blue topaz, for example) – just be sure you don't accidentally swallow it (the gemstone that is...).

Shopping

★ **Lily Pond Arts Centre** ARTS
(☎0702006501; www.lilypondartscentre.com; off Nairobi–Nanyuki Rd; ⏲8am-7.30pm Sun-Thu, to 11pm Fri & Sat) You could easily spend an afternoon here, browsing the galleries of contemporary art (p156), eating at its fine cafe (p157), then shopping for truly original African crafts. There's handcrafted furniture, beaded sandals, flip-flops made from recycled rubber, hand-sculpted animals and so much more. It's on the equator, 3km south of town and signposted off the main road.

Nanyuki Spinners & Weavers CLOTHING
(Laikipia Rd; ⏲hours vary) This women's craft cooperative specialises in high-quality woven woollen goods. The store is a short walk past the main market on Laikipia Rd. Opening hours vary.

Equator Curio Shops SOUVENIRS
(Kenyatta Ave; ⏲hours vary) The equator just wouldn't be the same without the 30 or so shops that cluster around its sign. Each

shop owner takes a turn at being the first to approach arriving tourists. After that, it's game on.

Information

Boma Holidays (Nairobi 020-2329683; www.bomaadventures.com; 2nd fl, Nakumart Centre, Kenyatta Ave) Travel agency that can arrange airline ticketing, car hire, airport transfers, hotel reservations and local safaris.

Getting There & Away

Nanyuki is well connected to all points north and south, as well as most major Rift Valley towns. Sample matatu fares include Nyeri (KSh250, one hour), Isiolo (KSh280, 1½ hours), Meru (KSh250, 1½ hours), Nakuru (KSh650, three hours) and Nairobi (KSh500, three hours).

Airkenya (Nairobi 020-3916000; www.airkenya.com; Nanyuki Airport; one way adult/child US$173.50/131.40) Flies once or twice daily between Nairobi's Wilson Airport and Nanyuki.

Safarilink (Nairobi 020-600777; www.flysafarilink.com; one way adult/child US$170/122) Flights at least daily between Wilson Airport in Nairobi and Nanyuki's airport.

Tropic Air (Nairobi 020-2033032; www.tropicairkenya.com; Nanyuki Airport) Charter helicopter and light-aircraft services from Nanyuki's airport.

Segera Ranch

North of Ol Pejeta Conservancy in southern Laikipia, this 202-sq-km (50,000-acre) ranch is a perfect example of how Laikipia works. It's a model cattle ranch, but wildlife is also prolific here, including the three big cats, elephants, buffaloes and endangered species such as Grevy's zebra (15 of them at last count), patas monkey (a small troop lives along the ranch's eastern border) and the reticulated giraffe.

The landscape here is classic Laikipia terrain – seemingly endless savannah country cut through with rocky river valleys and riverine woodland.

The ranch is owned by philanthropist Jochen Zeitz whose **Zeitz Foundation** (www.zeitzfoundation.org) is active in local community projects with local schools, women's groups and the Samuel Eto'o Soccer Academy for budding football stars. The foundation's philosophy is based around the 'Four Cs' – conservation, community, culture and commerce.

Sleeping

★ Segera Retreat LODGE

(www.segera.com; s/d all inclusive US$1940/2420; P ❄ ≋) Wow! We can be difficult to impress, but this place left us speechless. Six villas and a couple of houses inhabit an oasis in the heart of the ranch, looking out onto the savannah, yet enclosed within their own natural compound that keeps dangerous animals out. The villas are utterly magnificent – spacious, luxurious in every way and steeped in safari tradition.

It's no coincidence that the villas capture perfectly that *Out of Africa* longing that caused a generation of would-be travellers to fall in love with the continent – one of the bar areas is strewn with original letters and personal effects from Karen Blixen, and the Retreat even has the plane that was used in the movie; flights can be arranged. The food, too, is memorable, and there's a wine list to match. There's a spa, hi-tech gym and sculpture garden, and thought-provoking installations of African contemporary art fill the ranch's artfully converted stables.

Ol Pejeta Conservancy

Ol Pejeta Conservancy was once one of the largest cattle ranches in Kenya, but is now a 364-sq-km (90,000-acre), privately owned wildlife reserve. It markets itself as the closest place to Nairobi where you can see the Big Five (lions, elephants, rhinos, leopards and buffaloes) and possesses a full palette of African plains wildlife, including a healthy population of rhinos.

It's the rhinos that form the centrepiece of what the conservancy does here – the 102 (at last count) black rhinos are the largest population in East Africa. A reminder of the challenges the conservancy faces came when one of its rhinos was poached in March 2014, with another killed four months later.

It's not just about rhinos – Ol Pejeta's role in the wider Laikipia ecosystem extends beyond its boundaries thanks to its partner agreements and wildlife corridors that link it to other Laikipia ranches. Apart from its impressive conservation work, Ol Pejeta is, so far, the only one of the private conservancies open to the paying (but not necessarily staying) public – most other conservancies are accessible only for those who stay in one of their exclusive lodges. Ol Pejeta is also extremely active in local community projects from school infrastructure,

OL PEJETA CONSERVANCY

Why Go East Africa's largest black-rhino population; excellent wildlife viewing and activities; most accessible of the Laikipia conservancies.

When to Go Year-round, although you'll need a 4WD from late March to late May.

Practicalities Only the Serat and main Rongai gate (both in the conservancy's east) are open to visitors.

Budget Tips Rent a matatu (minibus transport) for the day with other travellers in Nanyuki; if staying overnight, stay in one of the campsites.

health care and the provision of clean water to local communities.

And as is more common in Laikipia than you might expect, the conservancy has over 5000 head of cattle, including the extravagantly horned Ankoli breed from Uganda.

Sights & Activities

The **conservancy** (☎0752325379, 0707187141, Nairobi 020-2033244; www.olpejetaconservancy.org; adult/child/student US$90/45/23, vehicle from KSh400; ⏲7am-7pm) has many sights and activities; you can also arrange at the park gate or through your accommodation for guided bush walks, bird walks and night wildlife drives; each costs US$40 per adult (US$20 per child).

★Chimpanzee Sanctuary ZOO
(⏲10am-4.30pm) Home to 39 profoundly damaged chimpanzees rescued from captivity across Africa and further afield, Ol Pejeta's Chimpanzee Sanctuary encompasses two large enclosures cut in two by the Ewaso Nyiro River. There's an elevated observation post and keepers are usually on hand to explain a little about each chimp's backstory; note the tiny replica cage in which one of the chimps was chained for years on end prior to being brought to the sanctuary.

There are plans to improve the small information centre, and you can even adopt a chimp.

★Endangered Species Enclosure ZOO
(adult/child US$40/20) This 283-sq-km (700-acre) drive-through enclosure next to the Morani Information Centre is home to three out of the world's last five remaining northern white rhinos, an ever-so-close-to-being-extinct subspecies. The rhinos were brought here from the Dvur Kralove Zoo in the Czech Republic in 2009, but have not yet bred successfully. Also in the enclosure are endangered Grevy's zebras and Jackson's hartebeests.

★Morani Information Centre MUSEUM
(⏲7am-6.30pm) FREE Part education or interpretation centre, part museum, this three-roomed structure is appealingly interactive and comes with the instructions to 'Please touch' the leopard skin, antelope horns and other similar objects. You'll also find displays and information on Ol Pejeta's predator-proof *bomas* (cattle enclosures designed to keep predators out) and the history of the conservancy's rhino conservation work.

★Lion Tracking WILDLIFE
(adult/child US$40/20) Easily our pick of the activities on offer, this nightly excursion trains you in the art of identifying individual lions and takes you out to find lions using radio receivers. The data you gather forms part of the conservancy's database on Ol Pejeta's estimated 65 to 70 resident lions.

Hippo Hide Walk GUIDED WALK
(⏲hide 7am-6.30pm) FREE This 20-minute meander along the river bank happens in the company of a knowledgable local ranger – hopefully you'll see hippos but it's worth doing even if you don't.

Rift Valley Adventures CYCLING, ADVENTURE
(☎0707734776, 0712426999; www.riftvalleyadventures.com; cycling per person half-/full day from US$70/120) This highly recommended operator runs cycling tours through Ol Pejeta, as well as other activities in the Mt Kenya area.

Sleeping & Eating

Booking ahead is highly recommended for all of the accommodation choices, including the campsites. Each of the campsites has toilets, water and firewood.

★Ewaso Campsite CAMPGROUND
(☎0707187141; info@olpejetaconservancy.org; camping adult/child KSh1000/500) Protected by dense foliage but with good river views, this is probably the pick of the sites in the park centre.

★**Ngobit Campsite** CAMPGROUND
(☎0707187141; info@olpejetaconservancy.org; camping adult/child KSh1000/500) Along the Ngobit River in the conservancy's far south, this is the quietest of Ol Pejeta's campsites.

Ol Lerai Campsite CAMPGROUND $
(☎0707187141; info@olpejetaconservancy.org; camping adult/child KSh1000/500) This attractive campsite on the Ewaso Nyiro is right in the conservancy's centre and you're likely to be visited by elephants and other wildlife.

★**Sweetwaters Serena Camp** TENTED CAMP
(☎0732123333; www.serenahotels.com; s/d full board from US$280/370; P@) The 39 large and beautifully appointed en suite tents by the reliable Serena chain are high end but with prices more accessible than other properties. The central location is a plus (handy for most of the conservancy) and a minus (things can get busy around here), depending on your perspective.

★**Kicheche Laikipia** TENTED CAMP $$$
(☎Nairobi 020-2493569; www.kicheche.com; s/d all inclusive US$800/1330; P) Close to the geographical centre of the park and overlooking a waterhole, this excellent tented camp has six stylishly furnished tents, an overall air of sophistication and impeccable service. It's Ol Pejeta's most exclusive accommodation.

Ol Pejeta House LODGE $$$
(☎0732123333; www.serenahotels.com; s/d full board US$360/495; P) As you'd expect from the former home of multibillionaire Adnan Khashoggi, this imposing lodge has over-the-top decor and high levels of comfort. Avoid coming here on weekends, when it tends to fill up with a Nairobi crowd that likes to party.

LAIKIPIA LODGES

Virtually all of Laikipia's lodges and camps (now numbering close to 50) fall squarely into the luxurious bracket and cater to the well heeled who visit as part of prepackaged tours. This list includes some of the options.

El Karama Eco Lodge (☎0720386616; www.laikipiasafaris.com; per person from US$370) One of few Laikipia places with modest prices (at least by Laikipia standards). The simple but pleasing *bandas* and cottages make use of natural materials such as stone and thatch. It's located on 56-sq-km (14,000-acre) El Karama Ranch, which is next to Segera Ranch. Watch out for African wild dogs and make sure you take a walking safari.

Loisaba Wilderness (s/d all inclusive US$594/990) Refined accommodation (including four-poster star beds under the stars) on a 250-sq-km (61,000-acre) ranch in northern Laikipia plus activities that range from walking safaris and wildlife drives to white-water rafting, horse riding and camel safaris; the latter two activities are not included in quoted rates.

Ol Malo (☎062-32715; www.olmalo.com; s/d all inclusive US$720/1220, plus conservation fee US$80) Posh rock and olive-wood cottages in a stunning setting close to the Ewaso Nyiro River make this a fine choice. The surrounding conservancy is quite small, but that's not how it feels from the swimming pool with views to the very distant horizon. The rooms have soaring thatched ceilings, stone-tiled floors and earth tones throughout. It's in northwestern Laikipia.

Sanctuary at Ol-Lentille (☎Nairobi 020-2047491; www.ol-lentille.com; s/d all inclusive US$1265/2110; @) Utter exclusivity is the aim on this 97-sq-km (24,000-acre) conservancy with a series of opulent digs with names such as 'The Sultan's House' and 'The Chief's House'; each comes with a private butler service, the ultimate in luxury safaris. It's in the northwestern reaches of Laikipia and wildlife in the area includes elephants, Grevy's zebras, lions, leopards, giraffes and African wild dogs.

Sosian (☎0704909355; www.sosian.com; per person US$700) Horse riding, fishing and even cattle ranching make a nice change from the usual wildlife drives it does these, too) on this 97-sq-km (24,000-acre) central Laikipia ranch which is home to lions, elephants, leopards and even African wild dogs. The lodge is centred around a colonial-era ranch house and accommodation is spacious and beautifully appointed.

Porini Rhino Camp TENTED CAMP **$$$**
(☎0774136523; www.porini.com; r from US$445; ⏲closed mid-Apr–May; 🅿) Out in the far east of Ol Pejeta, Porini Rhino Camp overlooks a small stream, nicely removed from the crowds of day trippers that visit the conservancy. The tents themselves are comfortable rather than luxurious, service is friendly, the food is excellent and, as with most Porini properties, the camp supports local conservation projects. Keep an eye for rhinos.

★**Morani's Restaurant** CAFE **$$**
(☎0706160114; www.moranisrestaurant.com; mains KSh675-875; ⏲10.30am-6pm) Next to the Morani Information Centre, this terrific little cafe with outdoor tables serves up excellent dishes that range from the Morani burger made from prime Ol Pejeta beef to Kenyan beef stew or a Mediterranean wrap. Fresh juices, fine smoothies and Kenyan coffee round out an excellent package.

Information

Pick up a copy of the *Ol Pejeta Conservancy* map (KSh700) from the entrance gate or download it for free from the website. Other useful (and free) resources include the *Mammal Checklist*, *Bird Checklist* and *Chimpanzee Factfile*.

Getting There & Away

Ol Pejeta is 15km southwest of Nanyuki, which also has the nearest airport.

Arid Adventures (☎0722692409, 0703149559; www.arid-adventures.com) This Nakuru-based company rents out 4WDs to self-drivers for single- or multiday trips, as well as camping equipment.

Lewa Wildlife Conservancy

Although technically not a part of Laikipia, Lewa Wildlife Conservancy, a vast region of open savannah grasslands that falls away from the Mt Kenya highlands, is very much a part of Laikipia's story. It was at Lewa that the conservancy idea was pioneered and it remains a leader in all of the elements – serious wildlife protection wedded to innovative community engagement – that have come to define the private conservancies of Laikipia and elsewhere. Apart from anything else, Lewa ranks among the premier wildlife-watching territories anywhere in Kenya. And unlike in Kenya's national parks where off-road driving is prohibited, Lewa's guides delight in taking visitors to almost within touching distance of rhinos, elephants and other species.

Sights & Activities

At **Lewa Wildlife Conservancy** (LWC; ☎0722203562, 064-31405; www.lewa.org; conservation fee per adult/child per night US$105/53), the following activities (with sample per-person prices) complement the day and night wildlife drives. Bookings are most easily made through your accommodation.

- Excursions to Il Ngwesi: US$40, half-day.
- Tour of Lewa Wildlife Conservancy's HQ: Free (US$10 if you visit the tracker dogs), one to two hours.
- Orphan Rhino Project: US$15, 30 minutes (this was where the moving final scene in Sir David Attenborough's Africa series was filmed).
- Visit to local school: US$50 donation.
- Horse-riding safari: US$55, one hour.
- Walking safari in Ndare Ndare Forest: US$30 conservation fee, one to three hours.
- Quad bike/buggy safari: Price on application.
- Flying safari: Price on application.

LEWA WILDLIFE CONSERVANCY

Why Go For some of the finest wildlife-viewing in Kenya; almost guaranteed sightings of all the Big Five (lions, elephants, rhinos, leopards and bufffaloes); walking safaris and night safaris. No minibus circus.

When to Go Year-round, but the dry season (June to March) is best.

Practicalities Lewa is closed to casual visitors: you must be staying at one of the (very expensive) lodges in order to enter. Most visitors fly in from Nairobi but road access is easy from Isiolo or the Central Highlands.

Budget Tips Not suitable for budget travellers.

THE LEWA STORY

Like so many Laikipia properties that later became wildlife conservancies, Lewa Downs was an expansive cattle ranch owned since colonial times by white settlers. In 1983 the owners, the Craig family, along with pioneering rhino conservationist Anna Merz, set aside 20-sq-km (5000 acres) of Lewa as the Ngare Sergoi Rhino Sanctuary. They received their first rhino a year later, and the numbers grew to 16 in 1988. The Craigs doubled the sanctuary's size, and by 1994 the entire cattle ranch (along with the adjacent Ngare Ndare Forest Reserve) was enclosed within an electric fence to create a 251-sq-km (62,000-acre) rhino sanctuary. The Lewa Wildlife Conservancy (LWC) in its current form was formed in 1995.

True to its origins as a sanctuary to save Kenya's rhinos, Lewa's primary conservation focus continues to be rhinos. Lewa suffered not a single poaching event between 1983 and 2009 – the joke doing the rounds of the conservation community for much of this time was that Lewa was 'State House' (Kenya's presidential palace) for rhinos. Sadly, poaching has been on the rise ever since, with six of Lewa's rhinos killed in 2013, prompting a massive investment in antipoaching operations.

At last count, Lewa was home to 66 black rhinos and 62 white rhinos (that's around 15% of the Kenyan total). And despite the poaching, the conservancy is close to its carrying capacity for rhinos. In 2014 the fence that separated Lewa from the 129-sq-km (32,000-acre) Borana Conservancy to the west was torn down, effectively increasing the size of the rhino sanctuary by 25%.

Rhinos aside, Lewa's conservation effort has been astounding and 20% of the world's Grevy's zebras call the reserve home.

Central to the Lewa model is a serious commitment to community development, fuelled by a recognition that local people are far more likely to protect wildlife if they have a stake (financial or otherwise) in its survival. LWC is a nonprofit organisation that invests around 70% of its annual US$2.5-million-plus budget into health care, education and various community projects for surrounding villages.

In 2013, Lewa Wildlife Conservancy, was inscribed on Unesco's World Heritage Sites list as an extension to the existing Mount Kenya National Park/Natural Forest site.

Festivals & Events

Lewa Safaricom Marathon MARATHON
(www.safaricom.co.ke/safaricommarathon; adult/child KSh5000/2000) It's one thing to run a marathon to the encouraging screams of people, it's entirely another to run it sharing the course with elephants, rhinos and the odd lion! Established in 2000 to raise funds for wildlife conservation and community development, the Safaricom Marathon, run within the Lewa Wildlife Conservancy in late June/early July, attracts world-record holders and is renowned as one of the planet's toughest marathons.

Thanks to experienced rangers, helicopters and spotter planes, your only worry should be the heat and the 1700m average elevation.

Sleeping & Eating

★**Lewa Safari Camp** TENTED CAMP $$$
(☎Nairobi 020-6003090; www.lewasafaricamp.com; s/d all inclusive US$708/1180;) This impressive property lies in the northwest corner of the conservancy, about one hour's drive from the main Matunda gate. Its safari tents are large and have that whole chic-bush-living thing down to a tee; they're arrayed around a shallow valley and large wildlife is kept out so you can walk around freely (although you get an escort at night). Service is impeccable.

And nothing beats an evening gin and tonic by the roaring log fire of the main building, a nostalgic ochre-hued homestead in the colonial style with lawns sweeping down into the valley. Prices include all safaris and activities.

Kifaru LODGE $$$
(☎Nairobi 020-2127844; www.kifaruhouse.com; per person US$1000;) Luxury hilltop *bandas* with no expense spared, not to mention fine views over the plains and an air of exclusivity with no more than 12 guests in camp at any one time.

Lewa House COTTAGES $$$
(☎0710781303; www.lewahouse.com; r/cottages from US$1590/3975;) Close to

the centre of the park. Apart from the main house, try the daringly designed 'earth pods' with curved walls, earth tones and superior levels of comfort.

Lewa Wilderness COTTAGES $$$
(☎0723273668; www.lewawilderness.com; r from US$1590;) Nine cottages owned and run by the Craig family in Lewa's east. Rooms are classic safari in style and faultlessly luxurious.

Sirikoi LODGE $$$
(☎0727232445; www.sirikoi.com; s/d tents US$1155/1930, 4-bed cottages US$4665, 6-person houses US$7000;) Stunning rooms in luxury tents, cottages and in the main house in the heart of the conservancy.

Getting There & Away

The turn-off to LWC is only 12km south of Isiolo (the entrance gate is another 5km on) and is well signposted on the A2 Hwy. Private vehicles are not generally allowed into Lewa. Those arriving by private vehicle will have to leave their car at the entrance gate and change to a lodge-provided jeep.

Airkenya (☎Nairobi 020-3916000; www.airkenya.com; adult/child one way US$238/175.30) Up to twice-daily flights between Lewa and Nairobi's Wilson Airport, sometimes via Nanyuki.

Safarilink (☎Nairobi 020-6000777; www.flysafarilink.com; adult/child one way US$230/164) Up to three daily flights between Lewa and Wilson Airport in Nairobi.

Il Ngwesi Group Ranch

Abutting the northwestern side of Lewa Wildlife Conservancy, Il Ngwesi is another fine example of a private conservation project linking wildlife conservation and community development, albeit on a smaller scale. The Maasai of Il Ngwesi (the name Il Ngwesi translates as 'people of wildlife'), with help from neighbour LWC, have transformed this undeveloped land, previously used for subsistence pastoralism, into a prime wildlife-conservation area hosting white and black rhinos, waterbucks, giraffes and other plains animals.

The south is quite steeply contoured in places, but the highest point (Sanga, at 1907m) lies on Il Ngwesi's western boundary. The northern lowlands mostly consist of light woodland. Just outside the eastern border of Il Ngwesi, Maasai, Turkana and Samburu villages line the trackside.

Il Ngwesi community supplements its herding income with tourist dollars gained from the award-winning **Il Ngwesi Eco Lodge** (☎Nairobi 020-2033122; www.ilngwesi.com; s/d all inclusive US$485/830;) . The divine open-fronted thatched cottages here boast views over the dramatic escarpment, and at night the beds in some rooms can be pulled out onto the private 'terraces', allowing you to snooze under the Milky Way. Profits go straight to the Maasai community.

Il Ngwesi is north of Lewa and accessed off the main Isiolo to Nairobi Rd. Lewa Safari Camp (p163) organises half-day visits to Il Ngwesi from Lewa, which includes visits to a Maasai *manyatta* (village), nature walks and explanations of Maasai tradition.

Borana Conservancy

One of the longest-standing conservancies in the area, the Borana cattle ranch, now the **Borana Conservancy** (www.borana.co.ke), owned by the Dyer family for three generations, turned its focus onto wildlife and community projects in 1992.

In the past couple of years this beautiful and already impressive 142-sq-km (35,000-acre) conservancy has suddenly become a whole lot more attractive. In 2013, rhinos from Lewa Wildlife Conservancy were translocated here, and the following year the fence between Borana and Lewa was torn down – Borana is now an integral part of one of Kenya's most important rhino sanctuaries. It's perfect rhino habitat and African wild dogs (as well as, at last count, 18 lions and other plains species) are also a possibility here.

As is something of a Laikipia trademark, Borana ploughs its money into antipoaching operations, community development and grasslands habitat management.

On a hill and overlooking a waterhole, the appealing, family-run **Borana Lodge** (www.borana.com; s/d all inclusive US$855/1490;) manages a perfect balance between rustic and luxurious. The eight thatched cottages have stone floors and walls and look down to a waterhole where wildlife is common. The main building is wonderfully colonial from its fireplace to stiff drinks.

Lekurruki Community Ranch

Ranged across almost 120-sq-km (12,000 hectares) north of Il Ngwesi and northwest of LWC, this community ranch is the homeland of the Mukogodo Maasai. With a good mix of habitats – the Mukogodo Forest covers 300-sq-km (74,000 acres) and is often said to be one of the largest indigenous forests in East Africa, while the remainder of the ranch is made up of open savannah – the ranch has a rich variety of both flora and fauna. Of the latter, you'll find predators and buffaloes here, but elephants are the main drawcard with one herd almost 500 strong. More than 200 bird species and over 100 butterfly species have been recorded on the ranch.

The immensity of African landscapes and the intimacy of the community lodge experience are perfectly combined at **Tassia Lodge** (☎0725972923; www.tassiasafaris.com; s/d all inclusive US$670/960;), high on a rocky bluff. Rooms are open sided and have an original handmade look with natural wood and stone used throughout. Views are splendid and activities include walking safaris and botanical walks.

MT KENYA NATIONAL PARK

Africa's second-highest mountain is also one of its most beautiful. Here, mere minutes from the equator, glaciers carve out the throne of Ngai, the old high god of the Kikuyu. To this day the tribe keeps its doors open to the face of the sacred mountain, and some still come to its lower slopes to offer prayers and the foreskins of their young men – this was the traditional place for holding circumcision ceremonies. Besides being venerated by the Kikuyu, Mt Kenya and **Mt Kenya National Park** (☎0722279502, Nairobi 020-3568763; www.kws.go.ke; adult/child day entry US$65/30, 4-/5-/6-day package adult US$255/315/380, child US$150/170/200), has the rare honour of being both a Unesco World Heritage Site and a Unesco Biosphere Reserve.

The highest peaks of Batian (5199m) and Nelion (5188m) can only be reached by mountaineers with technical skills, but Point Lenana (4985m), the third-highest peak, can be reached by trekkers and is the usual goal for most mortals. When the clouds part, the views are simply magnificent.

Mt Kenya National Park

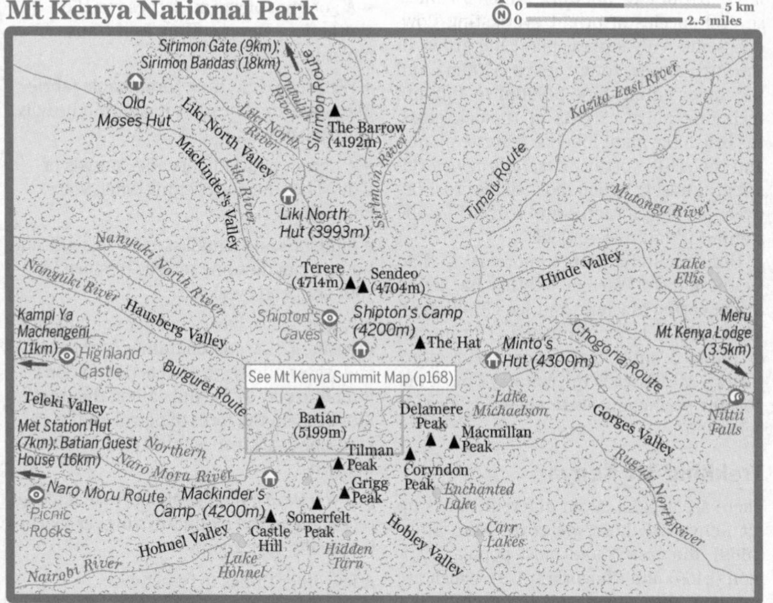

MT KENYA NATIONAL PARK

Why Go Awe-inspiring views from Africa's second-highest mountain; unlike Mt Kilimanjaro, it's possible to take different routes up and down, with arguably better scenery.

When to Go Climb during the driest months: mid-January to late February and late August to September.

Practicalities Don't underestimate the difficulty of this trek. You'd be flirting with death by not taking a guide.

Budget Tips Don't skimp on safety and length of acclimatisation; carry your own gear and cook your own meals; camp instead of staying in the huts.

Geography

There are ecosystems on the slopes of Mt Kenya that cannot be found anywhere else in the country.

This extinct volcano hosts, at various elevations, upland forest, bamboo forest (2500m), high-altitude equatorial heath (3000m to 3500m) and lower alpine moorland (3400m to 3800m), which includes several species of bright everlasting flowers. Some truly surreal plant life grows in the Afro-alpine zone (above 3500m) and the upper alpine zone (3800m to 4500m), including hairy carpets of tussock grass, the brushlike giant lobelias (rosette plants) and the sci-fi-worthy *Senecio brassica* (giant groundsel), which looks like a cross between an aloe, a cactus and a dwarf. At the summit it's all rock and ice.

Unfortunately, there's more rock than ice these days. Warmer weather has led to disappearing glaciers, and ice climbing on Mt Kenya is largely finished. The impact of reduced snow melt upon the region's rivers – Mt Kenya is the country's most important permanent watershed – is already being felt.

Trekking Mt Kenya

There are at least seven different routes up Mt Kenya. Of those, we cover Naro Moru (p169), the easiest and most popular; Sirimon (p169) and Chogoria (p170), which are excellent alternatives and the exciting but demanding Summit Circuit (p170), which circles Batian and Nelion, thus enabling you to mix and match ascending and descending routes. Other routes include the Timau Route and Burguret Route.

Safety

The trek to Point Lenana isn't an easy hike and people die on the mountain every year. Many people ascend the mountain too quickly and suffer from headaches, nausea and other (sometimes more serious) effects of altitude sickness. By spending at least three nights on the ascent, you'll enjoy yourself more. Be wary of hypothermia and dehydration; fluids and warm clothing go a long way towards preventing both. Unpredictable weather is another problem.

Clothing & Equipment

Consider the following to be a minimum checklist of necessary equipment. If you don't have your own equipment, items can be rented from some guiding associations. Prices vary, but expect to pay in the vicinity of KSh700/300/250/400 for a two-person tent/sleeping bag/pair of boots/stove per day:

- A good sleeping bag and a closed-cell foam mat or Therm-a-Rest if you're camping (nightly temperatures near the summit often drop to below -10°C).
- A good set of warm clothes (wool or synthetics – never cotton, as it traps moisture).
- Waterproof clothing (breathable fabric like Gore-Tex is best) as it can rain heavily any time of year.
- A decent pair of boots and sandals or light shoes (for the evening when your boots get wet).
- Sunblock and sunglasses (at this altitude the sun can do some serious damage to your skin and eyes).
- A tent, stove, basic cooking equipment, utensils, a 3L water container (per person) and water-purifying tablets (if you don't intend to stay in the huts along the way). Stove fuel in the form of petrol and kerosene (paraffin) is fairly easily found in towns.
- If you have a mobile phone, take it along; reception on the mountain's higher reaches is actually very good.

A few other things to remember:

- If a porter is carrying your backpack, always keep essential clothing (warm-

and wet-weather gear) in your day pack because you may become separated for hours at a time.

- Don't sleep in clothes you've worn during the day because the sweat your clothes absorbed keeps them moist at night, reducing their heat-retention capabilities.

- Fires are prohibited in the open except in an emergency; in any case, there's no wood once you get beyond 3300m.

Guides, Cooks & Porters

Having a porter for your gear is like travelling in a chauffeured Mercedes instead of a matatu. A good guide will help set a

ORGANISED TREKS

If you bargain hard, a package trek may end up costing only a little more than organising each logistical element of the trip separately. If you're keen to save money, think like a wildebeest and join a herd – the larger the group, the cheaper the per-person rate becomes. All prices listed here generally include guides, cooks and porters, park fees, meals and accommodation.

EWP (Executive Wilderness Programmes; ☎UK 1550-721319; www.ewpnet.com/kenya; 3-day trip per person US$590-985) Employs knowledgable local guides.

IntoAfrica (☎Nairobi 0722511752, UK 0797-4975723; www.intoafrica.co.uk; 7-day trip per person US$1385-2630) An environmentally and culturally sensitive company offering both scheduled and exclusive seven-day trips ascending Sirimon Route and descending Chogoria.

KG Mountain Expeditions (☎0733606338, Nairobi 020-2033874; www.kenyaexpeditions.com; 4-day treks per person around US$600) Run by a highly experienced mountaineer, KG offers all-inclusive scheduled treks.

Montana Trek & Information Centre (☎062-32731; www.montanatrekks.com; Lumumba Rd, Nanyuki; 4-day trip per person US$560-810) This community-based association in Nanyuki has friendly and knowledgeable guides. The centre is particularly useful for Sirimon trekkers.

Mountain Rock Safaris Resorts & Trekking Services (Bantu Mountain Lodge; ☎Nairobi 020-242133; www.mountainrockkenya.com; Naro Moru) Runs the Bantu Mountain Lodge near Naro Moru. Its popular four-day Naro Moru–Sirimon crossover trek costs US$650 per person.

Mountain View Tour Trekking Safaris (☎0722249439; mountainviewt@yahoo.com; Naro Moru; per person per day from US$120) An association of local guides working together who often approach independent travellers as they arrive in Naro Moru.

Mt Kenya Chogoria Guides & Porters Association (☎0733676970; anthonytreks@yahoo.com; Chogoria; per person per day from US$120) A small association of guides, cooks and porters based in Chogoria's Transit Motel, specialising in the Chogoria Route up the mountain.

Mt Kenya Guides & Porters Safari Club (☎0723112483, Nairobi 020-3524393; www.mtkenyaguides.com; Naro Moru; per person per day from US$120) The most organised association of guides, cooks and porters in Naro Moru.

Naro Moru River Lodge (☎0708984005, 0708984002; www.naromoruriverlodge.com; Naro Moru; 4-day trip per person US$719-1497) Runs a range of all-inclusive trips and operates Met Station Hut (p170) and Mackinder's Camp (p170) on the Naro Moru Route.

Rift Valley Adventures (☎0707734776, 0712426999; www.riftvalleyadventures.com) Based at Ol Pejeta Conservancy (p160) up on the Laikipia Plateau, this respected operator runs trekking and mountain-biking safaris on Mt Kenya, as well as climbing, canyoning and white-water rafting.

Sana Highlands Trekking Expeditions (Map p66; ☎0722243691, Nairobi 020-227820; www.sanatrekkingkenya.com; Contrust House, Moi Ave, Nairobi; 5-day trips per person from US$550) Sana Highlands Trekking Expeditions Operates five-day all-inclusive treks on the Sirimon, Naor Moru and Chogoria routes.

Mt Kenya Summit

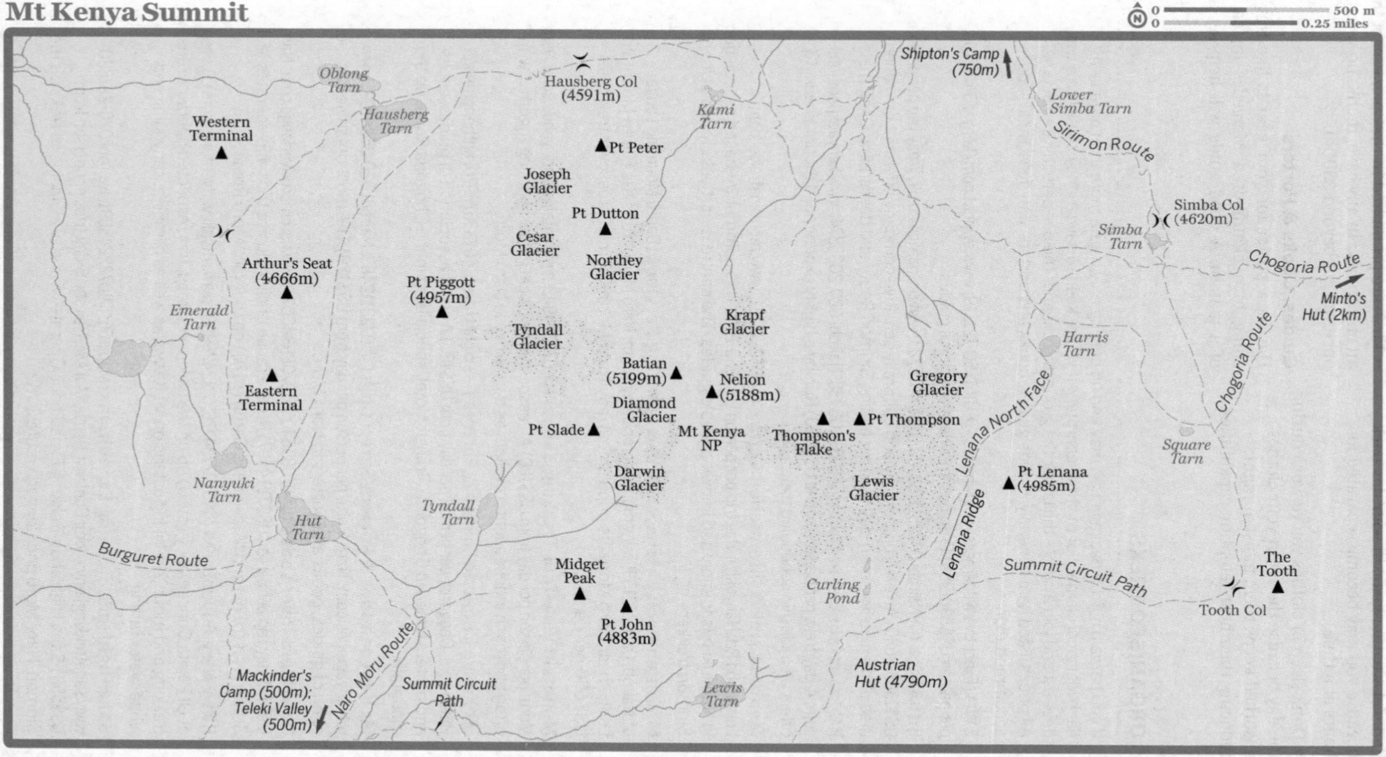

sustainable pace and hopefully dispense interesting information about Mt Kenya and its flora, fauna and wildlife. With both on your team, your appreciation of this mountain will be enhanced a hundredfold. If you hire a guide or porter who can also cook, you won't regret it.

The Kenya Wildlife Service (KWS) issues vouchers to all registered guides and porters, who should also hold identity cards; they won't be allowed into the park without them.

Costs

In addition to the following, park fees must be factored into the overall cost of climbing Mt Kenya.

- **Guides** The cost of guides varies depending on the qualifications of the guide, whatever the last party paid and your own negotiating skills. You should expect to pay a minimum of US$30/25/20 per day for a guide/cook/porter.
- **Tips** In addition to the actual cost of hiring guides, cooks and porters, tips are expected but these should only be paid for good service.

For a good guide who has completed the full trek with you, plan on a tip of about US$50 per group. Cook and porter tips should be around US$30 and US$20 respectively.

Naro Moru Route

Although the least scenic, this is the most straightforward and popular route and is still spectacular.

Starting in Naro Moru town, the first part of the route takes you along a gravel road through farmlands for some 13km (all the junctions are signposted) to the start of the forest. Another 5km brings you to the park entry gate (2400m), from where it's 8km to the road head and the Met Station Hut (3000m), where you stay for the night and acclimatise.

On the second day, set off through the forest (at about 3200m) and Teleki Valley to the moorland around so-called **Vertical Bog**; expect the going here to be, well, boggy. At a ridge the route divides into two. You can either take the higher path, which gives better views but is often wet, or the lower, which crosses the Naro Moru River and continues gently up to Mackinder's Camp (4200m). This part of the trek should take about 4½ hours. Here you can stay in the dormitories or camp.

On the third day you can either rest at Mackinder's Camp to acclimatise or aim for **Point Lenana** (4985m). This stretch takes three to six hours, so it is common to leave around 2am to reach the summit in time for sunrise. From the bunk-house, continue past the ranger station to a fork. Keep right, and go across a swampy area, followed by a moraine, and then up a long scree slope – this is a long, hard slog. The KWS **Austrian Hut** (dm KSh750), at 4790m high, is three to four hours from Mackinder's and about one hour below the summit of Lenana, so it's a good place to rest before the final push.

The section of the trek from Austrian Hut up to Point Lenana takes you up a narrow rocky path that traverses the southwest ridge parallel to the Lewis Glacier, which has shrunk more than 100m since the 1960s. Be careful, as the shrinkage has created serious danger of slippage along the path. A final climb or scramble brings you up onto the peak. In good weather it's fairly straightforward, but in bad weather you shouldn't attempt the summit unless you're experienced in mountain conditions or have a guide.

Sirimon Route

A popular alternative to Naro Moru, Sirimon has better scenery, greater flexibility and a gentler rate of ascent, but takes a day longer. It's well worth considering combining it with the Chogoria Route for a six- to seven-day traverse that really brings out the best of Mt Kenya.

The trek begins at the Sirimon gate, 23km from Nanyuki, from where it's about a 9km walk through forest to Old Moses Hut (3300m), where you spend the first night.

On the second day you could head straight through the moorland for Shipton's Camp, but it is worth taking an extra acclimatisation day via **Liki North Hut** (3993m), a tiny place on the floor of a classic glacial valley. The actual hut is in poor shape and meant for porters, but it's a good campsite with a toilet and stream nearby.

On the third day, head up the western side of Liki North Valley and over the ridge into Mackinder's Valley, joining the direct route about 1½ hours in. After crossing the Liki River, follow the path for another 30 minutes until you reach the bunk-house at Shipton's Camp (4200m), which is set in a fantastic location right below Batian and Nelion.

From Shipton's you can push straight for **Point Lenana** (4985m), a tough 3½- to five-hour slog via Harris Tarn and the tricky north-face approach, or take the Summit Circuit in either direction around the peaks to reach Austrian Hut (4790m), about one hour below the summit. The left-hand (east) route past Simba Col (4620m) is shorter but steeper, while the right-hand (west) option takes you on the Harris Tarn trail nearer the main peaks.

From Austrian Hut take the standard southwest traverse up to Point Lenana. If you're spending the night here, it's worth having a wander around to catch the views up to Batian and down the Lewis Glacier into the Teleki Valley.

Chogoria Route

This route crosses some of the most spectacular and varied scenery on Mt Kenya, and is often combined with the Sirimon Route (usually as the descent). The main reason this route is more popular as a descent is the 29km bottom stage. While not overly steep, climbing up that distance is much harder than descending it.

The only disadvantage with this route is the long distance between Chogoria and the park gate. These days most people drive, although it's a beautiful walk through farmland, rainforest and bamboo to the park gate. Most people spend the first night here, either camping at the gate or staying nearby in Meru Mt Kenya Lodge (3000m).

On the second day, head up through the forest to the trailhead (camping is possible here). From here it's another 7km over rolling foothills to the Hall Tarns area and **Minto's Hut** (4300m). Like Liki North, this place is only intended for porters, but makes for a decent campsite. Don't use the tarns here to wash anything, as careless trekkers have already polluted them.

From here follow the trail alongside the stunning **Gorges Valley** (another possible descent for the adventurous) and scramble up steep ridges to meet the Summit Circuit. It is possible to go straight for the north face or southwest ridge of Point Lenana, but stopping at Austrian Hut or detouring to Shipton's Camp gives you more time to enjoy the scenery; see Sirimon and Naro Moru routes for details.

Allow at least five days for the Chogoria Route, although a full week is better.

Summit Circuit

While everyone who summits Point Lenana gets a small taste of the spectacular Summit Circuit, few trekkers ever grab the beautiful beast by the horns and hike its entire length. The trail encircles the main peaks of Mt Kenya between the 4300m and 4800m contour lines and offers challenging terrain, fabulous views and a splendid opportunity to familiarise yourself with this complex mountain. It is also a fantastic way to acclimatise before bagging Point Lenana.

One of the many highlights along the route is a peek at Mt Kenya's southwest face, with the long, thin Diamond Couloir leading up to the **Gates of the Mists** between the summits of Batian and Nelion.

Depending on your level of fitness, this route can take between four and nine hours. Some fit souls can summit Point Lenana (from Austrian Hut or Shipton's Camp) and complete the Summit Circuit in the same day.

The trail can be deceptive at times, especially when fog rolls in, and some trekkers have become seriously lost between Tooth Col and Austrian Hut. It is imperative to take a guide.

Sleeping

As well as the sleeping options given for each route, it is possible to camp anywhere on the mountain; the cost of camping is included in the four- to six-day park-fee packages payable at any gate. Most people camp near the huts or bunk-houses, as there are often toilets and water nearby.

Naro Moru Route

Met Station Hut MOUNTAIN HUT
(dm US$23) One of three good bunk houses along the Naro Moru Route Route, at 3000m. Beds can be hard to come by; book through Naro Moru River Lodge (p173).

Mackinder's Camp MOUNTAIN HUT
(Map p165; dm US$30) At 4200m on the Naro Moru Route Route. Book through Naro Moru River Lodge (p173).

Batian Guest House GUESTHOUSE $
(www.kws.go.ke; 8-bed bandas US$180) Those needing more luxury than the mountain

huts can sleep in lovely, KWS-run Batian Guest House, which sleeps eight. It's around 1km from the Naro Moru gate.

Sirimon Route

Old Moses Hut MOUNTAIN HUT
(dm US$20) At 3300m and usually the first night's stop on the Sirimon Route. Book through Bantu Mountain Lodge (p173).

Shipton's Camp MOUNTAIN HUT
(Map p165; dm US$20) Bunk house at 4200m for the third night on the Sirimon Route. Book through Bantu Mountain Lodge (p173).

Sirimon Bandas BANDA $
(two-bed banda US$80) Many trekkers acclimatise by camping at Liki North Hut. If you'd like a little more comfort, book into the excellent KWS Sirimon Bandas, which are located 9km from the Sirimon gate. Each *banda* sleeps four.

Chogoria Route

Meru Mt Kenya Lodge CABINS
(per person KSh2500) The only option besides camping on the Chogoria Route, this group of comfortable cabins is administered by **Meru South County Council** (☎0729390686; Chuka). Ask your guide to reserve these in advance, as during peak season they can be booked out.

Eating

Increased altitude creates unique cooking conditions. The major consideration is that the boiling point of water is considerably reduced. At 4500m, for example, water boils at 85°C; this is too low to sufficiently cook rice or lentils (pasta is better) and you won't be able to brew a good cup of tea (instant coffee is the answer). Cooking times and fuel usage are considerably increased as a result, so plan accordingly.

Take plenty of citrus fruits and/or citrus drinks as well as chocolate, sweets or dried fruit to keep your blood-sugar level up.

To avoid severe headaches caused by dehydration or altitude sickness, drink at least 3L of fluid per day and bring rehydration sachets.

Water-purification tablets, available at most chemists, aren't a bad idea either (to purify water by boiling at this altitude would take close to 30 minutes).

Information

Mountain Club of Kenya (MCK; ☎Nairobi 020-602330; www.mck.or.ke) Technical climbers and mountaineers should get a copy of the MCK *Guide to Mt Kenya & Kilimanjaro*. MCK also has reasonably up-to-date mountain information posted on its website.

AROUND MT KENYA

Naro Moru

POP 9018

Naro Moru may be little more than a string of shops and houses, with a couple of very basic hotels and a market, but it's the most popular starting point for treks up Mt Kenya. There's a post office and internet but no banks.

Sights & Activities

In addition to gazing up at Mt Kenya (best before 6.30am, after which it is usually obscured by clouds) and starting the Naro Moru Route up to its summit, there are a number of interesting day excursions. Some guide associations can organise **nature walks** on Mt Kenya and hikes to the **Mau Mau caves**, which are impressive from both a physical and historical perspective.

Sleeping & Eating

As a general rule, the basic hotels are in town, while the more tourist-oriented options are in the surrounding countryside, particularly on the bumpy road between Naro Moru and the park gates. Eating options in town are slim, but you won't starve if you like greasy chips and dining on goats who have lived long and eventful lives.

Mt Kenya Guides & Porters Safari Club BANDA $
(☎Nairobi 020-3524393; www.mtkenyaguides.com; per person KSh2300) Principally in the business of supplying guides and porters, this association has branched out with a couple of excellent-value cottages with open fires. Meals can be arranged on request and, obviously, organising a trek here is a breeze.

Timberland Hotel HOTEL $
(Naro Moru; s/d excl breakfast KSh400/600) It doesn't get much cheaper or more basic than this. If you don't mind squat toilets, the

Around Mt Kenya

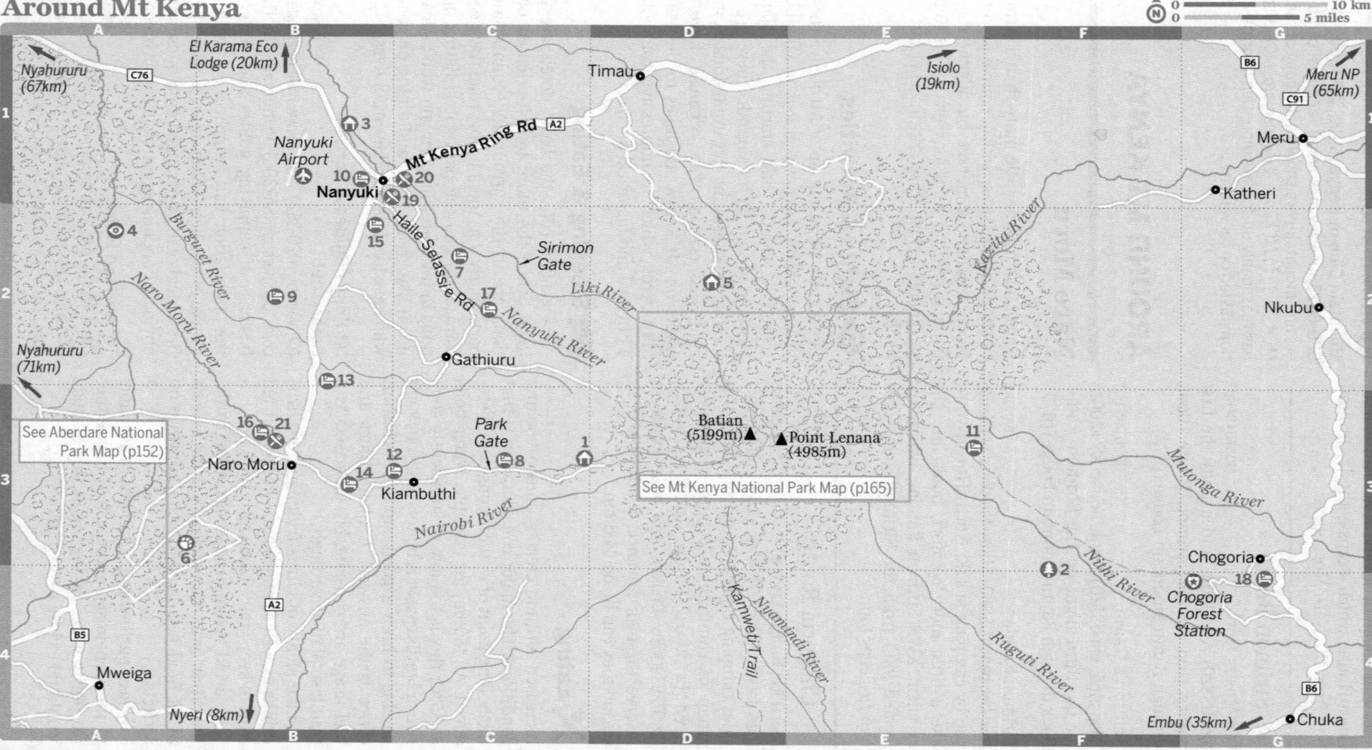

Around Mt Kenya

Sights

1 Met Station Hut C3
2 Mt Kenya Forest F3
Mt Kenya Wildlife Conservancy Animal Orphanage .... (see 12)
3 Nanyuki River Camel Camp B1
4 Ol Pejeta Conservancy A2
5 Old Moses Hut D2
6 Solio Game Reserve A3

Activities, Courses & Tours

Mt Kenya Chogoria Guides & Porters Association .... (see 18)
Mt Kenya Guides & Porters Safari Club .... (see 13)
Naro Moru River Lodge .... (see 16)

Sleeping

7 Bantu Mountain Lodge C2
8 Batian Guest House C3
9 Colobus Cottages B2
10 Kongoni Camp B1
11 Meru Mt Kenya Lodge E3
12 Mount Kenya Safari Club C3
13 Mt Kenya Guides & Porters Safari Club B2
14 Mt Kenya Leisure Lodge B3
15 Mt Kenya Royal Cottages B2
16 Naro Moru River Lodge B3
17 Sirimon Bandas C2
18 Transit Motel G4

Eating

19 Cape Chestnut B1
20 Le Rustique C1
21 Trout Tree Restaurant B3
Tusks Restaurant .... (see 12)

odd bug and a little late-night noise, you can save a packet.

★ Naro Moru River Lodge LODGE $$
(☎0708984005; www.naromoruriverlodge.com; campsites/dm US$15/30, s full board US$117-173, d & tw full board US$162-218; P📶🏊) A bit like a Swiss chalet, the River Lodge is a lovely collection of dark, cosy cottages and rooms embedded into a sloping hillside that overlooks the rushing Naro Moru River, 3km from town. All three classes of room are lovely, but the middle-of-the-road 'superior' option seems the best of the lot.

Those camping here or staying in the dorm have access to the pool, squash and tennis courts. The restaurants here are the best in town.

Bantu Mountain Lodge HOTEL $$
(Mountain Rock Lodge; ☎0722858972, 0722511752; www.mountainrockkenya.com; camping US$8, s/tw from KSh3500/5000) Formerly the Mountain Rock Lodge, this is a major base for Mt Kenya climbers and the operators of Old Moses Hut (p171) and Shipton's Camp (p171) on the mountain. There are three classes of rooms and like most hotels in this price bracket, the rooms are serviceable enough but in need of refurbishment. It's 9km north of Naro Moru, in woods that are occasionally frequented by elephants.

Colobus Cottages COTTAGES $$
(☎0722840195, 0753951720; www.colobuscottages.wordpress.com; per person KSh3500) These cottages, some almost completely enveloped by trees, are more impressive from the outside, but the simple interiors are spacious, tidy, self-contained and exceptional value. There's a fireplace in each, a barbecue area and a communal treetop bar. It's 2km off the main highway; the turn-off is 6km north of Naro Moru.

Mt Kenya Leisure Lodge HOTEL $$
(☎0715724381; www.mtkenyaleisurelodge.com; s/d from KSh4500/6930; P📶) Built in 2008 and already showing signs of wear, the spacious rooms (some with awfully frilly pink curtains and bedspreads) are in a large lodge reminiscent of an old English manor. It's a bit of rabbit warren inside but when you find it, there's a communal lounge with an open fire to fend off the chilly night air.

Mt Kenya Royal Cottages COTTAGES $$
(☎0721470008; per person from KSh3000) On a rise beside the highway, this relatively new place offers simple but well-priced cottages and a decent on-site restaurant. It's fine for a night – any longer and the proximity to the road will start to annoy. It's around 1km south of Nanyuki Airport.

★ Trout Tree Restaurant FISH $$
(☎0726281704; www.trout-tree.com; Naro Moru-Nanyuki Hwy; mains KSh750-945) Inhabiting a marvellous fig tree overlooking the Burguret River, alongside colobus monkeys and tree hyraxes, this place is one of the most original places to eat in Kenya's Central Highlands. It

doesn't do much else, but we never get tired of the trout combinations – hot smoked trout and cucumber salad, trout chowder, trout curry, tandoori trout, whole grilled trout…chargrilled is best of all.

If you're lucky, you might be able to fish for your supper and have it cooked for you afterwards. Ask about Creaky Cottage, the fabulous riverside, self-contained house that sleeps six. It's 3km south of Nanyuki Airport and well signposted off the main road.

Getting There & Away

There are plenty of buses and matatus heading to Nanyuki (KSh70, 30 minutes), Nyeri (KSh170, 45 minutes) and Nairobi (KSh500, three hours) from either the northbound or southbound 'stages'.

Meru

POP 240,900

Meru is the largest municipality in the Central Highlands and the epicentre of Kenyan production of *miraa*, a mild, leafy stimulant more widely known outside of Kenya as khat. The town itself is like a shot of the stuff: a briefly invigorating, slightly confusing head rush but you'll wonder what the point of it all was when the first effects wear off.

Sights

Meru National Museum MUSEUM
(0786559427; www.museums.or.ke; Kenyatta Hwy; adult/child KSh500/250; 8.30am-5.30pm) There's a series of faded exhibits, desultory stuffed and mounted wildlife and a small but informative section concerning the clothing, weapons, and agricultural and initiation practices (including clitoridectomies) of the Meru people. Out back is a small menagerie of disheartened animals that have had the misfortune of ending up here.

Sleeping

Blue Towers Hotel HOTEL $
(064-30309; bluetowershotel@yahoo.com; Kenyatta Hwy; s/d excl breakfast KSh2200/2700; P) The architects here have done themselves proud, managing the tricky task of incorporating both a petrol station and a couple of castlelike towers into an otherwise unmemorable building. Not to be outdone on the peculiarity stakes, the rooms all have windows facing the hall. For all that, it's pretty good budget value.

★ **Alba Hotel** HOTEL $$
(0705556677; www.albahotels.co.ke; Milimani Rd; s/d Mon-Thu US$130/160, Fri-Sun US$100/120; P@) Easily Meru's best

Meru

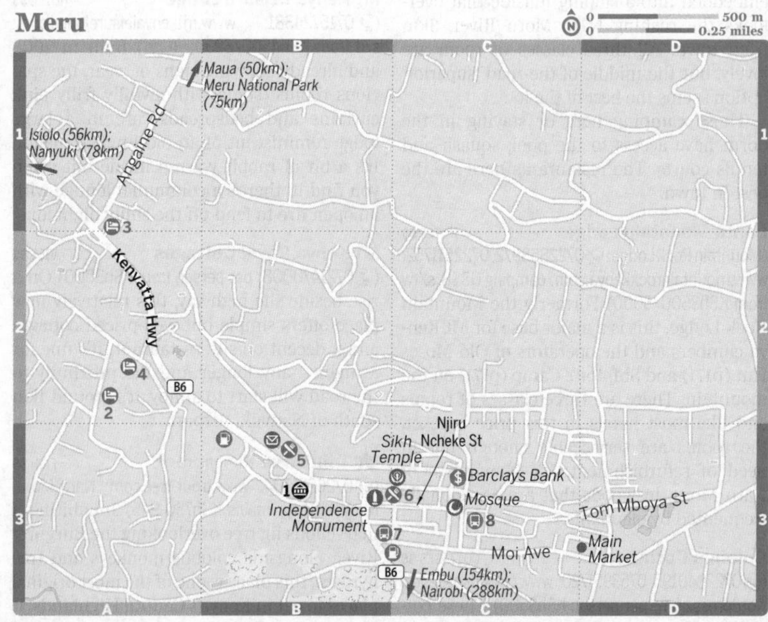

'YOU WILL BUILD CASTLES'

'What does this stuff do?' we ask our driver.

'It gives you energy. When you chew this thing, you will build castles.'

That was our introduction to *miraa*, the small shoots and leaves that are chewed throughout the Mt Kenya area and Muslim parts of the country.

Some of the best *miraa* in the world is grown around Meru. Much of the demand is from Somalia and, since *miraa*'s potency is diminished 48 hours after picking, massively overladen pick-up trucks race at breakneck speed to Wilson Airport in Nairobi for the next flight to Mogadishu – get out of their way if you see them coming.

Chewing *miraa* predates coffee drinking and is deeply rooted in the cultural traditions of some societies, especially in Muslim countries. It's usually chewed in company to encourage confidence, contentment and a flow of ideas. The active ingredient, cathinone, is closely related to amphetamine, and the euphoric effects can last for up to 24 hours, depending on how much is chewed.

Chewing too much can be habit-forming and has serious consequences, known as 'khat syndrome'. Aggressive behaviour, nightmares and hallucinations are common mental side effects, while reduced appetite, malnourishment, constipation and brown teeth are common physical consequences.

Meru is a good place for curious travellers to give *miraa* a go. It's bitter and gives a brief high, followed by a long come-down. Note that *miraa* is illegal in neighbouring Tanzania (and, more recently, the UK, which decreed it a Class C drug in June 2014), so best leave it out of the suitcase if you're heading that way.

rooms, this modern place has Western-style, Western-standard rooms with bright colours and modern furnishings. If you've only stayed here and in Nairobi, you might think this is the norm in Kenya – it's not.

Meru Slopes Hotel HOTEL $$
(0711620219; off Meru–Nairobi Hwy; r US$65-100; P @) A good choice in the town centre, Meru Slopes Hotel is behind the Nakumatt supermarket. It gets consistently good reviews from travellers – it's the sort of place that you won't remember years from now but won't hesitate to recommend it to others.

Eating & Drinking

Meru County Hotel KENYAN, INTERNATIONAL $
(Kenyatta Hwy; meals KSh350-800; 8am-9pm) Thatched umbrellas hover over each table on this pretty *nyama choma* terrace. If you want to give the flaming flesh a rest, try the Western, Kenyan and Indian meals on offer.

Royal Prince KENYAN $
(Tom Mboya St; mains KSh250-450; noon-10pm) There are two storeys of bustling eating goodness at this cheap hotel. The downstairs restaurant specialises in all things fried, while upstairs houses the '*choma* zone', where half a kilo of grilled flesh costs KSh450.

Getting There & Away

All transport leaves from the area between the main mosque and the market at the eastern end of the town centre.

You'll find regular bus departures throughout the day from 6.45am onwards to Embu (KSh400, two hours), Thika (KSh400, 3½ hours) and Nairobi (KSh500, five hours). There's also at least one late-afternoon departure to Mombasa (KSh1600, 12 hours).

Regular matatus also serve Nairobi (KSh750, four hours), Thika (KSh650, 3½ hours), Embu

Meru

Sights
1 Meru National Museum B3

Sleeping
2 Alba Hotel A2
3 Blue Towers Hotel A1
4 Meru Slopes Hotel A2

Eating
5 Meru County Hotel B3
6 Royal Prince C3

Transport
7 Matatu Stand B3
8 Matatu Stand C3

(KSh450, two hours), Nanyuki (KSh350, 1½ hours) and Isiolo (KSh300, 1½ hours).

Meru National Park

Welcome to one of Kenya's most underrated parks. Marred by serious poaching in the 1980s and the subsequent murder of George Adamson (of *Born Free* fame) in 1989, Meru National Park fell off the tourist map and has never quite managed to get back on. This is a pity, because it has all the essential ingredients for a classic safari destination, with some fine accommodation, excellent prospects for seeing lions and rhinos, and a landscape that incorporates Hemingway-esque green hills, arid, Tsavo-like savannah and fast-flowing streams bordered by riverine forests, baobab trees and doum palms. The advantage of being one of Kenya's best-kept secrets is plain to see – you're likely to have much of it all to yourself.

Other wildlife highlights include the endangered Grevy's zebra, but we were thwarted in our attempts to track down what the KWS website describes as a 'puff udder'.

Sights & Activities

Although a large **park** (061-2303094, Nairobi 020-2310443; www.kws.org; adult/child US$75/40; 6am-6pm) covering 870 sq km, most of the wildlife action is concentrated in the northern sector of the park. The triangle of largely open savannah between **Mururi Swamp**, **Leopard Rock Swamp** and **Mughwango Swamp** is easily the park's happiest hunting ground for lions and the herbivores they stalk.

> **MERU NATIONAL PARK**
>
> **Why Go** A pristine, seldom-visited park with rhinos and lions where you'll be guaranteed a 'congestion-free' experience.
>
> **When to Go** Because it falls within Mt Kenya's eastern rain shadow, the park is accessible year-round with a 4WD.
>
> **Practicalities** There is no public transport within the park but self-drive safaris are possible as park road junctions are numbered on the ground and labelled on park maps.
>
> **Budget Tips** Stay outside the park and try to join a larger group, perhaps from Ikweta Safari Camp.

The park's most significant waterway, **Rojewero River**, is a reliable place to view **hippos** and **crocodiles**. To the south you may want to check out **Elsa's Grave**, a stone memorial to the Adamson's star lioness. Access to the adjacent **Kora National Park** is via the bridge near **Adamson's Falls**.

Rhino Sanctuary NATIONAL PARK
(6am-6pm) A signposted hard right not long after entering Murera gate takes you to Meru's 48-sq-km Rhino Sanctuary, one of the best places in Kenya to see wild rhinos. At last count, this fenced portion of the park was home to 24 black and 56 white rhinos, many of whom were reintroduced here from Lake Nakuru National Park after the disastrous poaching of the '80s.

Sleeping

★**Ikweta Safari Camp** TENTED CAMP $$
(0705200050; www.ikwetasafaricamp.com; s/d full board US$100/165;) Opened in late 2011, this terrific place is outside the park, 2.5km from Murera gate on the road in from Meru, but you can be inside the park in minutes. The semiluxurious tents (with wi-fi) are outrageously good value and put to shame many tented camps that charge so much more for so much less. The food here is another highlight and Susana and John are engaging hosts.

The more-than-300 indigenous plants need a little time to mature, but when they do, this place will be even better. The name '*ikweta*' is Swahili for 'equator'.

Kinna Bandas BANDA $$
(061-2303094; www.kws.go.ke; bandas US$80;) These three *bandas* each sleep two and are stocked with kerosene lanterns that add the right romanticism to a star-studded bush night. Located in the heart of the park, you can't get closer to the wildlife without the risk of being eaten by it. There's also a 10-bed guesthouse (US$250), and one four-bed cottage (US$160).

Murera Bandas BANDA $$
(061-2303094; www.kws.go.ke; bandas US$80) The Murera camp, overflowing with plain wooden cottages and huts, isn't as charming as Kinna's, but it's a fine place to doss if everything is booked up. There's one two-bed *banda* with a TV, and six three-bed *bandas*.

Meru National Park

★**Elsa's Kopje** BANDA $$$
(☎0730127000; www.elsaskopje.com; s/d full board from US$648/1080;) Plenty of hotels claim to blend into their environment, but Elsa's did so in such a seamless manner that the bar on chic ecosuites was permanently raised. Carved into Mughwango Hill, these highly individualised 'three-walled' rooms open out onto views *The Lion King* animators would have killed for. Stone-hewn infinity pools plunge over the clifftops, while rock hyraxes play tag in your private garden.

These features come with intense luxury pampering, wildlife drives, walking safaris and an utterly marvellous sense of being in a stunning, exclusive, remote corner of wildest Africa.

Leopard Rock Lodge LODGE $$$
(☎Nairobi 0733333100, Nairobi 020-600031; www.leopardmico.com; per person full board US$240;) This beautiful unfenced lodge lets the wildlife right in; keep an eye on your possessions, as the baboons and/or Sykes' monkeys will nick your stuff. Accommodation is in massive yet extremely comfortable *bandas*, the food is good and the location puts you right in the heart of the wildlife action.

Information

Entrance to Meru National Park also entitles you to enter the adjacent Kora National Park, although visits into Kora must be prearranged with Meru's warden at the park headquarters.

The KWS *Meru National Park* map (KSh500), sometimes sold at the park gates, is essential if you want to find your way around. Even so you may want to hire a guide (six-hour/full-day tour KSh2000/4000).

Getting There & Away

Airkenya (☎Nairobi 020-3916000; www.airkenya.com; adult/child one way US$252/186) Twice-daily flights connecting Meru to Nairobi's Wilson Airport.

J Kirimi Safaris (☎0721683700; safari@bestkenyasafari.com) John Kirimi of J Kirimi Safaris, a small safari operator, sometimes has a 4WD based in Maua (a small town 31km from the main gate). A full-day safari, including pick-up and drop-off at Meru town, costs around US$150.

Chogoria

POP 6264

This town shares its name with the most difficult route up Mt Kenya. It's a friendly enough place but unless you're trekking, there's no real reason to stop here.

MERU'S LION STARS

When Joy Adamson wrote *Born Free* on her experience raising an orphaned lion cub called Elsa, few predicted the book would spend 13 weeks at the top of the *New York Times* best-seller list and go on to inspire a film that would become a worldwide hit.

Elsa, along with her two sisters, was orphaned when Joy's husband, George Adamson, was forced to kill their mother in self-defence while tracking a man-eater. But unlike her siblings, who were sent to European zoos, Elsa, the weakest of the litter, was kept by the Adamsons, who then spent two years educating her in the ways of lions before successfully releasing her into the wilds of what is today Meru National Park.

The story of freed lions was not, unfortunately, always so simple, and one of Adamson's formerly captive lions, Boy, who starred in the movie, mauled Adamson's assistant to death and Adamson was forced to shoot the lion. Similar maulings occurred with other lions.

Even so, it was the success of Elsa's rehabilitation that inspired John Rendall and Ace Bourke to have their own lion, Christian (www.alioncalledchristian.com.au), shipped to George Adamson's camp in 1969 in the hope that he too could be returned to the wild. Christian was originally bought from Harrods department store and lived in a London basement below their furniture shop. On learning that Christian had been successfully acclimatised, the boys returned to Kenya and their reunion with Christian was filmed for a 1971 documentary.

More than 30 years later, edited footage of this reunion went viral on YouTube. It's a real tear jerker, especially the part when Christian first recognises his old friends and comes bounding down a rocky slope and literally leaps into their arms, almost knocking the boys off their feet in a 150kg bundle of furry, lion love.

Sleeping & Eating

Transit Motel MOTEL $

(☎064-22096, 0721973133; www.transitmotelchogoria.com; camping with/without own tent KSh300/500, s/d/tr KSh1400/2400/2800) If you haven't arranged your accommodation with one of the many touts offering Mt Kenya climbs, head to Transit Motel, 2km south of town. This is a large, friendly lodge with pleasant rooms (some with small balconies) and a decent restaurant (meals KSh650). Mt Kenya Chogoria Guides and Porters Association (p167) is also based here.

Getting There & Away

Chogoria is 3km off the main B6 drag. In all likelihood an express matatu will drop you at either the Kiriani (southern) junction or the Kirurumwe (northern) junction, from where you will have to catch a *boda-boda* (motorcycle taxi) to town. Sample fares include Meru (KSh220, one hour), Embu (KSh300, 1½ hours) and Nairobi (KSh500, four hours).

Embu

POP 35,736

This sleepy town is the unlikely capital of Eastern Province, but despite its local significance there's not a lot to do, and it's a long way from the mountain. The only reason to pass through is en route between Meru and Nairobi along the quieter back road. The town is at its best around October/November, when the local jacaranda trees are in full, purple bloom.

Sleeping & Eating

Maina Highway Hotel HOTEL $

(☎068-31789, 0722827700; www.mainahighwayhotel.com; off Meru–Nairobi Hwy; s/d KSh1500/2000) Utterly unpromising from the outside, this simple place is the pick of the budget options. Rooms have mosquito nets and the central location is ideal, although noise can be a problem.

Izaak Walton Inn Hotel HOTEL $$

(☎0712781810; www.izaakwaltoninn.co.ke; Embu–Meru Rd; per person US$40-62;) Set in a mature garden on the northern edge of town, this once-fine establishment is running down fast and is in urgent need of renovations or, at the very least, some maintenance and tender loving care. Rooms are promising but many seem not to have been fussed over in a while.

Panesic Hotel INTERNATIONAL $

(mains KSh500-700; ⊙7am-9pm) The food here is great value and only a few shillings more than the town's cheap eateries. The steaks come with a soup starter, mounds

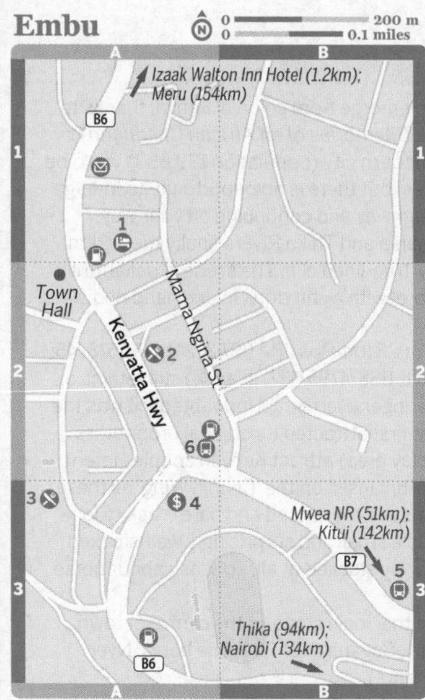

Embu

Sleeping

1 Maina Highway Hotel A1

Eating

2 Bomas Roasters & Pub A2
3 Panesic Hotel A3

Information

4 Barclays Bank A3

Transport

5 Bus & Matatu Stand B3
6 Buses A2

of vegies and *starch* (their phrasing) of your choice. The tri-coloured fruit cocktail is a vitamin-packed treat of layered avocado, mango and something-red juice. There is also a BBQ deck near the pool serving *nyama choma* and beer.

Bomas Roasters & Pub PUB $
(Kenyatta Hwy; mains KSh250-550; noon-10pm) From the 2nd-floor terrace, diners are afforded unadulterated views of downtown Embu, complete with acrid diesel fumes and views of the slightly depressing independence statue. Beers flow freely and good slabs of roast goat and *ugali* (a staple made from maize or cassava flour, or both) round out the experience.

Getting There & Away

Some buses call into the Shell petrol station in the centre of town on their way to and from Nairobi and Mombasa.

There are numerous matatus serving Chogoria (KSh300, 1½ hours), Meru (KSh450, two hours), Thika (KSh300, two hours), Nyeri (KSh320, two hours), Nanyuki (KSh400, 3½ hours), Nyahururu (KSh600, five hours), Nairobi (KSh400, three hours) and Nakuru (KS750, six hours).

Mwea National Reserve

In contrast to the rich greens that characterise so much of the highlands, this reserve is set in a dry depression that is nonetheless beautiful in a stony-scarp, thorn-bush and aloe-field kind of way. **Kamburu Dam**, at the meeting point of the Tana and Thiba Rivers, forms the focus for the 48-sq-km **Mwea National Reserve** (Nairobi 020-2052727; www.kws.go.ke; adult/child US$25/15; 6am-7pm). Enclosed by an electric fence, elephants, hippos, crocodiles, buffaloes, lesser kudus and endangered Rothschild giraffes are present here, as well as more than 200 bird species.

Sleeping

Public Campsite CAMPGROUND
(camping US$20) Mwea's most accessible campsite has the most basic facilities (no water) and is close to the reserve headquarters.

Hippo Point Public Campsite CAMPGROUND
(camping US$20) Little more than a open space cleared for camping, this campsite is basic but in a good location close to Hippo Point.

Getting There & Away

Mwea is best accessed from the 11km dirt road that's signposted off the B7 Hwy some 40km south of Embu. There's a signposted 27km dirt track to the park that's 14km south of Embu, but the going is very rough. A 4WD is essential to get to Mwea and around the park.

WORTH A TRIP

THIKA

Thika is one of the most recognisable names to emerge from colonial Kenya, thanks to the eloquent memoir *The Flame Trees of Thika (Memories of an African Childhood)* by Elspeth Huxley. These days, in this sprawling modern city (population 139,853) you'd be hard-pressed to find a tree, let alone a flame tree, but there is an opportunity to indulge in a little nostalgia before getting back on the highway and continuing on your way.

Both children of the Aberdare Range, the Chania and Thika Rivers finally meet 2km north of **town**, where they tumble over a rocky, tree-lined cliff. The scene is delightfully appreciated from the porch of the Blue Post Hotel with a stiff drink in one hand and a book in the other.

With a history that outdates the town itself, the **Blue Post** (067-22241, 0721578245; blueposthotel@africaonline.co.ke; Muranga Rd; s/d/tr US$74/95/132; P @) still retains a faint whiff of the colonial for those who want to linger overnight. Undoubtedly it was the prime location, opposite Thika's waterfalls, that first attracted its original proprietors in 1908. Today, the grounds (with a children's play area) attract Kenyan couples intent on tying the knot in all their polyester glory. Our tip: insist on the 'Chania Wing' as these rooms have views to the falls, although all rooms are overpriced and bare – ask to look at a few. Also located within the hotel grounds is a small and surprisingly well-stocked **craft village** and an equally surprising, but hardly stocked at all, **zoo**; ask about horse and ostrich rides.

Thika's steady stream of matatus leave from the 'main stage' in the centre of town. Destinations include Nairobi (KSh150, one hour), Sagana (KSh200, one hour), Nyeri (KSh300, two hours) and Embu (KSh300, 1½ hours).

Ol Donyo Sabuk National Park

The tiny **Ol Donyo Sabuk National Park** (Nairobi 020-2062503, Nairobi 020-600800; www.kws.go.ke; adult/child US$25/15; 6am-7pm) covers little more than 20 sq km and is built around the summit and slopes of **Ol Donyo Sabuk** (2146m), known by the Kikuyu as Kilimambongo (Buffalo Mountain). The name fits, as buffaloes are one of the few animals that you may actually encounter here, aside from primates such as baboons, colobus monkeys and Sykes' monkeys in the montane forest that covers all but the hill's summit.

Because of the death-by-buffalo-attack threat, it is only possible to explore on foot if accompanied by a ranger (per half-/full day KSh2000/4000). We found its signature 9km hike (three or four hours) to the summit on a dirt road to be disappointing and the views, while impressive, are slowly getting obscured by mobile-phone towers. More interesting was the weird Afro-alpine fauna that crowns the summit and which you'd otherwise have to climb Mt Kenya to see.

Sleeping

Public Campsite CAMPGROUND
(www.kws.co.ke; camping US$25) There's a pretty campsite just before the main gate. Facilities include one long-drop toilet, a rusty tap and free firewood.

Sabuk House BANDA $
(Nairobi 020-600800; www.kws.go.ke; 10-bed houses US$300) The most comfortable option in Ol Donyo Sabuk, this comfortable KWS *banda* is a little rundown but excellent value if you've enough people in your party to bring down per-person costs.

Getting There & Away

From Thika, take the same matatu you would for Fourteen Falls but continue to the village of Ol Donyo Sabuk (KSh150, 50 minutes), from where it's a 2km walk along a straight dirt road to the gate.

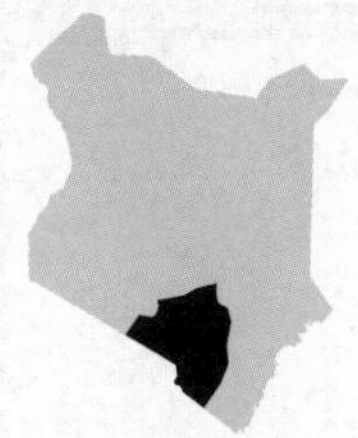

Southeastern Kenya

Includes ➡

Best of Nature

- Tsavo West National Park (p189)
- Tsavo East National Park (p196)
- Amboseli National Park (p183)
- Taita Hills Wildlife Sanctuary (p199)
- Mbulia Conservancy (p195)

Best Places to Stay

- Ol Donyo (p186)
- Campi ya Kanzi (p187)
- Tortilis Camp (p184)
- Rhino Valley Lodge (p193)
- Sarova Salt Lick Safari Lodge (p200)

Why Go?

Southern Kenya is one of the great wildlife-watching destinations in Africa. Here you'll find the triumvirate of epic Kenyan parks – Amboseli, Tsavo West and Tsavo East – that are home to the Big Five (lions, elephants, rhinos, leopards and buffaloes) and so much more. Big cats roam in relative abundance and large-tusked elephants pass by close enough to touch. It's all set against the backdrop of Africa's highest mountain, Mt Kilimanjaro, and a stirring backstory of wildlife surviving against the odds.

The region is also the scene for so many exciting initiatives that combine conservation with community engagement, and many of these ensure that the chances to get to know the Maasai – the soulful human inhabitants of this land – on equal terms are higher here than perhaps anywhere else in Kenya. In short, this is Kenya at its wildest and yet most accessible.

When to Go

Voi

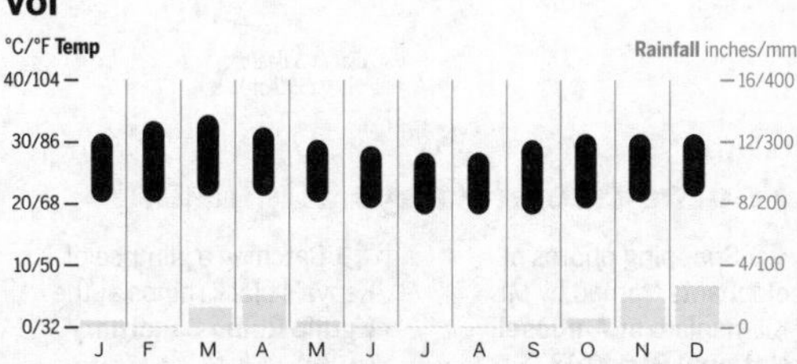

Jul–Oct Far from the Masai Mara, this is prime time for watching wildlife in southern Kenyan parks.

Nov–Feb Good for wildlife and birdwatching; November rains are a minor inconvenience.

Mar–May Rains here can make roads impassable and wildlife strays beyond Amboseli.

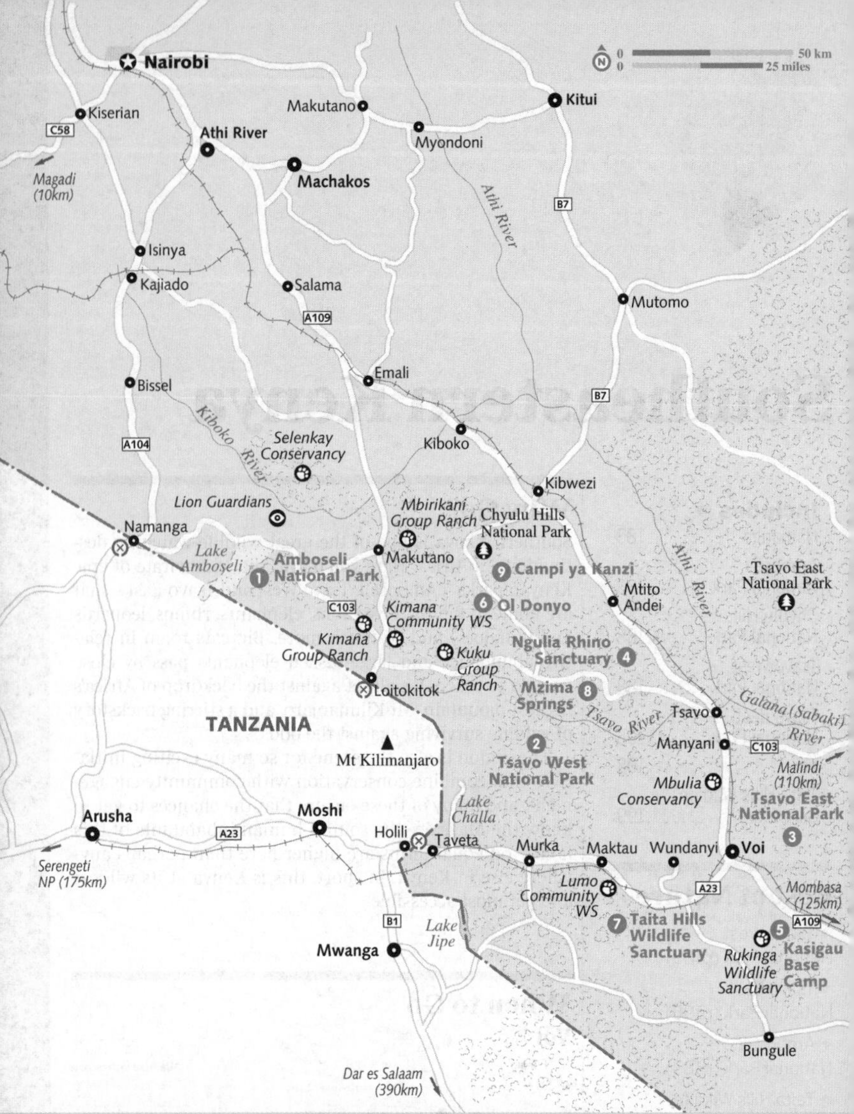

Southeastern Kenya Highlights

1. Snapping photos of elephants framed by Mt Kilimanjaro at **Amboseli National Park** (p183)
2. Roaming the wilderness in search of leopards in **Tsavo West National Park** (p189)
3. Braving lions and red elephants in the back country of **Tsavo East National Park** (p196)
4. Catching a glimpse of Kenya's black rhinos at the **Ngulia Rhino Sanctuary** (p189)
5. Getting your hands dirty while saving the forests at **Kasigau Base Camp** (p198)
6. Contemplating Maasailand's vast sweep from the heights of luxury at **Ol Donyo** (p186)
7. Learning about the region's WWI past at **Taita Hills Wildlife Sanctuary** (p199)
8. Spotting hippos, crocs and giant kingfishers at pristine **Mzima Springs** (p189)
9. Walking up into the Chyulu Hills in the company of a Maasai warrior at **Campi ya Kanzi** (p187)

SOUTH TO TANZANIA

Heading south from Nairobi, the A104 runs straight to the Tanzanian border en route to Arusha (Tanzania).

Namanga

The town of Namanga sits adjacent to one of the busiest border crossings in East Africa. That said, it has a surprisingly relaxed atmosphere away from the frontier itself. The border crossing is open 24 hours and the two posts are only a few hundred metres apart, so you can walk across. Money changers do a brisk trade on the Kenyan side of the border; don't believe anyone who says you can't take Kenyan shillings into Tanzania or vice versa!

Sleeping

Namanga River Hotel HOTEL $
(0724041375, 0721396851; www.riverhotelnamanga.blogspot.com; camping KSh750, s/d from KSh4000/5200; P) For one last night in Kenya or to otherwise break up your travels, consider this shady campsite that offers an attractive clutch of cabins that lie between basic and simple.

There's also a decent bar-restaurant that's often frequented by overland truck travellers.

Getting There & Away

Buses between Nairobi and Arusha pass through daily (KSh400 to KSh750, two hours). Matatus (minibus transport) and Peugeots (shared taxis) also run here from the junction of River Rd and Ronald Ngala St in Nairobi (KSh500).

On the Tanzanian side of the border, nine-seater minivans run from the border to Arusha (two hours).

SOUTHEAST TO TSAVO

Kenya's southeastern corner, set back from the coast, includes three of the country's most prestigious parks – Amboseli, Tsavo West and Tsavo East. Together, the latter two account for almost 4% of Kenya's surface area.

Less well known but nonetheless rewarding are the private, often community-run wildlife sanctuaries that lie beyond park borders, particularly around the picturesque Taita Hills.

Amboseli National Park

Amboseli belongs in the elite of Kenya's national parks, and it's easy to see why. Its signature attraction is the sight of hundreds of big-tusked elephants set against the backdrop of Africa's best views of Mt Kilimanjaro (5895m). Africa's highest peak broods over the southern boundary of the park, and while cloud cover can render the mountain's massive bulk invisible for much of the day, you'll be rewarded with stunning vistas when the weather clears, usually at dawn and/or dusk. Apart from guaranteed elephant sightings, you'll also see wildebeest and zebras, and you've a reasonable chance of spotting lions and hyenas. The park is also home to over 370 bird species.

Sights & Activities

The **park's** (0722992619, 0716493335, Nairobi 020-8029705; www.kws.org/parks/parks_reserves/AMNP; adult/child US$80/40; 6am-6pm) permanent swamps of **Enkongo Narok**, **Olokenya** and **Longinye** create a marshy belt across the middle of the park and this is where you'll encounter the most wildlife. Elephants love to wallow around in the muddy waters and you've a good chance of seeing hippos around the edge. For really close-up elephant encounters, **Sinet Causeway**, which crosses Enkongo Narok near Observation Hill, is often good. The surrounding grasslands are home to grazing antelope, zebras and wildebeest, with spotted hyenas, cheetahs and lions sometimes lurking nearby. Birdlife is especially rich in these swamps when the migrants arrive in November and stay until March.

Normatior (Observation Hill) LOOKOUT
This pyramid-shaped hill is one of the only places in the park where you can get out and walk. The summit provides an ideal lookout from which to orientate yourself to the plains, swamps and roads below. The views from here are also pretty special, whether south to Kilimanjaro or east across the swamps. Wildlife is generally a fair way off, but the views here put them in their context.

Sinet Delta LAKE
From Observation Hill, the northern route runs across the Sinet Delta, which is an excellent place for birdwatching. The vegetation is thicker the further south you go, providing fodder for giraffes and also framing some of the park's best Kilimanjaro views.

AMBOSELI NATIONAL PARK

Why Go To see big-tusked elephants, Africa's best Mt Kilimanjaro views, lions, wildebeest and zebras, and rich birdlife.

When to Go Year-round. The dry season (May to October and January to March) is best for spotting wildlife, while November to March is the best time to see migratory birds. Much of the wildlife moves beyond the park during and immediately after the rains.

Practicalities Drive in from Nairobi or Mombasa; flying is also possible.

Budget Tips Camp at a public campsite inside the park, or one of the private camps outside Kimana Gate.

Lake Amboseli LAKE
Away to the northwest from the delta, this 'lake' occupies a large swath of the park, but it's usually bone dry, except after extended rains. At other times it's worth a journey out here if you've time to spare, not least because few vehicles make it out this way.

Kimana Gate NATIONAL PARK
If you're taking the road that runs east across the park to the Kimana gate, watch for giraffes in the acacia woodlands; this is the best place inside the park for giraffe spotting. Here you may also find gerenuks, an unusual breed of gazelle that 'browse' by standing on their hind legs and stretching their necks, as if yearning to be giraffes. There are numerous lodges and campsites just outside the gate, while the unpaved road continues on to Tsavo West National Park.

Elephant Research Camp WILDLIFE RESERVE
(0714781699; www.elephanttrust.org; group of 10 or less US$800, group of more than 10 per person US$80; by prior appointment 3.30pm Mon-Fri) The elephants of Amboseli are among the most studied in the world, thanks largely to the work of Dr Cynthia Moss, whose books include *The Amboseli Elephants* and *Elephant Memories;* she was also behind the famous documentary DVD *Echo of the Elephants*. The research camp remains in operation in the heart of the park, under the guidance of the **Amboseli Trust for Elephants** (www.elephanttrust.org).

Although the camp is not open for casual visits, it is possible, with prior arrangement, to arrange a one-hour lecture at the camp, during which the researchers explain their work and other related issues of elephant conservation, with time for questions at the end. The visit doesn't come cheap. But this is one of the mother lodes for elephant research in Africa and a visit here is a rare opportunity to learn more about these soulful creatures. Bookings can be made via the Contact Us page of the website.

Sleeping & Eating

Inside the Park

KWS Campsite CAMPGROUND $
(www.kws.org; camping US$30) Just inside the southern boundary of the park, the Kenya Wildlife Service (KWS) campsite has toilets, an unreliable water supply (bring your own) and a small bar selling warm beer and soft drinks. It's fenced off from the wildlife, so you can walk around safely at night, though *don't* keep food in your tent, as baboons visit during the day looking for an uninvited feed.

★**Tortilis Camp** TENTED CAMP $$$
(045-622195; www.tortilis.com; s/d full board US$522/870, family tent US$1740, private house US$2175; P) This wonderfully conceived site is one of the most exclusive ecolodges in Kenya, commanding a superb elevated spot with perfect Kilimanjaro vistas. The luxurious canvas tents have recently been given a facelift; the family rooms have the biggest wow factor we found in southern Kenya. The lavish meals, which are based on north Italian traditional recipes, feature herbs and vegetables from the huge on-site organic garden.

★**Ol Tukai Lodge** LODGE $$$
(045-622275, Nairobi 020-4445514; www.oltukailodge.com; s/d full board US$350/450; P@) Lying at the heart of Amboseli, on the edge of a dense acacia forest, Ol Tukai is a splendidly refined lodge with soaring *makuti* (thatched roofs of palm leaves) and tranquil gardens defined by towering trees. Accommodation is in wooden chalets, which are brought to life with vibrant zebra prints, while the split-level bar has a sweeping view of Kili and a pervading atmosphere of peace and luxury.

Amboseli National Park

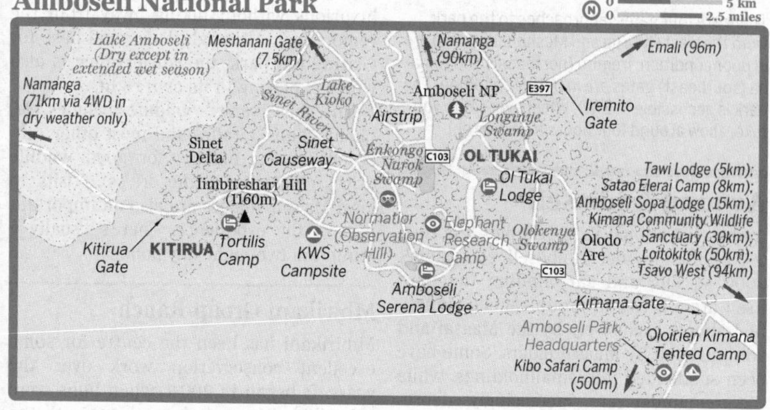

Amboseli Serena Lodge LODGE $$$
(☎0735522361, Nairobi 020-2842000; www.serenahotels.com; s/d US$285/386; @📶🏊) An elegant property in Amboseli, the Serena comprises of fiery red adobe cottages, some (rooms 68 to 75) overlook the wildlife-rich Enkongo Narok swamp and are fringed by lush tropical gardens of blooming flowers and manicured shrubs. There are no Kilimanjaro views from the lodge. Service is excellent.

Outside the Park

Oloirien Kimana Tented Camp CAMPGROUND $
(☎0720951500; per person tents/bandas KSh2500/3000; P) Just outside the park boundaries, 2.8km south of the Kimana gate, this camp is bare and dusty but friendly, with basic tents and simple *bandas* (thatched roof huts) with cold showers. There's a kitchen for DIY cooking.

★ **Tawi Lodge** LODGE $$$
(☎0722745552, Nairobi 020-2300943; www.tawilodge.com; s/d full board US$530/820; P📶🏊) Set on its own private 24-sq-km (6000-acre) conservancy close to Kimana gate and with its own airstrip, Tawi Lodge is our pick of the places southeast of the park. You've the choice of going into Amboseli or exploring Tawi's own wildlife-rich area, while the cottages are refined, beautifully furnished and most come with fine Kili views. There's even an on-site spa and night drives are possible.

Satao Elerai Camp TENTED CAMP $$$
(☎Nairobi 020-2434600; www.sataoelerai.com; s/d full board US$408/546; P📶🏊) The five lodge rooms are all well and good (and they are indeed very good), but we love this place for its nine supremely comfortable tents, each of which has its own private verandah and fabulous Kilimanjaro views when the weather's clear. It's signposted off the main track in from Loitokitok, and is around 10km from Kimana gate.

Kibo Safari Camp TENTED CAMP $$$
(☎0721380539; www.kibosafaricamp.com; per person from US$160; P) Around 2km from Kimana gate, Kibo Safari Camp gives you the experience of a tented camp without asking the prohibitive fees of the lodges. The tents, and indeed the whole property, could do with an overhaul, but it's a good deal that enables you to be inside the park soon after sunrise.

Amboseli Sopa Lodge LODGE $$$
(☎Nairobi 020-3750460; www.sopalodges.com; s/d US$223/314; P@📶🏊) Located 15km outside the park boundaries on the road to Tsavo West National Park, the Sopa Lodge offers clay huts that are decked out in safari spreads and a healthy smattering of Kenyan curios. You're a fair way from the park, and service is not quite up there with other top-end places, but nor are the prices.

Getting There & Away

AIR

Airkenya (www.airkenya.com; one way from $175) Has daily flights between Nairobi's Wilson Airport and Amboseli. You'll need to arrange with one of the lodges or a safari company for a vehicle to meet you at the airstrip, which is northwest of Ol Tukai.

CAR & 4WD

There are four gates; approaches to the park from the west (Kitirua and Meshanani gates) are in poor condition, Iremito (northeast) and Kimana (southeast) gates are in better condition. The park is accessible in 2WD. Whichever route you take, allow around four hours from Nairobi.

Around Amboseli

Amboseli National Park occupies less than 5% of the broader Amboseli ecosystem's 8000 sq km, and surrounding the park itself are a series of group ranches inhabited almost exclusively by the Maasai and administered by Maasai elders. Some have been subdivided into smallholdings, while the remainder are increasingly densely populated – by one estimate, around 30,000 Maasai live in the Amboseli ecosystem, along with upwards of a million of their livestock.

The ecosystem lies in Mount Kilimanjaro's rain shadow and the barren plains that emanate out from the park's swamps are typical of the region. The name 'Amboseli', after all, is a translation of the Maa word '*empusal*' which means 'salty dust' or 'barren place'. Droughts here hit hard – the heartbreaking scene of a dying baby elephant filmed as part of the BBC's *Africa* series was filmed in Amboseli.

This may be important for many reasons, but as it concerns wildlife it's worth remembering that the park effectively empties of wildlife during the rainy season when elephants, lions and all manner of species disperse out into the ecosystem, potentially bringing the wildlife into conflict with human populations. These ranches also occupy the ancient wildlife corridors that once connected Amboseli with northern Tanzania, the Athi Plains near Nairobi and even the Masai Mara.

At the same time, it is on these group ranches that some of the most exciting conservation work in Kenya is taking place.

Selenkay Conservancy

Far removed from the tourist lodges in the park itself, the deliciously remote **Porini Amboseli Camp** (☎0722509200, Nairobi 020-7123129; www.porini.com; per person incl full board from US$370; Ⓟ) inhabits the 748-sq-km Selenkay Conservancy (also known as Eselenkei Group Ranch) north of the national park. The tents are semi-luxurious without taking away from the remote feel. Although it's a good base for visiting the park, the conservancy is also worth exploring in its own right.

The conservancy's wildlife includes elephants, lions, giraffes and most other Amboseli species, making for good wildlife drives (including night drives). Visits to local Maasai villages are also an important part of the experience. There's usually a minimum two-night stay policy.

Mbirikani Group Ranch

Mibirikani has been the centre for some excellent conservation work over the years. It began in 2004 (when lions were being killed in record numbers) with the Predator Compensation Fund (PCF), a scheme run by the **Masailand Preservation Trust** (www.maasailand.wildlifedirect.org). Designed to reduce human-wildlife conflict by paying monetary compensation to local Maasai herders for livestock killed by predators, the PCF is largely credited with turning the situation around.

Another important initiative is the **Big Life Foundation** (www.biglife.org), which operates a paramilitary force of armed rangers who patrol the area to combat poaching. Run by veteran conservationist Richard Bonham, Big Life is widely touted as the reason why the poaching of elephants and rhinos – there's a small population of the latter on the western slopes of the Chyulu Hills – has largely passed Amboseli by.

Sleeping

★Ol Donyo LODGE $$$

(☎Nairobi 020-600457; www.greatplainsconservation.com; per person US$595-910; Ⓟ) Welcome to what could just be our favourite place to stay in Kenya. Built onto the foothills of Chyulu Hills at the remote eastern reaches of the 1113-sq-km (275,000-acre) Mbirikani Group Ranch, Ol Donyo is a temple to good taste grafted onto one of the loveliest corners of Africa.

The lodge is built entirely of local materials and employs advanced water recycling and solar-power systems. The rooms, each overlooking their own waterhole, are expansive and utterly gorgeous in both their scope and detail: private plunge pools, divinely comfortable four-poster beds with Kilimanjaro views, complete privacy and

LION GUARDIANS

Because lions are the easiest of the big cats to observe, few people realise that lions face an extremely uncertain future. A century ago, more than 200,000 lions roamed Africa. Now, fewer than 30,000 are thought to remain and lions have disappeared from 80% of their historical range, according to **Panthera** (www.panthera.org), the world's leading cat conservation NGO. In Kenya, lion numbers have reached critical levels: less than 2000 lions are thought to remain in the country. Fewer than 100 of these inhabit the Amboseli ecosystem and around half of these (many more in the rainy season) live outside park boundaries, sharing the land with the Maasai and their herds of livestock.

In Maasai culture, young male warriors (the *morran*) have traditionally killed lions and other wild animals to prove their bravery and as an initiation rite into manhood. But one organisation has come up with an innovative way of honouring Maasai tradition while protecting lions in the process. The **Lion Guardians** (www.lionguardians.org) has taken many of these young, traditional warriors and turned them into Lion Guardians, whose task is to protect the Maasai and the lions from each other. Each Lion Guardian, most of whom are former lion killers, patrols a territory, keeping track of the lions, and warning herders of lion locations and helping them to find lost livestock and even lost children. In areas where the Lion Guardians operate, lion-killings (and livestock lost to lions) have fallen dramatically.

roof beds are merely the beginning of an overwhelming sensory experience that takes safari chic to a whole new level. The meals are world-class as well.

Day or night wildlife drives are, of course, possible, but so, too, are walking safaris out onto the plains or up onto the Chyulu Hills, horse-riding safaris and even running safaris for those eager not to let their exercise regimen slip.

Kuku & Kimana Group Ranches

These ranches at the eastern end of the Amboseli ecosystem are crucially important corridors for wildlife moving between Tsavo West and Amboseli National Parks. Wildlife can be quite plentiful in this area, especially at the Tsavo West end of the corridor.

Kuku in particular is the base for the **Maasai Wilderness Conservation Trust** (www.maasaiwilderness.org), which is run partly out of Campi ya Kanzi and has Hollywood star Edward Norton as the president of its US board of directors.

The trust works closely with local communities in protecting these important wildlife habitats and corridors through programs such as Simba Scouts (local Maasai rangers), environmental education, and Wildlife Pays (payments are made to local communities for the wildlife that lives on their land, instead of paying compensation for livestock losses after the fact).

Sights

Maasai Cattle Market MARKET
(Tue) If you're in the Amboseli area on a Tuesday, consider stopping in the town of Kimana (along the paved road between Emali and Loitokitok) for its weekly Maasai livestock market.

Kimana Community Wildlife Sanctuary WILDLIFE RESERVE
(admission US$30) On Kimana Group Ranch, around halfway between Amboseli and Chyulu Hills National Parks, the 40-hectare Kimana Wildlife Sanctuary protects an impressive concentration of plains wildlife. More importantly, any money spent here directly supports the local community. Established in 1996 by United States Agency for International Development (USAID) and KWS, the sanctuary is now owned and managed by local Maasai.

Kimana is about 30km east of Amboseli, just off the road heading to Tsavo West National Park.

Sleeping

★**Campi ya Kanzi** TENTED CAMP $$$
(045-622516; www.campiyakanzi.com; s/d US$950/1500, conservation fee per person US$100; P) Campi ya Kanzi is, quite simply, an outstanding place to stay. Set upon the slopes of the Chyulu Hills (these were Ernest Hemingway's 'Green Hills of Africa' and that sobriquet means so much more here than it does in Chyulu Hills

National Park) accommodation here is in luxury tents scattered around an enormous ranch that is centred on a nostalgically decorated stone lodge.

Wildlife viewing (both the day and night), walking safaris up into the Chyulu Hills, transcendental meditation sessions and visits to Maasai villages are all possible, but you'll also be tempted to simply nurse a drink as you gaze out across Maasailand towards Mt Kilimanjaro in all its glory.

Campi ya Kanzi was begun and continues to be overseen by Italians Luca and Antonella. While they bring so much personality to this place, Campi ya Kanzi is very much a Maasai concern. The camp's environmental credentials are also impeccable and the camp directly supports education, health care and environmental conservation in local communities, quite apart from employing dozens of local Maasai staff.

Chyulu Hills National Park

One of Kenya's least visited parks, Chyulu Hills National Park is an oasis of green rising above the arid plains of southern Kenya. The park, just northwest of Tsavo West National Park, is dominated by extinct volcanoes that rank among the world's youngest range of mountains – some of the mountains here were formed perhaps no more than 500 years ago. There are fine views of Mt Kilimanjaro and the Amboseli plains of Maasailand to the east.

At the same time, you're likely to see more herders with their cattle than wildlife, and poaching remains a problem here. Not surprisingly, wildlife populations – elands, klipspringers, giraffes, zebras, baboons, Sykes' monkeys and wildebeest, plus a small number of elephants, lions, leopards and buffaloes – are small and generally shy, but you'll likely have them to yourself.

Sights & Activities

The most beautiful corner of the **park** (Nairobi 020-2153433; www.kws.org/parks/parks_reserves/CHNP; adult/child US$25/15; 6am-7pm) is at altitude, with some surprisingly dense **cloud forest** clinging (like the park border) to the ridgeline. The track into the hills from the headquarters is tough going, but should be passable in a 2WD if it hasn't rained in recent days. Ask at the park headquarters for the latest situation.

Leviathan CAVE

Some 15km from the park entrance and well signposted, the aptly named Leviathan, the second-longest lava tube in the world at 12km, was formed by hot lava flowing beneath a cooled crust. You'll need full caving equipment to explore it, and perhaps a bit of prior experience spelunking in claustrophobic conditions.

Savage Wilderness Safaris Ltd CAVING

(0737835963, Nairobi 020-7121590; www.whitewaterkenya.com) Caving and trekking trips in the hills are possible with Savage Wilderness Safaris Ltd. Otherwise, you're only allowed to enter the cave in the company of a KWS ranger and with prior permission from the warden.

Sleeping

There are no lodges within the park's boundaries.

KWS Campsite CAMPGROUND $

(camping US$20; P) If you're completely self-sufficient, you can spend the night at this basic but functional campsite near the park headquarters.

Getting There & Away

The park headquarters, signposted just outside Kibwezi about 41km northwest of Mtito Andei, is 1.3km inside the northwest gate, 9km off the Nairobi–Mombasa road.

Tsavo West National Park

Welcome to the wilderness. Tsavo West is one of Kenya's larger national parks (9065 sq km), covering a huge variety of landscapes from swamps, natural springs and rocky peaks to extinct volcanic cones, rolling plains and sharp outcrops dusted with greenery.

This is a park with a whiff of legend about it, first for its famous man-eating lions in the late 19th century and then for its devastating levels of poaching in the 1980s. Despite the latter, there's still plenty of wildlife here, although you'll have to work harder and be much more patient than in Amboseli or the Masai Mara to see them all; the foliage is generally denser and higher here. Put all of these things together, along with its dramatic scenery, fine lodges and sense of space and this is one of Kenya's most rewarding parks. If possible, come here with some time to spare to make the most of it.

Sights & Activities

The northern half of **Tsavo West** (043-30049, 0724954745, Nairobi 020-600800; www.kws.org/parks/parks_reserves/TWNP; adult/child per day US$75/40; 6am-6pm) is the most developed, with a number of excellent lodges, and the landscape is also striking and is largely comprised of volcanic hills and sweeping expanses of savannah. The southern part of the park, on the far side of the dirt road between Voi and Taveta on the Tanzanian border, is rarely visited.

Ngulia Rhino Sanctuary WILDLIFE RESERVE

(4-6pm) At the base of Ngulia Hills, this 90-sq-km area is surrounded by a 1m-high electric fence, and provides a measure of security for, at last count, 78 of the park's highly endangered black rhinos. There are driving tracks and waterholes within the enclosed area, but the rhinos are mainly nocturnal and the chances of seeing one are slim – black rhinos, apart from being understandably shy and more active at night, are browsers, not grazers and prefer to pass their time in thick undergrowth.

These archaic creatures are breeding successfully and around 15 have been released elsewhere in Tsavo West National Park. For all the security, one rhino was poached from inside the sanctuary in April 2014. Even so, there are plans to expand the boundaries of the sanctuary to the south.

Rhino Valley PARK

This is one of our favourite areas for wildlife watching, with plenty of antelope species keeping a careful eye out for the resident lions, leopards and cheetahs. You'll also see elephants, giraffes and, if you're lucky, black rhinos. Birdlife is also particularly diverse here. The signposted 'Rhino Valley Circuit' is a good place to start, while anywhere along the Mukui River's ponds and puddles is a place to watch and wait.

Ngulia Hills MOUNTAIN

Rising more than 600m above the valley floor and to a height over 1800m above sea level, this jagged ridgeline ranks among the prettiest of all Tsavo landforms, providing a backdrop to Rhino Valley. The hills can be climbed with permission from the warden, while the peaks are also a recognised flyway for migrating birds heading south from late September through to November.

TSAVO WEST NATIONAL PARK

Why Go For the dramatic scenery, wilderness and good mix of predators (lions, leopards, cheetahs and hyenas), prey (lesser kudus, gazelles, impalas) and other herbivores (elephants, rhinos, zebras, oryxes and giraffes).

When to Go Year-round. The dry season (May to October and January to March) is best for spotting wildlife. November to March is the best time to see migratory birds.

Practicalities Drive in from Mtito Andei or Tsavo gate along the Nairobi–Mombasa road. There is a campsite close to the park entrance and lodges throughout the park.

Budget Tips Rent a matatu (minibus transport) with other travellers in Mtito Andei; if staying in a lodge, June is much cheaper than July.

Mzima Springs SPRING

Mzima Springs is an oasis of green in the west of the park and produces an incredible 250 million litres of fresh water a day. The springs, the source of which rises in the Chyulu Hills, provides the bulk of Mombasa's fresh water. A walking trail leads along the shoreline. The drought in 2009 took a heavy toll on the springs' hippo population; the population is stable at around 20 individuals. There are also crocodiles and a wide variety of birdlife.

There's an underwater viewing chamber, which gives a creepy view of thousands of primeval-looking fish. Be careful here though, as both hippos and crocs are potentially dangerous. Impressive it may all be, but it's not quite up to the hyperbole of the inscription at the entrance to the site and which claims Mzima Springs to be 'undoubtedly the greatest attraction in Tsavo West National Park, if not the whole country'...

Chaimu Crater & Roaring Rocks LOOKOUT

Just southeast of Kilaguni Serena Lodge, these two natural features offer stunning views of the Chyulu Hills and birds of prey circling high above the plains. The Roaring Rocks can be climbed in about 15 minutes; the name comes from the wind whistling

Tsavo East & West National Parks

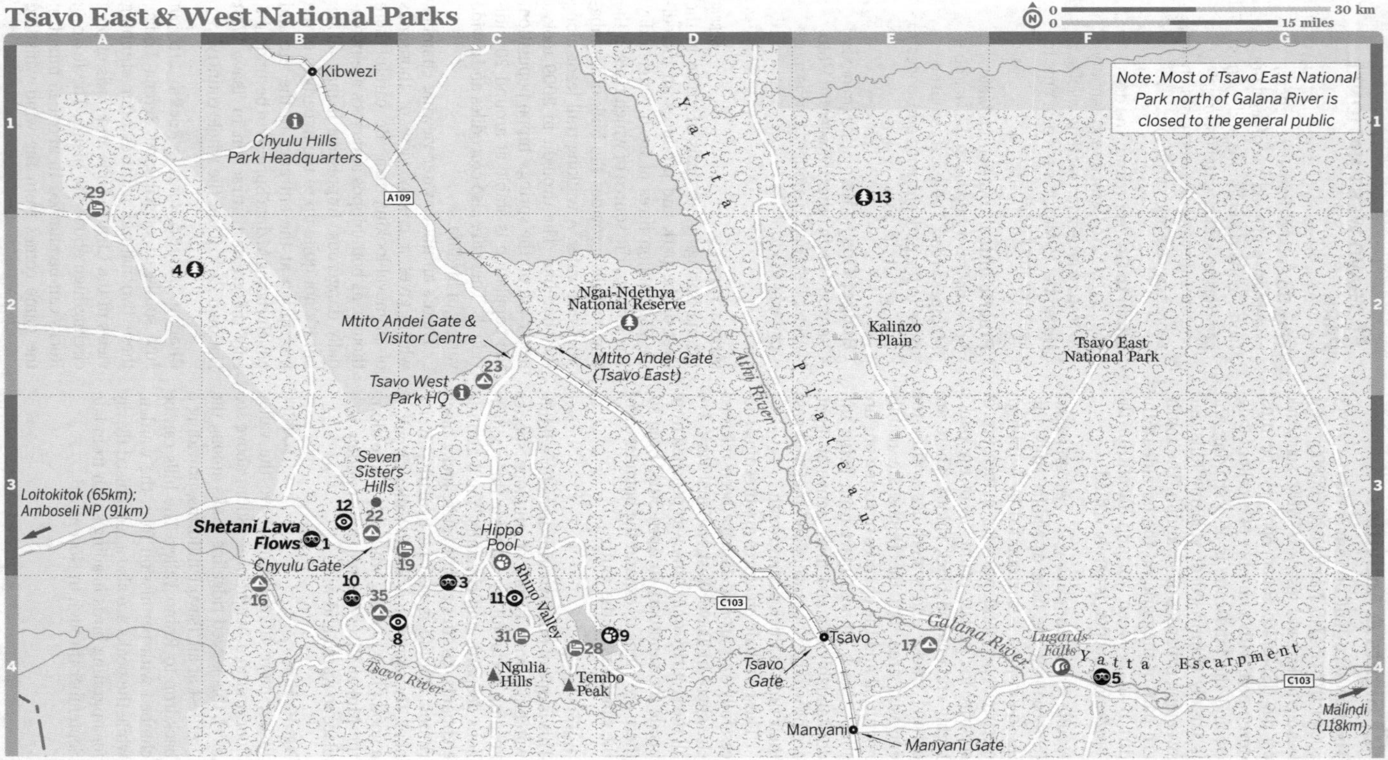

0 — 30 km
0 — 15 miles

Note: Most of Tsavo East National Park north of Galana River is closed to the general public

Kibwezi
Chyulu Hills Park Headquarters
A109
29
4
13
Yatta Plateau
Ngai-Ndethya National Reserve
Mtito Andei Gate & Visitor Centre
Mtito Andei Gate (Tsavo East)
Athi River
Kalinzo Plain
Tsavo East National Park
23
Tsavo West Park HQ
Seven Sisters Hills
Loitokitok (65km); Amboseli NP (91km)
12
22
Shetani Lava Flows 1
Chyulu Gate
19
Hippo Pool
Rhino Valley
16
10
35
3
11
C103
8
31
9
28
Tsavo
17
Galana River
Lugards Falls
Yatta Escarpment
5
C103
Tsavo Gate
Ngulia Hills
Tembo Peak
Tsavo River
Manyani
Manyani Gate
Malindi (118km)

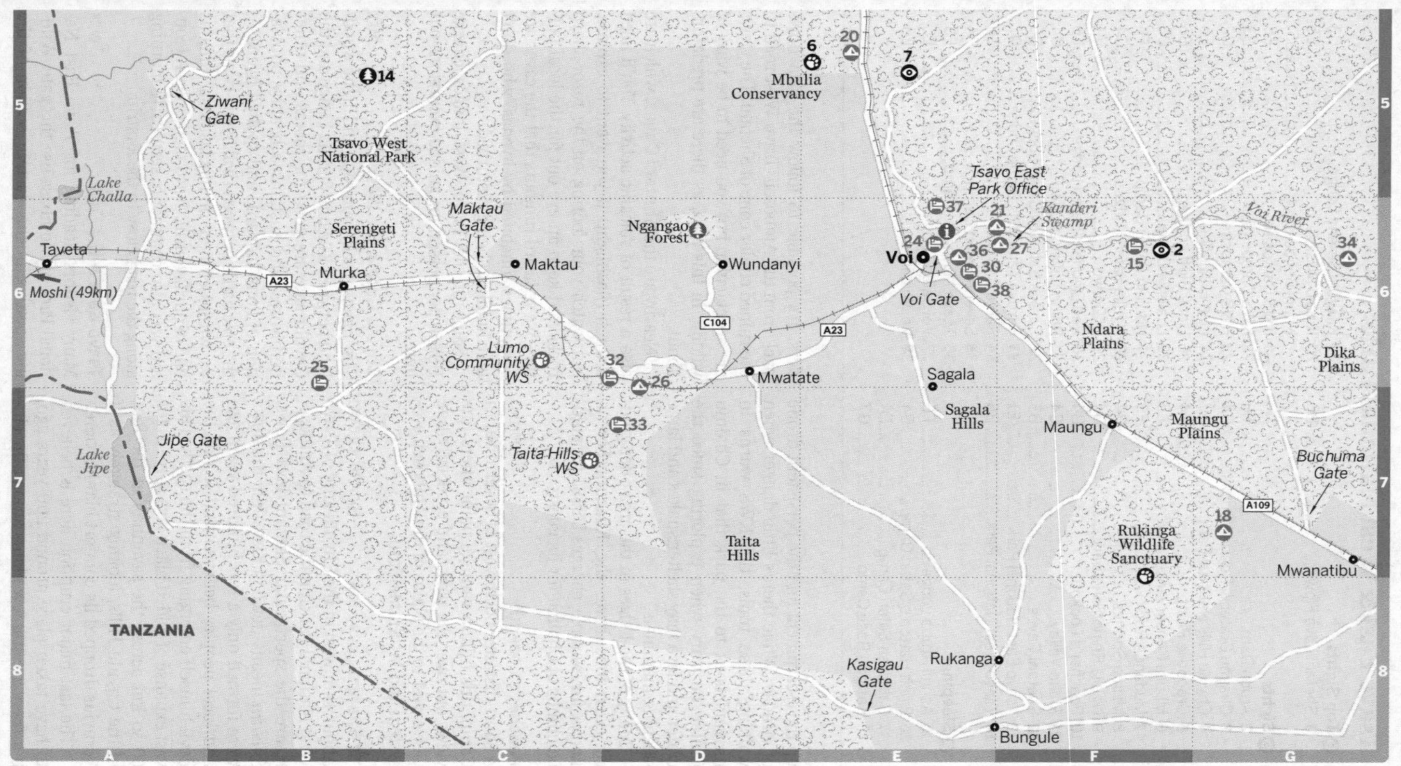
14
6
20
7
Mbulia Conservancy
Ziwani Gate
Tsavo West National Park
Lake Challa
Tsavo East Park Office
Maktau Gate
Serengeti Plains
37
21
Kanderi Swamp
Voi River
34
Ngangao Forest
24
Taveta
Maktau
Wundanyi
Voi
36
27
15
2
Murka
A23
30
Moshi (49km)
38
Voi Gate
C104
A23
Ndara Plains
Lumo Community WS
Dika Plains
32
25
Sagala
26
Mwatate
Sagala Hills
33
Maungu
Maungu Plains
Jipe Gate
Lake Jipe
Taita Hills WS
Buchuma Gate
A109
18
Taita Hills
Rukinga Wildlife Sanctuary
Mwanatibu
TANZANIA
Kasigau Gate
Rukanga
Bungule

Tsavo East & West National Parks

Top Sights

1 Shetani Lava Flows ... B3

Sights

2 Aruba Dam ... F6
3 Chaimu Crater & Roaring Rocks ... C4
4 Chyulu Hills National Park ... A2
5 Crocodile Point ... F4
6 Mbulia Conservancy ... E5
7 Mudanda Rock ... E5
8 Mzima Springs ... B4
9 Ngulia Rhino Sanctuary ... D4
10 Poacher's Lookout ... B4
11 Rhino Valley ... C4
12 Shetani Caves ... B3
13 Tsavo East National Park ... E1
14 Tsavo West National Park ... B5

Sleeping

15 Ashnil Aruba Lodge ... F6
16 Finch Hatton's Safari Camp ... B4
17 Galdessa Safari Camp ... E4
18 Kasigau Base Camp ... G7
19 Kilaguni Serena Lodge ... C3
20 Kipalo Hills ... E5
Kitani Bandas ... (see 35)
21 KWS Campsite ... E6
22 KWS Campsite ... B3
23 KWS Campsite ... C2
24 Lion Hill Lodge ... E6
25 Lions Bluff Lodge ... B6
26 Lualenyi Camp ... D6
27 Ndololo Safari Camp ... F6
28 Ngulia Safari Lodge ... C4
29 Ol Donyo ... A1
30 Red Elephant Safari Lodge ... E6
31 Rhino Valley Lodge ... C4
32 Sarova Salt Lick Safari Lodge ... D6
33 Sarova Taita Hills Game Lodge ... D7
34 Satao Camp ... G6
35 Severin Safari Camp ... B4
36 Tsavo Mashariki Camp ... E6
37 Voi Safari Lodge ... E6
38 Voi Wildlife Lodge ... E6

up the escarpment and the persistent drone of cicadas. While there's little danger when walking these trails, the KWS warns in its guidebook to the park that in Chaimu Crater 'be wary when exploring since the crater and lava may shelter snakes and large sleeping mammals'.

Many of the lodges in the area offer guided excursions here; the Kilaguni Serena Lodge, for example, charges US$35 for guided climbs of Chaimu for its guests.

Poacher's Lookout LOOKOUT

A short distance northwest of Severin Safari Camp, this hilltop vantage point offers fine views out over the park, and especially fine views west to the plains of the Amboseli ecosystem and Mt Kilimanjaro.

★ **Shetani Lava Flows** LOOKOUT, VOLCANO

About 4km west of the Chyulu gate of Tsavo West National Park, on the road to Amboseli, are the spectacular Shetani lava flows. *Shetani* means 'devil' in Kiswahili: the flows were formed only a few hundred years ago and local peoples believed that it was the devil himself emerging from the earth. This vast expanse of folded black lava spreads for 50 sq km across the savannah at the foot of the Chyulu Hills, looking strangely as if Vesuvius dropped its comfort blanket here.

The last major eruption here is believed to have taken place around 200 years ago, but there are still few plants among the cinders. It's possible to follow the lava flows back from the Amboseli–Tsavo West road to the ruined cinder cone of Shetani. The views are spectacular, but you need to be wary of wildlife in this area, as there are predators about.

Nearby are the **Shetani Caves**, which are also a result of volcanic activity. You'll need a torch (flashlight) if you want to explore, but watch your footing on the razor-sharp rocks and keep an eye out for the local fauna – we've heard rumours that the caves are sometimes inhabited by hyenas, who don't take kindly to being disturbed.

Some of the Tsavo West lodges charge US$50 per person for guided excursions out here.

Chyulu Gate & the West PARK

The plains, rocky outcrops and light woodland between Kilaguni Serena Lodge and the Chyulu gate are good for zebras and other herbivores, and sustains a healthy population of lions, leopards and spotted hyenas – the epic battle between rival hyena clans that we witnessed here on our last visit remains one of our favourite Tsavo memories. A leopard was also commonly seen early morning along the road close to the airstrip.

Tsavo Gate & the East PARK

Many visitors heading for Tsavo East National Park or Mombasa use this gate. Wildlife spotting in this eastern section of the park is challenging due to the dense foliage, but both leopards and lions are known to frequent the area.

Tsavo River & the South RIVER
Running west–east through the park, this lovely year-round river is green-shaded and surrounded for much of its path by doum palms. Along with Mzima Springs, the river provides aesthetic relief from the vast semiarid habitats that dominate the park. The trees all along the river are known to shelter leopards.

South of the river, running down to the Ziwani and Maktau gates, the foliage is less dense with cheetah sightings a small possibility. This area has seen problems with poaching and the encroachment into the park by local herders – the further south you go, the less you're likely to see.

Lake Jipe LAKE
Lake Jipe (ji-pay) lies at the extreme southwestern end of the park and is reached by a desperately dusty track from near Taveta. You can hire boats at the campsite to take you hippo and crocodile spotting on the lake (US$5). Huge herds of elephants come to the lake to drink, and it's particularly good for wildlife near the end of the dry season. Conversely, large flocks of migratory birds stop here from February to May.

Tembo Peak & Ngulia Hills ROCK CLIMBING
It's possible to go rock climbing at Tembo Peak and the Ngulia Hills, but you'll need to arrange this in advance with the **park warden** (043-30049; tsavowestnp@kws.go.ke). You'll also need a 4WD and a KWS park ranger to accompany you.

Sleeping & Eating

KWS Campsite CAMPGROUND $
(camping US$20) This public campsite is at Komboyo, near the Mtito Andei gate. Facilities are basic, so be prepared to be self-sufficient.

KWS Campsite CAMPGROUND $
(camping US$20) This basic public campsite is at Chyulu, just outside the Chyulu gate. Be prepared to be self-sufficient.

Kitani Bandas BANDA $$
(041-211000, Nairobi 020-2684247; www.severinsafaricamp.com; bandas s/d US$81/124; P) Run by the same people as Severin Safari Camp, Kitani is located next to a waterhole, about 2km past its sister site, and offers the cheapest Kili views in the park. These *bandas* (which have their own simple kitchens) have far more style than your average budget camp and you can use Severin's facilities (including the pool and free wi-fi). Great value.

★ **Rhino Valley Lodge** BANDA $$$
(Ngulia Bandas; 0721328567; www.tsavolodgesandcamps.com; bandas s/d US$150/200; P) This hillside camp is Tsavo's best bargain and one of the most reasonably priced choices in the parks of southern Kenya. The thatched stone cottages and tents perch on the lower slopes of the Ngulia Hills with sweeping views of Rhino Valley, overlooking a stream where leopards are known to hide out. The decor is designer rustic with plenty of space and private terraces.

The setting and standards outdo plenty of the more ambitious lodges, for a fraction of

POACHING IN TSAVO

As poaching reached epidemic proportions in Kenya in the 1980s, Tsavo was very much on the frontline – not surprising given the park's size and terrain. In a few short years, the elephant population dropped from 45,000 to just 5000, and rhinos were almost wiped out entirely; at the height of the crisis, an estimated 5000 elephants were being killed every year. Populations are slowly recovering to a high of 12,500 elephants in early 2011, but less than 100 rhinos, down from about 9000 in 1969.

Sadly, there has been a recent upsurge in poaching once again – a census in early 2014 found just 11,000 elephants, 1500 less than three years earlier. The northern half of Tsavo East (off limits to travellers) is of particular concern, as well as many areas bordering the two Tsavo parks; the area around Maktau gate at the southern edge of Tsavo West has been particularly hard hit.

As a result of all of this, if you're used to the human-habituated elephants of Amboseli, who'll scarcely move when approached in a vehicle, Tsavo's elephants may come as a surprise – they're skittish and prone to sudden retreats. Rhinos, too, can be difficult to see, not just because they're nocturnal.

ONE OF THE WORLD'S RAREST ANTELOPES

Until their partial translocation to Tsavo East, the sole surviving population of hirola antelope was found near the Kenya–Somalia border in the south Tana River and Garissa districts. Intense poaching (for meat) and habitat destruction have reduced their numbers from an estimated 14,000 in 1976 to a pitiful 450 today. At the time of writing, there were no more than 100 left (and probably far fewer) within the park confines, mostly in the little visited southern reaches of the park.

the price. It's still signposted throughout the park under its old name, Ngulia Bandas.

★Kilaguni Serena Lodge LODGE $$$
(☎045-622376; www.serenahotels.com; s/d US$240/320; @≋) As you'd expect from the upmarket Serena chain, this lodge is extremely comfortable with semiluxurious rooms, many of which have been recently renovated. The centrepiece here is a splendid bar and restaurant overlooking a busy illuminated waterhole – the vista stretches all the way from Mt Kilimanjaro to the Chyulu Hills.

The best watering-hole views are in rooms 14 to 39. The extravagant suites are practically cottages in their own right, boasting chintzy living rooms and epic balconies.

Severin Safari Camp TENTED CAMP $$$
(☎Nairobi 020-2684247; www.severinsafaricamp.com; s/d full board from US$240/370; P≋) This fantastic complex of thatched luxury tents just keeps getting better. The owners have recently overhauled the tents, added a luxury swimming pool and spa, and even a tented gym. The staff offer a personal touch, the food is outstanding and the tents are large and luxurious despite costing considerably less than others elsewhere in the park. Hippo and lion visits are fairly frequent and there are Kilimanjaro views from some points on the property.

Finch Hatton's Safari Camp TENTED CAMP $$$
(☎0716021818, Nairobi 020-8030936; www.finchhattons.com; s/d US$1000/1580, luxury family tent US$3360, presidential ste US$3750; P≋) This upmarket tented camp, which is distinguished by its signature bone china and gold shower taps (guests are requested to dress for dinner), was named after Denys Finch Hatton, the playboy hunter and lover of Karen Blixen. He died at Tsavo, despite his obsession with maintaining civility in the middle of the bush.

The camp is situated among springs and hippo pools in the west of the park, and is the height of exclusivity, especially since renovation works in mid-2014. The presidential suite has its own heated plunge pool, a kitchen pantry for butler service and a room for your nanny and/or bodyguard...

Ngulia Safari Lodge LODGE $$$
(☎043-30000; www.safari-hotels.com; s/d US$190/290; P≋) Tsavo vantage points don't come any better than this – the views are simply magnificent and there's a waterhole right by the restaurant. It's all enough to make you forget that the building itself is a monstrosity and the rooms (especially the bathrooms) are tired and in need of an overhaul; the balcony views from all rooms are wonderful, especially rooms 6 and 7.

Out the back there are sweeping views down off the escarpment and over the Ngulia Rhino Sanctuary.

The practice of baiting leopards each night for photo opportunities has, thankfully, been discontinued by other hotels in the area.

ℹ Information

Fuel is generally available at Kilaguni Serena Lodge and Severin Safari Camp; fill up before entering the park.

Tsavo West National Park map and guidebook is available from Mtito Andei gate.

ℹ Getting There & Away

There are six gates into Tsavo West, but the main access is off the Nairobi–Mombasa Highway at Mtito Andei and Tsavo gates.

Safarilink (☎Nairobi 020-6000777; www.flysafarilink.com; one way adult/child US$154/216) Daily flights between Nairobi's Wilson Airport and Tsavo West, with airstrips near Finch Hatton's Camp and Kilaguni Serena Lodge. You'll need to arrange with one of the lodges or a safari company for a vehicle to meet you at the airstrip.

Mbulia Conservancy

Welcome to one of the most exciting things to happen in the Tsavo area for years.

The 12,000-acre **Mbulia Conservancy** (conservation fee US$58), which borders the extreme southeastern corner of Tsavo West National Park, close to the Nairobi-Mombasa Highway, inhabits what was, until recently, a major hideout for poachers. While poaching continues in adjacent areas, Mbulia Conservancy uses a clever mix of carrot and stick – careful community engagement and an armed private ranger force – to ensure the poachers don't return.

Although the project is still in its infancy (it was launched in early 2012), wildlife has already begun to return, with elephants, African wild dogs and all three species of big cat passing through. There are advanced plans to provide permanent water points for wildlife throughout the conservancy, and the fencing of Tsavo West's southern border will actually go around Mbulia, effectively bringing the conservancy within the protected boundaries of the park itself. If plans to extend the boundaries of Ngulia Rhino Sanctuary (p189) down to Tsavo's southern border come to fruition, Mbulia's strategic importance will be further enhanced.

In the meantime, the views out over the plains towards the Taita and Ngulia Hills are some of the most splendid in southeastern Kenya. By night, you can have that rare experience of gazing out across the plains without a single light or sign of the human presence interrupting the silence and pristine darkness of the African night.

Sleeping & Eating

Kipalo Hills TENTED CAMP

(☎0718139359, Nairobi 020-2663397; www.africanterritories.co.ke; s/d full board US$400/600, all inclusive US$520/900; P 📶 ❄) 🍃 Inhabiting the rocky slopes of a kopje that rises above the Tsavo plains, Kipalo Hills is a wonderful hideaway with superlative views. The nicely spaced tents all have expansive views from their verandahs and have tastefully turned out interiors; they're extremely comfortable rather than luxurious. The public areas are utterly lovely and seem to emerge from the rocks themselves. From a distance, the camp is barely visible.

Possible activities included in the all-inclusive rates are guided walking safaris, perfectly located sundowners, visits to a local school and Taita cultural performances; excursions into Tsavo West are not included. A percentage of the profits go straight to the local community.

Getting There & Away

Many visitors fly into Tsavo West's Kilaguni airstrip with Safarilink, and combine their transfer here (three hours) with a wildlife drive through the national park.

If driving, ask for detailed directions; the turn-off is around 20km north of Voi.

Tsavo East National Park

Kenya's largest national park, Tsavo East National Park has an undeniable wild and primordial charm and is a terrific wildlife-watching destination. Although one of Kenya's largest rivers flows through the middle of the park and the contrast between the permanent greenery of the river and the endless grasses and thorn trees that characterise much of the park is visually arresting, the landscape here lacks the drama of Tsavo West. Tsavo East is markedly flatter and drier than its sister park. The flipside is that spotting wildlife is generally easier thanks to the thinly spread foliage.

Despite the size of the park, the area of most wildlife activity is actually quite compact – the northern section of the park is largely closed and can only be visited with advance permission due to the threat of banditry and ongoing campaigns against poachers. The demarcation point is the Galana River.

TSAVO EAST NATIONAL PARK

Why Go Wilderness, red elephants and leopards, lions and cheetahs. The park also has close to 500 bird species.

When to Go June to February. Wildlife concentrations are highest in the dry season (September to October and January to early March).

Practicalities Drive in from Voi, Mandanyi or Tsavo gates along the Nairobi–Mombasa road. The Sala and Buchuma gates are good for Mombasa. There are a small number of lodges and camps throughout the park or close to Voi Gate.

Budget Tips Rent a matatu (minibus transport) or organise a budget safari with other travellers in Voi or the coast; use public campsites.

Sights & Activities

Most people come to **Tsavo East** (☎0775563672, 0722290009, Nairobi 020-6000800; www.kws.org/parks/parks_reserves/TENP; adult/child per day US$75/40; ⌚6am-6pm) to see the famous red elephants of Tsavo – their colour comes from bathing in the red Tsavo mud (to keep the skin cool and prevent insect bites). The two Tsavo parks have the largest elephant populations of any Kenyan parks and include a third of the country's total, although herds are quite small. Lion and cheetah sightings are also common; unusually, the male lions are almost maneless.

Kanderi Swamp RIVER

Around 10km from Voi gate, the lovely area of green known as Kanderi Swamp is home to a resident pride of lions, and elephants also congregate near here; this is one of only two water sources in the park during the dry season. The landscape here has a lovely backdrop of distant hills. A number of vehicle tracks also follow the contours of the Voi River; keep an eye on the overhanging branches for leopards.

Aruba Dam LAKE

Some 30km east of Voi gate is the Aruba Dam, which spans the Voi River. It also attracts heavy concentrations of diverse wildlife; one of the park's regularly spotted lion prides ranges around here. Away to the east and southeast, all the way down to the Buchuma gate, the open grasslands provide the perfect habitat for cheetahs and sightings are more common here than anywhere else in southeastern Kenya.

Galana River RIVER

Running through the heart of the park and marking the northernmost point in the park that most visitors are allowed to visit, the Galana River, which combines the waters of the Tsavo and Athi Rivers, cuts a green gash across the dusty plains. Surprisingly few visitors make it even this far and sightings of crocs, hippos, lesser kudus, waterbucks, dikdiks and, to a lesser extent, lions and leopards, are relatively common.

Watch out also for the distinctive Somali ostrich. There are several places along the flat-topped escarpments lining the river where you can get out of your vehicle (with due caution, of course). Most scenic are **Lugards Falls**, a wonderful landscape of water-sculpted channels, and **Crocodile Point**, where you may see abundant crocs and hippos. The trail that runs from the falls back to Voi follows a river and is good for wildlife spotting, but the track is impassable after the rains.

The area north of the Galana River is dominated by the Yatta Escarpment, a vast prehistoric lava flow which is estimated by some to be the longest lava flow in the world at 300km.

Mudanda Rock MOUNTAIN

Towering over a natural dam near the Manyani gate, this towering natural formation runs for over 1.5km. It attracts elephants in the dry season and is reminiscent of Australia's Uluru (Ayers Rock), albeit on a smaller scale. Leopards and elephants are among the wildlife to watch out for here.

Sleeping & Eating

Inside the Park

KWS Campsite CAMPGROUND $

(camping US$20) Decent site with toilets, showers and a communal kitchen.

Voi Safari Lodge LODGE $$$

(☎Mombasa 041-471861; www.safari-hotels.com; s/d US$190/290;) Just 4km from Voi gate, this is a long, low complex perched on the edge of an escarpment overlooking an incredible sweep of savannah. There's an attractive rock-cut swimming pool, as well as a natural waterhole that draws elephants, buffaloes and the occasional predator; a photographers' hide sits at the level of the waterhole. Rooms are attractive and many have superlative views.

Satao Camp TENTED CAMP $$$

(☎Mombasa 041-475074, Nairobi 020-2434600; www.sataocamp.com; s/d US$337/436; P) Located on the banks of the Voi River, this luxury camp is run by the experienced safari operator Southern Cross Safaris (p39). There are 20 canopied tents, all of which are perfectly spaced within sight of a waterhole that's known to draw lions, cheetahs and elephants on occasion.

Ashnil Aruba Lodge LODGE $$$

(☎Nairobi 020-4971008; www.ashnilhotels.com; s/d full board US$262/350; P@) A stone's throw from the wildlife-rich Aruba Dam, this lodge has attractively decorated rooms decked out in safari prints. In the heart of the park, it's an ideal starting point for most

Tsavo East safaris. Wildlife wanders around the property's perimeter at regular intervals.

Ndololo Safari Camp TENTED CAMP **$$$**
(www.tsavolodgesandcamps.com; s/d US$150/200) A well-priced tented camp in a good location close to Kanderi Swamp, Ndololo Safari Camp has a tight cluster of tents that are far more reasonably priced than most in southern Kenya.

Galdessa Safari Camp TENTED CAMP **$$$**
(☎040-3202217; www.galdessa.com; s/d full board US$345/540; P 📶) Perched on the edge of the Galana River, approximately 15km west of Lugards Falls, this exclusive safari camp is by far the swishest property in Tsavo East; it's often booked out entirely by private parties. For a healthy dose of European sophistication in your bush camping experience (fine wines, gourmet dining, fashionable decor and impeccable service), look no further.

All-inclusive package rates are available and include many activities.

Outside the Park

★Tsavo Mashariki Camp TENTED CAMP **$$**
(☎0729179443; www.masharikicamp.com; s/d from US$131/185) The closest camp to Voi gate just outside the park, this charming little Italian-run place has some fine tents made out of all-natural local materials; the family tent is brilliant and there are also two stone-built cottages. Best of all, the prices here put many other tented camps to shame. Highly recommended.

Red Elephant Safari Lodge LODGE **$$**
(☎0727112175; www.red-elephant-lodge.com; r/bungalows per person full board €53/68; P @ 🏊) One of the better budget places bordering Tsavo East, close to Voi, Red Elephant is popular with German travellers for its reasonable prices and attractive accommodation. The standard rooms have stone furnishings while the bush houses are lighter, come with mosquito nets and attractive yet simple Maasai prints. It's signposted off the main road into the park from Voi.

MAN-EATERS OF TSAVO

Wild felines the world over are rightfully feared and respected, though the famed 'man-eaters of Tsavo' were among the most dangerous lions to ever roam the planet. During the building of the Kenya–Uganda Railway in 1898, efforts soon came to a halt when railway workers started being dragged from their tents at night and devoured by two maneless male lions.

The surviving workers soon decided that the lions had to be ghosts or devils, which put the future of the railway in jeopardy. Engineer Lt Col John Henry Patterson created a series of ever more ingenious traps, but each time the lions evaded them, striking unerringly at weak points in the camp defences. Patterson was finally able to bag the first man-eater by hiding on a flimsy wooden scaffold baited with the corpse of a donkey. The second man-eater was dispatched a short time later, although it took six bullets to bring the massive beast down.

According to Patterson's calculations, the two lions killed and ate around 135 workers in less than one year. He detailed his experiences in the best-selling book *The Man-Eaters of Tsavo* (1907), which was later rather freely filmed as *Bwana Devil* (1952) and *The Ghost and the Darkness* (1996).

Patterson turned the two man-eaters into floor rugs. In 1924 he finally rid himself of the lions by selling their skins to the Chicago Field Museum for the sum of US$5000. The man-eaters of Tsavo were then stuffed and placed on permanent display, where they remain to this day.

Hypotheses vary as to why these lions became man-eaters. Tsavo lions have noticeably elevated levels of the male sex hormone testosterone. The pair themselves also had badly damaged teeth, which may have driven them to abandon their normal prey and become man-eaters. An outbreak of rinderpest (an infectious viral disease) might have decimated the lions' usual prey, forcing them to find alternative food sources. One final theory is that the man-eaters may have developed their taste for human flesh after growing accustomed to finding human bodies at the Tsavo River crossing, where slave caravans often crossed en route to Zanzibar.

WORTH A TRIP

KASIGAU

South of Voi and signposted west off the Nairobi–Mombasa Highway, Kasigau is the epicentre of some pretty innovative conservation and community development work.

The **Rukinga Wildlife Sanctuary**, at the heart of the project, is reliable elephant country – Kasigau lies along a migration corridor between Tsavos East and West. But there's so much more happening here; the sanctuary, by employing local people and selling carbon credits, aims to prevent deforestation by making wildlife work for the local community. Check out www.wildlifeworks.com for more on this deceptively simple idea. Other projects include the use of village workshops to employ and train the local community in tailoring; this is also production (and carbon-neutral) home base and is the production site for the **African Shirt Company** (www.theafricanshirtcompany.com).

The work-in-progress **Kasigau Base Camp** (0721365768, 0710755225; www.malewa.com; camping per person in own/hired tent KSh500/750, cottages per person self-catering/full board KSh2500/6000; P) is an essential part of the Kasigau project, with good campsites, six attractive, locally built cottages and a range of activities that include hiking, abseiling and rock climbing in the surrounding hills. It can also arrange volunteering placements in local projects.

Lion Hill Lodge LODGE $$

(Nairobi 020-8030828; www.lionhilllodge.com; s/d US$80/120) Just before the park entrance, this quiet place sits atop an impossibly steep hill and the views that result from this location are extraordinary. The best views are in rooms 5 and 6, large rooms with balconies, or, failing that, rooms 7 to 10 also boast fine panoramas.

Voi Wildlife Lodge LODGE $$

(0733201240, 0722201240; www.voiwildlifelodge.com; s/d full board US$116/192; P) Close to Voi gate, this well-run place is actually three places in one, two of which were being substantially renovated when we passed through. From the main property, there are fine views into the park from some rooms as well as from the restaurant and viewing platform. At its Manyatta property, the tents have private plunge pools. Prices were under review at the time of writing.

Information

Fuel is available in Voi; fill up before entering park.

The *Tsavo East National Park* map and guidebook is available from Voi gate.

Getting There & Away

A track through the park follows the Galana River from the Tsavo gate to the Sala gate; others fan out from Voi gate.

To/from Nairobi or Tsavo West Voi, Tsavo and Manyani gates.

To/from Mombasa Sala or Buchuma gates.

Voi

POP 17,152

Voi is a key service town at the intersection of the Nairobi–Mombasa road, the road to Moshi in Tanzania and the access road to the main Voi gate of Tsavo East National Park. As such, much of its activity is designed around trying to catch the monetary crumbs that fall from the pockets of those changing transport, on safari or simply passing through. Think of it more as a place to get directions, fill up on petrol, change money and buy some snacks for the road, than as a place to linger.

Sights & Activities

Voi War Cemetery CEMETERY

(Commonwealth War Graves; hours vary) On the north side of the road just before the turn-off to Voi gate on the eastern outskirts of town, this well-tended cemetery contains 137 graves, including 70 South African, 44 British, 12 'Rhodesian', nine East African and two Indian graves. The area around Tsavo, particularly the railway, was a major theatre of war between Britain and Germany during WWI. The gate is usually padlocked shut, but ask around the nearest shops and soon enough they'll track down the custodian of the key.

Sleeping & Eating

You'll find simple places serving *nyama choma* (barbecued meat) in numerous places surrounding the main matatu park and market in the centre of town.

Fine Breeze Hotel HOTEL $
(☎043-2031041, 0722655753; Main Rd; s/d KSh3000/4000; P) Cheap hotels proliferate around Voi and this is one of the better places in the heart of town. Rooms are simple and generally clean, but there's a pub next door and noise can be a problem. Most beds have mosquito nets.

Tsavo Lodge LODGE $$
(☎0721328567; www.tsavolodgesandcamps.com; s/d full board US$55/90) About halfway between Voi and Tsavo East National Park's Voi gate, this simple place has rooms and tents arrayed around a green courtyard. Rooms are large and basic. If you can stay closer to (or inside) the park, do so.

Getting There & Away

Frequent buses and matatus run to/from Mombasa (KSh200 to KSh500, three hours), and there are buses to Nairobi (KSh500 to KSh1200, six hours). There are at least daily matatus to Wundanyi (KSh350, one hour), and Taveta (KSh600, two hours), on the Tanzanian border.

Voi also lies along the Nairobi–Mombasa railway line.

Taita Hills Wildlife Sanctuary

The Taita Hills, a fertile area of verdant hills and scrub forest, is a far cry from the semi-arid landscape of Tsavo. Within the hills is the private wildlife sanctuary, covering an area of 100 sq km – the landscape is dramatic and all the plains wildlife is here in abundance.

Sights & Activities

The **sanctuary** (admission US$30) has three main focal points for wildlife watching. First the **river valley** that runs east of the Sarova Taita Hills Game Lodge is good for birds of prey, while the open **grasslands** that rise gently south of the river and take up much of the park feed Grant's gazelles, impalas and hartebeests in numbers sufficient to sustain lions and cheetahs; elephants are also possible. At the southern

TAITA HILLS & WWI

There's a very good reason that they decided to put a museum dedicated to WWI in the Taita Hills Wildlife Sanctuary – the neighbouring area was one of the most important theatres of war in the early years of the East Africa Campaign.

The German interest in Britain's Kenyan territories was focused on two primary targets.

The first was Mzima Springs (p189) in Tsavo West National Park, one of East Africa's most important permanent water supplies. The second target for the German incursions was a major railway bridge over the Tsavo River – if they could sever the supply and general transport artery that was the Mombasa–Uganda Railway, the German argument ran, the British would be in trouble.

On 15 August 1914, the first German soldiers crossed the border at Taveta and seized the town. These were the first shots of the East African Campaign on Kenyan soil, although the outnumbered British troops retreated almost immediately. The first major battle took place at Mile 27 along the Voi–Taveta road, around 1.5km from the museum. The first airfield in British East Africa was at Maktau and the Allies built their first fort of the war 5km from the Taita Hills Wildlife Sanctuary.

Although little remains of these incidents (the Voi War Cemetery is one of the few easily accessible landmarks to WWI) the museum (p200) gives an excellent overview. And while these sites can be impossible to find on your own, those with a particular interest in the campaign should contact **Willie Mwadilo** (☎0733931036; willie.mwadilo@sarovahotels.com; per group per day US$200), lodge manager at the Sarova Taita Hills Game Lodge. With prior notice, he can show you around the museum for free, bringing to life many of its exhibits. With more advance warning he can guide you around the region's sites.

One other landmark is found on the neighbouring Lumo Community Wildlife Sanctuary (p200), scene of a battle that later formed part of the film *Shout at the Devil* starring Lee Marvin and Roger Moore. The sanctuary organises 'Battlefield Tours' which encompass the battlefield, as well as the ruins of a British wartime camp and a local WWI cemetery.

reaches of the sanctuary, **Lion Rock** provides sanctuary for klipspringer and resting predators.

Taita Hills WWI Museum MUSEUM
(24hr) FREE Occupying a corner of the lobby in the Sarova Taita Hills Game Lodge, this engaging little open-sided museum tells the story of World War I as it played out in East Africa. There are artefacts found on the nearby former battlefields (from bullets made in 1912 to glass shards from bottles of Indian hair oil), archival photos, informative and detailed panels on the course of the war and major personalities.

There are further artefacts outside, including railway sleepers and a vehicle chassis, between the main entrance and the car park.

Sleeping & Eating

★Sarova Salt Lick Safari Lodge LODGE $$$
(0728608765; www.sarovahotels.com; s/d full board from US$176/273; P ✻ @ ≋) The centrepiece of the sanctuary, this original lodge calls to mind a traditional village of beehive huts on stilts, all connected by a web of walkways and overlooking a waterhole where elephants often come to drink. Rooms are a touch old-fashioned but the views outweigh such minor details. Night drives are also possible.

There's a subterranean hide for wildlife viewing, an elevated bar where the drinks provide ambitious approximations of Western cocktails and an open-sided dining area with bats in the ceiling. Check-in is at the Sarova Taita Hills Game Lodge at the sanctuary gate.

Sarova Taita Hills Game Lodge LODGE $$$
(0728608765; www.sarovahotels.com; s/d full board from US$166/216; P ✻ @ ≋) The older of the two Sarova properties within the sanctuary, this place has marginally better rooms and the service is more switched on (this is the main reception for both properties), but it's closer to the road and lacks the waterhole proximity and architectural personality of the Salt Lick. Don't miss its fine little museum in the lobby.

Getting There & Away

You'll need your own vehicle to get to the sanctuary, which lies south of the dirt road from Voi to Taveta.

Lumo Community Wildlife Sanctuary

The innovative community-run Lumo Community Wildlife Sanctuary covers 657 sq km and was formed from three community-owned ranches in 1996, but only opened to the public in 2003. It's partly funded by the EU and involves local people at every stage of the project, from the park rangers to senior management.

Sights & Activities

You could easily spend three or four days taking in everything the **sanctuary** (0729265018; www.lumoconservancy.com; adult/child US$30/15) has to offer. In addition to the guided **WWI Tours** to local wartime landmarks (watch for spent shell casings and other relics), there are also **wildlife drives** – unlike in national parks, both day and night drives are possible as this is a private conservancy. The wildlife here is surprisingly varied – all the Big Five (elephants, rhinos, lions, leopards and buffaloes) are here, and the night drives are especially good for nocturnal specialists such as lions, leopards, melanistic servals and aardwolves.

Birdwatching is also rewarding here with more than half of Kenya's 1070 species recorded in the area. Endemics to watch out for include the Taita thrush, Taita white-eye, Taita apalis, Abbott's starling and the southern banded snake eagle.

Walking expeditions are another advantage of being on private land – these often have a focus on bush survival skills and the traditional plant and fauna knowledge of the Taita people, from edible and medicinal plants to insects and other wildlife.

Traditional local dances and visits to **local community projects** can also be arranged.

Sleeping & Eating

Cheetah Campsite CAMPGROUND $
(camping per person from US$15) Close to Lion Bluff Lodge, this shady, green-tinged campsite has levelled sites as well as running water, a communal kitchen, showers and toilets, and you can access the facilities at the lodge as required.

Lions Bluff Lodge LODGE $$$
(0717555498, 0733222420; www.lionsblufflodge.com; s/d full board US$231/330; P) Built by the local community, these timber-and-

WORTH A TRIP

WUNDANYI

The provincial capital of Wundanyi is set high in the Taita Hills. Numerous trails criss-cross the cultivated terraced slopes around town, leading to dramatic gorges, waterfalls, cliffs and jagged outcrops. It's easy to find someone to act as a guide, but stout walking boots and a head for heights are essential.

Other attractions in the hills include the butterflies of **Ngangao Forest**, a 6km matatu (minibus transport) ride northwest to Werugha (KSh70); the huge granite **Wesu Rock** that overlooks Wundanyi; and the **Cave of Skulls** where the Taita people once put the skulls of their ancestors (and where the original African violets were discovered).

Semifrequent matatu services run between Wundanyi and Voi (KSh200, one hour). Leave Wundanyi by around 8.30am if you want to connect with the morning buses to Nairobi from Voi.

Set up as a research station for Finnish scientists, the small and simple **Taita Research Station** (☎0722287486, 0733849103; dm KSh1200) rest house offers basic facilities. Wundanyi's best place to stay, **Lavender Garden Hotel** (lavendergarden.hotel@yahoo.com; r per person US$70) is a little overpriced, but rooms are comfortable and the views from the front-facing rooms are lovely. It's a good place to arrange excursions around the area.

canvas *bandas* with coconut-palm-thatched roofs get the balance right between being genuinely rustic yet supremely comfortable; most have exceptional views and there's a small waterhole. Food for the excellent meals is sourced almost exclusively from local farmers.

Lualenyi Camp TENTED CAMP **$$$**
(☎0729965409; www.lualenyi.com; price on application) Set on its own private game reserve (Lualenyi Ranch is part of the Lumo Community Wildlife Sanctuary) and signposted off the main Voi–Taveta road east of Taita Hills Wildlife Sanctuary, this Italian-run place consistently gets rave reviews from travellers. The tents are simple yet comfortable and all the usual activities are possible here, from day and night wildlife drives to walking safaris.

Wildlife is impressive, with particularly healthy lion, leopard and elephant populations. There's not a whole lot of English spoken here.

Getting There & Away

The sanctuary lies on the Voi–Taveta road.

The Road to Moshi

Heading west from Voi, the A23 runs straight to the Tanzanian border en route to the city of Moshi, Tanzania's gateway to Mount Kilimanjaro. On the way, there's a worthwhile detour to the rarely visited **Lake Chala**, a deep, spooky crater lake about 10km north of the town. There are grand views across the plains from the crater rim, with the mysterious waters shimmering hundreds of metres below. In early 2002 a gap-year student was killed by crocodiles here – although you *can* walk around the crater rim, be very careful near the water's edge and under no circumstances consider swimming. On market days (Wednesday and Saturday) in the dusty border town of **Taveta**, there are local buses to Challa village (KSh80), passing the turn-off to the crater rim.

A pastel-orange building conveniently situated on the main road, **Tripple J Paradise** (☎043-5352463; r from KSh850; P) is little more than a crash pad for drivers heading back and forth between Kenya and Tanzania, though it'll do in a pinch if you can't make it to Moshi in one go.

The **Tanzania border** is open 24 hours, but the border posts are 4km apart, so you'll have to take a *boda-boda* (bicycle taxi; KSh40) if you don't have your own wheels. From Holili on the Tanzanian side, there are matatus to Moshi (TSh1500), where you can change on to Arusha (TSh2500).

From Taveta, numerous matatus head to Voi (KSh450, 2½ hours) and Mombasa (KSh900, four hours) throughout the day.

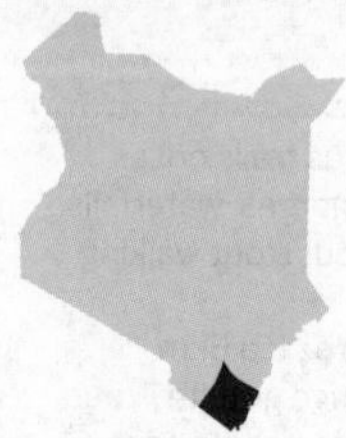

Mombasa & the South Coast

Includes ➡

Best of Nature

- ➡ Shimba Hills National Reserve (p218)
- ➡ Mwaluganje Elephant Sanctuary (p219)
- ➡ Kisite Marine National Park (p228)
- ➡ Haller Park (p233)
- ➡ Colobus Conservation Centre (p220)

Best of Culture

- ➡ Mombasa (p204)
- ➡ Wasini Island (p227)
- ➡ Jumba la Mtwana (p235)
- ➡ Kaya Kinondo (p222)

Why Go?

From the hypnotic port city of Mombasa south to the border with Tanzania, this stretch of Kenyan coast is anything but ordinary. Where else can you see snow white beaches framed by *kayas* (sacred forests), soft-sailed dhows and elephant watering holes, all in one day?

Governed by Swahili rhythms and the rise and fall of the tides, life here moves to its own beat. Duck into the Indian Ocean and you'll see there's far more going on beneath the surface than the simple pleasures of sun, sea and sand. Those waters hide dolphins, turtles, Swahili secrets and some of the best diving and kitesurfing in Africa.

Thanks to the long interplay of Africa, India and Arabia, this coast feels wildly different from the rest of Kenya. Its people, the Swahili, have created a distinctive Indian Ocean society – built on trade with distant shores – that lends real romance to the coast's beaches and to Mombasa, a city poets have embraced for as long as ivory has been traded for iron.

When to Go

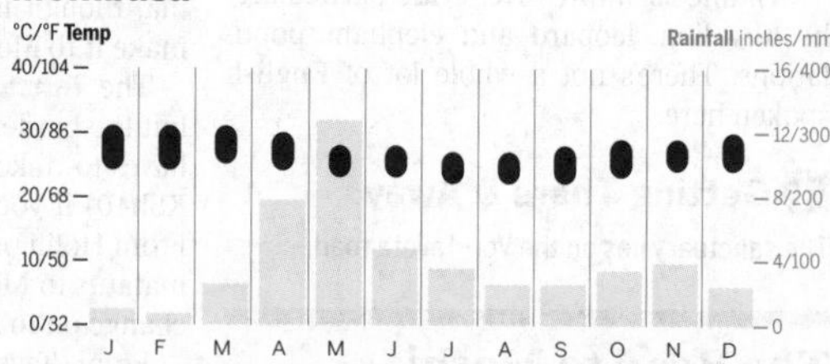

Jan–Mar Dolphins (and the occasional whale shark) fill the ocean and diving is at its best.

Apr–Aug The rainy season is the coolest time of year.

Sep School-holiday crowds are gone, accommodation is cheaper and beaches are quieter.

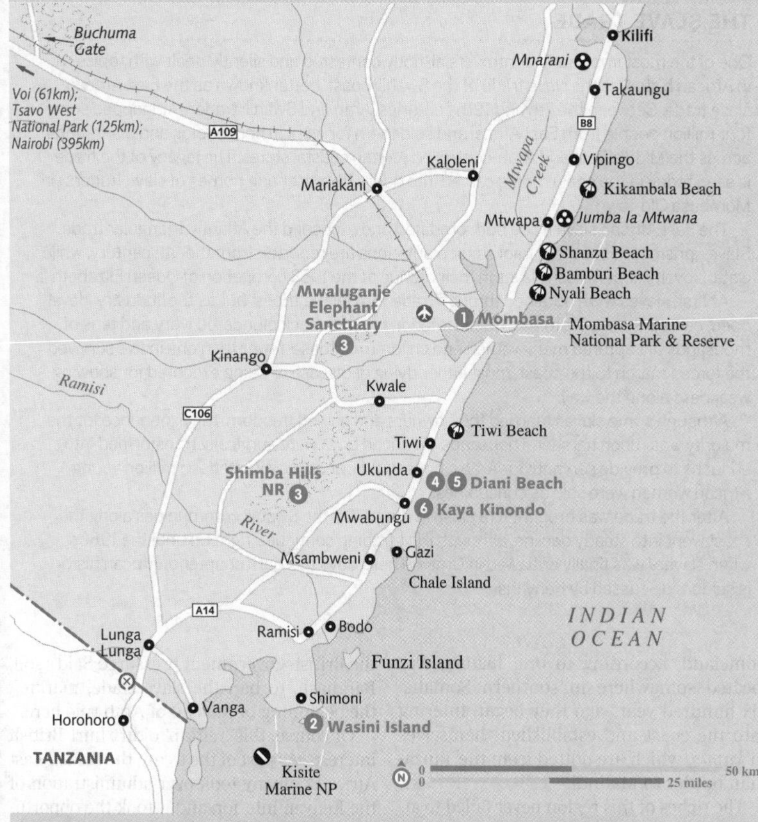

Mombasa & the South Coast Highlights

1. Trading for chilli and cardamom inside the skinny streets of **Mombasa Old Town** (p212)
2. Diving into the emerald reef at **Wasini Island** (p228) and soaking up the Swahili spirit
3. Tracking down elephants and sable antelope in **Shimba Hills National Reserve** (p218) and **Mwaluganje Elephant Sanctuary** (p219)
4. Stepping barefoot onto the soft white sand at **Diani Beach** (p220), and later kitesurfing its waves
5. Spending some one-on-one time with a baby colobus monkey at the **Colobus Conservation Centre** (p220)
6. Finding god in the greenery in **Kaya Kinondo** (p222)

History

The coast's written history stretches much further back than the history of the interior, and is essentially a tale of trade and conquest, with outside forces. By the 1st century AD, Yemeni traders were in East Africa, prompting one unidentified Greek observer to write about 'Arab captains and agents, who are familiar with the natives and intermarry with them, and who know the whole coast and understand the language'. Merchants traded spices, timber, gold, ivory, tortoise shell and rhinoceros horn, as well as slaves.

The mixture of Arabs, local Africans and Persian traders gave birth to the Swahili culture and language. But the Swahili were not the only inhabitants of the coast. Of particular note were the Mijikenda (Nine Homesteads), a Bantu tribe whose

THE SLAVE TRADE

One of the most important, controversial, hotly contested and silently dealt with topics in African history is the slave trade of the Swahili coast, better known as the East African slave trade. Between the 7th and 19th centuries, Arab and Swahili traders kidnapped some four million people from East Africa, and sold them for work in households and plantations across the Middle East and Arab-controlled African coastal states. The legacy of the trade is seen today in the chain motifs carved into doors (representing homes of slave traders) in Mombasa Old Town.

The East African slave trade both predated and exceeded the Atlantic triangular trade. Slave uprisings in southern Iraqi sugar plantations are reported from the 9th century, while Qatari royalty kept African slaves in their retinue at the 1953 coronation of Queen Elizabeth II.

At first, slaves were obtained through trade with inland tribes, but as the 'industry' developed, caravans set off into the African interior, bringing back plundered ivory and tens of thousands of captured men, women and children. Of these, fewer than one in five survived the forced march to the coast, most either dying of disease or being executed for showing weakness along the way.

Although some slaves married their owners and gained freedom, the experience for the majority was much harsher. Thousands of African boys were surgically transformed into eunuchs to provide servants for Arabic households, and an estimated 2.5 million young African women were sold as concubines.

After the trade was brought to a close in the 1870s, the Swahili communities along the coast went into steady decline, although illicit trading continued right up until the 1960s, when slavery was finally outlawed in Oman. These days this dark chapter of African history is seldom discussed by Kenyans.

homeland, according to oral history, was located somewhere in southern Somalia. Six hundred years ago they began filtering into the coast and established themselves in *kayas*, which are dotted from the Tanzanian border to Malindi.

The riches of this region never failed to attract attention, and in the early 16th century it was the Portuguese who took their turn at conquest. The Swahili did not take kindly to becoming slaves (even if they traded them), and rebellions were common throughout the 16th and 17th centuries. It's fashionable to portray the Portuguese as villains, but their replacements, the sultans of Oman, were no more popular. Despite their shared faith, the natives of this ribbon of land staged countless rebellions and passed Mombasa into British hands from 1824 to 1826 to keep it from the sultans. Things only really quietened down after Sultan Seyyid Said moved his capital from Muscat to Zanzibar in 1832.

Said's huge coastal clove plantations created a massive need for labour, and the slave caravans of the 19th century marked the peak of the trade in human cargo. News of massacres and human-rights abuses reached Europe, galvanising the British public to demand an end to slavery. Through a mixture of political savvy and implied force, the British government pressured Said's son, Barghash, to ban the slave trade, marking the beginning of the end of Arab rule here.

Of course, this 'reform' didn't hurt British interests. As part of the treaty, the British East Africa Company took over administration of the Kenyan interior, and it took the opportunity to start construction of the East African Railway. A 16km-wide coastal strip was recognised as the sultan's territory and leased by the British from 1887. Upon independence in 1963, the last sultan of Zanzibar gifted this land to the new Kenyan government.

The coast remains culturally and religiously distinct (most coastal people are Muslim) and there are calls by a separatist group in Mombasa for some autonomy from the rest of Kenya. In mid-2014 there were still concerns those calls might be reinforced by an ongoing spate of insecurity and violence along parts of the coast, fuelled by ethnic tensions within Kenya and political tension with Somalia.

MOMBASA

POP 939,000

Mombasa: city of salt and of spice, of dreams and of battles, of poetry, of seafaring stories and of wave upon wave of traders from faraway lands. 'It does not reveal the great secret it holds,' wrote the classical Swahili poet Muyaka about his hometown. 'Even those who are well-informed do not comprehend it.'

Indeed, the city dubbed Kisiwa Cha Mvita – the Island of War – in Swahili has many faces. It's muttered chants echoing over the flagstones of a Jain temple, the ecstatic passion of the call to prayer, the teal break of a vanishing wave and the sight of a Zanzibar-bound dhow slipping over the horizon. It's row upon row of purveyors of herbal medicine. It's cows dozing outside hair-braiding salons. It's birds swooping low over great piles of smoking rubbish, and buildings so scorched by the sun their burnt skin has peeled away, just like ours.

Mombasa has more in common with Dakar or Dar es Salaam than Nairobi – its blend of India, Arabia and Africa can be intoxicating. But it's also grimy and sleazy, with deep ethnic tensions and security concerns that threaten to boil over. But what would you expect from East Africa's largest port? Cities by the docks always attract mad characters, and Mombasa's come from all over the world.

Perhaps it's best to let the Swahili people themselves describe their city in their native tongue with an old line of poetry and proverb: *'Kongowea nda mvumo, maji maangavu. Male!'* ('Mombasa is famous, but its waters are dangerously deep. Beware!').

History

Unlike Nairobi, Mombasa, which sits over the best deep-water harbour in East Africa, has always been an important town.

Travellers who come here are walking in the footsteps of Ibn Battuta, Marco Polo and Zhang He, which says something of this town's trade importance. Modern Mombasa traces its heritage back to the Thenashara Taifa (Twelve Nations), a Swahili clan that maintains an unbroken chain of traditions and customs stretching from the city's founding to this day. The date when those customs began – ie when Mombasa was born – is a little muddy, although it was already a thriving port by the 12th century. Early in its life, Mombasa became a key link on Indian Ocean trade routes.

In 1498 Vasco da Gama became Mombasa's first Portuguese visitor. Two years later his countrymen returned and sacked the town, a habit they repeated in 1505 and 1528, when Nuña da Cunha captured Mombasa using what would become a time-honoured tactic: slick 'em up with diplomacy (offering to act as an ally in disputes with Malindi, Pemba and Zanzibar) then slap 'em down by force. Once again Mombasa was burnt to the ground.

In 1593 the Portuguese constructed the coral edifice of Fort Jesus as a way of saying, 'We're staying'. This act of architectural hubris led to frequent attacks by rebel forces and the ultimate expulsion of the Portuguese by Omani Arabs in 1698. But the Omanis were never that popular either, and the British, using a series of shifting alliances and brute force, turfed them out in 1870. All these power struggles, by the way, are the source of Mombasa's Island of War nickname.

Mombasa subsequently became the railhead for the Uganda railway and the most important city in British East Africa. In

INSECURITY IN MOMBASA

Although most of the sporadic attacks linked to the al-Qaeda affiliate al-Shabaab affected sections of Nairobi (the biggest being the one at Westgate Mall in September 2013), Mombasa and the south coast have borne the brunt of the effect on tourism. Following two small-scale bomb blasts that killed four people at a bus station and a hotel in May 2014, several countries, including the UK, USA and Australia, issued warnings against travelling to Mombasa island and sections of the coast between Mtwapa Creek in the north and Tiwi in the south. Although this area didn't include popular Diani Beach or Moi International Airport, British tour operators Thomson and First Choice pulled all guests out of the area as a precaution.

Although tourists are not typically targeted during periods of insecurity along the coast, robberies and violent attacks are more common during such periods, fuelled by anger, fear and the impact on unemployment levels. In the month following the bombings, two foreign female tourists and a Ugandan guide were shot dead in separate incidents in the vicinity of Fort Jesus.

Mombasa

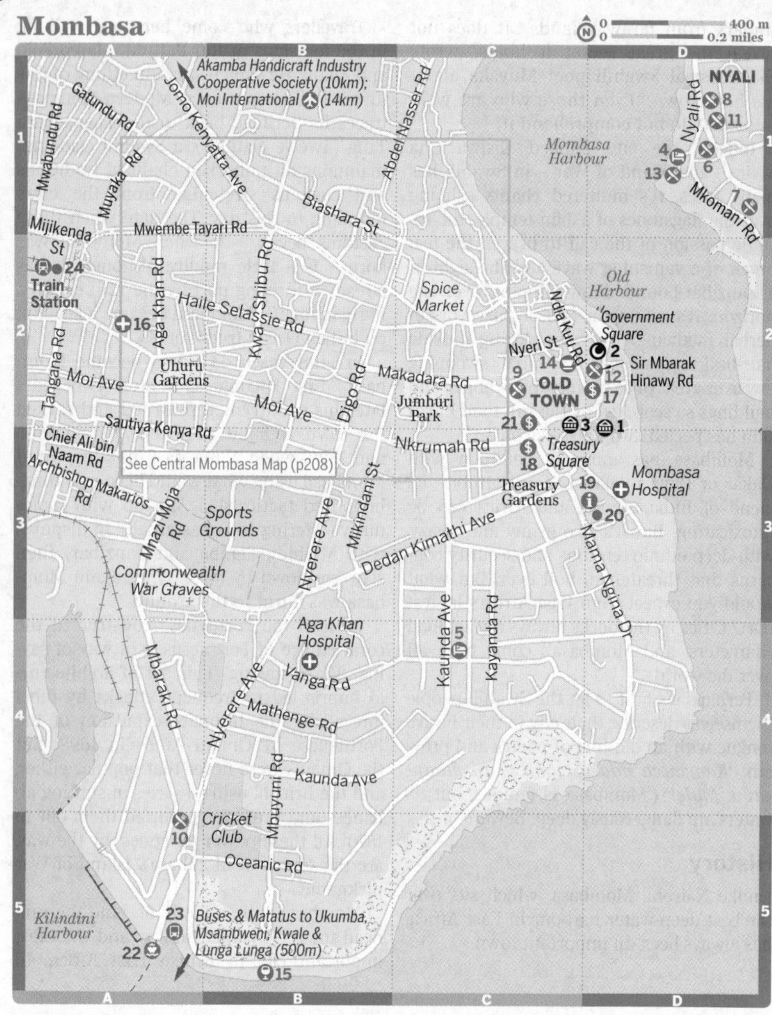

1920, when Kenya became a fully fledged British colony, Mombasa was made capital of the separate British Coast Protectorate. Following Kenyan independence in 1963 the city fell into a torpor. It was the most important city in the region and the second largest in the country, but it was removed from the cut and thrust of Kenyan politics, the focus of which had turned inland.

In the early 1990s violence briefly engulfed the city as supporters and opponents of the Islamic Party of Kenya clashed, but this has long since died down. During the 2007 elections the coast, and Mombasa in particular, provided a rare peek into the policy platforms, rather than communal politics, of Raila Odinga and Mwai Kibaki. Neither politician could rely on a Kikuyu or Luo base here, and both campaigned on ideas, rather than appeals to tribalism. Odinga won the province by promising, in effect, a form of limited federation, which remains a hope of many Mombasan politicians who consider the coast culturally, economically and religiously distinct enough to warrant some form of self-governance.

Mombasa's outlawed separatist movement, known as the Mombasa Republican

Mombasa

Sights
1 Fort Jesus D2
2 Mandhry Mosque D2
3 Old Law Courts C2

Activities, Courses & Tours
Tamarind Dhow .... (see 13)

Sleeping
4 Tamarind Village D1
5 YWCA Mombasa C4

Eating
6 Cafesserie D1
7 Hunter's Steak House D1
8 Misono D1
9 MN Kafe C2
10 Nakumatt Supermarket A5
11 Ooh! Ice-Cream D1
12 Rozina D2
13 Tamarind Restaurant D1

Drinking & Nightlife
14 Jahazi Coffee House C2
15 New Florida Nightclub B5

Information
16 AAR Health Services A2
17 Fort Jesus Forex Bureau D2
18 Kenya Commercial Bank C3
19 KWS Office D3
20 Mombasa Immigration Office D3
21 Standard Chartered Bank C2

Transport
22 Ferry A5
23 Local Bus & Matatu Stand A5
24 Mombasa–Nairobi Train A2

Council (MRC), listed grievances from land reform issues to economic marginalisation among reasons when it called for voters to boycott Kenya's 2013 presidential election. Nairobi imprisoned several of its key members over the years, and was jarred by its slogan, 'Pwani si Kenya' ('The coast is not Kenya'). Still, it continues to operate.

Mombasa's tensions were exacerbated in October 2013, when radical Muslim cleric Sheikh Ibrahim Rogo was killed by gunmen in the city. His supporters alleged that Kenyan security forces were involved in his murder. A second cleric, Sheikh Abubakar Shariff Ahmed, was killed in April 2014 under similar circumstances.

Sights

Fort Jesus
MUSEUM

(Map p206; adult/child KSh800/400; 8am-6pm) Fort Jesus, a Unesco World Heritage treasure, is Mombasa's most visited site. The metre-thick walls, frescoed interiors, traces of European graffiti, Arabic inscriptions and Swahili embellishment aren't just evocative, they're a record of the history of Mombasa and the coast writ in stone. The fort was built by the Portuguese in 1593 to serve as both symbol and headquarters of their permanent presence in this corner of the Indian Ocean.

It's ironic, then, that the construction of the fort marked the beginning of the end of local Portuguese hegemony. Between Portuguese sailors, Omani soldiers and Swahili rebellions, the fort changed hands at least nine times between 1631 and the early 1870s, when it finally fell under British control and was used as a jail.

The fort was the final project completed by Joao Batista Cairato, whose buildings can be found throughout Portugal's eastern colonies, from Old Goa to Old Mombasa. The building is an opus of period military design – assuming the structure was well manned, it would have been impossible to approach its walls without falling under the cone of interlocking fields of fire.

These days the fort houses a **museum** built over the former barracks. The exhibits should give a good insight into Swahili life and culture but, like the rest of the complex, it's all poorly labelled and woefully displayed, which, considering it's the city's number-one tourist attraction, is fairly scandalous.

Elsewhere within the fort compound, the **Mazrui Hall**, where flowery spirals fade across a wall topped with wooden lintels left by the Omani Arabs, is worthy of note. In another room, Portuguese sailors scratched graffiti that illustrates the multicultural naval identity of the Indian Ocean, leaving walls covered with four-pointed European frigates, three-pointed Arabic dhows and the coir-sewn 'camels of the ocean': the elegant Swahili *mtepe* (traditional sailing vessel). Nearby, a pair of whale bones serves in the undignified role of children's seesaw. The **Omani house**, in the San Felipe bastion in the northwestern corner of the fort, was built in the late 18th century. It was closed at the time of writing, but used

Central Mombasa

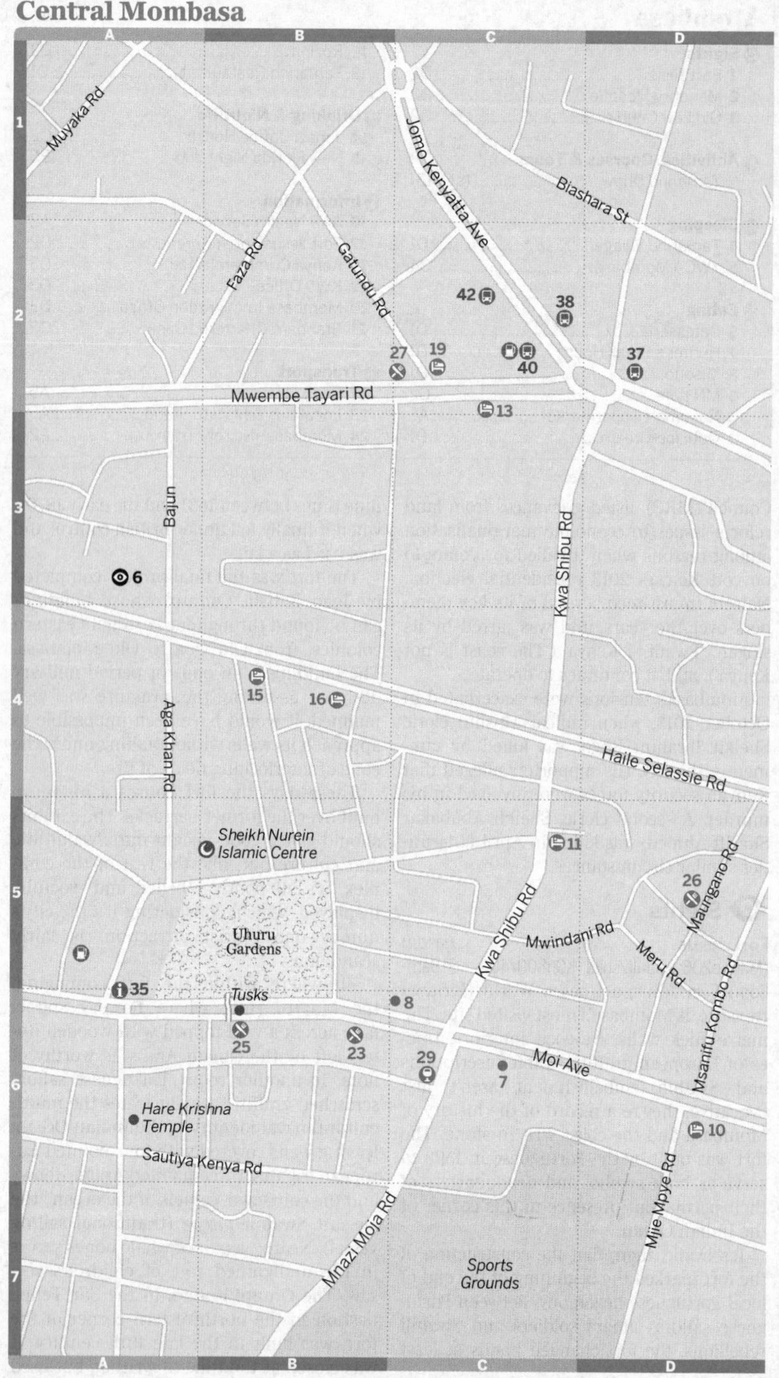

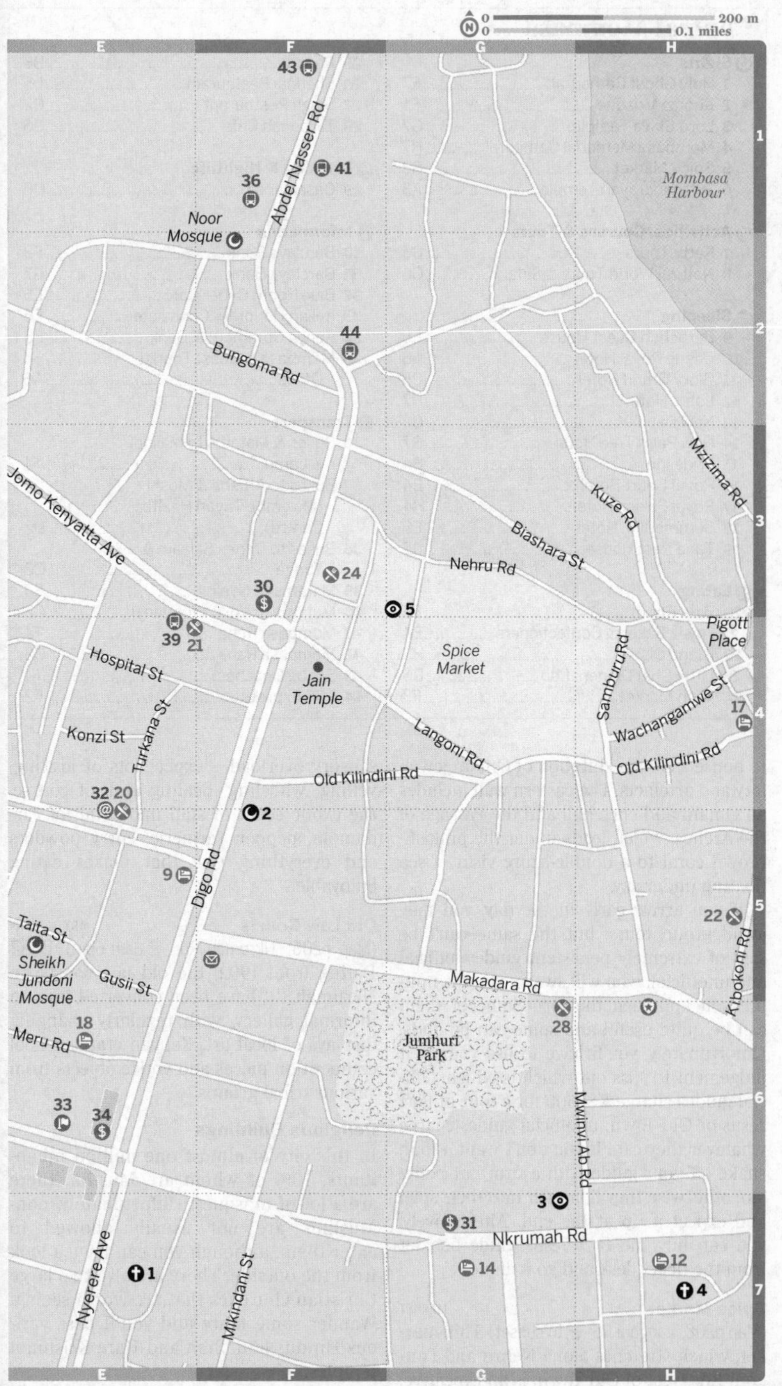
0 200 m
0 0.1 miles
Abdel Nasser Rd
Noor Mosque
Bungoma Rd
Mombasa Harbour
Jomo Kenyatta Ave
Biashara St
Nehru Rd
Kuze Rd
Mzizima Rd
Spice Market
Jain Temple
Pigott Place
Hospital St
Konzi St
Turkana St
Langoni Rd
Samburu Rd
Wachangamwe St
Old Kilindini Rd
Old Kilindini Rd
Digo Rd
Taita St
Sheikh Jundoni Mosque
Gusii St
Makadara Rd
Kibokoni Rd
Meru Rd
Jumhuri Park
Mwinyi Ab Rd
Nkrumah Rd
Nyerere Ave
Mikindani St
43
41
36
44
24
30
5
39
21
32
20
2
9
22
17
18
28
33
34
3
31
14
12
1
4

Central Mombasa

Sights
1 Holy Ghost Cathedral E7
2 Khonzi Mosque F5
3 Lord Shiva Temple G7
4 Mombasa Memorial Cathedral H7
5 Spice Market G3
6 Swaminarayan Temple A3

Activities, Courses & Tours
7 Ketty Tours C6
8 Natural World Tours & Safaris C6

Sleeping
9 Berachah Guest House E5
10 Castle Royal Hotel D6
11 Glory Grand Hotel C5
12 Lotus Hotel H7
13 New Daba C2
14 New Palm Tree Hotel G7
15 Pride Inn B4
16 Royal Court Hotel B4
17 Royal Palace Hotel H4
18 Summerlink Hotel E6
19 Tana Rest House C2

Eating
20 Blue Room E5
21 Fayaz Baker & Confectioners E4
22 Island Dishes H5
23 Little Chef Dinners Pub B6
24 Main Market F3
25 Recoda B6
26 Shehnai Restaurant D5
27 Singh Restaurant C2
28 Tarboush Cafe G6

Drinking & Nightlife
29 Casablanca C6

Information
30 Barclays Bank F3
31 Barclays Bank G7
32 Blue Room Cyber Café E5
33 Italian Honorary Consulate E6
34 Kenya Commercial Bank E6
35 Mombasa & Coast Tourist Office A6

Transport
36 Buses & Matatus to Malindi & Lamu F1
37 Buses to Arusha & Moshi (Mwembe Tayari Health Centre) D2
38 Buses to Dar es Salaam & Tanga C2
39 Matatus to Nyali E4
40 Matatus to Voi & Wundanyi C2
41 Mombasa Raha F1
42 Mombasa Raha C2
43 Simba Coaches F1
44 TSS Express F2

to house a small exhibition of Omani jewellery and artefacts. The eastern wall includes an Omani audience hall and the Passage of the Arches, which leads under the pinkish-brown coral to a double-azure vista of sea floating under sky.

If you arrive early in the day, you may avoid group tours, but the same can't be said of extremely persistent guides, official and unofficial, who will swarm you the minute you approach the fort. Some of them can be quite useful and some can be duds. Unfortunately, you'll have to use your best judgement to suss out which is which. Official guides charge KSh500 for a tour of Fort Jesus or Old Town; unofficial guides charge whatever they can. If you don't want a tour, shake off your guide with a firm but polite 'no', otherwise they'll launch into their spiel and expect a tip at the end. Alternatively, you can buy the Fort Jesus guide booklet from the ticket desk and go it alone.

Spice Market MARKET

(Map p208; Langoni Rd; ⏲to sunset) This market, which stretches along Nehru and Langoni Rds west of Old Town, is an evocative, sensory overload – expect lots of jostling, yelling, wheeling, dealing and, of course, the exotic scent of stall upon stall of cardamom, pepper, turmeric, curry powders and everything else that makes eating enjoyable.

Old Law Courts ART GALLERY

(Map p206; Nkrumah Rd; ⏲8am-6pm) FREE Dating from 1902, the old law courts on Nkrumah Rd have been converted into an informal gallery, with regularly changing displays of local art, Kenyan crafts, school competition pieces and votive objects from various tribal groups.

Religious Buildings

In this city of almost one million inhabitants, 70% of whom are Muslim, there are a lot of mosques. Unfortunately, non-Muslims are not usually allowed to enter them, although you can have a look from the outside. There are also two large Christian churches that are worth seeing. Wander some more and you'll pass various Hindu, Jain, Sikh and Hare Krishnan temples.

Mandhry Mosque MOSQUE

(Map p206; Sir Mbarak Hinawy Rd) Mandhry Mosque in Old Town is an excellent example of Swahili architecture, which combines the elegant flourishes of Arabic style with the comforting, geometric patterns of African design; note, for example, the gently rounded minaret.

Khonzi Mosque MOSQUE

(Map p208; Digo Rd) One of the more modern Islamic buildings in Mombasa.

Holy Ghost Cathedral CHURCH

(Map p208; Nkrumah Rd) The Christian Holy Ghost Cathedral is a very European hunk of neo-Gothic buttressed architecture, with massive fans in the walls to cool its former colonial congregations.

Mombasa Memorial Cathedral CHURCH

(Map p208; Nkrumah Rd) This cathedral tries almost too hard to fit in, resembling a mosque with its white walls, arches and cupola.

Lord Shiva Temple TEMPLE

(Map p208; Mwinyi Ab Rd) Mombasa's large Hindu population doesn't lack for places of worship. The enormous Lord Shiva Temple is airy, open and set off by an interesting sculpture garden.

Swaminarayan Temple TEMPLE

(Map p208; Haile Selassie Rd) The Swaminarayan Temple is stuffed with highlighter-bright murals that'll make you feel as if you've been transported to Mumbai.

Activities

Tamarind Dhow BOAT TOUR

(Map p206; 041-4471747; www.tamarind.co.ke; lunch/dinner cruise per person US$50/75; lunch/dinner cruise departs 1pm/6.30pm) This top-billing cruise is run by the posh Tamarind restaurant chain. It embarks from the jetty below Tamarind restaurant in Nyali and includes a harbour tour and fantastic meal. Prices include a complimentary cocktail and transport to and from your hotel, and the dhow itself is a beautiful piece of work.

Jahazi Marine BOAT TOUR

(01714967717; adult/child from €60/30) This other big operator offers a range of dhow trips.

Festivals & Events

Mombasa Triathlon SPORTS

(www.kenyatriathlon.org) Sporty types or keen spectators will enjoy this open competition, with men's, women's and children's races. It's held in November.

Sleeping

★ **Berachah Guest House** GUESTHOUSE $

(Map p208; 0725864704; Haile Selassie Rd; s/d KSh1000/1600) This popular central choice is located in the heart of Mombasa's best eat streets. It has variable but clean rooms in a range of unusual shapes. It's on the 2nd floor – on the stair landing, turn right into the hotel, not left into the evangelical church.

TOURS & SAFARIS FROM MOMBASA

A number of tour companies offer standard tours of Old Town and Fort Jesus (per person from US$45), plus safaris to Shimba Hills National Reserve and Tsavo East and Tsavo West National Parks. Most safaris are expensive lodge-based affairs, but there are a few camping safaris to Tsavo East and West.

The most popular safari is an overnight tour to Tsavo, and though most people enjoy these, be warned that a typical two-day, one-night safari barely gives you time to get there and back, and that your animal-spotting time will be very limited. It's much better to add in at least one extra night.

We receive a constant stream of emails from travellers who feel that their promised safari hasn't lived up to expectations, but these companies have received positive feedback.

Natural World Tours & Safaris (Map p208; 041-2226715; www.naturaltoursandsafaris.com; Jeneby House, Moi Ave) The hard sell prattled by the company 'representatives' on the street can quickly put you off, but otherwise it has a reputation for delivering what it promises.

Ketty Tours (Map p208; 041-2315178; www.kettysafari.com; Ketty Plaza, Moi Ave) Organised and reliable.

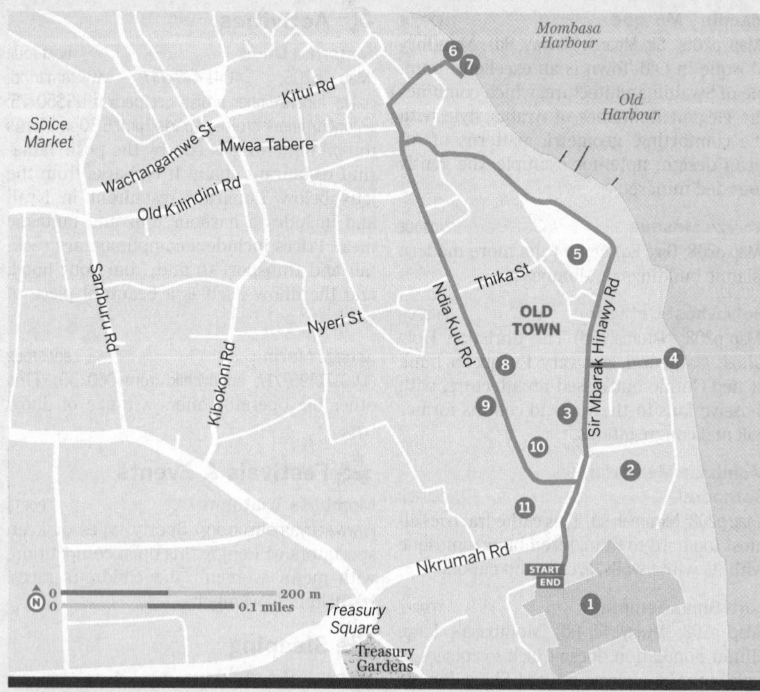

City Walk Mombasa Old Town

START FORT JESUS
FINISH FORT JESUS
LENGTH ABOUT 1.5KM
DURATION ONE HOUR

Mombasa may not have the medieval charm of Lamu or Zanzibar, but Old Town is a unique architectural blend of all who've influenced Swahili history and culture.

Start at 1 **Fort Jesus** (p207). From here head past the colonial 2 **Mombasa Club** onto Sir Mbarak Hinawy Rd, once the main access road to the port and still a lively thoroughfare.

On the left, 3 **Africa Hotel** was one of only three hotels in the city at the turn of the 20th century. If you take a quick jaunt to your right you'll hit the water and see the restored facades of 4 **old houses**.

Turn the corner at the end of the street and you'll enter 5 **Government Square**, the largest open space in Old Town. The buildings lining the square used to hold some of the city's key administrative offices.

Heading out of the square you'll need to hang a right towards Mombasa harbour. Here you'll find the 6 **Leven Steps**, which lead down past a great view of the ships docking in the harbour to 7 **Vasco da Gama's Well**, a reservoir that supposedly never dries.

Returning to Ndia Kuu Rd, the final stages of your route can be as direct or as tangential as you wish – diverting into side streets is highly recommended.

The winding alleyways linking Old Town towards Digo Rd are lively with market traders. Heading this way will eventually land you in the city spice market.

If you do stick to Ndia Kuu Rd, you'll see a lot of nicely restored traditional buildings, including the 8 **Balcony House**, so named for obvious reasons; 9 **Edward St Rose**, the former chemist, which retains its original engraved glass panel; and 10 **Ali's Curio Market**, one of the better-preserved balcony houses. Pass the Muslim 11 **cemetery** and you're back at Fort Jesus.

YWCA Mombasa HOSTEL $
(Map p206; ☎0412229856; cnr Kaunda & Kiambu Aves; r from KSh1600) If you're not already a member, you'll have to sign up (KSh300) to use this YWCA. It's primarily for women, but there is a men's floor as well. Rooms can also be split between mixed-sex couples or groups. There's a cheap restaurant that's popular with Kenyan students.

New Palm Tree Hotel HOTEL $
(Map p208; ☎Nairobi 020-8025682; www.newpalmtreehotel.com; Nkrumah Rd; s/d US$33/45) If you're looking for budget-friendly but reasonably comfortable digs, this place delivers. Rooms are arranged around a spick-and-span courtyard and while the amenities (such as hot water) aren't always reliable, the service is fine, it's generally well cared for and there's a good vibe about the place.

Tana Rest House GUESTHOUSE $
(Map p208; ☎041-490550; cnr Mwembe Tayari & Gatundu Rds; s/d KSh400/500) Probably the cheapest of Mombasa's safe guesthouses, this place isn't pretty on the outside (the name looks like it's been scrawled with a felt-tip pen), but the rooms are clean and your purse will thank you. Perfectly fine for a night or two.

New Daba GUESTHOUSE $
(Map p208; ☎0722472982; Mwembe Tayari Rd; r from KSh1200) The distinctly functional (ie ugly) New Daba is nonetheless one of the cleaner options if you're on a budget, or you've just arrived on a night bus and need a place to crash.

Glory Grand Hotel BUSINESS HOTEL $
(Map p208; ☎041-2313564; Kwa Shibu Rd; s/d from KSh3200/4000) Neither glorious nor grand, this hotel is instead excellent value, with spruced-up rooms that hint at business-hotel style – minus the cost. Breakfast is simple, but it's a safe, convenient place to sleep and is located in a quiet(ish) area.

Summerlink Hotel HOTEL $
(Map p208; ☎041-2317895; www.summerlinkhotel.blogspot.com; Meru Rd; s/d KSh1700/2300; ❄🏋) Another midrange place with a lovely rooftop terrace (sometimes Mombasa is just better experienced from up high). It's a clean place with excellent security, good service and loads of Kenyan businessmen. There's also an on-site gym and karate classes, which is obviously what you came here for.

Royal Palace Hotel HOTEL $
(Map p208; ☎0717620602, 0736663011; www.royalpalacehotelmombasa.com; cnr Old Kilindini & Kibokoni Rds; s/d from KSh1300/2500) The style here is a bit Nigerian chic and some of the rooms could do with a lick of paint, but there's a lovely rooftop terrace and the staff are welcoming. A perfectly fine budget option.

★**Lotus Hotel** HOTEL $$
(Map p208; ☎041-2313207; www.lotushotelmombasa.com; Cathedral Lane, off Nkrumah Rd; s/d KSh4300/5000) Close to the cathedral, this hotel is a reliable midrange bet. Both the hot water and air-conditioning were working when we took up residence, and the breakfasts set us up for the day. Plus, it's clean and slightly quieter than most other city-centre options.

★**Castle Royal Hotel** HISTORIC HOTEL $$
(Map p208; ☎Nairobi 020-315680; www.sentrimhotels.net; Moi Ave; s/d US$95/130; ❄@📶) With old-fashioned balconies and a dated, colonial exterior, this place scrubs up pretty well on the inside. The rooms have had a makeover and are rather nice indeed, plus there's a beautiful terrace looking out over the city. Breakfast includes coconut beans and *mandazi* (semisweet doughnuts), or bacon and croissants.

★**Pride Inn** BUSINESS HOTEL $$
(Map p208; ☎041-2317895; www.prideinn.co.ke; Haile Selassie Rd; s/d US$80/$105; ❄@📶) Right on Haile Selassie Rd, this hotel makes up in convenience what it lacks in soundproofing. The rooms are business quality and well cared for, but they're not fancy. A solid, mildly stylish option for a short Mombasa stay.

Royal Court Hotel BUSINESS HOTEL $$
(Map p208; ☎0733412867; Haile Selassie Rd; s/d KSh6500/7750; ❄@📶🏊) The swish lobby is the highlight of this stylish business hotel. Still, service and facilities are good, disabled access is a breeze and you get great views and food at the Tawa Terrace restaurant on the roof, which also has a pool. It wins points for charging tourists and residents (expatriates) the same, but loses points for charging to use the wi-fi.

Eating

★ Shehnai Restaurant INDIAN $

(Map p208; ☎041-2224801; Fatemi House, Maungano Rd; mains from KSh500; ⏲noon-2pm & 7.30-10.30pm Tue-Sun) This reputable *mughlai* (north Indian) curry house does delicious things such as *gosht palakwalla* (lamb with masala and spinach) and scrambled eggs tossed with green chillies and cumin. It's complemented by nice decor that's been copied from Indian restaurants the world over (pumped-in sitar music thrown in for free). It's very popular with well-heeled Indian families, probably because the food is authentic and very good. Add 25% in various taxes to all prices.

Tarboush Cafe INTERNATIONAL $

(Map p208; Makadara Rd; mains KSh150-350) Most people come to this open-air, parkside restaurant for the chicken tikka, and rightfully so. Eat it with lovely soft naan bread, rice or chips. There's also a good range of Swahili staples and some curries. Despite being packed at all hours, the service remains fast and friendly.

Blue Room SANDWICHES $

(Map p208; ☎0721786868; www.blueroomonline.com; Haile Selassie Rd; mains KSh200-450) There's nothing to bring on the blues at this cheap-and-cheerful fast (well, sometimes) food diner. On the menu, there's a long list of sandwich options, plus wood-fired pizzas (the chicken tikka option goes down well in these Swahili parts) and, of course, hot bowls of masala chips. Delivery is also possible.

Recoda KENYAN $

(Map p208; Moi Ave; mains KSh150-400; ⏲lunch & dinner) Fifty years ago this legendary Mombasa eatery must have been wondrous. Sadly, all that remains from those days are stories and recipes – the kebabs are grilled to fat-dripping perfection. Service is a bit sharp, but take it with a spoonful of sugar, because the food is worth your patience.

Island Dishes KENYAN $

(Map p208; Kibokoni Rd; mains KSh80-220) Once your eyes have adjusted to the dazzling strip lights, feast them on the tasty menu at this very popular Swahili restaurant. *Mishikaki* (marinated, grilled meat kebabs), chicken tikka, fish, fresh juices and all the usual favourites are on offer to eat in or take away, though the biryani is only available at lunchtime.

Little Chef Dinners Pub KENYAN $

(Map p208; Moi Ave; mains KSh120-300; ⏲lunch & dinner) This funky, green-hued pub-restaurant has no relation to the British motorway diners of the same name. Little Chef dishes up big, tasty portions of Kenyan and international dishes (as long as those dishes are fried, anyway). There are a couple more outlets in the area, but this is by far the nicest.

Ooh! Ice-Cream ICE CREAM $

(Map p206; Nyali Rd, Nyali; ice cream KSh60-100) Even if this glossy, air-conditioned place didn't serve fantastic ice creams, cakes and snacks, we'd still consider including it just because of the name!

Fayaz Baker & Confectioners BAKERY $

(Map p208; Jomo Kenyatta Ave) Mombasa's 'Master Baker' cooks up excellent cakes and muffins in several locations around town.

Main Market MARKET $

(Map p208; Digo Rd) Mombasa's dilapidated 'covered' market is packed with stalls selling fresh fruit and vegetables. Roaming produce carts also congregate in the surrounding streets, and dozens of *miraa* (twigs and shoots that are chewed as a stimulant) sellers join the fray when the regular deliveries come in. Remember, if you're chewing, you chew the peeled stalks and not the leaves like in Ethiopia and Yemen.

Nakumatt Supermarket SUPERMARKET $

(Map p206; ☎0733632134; Nyerere Ave) Close to the Likoni ferry jetty, this place has a good selection of provisions, drinks and hardware items – just in case you need a TV, bicycle or lawnmower to take on safari.

★ Rozina KENYAN $$

(Map p206; ☎041-2312642; Africa Hotel, Sir Mbarak Hinawy Rd; mains around KSh800) Rozina makes for a good lunch stop after a morning exploring Fort Jesus (it's a short walk away). Locals will tell you it's been around almost as long as the fort itself, and it retains a dose of old Swahili charm. The ginger-infused seafood grills are excellent.

★ Hunter's Steak House STEAKHOUSE $$

(Map p206; ☎041-4474759; Mkomani Rd, 'Königsallee', Nyali; mains KSh450-2000; ⏲Wed-Mon) *Nyama choma* (barbecued meat) this isn't.

Instead you'll find thick sizzling steaks, served with serious comfort food such as garlic mushrooms, crunchy fries and husks of toasted bread. In fact, if you squint a little and stare at the decor you could almost be in the American Midwest. There's a nice range of beers, too.

★MN Kafe CAFE $$
(Map p206; ☎0711665233; Makadara Rd) Between the narrow alleys of Old Town, this sleek gem serves up the best international breakfasts in Mombasa. The Mexican version – bacon and eggs served with chilli-lime salsa and spiced waffles – couldn't be more irrelevant here, but damn, it's good. The cakes are just as good.

★Singh Restaurant INDIAN $$
(Map p208; ☎0733702145; Mwembe Tayari Rd; mains KSh350-850) Another great Indian restaurant steeped in Mombasa history: the owner first opened the doors in 1962 to serve arriving and departing railway passengers. The decor is plain, but your taste buds won't notice. Even things that don't sound great on paper, such as egg curry, are divine here. We rate the aubergine dishes highly.

Drinking & Nightlife

★Jahazi Coffee House CAFE
(Map p206; ☎0720777313; Ndia Kuu Rd; ⏲8am-8pm) With lashings of sexy Mombasa style, this lounge cafe is the perfect spot to chill out in arty surrounds. Did we mention that it has great coffee? The Swahili pot, if you're after something different, turns the grind into a ritual. You won't want to leave.

Casablanca BAR
(Map p208; Mnazi Moja Rd; ⏲noon-late) Of all the gin joints, in all the towns...walking into this one isn't the worst thing you could do. Classy but still cheeky, Casablanca is wildly popular. And yes, it's brimming with ladies of the night, but rumour has it that the late owner treated his resident girls so well, 300 of them turned up at his funeral.

New Florida Nightclub CLUB
(Map p206; Mama Ngina Dr; entry after 7.30pm KSh500; ⏲6pm-6am) We know why this place was named after the Disney state. Like a theme park for grown-ups, there's all sorts to get into here: an outdoor pool, a 'crazy' blue bar, fluorescent palm trees and Vegas-style floor shows.

Shopping

Akamba Handicraft Industry Cooperative Society HANDICRAFTS
(www.akambahandicraftcoop.com; Port Reitz Rd; ⏲8am-5pm Mon-Fri, to noon Sun) This cooperative employs an incredible 10,000 people from the local area. It's also a non-profit organisation and produces fine woodcarvings. Kwa Hola/Magongo matatus run right past the gates from the Kobil petrol

SHOPPING MOMBASA

What else to do in a centuries-old trading port than hit the shops? Mombasa's shopping scene blends markets with artisanal co-ops, and food with fashion. Here are a few things to look out for.

Kikois and kangas are brightly coloured woven sarongs (the former, for men) and wraps (the latter, for women). They come as a pair, one for the top half of the body and one for the bottom, and are marked with Swahili proverbs. Head to Biashara St, west of the Digo Rd intersection (just north of the spice market). You may need to bargain, but what you get is generally what you pay for – bank on about KSh500 for a pair of cheap kangas or a *kikoi*. *Kofia*, the handmade caps worn by Muslim men, are also crafted here; a really excellent one can cost up to KSh2500.

Tailored outfits are easy to come by, as long as you have a few days with which to play. Try the tailors on Nehru Rd, behind the spice market. You can either buy some stylish printed fabric beforehand or have your tailor assist.

Moi Ave has loads of souvenir shops, but prices are high and every shop seems to stock exactly the same stuff. Instead, head to the quieter Chembe Rd, where the touts are less aggressive and you'll be able to take your time over your big decisions.

Saffron, cinnamon, cloves, cardamom, curry powder from India...no visit to Mombasa is complete without a stop at the famous spice market (p210). Prices aren't fixed, so start bargaining only once you're sure you want to buy something. You'll also likely be offered other kinds of 'spices', such as *miraa* (twigs and shoots that are chewed as a stimulant) and pan.

station on Jomo Kenyatta Ave. Many coach tours from Mombasa also stop here.

Information

DANGERS & ANNOYANCES

Rising crime levels and security issues can make it unwise to walk around alone after dark. During the day, you shouldn't have a problem, although women in particular can expect to be hassled when walking alone through Old Town. When in doubt, hailing a tuk-tuk is an easy (and cheap) answer. Wrapping a headscarf around your hair is also a quick solution to unwanted male attention.

Most visits to Mombasa are free from crime and violence, but we advise not to fight back if muggers do appear – at least one of the two women shot and killed near Fort Jesus in May 2014 was believed to be the victim of a botched robbery.

EMERGENCY

Central Police Station (Map p208; ☎999; Makadara Rd)

INTERNET ACCESS

Blue Room Cyber Café (Map p208; ☎041-224021; www.blueroomonline.com; Haile Selassie Rd; per min KSh2; ⊙9am-10pm)

MEDICAL SERVICES

AAR Health Services (Map p206; ☎0731191067; www.aarhealth.com; Pereira Bldg, Machakos St, off Moi Ave; ⊙24hr) Medical clinic.

Aga Khan Hospital (Map p206; ☎041-222771; www.agakhanhospitals.org; Vanga Rd)

Mombasa Hospital (Map p206; ☎041-2312191; www.mombasahospital.com; off Mama Ngina Dr)

MONEY

Barclays Bank (Map p208; ☎041-311660; Digo Rd) Has an ATM, as does another branch on Nkrumah Rd (Map p208; Nkrumah Rd).

Fort Jesus Forex Bureau (Map p206; ☎041-316717; Ndia Kuu Rd) Currency exchange.

Standard Chartered Bank (Map p206; ☎041-224614; Treasury Sq, Nkrumah Rd) With ATM.

POST

Post office (Map p208; ☎041-227705; Digo Rd)

TOURIST INFORMATION

Mombasa & Coast Tourist Office (Map p208; ☎041-2228722; Moi Ave; ⊙8am-4.30pm) Provides information and can organise accommodation, tours, guides and transport.

Getting There & Away

AIR

Fly540 (☎Mombasa 041-2319078, booking 0710540540; www.fly540.com; Moi International Airport) Flies between Nairobi and Mombasa at least five times daily (one way from KSh4200), as well as between Mombasa and Zanzibar. Malindi and Lamu flights go through Nairobi.

Kenya Airways (☎Mombasa 041-2125251, Nairobi 020-3274747; www.kenya-airways.com; Nyali City Mall) Book online or in person at the ticket office in Nyali City Mall (next to Nakumatt). Nairobi–Mombasa return flights cost around KSh10,000.

BUS & MATATU

Most bus offices are on either Jomo Kenyatta Ave or Abdel Nasser Rd. Services to Malindi and Lamu leave from Abdel Nasser Rd, while buses to destinations in Tanzania leave from the junction of Jomo Kenyatta Ave and Mwembe Tayari Rd.

For buses and matatus to the beaches and towns south of Mombasa, you first need to get off the island on the Likoni ferry. Frequent matatus run from Nyerere Ave to the transport stand by the ferry terminal.

Note that as with most bus and matatu fares in Kenya, fares vary depending on demand (and fuel prices).

Nairobi

There are dozens of daily departures in both directions (mostly in the early morning and late evening). Daytime services take at least six hours, and overnight trips eight to 10 hours, and include a meal/smoking break about halfway.

The trip isn't particularly comfortable, although it's not bad for an African bus ride, but note that the Nairobi–Mombasa highway is accident prone. Speedometers with an 80km/h limit fitted on buses and matatus have eased the problem somewhat, but some drivers continue to flout rules. Theft is also an issue on this route – as much as it disappoints us to say so, don't accept food and drink from fellow travellers. We've heard too many stories of *mzungus* (both tourists and white Kenyans) being drugged and mugged on this route. Most trips, however, are crime and accident free.

Fares vary from KSh500 to KSh3000, with Modern Coast the swishest (and most expensive) of the lot. Most companies have at least four departures daily. Most buses to Nairobi travel via Voi (KSh300 to KSh500), which is also served by frequent matatus from the Kobil petrol station on Jomo Kenyatta Ave (KSh200). Several companies go to Kisumu and Lake Victoria, but all go via Nairobi.

WORTH A TRIP

LUNATIC LINE: NAIROBI–MOMBASA RAILWAY

Few subjects divide our readers' letters more fiercely than the train from Nairobi to Mombasa. Once one of the most famous rail lines in Africa, the train is today, depending on who you speak to, either a sociable way of avoiding the rutted highway and a way of spotting wildlife from the clackety comfort of a sleeping car, or a ratty, tatty, overrated waste of time. The truth lies somewhere in the middle. The train's condition could be described as 'faded glory', occasionally bumping up to 'romantically dishevelled', or slipping into 'frustrating mediocrity'. The latter isn't helped by spotty scheduling and lax timetable enforcement. At the time of writing, it wasn't uncommon for the Mombasa–Nairobi leg to take up to three days longer than planned. Still, if you're up for an adventure...

Currently then, the 'iron snake' departs Mombasa train station at 7pm on Tuesday, Thursday and Sunday, arriving (in theory) in Nairobi the next day somewhere between 9.30am and 1pm. Fares are US$75 for 1st class (two-bed compartments) and US$65 for 2nd class (four-bed), including breakfast (you get dinner with a 1st-class fare); reserve as far in advance as possible.

Heading North

There are numerous daily buses and matatus (Map p208) up the coast to Malindi, leaving from in front of the Noor Mosque on Abdel Nasser Rd. Buses take up to three hours (around KSh500) and matatus take about two hours (KSh350 rising to KSh600 during holidays and very busy periods).

Tawakal, Simba and **TSS Express** (Map p208; Abdel Nasser Rd) have buses to Lamu, most leaving at around 7am (report 30 minutes early) from its offices on Abdel Nasser Rd. Buses take around seven hours to reach the Lamu ferry at Mokoke (KSh600 to KSh800) and travel via Malindi.

Heading South

Regular buses and matatus leave from the Likoni ferry terminal and travel along the southern coast.

Tanzania

Simba and a handful of other companies have daily departures to Dar es Salaam (KSh1200 to KSh1600, 10 to 12 hours) via Tanga from their offices on Jomo Kenyatta Ave, near the junction with Mwembe Tayari Rd (Map p208).

Dubious-looking buses to Moshi and Arusha leave from in front of the Mwembe Tayari Health Centre (Map p208) in the morning or evening.

Coast (☎041-3433166; www.coastbus.com)
Mash (☎041-3432471)
Simba Coaches (Map p208; Abdel Nasser Rd)

TRAIN

Mombasa–Nairobi Train (Map p206; ☎Nairobi 020-3596750, 0722106395, 0733681061; www.kenyatrainbooking.com; Mombasa Railway Station) You can reserve online, by phone or in person at the station from Monday to Friday (9am to 5pm).

Getting Around

TO/FROM THE AIRPORT

There is currently no public transport to or from the airport, so you'll need to hop in a taxi. The fare to central Mombasa is around KSh1200.

BOAT

The two Likoni ferries connect Mombasa island with the southern mainland. There's a crossing roughly every 20 minutes between 5am and 12.30am, and less frequently outside these times. It's free for pedestrians, KSh75 per small car and KSh165 for a safari jeep. To get to the jetty from the centre of town, take a Likoni matatu from Digo Rd (Map p206) .

MATATU, TAXI & TUK-TUK

Matatus charge between KSh30 and KSh50 for short trips. Mombasa taxis are as expensive as those in Nairobi, and harder to find; a good place to look is in front of Express Travel on Nkrumah Rd. Assume it'll cost KSh250 to KSh400 from the train station to the city centre. There are also plenty of three-wheeled tuk-tuks about, which run from about KSh50 to KSh200 for a bit of open-air transit.

SOUTH OF MOMBASA

From Mombasa to the Tanzanian border there's some serious sand. And not just any sand; oh no, these beaches are some of Africa's most splendid. Think sweeping coves buttered with lashings of white sand, framed by emerald waters and topped with buff kitesurfers. There are far worse places to spend a few days.

And yet, this stretch of Kenya is about more than just beach life. Slip into the sea and lay out under those coconut fronds, but, while you're at it, try walking through a 600-year-old sacred forest, scouting for mudskippers in a forest of mangroves, snorkelling in the jewel-box waters of a marine park, or feeling the salty wind curl off a dhow's prow as you head to a new island.

Shimba Hills National Reserve

Cool and grassy, this 320-sq-km **national reserve** (☎0704467855; www.kws.org; adult/child US$20/10; ⏲6am-6pm) makes an easy day trip from Diani Beach. Its lush hills are home to sable antelope, elephants, warthogs, baboons, buffaloes and Masai giraffes, as well as 300 species of butterfly. The sable antelope have made a stunning recovery here after their numbers dropped to less than 120 in 1970.

In 2005 the elephant population reached an amazing 600 – far too many for this tiny space. Instead of culling the herds, Kenya Wildlife Service (KWS) organised an unprecedented US$3.2-million translocation operation to reduce the pressure on the habitat, capturing no fewer than 400 elephants and moving them to Tsavo East National Park.

There are more than 150km of 4WD tracks that criss-cross the reserve.

Sights

Sheldrick Falls WATERFALL

These pretty 21m-high falls are laced with lianas and greenery, and have a natural plunge pool. KWS-organised walks, lasting one to two hours, depart from the Sheldrick Falls ranger post several times a day.

Marere Dam VIEWPOINT

A watering hole that attracts animals, including elephants. Also a great birdwatching spot.

Elephant Hill VIEWPOINT

The best viewpoint in the reserve, this hill is the place to see elephants and affords lovely views out over the valley towards the ocean. Armed rangers will escort you once you reach the entry point to the hill.

Sleeping

There are four public campsites (camping US$15) within the reserve, included one located on the way to Sheldrick Falls. Most of the camps are large, with a capacity for around 50 tents, and all are basic with limited facilities. KWS also has two *bandas* (thatched huts; US$70) available, each fitted with twin beds.

Shimba Lodge LODGE $$

(☎0722200952; www.aberdaresafarihotels.com; Kinango Rd; r from US$140) Staying here is quite an experience, although not one as luxurious as the price might suggest. The rooms are simple but clean and come with character; the highlight is the wildlife seen from the canopy tree platform, which looks out over a forest clearing. The restaurant is open until midnight and serves simple, hearty meals.

Getting There & Away

You'll need a 4WD to enter the reserve, but hitching may be possible at the main gate. From Likoni, small lorry-buses to Kwale pass the main gate (KSh80) or nearby; be prepared to walk or find alternative transport if routes vary.

SHIMBA HILLS NATIONAL RESERVE

Why Go It's an easy day trip from the coast, has good elephant spotting and is the only Kenyan home of the sable antelope.

When to Go Year-round, but the dry season from November to March is best.

Practicalities Diani Beach, 45 minutes' drive away, is the most popular base, and numerous safari companies and hotels there offer trips to Shimba Hills. With good roads, short distances and ease of access, this is a perfect family-friendly park.

Budget Tips Some of the package deals offered by Diani Beach hotels (starting at US$50 per person) actually represent the best value for a trip to Shimba Hills.

If you prefer to go your own way, matatus (minibus transport) run from the Likoni ferry to the town of Kwale, 3km from the reserve gate. From there you can walk to the main gate or board a matatu (KSh70). You may be able to link up with other travellers at the gate, but be prepared to wait around.

DON'T MISS

MWALUGANJE ELEPHANT SANCTUARY

This **sanctuary** (☎040-41121; www.kws.org; adult/child US$15/2, vehicles KSh150-500; ⊙6am-6pm) is a good example of community-based conservation, with local people acting as stakeholders in the project. It was opened in October 1995 to create a corridor along an elephant-migration route between Shimba Hills and Mwaluganje Forest Reserve, and comprises 24 sq km (2400 hectares) of rugged, beautiful country along the valley of the Cha Shimba River.

Other than the 150-or-so elephants, the big-ticket wildlife can be a little limited. However, you're likely to have the place to yourself, the scenery is almost a cliché of what East Africa should look like and there's plenty of little stuff to see. All this makes Mwaluganje more suitable for those who've done a few safaris elsewhere and are after a wilder, more pristine experience. The drier country means the wildlife in Mwaluganje differs slightly from that of wetter and greener Shimba Hills. This is especially noticeable when it comes to the birds, with many species found here that aren't seen anywhere else on the coast.

The main entrance to the sanctuary is about 13km northeast of Shimba Hills National Reserve, on the road to Kinango. A shorter route runs from Kwale to the Golini gate, passing the Mwaluganje ticket office. It's only 5km but the track is 4WD only. The roads inside the park are pretty rough and a 4WD is the way to go.

You can stay at the **Mwaluganje Elephant Camp** (☎0115486121; camping KSh600, s/d US$160/225), a rather fine place with very plush safari tents overlooking a waterhole. If you can't afford the fancy-pants tents then camping in your own tent is possible at the campsite, located near the main gate. The setting is sublime (though the rocky surface makes things tricky for tent pegs!). It's as genuine an African wilderness experience as you can ask for.

Every safari company in Mombasa and Diani Beach offers trips to Shimba Hills (half-day tours start from US$50 per person).

Tiwi Beach

More sleepy, shaded and secluded than Diani Beach, Tiwi makes a lovely, quiet, cottage-style escape by the ocean. The sand isn't that same peroxide shade, but the pretty beach is studded with skinny palms and there are fewer hassles. Tiwi also has a beautiful coral reef, part of which teems with starfish of all shapes and colours. A stable, pool-like area between the shore and the coral is great for swimming.

Sleeping & Eating

Twiga Lodge HOTEL $
(☎0721577614; twigakenya@gmail.com; camping KSh500, s/d KSh1500/2500, new wing s/d KSh3000/4800) Overlanders' favourite Twiga is great fun when there's a crowd staying, with the palpable sense of isolation alleviated by the sheer tropical exuberance of the place. The older rooms are set off from the beach – opt for one of the nicer, newer rooms if you can. The on-site restaurant is OK, but having a drink under thatch while stars spill over the sea is as perfect as moments come.

★**Sand Island Beach Cottages** COTTAGES $$
(☎0722395005; www.sandislandbeach.com; cottages US$120-200) A favourite among worn-out Nairobians, Sand Island occupies a peaceful, blissful spot swathed in green and gold. Accommodation is in homely cottages nestled on the edge of the sand; each has its own style. The newest, Pweza cottage, features furniture made from salvaged Swahili doors. The cottages are self-catering, but you can hire your own cook for KSh1000 per day.

It's signposted from the main Tiwi Beach road, and lies 3.5km along a dirt track.

Coral Cove Cottages COTTAGES $$
(☎0722732797; www.coralcove.tiwibeach.com; cottages KSh5500-8600) Another good self-catering option, offering simple, colourful cottages within sight of the ocean. Expect a warm welcome – from the menagerie of animals as well as from host Kerstin – and cottages furnished with everything you might need for a weekend hideaway.

Amani RESORT $$
(☎Nairobi 020-2120192; www.amanitiwibeachresort.com; d from KSh8000; ≋) If your dreams run bigger and shinier than Tiwi's other

offerings, there's always Amani. This huge resort looks somewhat monstrous in comparison to the other accommodation options, but its seafood buffet is apparently quite good, and the rooms are nice. It's clad in peach and has several pools, plus a spa, large restaurant and bar.

Getting There & Away

To get to Tiwi, turn left off the main highway (A14) about 18km south of Mombasa (or right if you're coming from Diani) and follow the track until it terminates at a north–south T-junction.

Buses and matatus on the Likoni–Ukunda road can drop you at the start of either track down to Tiwi (KSh50). The southern turn-off, known locally as Tiwi 'spot', is much easier to find. Although it's only 3.5km to the beach, both access roads are notorious for muggings, so take a taxi or hang around for a lift. If you're heading back to the highway, any of the accommodation places can call ahead for a taxi.

Diani Beach

With a flawless stretch of white-sand beach hugged by lush forest and kissed by surfable waves, it's no wonder Diani Beach is so popular. This resort town scores points with a diverse crowd: party people, families, honeymooners, backpackers and water-sports enthusiasts.

But if that sounds like your typical resort town, think again. Diani has some of the best accommodation in Kenya, from budget tree houses to funky kitesurfing lodges and intimate honeymoon spots. Most places are spread along the beach road, hidden behind a line of forest.

When lazing in a hammock gets tiring, visit the coral mosques with their archways that overlook the open ocean, venture into the sacred forests where guides hug trees that speak in their ancestors' voices, or take in the monkey sanctuary – all are good ways to experience more of the coast than the considerable charms of sun and sand.

Sights

★Colobus Conservation Centre

WILDLIFE RESERVE

(0711479453; www.colobusconservation.org; Diani Beach Rd; tours adult/child KSh750/250; 8am-5pm Mon-Sat) Notice the monkeys clambering on rope ladders over the road? The ladders are the work of the Colobus Conservation Centre, which aims to protect the Angolan black-and-white colobus monkey, a once-common species now restricted to a few isolated pockets of forest south of Mombasa. It runs excellent tours of its headquarters, where you'll likely get to see a few orphaned or injured colobus and other monkeys undergoing the process of rehabilitation to the wild.

With advance notice it can organise forest walks (per person KSh1000) in search of wilder primates and other creatures. There's also a wildly popular volunteer program, costing from €750 for three weeks.

Tiwi & Diani Beaches

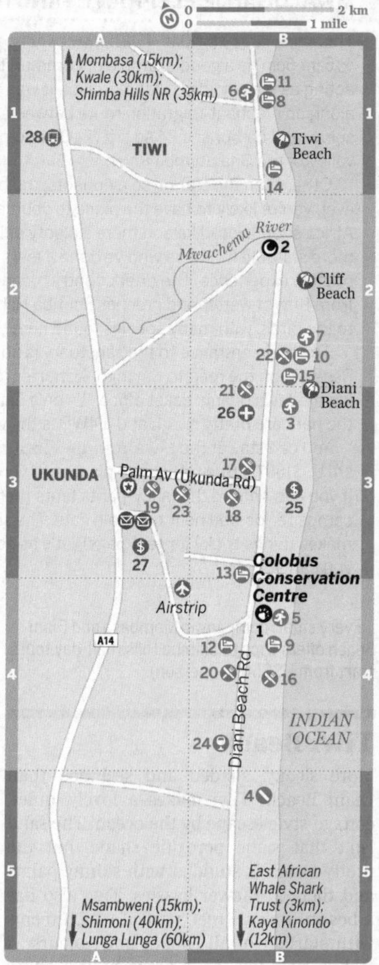

Tiwi & Diani Beaches

Top Sights
1 Colobus Conservation Centre B4

Sights
2 Kongo Mosque B2

Activities, Courses & Tours
3 Chui Adventure Centre B3
Diani Marine .... (see 9)
4 Diving the Crab B5
5 Fredlink Tours B4
H_2O Extreme .... (see 9)
6 Pilli Pipa B1
7 Skydive Diani B2

Sleeping
8 Amani B1
Coral Cove Cottages .... (see 14)
9 Diani Marine Village B4
Flamboyant .... (see 16)
10 Leopard Beach Resort & Spa B2
11 Sand Island Beach Cottages B1
12 Stilts Eco-Lodge B4
13 The Maji B3
14 Twiga Lodge B1
15 Water Lovers B2

Eating
16 Ali Barbour's Cave Restaurant B4
17 Aniello's B3
18 Coast Dishes B3
19 Rongai A3
20 Sails B4
21 Shan-e-Punjab Restaurant B3
22 Swahili Beach Restaurant B2
23 Swahili Pot A3

Drinking & Nightlife
Forty Thieves Beach Bar .... (see 16)
24 Shakatak B4

Information
25 Barclays Bank B3
26 Diani Beach Hospital B3
27 Kenya Commercial Bank A3

Transport
28 Bus Stop A1

Kongo Mosque MOSQUE
At the far northern end of the beach road (turn right at the three-way intersection where the sealed road ends) is the 16th-century Kongo Mosque, Diani's last-surviving relic of the ancient Swahili civilisations that once controlled the coast, and one of a tiny handful of coral mosques still in use in Kenya.

Activities

★ **Pilli Pipa** WATER SPORTS
(☎0722205120, 0724442555; www.pillipipa.com; Colliers Centre, Diani Beach Rd; from KSh7500) The most reputable dive school in Diani, Pilli Pipa also offers dhow safaris, dolphin-spotting trips, whale watching, night dives and snorkelling trips to Wasini island.

Diani Marine DIVING
(☎0707629061; www.dianimarine.com; Diani Marine Village) This highly regarded, German-run centre provides its own accommodation. Open-water diving courses cost €495, with single dives from €90.

Chui Adventure Centre WATER SPORTS
(☎0708358095; www.chuiadventurecentre.com; Leopard Beach Resort & Spa) A reputable water-sports outfit, also offering mountain biking, kitesurfing and diving or snorkelling trips to Wasini island.

Diving the Crab DIVING
(☎0723108108; www.divingthecrab.com; Sands at Nomad) A diving outfit used by the big hotels. Open-water courses cost €480, with kiddy dives from €30.

Whaleshark Adventures DIVING
(☎0726775047; Diani Beach Rd; dive courses from €399) The most budget friendly of all the dive outfits, this one specialises in viewing whale sharks, housed inside its enormous seaquarium between Diani and Mombasa. The creatures are released every six months.

★ **H_2O Extreme** KITESURFING
(☎0721495876; www.h2o-extreme.com) The best-regarded kitesurfing outfit in Diani offers half-day beginner courses for €100. It has locations at Sands at Nomad, Kenyaways Kite Village and Forty Thieves Beach Bar.

Skydive Diani ADVENTURE SPORTS
(☎040-3204320; www.skydivediani.com; Diani Beach Rd, next to Forty Thieves Beach Bar) Set up by a British Army parachutist and a professional skydiver (among others), this school offers dives of a different kind: through the sky, not the sea. Tandem jumps cost US$350, or you can sign up for the Accelerated Freefall course for US$2200.

DON'T MISS

ENTERING THE SACRED FOREST

The *kaya* (sacred forests) of the Mijikenda are typically closed to visitors, with just a handful of exceptions: **Kaya Kinondo** (www.kaya-kinondo-kenya.com; admission KSh1500), near Diani Beach, is among them.

Visiting this small but sacred grove includes elements of a nature walk, historical journey and cultural experience.

Before entering the Kaya Kinondo you have to remove headwear, promise not to kiss anyone inside the grove, wrap a black *kaniki* (sarong) around your waist and go with a guide, who will explain the significance of some of the 187 plant species inside. They include the 'pimple tree', a known cure for acne; a palm believed to be 1050 years old; snatches of coral and the rather self-explanatory 'Viagra tree'. Enormous liana swings (go on, try it) and strangling fig trees abound.

The Mijikenda (Nine Homesteads) are actually nine subtribes – Chonyi, Digo, Duruma, Giriama, Jibana, Kambe, Kauma, Rabai and Ribe – united, to a degree, by culture, history and language. Yet each of the tribes remains distinct and speaks its own dialect of the Mijikenda language. Still, there's a binding similarity between the Nine Homesteads, and between the modern Mijikenda and their ancestors – their shared veneration of the *kaya*.

This historical connection becomes concrete when you enter the woods and realise – and there's no other word that fits here – they simply feel *old*.

Many trees are about 600 years old, which corresponds to the arrival of the first Mijikenda from Singwaya, their semilegendary homeland in southern Somalia. Cutting vegetation within the *kaya* is strictly prohibited – visitors may not even take a stray twig or leaf from the forest.

The preserved forests do not just facilitate dialogue with the ancestors; they provide a direct link to ecosystems that have been clear felled out of existence elsewhere. Kaya Kinondo contains five possible endemic species, and 140 tree species classified as 'rare', within its 30 hectares – the space of a suburban residential block.

The main purpose of the *kaya* was to house the villages of the Mijikenda, which were located in a large central clearing. Entering the centre of a *kaya* required ritual knowledge to proceed through concentric circles of sacredness surrounding the node of the village. Sacred talismans and spells were supposed to cause hallucinations that disoriented enemies who attacked the forest.

The *kaya* were largely abandoned in the 1940s and conservative strains of Islam and Christianity have denigrated their value to the Mijikenda, but thanks to Unesco World Heritage status, they will hopefully be preserved for future visitors. The *kaya* have lasted 600 years; with luck, the wind will speak through their branches for much longer.

Kenya Wild ADVENTURE SPORTS

(www.kenyawild.com; Diani Beach Rd) A small outfit offering microlight flights and Aquilla triking adventures.

Festivals & Events

Diani Rules SPORTS

(www.dianirules.com) This entertaining charity sports tournament, in aid of the Kwale District Eye Centre, is held at Diani Sea Lodge around the first weekend of June. It's more an expat event than a tourist attraction, but if you're staying locally there's every chance you'll be invited to watch or asked to join a team. Games include football (played with a rugby ball) and blindfold target throwing, but the real endurance event is the three days of partying that accompanies proceedings.

Sleeping

★South Coast Backpackers BACKPACKERS $

(☎0715614038; www.dianibackpackers.com; off Diani Beach Rd; camping KSh600, dm KSh1200, s/d KSh 2600/3600; P 📶 🏊) More stylish and security conscious than the average backpackers, South Coast has dorms and privates in a lovely house. Come to party at the 24-hour bar and pool, chill out in the lush garden, or catch up on sleep in the baobab dorm, where beds wrap around the trunk of a tree. There's a communal kitchen, great daily menu and lockers. Turn right after KFI supermarket.

Stilts Eco-Lodge LODGE $
(☎0722523278; www.stiltsdianibeach.com; Diani Beach Rd; s/d KSh 1800/2400; P 📶) Tree-house heaven. Stilts has a handful of simple wooden tree houses, each in its own private cove in a swath of coastal forest. A stilted lounge offers sofas, wi-fi, food and drinks, plus visits from the resident bush babies. Popular with backpackers and an eco-conscious crowd.

★ **Kenyaways Kite Village** BOUTIQUE HOTEL $$
(☎calls 8am-4.30pm only 0728886821; www.thekenyaway.com; Diani Beach Rd; s/d US$64/151; 📶🏊) 🍃 This small, stylish kitesurfing lodge is our favourite place to stay in Diani. Rooms are simple but lovely, with driftwood bed frames, whitewashed walls and a sea breeze. Downstairs, there's an atmospheric bar-restaurant that attracts surfers, foodies and a chilled-out crowd. Throw in free wi-fi, cushion-strewn couches and lots of local info, and everyone's happy.

Flamboyant BOUTIQUE HOTEL $$
(☎0720843585, 0733411110; www.flamboyant.co; Diani Beach Rd; r from US$85; ❄@📶🏊) This intimate boutique hotel has breathtaking beach views, subtly decorated rooms with some of the nicest bathrooms this side of the Indian Ocean and a fantastic pool complex.

Diani Marine Village BOUTIQUE HOTEL $$
(☎Nairobi 020-2650426, 0707629060; www.dianimarine.com/village; Diani Beach Rd; s/d €55/100; 📶🏊) The huge rooms at this dive resort are more than just a little appealing. With stone floors, a modern Swahili style and a beautiful pool and gardens, this place represents superb value for money. The complimentary breakfast is fit for a king.

Blue Marlin HOTEL $$
(☎0724100629; www.bluemarlin.co.ke; Diani Beach Rd; s/d €75/90; P📶🏊) You'll hear waves lapping and monkeys dancing on the roofs at this beachfront spot, next door to Kenyaways kitesurf school. Rooms are spacious, while sandstone walkways lead through the garden and down to the restaurant, where you'll be greeted by a salty breeze and great breakfasts.

Galu Inn HOTEL $$
(☎022-6649909; www.galuinn.com; Diani Beach Rd; r Ksh5250-8500; ❄🏊) A good option if the beach hotels are full, this well-maintained hotel is on the other side of the road, opposite Kenyaways. It has 13 rooms equipped with air-conditioning and televisions, plus a nice garden pool.

★ **Water Lovers** HOTEL $$$
(☎0735790535; www.waterlovers.it; Diani Beach Rd; r €250-569; P📶🏊) Beautiful, peaceful and intimate, Water Lovers has eight rooms and one villa, all designed with aesthetics, sustainability and love in mind. The furniture is a mix of Swahili wood and Italian pottery, and the wonderful staff will cater for every need. As you might expect from Italian owners, there's a great private restaurant serving organic fare and homemade gelato.

Snorkelling, kayaking and kitesurfing can be arranged, and there's a spa next door.

The Maji HOTEL $$$
(☎0773178873/4; http://themaji-com; Diani Beach Rd; r from KSh34,000; P📶🏊) The newest of Diani's beachfront boutique hotels, the Maji – which means 'water' in Swahili – is simply gorgeous. The beautiful Swahili lobby is cut by bubbling streams, while huge open windows light up honeymoon coves. Each room has its own vibe, but all have enormous beds and lovely bathrooms. Bliss.

Four Twenty South COTTAGES $$$
(www.fourtwentysouth.com; Diani Beach Rd, Galu; beach houses US$262-880; P) Named after the

WILDLIFE ON THE SOUTH COAST

While you wouldn't come to the south Kenyan coastline in search of the Big Five (lions, elephants, rhinos, leopards and buffaloes), it doesn't mean that bringing a pair of binoculars is a waste of time. Quite the contrary. If you want to see elephants, giraffes, buffaloes and more, Shimba Hills National Reserve (p218) and the neighbouring Mwaluganje Elephant Sanctuary (p219) should put a smile on your face. Diani Beach has a unique subspecies of beautiful **colobus monkeys**, and coral reefs everywhere are alive with sea creatures, big and small – some of them really big: **dolphins** are common and **whale sharks** occasionally cruise by. But it's the **birds** that are the real standout wildlife event. The Kenyan coast features many birds that can't be seen anywhere else in the country, and from October to March it also plays host to thousands of **winter migrants** escaping the cold of northern latitudes. Pack those binoculars!

latitude of this gorgeous, remote beach, Four Twenty South has six rustic-chic cottages. Each comes with a personal chef (who may have cordon bleu credentials), stylish beach furniture, fresh flowers and creative decor. The welcome is warm and there's attention to detail. Great for groups. Turn left after KFI supermarket and follow the signs.

Leopard Beach Resort & Spa RESORT **$$$**
(Nairobi 020-2049270; www.leopardbeachresort.com; Diani Beach Rd; s/d US$185/260;) As beach resorts go, Leopard is among Diani's best. Although it's so huge you'll have to get around by golf buggy, the newest rooms are gorgeous and the sleek villas come with spas. Trees and lianas give it a forest feel, swimming pools abound and the restaurants (yes, there are several) serve excellent fusion fare.

Strangely, it's also home to the Slovak consulate, should that be helpful.

Eating

Rongai KENYAN **$**
(Palm Ave, Ukunda; mains KSh200; lunch & dinner) This rowdy joint is a popular place for *nyama choma* – if you've been missing your roast meat and boiled maize, Rongai's here for you.

Coast Dishes KENYAN **$**
(Palm Ave, Ukunda; mains KSh300; lunch & dinner) Want to give the overpriced tourist restaurants a miss? Want to eat where the locals eat? Coast Dishes ticks both of these boxes and, if you're sensible, you'll opt for a steaming great bowl of biryani, the house special.

Travellers' Cafe KENYAN **$**
(meals from KSh150) Handy if you're waiting for a matatu, this local cafe is right next to the stage. It serves up *sukumawiki* (leafy greens), *nyama choma,* potatoes, cabbage and other coast staples.

Swahili Pot KENYAN **$**
(Coral Beach Cottages; mains KSh150-230; lunch & dinner) This place and its culinary siblings (there are two other branches, one about halfway down the beach-access road and another at Ukunda junction) do excellent traditional African and Swahili dishes. The title comes from the gimmick of selecting a meat and having it cooked in a variety of sauces and marinades, all of which are

SWA-WHO-LI?

'So you are a Swahili?' we ask the Mombasa shop owner, who's dressed like all the Swahili in the streets and shares their caramel skin colour. 'No! No, I am Kenyan, but my roots are in Gujarat,' he says.

In the village, watching a man walk by, we turn to our guide: 'He's a Digo, right?'

'No!' says the guide. 'His father and his mother are Digo. His mother is so traditional she won't wear shoes. But he was sent to work in a Swahili house when he was young and converted to Islam, married a Muslim girl, made the haj (pilgrimage to Mecca) and would be insulted to be called anything but Swahili.'

Just who the Swahili are is a complex question, and not just for anthropologists. For many people on the Kenyan coast, being Swahili is the most important marker of their identity. This is not a unique set of affairs – the same emphasis on tribe can be noted in many groups in Kenya – but what sets the Swahili apart is their connection to the Muslim, particularly Arab, world.

To put it plainly: there are Swahili who believe the presence, real or imagined, of Arab and Persian blood sets them apart from 'black' Africans (this despite the fact many Swahili are as dark as any inland Kenyans). This attitude is not shared by all Swahili by any stretch, but it is present. It stems from Swahili cosmopolitanism, the Kiswahili language (generally considered to be spoken at its 'purest' on the coast) and the fact the Swahili were the area's original converts to Islam. A stronger link to the Arab world (which may be arbitrarily measured or fancifully concocted, much like white Americans claiming descent from European nobility) is often taken to mean a weaker tie to black Africa and, by extension, a stronger tie to Islam.

Due to its mixed nature, Swahili identity has been, and remains in some ways, a malleable thing. At its uglier edges, it still draws influence from the Arab imperialism that once dominated the coast. With that said, many thousands of Swahili cheerfully acknowledge they are black and something else – something quintessentially 'coast'.

highly rated. Note that the three branches are also trading under their old name of African Pot Restaurant.

Shan-e-Punjab Restaurant INDIAN $
(Diani Complex; mains KSh350-800; ⌚lunch & dinner) One of the only dedicated Indian options in town, this restaurant could easily hold its own against any high-class curry house in the world. The food is well spiced, rich and delicious. It often closes in the low season.

Avanti CAFE $$
(Nakumatt Diani; meals from KSh450; P ❄ 📶) Good for a quick bite or a coffee, Avanti has an outdoor terrace and indoor booths. On the menu, there's freshly squeezed juice, posh hot dogs, salads and sandwiches. It's in the same strip mall as Nakumatt supermarket.

★**Madafoos** KENYAN $$
(☎0714632801; www.thekenyaway.com; Diani Beach Rd) Fresh and funky, Madafoos sits right on the beach, in the same grounds as Kenyaways. Lounge on the sofas and order a plate of feta-coriander samosas, a chocolatey dessert, or a bowl of steaming pumpkin soup to replenish after a day in the ocean. Don't miss the cocktails, or the chance to ask owner Bruce how he came up with the name.

After dark, the place fills with a lively crowd, and has occasional live-music acts.

★**Aniello's** ITALIAN $$
(☎0733740408; Colliers Centre; mains KSh400-1000; ⌚lunch & dinner; P) Nurse a glass of red and peruse the long list of good pizzas and pastas at this thoroughly authentic Italian restaurant. As you eat, the ageing patron will do the rounds, as cries of '*buonissimo*' erupt from nearby tables. It is indeed.

Swahili Beach Restaurant SEAFOOD $$
(☎040-3201130; Swahili Beach Resort, Diani Rd; mains from KSh600; P) At once smart and laid-back, this alfresco restaurant spills towards the ocean and features funky lighting and intimate, salt-kissed tables. The pizzas, pastas and salads are pretty good and there's a nice bar with stools to perch at as the sun goes down.

★**Sails** SEAFOOD $$$
(☎0717010670; www.villasdiani.com; Almanara Luxury Villas Resort, Diani Beach Rd; mains KSh850-3800; P 📶 ✎) By far the most stylish place to eat in Diani, Sails is gorgeous: a canopy of billowing white canvas separates the restaurant from the stars, while waiters serve up fine food, including fresh salads and seafood. After dark, fairy lights twinkle and the style set emerges. We've only ever heard good things.

Ali Barbour's Cave Restaurant SEAFOOD $$$
(☎0714456131; www.alibarbours.co; Diani Beach Rd; mains KSh1550-3200; ⌚from 7pm) For a theme restaurant set in a coral cave, this is actually quite good and not cheesy at all. The focus is seafood and steak, cooked up poshly and perfect for a special dinner. It's served under the stars, jagged rocks and fairy lights.

Drinking & Nightlife

★**Forty Thieves Beach Bar** BAR
(☎0712294873; Diani Beach Rd; 📶) Of all the phrases you'll hear in Diani, 'Meet you at Forty's?' is probably the most common, and the most welcome. A legendary boozer, it has movie nights, a pool table, live bands, there's a pub quiz at least once a week and it's open until the last guest leaves. It's a popular place to eat as well, dishing out comfort food (meals KSh700 to KSh1500) such as burgers and scampi. The Sunday roast is a big hit.

Shakatak CLUB
(Diani Beach Rd) The only full-on nightclub in Diani not attached to a hotel is Shakatak. It's quite hilariously seedy, but can be fun once you know what to expect. Like most big Kenyan clubs, food is served at all hours.

Information

DANGERS & ANNOYANCES

Take taxis at night and try not to be on the beach by yourself after dark. Souvenir sellers are an everyday nuisance, sex tourism is pretty evident and beach boys are a hassle – you'll hear a lot of, 'Hey, one love, one love' Rasta-speak spouted by guys trying to sell you drugs or scam you into supporting fake charities for 'local schools'. Yes, very 'one love'.

EMERGENCY

Diani Beach Hospital (☎040-3300150, 0722569261; www.dianibeachhospital.com; Diani Beach Rd; ⌚24hr)
Police (☎999; Ukunda)

MONEY

Barclays Bank (Barclays Centre) With ATM.

IT'S A SAILOR'S LIFE

The salty breeze and the high seas, it's a sailor's life for you and me. There's no more romantic way to explore the Kenyan coast than sailing by dhow (a traditional sailing boat that's been used here for centuries) past slivers of sand, offshore coral islands and reefs bubbling with colourful fish. Several companies offer dhow trips down the coast to Funzi and Wasini islands. Pilli Pipa (p221) is probably the best known, but there are several other operators in Diani.

The **East African Whale Shark Trust** (☎0720293156; www.giantsharks.org; Aqualand) is an excellent conservation body, monitoring populations of the world's largest fish – the harmless, plankton-feeding whale shark. In February and March (the busiest time for whale sharks) it occasionally opens survey and shark-tagging expeditions to paying guests. Trip costs vary, depending on how much sponsorship money has been raised, but averages US$150 per person, with a minimum of six people needed for a trip. Its offices are located in the Aqualand centre, about 4km south of Diani.

Kenya Commercial Bank (Ukunda) With ATM.

POST

Diani Beach Post Office (Diani Beach Rd)
Ukunda Post Office (Ukunda)

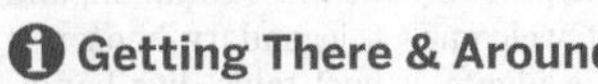

Getting There & Around

The town of Ukunda, which is basically a traffic junction on the main Mombasa–Tanzania road, is the turn-off point for Diani Beach. From here a sealed road runs about 2.5km to a T-junction with the beach road, where you'll find everything Diani has to offer.

AIR

Air Kenya (☎Nairobi 020-3916000; www.airkenya.com) Is a charter company unrelated to Kenya Airways. It flies between Nairobi and Diani Beach most days, from US$118.

BUS & MATATU

Numerous matatus run south from the Likoni ferry in Mombasa directly to Ukunda (KSh100, 30 minutes), the junction for Diani, and onwards to Msambweni and Lunga Lunga.

From Ukunda, matatus run to the beach (KSh50) all day; check before boarding to see if it's a 'Reef' (heading north along the strip, then south) or 'Neptune' (south beach only) service.

CAR & TAXI

Taxis and tuk-tuks hang around Ukunda junction and all the main shopping centres, and most hotels and restaurants will also have a couple waiting at night.

Fares should be between KSh150 and KSh800, depending on the distance.

From Diani to Mombasa, via the Likoni ferry, bank on one to two hours' driving time, depending on traffic.

Gazi & Chale Island

About 20km south of Diani (and a world away from its international resort scene) is Gazi, where you'll find a village of friendly Digo Mijikenda folk, a big dollop of African rural life and an excellent **mangrove boardwalk** (KSh150) run by a local women's group. The boardwalk is a sun-blanched, pleasantly rickety affair that winds back into a wine-dark lagoon webbed over by red, orange, green and grey mangrove trees as, nearby, the husks of old dhows bake into driftwood on the sand. Previously, the mangroves were cut for timber, which led to extreme beach erosion; today, both the shore and the mangroves are being restored and a glut of entrepreneurial activities has grown around the boardwalk, including oyster farming and bee-keeping. The fee for the walk goes into improving the boardwalk, buying school textbooks and paying teachers at local schools.

To the north of Gazi, the island of Chale is a small slice of tropical paradise purportedly bestowed with healing powers. Much of the island is a *kaya*, or sacred woodland, closed to visitors, but its sulphur springs and therapeutic mud ponds are very much open. You can, in theory, visit for the day, hiring a local boatman from Gazi.

Sleeping

Homestay accommodation is available in Gazi in the house just behind the telephone mast (ask around – everyone knows it). The accommodation is much more swish than you'd expect from muddy old Gazi.

The Sands at Chale Island RESORT $$$

(☎040-3300269, 0725699910; www.thesandsatchaleisland.com; r from US$350) A plush resort on the tip of a sacred island? Not everyone on this stretch of the coast is in favour of the Sands' presence here, but if you do choose to stay, you can expect spacious rooms, a large restaurant and all the mod cons you'd expect at such a resort.

Funzi Island

Funzi is a small mangrove island about 35km south of Diani that tends to be visited as part of package tours organised through agencies and hotels to the north. The main attraction (besides the beaches and palm trees) is birdwatching and croc spotting.

Arranging your own boat trip is easy if you're in a group: boatmen in the mainland village of Bodo ask around KSh3500 per person with a minimum of three people required (or one person with a really big wallet!), or you can negotiate individual dolphin- and crocodile-spotting trips up the Ramisi River.

If you arrive independently, you can generally count on the permanent presence of an accompanying guide from the moment you land, which is actually no bad thing, as he'll show you around the island and can arrange a homestay package in the village for around KSh1000 to KSh1500.

To get to Bodo, take a matatu from Ukunda towards Lunga Lunga and ask for the Bodo turn-off (KSh100). The village lies another 1.5km along a sandy track; you can take a *boda-boda* (bicycle taxi), though the rider will try to charge you KSh150, or get someone to show you the way.

Sleeping

Funzi Keys Lodge LODGE $$$

(☎0733900446; www.thefunzikeys.com; full board US$270-460; ❄☒) Rustic, chic and dripping with honeymoon appeal, this mangrove-creek resort gets consistently good reviews. The cottages are spacious and some have sunken bath-tubs that look out over the ocean. Expect a warm welcome, good food and few distractions that don't involve the natural surroundings.

Shimoni & Wasini Island

The final pearls in the tropical-beach necklace that stretches south of Mombasa are the mainland village of Shimoni and the idyllic island of Wasini, located about 76km south of Likoni.

Shimoni and Wasini (the name of the island's main village and the island) are usually visited as part of a package tour that includes a dhow trip to Kisite Marine National Park. Every morning in high season a convoy of coaches arrives, carrying tourists from Diani Beach. Independent travellers are still fairly rare in these parts.

Wasini, in particular, is ripe with the ingredients required for a perfect backpacker beachside hideaway: it has that sit-under-a-mango-tree-and-do-nothing-all-day vibe, a coastline licked with pockets of white sand and the most gorgeous snorkelling reef on the coast. In fact, the only things it doesn't have are banana-pancake traveller cafes and backpacker hostels, and it's all the better for it.

JOIN THE DOTS: ON THE COASTAL BACKPACKER TRAIL

There's so much to see along Kenya's stunning coastline. If you're travelling on a budget and after cheap, safe and fun digs, there's no better option than to follow the backpacker trail.

Starting in **Diani Beach**, bunk down at South Coast Backpackers (p222), inside a lovely house with a lush garden. You'll meet the owners behind the 24-hour bar. Next stop is the beachside Mombasa suburb of **Nyali**, where you can take your pick from the lively Tulia House Backpackers (p230), quiet Backpackers' Nirvana (p230) or legendary Mombasa Backpackers (p230). All make good bases for exploring Mombasa island.

From there, board a bus to **Kilifi**, home of Distant Relatives (p238) ecolodge, where there's always a good crowd and some beautiful gardens in which to chill out. At the time of writing, **Malindi** and **Watamu** still lacked good backpacker hostels, but Kite Watamu (p244) is a kitesurf school with a small and lovely guesthouse. On **Lamu** island, Baitul Noor House (p258) marks the end of the line.

Shimoni

The mainland village of Shimoni is the departure point for boats to Wasini, and can be a bit of a circus when the tour buses rock up. But after sunset, when the day trippers go home, a tranquil Swahili vibe returns.

Sights & Activities

Slave Caves HISTORIC SITE

(KSh400; 8.30-10.30am & 1.30-6pm) These caves, where slaves were supposedly kept before being loaded onto boats, are the main attraction in Shimoni. A custodian takes you around the dank caverns to illustrate this little-discussed part of East African history. Actual evidence that slaves were kept here is a little thin, but as piles of empty votive rose water bottles indicate, the site definitely has significance for believing locals.

Shimoni Reef FISHING

(Nairobi 725643733; www.shimonireeflodge.com; trips per day from US$600) The Pemba Channel is famous for deep-sea fishing, and Shimoni Reef can arrange a variety of offshore fishing trips.

Sleeping & Eating

Shimoni Cottages COTTAGES $

(Nairobi 020-3549520; www.kws.org; cottages KSh3500) These seven basic but cosy *bandas* are owned and managed by the KWS. There's a kitchen (with some cooking equipment) and shared bathroom facilities. The compound is located about 200m south of Shimoni pier, and there's usually a ranger around to assist if you haven't managed to make a booking ahead of time.

You can also camp in the grounds.

Shimoni Gardens BANDA $

(0722117900; bandas KSh4000) The unkempt *bandas* at this place, 2.5km west of Shimoni, would be overpriced anywhere else in Kenya, but in expensive Shimoni they come out at quite good value. If the *bandas* themselves can be faulted, the peaceful setting certainly can't.

Betty's Camp LODGE $$

(0722434709; r US$70-110) This small, pretty fishing camp usually attracts serious deep-sea-fishing types, so expect lots of chat about such things. The rooms are simple, but nicely furnished and there's always a friendly welcome and some good seafood on the grill.

Shimoni Reef Lodge LODGE $$$

(0725643733; www.shimonireeflodge.com; s/d US$180/300;) This waterfront fishing camp is a lovely place to while away a few days. It's also a good base for diving. The rooms, although spacious and colourful, aren't luxurious – they're best enjoyed after a day on the ocean wave.

Getting There & Away

There are matatus every hour or so between Likoni and Shimoni (KSh300, 1½ hours) until about 6pm. Matatus heading to the Tanzanian border from Ukunda (for Diani Beach) can also drop you at Shimoni.

Wasini Island

With its faded white alleyways, Swahili fishing vibe and fat, mottled trees, tiny Wasini Island (it's only 5km long) feels like a distant relative of Lamu and Zanzibar. There are no cars, and most electricity comes from generators. But who needs such luxuries when the nearby marine park has some of the best snorkelling in Kenya?

It's worth poking about the ancient Swahili ruins and the **coral gardens**, a bizarre landscape of exposed coral reefs with a boardwalk for viewing, on the edge of Wasini village.

Most visitors come to Wasini on organised dhow tours from Mombasa or Diani Beach, but with a bit of bargaining power you can charter a simple motorboat from Shimoni pier and spend the day chilling on the beach or chowing on seafood.

Sights & Activities

Kisite Marine National Park PARK

(www.kws.org; adult/child US$20/10) Off the south coast of Wasini, this gorgeous marine park, which also incorporates the Mpunguti Marine National Reserve and the two tiny Penguti islands, is one of the best in Kenya. The park covers 28 sq km of pristine coral reefs and offers colourful diving and snorkelling. You have a reasonable chance of seeing dolphins and sea turtles. You can organise your own boat trip; the going rate is between KSh2000 and KSh3000 per person for a group.

The best time to dive and snorkel is between October and March. Avoid diving in June, July and August because of rough seas, silt and poor visibility. During the monsoon season you can snorkel over the coral gardens; enquire about prices opposite the pier in Wasini.

Mkwiro Village VILLAGE
Mkwiro is a small village on the unvisited eastern end of Wasini Island. There are few facilities here and there's not a lot to do, but the gorgeous hour-long walk from Wasini village, through woodlands, past tiny hamlets and along the edge of mangrove forests, is more than reason enough to visit. There are some wonderful, calm swimming spots around the village. Local children are sure to take you by the hand and show you the best swimming places.

The Mkwiro Youth Group can help you dig a little deeper into village life by organising village tours and cooking classes. It's all a little vague and prices are highly flexible, but the man you need to speak to about organising these is Shafii Vuyaa.

You can arrange homestays in Mkwiro for roughly KSh800, which should include a nice home-cooked coastal dinner.

Tours

Besides Wasini-based operators, Pilli Pipa (p221) and Chui Adventure Centre (p221) in Diani Beach also operate snorkelling and diving tours to Kisite Marine National Park.

★Charlie Claw's WATER SPORTS
(☎0722205155/6; www.wasini.com) This highly regarded outfit, based on Wasini, offers diving and snorkelling trips to Kisite, as well as to Mako Koko reef a few kilometres west. Dhow sunset cruises are also on offer. Some of the day excursions include lunch at its eponymous restaurant on Wasini island.

Paradise Divers WATER SPORTS
(☎0718778372; www.paradisediver.net) On the eastern side of Wasini, this dive outfit offers diving and snorkelling trips to the marine park, starting at €45 per day, as well as full PADI certification courses. It also has a small lodge (p229) at which you can stay.

Sleeping & Eating

Mpunguti Lodge HOTEL $
(☎0722566623, 0710562494; r from KSh2500) The rooms here, which overlook the delicious turquoise ocean, are uncomplicated, with mosquito nets and small verandahs. Running water is collected in barrels. The food is excellent (ask for the seagrass starter, possibly the nicest thing we ate on the Kenyan coast) and it's a common lunch stop for boat trips. It's on the edge of Wasini village.

★Paradise Lodge LODGE $$
(☎0718778372; www.paradisediver.net; per person €44-85) This friendly little dive lodge on the eastern side of Wasini has a range of simple but colourful rooms, plus two furnished safari tents. Diving trips can also be arranged. You can sleep here independently, or as part of a diving tour.

★Charlie Claw's Restaurant SEAFOOD $$
(mains from KSh850) After a tiring morning watching fish in their natural habitat, what else to do but tuck in? Charlie's cooks up a seafood feast at lunch and dinner, including grilled crab and seared Swahili beef steaks. Afterwards, you can relax in the gardens and ocean nooks.

Coral Spirit SEAFOOD $$
(☎0770841924; mains from KSh750) Opened in 2014, Coral Spirit has a cute restaurant with decent seafood. Rooms might become

FISHING: TAG & BRAG

While the idea of wrestling a huge marlin on the open sea has macho allure, catches of billfish in the Indian Ocean are getting smaller all the time. The biggest threat to game fish is overfishing by commercial tuna companies, which routinely hook other pelagic fish as so-called 'bycatch'. Pollution and falling stocks of prey are also having a serious knock-on effect. Some large species are believed to have declined by as much as 80% since the 1970s. Sharks are particularly vulnerable.

You can do your bit to help sustain shark and billfish populations by tagging your catch and releasing it back into the ocean. Most deep-sea-fishing companies provide anglers with a souvenir photo and official recognition of their catch, then release the fish to fight another day, carrying tags that will allow scientists to discover more about these magnificent predators.

available here in the future. The owners can also organise diving and snorkelling trips.

Getting There & Away

Although most people come to Wasini on organised tours, you can cross the ocean by motorboat (from KSh2000 per passenger) or by simple wooden vessel with the islanders (KSh300). Head to Shimoni pier to assess your options.

Lunga Lunga

There isn't much at Lunga Lunga apart from the Tanzanian border crossing, which is open 24 hours. It's 6.5km from the Kenyan border post to the Tanzanian border post at Horohoro; *boda-bodas* run between the two border posts throughout the day (KSh100, if you're lucky). From Horohoro, there are numerous matatus (KSh1500) and buses (KSh2000) to Tanga. Matatus from Lunga Lunga to Likoni cost KSh300.

NORTH OF MOMBASA

From Nyali to Shanzu, it's all big-box beach resorts, highway junctions, bottle green palms and acres of sisal. But there are sights of interest for independent travellers. These include the stunning Swahili ruins of Jumba la Mtwana, the raucous fishing village of Mtwapa and some nice nature parks. Beyond that, the high-end resorts are hardly the 'real Kenya' and from December to April, seaweed often clogs the sand. Still, for most of the year this is tropical pleasantness, if not paradise. Expect lots of *makuti* (thatched roof) chic.

Nyali Beach

Mombasa's most popular northern beach suburb, Nyali is a good alternative to staying on Mombasa island. What it lacks in charm it makes up for in amenities; there's a nice selection of places to sleep and eat, and the sand is but a hop, skip and jump away.

Sights & Activities

Mamba Village Crocodile Farm ZOO
(Links Rd; adult/child KSh650/350; 8.30am-7pm) This is the largest reptile farm in Kenya, but be aware that some of the crocodiles here become handbags and fried reptile bites. Crocodile feeding time is at 5pm.

Sleeping

★ Tulia House Backpackers BACKPACKERS $
(0711955999; www.tuliahouse.com; off Links Rd; camping KSh500, hammock/dm/s/d KSh700/1000/3300/4000;) Backpackers seem to love Tulia. It's new, clean and knows how to party. Accommodation is in well-kept dorms, *funzi* hammocks or good private rooms, while the emerald green pool is the setting for BBQs, swimwear contests and games of beer pong. Expect a warm welcome, tonnes of local info and just as much fun.

★ Backpackers' Nirvana BACKPACKERS $
(0705312019; www.backpackersnirvana.com; off Mt Kenya Rd, Mombasa Beach; dm/hammock/s/d KSh700/800/1300/2500;) Some backpackers want to relax, not party. If that's you, this is your spot. Set in a private house, Nirvana is small and homely, infused with a healing vibe and overseen by the lovely Leslie, who offers holistic therapies and free tea. There's a pool, small gym (let out that stress) and a chilled-out conservatory in which to relax.

There's a choice of basic rooms, as well as more upmarket doubles. Best of all, it's located inside the army barracks, so it feels very secure. Ask any taxi or tuk-tuk to turn left inside the barracks, after the 'Kenya rifles' sign.

Mombasa Backpackers BACKPACKERS $
(0701561233; www.mombasabackpackers.com; 69 Mwamba Dr; camping KSh300, dm/d excl breakfast KSh1000/1500;) Set in a rundown house flanked by pretty gardens, this place has recently undergone a change in management. Some say it's lost its spirit, but the dorms and doubles are still OK value, and you can camp in the garden. There's usually a party vibe in the lounge and around the pool. Adventurous couples can opt for the doubles dorm.

★ Tamarind Village APARTMENT $$
(Map p206; 041-4474600; Cement Silo Rd; r from KSh13,000;) These beautiful self-catering apartments are brought to you by the owners of the excellent Tamarind restaurant (right next door) and Nairobi's Carnivore (p75). Whitewashed, spacious and stylish; if your budget allows, there's no lovelier place to sleep in the Mombasa area. And you won't beat the view from those balconies, which stretches all the way to Mombasa's Old Town.

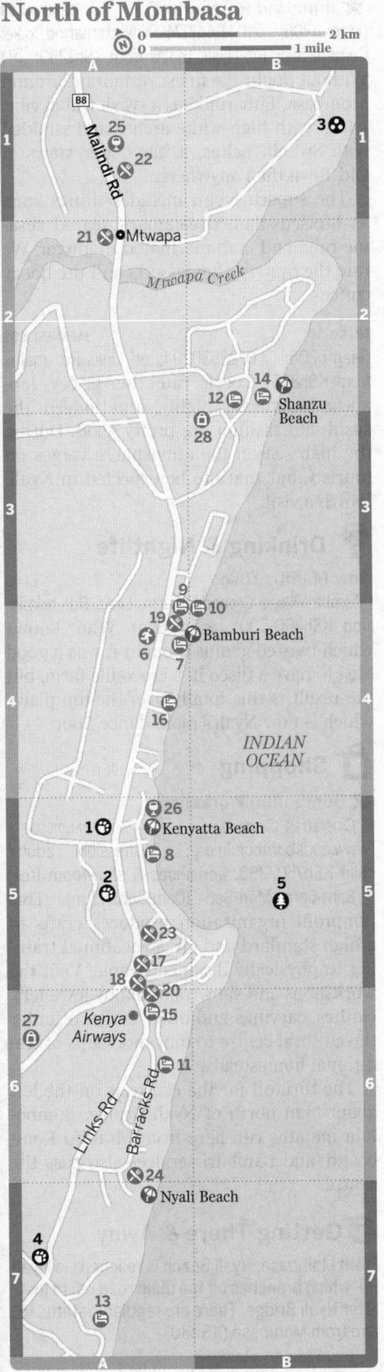

North of Mombasa

Sights

1 Baobab Adventure A5
2 Haller Park A5
3 Jumba la Mtwana B1
4 Mamba Village Crocodile Farm A7
5 Mombasa Marine National Park & Reserve B5
Ngomongo Villages .... (see 28)

Activities, Courses & Tours

6 Bamburi Forest Trails A4

Sleeping

7 Bamburi Beach Hotel A4
8 Camper's Haven Beach Resort A5
9 Kahama Hotel A4
10 Kenya Bay B4
11 Mombasa Beach Hotel A6
12 Mombasa Safari Inn B2
13 Nyali Beach Hotel A7
14 Serena Beach Hotel & Spa Kenya B2
15 Tulia House Backpackers A6
16 Whitesands Sarova Hotel A4

Eating

Il Covo .... (see 10)
17 Java House Nyali A5
18 La Veranda A5
19 Maharajah Restaurant A4
20 Mamma Sitty A6
21 Moorings Restaurant A2
22 Mumtaz A1
23 Splendid View Restaurant A5
24 Yul's A6

Drinking & Nightlife

25 Casuarina A1
Kahama Sports Bar .... (see 9)
New Mamba Disco .... (see 4)
26 Pirates A5

Shopping

27 Bombolulu Workshops & Cultural Centre A6
28 Shanzu Transitional Workshop B3

Mombasa Beach Hotel HOTEL **$$**

(☎041-44718615; www.safari-hotels.com; Mt Kenya Rd; r from US$150; P ❄ 📶 🏊) A slow makeover is underway at this hotel, and if the room refits are anything like the pool renovations, it should look pretty good once completed.

In the meantime, the doubles are perfectly fine for the price and there are two pools and some nice lounge areas. There's air-con in every room.

Nyali Beach Hotel RESORT $$
(Nairobi 020-2648100; www.nyali-international.com; Beach Rd; r from US$95;) At the southern end of the beach is the oldest resort in Nyali. If you like small and intimate then you'll hate this place – it's HUGE. Plus points are the beautiful (and yes, huge) pool, the equally beautiful (and huge) gardens and the even more beautiful (and really huge) beach it fronts. Minus points are that the room designs lack flair and imagination. The price is about right, though.

Eating

Mamma Sitty KENYAN $
(Malindi Rd; mains from KSh150) Mamma Sitty is generally the best regarded of the eating shacks. You'll probably need locals to point it out to you, but you won't need them to point you to the fried fish with coconut rice. It's the ultimate cultural contrast to the big resort hotels.

★**Cafesserie** CAFE $$
(Map p206; 041-5486933; mains from KSh650;) Next door to Nakumatt, inside Nyali City mall, Cafesserie has the best selection of cakes on the coast. We could stand for hours gazing at that mouth-watering counter, but far better to grab a seat on the terrace and order a double cappuccino and a healthy salad. Wait, those are delicious too! It's a winner.

Yul's PIZZERIA $$
(Mombasa-Malindi Rd; mains from KSh850) This beachfront pizzeria makes *the* best ice cream in town (we've never heard anyone disagree.) The pizzas are pretty good too, only rivalled by the views out to sea. Good for an atmospheric dinner or a long lunch.

La Veranda ITALIAN $$
(0733774436; mains KSh800-1400; Tue-Sun) This reliable Italian restaurant is behind Nakumatt Nyali shopping centre, with a big pizza oven, alfresco verandah dining and reasonable prices.

Java House Nyali CAFE $$
(www.nairobijavahouse.com; Nyali Centre, Links Rd;) We know, we know. It's a chain, but at least it's Kenyan. Java House's coffee always goes down a treat, and we're big fans of its BLT sandwiches. The Nyali branch has enough in the way of hot drinks, pastries, burgers and salads to cure the worst bout of homesickness.

★**Tamarind Restaurant** KENYAN $$$
(Map p206; 041-447174; www.tamarind.co.ke; Cement Silos Rd, Nyali; mains from KSh1250;) Without doubt the finest restaurant around Mombasa, Tamarind has a swish Dubai vibe. Laced with high white arches and studded with Swahili palms, it has better views of Old Town than anywhere.

The superb menu includes things such as hibiscus-flamed calamari, seared sesame tuna and crab marinated in ginger. We rate the oysters, the desserts and the boozy coffees.

Misono JAPANESE $$$
(Map p206; 0722530204; off Links Rd; mains from KSh850) Locals rate this pricey Japanese restaurant highly, and indeed the sushi and sashimi are pretty good. During the high season the atmosphere verges on touristy, but that's to be expected in Nyali. Worth a visit.

Drinking & Nightlife

New Mamba Disco CLUB
(Mamba Village Crocodile Farm, Links Rd; admission KSh200-500; Thu-Sun) Who knows which twisted genius thought it was a good idea to have a disco in a crocodile farm, but the result is this totally over-the-top place, which is now Nyali's main dance floor.

Shopping

★**Bombolulu Workshops & Cultural Centre** HANDICRAFTS
(www.apdkbombolulu.org; admission adult/child KSh750/350, workshops & showroom free; 8am-6pm Mon-Sat, 10am-3pm Sun) This nonprofit organisation produces crafts of a high standard and gives vocational training to physically disabled people. Visit the workshops and showroom to buy jewellery, clothes, carvings and other crafts, or enter the cultural centre to tour mock-ups of traditional homesteads.

The turn-off for the centre is on the left about 3km north of Nyali Bridge. Bombolulu matatus run here from Msanifu Kombo Rd, and Bamburi services also pass the centre.

Getting There & Away

From Mombasa, Nyali Beach is reached via Nyali Rd, which branches off the main road north just after Nyali Bridge. There are regular matatus to and from Mombasa (KSh30).

Bamburi Beach

Bamburi merges with neighbouring Nyali to create one long Mombasa holiday strip. Either place works fine as a base for exploring Old Town. Kenyatta Beach, near the south end of Bamburi, thumps to the beat of holidaying Kenyans.

Sights & Activities

Baobab Adventure WILDLIFE RESERVE
(Malindi Rd) Funnily enough, one of the prettiest nature reserves on the Mombasa north coast has been carved out by a cement company. In a nice example of environmentalism and entrepreneurship finding common ground, Baobab Adventure is the child of seemingly unlikely parents: Bamburi Cement and a group of conservationists. The various parts of the Baobab Adventure, including forest trails, are well signposted from the highway north of Mombasa and have well-marked bus stops.

Haller Park WILDLIFE RESERVE
(adult/child KSh800/400; 8am-5pm) This lovely wildlife sanctuary, part of the Baobab Adventure complex, includes a fish farm, reptile park and other green goodness. Guided walks around the park last about 1½ hours.

Bamburi Forest Trails NATURE RESERVE
(adult/child KSh300/150; 7am-6pm) This network of walking and cycling trails passes through reforested cement workings, with a butterfly pavilion and terrace (it's also known as the Butterfly Pavilion) from which to catch the sunset. It's located within the Baobab Adventure site.

Mombasa Marine National Park & Reserve PARK
(0412312744; www.kws.org; adult/child US$15/10) The offshore Mombasa Marine National Park and Reserve has impressive marine life, although it cops some pollution from industry in the area. You can hire glass-bottomed boats for a couple of hours for around KSh2500 (excluding park fees), but you'll need to be seriously silver-tongued to whittle the price down that low.

Sleeping

★**Kahama Hotel** HOTEL $$
(041-5485395, 0725961791; www.kahamahotel.co.ke; s/d from KSh4500/5750;) Sometimes business hotels seem too impersonal, holiday resorts seem too packagey and boutique hotels seem too expensive. Thankfully, there's the Kahama, which marries all three and does a mighty fine job of it. This Bamburi branch of the Kenyan chain has the most spacious rooms of the lot, with stylish touches, wi-fi and an on-site bar-restaurant. It gets our vote.

Kenya Bay RESORT $$
(041-5487600; www.kenyabay.com; r from KSh6500;) Between the Kahama Hotel and the excellent Il Covo restaurant, Kenya Bay is one of the oldest resorts on the block, but it's still in decent shape. Air-conditioned rooms spill out around the gardens and pool and have glass doors for ocean views. There's a small spa, a beach bar and a decent breakfast buffet.

Camper's Haven Beach Resort HOTEL $$
(0720240991; campers_haven@yahoo.com; camping per tent KSh400-800, s/d KSh3600/5400) About the closest the Bamburi strip gets to a cheap beach hotel. The rooms are pleasant, but nothing more, and be warned that the place has a disco, and it's loud. We're not sure how anyone can sleep in the rooms, let alone the tents, given the party raging outside. All that said, if you're looking for fun, it's a good party to join.

Whitesands Sarova Hotel RESORT $$$
(041-2128000; www.sarovahotels.com; s/d half board from US$180/260;) Whitesands is beautiful: a seafront Swahili castle of airy corridors, marble accents and wooden detailing uplifted by every flash, modern amenity you can imagine. It's considered one of the best high-end resorts on the coast, and with good reason. It's also big. Really big.

Bamburi Beach Hotel RESORT $$$
(041-5485611; www.bamburibeachkenya.com; s/d half board €130/170;) This tidy little complex has direct access to the beach and a choice of appealing, bamboo-finished hotel rooms and self-catering rooms (with outdoor kitchens). There's a nice beachfront bar with a big, shaggy *makuti* thatch.

Eating

Splendid View Restaurant INDIAN $
(Malindi Rd; mains KSh350-800; lunch & dinner, closed Mon) Sister to the original branch in Mombasa, this place has a wide menu, serving customary Indian cuisine and a handful of Western dishes. Ironically, the views aren't all that splendid.

Maharajah Restaurant INDIAN $
(Indiana Beach Hotel; mains KSh350-600; ⊙dinner Wed-Mon, plus lunch Sat & Sun) A stylish Indian restaurant with good veg and nonveg food.

★**Il Covo** ITALIAN $$
(☎041-470752; www.ilcovo.net; mains KSh600-1200; P) You'll find salt-licked walls, white tablecloths and – if you eat in the intimate little cove at the end – breakers crashing beneath your feet at this charming Italian/Japanese spot. The tuna carpaccio starter, served with rosemary focaccia, is pretty good. We rate the fish more highly than the pasta. After dark, the attached nightclub gets going.

Drinking & Nightlife

From here to Malindi, the nightlife can be dodgy, with lots of sex tourism evident.

Kahama Sports Bar SPORTS BAR
(Kahama Hotel;) This sleek sports bar, part of the same complex as the Kahama Hotel, has more big screens than you can count, plus disco-ball lighting, burgers and beers on tap. It attracts a mixed local and foreign crowd. The couches inside the gazebo are quieter than the main bar.

Pirates CLUB
(Kenyatta Beach; Fri & Sat KSh200; ⊙Wed-Sat) A huge complex of water slides and bars transforms into the strip's rowdiest nightclub in high season, blazing into the small hours. During the day it's surprisingly wholesome, with family 'fun shows' every Saturday.

Getting There & Away

Matatus run from Mombasa to Bamburi for KSh70. If you're driving yourself, be aware that the roads near Kenyatta Beach can get *insane* with a combination of matatus and drunk holidaymakers – never a good mix.

Shanzu Beach

Just north of Bamburi is Shanzu Beach. The coastline here is beautiful, but it's dominated by all-inclusive resorts. Outside of these areas, Shanzu is not much more than a highway fuel stop and string of seedy bars.

Sights & Activities

Ngomongo Villages CULTURAL CENTRE
(adult/child KSh850/425; ⊙9am-5pm Tue-Sun) Maybe best described as a 'tribal theme park', this place attempts to give visitors a glimpse of eight of Kenya's different tribal groups in one place. Although it's touristy, the tours are good fun and you can try your hand at various tribal activities, such as dancing, archery and pounding maize.

Sleeping & Eating

Mombasa Safari Inn HOTEL $
(☎0733925736, 0736417575; s/d KSh950/1450) This small, cheerful and authentically Kenyan place has a few basic but adequate rooms set behind a busy bar that may as well be sponsored by Tusker, so many advertising posters does it have.

SEX ON THE BEACH

Visitors to Kenya will soon notice that sex tourism is very common on parts of the coast, and occurs in different contexts, from petrol stations to high-end restaurants.

There's a sizeable number of Western men with younger Kenyan boys and girls, and Western women with younger Kenyan boys. Assuming nobody is actually under age (which does happen), there's nothing illegal in this. It's difficult to judge how many Westerners visit Kenya to seek brief, beachside affairs – one Reuters article quoted the figure as one in five Western women who visit the coast.

Many Kenyans are scandalised by the sight of older Western men with teenage Kenyans, and Western women with significantly younger Kenyan men. While they may recognise these relationships are legal, many also find them extremely distasteful and feel that sex tourism destroys the fabric of their society.

It's often assumed by both foreign tourists and Kenyans that it's the Westerner who's in the wrong, but of course nothing is clear cut. A major exposé in a big Kenyan newspaper a couple of years ago revealed that some married Kenyan couples in Malindi actually choose to 'break up' during the tourist season and seek foreign lovers for financial gain.

Areas such as Bamburi, Shanzu, Malindi and Mtwapa attract the largest number of sex tourists.

Serena Beach Hotel & Spa Kenya RESORT $$$

(Nairobi 020-3548771; www.serenahotels.com; r from US$240;) This lovely, polished resort is extensive and is styled on a traditional Swahili village – the pathways around the tree-filled complex even have street names. The split-level rooms are equally impressive and the design lends an incongruous intimacy.

Shopping

Shanzu Transitional Workshop ARTS & CRAFTS

(shanzuworkshop@yahoo.com; 8am-12.30pm & 2-5.30pm Mon-Fri, 8am-12.30pm Sat) Run by the Girl Guides Association, this centre provides training for handicapped women and sells their crafts for them.

Getting There & Away

Public transport plying the route between Mombasa and Malindi or Mtwapa passes the turn-off to Shanzu (KSh50), where a crowd of *boda-bodas* touts for rides to the hotels (KSh50). Hourly matatus from Mtwapa stop at the resorts (KSh100) before heading to Mombasa. The Metro Mombasa bus 31 to Mtwapa also comes through here; look for the yellow 'Via Serena' sign in the windscreen.

Mtwapa

Locals call Mtwapa the Las Vegas of Kenya, suppressing a smirk as they do so. This roadside town certainly knows how to party, although its bars are far more seedy than they are shiny. Both Mombasa (to the south) and Kilifi (to the north) are more pleasant than Mtwapa, and there's little reason to spend the night here. But the creek makes a good stop for a scenic supper. The businesses with red mood lighting and names such as 'Escort Lodge' and 'Best Lady Bar' are probably best avoided.

Sights

Jumba la Mtwana RUINS

(adult/child KSh500/100; 8am-6pm) These Swahili ruins, just north of Mtwapa Creek, have as much archaeological grandeur as the more famous Gede Ruins (see p245). Jumba la Mtwana means 'Big House of Slaves' and locals believe the town was once an important slave port. Notice the Arabic inscription on the stela adjacent to the nearby graveyard: 'Every Soul Shall Taste Death'. Underneath is a small hole representing the opening all humans must pass through on the way to paradise.

In the dying evening light, your imagination will be able to run riot with thoughts of lost treasures, ghosts, pirates and abandoned cities. The remains of buildings, with their exposed foundations for mangrove beam poles, ablution tanks, floors caked with millipedes and swarms of safari ants, and the twisting arms of 600-year-old trees – leftover from what may have been a nearby *kaya* – are quite magical.

Slaves may or may not have been traded here, but turtle shell, rhino horn and ambergris (sperm-whale intestinal secretions, used for perfume – mmm) all were. In return, Jumba received goods such as Chinese dishes, the fragments of which can be seen in the floors of some buildings today. While here, keep your eyes peeled for the upper-wall holes that mark where mangrove support beams were affixed; the **House of Many Doors**, which is believed to have been a guesthouse (no breakfast included); and dried-out, 40m-deep wells. You'd be remiss to miss the **Mosque by the Sea**, which overlooks a crystal-sharp vista of the Indian Ocean (and don't forget your swimmers for a splash in the empty waters here).

The custodian gives excellent tours for a small gratuity.

Eating & Drinking

Mumtaz KENYAN $

(near Mtwapa main stage; meals KSh250) The best value *nyama choma* joint in town, this spot also offers big plates of chicken and chapati, served with a soda. A popular local hang-out.

Moorings Restaurant SEAFOOD $$

(041-5485260, 0723032536; mains KSh500-1000) This legendary restaurant is on a floating pontoon on the north bank of Mtwapa Creek. It's a fine place for a beer and serves great seafood with a view. The turn-off is just after the Mtwapa bridge; follow the signs down to the water's edge.

Casuarina BAR

(near Mtwapa main stage) The first bar to get going in Mtwapa, Casuarina always makes for a fun night out. Everyone from prostitutes to fishing tourists to mosquitoes seems to agree.

Getting There & Away

Regular matatus run from Mtwapa to Mombasa (KSh150) and Kilifi (KSh100).

Lamu & the North Coast

Includes ➡

Best of Nature

- ➡ Arabuko Sokoke Forest Reserve (p244)
- ➡ Mida Creek (p245)
- ➡ Malindi Marine National Park (p246)
- ➡ Distant Relatives (p238)
- ➡ Bio-Ken Snake Farm and Laboratory (p241)

Best of Culture

- ➡ Lamu (p254)
- ➡ Paté Island (p265)
- ➡ Malindi (p246)
- ➡ Gede Ruins (p245)

Why Go?

Prepare to fall under the spell of this hypnotic part of the coast. The exotic permeates everything here, blending spice and soul and cramming your head with the accents that equal adventure. Here you'll find honey-gathering crocodile hunters; ghost crabs, tree crabs and elephant shrews; the Vain Island and the Island of Wailing; and a stone city divided into halves, the Beauteous and the Fortunate.

You'll taste spice in fine Swahili cooking, catch it on the bow of a dhow, feel it as you slip into the salty emerald ocean. You'll hear it in the songs of village children in Malindi, chanting 'ciao!' in place of the familiar refrain of '*mzungu*!' This land belongs to no single group. It's been seasoned by Cushitic Somalis, Bantu-speaking Mijikenda, cattle-herding Orma, Italians, Indians, the Bajun, who once sewed their boats together with coconut fibre, and, of course, the Swahili. This land is their land. And it can be yours, too.

When to Go

Lamu

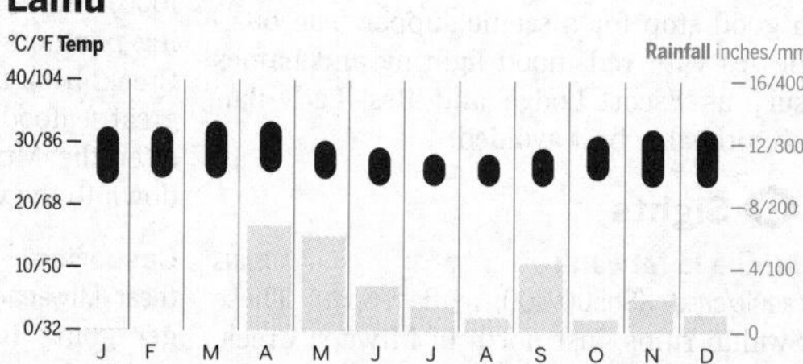

Jul–Sep Lamu is aglow in the wake of Eid; satisfy your sweet tooth with a visit to the island's night markets.

Oct The light *matilai* wind blows softly, clearing the water for fantastic snorkelling and diving.

Nov–Feb The sky is ablaze with migrating birds and the sea is still.

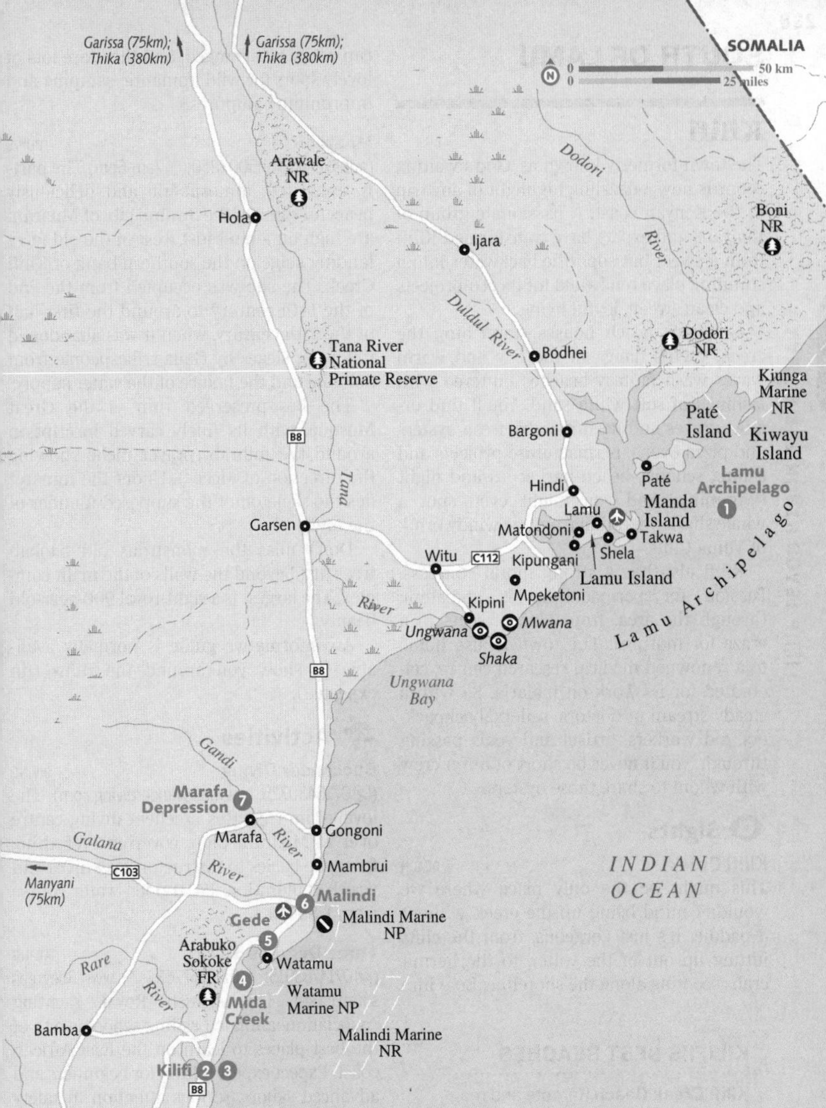

Lamu & the North Coast Highlights

1. Island-hopping by dhow through the stunning **Lamu archipelago** (p253)
2. High-fiving Mother Nature on the bank of **Kilifi Creek** (p238)
3. Losing your bearings and doubting your map atop the otherworldly **Vuma Cliffs** (p240) in Kilifi
4. Watching shooting stars tear open the sky while camping at **Mida Creek** (p245)
5. Exploring the ruined city of **Gede** (p245)
6. Biting into the perfect slice of pizza in the Little Napoli of **Malindi** (p246)
7. Discovering the jagged Mars-like landscape of the **Marafa Depression** (p252)

SOUTH OF LAMU

Kilifi

The town formerly known as 'God's waiting room' is now a dazzling highlight of any trip to the Kenyan coast. A passionate group of Kenyans and expats have transformed Kilifi from a sweet but soporific backwater into a stunning place renowned for its eco-projects and clean, green, joyful living.

Gorgeous beach houses stand atop the creek, yachts dance in the bay and warm waves wash fantasy beaches buttered with lashings of soft white sand. You'll find orange groves and hermit crabs, fresh oysters and pizza ovens, permaculture projects and sailing schools, beach barbecues and night swimming. And you might even spot a whale shark migration from the windy brink of Vuma Cliffs.

Kilifi also has a strong moral compass. Passion for permaculture is spreading through the area, from aloe projects to a craze for moringa. The town is also home to a renowned medical research centre, celebrated for its work on malaria. So with a steady stream of doctors, sailors, backpackers, aid workers, artists and yogis passing through, you'll never be short of a fun crew with whom to share those oysters.

Sights

Kilifi Creek BEACH

This might be the only place where we wouldn't mind being up the creek without a paddle. It's just gorgeous, from the cliffs jutting up out of the water, to the hermit crabs scooting along the shoreline. Boat hire can easily be arranged, and there are lots of lovely spots for wild, romantic camping and impromptu campfires.

Mnarani RUINS

(adult/child KSh500/250; 7am-6pm) The partly excavated, atmospheric and deliciously peaceful ruins of the Swahili city of Mnarani are high on a bluff just west of the old ferry landing stage on the southern bank of Kilifi Creek. The site was occupied from the end of the 14th century to around the first half of the 17th century, when it was abandoned following sieges by Galla tribespeople from Somalia and the failure of the water supply.

The best-preserved ruin is the Great Mosque, with its finely carved inscription around the mihrab (prayer niche showing the direction of Mecca). Under the minaret lies the skeleton of the supposed founder of the town.

Don't miss the monstrous old baobab trees just beyond the walls of the main complex. The largest is a right-royal 900-year-old beauty.

An informative guide is normally available to show you around the ruins (tip expected).

> **KILIFI'S BEST BEACHES**
>
> **Kilifi Creek Beach** Remote and magic, and a lovely spot for a bit of wild camping.
>
> **Bofa Beach** All white sand, swaying palms and soft, pure water. The stuff of which fantasies are made.
>
> **Kitangani Beach** All but abandoned a few years ago when the owner of a landmark Italian restaurant went out for swim and never came back. Today its golden sands are popular for barbecues and as a training ground for a local acrobatic troupe. Beware of the tides.

Activities

Buccaneer Diving DIVING

(0716430725; www.buccaneerdiving.com) The lovely Tim runs this excellent diving centre over at Mnarani Club, covering everything from the basics to instructor-level dives and wreck exploration. PADI open-water course from US$550.

Three Degrees South SAILING

(0714783915, 0714757763; www.3degreessouth.co.ke) This British Royal Yachting Association–affiliated sailing school is one of the best places to learn on the East African coast. Expect expert tuition for beginners and advanced sailors, serious attention to safety and a vast expanse of (beautiful) empty space.

Sleeping

★**Distant Relatives** LODGE, BACKPACKERS $

(0787535145, 0770885164; www.kilifibackpackers.com; dm/r/bandas KSh1000/3000/4000, safari tents KSh1500;) If you need a reason to come to Kilifi, this is it. Both an ecolodge and a backpackers, this place gets it so right. The fantastic owners, staff and guests have created a living, breathing space that's a haven for everyone. Expect good cheer, good people and good conscience. We love the pizza oven and the amazing bamboo showers.

Pretty pathways lead down to the creek, where you can climb aboard a dinghy bound for remote, starfish-studded beaches. Or you can hire a bike, laze in a hammock, or muck in at the vegetable garden.

★Takashack COTTAGES $
(bruceryrie@yahoo.com; Takaungu beach; P) On gorgeous Takaungu beach and off the electricity grid, this eclectic, relaxed house makes a great budget escape when split among friends. Catch the sunrise from the top floor, buy fresh fish every morning, jump in the ocean and, after dark, watch the house light up from the glow of amber hurricane lanterns. Email bookings only.

Hotel Titanic HOTEL $
(041-522370, 0726363437; www.hoteltitanic-kenya.com; Biashara St; s/d KSh2000/3000) We don't know why you'd want to stay in Kilifi town when there's all this beach but, if you did, you could stay at this oddly named hotel. It's right opposite Coffee Pub and the rooms are small but clean. Business seems fairly brisk; it certainly doesn't appear to be a sinking ship.

Bofa Bay Beach Resort RESORT $$
(0703110995; www.bofabaybeachresort.com; tents KSh3500, r from KSh4500; P) A little jungle oasis not far from the blindingly beautiful beach of the same name, Bofa Bay has some posh safari tents with fancy showers and showy rugs. There's a lovely garden restaurant and free wi-fi.

Mnarani Club RESORT $$
(Nairobi 020-8070501/2; www.mnarani.co.za; s/d from US$75/118; P @) This big resort sits on the edge of Kilifi Creek, close to Mnarani ruins. There's a gorgeous curved infinity pool, a decent restaurant, a spa and lots of extras, such as diving and sailing schools, on-site. The creek rooms are the nicest.

Kilifi Bay Beach Resort RESORT $$$
(0722202564; www.madahotels.com; s/d from €135/170;) This polished place sits right on the beach (until high tide, that is) and has a series of comfortable, Swahili-themed rooms with flowing mosquito nets. It's about 5km north of Kilifi, on the coast road.

ECO-TISTICAL: THE BEST GREEN PROJECTS IN KILIFI

Distant Relatives, a backpackers and ecolodge in Kilifi, is an ecosystem in its own right, with a beautiful garden that serves as the basis for permaculture projects. Beds are made from neem trees, mattresses stuffed with cotton from kapok trees, and coat hangers are made from empty wine bottles. Permaculture design courses, taught by big East African names, are held here frequently, covering everything from grafting to composting toilets.

Wild Living (p240) conservation centre is a beautiful 53-hectare conservancy on the outskirts of Kilifi. It serves as a training centre for farmers interested in eco-charcoal production and aloe farming. The shop can arrange tours of the site.

Eating

Village Dishes KENYAN $
(mains KSh200) Inside the petrol station (of all places) in the centre of town, this is the popular cheap cafe in town. It does a tasty fried fish with coconut rice.

Kilifi Members Club KENYAN $
(mains KSh150-400) Atop a cliff on the edge of the bay, this restaurant/bar has the best location in Kilifi. Unfortunately, not all of the staff seem so thrilled to be here. But never mind that; chow down on some good chicken and chips or stop by for sundowners.

Tusky's SUPERMARKET $
The Kenyan supermarket chain has a large-ish Kilifi store that sells plenty of self-catering supplies.

★Distant Relatives Restaurant INTERNATIONAL $$
(0787535145, 0770885164; www.kilifibackpackers.com; mains KSh500-900) Even if you're not staying here, join your distant relatives for dinner at this great, laid-back eatery atop Kilifi Creek. We rate the bacon-and-avo sandwiches, the beetroot-and-hummus veggie bowls and the steaks. Friday is pizza night (there's a pizza oven) and Tuesday is burger night. The breakfast smoothies are the best we tried on the coast.

DON'T MISS

VUMA CLIFFS

'Just you wait, this place looks like another country,' our motorbike driver yells into the wind as we leave the pretty Muslim village of Takaungu and zoom towards Vuma Cliffs. We pass the ruins of a former slave-owner's home, fly through clouds of butterflies and skirt mango and banana plantations.

And then the scenery starts to change. The ground grows rough and is pockmarked and cut by gaping craters. 'Artisanal coral quarries,' our driver says. 'The land here is not very fertile, so coral mining is how people get by.'

We climb higher. The grey coral quarries are soon replaced by heavy granite rocks, interspersed with patches of grass and dewy shrubs. The air cools and darkens, and crows squawk overhead. We feel the bite of thistles against ankles, spot a small fishing shack and clumps of black coral. In the distance, way down below, a perfect wave rolls to shore.

'This place is full of wind and loneliness,' our driver says as he jumps down from the bike and wanders to the edge of the Vuma Cliffs. And yet it's beautiful. We hop rocks, look out for humpback whales and wonder if we've entered a secret portal for Scotland or Norway. But no, this too, it seems, is Kenya.

To reach Vuma, charter a motorbike from Kilifi or ask about organised trips from Distant Relatives (p238). The journey takes about 40 minutes each way.

★ Boatyard SEAFOOD $$

(☎0721590502; mains from KSh600; ⏰7am-7pm) Jetties and boats, fresh crab and fries, old ropes and salty air…there's nothing better than a long, lazy meal at the Boatyard, especially when it involves fresh oysters (oyster night is Saturday). A boatman can pick you up from the other side of the creek for KSh300, or it's a 20-minute motorbike ride along tracks fringed by forest.

★ Nautilus SEAFOOD $$$

(Seahorse Rd; mains KSh850-2500) We're still dining out on our last memory of dinner at Nautilus. This Swiss-owned restaurant offers fine, romantic dining with gorgeous views over the water and a warm welcome. The wine is good, the oysters are even better and the pastas top the lot.

Drinking & Nightlife

Felix Unique Collection JUICE BAR

(Kibaoni St) Felix Unique Collection might not be what we would name our juice bar if we had one – especially if we wanted to make it into an acronym – but the blender geniuses here turn out fantastic avocado, passionfruit, tamarind and mango juice, which is probably why they have a juice bar and we don't. The name, by the way, comes from the owner's clothing store next door.

Dancing Elephant JUICE BAR

(Mombasa-Malindi hwy, next to Wild Living) Even if this tiny, informal place didn't make the best mango juice in Kilifi, we'd still rate it for its name. But during mango season it does – probably because it's right next to a fruit shop.

Coffee Pub PUB

(Biashara St; ⏰8am-late; wi-fi) You can disco dance on caffeine (and alcoholic things) at this popular nightspot. *Nyama choma* (barbecued meat) is on the grill, wi-fi is on the house and drinks are on (well, actually behind) the bar. There's a slightly posh VIP area.

Da Pot CLUB

(Kibaoni St) Da Pot is da bomb, or you might think it is after a few too many Tusker's. This thatched club is open 24/7, which probably says it all.

Shopping

★ Zinj ACCESSORIES

(☎0736808464; www.zinjdesign.com; Takaungu village; ⏰8am-4.30pm Mon-Fri, to 1pm Sat) Walk through a field of donkeys to reach this home-run design store of international reputation. You'll find stylish leather bags adorned with Maasai-style beading (from KSh9860), belts (from KSh3500) and sandals. Pretty and also convenient, in case you follow our lead and break your flip-flops on the Vuma Cliffs.

Wild Living ACCESSORIES

(☎Nairobi 020-2330538; Mombasa-Malindi hwy) Stock up on baobab oil, moringa powder, charcoal briquettes for the barbecue and hats made from soft Ugandan bark at this innovative eco-shop on the edge of Kilifi.

Tours of its excellent conservation centre can also be arranged.

Watamu

Like Malindi to its north, Watamu is something of a Janus – it has two faces, both completely different. The prettiest looks out over the ocean and is plastered with soft white sand and blessed by a soft breeze. The other looks out onto the main road, and is strewn with litter, stones, stores and tourist haunts. Whichever you choose, Watamu does make a good base for explorations between Malindi and Kilif.

Sights & Activities

★Bio-Ken Snake Farm & Laboratory ZOO

(Map p242; ☎042-2332303; www.bio-ken.com; adult/child KSh750/250; ⏲10am-noon & 2-5pm) Don't be fooled by the wooden turquoise cages; this humble-looking place is one of the world's most renowned snake research centres. It specialises in antivenin research, and also acts as an emergency service for snake-bite victims throughout the region. Passionate guides lead excellent 45-minute tours (included in the price); they're highly recommended if you're heading into the bush and want to identify the most deadly serpents. Pricey snake safaris can also be organised.

Watamu Marine National Park PARK

(Map p242; adult/child US$15/10) The southern part of Malindi Marine National Reserve, this park includes some magnificent coral reefs, abundant fish life and sea turtles. To get here to snorkel and dive, you'll need a boat, which is easy enough to hire at the Kenyan Wildlife Service (KWS) office, where you pay the park fees, at the end of the coast road. Boat operators ask anywhere from KSh2500 to KSh4000 for two people for two hours; it's all negotiable.

Watamu Turtle Watch WILDLIFE RESERVE

(Map p242; www.watamuturtles.com; ⏲2.30-4pm Mon, 9.30am-noon & 2.30-4pm Tue-Fri, 9.30am-noon Sat) All credit to the good guys: Watamu Turtle Watch provides a service protecting the marine turtles that come here to lay eggs on the beach. You can get up close and personal with various cutesy turtles at the trust's rehabilitation centre.

Sleeping

Most of Watamu's major hotels close from May to mid-July for the low, rainy season.

★Mwamba Field Study Centre GUESTHOUSE $

(Map p242; ☎042-2332023, Nairobi 020-2335865; www.arocha.org; Watamu Beach; r full board from US$25) This lovely guesthouse and eco-study centre has had a recent makeover. The rooms are bright and serene, with nice touches such as fresh flowers. Run by a Christian conservation society, it offers plenty of opportunities to learn and volunteer. And it's only 50m from the beach; you'll hear the waves crashing as you drift off to sleep.

Hossana Guesthouse GUESTHOUSE $

(☎0721765162; s/d excl breakfast from KSh1200/2400) Pretty in pink (and turquoise) on Watamu's main road, this female-run Christian guesthouse is a good bet for budget travellers. The friendly, no-nonsense owner, Priscilla, has eight simple

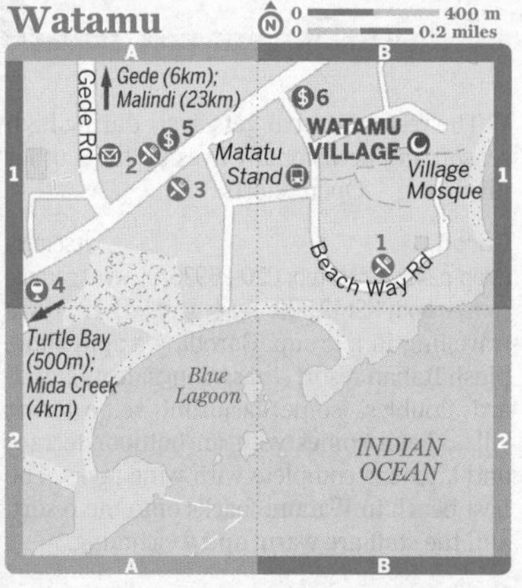

Watamu

Eating

1	Ascot Pizzeria	B1
2	Bistro Coffee Shop	A1
3	That's Amore	A1
	Watamu Supermarket	(see 2)

Drinking & Nightlife

4	Kalahari Club	A1

Information

5	Barclays Bank	A1
6	Kenya Commercial Bank	B1

Around Watamu

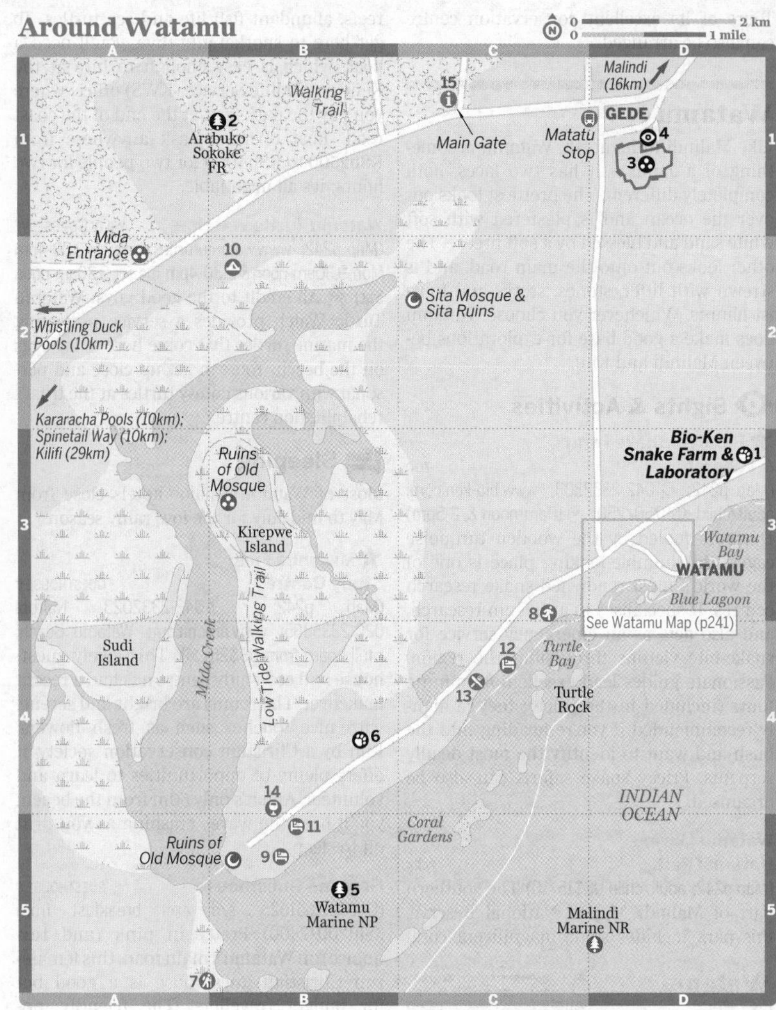

but clean rooms (and is planning an extension) equipped with fans and nets. Breakfast costs an extra KSh300, and the basic cafe serves up Swahili food.

Ocean Sports RESORT **$$**
(Map p242; ☎0734195227; www.oceansports.net; r from US$110;) In the same complex as Hemingway's, Ocean Sports is true to its name. There's a pool and diving trips, as well as a tennis court and ultimate frisbee. It has pretty, breeze-blown rooms in a garden setting, which can get noisy on weekends.

The restaurant-bar gets lively during high season and occasionally lives up to its other nickname – 'Open Shorts.'

Garoda RESORT **$$**
(Map p242; ☎Nairobi 020-2692679; www.garoda.com; r from KSh12,500;) If you're travelling in a group, Garoda – a sprawling, plush Italian resort – has, alongside its standard doubles, some beautiful self-catering villas. Each comes with an outdoor terrace and kitchens complete with wine racks. The best beach in Watamu backs onto the resort, and the staff are warm and welcoming.

Around Watamu

Top Sights

Sights

Activities, Courses & Tours

Sleeping

Eating

Drinking & Nightlife

Information

★Kobe Suite Resort BOUTIQUE HOTEL $$$
(Map p242; ☎Nairobi 020-2692679; www.kobesuiteresort.com) With just five rooms inside a lush villa that once belonged to a motocross champion, this new boutique hotel works a sleek, dreamy vibe. Expect Swahili archways, bougainvillea window frames and a beautiful rooftop terrace. The garden hides intimate coves and a firepit, while the restaurant serves fine food. Sweet indeed.

Hemingway's HOTEL $$$
(Map p242; ☎042-32624; www.hemingways-watamu.com; s/d US$170/390; P❄☜≋) Hemingway spent his gin-fuelled holidays along this part of the Kenyan coast, and this namesake hotel blends exclusive touches with everything you'd expect from a standard coastal resort. Plush beds face the ocean, and the deluxe doubles come with large tubs. The pool (KSh1600 for nonguests) and the atmospheric bar are highlights.

Turtle Bay Beach Club RESORT $$$
(Map p242; ☎042-2332003, 042-2332226; www.turtlebaykenya.com; d from KSh18,000; ❄@≋) With a silver ecotourism rating, this is easily one of Watamu's best top-end resorts. The hotel uses managed tree cover to reduce its environmental imprint, runs enough ecotourism ventures to fill a book (including birdwatching safaris and turtle-protection programs) and contributes to local charities.

Eating

Bistro Coffee Shop CAFE $
(Map p241; cakes from KSh150; ⊙8am-5pm) Opening onto a little garden area (and also a car park), this pretty coffee shop has freshly baked cakes, gooey brownies, pastries and quiches, plus decent coffee.

Watamu Supermarket SUPERMARKET $
(Map p241; Jacaranda Rd) This friendly supermarket is the best stocked in Watamu.

★Ocean Sports Restaurant INTERNATIONAL $$
(Map p242; ☎0734195227; Ocean Sports Hotel; mains from KSh750; P☜) This popular place is spread along a breeze-blown terrace and has some plusher seating inside. Expect sandwiches, burgers, great salads and finer dining such as seared tuna and other seafood creations. It's atmospheric at night, when the ocean rock formations glow under the moon. That's also when the music gets louder and the party starts.

That's Amore INTERNATIONAL $$
(Map p241; Jacaranda Rd; mains from KSh450; ☜) From the owners of the Garoda and Kobe resorts, this cute little Italian cafe sits opposite Watamu supermarket. It looks fresh and modern, and serves delicious breakfasts and good coffee (but, surprisingly, no pizza). Free wi-fi.

Ascot Pizzeria ITALIAN $$
(Map p241; Ascot Hotel, Beach Way Rd; mains KSh500-1250) A favourite for romantic dinners, Ascot consistently gets good feedback and is famous for its pizzas. It occasionally closes during the low season.

★Pili Pan INTERNATIONAL $$$
(Map p242; ☎0734622578, 0736724099; mains KSh900-1400; ⊙Tue-Sun; P) Set in a breezy Swahili-style outdoor terrace, Pili Pan turns up Watamu's chic factor. The menu includes things such as salt-and-pepper squid, tikka

DON'T MISS

DIVING, FISHING & WINDSURFING

There are plenty of waterborne activities on offer at Watamu, including diving, deep-sea fishing and windsurfing.

Alleycat Big Game Fishing (Map p242; ☎0722734788; www.alleycatfishing.com; Ocean Sports Resort, Turtle Bay) Runs dedicated, tailored deep-sea fishing safaris.

Aqua Ventures (Map p242; ☎0703628102, 0422332420; www.diveinkenya.com; Ocean Sports Resort; dives from €85) Offers guided dives in the marine park, as well as trail biking and kayaking.

Kite Watamu (Map p242; www.kitewatamu.com; kitesurfing from €30) Offers highly recommended kitesurfing sessions. It's run by a group of passionate young guys who care about the future of Watamu. The owners were also in the process of opening the Kite House, a low-budget, stylish guesthouse, at the time of writing.

Ocean Sports (Map p242; ☎0734195227; www.oceansports.net) Offers windsurfing courses from €20, which is about as cheap as you'll find in Kenya.

skewers with tamarind and tuna carpaccio. Service is good and there's a stylish bar area for aperitifs.

Drinking

Kalahari Club BAR
(Map p241; off Jacaranda Rd) A joint where you can do everything from eating (*nyama choma* and fries; mains from KSh250) to watching sport, singing (karaoke night is Tuesday) and dancing.

Radio Maria BAR
(Map p242; ☎0722160827; Turtle Bay Rd) Come for cocktails and seafood at this quirky, Virgin Mary (the biblical figure, not the drink) themed bar. Open late during high season.

Information

Barclays Bank (Map p241; Watamu Supermarket, Jacaranda Rd)

Kenya Commercial Bank (Map p241; Beach Way Rd)

Getting There & Around

Watamu is about an hour's drive north of Kilifi and about 40 minutes' drive south of Malindi. Matatus (minibus transport) run regularly between the three destinations. Heading north, they depart from Watamu village; southbound vans leave from Gede ruins. Matatus to Malindi charge KSh100. Matatus to Kilifi charge KSh200.

Arabuko Sokoke Forest Reserve

This 420-sq-km tract of natural forest – the largest indigenous coastal forest remaining in East Africa – is most famous as the home of the golden-rumped elephant shrew. Yes, you read that right – it's a guinea-pig-sized rodent with a long furry trunk and a monogamous streak, and the **Arabuko Sokoke Forest Reserve** (Map p242; adult/child US$20/10; ⏲6am-6pm) is its only natural habitat.

Besides this marvellous creature, the forest is home to about 240 bird species, including the Amani sunbird, the Clarke's weaver and the Sokoko scoops owl – Africa's smallest owl. More than 33 species of snakes slither through the undergrowth and shy waterbucks hide behind mahogany trees.

The **visitor centre** (Map p242; www.kws.org; Malindi Rd; ⏲8am-4pm) is at Gede Forest Station and has displays on the various species found here. Three-hour guided walking tours (Ksh1500) leave from here. Night walks can also be arranged in advance.

From the visitor centre, nature trails and 4WD tracks cut through the forest. There are bird trails at Whistling Duck Pools, Kararacha Pools and Spinetail Way, located 16km south. It's possible to spend the night in the forest, setting up camp (US$10) on a tall tree platform with a spectacular view of the species below.

The forest is just off the main Malindi–Mombasa road. The main gate is about 1.5km west of the turn-off to Gede and Watamu, while the Mida entrance is about 3km further south. Buses and matatus between Mombasa and Malindi can drop you at either entrance. From Watamu, matatus to Malindi can drop you at the main junction.

Mida Creek

Mida Creek is a quiet and gentle place. Hugged by silver-tinged mudflats flowing with ghost crabs and long tides, it's a place where the creeping marriage of land and water is epitomised by a mangrove forest and the salty, fresh scent of wind over an estuary. Mida Creek saves its real appeal for evening, when the stars rain down on you.

Any bus travelling between Mombasa and Malindi can drop you on the main road near Mida Creek, from where it's a pleasant, leafy, 20-minute walk to the camp.

Sights & Activities

Kirepwe Island ISLAND

Mida Eco-camp organises day trips (KSh3500) to this quiet island just across the estuary. The ruins are atmospheric and you can visit a Giriama village and stop for a fisherman's lunch.

Green Island ISLAND

This uninhabited island on the other side of Mida Creek makes an interesting excursion. It is, as you'd imagine, very green (at least during the rainy season) and there are all sorts of curious creatures around. Local fisherpeople can ferry you across, or the eco-camp can organise a trip.

Mida Creek Boardwalk WALKING

(Map p242; adult/child KSh250/150, guides KSh500) Excellent Giriama guides will take you through the water-laced landscape of the creek and through the mangroves on a rickety walkway. At the end of the walkway, a bird hide looks out over the surrounding wetlands. Of all Kenya's mangrove walkways, this one is by far the best. You can also organise canoe trips (from KSh700) from here. Best of all, this is a community project, so your visit helps the local Giriama people.

Sleeping

★ **Mida Eco-camp** CAMPGROUND $

(Map p242; ✆0729213042; www.midaecocamp.com; camping KSh500, huts per person KSh1400) This relaxed, budget-minded eco-camp has *the* most perfect position, between the forest, the creek and the stars. Accommodation is in rickety but atmospheric huts – choose from Zanzibar (an antiquey duplex hut with a rooftop), Giriama (with raised platform beds) and Bamboo (self-explanatory). The eco-credentials stretch to solar panels, renewable materials and a serious Giriama community focus.

The sofas in the restaurant, which serves delicious Kenyan dishes, are made from old fishing canoes. All manner of great excursions can be arranged here.

Gede Ruins

If you thought Kenya was all about nature, you're missing an important component of its charm: lost cities. The remains of medieval Swahili towns dot the coast, and many would say the most impressive of the bunch

ON THE TRAIL OF THE ELEPHANT SHREW

'The most interesting thing about the golden-rumped elephant shrew,' says our guide, pausing for effect as we push back lianas inside the Arabuko Sokoke Forest Reserve, 'is its forgetfulness.' We're surprised. We thought perhaps it would be its shiny golden bum, its elephantine trunk, or the fact that the male lives in mixed-sex couples but frequents other females on the side.

But no. 'Here in the forest, the shrew's forgetfulness has saved its life. It's the reason it continues to thrive here,' he says. 'People say that if they catch and kill an elephant shrew, they will lose their memory, too. So nobody touches them.'

We walk past tall tamarind trees (an accidental import from India), medicinal plants and briliant blue-and-orange African tiger moths. We spot flying handkerchief butterflies and tiny duikers, prehistoric zamia plants and parasitic trees that have squeezed all life from their reluctant hosts. We see gigantic termite mounds and deadly orange fungus. But still no golden-rumped elephant shrews.

And then, a red-capped robin flutters into view. 'Aha,' whispers our guide, explaining that this small bird has a symbiotic relationship with the shrew, feeding on the insects that escape its nozzle and, in turn, alerting the rodent to predators. 'A shrew must be nearby...' And then we see it, scooting across the forest floor, its glorious golden rump reflecting the afternoon sun.

are the **Gede Ruins** (Map p242; adult/child KSh500/250; ⏲7am-6pm).

Guided tours are available from the gate for KSh300 to KSh500.

This series of coral palaces, mosques and townhouses, which once housed 3000 people, lies quietly in the jungle's green grip. Here, archaeologists found evidence of the cosmopolitan nature of Swahili society: silver necklaces decorated with Maria Teresa coins (from Europe) and Arabic calligraphy (from the Middle East), vermicelli makers from Asia that would become pasta moulds in the Mediterranean, Persian sabres, Arab coffee pots, Indian lamps, Egyptian or Syrian cobalt glass, Spanish scissors and Ming porcelain.

But the good times were not to last. Gede, which reached its peak in the 15th century, was inexplicably abandoned in the 17th or 18th century. Some theories point to disease and famine, others blame guerrilla attacks by Somalian Gallas and cannibalistic Zimba from near Malawi, or punitive expeditions from Mombasa. Or Gede ran out of water – at some stage the water table here dropped rapidly and the 40m-deep wells dried up.

Entry to the dusty **museum** is included in the site ticket. There's a small collection of excavated Chinese coins, porcelain bowls, weapons, terracotta pots and other items found here.

Malindi

With an Italian-sounding name, some of the best pizza in all of Africa and, well, plenty of Italian tourists, it would be easy to dismiss Malindi as just another European holiday resort. Until, that is, you wander through the alleys of the atmospheric old town, stop for fresh oysters beside the Indian Ocean and pause for Swahili cakes on Jamhuri St. Malindi, it turns out, is quite the charmer.

Sights & Activities

Malindi Marine National Park PARK

(adult/child US$20/15, boats KSh3000; ⏲6am-6pm) The oldest marine park in Kenya covers 213 sq km of powder blue fish, organ-pipe coral, green sea-turtles and beds of Thalassia seagrass. If you're extremely lucky, you may spot mako and whale sharks. Unfortunately, these reefs have suffered (and continue to suffer) extensive damage, evidenced by the piles of seashells on sale in Malindi. Note that monsoon-generated waves can reduce visibility from June to September.

Malindi Historic Circuit HISTORIC SITE

(adult/child KSh500/250; ⏲8am-6pm) National Museums of Kenya has smartly grouped the major cultural sites of Malindi under the one general ticket of this circuit.

The most compelling attraction covered in the Historic Circuit is the **House of Columns** (Mama Ngina Rd). The structure itself is a good example of traditional Swahili architecture and, more pertinently, contains great exhibits of all sorts of archaeological finds dug up around the coast.

The **Vasco da Gama pillar** is admittedly more impressive for what it represents (the genesis of the Age of Exploration) than the edifice itself. Erected by Vasco da Gama as a navigational aid in 1498, the coral column is topped by a cross made of Lisbon stone, which almost certainly dates from the explorer's time. There are good views from here down the coast and out over the ocean. To get here, turn off Mama Ngina Rd, by Scorpio Villas.

The tiny thatched **Portuguese church** (Mama Ngina Rd) is so called because da Gama is reputed to have erected it, and two of his crew are supposedly buried here. It's certainly true that St Francis Xavier visited on his way to India.

Malindi Pier LANDMARK

This long tongue flicks out into the Indian Ocean. It's a low-key highlight of a stroll along Mama Ngina Rd. On weekends, families wander arm in arm and kids dress up and pose in makeshift photo studios.

Sleeping

Moonlight Bandas & Campsite CAMPGROUND $

(☎0721652416, 0720288719; Marine Park Rd; camping KSh600-1000, bandas KSh1500-3000) This small, well-kept campground is overseen by friendly manager Abdul. There are five simple raised-platform tents and a few basic but neat *bandas* (thatched huts). The wooden bar doesn't have a kitchen, but takeaways can be arranged.

Marine Park Bandas & Camping CAMPGROUND $

(☎Nairobi 020-6000800; Marine Park; camping KSh800, bandas KSh3000; Ⓟ) Malindi Marine National Park has set aside a small area for pitching tents. It also has a handful of

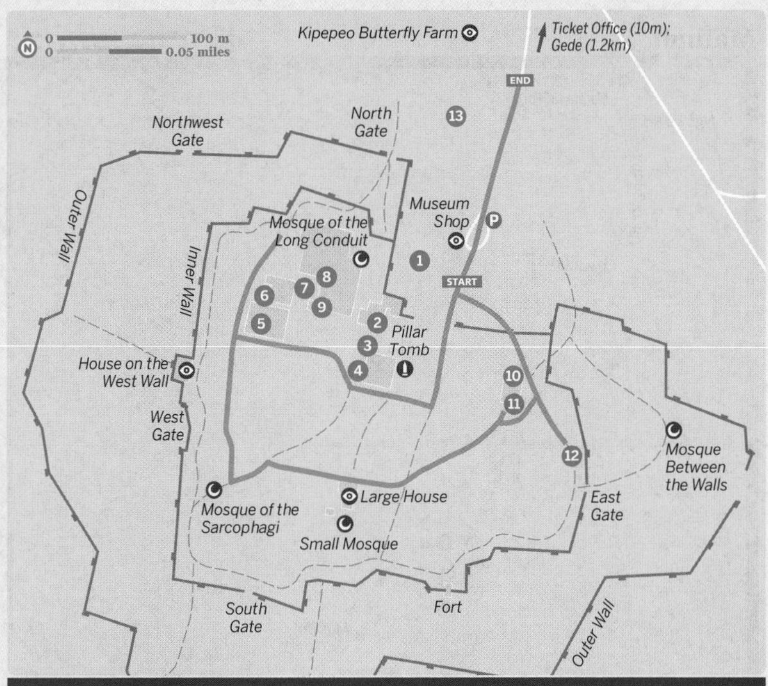

Walking Tour Gede Ruins

START GEDE RUINS ENTRANCE
FINISH GEDE RUINS MUSEUM
LENGTH 1.5KM
DURATION ONE TO 1½ HOURS

Gede is Kenya's most visitor-friendly archaeological site. Most of the excavated buildings are concentrated near the entrance, but there are dozens of other ruins scattered through the forest. On your right as you enter the compound is the 1 **Dated Tomb**, so called because of the wall inscription featuring the Muslim date corresponding to 1399. Near it, inside the wall, is the 2 **Tomb of the Fluted Pillar**, which is characteristic of such pillar designs found along the East African coast. Past the tomb, next to the 3 **House of the Long Court**, the 4 **Great Mosque** is one of Gede's most significant buildings. The entrance was on the side of a long rectangular prayer hall, with the mihrab (prayer niche that faces Mecca) obscured behind rows of stone pillars. Behind the mosque are the ruins of an extensive 5 **palace**. One of the interesting things found within the ruins was an earthenware jar containing a *fingo* (charm), thought to attract jinn (guardian spirits) who would drive trespassers insane. The palace also has a particularly fine 6 **pillar tomb**; its hexagonal shape is unique to East Africa. Just off to the right from the palace is a 7 **tree** with steps leading high up into its canopy for a bird's-eye view of the site. Along the path past the tomb are around 11 old 8 **Swahili houses**. They're each named after particular features of their design, or objects found in them by archaeologists, such as the House of Scissors and the House of the Iron Lamp. The 9 **House of the Cistern** is particularly interesting, with ancient illustrations incised into the plaster walls. The other excavations include the 10 **House of the Dhow**, 11 **House of the Double Court** and the nearby 12 **Mosque of the Three Aisles**, which has the largest well at Gede. On the way out you'll find an excellent little 13 **museum**.

The ruins lie off the main highway, on the access road to Watamu. The easiest way here is on any matatu (minibus transport) plying the main highway between Mombasa and Malindi. Get off at the village of Gede and follow the well-signposted dirt road from there; it's about a 10-minute walk.

Malindi

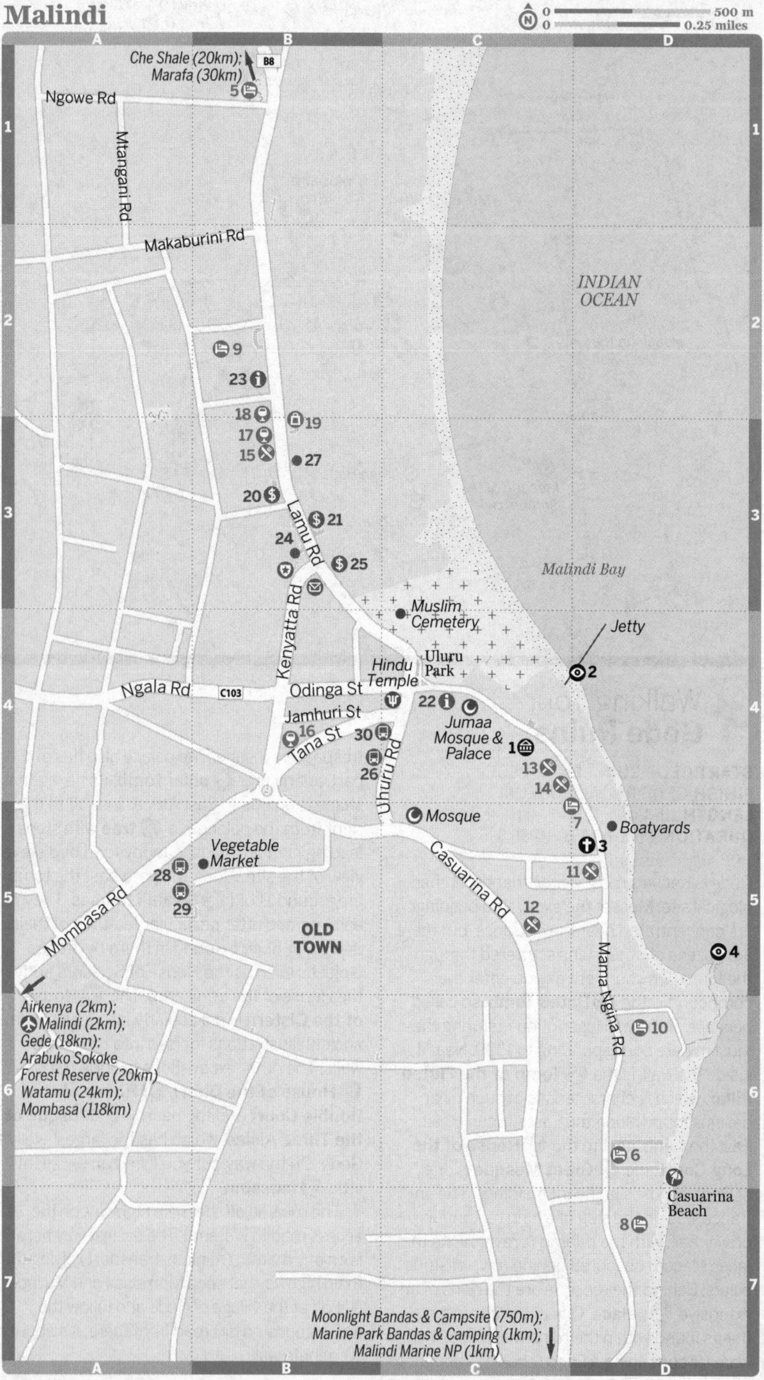

0 500 m
0 0.25 miles
A
B
C
D
1
2
3
4
5
6
7
Che Shale (20km); Marafa (30km)
B8
Ngowe Rd
Mtangani Rd
Makaburini Rd
INDIAN OCEAN
Lamu Rd
Malindi Bay
Muslim Cemetery
Jetty
Kenyatta Rd
Uluru Park
Hindu Temple
Ngala Rd
C103
Odinga St
Jamhuri St
Tana St
Uhuru Rd
Jumaa Mosque & Palace
Mosque
Boatyards
Vegetable Market
Casuarina Rd
Mombasa Rd
OLD TOWN
Mama Ngina Rd
Airkenya (2km); Malindi (2km); Gede (18km); Arabuko Sokoke Forest Reserve (20km) Watamu (24km); Mombasa (118km)
Casuarina Beach
Moonlight Bandas & Campsite (750m); Marine Park Bandas & Camping (1km); Malindi Marine NP (1km)
1
2
3
4
5
6
7
8
9
10
11
12
13
14
15
16
17
18
19
20
21
22
23
24
25
26
27
28
29
30

Malindi

Sights

1 House of Columns C4
2 Malindi Pier D4
3 Portuguese Church D5
4 Vasco da Gama Pillar D5

Sleeping

5 African Pearl Hotel B1
6 Coral Key Beach Resort D6
7 Dagama's Inn D5
8 Driftwood Beach Club D7
9 Lutheran Guest House B2
10 Scorpio Villas D6

Eating

11 Baby Marrow D5
12 Dreamland Cafe C5
13 I Love Pizza C4
14 Jahizi C4
15 Kako B3
Karen Blixen Restaurant & Coffee Shop .... (see 19)
Old Man & the Sea .... (see 7)

Drinking & Nightlife

16 Cheers B4
Fermento Piano Bar .... (see 19)
17 Putipo B3
18 Stars & Garters B2

Shopping

19 Karen Blixen Vintage Shop B3
Kipepeo .... (see 19)
Mizizi Ya Afrika .... (see 15)

Information

20 Barclays Bank B3
21 Dollar Forex Bureau B3
22 Immigration Office C4
23 Malindi Tourist Office B2
24 North Coast Travel Services B3
25 Standard Chartered Bank B3

Transport

26 Buses to Lamu B4
27 Kenya Airways B3
28 Matatus to Mombasa & Nairobi A5
29 New Malindi Bus Station A5
30 Simba Coaches C4
Tawakal Office .... (see 30)
TSS Buses Office .... (see 26)

simple *bandas*. A good option if you're planning on exploring the park bright and early.

Dagama's Inn INN $
(☎0701864446, 0722357591; Mama Ngina Rd; s/d excl breakfast KSh1000/1200) This friendly little place is a real seaside travellers' inn – that's to say that seamen prop up the bar with mermaid stories, and drunken sailors make eyes at the barmaid. The rooms are spacious but simple. If you can get hot water out of those rusty water-storage tanks, you're a better person than us.

Lutheran Guest House GUESTHOUSE $
(☎042-30098; s/d KSh1200/2000) If you need quiet, this religious centre (which accepts guests of all stripes) is a nice option. Like most church-run places in Kenya, everything here is a little cleaner, staff are earnestly friendly and alcohol is strictly prohibited.

African Pearl Hotel RESORT $
(☎0725131956; www.africanpearlhotel.com; Lamu Rd; r from KSh3500;) Not as fancy as the name suggests, this resort is handy if you're after all the resort trimmings without the price tag. In theory there's everything you could want here, but in practice not all of it works.

★ **Scorpio Villas** RESORT $$
(☎042-2120194; www.scorpio-villas.com; Mnarani Rd; s/d KSh4600/7200;) Pretty and great value, Scorpio Villas is a winner. It's right by the ocean and within walking distance of some good restaurants. The 40-or-so rooms follow the hotel theme: gorgeous dark wood, white linen sofas and Swahili carvings. The bathrooms have huge monsoon showers. What's not to love?

Coral Key Beach Resort RESORT $$
(☎042-30717; www.malindikey.com; Mama Ngina Rd; s/d from €70/140; @) It's a bit bling and full of, well, we're not really sure what they are – possibly swimming pools, or maybe ponds or water features? Whatever, they're certainly memorable. The rooms, though, are comfortable, clean and good bang for your shillings.

★ **Driftwood Beach Club** RESORT $$$
(☎042-2120155, 042-2130845; www.driftwoodclub.com; Mama Ngina Rd; r from KSh14,000;) Somewhere between fancy pants and seaside chic, this place sees plenty of expat and Anglo-Kenyan traffic. The rooms are smart, but the hotel pulls off a relaxed vibe. The ambience is closer to palm-breezed

KENYA'S SNAKES: GEOGRAPHY & HISSS-TORY

- Most of the snakes on the Kenyan coast are shy and attack only in self-defence. But they do include black mambas, grass snakes (known as Kenyan spaghetti in Italian-influenced Malindi) and even deadly twig snakes, for which there is no antivenin.
- Snakes with horizontal patterns are generally more deadly than those with patterns that stretch lengthways along their bodies.
- When poured into a glass, cobra venom looks remarkably like Tusker beer. Do not confuse the two.
- After a sexual encounter, some female snakes have the lucky option of storing sperm for up to three years until they're ready for motherhood.
- If you're bitten by a snake, whip out your camera before you rush to hospital or call the guys at Bio-Ken Snake Farm (p241). Identifying the snake will speed treatment. Oh, and don't panic or try to calm your nerves with a stiff drink: both adrenalin and alcohol will worsen your painful symptoms.

serenity than the party atmosphere at similar hotels.

Eating

With great seafood and strong Italian influences, there's a reason Malindi is known as Little Napoli. Street-food heaven is Jamhuri St, where stalls line both sides of the road selling deep-fried goodies, bhajis, dates and chapatis.

Dreamland Cafe KENYAN $
(Casuarina Rd; mains around KSh250) The outer walls look a bit like the children's ward of a hospital, but there's nothing sterile about this circular roadside lunch spot. Expect friendly service, local banter and a blaring TV. The fresh juice is good.

Kako FAST FOOD $
(Lamu Rd; mains from KSh250) Chicken, chips and chapatis from this shiny hole-in-the-wall joint.

★Karen Blixen Restaurant & Coffee Shop CAFE $$
(www.karenblixen.net; Lamu Rd; meals KSh500-1500; P 🛜) Everyone in Kenya, it seems, wants to be Karen Blixen these days. This place isn't sure if it's a shabby-chic Karen Blixen or a blinging Karen Blixen, so it's gone for both looks, with scruffy leather seats and blinding gold lampshades. The pizza is as good as the coffee, and the place acts as Malindi's expat epicentre.

★I Love Pizza ITALIAN $$
(☎042-20672; nwright@africaonline.co.ke; Mama Ngina Rd; pizzas around KSh900, pastas KSh400-600) We do too, and the pizza is done really well here – way better than you might expect this far from Naples. No matter how good the pizza, many people come instead for the seafood and pasta. The hip, renovated colonial building, with a lovely terrace, seals the deal.

★Jahizi SEAFOOD $$
(☎0720747180, 0720178982; Mama Ngina Rd) Another breeze-kissed Mama Ngina Rd hang-out, this time with a hip slant on a fishing theme. Think big oysters, fish, juices, a long wine list and plenty of pizza. You could be in Sicily. Popular with everyone from waistcoated elderly gentlemen to stylish Malindians.

Old Man & the Sea SEAFOOD $$
(☎042-31106; Mama Ngina Rd; mains KSh400-750, seafood KSh550-1100) This Old Man's been serving elegant, excellent seafood, using a combination of local ingredients and fresh recipes, for years. The classy waitstaff and wicker-chic ambience combine for some nice colonial-style, candlelit meals under the stars. The menu also contains a small selection of vegetarian options.

★Baby Marrow ITALIAN, SEAFOOD $$$
(☎0733542584; Mama Ngina Rd; mains KSh500-2000) Imagine an intimate honeymoon lodge restaurant, minus the lodge. That's what Baby Marrow is like. You can feast on smoked sailfish, pizza bianca, vodka sorbet or Sicilian ice cream (and plenty of other things) beneath the bamboo eaves. The jungle bar is a good spot for a *digestif.*

Drinking & Nightlife

Cheers JUICE BAR
(☎0716030379; Kenyatta Ave) This tiny roadside bar deserves a mention for its lovely garden and fresh carrot juice. Who needs alcohol to clink glasses?

Rosada BAR
Right on the sand, Rosada is a chilled beach bar with some nice views out to the marine park.

Stars & Garters BAR
You can count on seeing both – stars and garters – during a night out here. Enough said.

Putipo BAR
(Lamu Rd) Posh bar Putipo sits opposite the Karen Blixen Restaurant and Coffee Shop. Happy hour is every evening from 5.30pm to 7.30pm.

Fermento Piano Bar LOUNGE
(☎042-31780; Galana Centre, Lamu Rd; admission KSh200; ⏲from 10pm Wed, Fri & Sat) Fermento, for 'your endless night'…or so the slogan goes. The dance floor was apparently once frequented by Naomi Campbell. It's young and trendy, so try to look so yourself.

Shopping

Karen Blixen Vintage Shop CLOTHING
(Lamu Rd) There's everything from silk purses to sows' ears inside this vintage treasure trove. We spied an orginal sax, old Kenyan irons (actually made from iron), hipster trousers and sundresses.

Kipepeo CLOTHING
(Lamu Rd) Imported Italian bikinis, kaftans, sandals and lingerie: everything you need to pretend you're lovestruck in Napoli.

Mizizi Ya Afrika SOUVENIRS
(Lamu Rd) This boutique take on a souvenir shop sells some bigger, more artistic (and pricier) carvings and beads than other places.

Information

DANGERS & ANNOYANCES

Being on the beach alone at night is asking for trouble, as is walking along any quiet beach back road at night. Also, avoid the far northern end of the beach, or any deserted patches of sand, as muggings are common. There are lots of guys selling drugs, so remember: everything from marijuana up is illegal. Drug sales often turn into stings, with the collusive druggie getting a cut of whatever fee police demand from you (if they don't throw you in jail). There's also a lot of prostitution here.

EMERGENCY

Ambulance (☎999)
Police (☎042-2120485, 999; Kenyatta Rd)

MONEY

Barclays Bank (☎042-2120036; Lamu Rd) With ATM.
Dollar Forex Bureau (☎042-30602; Lamu Rd) Rates may be slightly better here than at the banks.
Standard Chartered Bank (☎042-20130; Stanchart Arcade, Lamu Rd) With ATM.

POST

Post office (Kenyatta Rd)

TOURIST INFORMATION

Malindi Tourist Office (☎042-20689; Malindi Complex, Lamu Rd, Malindi; ⏲8am-12.30pm & 2-4.30pm Mon-Fri)

TRAVEL AGENCIES

North Coast Travel Services (☎042-20370; Lamu Rd) Agent for Fly540.

Getting There & Away

AIR

Airkenya (☎042-30646; Malindi Airport) Daily afternoon/evening flights to Nairobi (US$100, two hours).
Kenya Airways (☎042-20237; Lamu Rd) Flies to Nairobi at least once a day (US$134).

BUS & MATATU

Bus-company offices are found opposite the old market in the centre of Malindi.

There are usually at least six buses a day to Lamu (KSh800 but can rise in periods of high demand, four to five hours). Most leave around 9am. TSS Buses and Tawakal are the biggest operators.

There are numerous daily buses and matatus to Mombasa (bus/matatu KSh300/350, two hours). During periods of high demand, fares can rise to KSh600.

All the main bus companies have daily departures to Nairobi, via Mombasa, at around 7am and/or 7pm (KSh500 to KSh3000, 10 to 12 hours).

Matatus to Watamu (KSh100, one hour) leave from the not-very-new New Malindi Bus Station on the edge of town.

DON'T MISS

MARAFA

Away from the hedonistic delights of sun and sand, one of the more intriguing sights along the north Kenyan coast is the **Marafa Depression**, also known as Hell's Kitchen or Nyari ('the place broken by itself'). About 30km northeast of Malindi, it's an eroded sandstone gorge where jungle, red rock and cliffs heave themselves into a single stunning Mars-like landscape.

The Depression is currently managed as a local tourism concern by Marafa village. It costs a steep KSh600 (which goes into village programs) to walk around the lip of the gorge, and KSh400 for a guide who can walk you into its sandstone heart and tell Hell's Kitchen's story. Which goes like so: a rich family was so careless with their wealth that they bathed themselves in the valuable milk of their cows. God became angry with this excess and sank the family homestead into the earth. The white and red walls of the Depression mark the milk and blood of the family painted over the gorge walls. The more mundane explanation? The Depression is a chunk of sandstone that's geologically distinct from the surrounding rock and more susceptible to wind and rain erosion.

Most people visit here on organised tours, with a self-drive car or by taxi (KSh7000). Alternatively, there are one or two morning matatus from Mombasa Rd in Malindi to Marafa village (KSh150, three hours) and from there it's a 20-minute walk to Hell's Kitchen. There are two very basic places to stay if needed.

If you come by private transport, it's worth making a day trip of it and enjoying the beautiful African countryside, stopping for a chat in any of the numerous villages that line the route.

Getting Around

You can rent bicycles from most hotels for around KSh500 per day. Cycling at night is not permitted. Tuk-tuks are ubiquitous; a short hop through town should cost around KSh150 to KSh250. A taxi to the airport is at least KSh300 and a tuk-tuk is KSh150. However, these are official prices and you'll need the gift of the gab to actually bargain them down to this.

Around Malindi

North of Malindi, the road winds westwards towards the stunning Marafa Depression. Or follow the coast road instead and you'll hit waves made for kitesurfing.

Sleeping

★**Che Shale** TENTED CAMP $$
(☎0722230931; www.cheshale.com; s/d from €80/160) Live out your castaway fantasties at this gorgeous, peaceful spot that's perfectly isolated from the rest of the world (and yet only 30km from Malindi). Kitesurfers swear by the place, as do foodies and those who know their eco-design. Simple perfection.

★**Barefoot Beach Camp** TENTED CAMP $$$
(☎0723564258, 0722421351; www.barefootbeachcampkenya.com; per person US$120-$200) If you venture 25km from Malindi, you can have Mambrui North beach to yourselves (well, almost) at this intimate and relaxed tented camp, run by fantastic hosts. The food is delicious, the atmosphere casual and the style is beachy hip.

Tana River

The Tana River delta is regarded by most travellers as an inconvenient stretch of road between Malindi and Lamu. It's true that the delta marks the fall line, as it were, of resorts – past here, Sir David Attenborough might say, the hotels simply cannot survive (well, until Lamu).

But there are some fantastic areas of exploration here for intrepid travellers. The delta country is a long, low marshland dotted with domes of jungle sprouting over a wet prairie. Cooking smoke from the thin houses of the Orma people and the mud-and-thatch huts of the Pokomo floats over the sedge, while black herons flap over the slow water. In the tall grass, hippos and crocodiles warily circle one another. This is one of those parts of Kenya where hippos are a viable traffic hazard! It's also prime dhow-building turf; huge boats, including the **Musafir** (www.musafir.org), have been conceived and built here.

Sights & Activities

Kipini Wildlife Conservancy WILDLIFE CONSERVANCY
(☎0705133509; www.kipiniconservancy.wildlifedirect.org; admission US$10) This low-key private coastal conservancy is home to turtles and dolphins, as well as a trickle of international volunteers.

Boat Safaris
The most obvious thing to do is a boat safari onto the great, greasy, green Tana River. There's no thrill like that of being in a small boat, looking at a tree, then watching said tree slide into the water and realising it's a crocodile. Canoe safaris are about KSh2000 for the day, but the problem is that most of the crocs and hippos are a fair way upriver and you won't get very far very quickly in a canoe.

Therefore it's better to hire a motor boat, but that's going to cost you. We were quoted KSh6000 per hour with fuel and you'd best allow three hours to make it worthwhile.

Sleeping & Eating

Mamba Campsite & Lodging COTTAGES $
(Kipini; cottages excl breakfast KSh500) Very basic cottages with smelly shared toilets, but it's about the only 'formal' accommodation in Kipini village.

Delta Dunes LODGE $$$
(☎0718139359; www.deltadunes.co.ke; s/d full board US$590/1000, plus conservation fee per person US$60;) This remote, exclusive lodge sits at the scenic mouth of the Tana River and offers walking and canoe safaris (included in the price) amid the marshes. It's at least three hours from Malindi by road and canoe, but if you can afford the sky-high rates then you can also afford the private helicopter transfer.

Getting There & Around

If you'd like to explore this region on your own, disembark Lamu–Malindi buses at little Witu and catch a bus/matatu (KSh70/100) to smaller Kipini, at the mouth of the delta (when you're ready to leave, you can board Lamu–Malindi buses in Witu up to about 2.30pm). You can also hop on a *boda-boda* (motorcycle taxi) to Mpeketoni (KSh500 to KSh700, 45 minutes) and then take a matatu to the Lamu jetty (KSh150). On the latter route, the scenery is stunning, broken up by buffaloes, zebras, giraffes and large cattle herds.

LAMU ARCHIPELAGO

The Arabs called them the 'Seven Isles of Eryaya', while sailors called them a welcome port of call when en route to, or from, India.

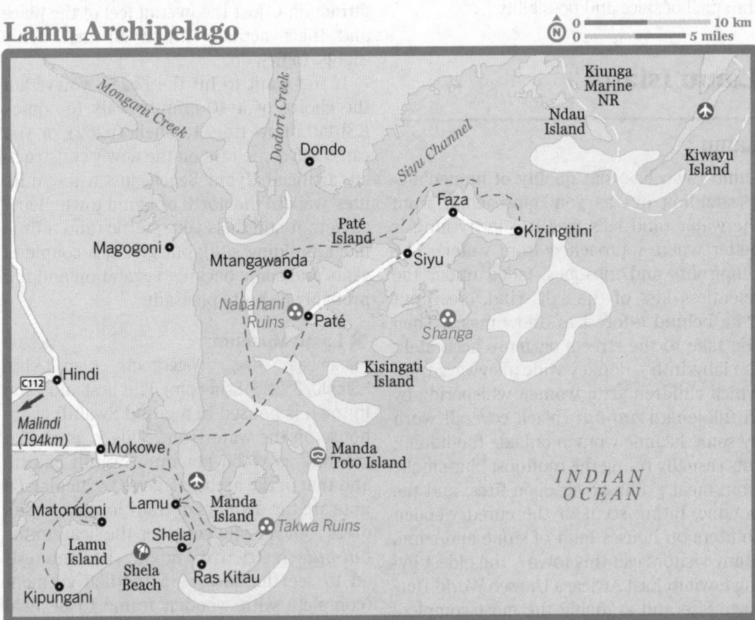

WILDLIFE ON THE NORTH COAST

The aquatic life on the north coast is very impressive and the Watamu and Malindi marine parks offer world-class diving and snorkelling. The most noteworthy terrestrial protected area is the Arabuko Sokoke Forest Reserve (p244), a rare slab of coastal forest filled with endemic bird species, a few elephants and the much smaller, but equally impressive, golden-rumped elephant shrew. The Tana River estuary offers adventurous canoe safaris in search of hippos and crocodiles. It's the birds that rule the roost, though – Mida Creek offers outstanding birdwatching.

Hundreds of expats who've fallen irrevocably in love with these islands call them home, as do the Swahili, who trace the deepest roots of their culture here.

Few would dispute the Lamu archipelago forms the most evocative destination on the Kenyan coast. It's the best of several travelling worlds: medieval stone towns of narrow streets *and* charming architecture *and* tropical-island paradise *and* delicious local cuisine *and* star-heavy nights that are pregnant with the smell of spice and possibility.

Lamu Island

Lamu

Lamu town has that quality of immediately standing out as you approach it from the water (and let's face it – everything is better when approached from water). The shopfronts and mosques, faded under the relentless kiss of the salt wind, creep out from behind a forest of dhow masts. Then you take to the streets or, more accurately, the labyrinth – donkey-wide alleyways from which children grin; women whispering by in full-length *bui-bui* (black coverall worn by some Islamic women outside the home); cats casually ruling the rooftops; blue smoke from meat grilling over open fires; and the organic, biting scent of the cured wooden shutters on houses built of stone and coral. Many visitors call this town – the oldest living town in East Africa, a Unesco World Heritage Site and arguably the most complete Swahili town in existence – the highlight of their trip to Kenya. Residents call it Kiwa Ndeo (the Vain Island) and, to be fair, there's plenty for them to be vain about.

History

In pre-Arab times the islands were home to the Bajun, but their traditions vanished almost entirely with the arrival of the Arabs.

In the 19th century the soldiers of Lamu caught the warriors of Paté on open mud at low tide and slaughtered them. This victory, plus the cash cows of ivory and slavery, made Lamu a splendidly wealthy place, and most of the fine Swahili houses that survive today were built during this period.

It all came to an end in 1873, when the British forced Sultan Barghash of Zanzibar to close down the slave markets. With the abolition of slavery, the economy went into rapid decline. The city-state was incorporated into the British Protectorate from 1890, and became part of Kenya with independence in 1963.

Until it was 'rediscovered' by travellers in the 1970s, Lamu existed in a state of humble obscurity, which has allowed it to remain well preserved for tourists today.

Sights

Lamu is one of those places where the real attraction is just the overall feel of the place and there actually aren't all that many 'sights' to tick off.

If you want to hit the beach, you've got the choice of a 40-minute walk (or quick KSh150 dhow ride) to Shela (p262), or you can catch some rays on the newly constructed, artificial Uyoni Beach, just a few minutes' walk to the north of Lamu town. Being so new, it still feels very sterile (and a little like a building site), but give it a couple of years and some backing vegetation and it'll probably be quite pleasant.

★Lamu Museum MUSEUM
(Harambee Ave, Waterfront; adult/child KSh500/250; ⌚8am-6pm) The best museum in town is housed in a grand Swahili warehouse on the waterfront. This is as good a gateway as you'll get into Swahili culture and that of the archipelago in particular. Of note are the displays of traditional women's dress – those who consider the head-to-toe *bui-bui* restrictive might be interested to see the *shiraa,* a tentlike garment (complete with wooden frame to be held

Town Walk
Lamu Town

START LAMU MAIN JETTY
FINISH LAMU MAIN JETTY
LENGTH ABOUT 4KM
DURATION ONE TO 1½ HOURS

The best, indeed only, way to see Lamu town is on foot. Few experiences compare with exploring the far backstreets, where you can wander amid wafts of cardamom and carbolic and watch the town's agile cats scaling the coral walls. There are so many wonderful Swahili houses that it's pointless for us to recommend specific examples – keep your eyes open wherever you go, and don't forget to look up.

Starting at the 1 **main jetty**, head north past the 2 **Lamu Museum** (p254) and along the waterfront until you reach the 3 **door-carving workshops**.

From here head onto Kenyatta Rd, passing an original Swahili 4 **well**, and into the alleys towards the 5 **Swahili House Museum** (p257). Once you've had your fill of domestic insights, take any route back towards the main street.

Once you've hit the main square and the 6 **fort**, take a right to see the crumbled remains of the 14th-century 7 **Pwani Mosque**, one of Lamu's oldest buildings – an Arabic inscription is still visible on the wall. From here you can head round and browse the covered 8 **market** (p257) then negotiate your way towards the bright, Saudi-funded 9 **Riyadha Mosque**, the centre of Lamu's religious scene.

Now you can take as long or as short a route as you like back to the waterfront. Stroll along the promenade, diverting for the 10 **German Post Office Museum** (p257) – the door is another amazing example of Swahili carving. If you're feeling the pace, take a rest and shoot the breeze on the 11 **baraza ya wazee** (old men's bench) outside the stucco minarets of the 12 **Shiaithna-Asheri Mosque**.

Carrying on up Harambee Ave will bring you back to the main jetty.

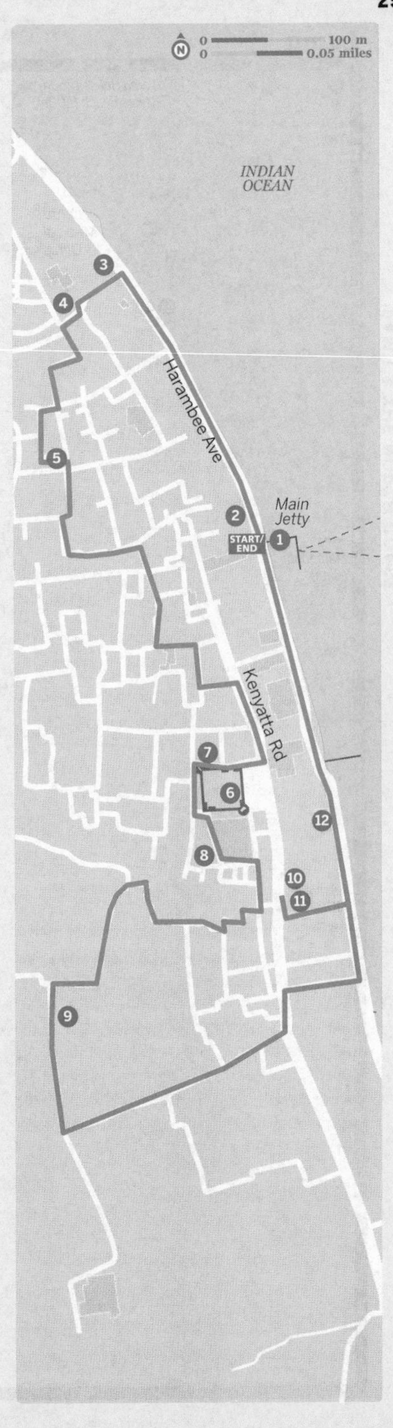

Lamu

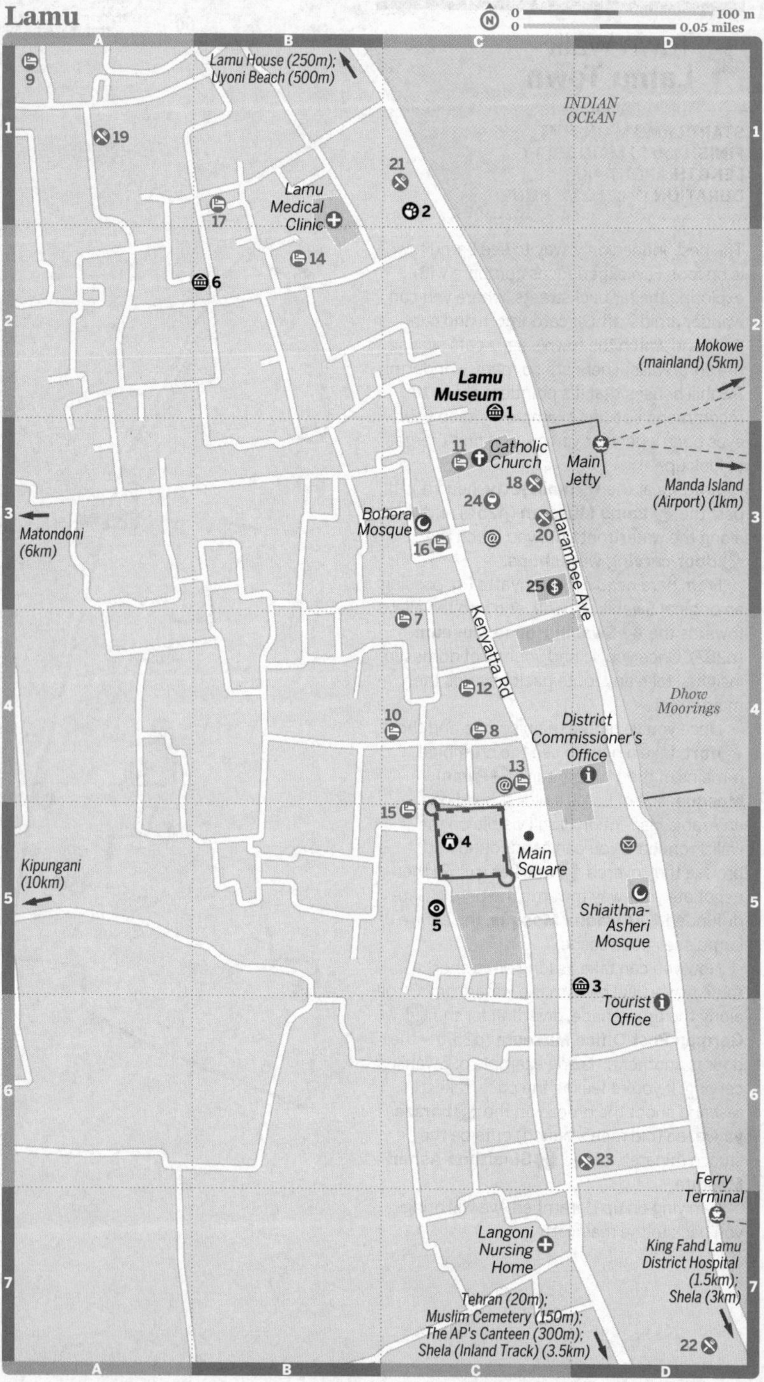

0 100 m
0 0.05 miles

Lamu House (250m); Uyoni Beach (500m)

INDIAN OCEAN

Lamu Medical Clinic

Lamu Museum

Catholic Church

Main Jetty

Mokowe (mainland) (5km)

Manda Island (Airport) (1km)

Matondoni (6km)

Bohora Mosque

Harambee Ave

Kenyatta Rd

Dhow Moorings

District Commissioner's Office

Main Square

Kipungani (10km)

Shiaithna-Asheri Mosque

Tourist Office

Ferry Terminal

Langoni Nursing Home

King Fahd Lamu District Hospital (1.5km); Shela (3km)

Tehran (20m); Muslim Cemetery (150m); The AP's Canteen (300m); Shela (Inland Track) (3.5km)

Lamu

Top Sights
1 Lamu Museum C2

Sights
2 Donkey Sanctuary C1
3 German Post Office Museum D5
4 Lamu Fort C5
5 Lamu Market C5
6 Swahili House B2

Sleeping
7 Amu House C4
8 Baitul Noor House C4
9 Jannat House A1
10 Kilimanjaro House C4
11 Lamu Guest House C3
12 New Bahati Lodge C4
13 New Mahrus Hotel C4
14 Stone House Hotel B2
15 Subira House C5
16 Sultan Palace Hotel C3
17 Yumbe House B1

Eating
18 Bush Gardens Restaurant C3
19 Bustani Café A1
20 Hapa Hapa C3
21 Mwana Arafa Restaurant Gardens C1
22 Olympic Restaurant D7
23 Whispers Coffeeshop D6

Drinking & Nightlife
24 Petley's Inn C3

Shopping
Baraka Gallery .... (see 23)
Black & White Gallery .... (see 7)
Lamu Museum Shop .... (see 1)

Information
25 Kenya Commercial Bank C3

Transport
Airkenya .... (see 23)

over the head) that was once the respectable dress of local ladies. There are also exhibits dedicated to artefacts from Swahili ruins, the bric-a-brac of local tribes and the nautical heritage of the coast (including the *mtepe,* a traditional coir-sewn boat meant to resemble the Prophet Mohammed's camel – hence the nickname, 'camels of the sea'). Guides are available to show you around.

Lamu Fort FORTRESS
(Main Sq) This squat castle was built by the Sultan of Paté from 1810 and completed in 1823. From 1910 to 1984 it was used as a prison. It now houses the island's library, which holds one of the best collections of Swahili poetry and Lamu reference work in Kenya. Entrance is free with a ticket to the Lamu Museum.

Lamu Market MARKET
(opposite Lamu Fort) Atmospheric and chaotic, this quintessential Lamu market is best visited early in the morning. Bargain for stonkingly fresh tuna and sailfish, wade through alleys teeming with stray cats, dogs and goats, and experience Lamu at its craziest. If you're sick of seafood, this is the place to find your five-a-day.

Swahili House MUSEUM
(adult/child KSh500/250; 8am-6pm) This preserved Swahili house, tucked away to the side of Yumbe House hotel, is beautiful, but the entry fee is very hard to justify, especially as half the hotels in Lamu are as well preserved as this small house.

German Post Office Museum MUSEUM
(Kenyatta Rd; adult/child KSh500/250; 8am-6pm) In the late 1800s, before the British decided to nip German expansion into Tanganyika in the bud, the Germans regarded Lamu as an ideal base from which to exploit the interior. As part of their efforts, the German East Africa Company set up a post office, and the old building is now a museum exhibiting photographs and memorabilia from that fleeting period when Lamu had the chance of being spelt with an umlaut.

Donkey Sanctuary WILDLIFE CONSERVANCY
(042-633303; Harambee Ave; 9am-1pm Mon-Fri) FREE A man without a donkey *is* a donkey, claims one Swahili proverb. Or, as the staff of this sanctuary might tell you, a man who doesn't look after his donkey *is* a donkey. With around 3000 donkeys (and a couple of cars) active on Lamu, *Equus asinus* is the main form of transport here. This sanctuary was established by the International Donkey Protection Trust of Sidmouth, UK, to improve the lot of the island's hard-working beasts of burden. Visitors are free to visit the sanctuary

and learn about its work – donations appreciated.

Festivals & Events

Lamu Painters' Festival ART
(www.lamupaintersfestival.org) Draws contemporary artists and work from across Africa and Europe. Often held in February.

Lamu Cultural Festival CULTURAL
Exact dates for this colourful carnival vary each year, but it often falls in November. Expect donkey and dhow races, Swahili poets and island dancing.

Maulid Festival RELIGIOUS
(www.lamu.org/maulid-celebration.html) The Maulid Festival celebrates the birth of the Prophet Mohammed. Its date shifts according to the Muslim calendar (see p374). The festival has been celebrated on the island for over 100 years and much singing, dancing and general jollity takes place around this time. On the final day a procession heads down to the tomb of the man who started it all, Ali Habib Swaleh.

Lamu Yoga Festival SPORTS
(www.lamuyoga.org) Can't make it to India? Practice yoga near the Indian Ocean instead. First held in 2014, this festival spills across Shela, Manda and Lamu and includes workshops and classes. It culminates in one big beach party featuring drummers and acrobats. Dates vary each year.

Sleeping

★ **New Bahati Lodge** GUESTHOUSE $
(☎0726732746; www.lamuguesthouse.com; d/tr KSh1400/2500) This newly renovated budget house occupies prime position in Lamu's old town and pulls in plenty of budget travellers. The rooms are clean, fresh and spacious, but you'll probably spend most of your time in the loungey chill-out areas. The master bedroom at the top of the house has the best ocean view.

★ **Baitul Noor House** BACKPACKERS $
(☎0725220271, 0723760296; www.lamubackpackers.com; dm/s/d KSh1000/1500/2500) From the Arabic for 'house of light', this 16th-century town house is the stylish new backpackers on the block. The dorms are lovely and ecofriendly, featuring 2.1m beds, homemade soaps and solar reading lamps. Don't miss the stylish roof terrace and the downstairs restaurant, which does lobster suppers for lemonade pockets. Helpful staff can arrange all manner of excursions.

Amu House APARTMENT $
(☎0718196286; s/d/tr KSh2500/3500/5000) A winner during the hottest months of February and March, Amu is the coolest house on the island. It sits above the Black & White Gallery and had a fresh lick of paint at the time of writing.

Yumbe House BOUTIQUE HOTEL $
(☎0726732746; www.lamuguesthouse.com; s/d KSh2500/3200) This beautiful 17th-century house is made from coral, which is reason enough to stay here. Add spacious rooms decorated with pleasant Swahili accents, verandahs that are open to the stars and the breeze, and a ridiculously romantic top-floor suite. Top value for your shilling.

Stone House Hotel BOUTIQUE HOTEL $
(☎042-4633544; www.stonehousehotellamu.com; r KSh1700-4000) This Swahili mansion is set into a tourist-free backstreet and is notable for its fine, whitewashed walls and fantastic rooftop, which includes a superb restaurant (no alcohol) with excellent views over the town and waterfront. The rooms are spacious and nicely decorated and it's easily one of the better-value midrange options in town.

New Mahrus Hotel BUSINESS HOTEL $
(☎0721124421; Kenyatta Rd; r KSh2500; ❄) Blending Lamu style with business amenities, New Mahrus fills a gap in the Lamu market. Most of its guests are Kenyan business travellers, but should you be lusting after functioning air-conditioning and satellite TV, you can join them. There's also a speedy internet cafe and a brilliant budget restaurant (offering seriously big portions) overlooking the fort.

Kilimanjaro House BOUTIQUE HOTEL $
(☎0721141924; www.kilimanjaro-lamu.com; s/d KSh2600/3300) Another nicely restored Swahili house, this is a smallish place, but friendly and cosy. It's across from the Stone House Hotel on a pleasantly quiet side street. It's a little overpriced, though.

Jannat House HOTEL $
(☎0714969831, 0708569892; www.jannathouselamu.com; s/d KSh2500/4000; ≋) The main draws here are the pool and the bar, both rare luxuries on the Lamu guesthouse scene. Otherwise this multiterraced option is a lit-

tle rundown. Rooms on the upper floors are much better than those lower down.

Lamu Guest House HOTEL $

(☎0726732746; Kenyatta Rd; s/d excl breakfast KSh1000/1750, with shared bathroom KSh800/1600) The basic rooms here are very plain, but the upper-floor ones are better and catch the sea breeze. The 'official' rates quoted here are a good KSh500 more than you'll end up paying. Abdul, the boss, is a real character – check out his shell-picture collection.

★Subira House GUESTHOUSE $$

(☎0726916686; www.subirahouse.com; r KSh5000-8000) This beautiful house features graceful arches and twin gardens with wells. The Swedish owners certainly know a thing or two about style, as did the Sultan of Zanzibar when he built the house 200 years ago. As well as seven stylish bedrooms, there are galleries in which to relax and serious eco-credentials. We rate the restaurant highly.

Sultan Palace Hotel APARTMENT $$

(☎0723593292; Kenyatta Rd; apt/penthouse KSh6600/9000) The Mediterranean style feels like a strange choice here, when there's so much Swahili style on offer elsewhere. Still, this century-old house has had a recent makeover and its rooms feature gorgeous four-poster beds.

★Lamu House BOUTIQUE HOTEL $$$

(☎0708073164, 0708279905; www.lamuhouse.com; Harambee Ave; r US$230-490) In a town where every building wants to top the preservation stakes, Lamu House stands out. It looks like an old Swahili villa, but it feels like a stylish boutique hotel, blending the pale, breezy romance of the Greek islands into an African palace, with predictably awesome results. The excellent Moonlight restaurant serves fine Swahili cuisine.

A free boat service to Manda Island leaves from here every morning at 8am.

Eating

Many of Lamu's cheap eating places close until after sunset during Ramadan.

The restaurants at New Mahrus Hotel, Subira House, Lamu House and Baitul Noor House are all well worth a visit.

Lamu's fruit juices, which are sold in almost every restaurant, are good. Really, really good.

Self-caterers can head to the main market (p257) next to the fort.

★Tehran KENYAN $

(Kenyatta Rd; mains from KSh100) This very atmospheric but basic place doesn't even have a sign, but it does serve dirt-cheap meals of fish, beans (the best is *maharagwe ya chumvi* – with coconut milk) and chapatis. It's consistently packed with locals and is pretty much open all the time.

Bustani Café CAFE $

(meals KSh320-500) This pretty garden cafe has tables set about a lily-bedecked pond. The small menu includes lots of healthy salads and various snack foods. It also contains a decent bookshop and an evening-only internet cafe (KSh240 per hour).

Olympic Restaurant AFRICAN $

(Harambee Ave; mains KSh450-900) The family that runs the Olympic makes you feel as if you've come home every time you enter, and their food, particularly the curries and biryani, is excellent. There are few better ways to spend a Lamu night than with a cold mug of passionfruit juice and the noirish view of the docks you get here, at the ramshackle end of town.

Bush Gardens Restaurant INTERNATIONAL $

(☎021-633285; Harambee Ave; mains KSh280-1000; ⊙breakfast, lunch & dinner) This place is a backpacker institution, but reputation alone doesn't make a meal. The food isn't quite as good as it's supposed to be, and some say that standards have slipped. It offers breakfast, seafood (including 'monster crab' and the inevitable lobster in Swahili sauce) and good juices and shakes mixed up in panelled British pint mugs.

Hapa Hapa INTERNATIONAL $

(Harambee Ave; mains around KSh300) For a decent but cheap feed right on the seafront, Hapa Hapa is a safe bet. It offers substandard international fare, but the kitchen is clean and there's always a good crowd around.

★Mwana Arafa Restaurant Gardens SEAFOOD $$

(Harambee Ave; meals KSh350-1200) Everyone loves Mwana Arafa. It has the perfect combination of garden seating and views over the dhows bobbing about under the moonlight. With barbequed giant prawns, grilled calamari, lobster or a seafood platter on offer, we guess you'll be eating the fruits of the sea tonight.

Whispers Coffeeshop CAFE $$
(Kenyatta Rd; mains KSh340-950; ⏰9am-9pm) You know how sometimes you just need that escape into the world of magazines and fresh pastries? Welcome to Whispers. For a real cappuccino or the best desserts in town, this garden cafe, set in the same building as the Baraka Gallery, is highly recommended.

Drinking & Nightlife

As a Muslim town, Lamu has few options for drinkers and local sensibilities should be respected.

Full-moon parties, organised by the local beach boys, take place regularly, alternating between the islands. Entry (including boat access) costs KSh100, and you can expect bongo drums and copious amounts of coconut-palm wine. You might want to leave before the crowd gets rowdy, though – fights and sexual harrassment are not uncommon as dawn slips closer.

The AP's Canteen CLUB
The administrative police canteen may seem an unlikely place to drink and dance, but on Muslim Lamu, where the supply of alcohol is controlled by the police department, it actually makes sense. It's small, loud and dingy. Lone women should run for cover and lone men should expect working-girl attention.

Petley's Inn BAR
(Harambee Ave) Right in front of the main jetty, Petley's seems to be the local watering hole for just about everyone. Expect almost anything, from good fun and merriment to enough hassle to speed you through the doors.

Shopping

There's a huge international market for traditional doors, furniture and window frames and many families have actually sold off their doors and other furnishings. If you want something custom-made, carvers tend to concentrate on the north side of the waterfront. Woodwork that's slightly more friendly to your airline baggage allowance includes picture frames, *bao* (a traditional board game) sets, Quran stands and *ito* – round painted 'eyes' from Swahili dhows, originally used as talismans to avoid underwater obstacles and protect against the evil eye.

If you have an eye for antiques, you can also pick up some interesting pieces (from street sellers) such as brass trumpets and copper lanterns.

If you're into unusual fabrics, you can pick up bags made from the recycled cotton of dhow sails. Often they're decorated with iconic Lamu images. Textile fans will also enjoy shopping for material sourced from Oman and Somalia. Head north along Kenyatta Rd from the fort and you'll find a scattering of places selling such wares, as well as some high-quality silversmiths. Perhaps the most charismatic among them is a chap called Slim, whose silversmith shop – with the original name of Slim Silversmith – sells beautiful rings created from ancient cuttings of coloured tiles.

Lamu is also a good place to buy *kikois,* the patterned wraps traditionally worn by Swahili men. The standard price is around KSh350, more for the heavier Somali style.

Baraka Gallery ARTS & CRAFTS
(Kenyatta Rd) For upmarket Africana, Baraka Gallery has a fine selection, but stratospheric prices.

Black & White Gallery ARTS & CRAFTS
Spanish-run art shop with some beautiful tribal-inspired crafts and paintings.

Lamu Museum Shop BOOKS
(Harambee Ave) Specialists in Lamu and Swahili cultural books.

ℹ Information

DANGERS & ANNOYANCES

At the time of writing, some governments were advising against travel to Lamu and the wider region (see box opposite for more information).

When times are normal, the biggest real issue is the beach boys. They'll come at you the minute you step off the boat, offering drugs, tours and hotel bookings (the last can be useful if you're disoriented).

Lamu has long been popular for its relaxed, tolerant atmosphere, but it does have Muslim views of what's acceptable behaviour. Whatever your sexuality, it's best to keep public displays of affection to a minimum and respect local attitudes to modesty.

Female travellers should note that most Lamurians hold strong religious and cultural values and may be deeply offended by revealing clothing. There have been some isolated incidents of rape, which locals say were sparked by tourists refusing to cover up. That may outrage some Western ears, but the fact remains that

SAFETY ON LAMU ARCHIPELAGO

In September 2011 an English couple staying on the island of Kiwayu, north of Lamu, were attacked by Somali pirates/militants. The husband was killed and the wife was kidnapped and taken to Somalia (she was subsequently released in March 2012). It was widely thought this was a one-off attack and that Lamu itself was not at risk. However, despite a massive beefing up of security, just over two weeks later another attack occurred. This time a French woman was kidnapped from her home on Manda Island and taken to Somalia (where she later died from a diabetic incident).

Following a series of armed attacks in Mombasa in mid-2014, more than 60 Kenyans were killed in two attacks near the town of Mpeketoni (54km by road from Lamu town). Although Al-Shabaab militants claimed responsibility for one of the attacks (as revenge for Kenya's military presence in Somalia), Kenya's president controversially shifted the blame to well-organised local political networks. Regardless of who was to blame, many countries advised against travel to Lamu in the wake of these attacks.

While Al-Shabaab may indeed have a presence in the area, most Lamu residents believe that Western tourists have never been a target. That said, a curfew was in place on Lamu at the time of writing and we urge you to check the latest on the security situation before travelling. Those who do travel may be reassured by the presence of the large US naval base on Manda Island.

you risk getting into trouble if you walk around in small shorts and low-cut tops. There are kilometres of deserted beaches on which you can walk around butt naked if you choose, but we urge you to respect cultural norms in built-up areas.

INTERNET ACCESS

Cyberwings (per hour KSh40; ⏲8am-8pm) Across from Petley's Inn.

Rose of Sharon (☎0724966799; roseofsharonlamu@yahoo.com; New Mahrus Hotel, Kenyatta Rd) This friendly internet cafe has speedy service.

MEDICAL SERVICES

King Fahd Lamu District Hospital (☎012-633075) This government-run hospital is rundown but has competent medical staff.

Lamu Medical Clinic (☎012-633438; Kenyatta Rd; ⏲8am-9pm) Medical clinic.

Langoni Nursing Home (☎012-633349; Kenyatta Rd; ⏲24hr) Don't be put off by the name; this clinic offers GP services.

MONEY

Kenya Commercial Bank (☎012-633327; Harambee Ave) The main bank on Lamu, with an ATM (Visa only).

POST

Post office (Harambee Ave) Postal services and phonecards.

TOURIST INFORMATION

Tourist office (☎012-633132; lamu@tourism.go.ke; Harambee Ave; ⏲9am-1pm & 2-4pm) A commercial tour and accommodation agency that also provides tourist information.

Getting There & Away

AIR

The airport at Lamu is on Manda Island, and the ferry across the channel to Lamu costs KSh150. You'll be met by 'guides' at the airport who will offer to carry your bags to the hotel of your choice for a small consideration (about KSh200). Many double as touts, so be cautious about accepting the first price you're quoted when you get to your hotel.

Airkenya (☎042-633445; www.airkenya.com; Baraka House, Kenyatta Rd) Daily afternoon flights between Lamu and Wilson Airport in Nairobi (US$195).

Fly540 (☎042-632054; www.fly540.com) Flies twice daily to Malindi (around US$45) and Nairobi (around US$170).

Safarilink (www.flysafarilink.com) Daily flights to Nairobi Wilson airport (around US$185).

BUS

There are booking offices for several bus companies on Kenyatta Rd. Buses leave from the jetty on the mainland; you'll see the spot after you dock. The going rate for a trip to Mombasa (eight to nine hours) is KSh800 to KSh900. Most buses leave between 7am and 8am, so you'll need to be at the jetty at 6.30am to catch the boat to the mainland. Book early and be on time. Buses deliberately leave on the dot in order to resell the seats of latecoming passengers further up the line. The most reliable companies are **Simba** (☎0707471110, 0707471111), **Tahmeed** (☎0724581015, 0724581004) and **Tawakal** (☎0705090122). Note that prices tend to increase by KSh100 to KSh200 during the high season.

At the time of writing, armed guards were on every Lamu-bound bus from Mombasa. Matatus have no such security measures.

Coming from Mombasa to Lamu, buses will drop you at the mainland jetty at Mokowe. From there you can either catch the passenger ferry (KSh100, 30 to 40 minutes) or a speedboat (KSh150, 10 minutes). If you're laden with bags, it's easy to find a porter to carry them all the way from the Mokowe bus stop to your hotel doorstep for around KSh300.

Getting Around

Ferries to the airstrip on Manda Island (KSh150) leave about half an hour before the flights leave (yes, in case you're wondering, all the airline companies are aware of this and it's sufficient time).

Between Lamu village and Shela there are plenty of motorised dhows throughout the day until around sunset; these cost about KSh150 per person and leave when full.

There are also regular ferries between Lamu and Paté Island.

Shela

Shela has undergone a severe case of gentrification and is sort of like Lamu put through a high-end wringer. It's cleaner, more sterile, has less character and a lot more expats. On the plus side, there's a long, lovely stretch of beach and a link to a specific slice of coast culture – the locals speak a distinct dialect, of which they're quite proud.

Sights & Activities

There's reasonable windsurfing in the channel between Shela and Manda Island, while the water-sports centre at Peponi Hotel runs all kinds of activities of the damp sort, including diving, snorkelling, windsurfing and kayaking.

Beach BEACH
Most people are here for the beach – a 12km-long sweep of sand where you're guaranteed an isolated spot (at least if you're prepared to walk some way) to catch some rays. But as locals say, '*Yana vuta kwa kasi*' (There's a violent current there). And no lifeguards. Tourists drown every year, so don't swim out too far.

It should be pointed out that, beautiful as Shela beach is, it's more of a wild, windy, empty kind of beauty rather than an intimate, palm-tree-backed, tropical beauty.

Sleeping

Many houses in Shela are owned by expats who only live here part-time, and there's a huge amount of accommodation available, very little of which is widely advertised outside the island. The best place to check these out and book ahead of time is through **Lamu Retreats** (www.lamuretreats.com), which will help you into 11 posh houses situated between Shela and Lamu town.

★ Stopover Guest House GUESTHOUSE $$
(☎ Nairobi 020-2638719, 0720127222; r from US$50) The first place you come to on the waterfront is this beautiful guesthouse of pure-white unfussy lines. Rooms are spacious, airy, bright and crisp, and a salt wind through your carved window shutters is the best alarm clock imaginable. It's above the popular restaurant of the same name.

Kijani House Hotel BOUTIQUE HOTEL $$
(☎ Nairobi 020-2435700; www.kijani-lamu.com; s/d US$135/175; @ 🛜 🏊) This villa complex is enormous, yet the design is elegantly understated, achieving a sort of Zen or Swahili aesthetic even as it spoils you with luxuriant tropical gardens, the nicest pool on Lamu and palace-sized – and equally palatially decorated – rooms. It's one of the best midrange deals on the island.

Bahari Guest House GUESTHOUSE $$
(☎ 0722901643; info@shellabahari.com; r KSh3000-5500) Right on the seafront as you round the corner to Peponi, Bahari Guest House is clean and spacious. The rooms are whitewashed and self-contained and during the low season prices are negotiable. A rare Shela gem.

★ Fort BOUTIQUE HOTEL $$$
(www.thefortshela.com; d from US$237) This swish boutique hotel is one of the most beautiful places to sleep in Shela. The entire place is faithful to Lamu style, with some lovely touches, including intricate rugs and cushions. During low season you can sometimes bag a luxurious double for somewhere in the realm of KSh5000. Email bookings only.

Peponi Hotel HOTEL $$$
(☎ Nairobi 020-2435033, 020-8023655; www.peponilamu.com; s/d from €175/215; ⏲ closed May & Jun; 🏊) If there was a capital of Shela, it would be here. This resort has a grip on everything in the village, from

DON'T MISS

DHOW TRIPS

More than the bustle of markets or the call to prayer, the pitch of 'We take dhow trip, see mangroves, eat fish and coconut rice' is the unyielding chorus of Lamu's voices when you first arrive. That said, taking a dhow trip (and seeing the mangroves and eating fish and coconut rice) is almost obligatory and generally fun besides, though this depends to a large degree on your captain. There's a real joy to kicking it on the boards under the sunny sky, with the mangroves drifting by in island time while snacking on spiced fish.

Trips include dhow-racing excursions (learning how to tack and race these amazingly agile vessels is quite something), sunset sails, adventures to Kipungani and Manda, deep-reef fishing and even three-day trips south along the coast to Kilifi (from US$100 per person).

Prices vary, depending on where you want to go, who you go with and how long you go for. **Bwana Dolphin** (☎0726732746) is a recommended local captain. With bargaining you could pay around KSh2500 per person in a group of four or five people, on a half-day basis. Don't hand over any money until the day of departure, except perhaps a small advance for food. On long trips, it's best to organise your own drinks. A hat and sunscreen are essential.

tours to water sports to whatever else you can imagine. Sleepingwise it's a winner, but then for the price it's charging, you'd hope so! The fairly lavish rooms are decorated in the usual Swahili styles of light colours set off by dark embellishments.

Shella Pwani Guest House HOTEL $$

(☎0712506778; r from KSh4500) This lovely Swahili house, located a little east of Stopover Guest House, is decked out with carved plasterwork and pastel accents. Some rooms have fine sea views, as does the airy roof terrace, and some of the bathrooms are modelled to look like *qiblahs* (prayer walls in mosques). The Muslim owner doesn't seem to find this offensive, if you were wondering.

Eating & Drinking

Rangaleni Café KENYAN $

(meals KSh160-200) The best of the Shela cheapies. Hidden away in the alleys behind the shorefront mosque, this tiny greeny-turquoise cafe does the usual stews and *ugali* (maize- or cassava-baked staple).

★**Stopover Restaurant** SEAFOOD $$

(☎012-633459; mains KSh550-1500) There are waterfront restaurants all over the place, but the Stopover's friendly staff and excellent grub (of the spicy Swahili-seafood sort) make it a cut above the competition. Oh, and it's a big call, but its fruit juices might just be the best around...

Peponi's Bar BAR

(Peponi Hotel; KSh1500-3000) Naturally, the bar at a Swiss-owned Kenyan hotel with an Italian name has to resemble an English pub. Pretty much everyone on Shela comes to this terrace for a (ridiculously expensive) sundowner as evening sets in.

Getting There & Away

You can take a motorised dhow here from the moorings in Lamu (KSh150 per person). Alternatively, you can walk it in about 40 minutes. The easiest way is to take Harambee Ave (the waterfront road) and follow the shoreline, though this may be partly flooded at high tide. If that's the case, wade through the sunken bits or cut across to the inland track, which starts near the Muslim cemetery in Lamu. If you need to get back to Lamu (or Shela) after dark, find someone to walk with (restaurant staff are often happy to accompany solo travellers once they get off their shift) and bring a torch as the tides are unpredictable and there have been muggings in the past, especially on the inland track. Boat captains, for all their 'brother, we are one' prattle, will rip you off if you want a ride back at night. You won't get back for anything less than KSh1000.

Matondoni & Kipungani

The best place to see dhows being built is the village of Matondoni, in the island's northwest. It's a peaceful little fishing village that receives few visitors, so the welcome is always warm. To get there from Lamu town, you have a choice of walking (6km, about

DON'T MISS

BEST BEACHES

Lay down a towel on one of these beauties and feel the smile spread over your face.

➡ **Manda Island** It's a desert island in the Indian Ocean. Of course it's good.

➡ **Shela Beach** Vast, wild and empty (if you walk a bit).

➡ **Manda Toto** Bright-blue water, white sand and top snorkelling.

two hours; ask for directions from the back of town and follow the telephone poles), hiring a donkey or taking an organised dhow trip (which normally continues onto Kipungani for a swim and, sea conditions depending, then loops around the island and back to Lamu town via Shela).

Kipungani, 'the place of fresh air', is a small village at the island's southwest tip where locals make straw mats, baskets, hats and *kifumbu*, used to squeeze milk from mashed coconut. Tea and snacks can be arranged and there's a beautiful empty beach nearby, but it's a long, hot walk to get here from Lamu or Shela and the path is very hard to find.

This part of the island also offers some of Kenya's best kitesurfing, though you'll have to bring your own gear. There's no backdrop quite like it.

Sleeping

★Kizingo RESORT $$$
(0722901544, 0733954770; www.kizingo.com; s/d US$250/440; P@) The owners describe this beautiful spot as 'no news, no shoes', which says it all really. It's at the end of the 12km stretch of beach that begins in Shela (a little beyond Kipungani). The bar serves up refreshing cocktails, the food is healthy and hip, and hostess Mary-Jo always has great stories to tell. Rooms are simple but chic.

Kipungani Explorer RESORT $$$
(Nairobi 020-4446651; www.heritage-eastafrica.com; s/d full board from US$247/380; Jul-Mar) This exclusive resort is quite luxurious, in a rustic, end-of-the-world, *banda*-on-the-beach kind of way, which is probably what you're looking for if you come this far. The resort deserves a shout-out for employing local villagers as staff, funding school projects, experimenting with solar and wind power and sourcing food from village fishers.

Manda Island

Manda is a quiet lattice of dune and mangroves a short hop and jump (OK, a 30-minute boat ride) from Lamu. The island has just started to feel the claws of development, and the shoreline facing Lamu is now backed by a couple of places to stay and several huge private villas. Away from here, though, the island quickly starts to feel like a deserted fleck – an impression that extends with the shadows as they grow with the setting sun in the thornbush-lined alleyways of the once-great city of Takwa.

Sights & Activities

The island is ringed by beaches (and in places mangrove swamps and mudflats) and it's easy to find a quiet patch of sand on which to lay your towel. The most popular beach (but still virtually deserted) is the one facing Lamu.

Takwa Ruins RUIN
(adult/child KSh500/250; 6.30am-6pm) What sets the Takwa ruins, the remains of a city that existed between the 15th and 17th centuries, apart from other archaeological sites on the coast? Quiet. When you're here and the light shatters in the trees, which have grown over some 100 ruined Mecca-aligned houses, you feel as if the ruins are speaking to you in the breeze.

As you're likely to have Takwa to yourself, it's a good spot to enter an abandoned home and ponder the lives of whoever inhabited it without the buzz of a guide. The seminal structure here is the **Jamaa mosque**, with its unusually tall pillar facade. You can arrange camping here for about US$10 – it's a supremely peaceful way to spend a star-heavy evening.

Manda Toto Island SNORKELLING
Just off the northeast coast of Manda is Manda Toto Island, which offers some of the best snorkelling possibilities in the archipelago. The only way to get here is by dhow – a full day (there and back) from Lamu.

Sleeping & Eating

All places to stay at Manda have in-house restaurants, which is handy because there aren't any other eating options.

Diamond Beach Village HUT $$
(☎0720915001; www.diamondbeachvillage.com; s/d UK£50/100;) This is one of those Robinson Crusoe–style beach-shack hideouts; but don't worry, that doesn't mean it's basic. The thatched huts stand out, thanks to the judicious use of driftwood and shell art, and there are lots of cosy nooks and crannies. If you want a different view of the world, opt for the eccentric tree house perched in the branches of an old baobab tree. The beach out front is glorious. It's a little overpriced, though.

★**Majlis** RESORT $$$
(☎0770275546, Nairobi 020-7123300; www.themajlisresorts.com; per person full board from US$275;) This spectacular resort is the newest to emerge here and looks like something out of the pages of a glossy design magazine. It offers everything you'd expect from a luxury boutique hotel. Each room has a different view of Shela town on the other side of the creek.

Manda Bay RESORT $$$
(☎Nairobi 020-2115453; www.mandabay.com; r from US$200) This luxury resort on the northern end of the island is most famous as the site of a Somali pirate kidnapping in 2011. However, that shouldn't put you off. Security has been boosted, there's an American base nearby and lightning rarely strikes twice. Plus the food and accommodation are out of this world.

Getting There & Away

The trip across to Manda from Lamu takes about half an hour by boat (to the beach opposite Lamu). Once in a blue moon a boatman will take you for just KSh350, but somewhere between KSh450 and KSh600 is much more realistic. It can sometimes be cheaper if you take a boat to Shela first and then another from there across the channel. To the Takwa ruins takes around 1½ hours by boat from Lamu and can only be done at high tide. Since you have to catch the outgoing tide, your time at Takwa will probably be an hour or less.

Paté Island

Paté is a low island of green brush, silver tidal flats, coconut trees like thin legs dancing in the wind and a red track slithering over dust-embedded ridges and rivers. And it's quiet. Not like small-town quiet, but utter-auditory-void quiet. You can walk over the island in about seven hours (excluding lots of stopping time for chats and cups of tea with locals), or ride across in one of the jeeps that act as an informal bus service.

As isolated from the modern world as Paté is, this was once the dominant island of the archipelago. 'None who go to Paté returns;

SWAHILI ARCHITECTURE

The Swahili culture has produced one of the most distinctive architectural styles in Africa, if not the world. Once considered a stepchild of Arabic building styles, Swahili architecture, while owing some of its aesthetic to the Middle East, is more accurately a reflection of African design partly influenced by the Arab (and Persian, Indian and even Mediterranean) worlds.

One of the most important concepts of Swahili space is marking the line between the public and private, while also occasionally blurring those borders. So, for example, you'll see Lamu stoops (semicovered doorway areas or porches) that exist in the public arena of the street but also serve as a pathway into the private realm of the home. The use of stoops as a place for conversation further blends these inner and outer worlds. Inside the home the emphasis is on creating an airy, natural interior that contrasts with the exterior's constricting network of narrow streets. The use of open space also facilitates breezes that serve as natural air-conditioning.

You will find large courtyards, day beds placed on balconies and porches that all provide a sense of horizon within a town where the streets can only accommodate a single donkey. Other elements include *dakas* (verandahs), which again sit in the transitional zone between the street and home and also provide open areas; *vidaka*, wall niches that either contain a small decorative curio or serve a decorative purpose in their own right; and *mambrui* (pillars), which are used extensively in Swahili mosques.

what returns is wailing', goes one archipelago song. Whether this refers to military battles or the slave trade that was conducted through here is unknown, but the warning certainly doesn't apply now – most people return from Paté with a peaceful smile.

You're likely to experience great hospitality here – residents are either not used to tourists and consider them a happy novelty, or work in the tourism industry in Lamu and appreciate you making the effort to come all the way out here.

Sights & Activities

Siyu & Shanga

VILLAGE, RUIN

It's hard to believe today that Siyu was once the major city of the Lamu archipelago, with 30,000 inhabitants and several major universities. The only remnant of this glory is an enormous **fort**, which, given its emergence from the abandoned mangrove and coconut forest, is quite dramatic. Today Siyu is a small village with a whole lot of donkeys. Locals will happily put you up with a meal for about KSh400 to KSh600.

South of Siyu is Shanga, arguably the oldest archaeological site on the Kenyan coast. Legend says it was originally settled by stranded Chinese traders (the name being a corruption of 'China'), but this version of events is disputed. We can say this for sure, though: getting here requires a rewarding slog through a mangrove swamp and under swaying palm groves and, once you arrive, there's a real feeling of discovery. That's probably because Shanga is, despite its obscurity, the world's most complete example of a medieval Swahili town. You may be able to hire a guide in Siyu (several men here helped dig Shanga out in the 1980s), but otherwise you're on your own and, if you have any sense of imagination, feeling very Indiana Jones.

Be on the lookout for a 21-sided pillar tomb topped by a 15th-century celadon bowl, five town gates, 'Lamu' arches constructed of sandstone bedrock, coral ragstone and sand gathered from the nearby dunes, tablets marked with Arabic inscriptions and the ruins or foundations of some 130 houses and 300 tombs. There's no official Museums of Kenya presence here, so your visit is free, but remember not to remove anything from the site.

> **A GUIDE TO PATÉ**
>
> To get the most out of a trip to Paté Island it's well worth having a little local help. **Mansur Ile** (☎0717165311) is a top guide to the island's historical sites. He worked on many of the original excavations, knows the island intimately and speaks superb English.

Faza

VILLAGE

The biggest settlement on the island has a chequered history. Faza was almost totally destroyed by Paté in the 13th century, then again by the Portuguese in 1586 or 1587 (accounts differ, but it is known that the Portuguese chopped off the local sheik's head and preserved it in salt). With the demise of slavery, Faza faded away, but its new status as an administrative centre is breathing some life back into the place.

The modern town is quite extensive, if not terribly interesting. A major fire in 2010 largely gutted the town and destroyed what old buildings there were (amazingly, nobody died). Today the town has been totally rebuilt and you'd hardly know that a fire had taken place. The only remaining historical relics are rotting Portuguese offices on the waterfront, the ruined **Kunjanja Mosque** on the creek next to the district headquarters, and the **Mbwarashally Mosque**, also ruined, with a mihrab containing beautiful heart motifs, including the shahada (Muslim declaration of faith) written in an inverted heart pattern. Outside town is the **tomb of Amir Hamad**, commander of the sultan of Zanzibar's forces, who was killed here in 1844 while campaigning against Siyu and Paté.

Paté Town

VILLAGE

Paté town, on the west side of the island, is a functioning village carved out of orange and brown coral ragstone. The **Nabahani ruins**, which are slowly vanishing under a riot of tropical vegetation and banana plantations, are just outside town. They've never been seriously excavated, yet National Museums of Kenya still manages to charge you KSh500 to enter! A lot of locals will tell you to go after sunset for free – we plead silence on passing moral judgement on this activity.

The modern village itself is almost identical in design and construction to the ruins and, in fact, the two merge almost seamlessly into one another. Paté, with its tall coral-ragstone houses and narrow streets leading to a small port among the mangroves, is a fascinating place to wander around.

Sleeping & Eating

Accommodation and food are easy to arrange with local families, and there are one or two simple restaurants offering basic meals and tea. The only formal accommodation is in Faza town. Lamu-based **Mohamed** (☎0702080777), who also works as a guide, organises homestays with his extended family.

Peponi Hotel HOTEL $
(Faza; r excl breakfast KSh500) You know the Hilton and Sheraton hotel chains? Well, this is nothing like those. Not even slightly. It is a bed for the night though, and the family who runs it (and can provide meals) are lovely. It's also known as the Thuerya Hotel.

Getting There & Away

A motor launch leaves Lamu more or less daily for Mtangawanda (diesel/petrol boat KSh350/400, about two hours). Boats continue to Faza (KSh150, about another two hours) and Kizingitini (an additional KSh150, another hour), also stopping at the mouth of the channel to Siyu (KSh100), where small boats transfer passengers to shore. Boats leave from the main jetty in Lamu town. Times depend on the tides, but it can be tricky finding out when they go, as everyone you ask will tell you something different! It's normally around one or two hours before high tide. Note that the boats can't always get very close to shore so you might need to wade ashore.

Coming back from Paté, make sure the boat will be calling at Mtangawanda on the return trip. If not, you may have to wait an extra day.

A bunch of old British military Land Rover taxis meet the boats and link the three main settlements on the island together. Taxis from Mtangawanda can run you to Paté Town (KSh150), Siyu (KSh350) and Faza (KSh500).

Kiwayu Island

Cut by a dazzling white sandbar and stippled with rocks that are home to huge oysters, Kiwayu is a wonder. You can't possibly make it this far without singing about it for years to come. At the far northeast end of the archipelago, Kiwayu has a population of just a few hundred people and is part of the **Kiunga Marine National Reserve** (adult/child US$15/10). Gloriously remote, it's a long, narrow ridge of sand and baobab trees surrounded by reefs, with a long beach stretching down the eastern side of the island. Standing at the tallest point and surveying your surroundings at sunset will probably be one of the defining experiences of your time on the coast.

The main reason to come here is for a three-day dhow trip, and to explore the coral reefs off the eastern side of the island, rated as some of the best along the Kenyan coast. Dugongs, dolphins, whale sharks and sea turtles are a common sight. A day out fishing on the reef will have you fighting anything from yellowfin tuna to black marlin, sailfish, dorado, koli koli (trevally) and barracuda.

The village on the western side of the island, where the dhows drop anchor, is very small, but it does have a general store with a few basics.

Sleeping & Eating

The two high-end accommodation options on Kiwayu Island have reopened after two years of closure. If you're travelling on a budget, lovely locals **Aswar and Zena** (☎0704953979) organise homestays from Ksh500. Mzee Omari also offers highly recommended stays for groups (including his services as a chef and guard) in basic *bandas* on the baobab-strewen patch of beach that he owns. He has no phone number but is well known; ask around in the village for him.

★ **Mike's Camp** RESORT $$$
(www.mikescampkiwayu.com; r per person from US$200) Seven glorious *bandas*, a gorgeous deck looking out over the ocean, great seafood and every activity under the sun, including ocean kayaking.

Getting There & Away

If you'd like to travel (slowly, slowly) by dhow, you can arrange this from the jetty on Lamu. Three-night trips cost between KSh50,000 and KSh70,000, including food, fuel, snorkelling gear and two nights on Kiwayu. A public ferry also operates between Kiwayu and Lamu (stopping at Mtangawanda, Faza and Kizingitini on Paté Island). It's run by the marvellously named 'Captain Ship' – he leaves every three or four days and charges Ksh400 each way. Check at the jetty when he plans to return, otherwise you'll be stuck on Kiwayu without a paddle.

Northern Kenya

Includes ➡

Best of Nature

- ➡ Samburu, Buffalo Springs and Shaba National Reserves (p274)
- ➡ Matthews Range (p278)
- ➡ West Gate Community Conservancy (p277)
- ➡ Kalama Community Wildlife Conservancy (p277)
- ➡ Central Island National Park (p292)

Best of Culture

- ➡ Loyangalani (p288)
- ➡ Marsabit (p278)
- ➡ South Horr (p287)
- ➡ Moyale (p282)

Why Go?

Calling all explorers! We dare you to challenge yourself against some of the most exciting wilderness in Africa. Step forward only if you're able to withstand appalling roads, searing heat, clouds of dust torn by relentless winds, primitive food and accommodation, vast distances and more than a hint of danger.

The rewards include memories of vast, shattered lava deserts, camel herders walking their animals to lost oases, fog-shrouded mountains full of mysterious creatures, prehistoric islands crawling with massive reptiles and jokes shared with traditionally dressed warriors. Additional perks include camel trekking through piles of peachy dunes, elephant encounters in scrubby acacia woodlands and the chance to walk barefoot along the fabled shores of a sea of jade.

In our 21st-century world of wireless internet and dumbed-down TV, northern Kenya is an opportunity to leave behind all that is familiar and fall completely off the radar.

When to Go

Loyangalani

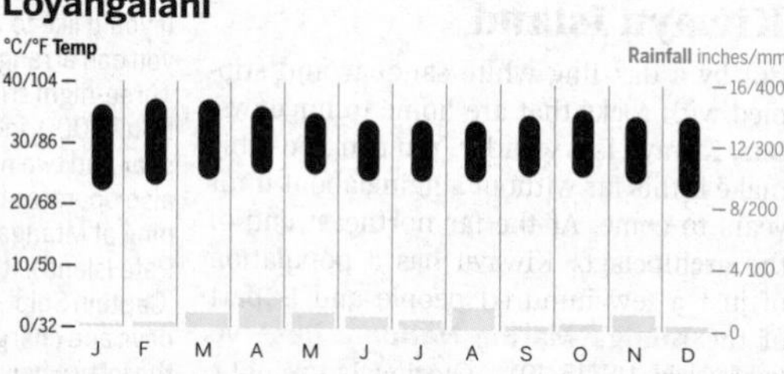

Jun Head to Loyangalani for the Lake Turkana Festival.

Aug Saddle up a camel and race through the Maralal International Camel Derby.

Nov–Dec It's marginally cooler in the northern deserts.

ISIOLO TO MOYALE

For most people this route means one of two things: the wildlife riches of the Samburu ecosystem, or the road to the cultural riches of Ethiopia. But in between and beyond, this area has much more to offer. You can drink tea and track wildlife with the Samburu people, climb mist-shrouded volcanoes in the desert, blaze trails in untrammelled mountains and get so far off the beaten track you'll start to wonder whether you're still on the same planet. All told, this massive wilderness offers something to anyone whose heart sings with adventure.

Isiolo

Isiolo is where anticipation and excitement start to send your heart aflutter. This vital pit stop on the long road north is a true frontier town, a place on the edge between the cool, verdant highlands just to the south and the scorching badlands – home of nomads and explorers – to the north. On a more practical note, it's also the last place with decent facilities until Maralal or Marsabit.

Among the first things you'll undoubtedly notice is the large Somali population (descendants of WWI veterans who settled here) and the striking faces of Boran, Samburu and Turkana people walking the streets. It's this mix of people, cultures and religions that is the most interesting thing about Isiolo. Nowhere is this mixture better illustrated than in the hectic **market**.

Sleeping

Isiolo has happy homes for budget and midrange travellers, but desperately lacks decent top-end options.

★Range Land Hotel COTTAGES $
(0710114030; www.rangelandhotels.com; A2 Hwy; campsite per person KSh1000, s/d cottages KSh3000/4000; P) About 4km south of town, this is a nice option for those with their own set of wheels. The sunny camping ground has bickering weaver birds and busy rock hyraxes in abundance, as well as neat-and-tidy stone bungalows with hot showers. Many people come to laze around in the gardens at the weekend, but during the week it's quiet.

Excellent meals are available and the house special is rabbit (KSh1200), a delicious rarity in Kenyan cuisine.

Moti Peal Hotel HOTEL $
(064-52400; s/d KSh2500/3500;) This smart place markets itself as the 'Pearl of Isiolo'. This actually says more about the state of Isiolo than the quality of the hotel, but even so it's shockingly clean, well run and has friendly management.

Bomen Hotel HOTEL $
(064-52389; near the Mansile Hospital; s/tw KSh2500/3500; P) The NGOs' favourite home, the Bomen Hotel has the town's most toe-curlingly frilly pink bedsheets! It also has TVs, shared terraces with views and unfailingly polite staff.

Josera Guest House HOTEL $
(0728059274; r KSh800-1200) Excellent-value sky blue rooms that range from tiny cubes to those large enough to swing a backpack. All have hot showers and there's a decent in-house restaurant.

Eating

There are numerous cheap eating establishments throughout the town, but hotel restaurants tend to offer more variety, as well as a more salubrious environment.

Bomen Hotel KENYAN $$
(meals KSh400-650; 7am-11pm) A rare place serving more than the local usuals, with fried tilapia, pepper steak, goulash and curries up for grabs.

WILDLIFE IN NORTHERN KENYA

Northern Kenya is one vast wilderness and one of the few areas in East Africa where close encounters with large mammals outside protected areas are almost a given. The area contains almost a full hand of Kenya's iconic animals, but many that you know and love from the south are here in different forms. Grevy's zebras, elegant thin-striped animals, patrol the plains, as do the beautifully blotchy subspecies of giraffe known as the reticulated giraffe. Then there are all the creatures that don't tend to occur elsewhere: the gerenuk, a type of long-necked antelope, and the beisa oryx are the most obvious. The birdlife, with numerous species not found elsewhere in Kenya, is possibly even more impressive than the roll call of large mammals.

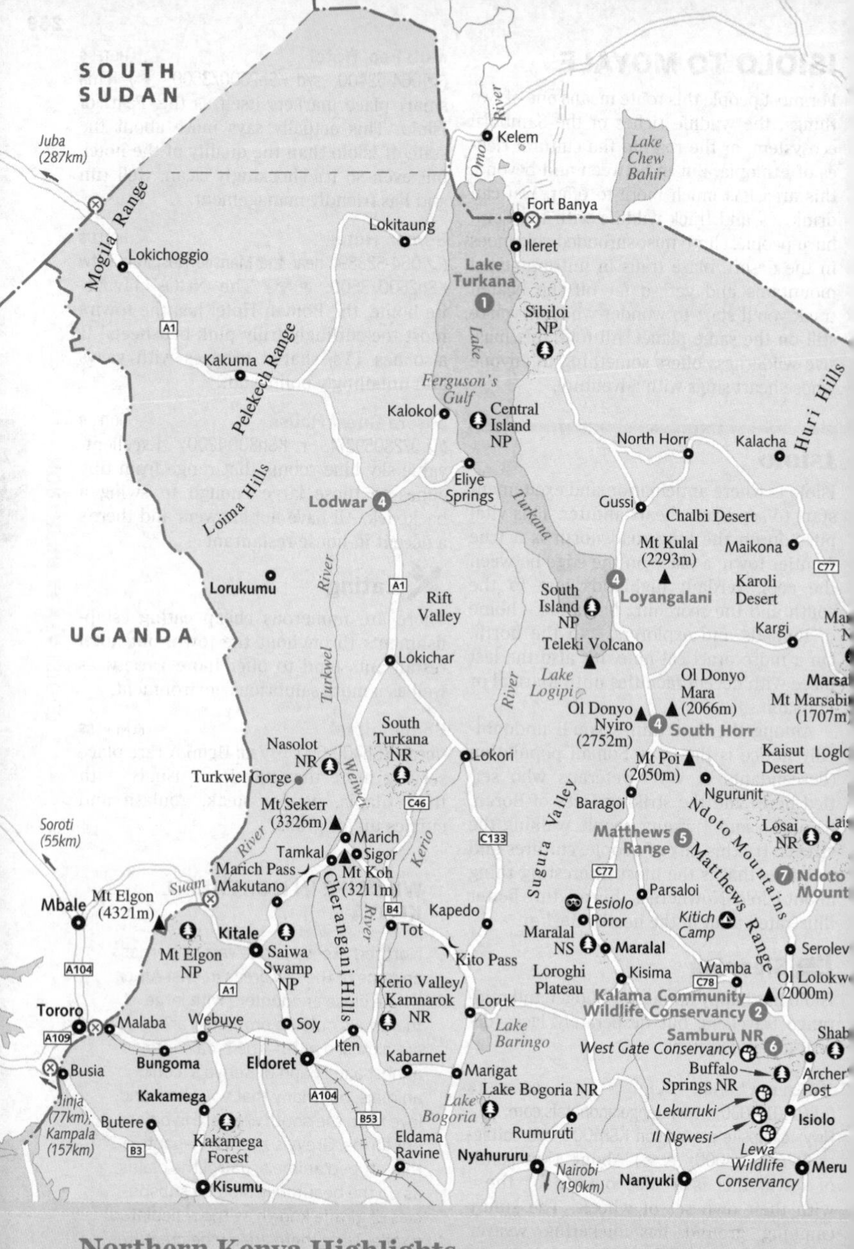

Northern Kenya Highlights

1 Blasting over the plains of darkness, destined for a sea of jade at **Lake Turkana** (p287)

2 Enjoying a private slab of wild Africa in **Kalama Community Wildlife Conservancy** (p277)

3 Searching for forest elephants in an ocean of sand in **Marsabit National Park** (p281)

4 Shaking hands with the Samburu in **South Horr** (p287), crocodile fishing with the El Molo north of **Loyangalani** (p288) and

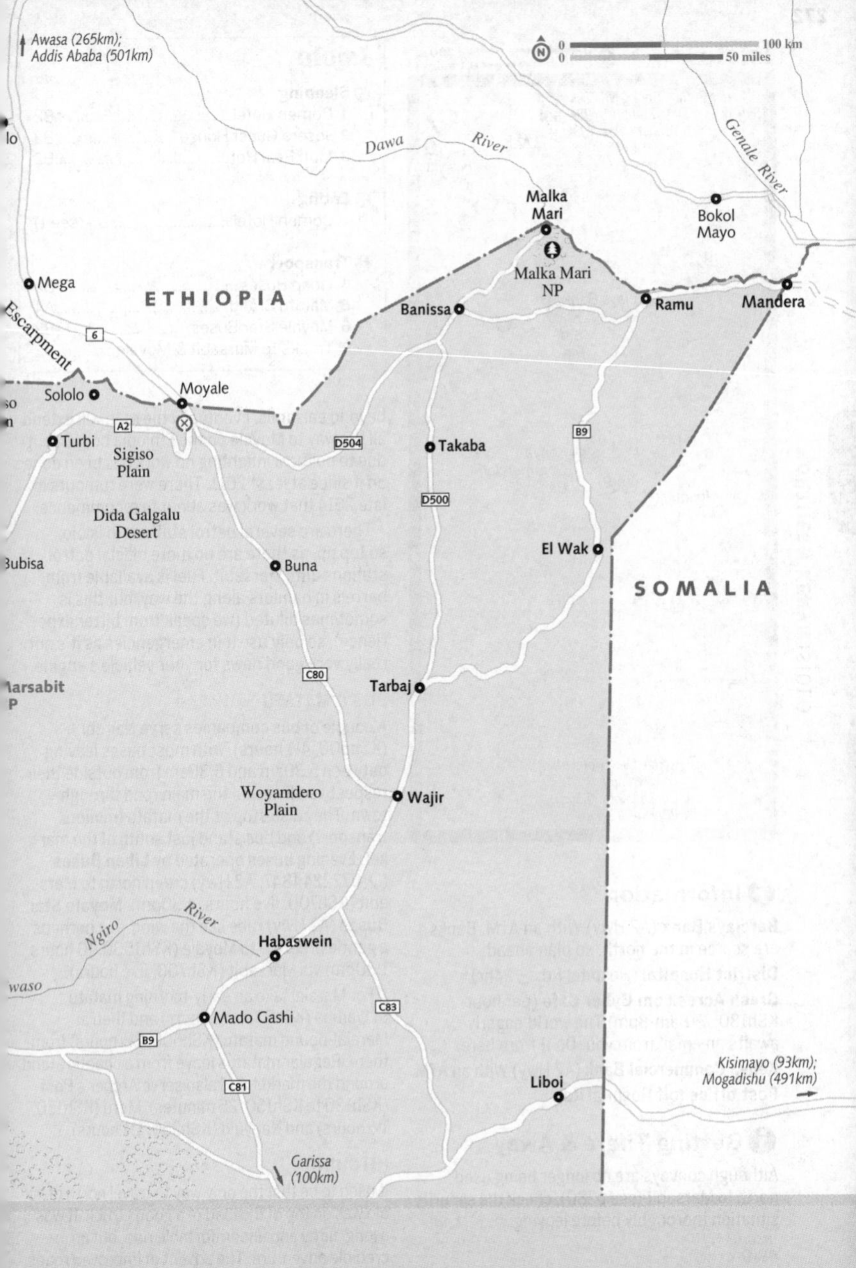

passing the time of day with the Turkana in **Lodwar** (p293)

5 Exploring the remote and little-visited highland forests of the **Matthews Range** (p278)

6 Realising that not only do zebras change their stripes in **Samburu National Reserve** (p274), but that giraffes change their spots and ostriches their legs

7 Leading your camels to water during a camel safari in the **Ndoto Mountains** (p278)

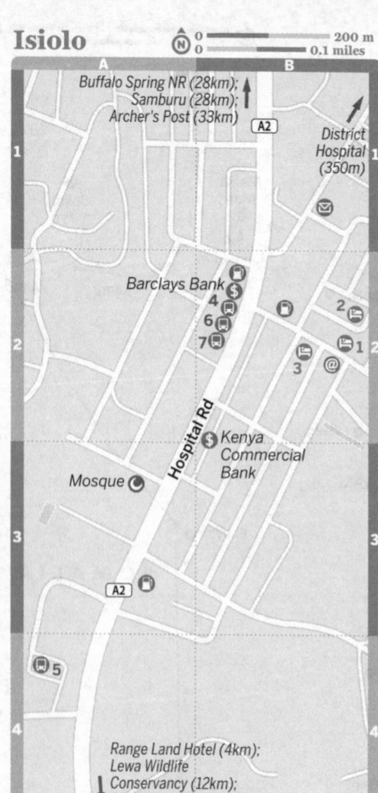

Isiolo

Sleeping

1 Bomen Hotel.....B2
2 Josera Guest House.....B2
3 Moti Peal Hotel.....B2

Eating

Bomen Hotel.....(see 1)

Transport

4 Liban Buses.....B2
5 Matatu Stand.....A4
6 Moyale Star Buses.....B2
7 Trucks to Marsabit & Moyale.....B2

Information

Barclays Bank (A2 Hwy) With an ATM. Banks are scarce in the north, so plan ahead.

District Hospital (Hospital Rd; 24hr)

Green Acres.com Cyber Cafe (per hour KSh180; 8am-8pm) The world eagerly awaits an email from you. Do it from here.

Kenya Commercial Bank (A2 Hwy) With an ATM.

Post office (off Hospital Rd)

Getting There & Away

Although convoys are no longer being used north to Marsabit (see p280), check the security situation thoroughly before leaving.

4WD

Isiolo long marked the northern terminus of the sealed road system, but the Chinese have, or rather had, been busy building roads here. A pristine sealed road runs about halfway to Marsabit before reverting to a rutted mess that will shake the guts out of you and your vehicle just beyond Laisamis. Eventually the road will extend all the way to Moyale on the Ethiopia border, but due to political infighting no work has been done on it since at least 2011. There were rumours in late 2014 that work was about to recommence.

There are several petrol stations in Isiolo, so top up, as there are no more official petrol stations until Marsabit. Fuel is available from barrels in hamlets along the way, but this is sometimes diluted (we speak from bitter experience), so only use it in emergencies as it's not really very good news for your vehicle's engine.

BUS & MATATU

A couple of bus companies serve Nairobi (KSh500, 4½ hours), with most buses leaving between 5.30am and 6.30am from outside their respective offices on the main road through town. They also stop at the matatu (minibus transport) and bus stand just south of the market. Evening buses operated by **Liban Buses** (0722244847; A2 Hwy) creep north to Marsabit (KSh700, five hours, 4.30pm). **Moyale Star Buses** (A2 Hwy) race like the wind – or perhaps a gentle breeze – to Moyale (KSh1500, 10 hours, 1.30pm) via Marsabit (KSh700, five hours).

For Maralal take an early-morning matatu to Wamba (KSh330, 2½ hours) and then a Maralal-bound matatu (KSh500, 2½ hours) from there. Regular matatus leave from a chaotic stand around the market and also serve Archer's Post (KSh130 to KSh150, 25 minutes), Meru (KSh150, 1½ hours) and Nanyuki (KSh250, 1¾ hours).

HITCHING

It used to be that the only way to travel north of Isiolo was on top of the load of a goods truck. It was a long, filthy and uncomfortable ride, but an incredible adventure. The advent of improved roads and a bus service means that few people use the trucks today, but should you want to relive the dusty, bumpy old days, trucks pick up passengers along the main road through town near the bus offices. Drain your bladder, purchase enough food, water and sunscreen, and hop aboard. Prices are negotiable, but if you sit atop the load reckon

GETTING AROUND NORTH KENYA

4WD Having your own 4WD gives you flexibility, but comes with its own challenges, due to wide-ranging road conditions. For starters, you'll need a large 4WD with high ground clearance and a skid plate to protect the undercarriage (a Toyota RAV4 or Suzuki won't do). You should have a high-rise jack, sand ladders, a shovel, a long strong rope or chain (to hitch up to camels or other vehicles), a tool kit, plus enough fuel, water and spare tyres (one is rarely enough). A compass and good map are also invaluable.

Do not underestimate how bad the roads are up here – on the three most recent research trips, we have twice snapped drive shafts, replaced more springs and tyres than we care to remember, destroyed three suspension systems and shattered two radiators (thank you to the two Samburu warriors with spears who, during our latest research trip, fixed the radiator at 2am somewhere south of Marsabit using a bar of soap and some tea leaves!). Unsurprisingly, many car-rental companies will not allow their vehicles to be taken north of Samburu National Reserve. If you do come up here, it's sensible to take an experienced driver and, if possible, travel in company with another 4WD.

Bus and matatu There's regular public transport as far north as Kalokol and Lokichoggio on Turkana's west side, but it's more limited up the lake's east side, only reaching Baragoi via Maralal, or North Horr via Marsabit. Buses run from Isiolo to Moyale, on the Ethiopian border, via Marsabit.

Hitching For the ultimate Kenyan adventure, hop aboard a dusty transport truck with the locals. It's an uncomfortable and dirty, but utterly enchanting, way to travel around northern Kenya. Improved bus services mean that Loyangalani is the only major destination, however, that still requires hitching.

Safaris Few organised safaris and overland trucks go to Lake Turkana's west side, with most still sticking to the east. Trips average seven to 10 days in length and typically follow identical routes. The main player on this route is Gametrackers (p38), which runs weekly overland safaris to Lake Turkana that generally depart from Nairobi on Wednesday and Friday.

on KSh500 to Marsabit and KSh1000 to Moyale. Double these prices for a seat in the cab.

Archer's Post

When the sealed road first reached Archer's Post, 33km north of Isiolo, the ramshackle village started to expand rapidly and the once forgotten-world feel of the place disappeared with the dust of the dying dirt road. Despite this loss of charm the village still makes an excellent base for budget travellers searching for elephants and lions in the neighbouring Samburu, Buffalo Springs and Shaba national reserves.

Sights & Activities

Umoja Village VILLAGE

(admission KSh1000) There are a number of Samburu villages in the area that welcome paying visitors. Probably the best one is Umoja, which was originally founded as a refuge for abused women and has now budded into a viable village in its own right. It might not be completely authentic, but admission fees go to a good cause. It's located next to the Umoja Campground (p274).

Ol Lolokwe HIKING

(conservancy fee per person US$40, guide per group US$50) About 30km north of town, and shrouded in Samburu folklore, is the massive mesa of Ol Lolokwe. It's a very tough, but rewarding, day hike (five hours just to climb it) and, at sunset, light radiating off its rusty bluffs is seen for kilometres around. The mountain is renowned for its raptors and has Kenya's highest population of Ruppell's vultures. It's now managed by the Namunyak Wildlife Conservation Trust, a locally run, community-based conservation effort.

Mohamed Leeresh WALKING

(☎0724143080; leeresh@yahoo.com; group per day US$50) A number of locals can take you on wildlife-tracking walks in the surrounding wilderness. Mohamed Leeresh is recommended. He can organise jeep rental for US$100 per half-day.

Sleeping & Eating

Don't want to camp with the lions and leopards in the national reserves? Want to save some moolah? Archer's Post can sort you out.

UMOJA UNITY

In 1990, 15 women who were allegedly raped by British military personnel who train in the area, and then suffered further abuse from violent husbands, abandoned their homes and started the village of Umoja (meaning 'unity' in Kiswahili), just outside Archer's Post. They hoped to survive together by producing and selling traditional Samburu jewellery to tourists. It all proved rather successful and Umoja thrived, even opening a camping ground a few years later. Boosted by its success, dozens more women left unhappy situations and now call the women-only village home.

At first, things weren't quite perfect in this female paradise and the success of Umoja spawned jealousy and even reports of violence directed at Umoja from local men. Today, things have calmed down considerably and there are few such problems. Find out more at www.umojawomen.net.

Umoja Campground CAMPGROUND $
(☎0718916247, 0721659717; www.umojawomen.net; camping KSh800, bandas KSh3000) Sitting on the Ewaso Ngiro's banks between town and Archer's Post gate, this fantastic option has clean and comfortable *bandas* (thatched-roof huts), but bring your own mosquito net because the campground's have seen better days, great camping, a chilled cafe (meals available on request) and occasional big-nosed, big-eared visitors coming in from the reserves.

Getting There & Away

There are matatus (KSh300, 1½ hours) and buses (KSh200, 1¾ hours) to Wamba that leave when full (most departures are in the morning). Matatus go to Isiolo (KSh130, 25 minutes) throughout the day. Transport to Marsabit is often full when it passes through Archer's – to be safe, return to Isiolo and catch the bus from there.

Samburu, Buffalo Springs & Shaba National Reserves

Blistered with termite skyscrapers, cleaved by the muddy Ewaso Ngiro River and heaving with heavyweight animals, this trio of national reserves has a beauty that is unsurpassed, as well as a population of creatures that occurs in no other major Kenyan park. These species include blue-legged Somali ostrich, endangered Grevy's zebra, beisa oryx, reticulated giraffe and gerenuk – gazelles that dearly wish to be giraffes. Despite covering just 300 sq km, the reserves' variety of landscapes and vegetation is amazing.

Sights

Shaba National Reserve (adult/child US$70/40, vehicle KSh1000), with its great rocky kopjes (isolated hills), natural springs and doum palms, is the most physically beautiful of the reserves, and you'll have it almost to yourself, but it often has less visible wildlife.

The open savannahs, scrub desert and verdant river foliage in **Samburu** (adult/child US$70/40, vehicle KSh1000) and **Buffalo Springs** (adult/child US$70/40, vehicle KSh1000) virtually guarantee close encounters with elephants and all the others.

The best wildlife viewing is almost always along the banks of the Ewaso Ngiro in Samburu.

Sleeping & Eating

Each reserve is blessed with at least two luxury lodges and several campsites. For campers and day visitors, some of the larger, less-exclusive luxury lodges have buffet meals.

Samburu National Reserve

Riverside Camp TENTED CAMP $
(Edwards Camp; ☎0721108032, 0721252737; per person KSh1500, per person full board KSh3500) On the northern bank of the Ewaso Ngiro River, the scrappy (and hot) dark canvas safari tents here might not climb as luxuriously high as some of the big-boy lodges but, let's face it, this is much more authentic Africa. Meals can be prepared on request. Vervet monkeys and baboons can be a menace, though. It's very close to the park headquarters.

Samburu Public Campsite CAMPGROUND $
(camping US$30) The main public camping site is close to the park headquarters. It lacks even the most basic facilities and there are lots of baboons with light fingers. Arrange your stay through the park ticket office.

Samburu & Buffalo Springs National Reserves

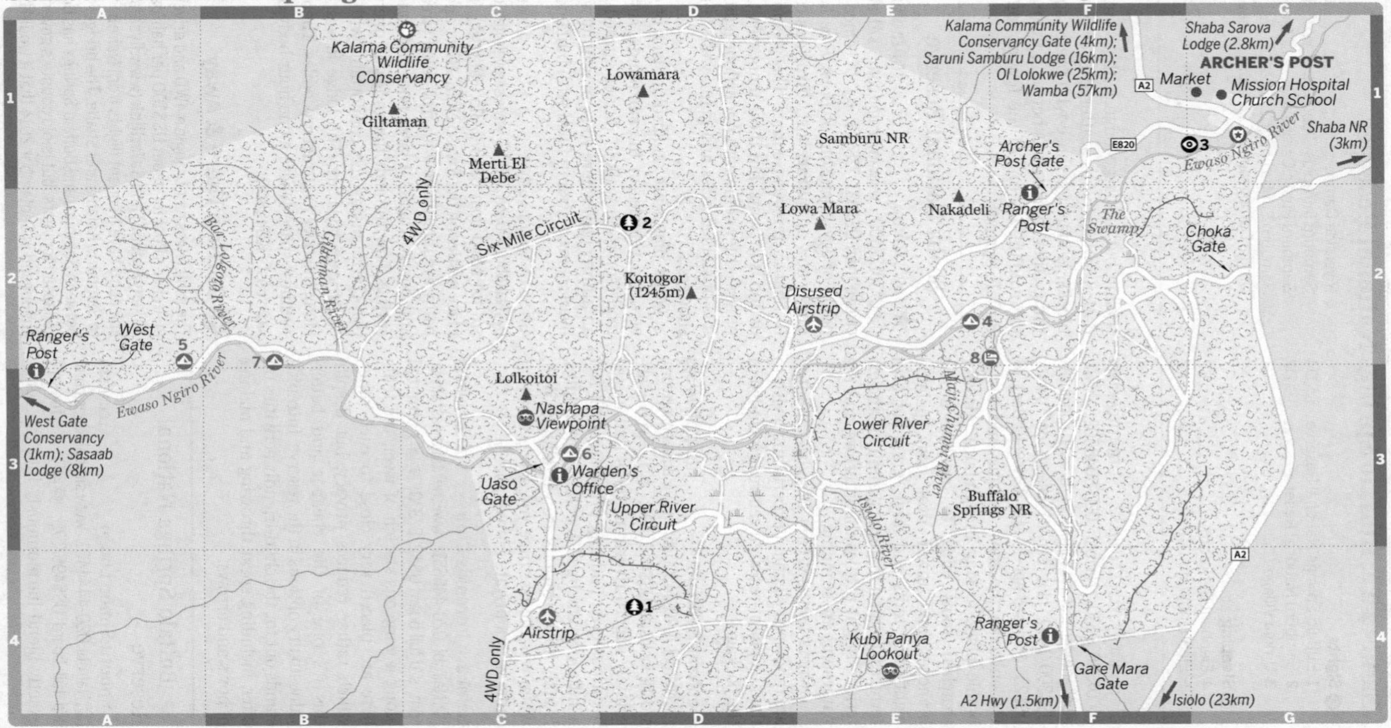

Samburu & Buffalo Springs National Reserves

Sights

1 Buffalo Springs National Reserve D4
2 Samburu National Reserve D2
3 Umoja Village G1

Sleeping

4 Elephant Bedroom E2
5 Elephant Watch Camp A2
6 Riverside Camp C3
7 Samburu Intrepids Club B2
Samburu Public Campsite .... (see 6)
8 Samburu Simba Lodge E2
Umoja Campground .... (see 3)

Elephant Watch Camp TENTED CAMP **$$$**
(0733639630, Nairobi 020-8048602; www.elephantwatchsafaris.com; s/d all inclusive US$800/1440, plus service charge per person US$25; closed Apr–10 May & Nov–10 Dec) Undoubtedly the most unique and memorable place to stay in Samburu. Massive thatched roofs cling to crooked acacia branches and tower over cosy, palatial eight-sided tents and large, grass-mat-clad terraces. Natural materials dominate the exteriors, bright textiles the interiors, and the bathrooms are stunning.

Owners Iain and Oria Douglas-Hamilton are renowned elephant experts and a visit to their elephant-research centre is included in the package.

Elephant Bedroom TENTED CAMP **$$$**
(Nairobi 020-4450035; www.atua-enkop.com; s/d all inclusive US$440/690;) Twelve absolutely superb riverfront tents that are so luxurious even budding princesses will feel a little overwhelmed by the surroundings. Exactly how luxurious are we talking? Well, when was the last time you saw a tent that came with a private plunge pool?

Samburu Intrepids Club TENTED CAMP **$$$**
(Nairobi 020-446651; www.heritage-eastafrica.com; s/d full board US$278/370;) Situated along a gorgeous stretch of river, the tents here are placed very close to each other, which rather reduces privacy, but despite this it's one of the cheaper and better-value luxury options in the reserve. Intrepids stands out for the child-friendly activities on offer, including spear throwing and making of bows and arrows.

Buffalo Springs National Reserve

Samburu Simba Lodge LODGE **$$$**
(Nairobi 020-4444401; www.simbalodges.com; s/d full board US$495/575;) It doesn't exactly blend harmoniously into the countryside, but this large lodge, with accommodation in big rooms scattered over several blocks, is ideal for those who prefer something other than canvas between them and the wildlife. It's one of the few options in Buffalo Springs.

Shaba National Reserve

★ **Joy's Camp** TENTED CAMP **$$$**
(0730127000; www.joyscamp.com; s/d all inclusive from US$437/728;) Once the home of Joy Adamson, of *Born Free* fame, this is now an outrageously luxurious camp in Shaba's remotest corner. The accommodation is in 'tents', but these tents aren't like others – they come with underfloor lighting, lots of stained glass and giant, walk-in rain showers.

Other pluses are an absolute lack of other safari vehicles in the surrounds, superb food (sorry, no walk-in dinner guests) and an infinity pool where you can wallow while overlooking a swamp filled with buffaloes.

Shaba Sarova Lodge LODGE **$$$**
(Nairobi 020-2767000; www.sarovahotels.com; s/d full board from US$270/315; @) This place nestles on the Ewaso Ngiro River and its pathways intertwine with frog-filled streams and ponds. There's a large pool and natural springs flow through the gorgeous open-air bar. The rooms are very comfortable with lots of Africana-style art. The lodge leaves bait along the river to attract crocodiles. There's a 'wellness space' where a one-hour body massage costs KSh2800.

Getting There & Away

The vehicleless can wrangle a 4WD and driver in Archer's Post for about US$100 per half-day. Airkenya (p385) and **Safarilink** (www.flysafarilink.com) have frequent flights from Nairobi to Samburu, Kalama and Shaba. The bridge between Samburu and Buffalo Springs has been collapsed for years, but Isiolo county's governor announced in September 2014 that it would be

SAMBURU, BUFFALO SPRINGS & SHABA NATIONAL RESERVES

Why Go To see some of Kenya's most unique creatures in a compelling and beautiful desert landscape. Samburu is also one of the best places in the country to see elephants. Crowds of visitors are nonexistent.

When to Go There's little rain in these parts, so it's possible to visit year-round, but between November and March, animals congregate near the Ewaso Ngiro River.

Practicalities Isiolo is the main gateway town. Conveniently, for the moment at least, Buffalo Springs, Shaba and Samburu entries are interchangeable, so you only pay once, even if you're visiting all three in one day. You must buy your ticket at the gate to the park in which you're staying. Petrol is available in Archer's Post.

Budget Tips You can camp in any of the reserves (but you mostly need to be self-sufficient). However, you'll still need a vehicle to get around. These can be hired by the half-day in Archers Post.

rebuilt soon. If it is still in pieces, and you want to visit both Samburu and Buffalo Springs, you'll need to make a long detour back to Archer's Post and the main A2 road, which can take up to three hours.

Samburu Area Conservancies

Kalama Community Wildlife Conservancy

Eight kilometres north of Archer's Post, and abutting the northern boundary of Samburu National Reserve, is the 384-sq-km Kalama Community Wildlife Conservancy, which opened in 2004. Although the conservancy is home to Grevy's zebras, elephants and reticulated giraffes, among others, and acts as a vital wildlife corridor for animals migrating between the Samburu and Marsabit areas, its drier habitat means animals are considerably less visible than in Samburu reserve. On a more positive note, you will pretty much have the place to yourself. It can also be used as a base for safaris in nearby reserves and, best of all, walking is allowed, unlike in Samburu.

Only guests of the lodge are allowed to enter the conservancy.

Sleeping

Saruni Samburu Lodge LODGE $$$

(☎0735950903; www.sarunisamburu.com; s/d all inclusive US$910/1520;) So perfectly designed is Saruni Samburu Lodge, the only accommodation within the conservancy, that its 'tents' virtually melt into the rocky bluff on which it's located. And when we say tents we do, of course, mean tents with stone bath-tubs, designer-chic furnishings and views that are quite simply out of this world.

Throw in an infinity pool, superb Italian-Kenyan fusion cooking and attentive staff and you get a place that gives any hotel in the world a run for its money. Prices include safaris, most drinks, airstrip transfers and almost anything else you can imagine.

West Gate Community Conservancy

West of Samburu National Reserve is the 400-sq-km **West Gate Community Conservancy** (www.nrt-kenya.org; adult/child US$58/40). The thorny acacia scrub that makes up much of the conservancy is home to several thousand Samburu people and a healthy, and growing, population of large mammals, including up to 500 Grevy's zebras. As in Samburu, the Ewaso Ngiro River flows through the conservancy and is the focus of interest for the area's wildlife. However, most of the animals here are much more jumpy and elusive than those in the reserve proper. Regardless, this conservancy is a brilliant example of how conservation and the needs of local people can facilitate each other.

There's no budget or midrange accommodation within the conservancy.

Sleeping

★**Sasaab Lodge** LODGE $$$

(☎Nairobi 020-5020888; www.thesafaricollection.com; s/d all inclusive US$1045/1740;) Quite possibly the most extravagant, yet serene, place to stay in northern Kenya. Its half-dozen Moorish-style 'tents' (each the size of a small house) have high-thatched roofs, private plunge pools, stunning river

WORTH A TRIP

NDOTO MOUNTAINS

Climbing from the Korante Plain's sands are the magnificent rusty bluffs and ridges of the Ndoto Mountains. Kept a virtual secret from the travelling world by their remote location, the Ndotos abound with hiking, climbing and bouldering potential. **Mt Poi** (2050m), which resembles the world's largest bread loaf from some angles, is a technical-climber's dream – its sheer 800m north face begs to be bagged. If you're fit and have a whole day to spare, it's a great hike to the summit and the views are extraordinary.

The tiny village of **Ngurunit** is the best base for your adventures and is interesting in its own right, with captivating, traditionally dressed Samburu people living in simple, yet elegantly woven, grass huts. Ngurunit is best accessed from Loglogo, 47km south of Marsabit and 233km north of Archer's Post. From Loglogo it's a tricky 79km drive with many forks; offer a lift to a local in Loglogo who can act as a guide. You can also get there from Baragoi.

views from the beds…and the showers…and the toilets…

The food is some of the best in any of the top lodges and there's a breathtaking infinity pool that seems to merge seamlessly into river and savannah views.

Matthews Range

West of the remarkable flat-topped Ol Lolokwe (p273) mountain, and north of Wamba, is the Matthews Range. The name might sound tame but, rest assured, this is real African wilderness, full of 1000 adventures. These forests and dramatic slopes support a wealth of wildlife, including elephants, lions, buffaloes and Kenya's most important wild-dog population. With few roads and almost no facilities, the mountains reward only those willing to go the extra kilometre on foot.

In 1995 the local Samburu communities collectively formed the Namunyak Wildlife Conservation Trust, now one of Kenya's most successful community conservation programs.

Sleeping

There's no budget accommodation within the conservancy, but it shouldn't be too hard to organise a camping trip here. Otherwise, the small town of Wamba (a couple of hours' drive from the heart of the Matthews) has a couple of grubby options.

Kitich Camp TENTED CAMP **$$$**
(☎0730127000; www.kitichcamp.com; s/d all inclusive US$562/936; ⊙closed Apr–mid-Jun & Nov–mid-Dec; P 📶) One of the remotest camps in Kenya, Kitich falls squarely into the luxury-tented-camp category, but staying here is unquestionably a wild-Africa experience. Elephants pass through the camp almost daily, and exploration of the thick forests is done on foot with expert Samburu trackers. This is a unique safari experience and is one of the most exciting places to stay in the country.

Marsabit

The road from Isiolo may be smooth tarmac for about half the distance, but Marsabit is still a long way from anywhere. For hour after scorching hour you'll pass a monotonous landscape of scrubby bush, and encounter wildlife and elegant Samburu people walking their herds of camels and goats. As the afternoon heats up and your brain starts to cook, you'll find the world around you sliding in and out of focus as mirages flicker on the horizon. Then, as evening comes, a final one appears: a massive wall of forested mountains where mammoth tusked elephants roam. This is no mirage. This is Marsabit.

The small town sits on the side of a 6300-sq-km shield volcano. Its surface is peppered with 180 cinder cones and 22 volcanic craters (*gofs* or *maars*), many of which house lakes – or at least they do when the rains have been kind. The terrible drought of 2009 and 2010 hit Marsabit very hard and the once-green mountain slopes were parched and dust-shrouded. Since then the rains have been a little more favourable (although the wet season of 2014 was another nonevent) and Marsabit has pretty much sprung back to green life. While the town is less attractive than its surrounds, which comprise the enormous 1500-sq-km Marsabit National Reserve and the smaller Marsabit National Park, it's an interesting and lively place, thanks to

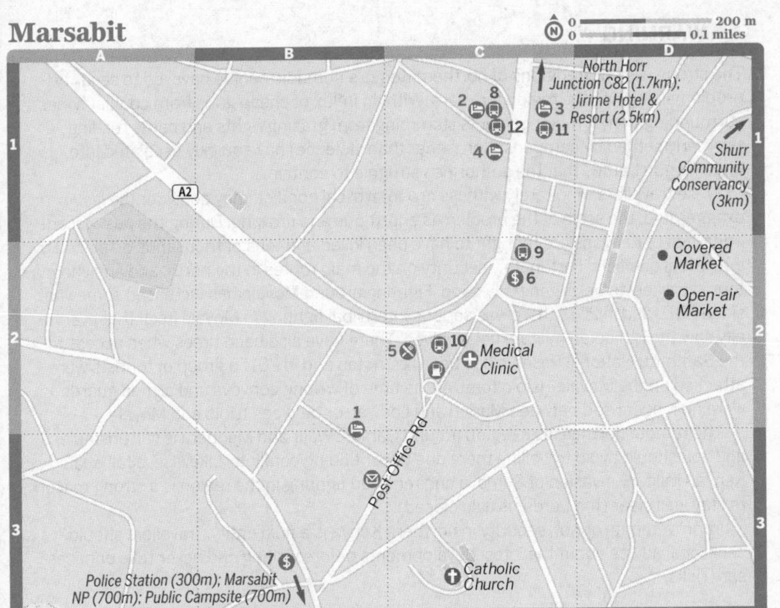

colourful nomads passing through. The best place to take in the cornucopia of culture is the lively **market**.

In 2013 the **Shurr Community Conservancy** (www.nrt-kenya.org) was established immediately to the east of Marsabit. The conservancy has a lot of potential and there's more wildlife around here than many people realise but, despite the advertising signs, there are currently no visitor facilities.

Sleeping

Water is a very scarce commodity in Marsabit and all the guesthouses have to truck it in from more H_2O-blessed parts of the country, so use it sparingly.

Nomads Trail Hotel HOTEL $
(☎0726560846, Nairobi 020-8004454; A2 Hwy; s/d old rooms KSh1800/2700, new rooms KSh3000/4500; Ⓟ 📶) The rooms here are prim and proper and all have attached bathrooms that come with – wait for it – real hot water from a real shower! Upstairs are some newer rooms that, for Marsabit, are shockingly posh.

JeyJey Centre HOTEL $
(☎0728808801/2; A2 Hwy; camping KSh300, s/d/tw KSh600/1000/1500 with shared bathroom, d KSh1200; Ⓟ 📶) This mudbrick castle bedecked in flowers is something of a travellers centre and is always bursting with road-hardened souls. Basic rooms with mosquito nets surround a courtyard, and bathrooms (even shared ones) sport on-demand hot water. There's also an unattractive camping ground.

Marsabit

Sleeping
1 Chicho B2
2 Horr Guest House C1
3 JeyJey Centre C1
4 Nomads Trail Hotel C1

Eating
5 Five Steers Hotel C2
JeyJey Centre .... (see 3)

Information
6 Co-operative Bank C2
7 Kenya Commercial Bank B3

Transport
8 Chalbi Buses C1
9 Liban Buses C2
10 Local Matatus C2
11 Moyale Raha Buses C1
12 Truck Pick-up Area C1

Horr Guest House HOTEL $
(☎0726147226; A2 Hwy; s/d excl breakfast with shared bathroom KSh500/1000) Alright, so we

WARNING

The strong warrior traditions of northern Kenya's nomadic people have led to security problems plaguing the region for years. With an influx of cheap guns from conflict zones surrounding Kenya, minor conflicts stemming from grazing rights and cattle rustling (formerly settled by compensation rather than violence) have quickly escalated into ongoing gun battles that the authorities struggle to contain.

While travellers, who rarely witness any intertribal conflict, may consider the issue exaggerated, the scale of the problem is enormous and growing. During the past decade hundreds of Kenyans are thought to have been killed and tens of thousands displaced by intertribal conflicts. Fortunately security on the main routes in the north, and anywhere a tourist is likely to be, is generally good. Fighting around Moyale has increased somewhat since 2011, and in 2012 there was serious intertribal fighting in Moyale itself that eventually saw the Ethiopian military get involved. There have also been times when access to the Samburu National Reserve has been restricted and in 2011 a group of tourists were attacked on the Moyale–Isiolo road. At the time of writing convoys and armed guards were no longer used between Marich and Lodwar, or between Isiolo and Moyale.

The remote northeastern region around Garsen, Wajir and Mandera is still unstable and you should avoid travelling there due to continuing conflicts. Likewise, a full-scale Kenyan military invasion of Somalia and renewed fighting in the region is a strong reason to stay well clear (the border is also closed).

Improvements or not, security in northern Kenya is a fluid entity. Travellers should seek local advice about the latest developments before visiting and never take unnecessary risks.

have a juvenile sense of humour but, honestly, how could we not include a place with a name like this? Despite the name, ladies of the night are not a part of the furniture and it's actually one of the better maintained cheapies in town.

Chicho GUESTHOUSE $
(☎0706153827; www.chichohotel.com; Post Office Rd; s/d KSh2000/3500; P 📶) Located very close to the post office, but up a quiet side road, this place has a helpful manager, colourful rooms with some character, small bathrooms with hot water and bedsheets that will shock you with their absence of dubious stains! All up it's the best bet in the town centre. Book ahead.

Jirime Hotel & Resort HOTEL $$
(☎0770834050; www.jirimehotel.com; A2 Hwy; camping KSh500, s/d KSh3000/5000; P 📶) The smartest option in Marsabit is this new place, 2.5km north of town on the road to Moyale. It has little in the way of character but has big, tiled en suite rooms, lots of peace and quiet, a decent in-house restaurant and pretty good wi-fi. Camping is also possible.

Eating & Drinking

While not having as many Michelin stars as Paris, you won't go to bed hungry here.

Five Steers Hotel KENYAN $
(A2 Hwy; meals KSh250-400; ⏰8am-8pm) With a wooden fenced-off terrace, this place is the height of Marsabit style. The '½ Federation' meal (a bulging pile of rice, spaghetti, beef, vegetables and chapatti) is filling and tasty. The owner is a good source of information on onward transport.

JeyJey Centre KENYAN $
(A2 Hwy; meals KSh300-500; ⏰lunch & dinner) Inside the popular hotel, JeyJey serves local favourites as well as the odd curry. Take a good book to read while you wait if you order anything out of the ordinary.

Information

Co-operative Bank With an ATM that works with foreign Visa cards.

Kenya Commercial Bank (off Post Office Rd) With ATM.

Medical Clinic (Post Office Rd; ⏰8am-7pm Mon-Sat, noon-7pm Sun)

Post Office (Post Office Rd)

Getting There & Away

Although improved security means convoys and armed guards are no longer being used to Moyale or Isiolo, it's still wise to get the latest security and Ethiopian border information from locals and the police station before leaving town.

As a rule, if buses and trucks travel in a convoy, or take armed soldiers on board, you should too!

4WD

The road from Marsabit to Moyale has long been renowned as a rutted, dusty, car-destroying mess, but work is underway to surface the route. A good chunk of the route is now completed, but it's not one long continuous stretch of tarmac. Rather it's a stretch of beautifully smooth tarmac road followed by a section of bone-shattering dirt road and then another stretch of tarmac and so on. It's very possible the road will soon be completely surfaced. The only fuel north is in Moyale, so stock up in Marsabit.

BUS

Moyale Raha Buses connects Marsabit to Moyale daily (KSh800, six hours, 5.30pm). The bus picks up passengers outside the JeyJey Centre. Heading south, both Moyale Raha and Liban Buses run to Isiolo (KSh700, six hours) at 6am (Liban Buses) and a flexible 11am (Moyale Raha Buses). Journey times will fall as the sealed road extends. If you're one of the really adventurous souls off to Lake Turkana, your journey out of Marsabit has recently become a little easier with the introduction of buses ('bus' is actually something of a misnomer; instead try to picture the offspring of a truck that slept with a bus!) to North Horr via Kalacha by **Chalbi Buses** (☎ 0705095511; County Guest House Bldg). Buses leave at 5pm every other day and take at least 10 very hot, sandy hours to North Horr. Take note that there's no reliable transport onward to the lake from North Horr.

HITCHING

Trucks regularly ply the bus routes for about KSh500, but balancing on a metal bar above discontented cows for eight hours, while simultaneously battling the sun, wind and dust, is one tricky, tiring act and few people use trucks along the road to Moyale nowadays. There are also some very rare trucks to Loyangalani (very negotiable KSh1000, hours and hours), travelling either the northern route via Kalacha and North Horr, or the southern one via Kargai. Most trucks pick up opposite JeyJey Centre.

Marsabit National Park

Within the larger national reserve, this small **park** (adult/child US$25/15; ⏲6.30am-6pm), nestled on Mt Marsabit's upper slopes, is coated in thick forests and contains a wide variety of wildlife, including leopards, elephants (some with huge tusks) and buffaloes. The park forms a key point on an elephant-migration route that extends as far as the slopes of Mt Kenya. The dense forest makes spotting wildlife very difficult, but fortunately help is at hand in the form of a couple of natural clearings with semi-permanent lakes, where animal sightings are almost guaranteed. Even if the larger mammals are playing shy, there are loads of birds and butterflies around but, perhaps surprisingly, few monkeys.

This is a very climate-affected park. In the increasingly common years when the rains fail, the park very quickly turns brown, parched and apparently lifeless. In more generous years the vegetation positively glows green, the lakes fill with water and animals seem to reappear from nowhere. At the time of writing the park was looking the best we've seen it in years and visiting was a real treat.

If you're without transport it's possible to walk to Marsabit Lodge from the park gate with an armed ranger (per person KSh1500; organise this through the park office the day before if possible). With luck you'll have some exciting encounters with buffaloes and elephants.

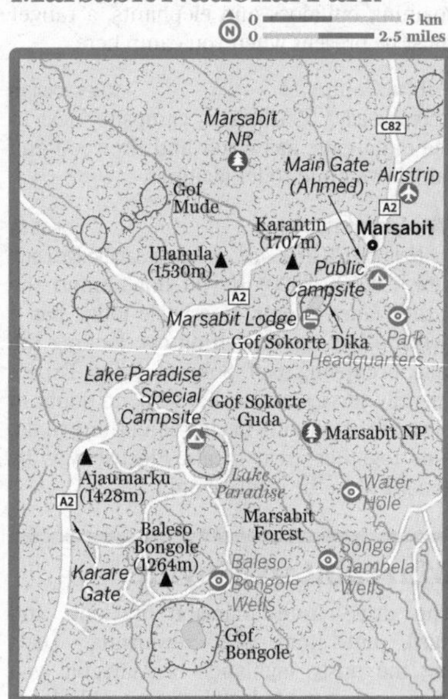

Sleeping & Eating

Lake Paradise Special Campsite CAMPGROUND **$**
(camping adult US$35, plus set-up fee US$20) Although there's nothing except a dried-up lake bed and firewood, this picturesque site

is the best place to camp in the park. Due to roaming buffaloes and elephants, a ranger must be present when you camp here.

Public Campsite CAMPGROUND $
(camping adult US$25) This campsite, next to the main gate, has water and firewood and fair shower and toilet facilities.

★ **Marsabit Lodge** LODGE $$
(☎ Nairobi 020-2695468; www.marsabitlodge.com; s/tw KSh6500/8500) If you don't mind the rather faded rooms, this basic lodge has a deliciously peaceful setting overlooking the lake occupying Gof Sokorte Dika. Expect friendly service and a chef who, no doubt in pleasure at actually having something to do, puts together great meals. Electricity is by generator in the evening only.

Marsabit to Moyale

The drive from Marsabit is long and hard, but immensely rewarding. Leaving the misty highlands of Marsabit, you drop onto the bleak-by-name, bleak-by-nature **Dida Galgalu Desert** (Plains of Darkness) and trundle for endless hours through a magnificent monotony of black, sunburnt lava rock. The only sign of life, aside from the odd nomad and his camels, is the hamlet of **Bubisa**, a fly-blown place marked on few maps, where bored-looking Gabbra, Somali and Ethiopians sit day after day chewing *miraa* (leaves and shoots that are chewed as a stimulant). Then it's onwards over an empty landscape until you reach the tiny village of **Turbi**, sheltered by two small, forested peaks. These can be climbed in half a day, but take a guide as there's a lot of wildlife and wild people in these parts. If you were to get stuck here for the night, there are a couple of very meagre places to stay. For security's sake, however, it's best to push onto Moyale. After Turbi, scrubby thorn bushes replace lava desert and, in the distance, the mountain vastness of Ethiopia springs up and tantalises.

Moyale

Let's be honest. Nobody comes to Moyale to see Moyale; people come because it's the gateway to one of the world's most fascinating countries – Ethiopia.

In stark contrast to the solitary journey here, Moyale's small, sandy streets burst with activity. The town's Ethiopian half

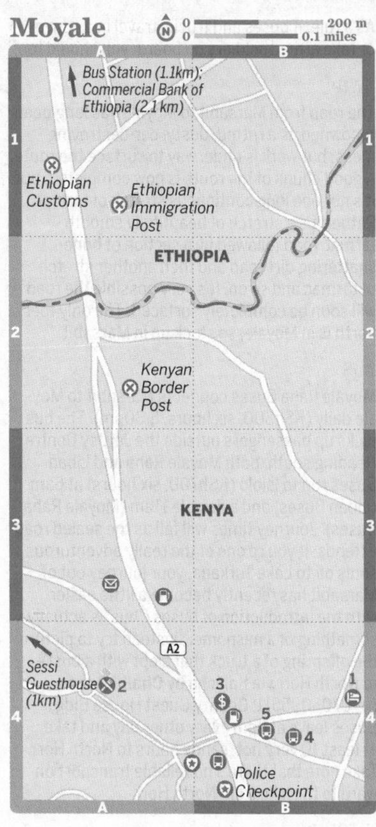

Moyale

Sleeping
1 Al-Yusra Hotel B4

Eating
2 Prison Canteen A4

Information
3 Kenya Commercial Bank B4

Transport
4 Moyale Raha Buses B4
5 Truck Pick-up Area B4

is more developed, complete with sealed roads, and there's a palpable difference in its atmosphere.

Sleeping & Eating

For years the hardy few travellers who passed through Moyale had to put up with some truly nasty accommodation. While 99% of places to stay on both sides of the border maintain this tradition, there is now one option that seems keen to break the mould. Be aware that prostitution here is almost unavoidable, as most cheap hotels and bars double as brothels.

Accommodation on the Ethiopian side of the border is generally of a (slightly) higher standard.

Al-Yusra Hotel HOTEL $
(☎0722257028; s/d KSh2500/3000; 📶) Big news, folks! Kenyan Moyale finally has a decent place to stay! OK, let's not go overboard. It's hardly fantastic, but it does have running water that's sometimes even hot and no strange creatures sharing your bed. You can't miss it. It's by far the town's tallest building, which also houses a clinic.

Sessi Guesthouse HOTEL $
(r per person with shared bathroom KSh750; P) This place, a short way out of the centre, is clean (well, clean for Moyale) and fairly quiet, and the best thing about it is that it's not even a brothel!

Prison Canteen KENYAN $
(meals KSh150-350; ⏰10am-late) It says a lot about the quality of life here when the best place to eat, drink and party is inside the town jail. Not only do you get a great atmosphere and an excellent *nyama choma* (barbecued meat), but you also get to tell your friends you went to prison on the Ethiopia-Kenya border!

ℹ Information

It used to be possible to cross to the Ethiopian side of Moyale without a visa for a few hours to see what you were missing (which isn't really very much at all), but this is generally no longer permitted. Be aware that visas aren't available at the border, nor at the Ethiopian embassy in Nairobi for nonresidents of Kenya. If you're coming the other way, three-month Kenyan tourist visas (US$50) are available at the border for most Western nationalities. The border is open from 6am to 6pm daily.

The Commercial Bank of Ethiopia, 2km from the border, changes travellers cheques as well as US dollars and euros. While it doesn't exchange Kenyan shillings, the Tourist Hotel will swap them for Ethiopian birr.

Kenya Commercial Bank (A2 Hwy) With ATM.

ℹ Getting There & Away

Onward transport from both sides of the frontier leaves before the border opens, so cross straight to the other side if you arrive early enough. Otherwise you'll get stuck here for an extra day.

Moyale Raha Buses leave town daily at 6am for Marsabit (KSh800, five to six hours). With the recent improvements in the road between Moyale and Marsabit, it's now possible to get from Moyale to Isiolo, or even Nariobi, in one very long, exhausting day. With the arrival of buses in northern Kenya, few people hitch a ride on trucks these days, but should you want to, trucks for Marsabit (KSh500) pick up passengers near the main intersection in town and generally leave around 6am. Drivers should note that petrol on the Ethiopian side of Moyale is half the cost of that in Kenya.

On the Ethiopian side, a bus leaves for Addis Ababa each morning at around 5am, though it takes two days, so you might want to break the journey at any number of fascinating places in southern Ethiopia.

MARALAL TO TURKANA'S EASTERN SHORE

Journeying to a sea of jade shouldn't be something that's easy to do, and this route, the ultimate Kenyan adventure, is certainly not easy. Your backside will take a battering, but you'll be rewarded 1000 times over with memories of vibrant tribes, camel caravans running into a red sunset, mesmerising volcanic landscapes and, of course, the north's greatest jewel – Lake Turkana.

Maralal

Walking down Maralal's dusty streets, with their swinging doors and camels tied up outside colourful wooden shopfronts, it's impossible not to think you've somehow been transported to the Wild West. It wouldn't come as much of a surprise to see Clint Eastwood stride slowly from a bar and proclaim that the town is not big enough for the two of you.

Maralal has gained an international reputation for its fantastically frenetic International Camel Derby (p285) and a visit over its duration is truly unforgettable. Less crazy, but almost as memorable, are the year-round camel safaris and treks that are offered here.

Many visitors don't delve into Maralal, stopping only for a night en route to Lake Turkana. The same can't be said for those relying on very erratic local transport north; they often end up spending more time here than planned. Lucky for them, Maralal is the kind of place where you should spend

Maralal

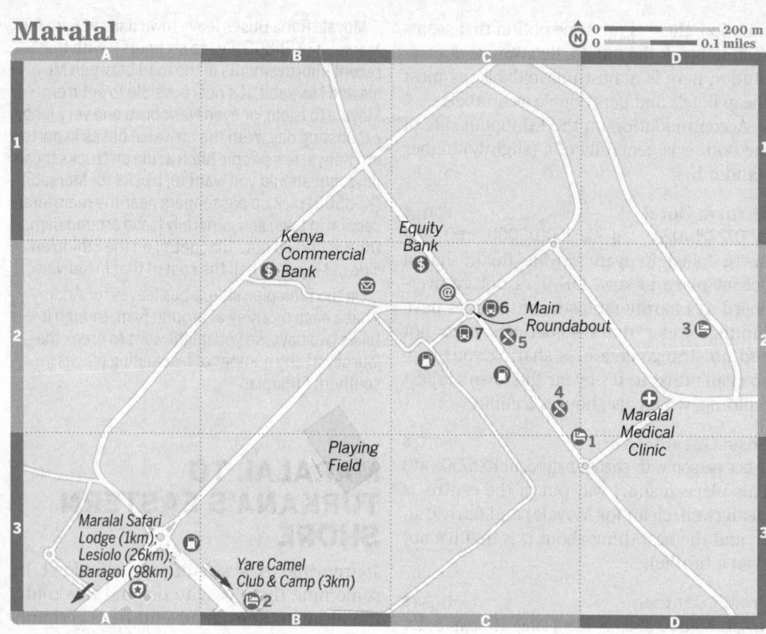

Maralal

Sleeping
1 Cheers Guest House C3
2 Samburu Guest House B3
3 Sunbird Guest House D2

Eating
4 Coast Dishes C2
5 Pop Inn Hotel C2

Transport
6 4WD Matatus & Land Rover Taxis C2
7 Matatus C2

some time. After all, the town's most famous former resident was one of the greatest explorers of the 20th century, Wilfred Thesiger, and if he decided that Maralal was the perfect place for retirement, then it must be doing something right.

Sights & Activities

Maralal National Sanctuary WILDLIFE RESERVE
FREE This sanctuary, home to zebras, impalas, hyenas and others, once completely surrounded the town. Today it only covers a small patch of land around what's left of the Maralal Safari Lodge. With nowhere really to drive or walk on a safari, one of the only ways to take in the animals is with a cold beverage in hand at Maralal Safari Lodge's bar. You may need to bring your own beer, though, as this place may be on its last legs.

Loroghi Hills Circuit TREKKING
The Loroghi Hills Circuit, which takes in one of Kenya's most astounding vistas, Lesiolo, is a rewarding five-day (78km) trek. It's detailed in Lonely Planet's *Trekking in East Africa*. It should be possible to organise a guide through Yare Camel Club and Camp. Somewhat shorter walks are possible by just strolling aimlessly around the high country and down the paths linking *shambas* (small plots) that surround the town.

Yare Camel Club & Camp SAFARIS
(0729322500) Organises guides and camels for independent camel safaris in the region. Half-day camel hire is US$20, while an overnight trip with guides, camping equipment, food and cook costs US$120 per person.

Sleeping

Advance booking is absolutely essential during the camel derby.

Sunbird Guest House GUESTHOUSE $
(0720654567; s/d KSh1000/1200; P) The single rooms are starting to look a little old and damp but, by and large, this very friend-

DON'T MISS

MARALAL INTERNATIONAL CAMEL DERBY

Inaugurated by Yare Safaris in 1990, the annual Maralal International Camel Derby, held in mid- to late August, is one of the biggest events in Kenya, attracting riders and spectators from around the world. The races are open to anyone, and the extended after-parties at Yare Camel Club and Camp are notorious – you're likely to bump into some genuine characters here.

Not interested in parties and just want some fast-moving camel action? Then the derby's first race has your name written all over it – it's for amateur camel riders. It's a butt-jarring 11km journey. Don't even start feeling sorry for your backside – the professional riders cover 42km.

For further information contact Yare Camel Club and Camp.

ly place has quiet, clean and comfortable rooms with nice linen, mosquito nets and hot water in the bathrooms. The courtyard has a sunny, garden vibe and there's a pleasant restaurant serving healthy fried stuff.

Samburu Guest House HOTEL $
(☎0725363471; www.samburuguesthouse.com; s/d KSh800/2000; P 📶) Large, outrageously pink cube of a building on the edge of town with spacious rooms that take the cleanliness award for Maralal. The design of the building, though, is such that noise echoes through the rooms.

Cheers Guest House GUESTHOUSE $
(☎065-62204, 0722655877; s/d KSh700/1000; P 📶) A long-time favourite, this well-run place has small single rooms and smart doubles with friendly staff and safe parking in the courtyard. The in-house restaurant (mains KSh150 to KSh250), which serves all your fried Kenyan favourites, is one of the town's better places to eat.

Yare Camel Club & Camp CAMPGROUND, CABINS $
(☎0729322500; camping KSh500, s/tw/tr US$23/38/55; P @) This long-standing travellers' hang-out, 3km south of town, has dreary and overpriced cabins, but it's a good spot for overlanders thanks to grassy lawns perfect for camping and a sociable bar.

Maralal Safari Lodge LODGE $$
(☎0715132640; s/d Ksh3000/6000; P 🏊) The wooden cottages are quite dark and dim and certainly show their age, plus the whole place is borderline closed down, but if all that doesn't put you off, the price is good and the setting a delight. You must call ahead though and bring your own food, but there's a cook on hand.

Eating

Unless you've got the *ugali* (a staple made from maize of cassava flour) or *nyama choma* itch, few of your taste buds will be scratched here. That said, a few places hammer out quality local eats, and the restaurants of the Sunbird, Cheers and Samburu guesthouses all have menus that are (for Maralal) positively cosmopolitan. Stock up at the market or the Sunguia Supermarket if you're heading north by public transport.

Coast Dishes KENYAN $
(mains KSh80-240) 'The neighbourhood will never be the same again', the sign outside this place confidently reads. In fact the neighbourhood hasn't changed one jot in years, but even so this place, which is run by a couple from the sultry coast, does bring a flavour of other places to Maralal with coastal staples such as pilau, though made with goat rather than fish.

Pop Inn Hotel KENYAN $
(meals KSh120-200; ⏲7am-8pm) This zebra-striped building has decent Kenyan staples, but its claim to have the 'best food south of the Sahara – and that's a fact' might not be a 'fact' at all – south of the roundabout seems more realistic.

Information

Equity Bank A more reliable ATM than that at Kenya Commercial Bank.

Kenya Commercial Bank Behind the market, with an ATM (the last one going north), but it can be a bit stroppy when presented with foreign Visa cards.

Links Cyber Café (per hour KSh120; ⏲8am-8pm Mon-Sat, 2-8pm Sun)

Maralal Medical Clinic

Post office Next to the market.

DON'T MISS

CAMEL SAFARIS IN NORTHERN KENYA

Days spent moving at the pace of a camel, and campfire nights under a star-spangled sky: a camel safari through the wild lands of northern Kenya will likely be the highlight of any trip to the country. One of the best-regarded camel safari operators is **Wild Frontiers** (satellite phone 088216-43334103; www.wildfrontierskenya.com). Safaris can be as tough or lazy as you want and while there's plenty of wildlife around, most of your animal sightings will, at best, be a fleeting glimpse of a fleeing animal. There will be lots of cultural interactions, though, as you pass by remote villages and herders with their livestock. The typical safari takes place in and around the magnificent Matthews and Ndoto mountains and lasts six nights, but much longer ones going all the way to Lake Turkana can be organised.

Wild Frontiers safaris help support the **Milgis Trust** (www.milgistrustkenya.com), which works with local communities to preserve the pastoral way of life and the wildlife of northern Kenya.

Getting There & Away

Matatus serve Nyahururu (KSh500, three to four hours), Rumuruti (KSh300 to KSh400, 2½ hours) and Wamba (KSh500, 3½ hours). For Nairobi you need to change in Nyahururu. Reaching Isiolo involves staying overnight in Wamba to catch the early-morning southbound matatu.

Access to the north has got a little easier since 2012, with the road out of Maralal, which used to be one of the worst in the country, being regraded (though it's still heavy going and drivers require a good 4WD with high clearance). There are buses too, which look like they're crossed with a tank, heading to Baragoi (KSh500) at around 11am every morning. As there is still no regular transport north from there, it's more pleasant to wait in Maralal for something heading further north.

Waits for trucks to Loyangalani (KSh1000 to KSh1500, nine to 12 hours), on the shore of Lake Turkana, might last from a few days to a week. Start asking around as soon as you arrive in town and remember that while breaking the truck journey in Baragoi or South Horr may seem like a good idea, you might have to wait there for a week before another truck trundles through. After rain you can expect prices for all transport to rise.

Most transport leaves from the main roundabout, while trucks usually pick up passengers at the former BP station.

Lesiolo

There are views and then there are views. Lesiolo (meaning 'world's view'), which perches atop an escarpment marking the Loroghi Plateau's dramatic end, offers an outrageous 120km-deep panoramic view over the Rift Valley and serrated Taita Hills. Lesiolo is part of the Malasso Ecotourism Project and a viewing fee (KSh500) is now charged – pricey, but worth every penny.

The Lesiolo Loop is a spectacular and gruelling 12km trek (four to five hours) that takes you down the escarpment to the valley floor and then slowly brings you back up again. A local guide (Malasso Ecotourism Project guides cost KSh1000 per day) is essential for this trek.

Sleeping

It's possible to **camp** (US$10 per adult) at Lesiolo and the viewing fee is waived if you do so. There's water (collected rain), crude toilets and a whole lot of cow patties to go with the astounding view.

Getting There & Away

Head north from Maralal towards Baragoi for 17km and the Malasso Ecotourism Project sign marks the turn-off for Lesiolo. Several more signs and helpful locals will point you the rest of the way. Patience and erratic transport can get you to the village of Poror, an easy 9km walk (two to three hours) from Lesiolo. You'll need a 4WD if driving in the wet season.

Baragoi

The long descent off the Loroghi Plateau towards Baragoi serves up some sweet vistas, and for kilometre after gorgeous kilometre you'll literally see nothing but tree-studded grasslands. For years this area looked like it should be wall to wall with grazing antelope, but the reality was that very few things larger than a dik-dik lived here. With wildlife conservancies stretching ever further northward that's changing and we've seen herds of Grevy's zebra out here – locals tell us that wildlife numbers are building rapidly. Despite all this good news, reaching Baragoi is a bit of an anticlimax, as the dusty, diminutive town is clearly outdone by its surroundings.

Sleeping

Morning Star Guest House HOTEL $
(s/d with shared bathroom KSh300/600) The bougainvillea-dressed Morning Star Guest House provides for a night's kip – though it doesn't supply the peg you'll need to place over your nose before entering the communal toilets.

Getting There & Away

The dirt track from Maralal to Baragoi is very rocky in places, but inifinitely better than it was in 2012. Even so, if there has been any rain it becomes treacherous. The drive takes a minimum of three hours.There are now daily buses to Maralal (KSh500), but heading north you're reliant on infrequent trucks. The Star Station Filling sells pricey petrol.

South Horr

South Horr, surrounded by flowering trees, is the next village north of Baragoi and sits in an acacia-lined valley beneath the towering peaks of **Ol Donyo Nyiro** (2752m) and **Ol Donyo Mara** (2066m). Despite the delightful craggy scenery, your eyes will rarely look up from the enchanting Samburu herders who gather in the wavering trees' shadows.

This is fantastic walking country; easy hikes are possible on the valley's forested lower slopes, while more motivated souls can try to bag Ol Donyo Nyiro's peak. In either case take a guide (around KSh1000 per day) because these woodlands are haunted by all manner of large, toothy creatures who'd love a passing hiker for lunch.

Sleeping & Eating

There are several camping 'sites' around the village, all of which consist of nothing but a patch of ground with the odd tap. All charge between KSh300 and KSh500 per person. There's also a jolly nice sign for the Lesamurei Top Hill View Lodge at the southern entrance to the village. However, it's only a sign. There are a couple of basic snack joints.

★ **Samburu Sports Centre Guesthouse** BANDA $
(0720334561; stockwellee@yahoo.com; per person tents KSh500, huts KSh1000, bandas KSh1500; wi-fi) If we told you there was a place to stay in South Horr with plush *banda*-style accommodation complete with art on the walls, twisted-branch bookcases and wardrobes, great traditional food, a basketball court and (occasionally working) wi-fi, you wouldn't believe us, would you? Well, prepare to be surprised!

Getting There & Away

The road between Baragoi and South Horr is in reasonable shape (for northern Kenya). There's no scheduled public transport in or out of South Horr, but there are worse places to be stuck.

North to Lake Turkana

Travelling north from South Horr, the scrub desert suddenly scatters and you're greeted by vast volcanic armies of shimmering bowling-ball-sized boulders, cinder cones and reddish-purple hues. If this arresting and barren Martian landscape doesn't take your breath away, the first sight of the sparkling Jade Sea a few kilometres north certainly will.

As you descend to the lake, South Island stands proudly before you, while Teleki Volcano's geometrically perfect cone lurks on Turkana's southern shore. Since you've probably pulled over for the moment, looking for your swimming kit, we thought we'd warn

LAKE TURKANA FACTS

- Lake Turkana, the world's largest permanent desert lake, has a shoreline that's longer than Kenya's entire Indian Ocean coast.
- The lake's water level was over 100m higher some 10,000 years ago and used to feed the mighty Nile. If the Gibe 3 Dam in Ethiopia is completed, the lake's waters may drop a further 10m.
- The first Europeans to reach the lake were Austrian explorers Teleki and von Höhnel in 1888. They proudly named it Lake Rudolf, after the Austrian Crown Prince at the time. It wasn't until the 1970s that the Kiswahili name Turkana was adopted.

OFF THE BEATEN TRACK

DESERT ROSE

First thought on seeing the incredible lodge **Desert Rose** (Nairobi 020-3864831; www.desertrosekenya.com; s/d all inclusive US$735/1250;) is likely to be 'How?'. How did anyone find this location, about as far as you can get from Nairobi and yet still in Kenya? How did anyone conjure up the idea of building a lodge here? And how on earth did they manage to do it?

We don't know the answers, but we're certainly glad someone did because this lodge, which seems to have grown out of the mountainside, is probably the most architecturally impressive lodge in Kenya and certainly the remotest. Heavy hardwood and the local rock have been chipped and carved into furnishings, and many of the rooms are totally open plan with nothing but a mosquito net protecting you from the elements. A stay here isn't about classic safaris but, rather, it's about easy relaxation, great food and, most importantly, getting to know the beautiful Samburu people and going on wild fly-in adventures to the terrifyingly forbidding Sugata Valley or up to Lake Turkana.

Most guests fly in by private charter or helicopter, but the adventurous can drive in up an almost-vertical section of the mountain. All visitors must give advance notice.

you that Turkana has the world's largest crocodile population.

LAKE TURKANA'S EASTERN SHORE

Loyangalani

Standing in utter contrast to the dour desert shades surrounding it, tiny Loyangalani assaults all your senses in one crazy explosion of clashing colours, feather headdresses and blood red robes. Overlooking Lake Turkana and surrounded by small ridges of pillow lava (evidence that this area used to be underwater), the sandy streets of this one-camel town are a meeting point of the great northern tribes: Turkana and Samburu, Gabbra and El Molo. It's one of the most exotic corners of Kenya and a fitting reward after the hard journey here.

Sights & Activities

South Island National Park PARK

(adult/child US$25/15) Designated a World Heritage Site by Unesco in 1997, this 39-sq-km purplish volcanic island is completely barren and uninhabited, apart from large populations of crocodiles, venomous snakes and feral goats. Spending the night at a **special campsite** (US$35) makes for an even eerier trip.

In calm weather a speedboat can reach the island in 30 minutes and circumnavigate it in another hour. If winds crop up, trip times can easily double. As speedboats are somewhat limited in number, you will probably end up in something much more sedate: reckon on a six-hour return trip, for which you will pay about KSh20,000 at a minimum. Ask at the Kenya Wildlife Service office in town, Palm Shade Camp or Malabo Resort about hiring boats.

Mt Kulal MOUNTAIN

Mt Kulal (2293m) dominates Lake Turkana's eastern horizon and its forested volcanic flanks offer some serious hiking possibilities. This fertile lost world in the middle of the desert is home to some unique creatures, including the Mt Kulal chameleon, a beautiful lizard first recorded in only 2003.

No matter what the local guides tell you, trekking to the summit from Loyangalani in a day isn't feasible. Plan on several days for a return trip. Guides (KSh1000 per day) and donkeys (KSh500 per day) to carry your gear can be hired in Loyangalani, or you can part with considerable sums of cash (KSh30,000 to KSh40,000) for a lift up Mt Kulal to the villages of Arapal or Gatab. From there you can head for the summit and spend a long day (eight to 10 hours) hiking back down to the base of the mountain.

If you pass by Arapal, be sure to whistle a tune at the **singing wells**, where the Samburu gather water (and sing while doing so – hence the name).

Loyangalani Desert Museum MUSEUM
(adult/child KSh500/250) Standing on a bluff above the lake several kilometres north of town, this museum contains lots of photo-heavy displays, but it's seriously overpriced. Opening hours are basically whenever an interested person comes along.

El Molo Villages

The El Molo tribe, which is one of Africa's smallest, lives on the lake shore just north of Loyangalani in the villages of **Layeni** and **Komote**. Although outwardly similar to the Turkana, the El Molo are linguistically linked to the Somali and Rendille people. Unfortunately, the last speaker of their traditional language died before the turn of the millennium. Visiting their villages (KSh1000 per person, negotiable) is something of a circus and don't expect to see many people traditionally dressed.

Sleeping & Eating

Let's face it, you came north for adventure, not comfort. If you're camping, remember to tie down your tent as early evening winds pick up tremendously – it can be blowing at 60km/h by 8pm.

Malabo Resort BANDA $
(0724705800; resortmalabo@yahoo.com; camping KSh2000, huts from KSh2000, bandas KSh3000-4000; P) The newest, and best, place to stay in Loyangalani is a few hundred metres north of the village and has slight lake views. There's a range of decent *bandas* with arty wooden beds and attached bathrooms, or there are thatched huts based on a traditional Turkana design. The bar-restaurant area is a good place to hang out.

BLACK GOLD

Northern Kenya has long been ignored by Kenya's rulers. However, black gold, a new nation and Turkana's relentless winds may soon change life in these parts forever – perhaps...

When South Sudan became the world's newest nation in July 2011, it faced a problem. It had oil and natural gas, but no reliable way of getting it out of the country since all the oil pipelines headed north to the Red Sea through its former partner, Sudan. Relations between Juba and Khartoum were so tense that access couldn't be guaranteed, so the plan was to build a new set of pipelines from South Sudan to Lamu, on the Kenyan coast. Riding on the back of this pipeline would be a major new port and oil refinery in Lamu, surfaced two-lane highways linking all the main towns of the north, and new airports and tourist resorts in Lamu, Isiolo and on the shores of Lake Turkana. The plan even included a new rail system that would stretch from Lamu to South Sudan, with another line to Ethiopia, along which dozens of daily trains would hurtle at up to 160km/h. It was certainly an ambitious project – so ambitious, some would say, that it was nothing but a white elephant.

As if to prove the sceptics right, in October 2011 it was announced by the European Coalition on Oil in Sudan that the pipeline project was unviable due to insufficient oil-reserve estimates in South Sudan and general insecurity. As it happened, insuffcient oil was to prove to be the least of South Sudan's, and the project's, problems. When a political dispute in Juba turned into a general implosion of the new country in 2013, Kenya's ambitious plans suddenly started to seem less likely...except that, almost bang on cue, oil was also discovered in Kenya's Lake Turkana region. It will also need pumping down to the coast.

Oil isn't northern Kenya's only energy generator. It has wind. Lots of it – and that may result in Africa's biggest wind farm. The Dutch consortium behind the proposed Lake Turkana Wind Power project aims to build 365 giant wind turbines on the southeast corner of Lake Turkana, which will generate 300MW, or a quarter of Kenya's current installed power. Although less ambitious than the other projects, the wind farm plan came to a grinding halt in 2010 for financial reasons. By early 2014 though, all the financial papers had been signed, work had started and the project is expected to be completed by 2016.

Meanwhile, over the border in Ethiopia, a massive dam project, Gibe 3, is underway on the Omo River. Opponents say it could lower Turkana's waters by up to 10m when completed.

Steve, the owner, can hep with organising boats, jeeps and general onward transport.

Palm Shade Camp BANDA $
(☎0726714768; camping KSh500, s/tw bandas KSh1000/1500 with shared bathroom, r KSh3000; P) Drop your tent on the grass beneath acacias and doum palms, lie back in one of the clean, tiled, newly constructed rooms, or crash in the tidy domed huts with their unique meshed cut-out walls that let in light and heavenly evening breezes. The manager is an endless source of information on travel in the area.

Cold Drink Hotel KENYAN $
(meals KSh100-150; ⏲7am-8pm) Not just cold drinks but also, according to locals, the finest eating experience in all of Turkana country, which sadly might actually be true.

Information

Other than the post office and the Catholic mission, which occasionally sells petrol out of the barrel at exorbitant prices, there's nothing in the way of services or banking.

Located towards the lake and tiny 'port', the KWS office doesn't recieve many tourists but it will try to help with information on local sights and activities and can arrange a boat for trips to South Island.

Getting There & Away

Trucks loaded with fish (and soon-to-be-smelly passengers) leave Loyangalani for Maralal (around KSh1000, nine to 12 hours) once or twice a week at best. Trucks heading in any other direction are even rarer and locals talk of waits of between a week and a month for transport to North Horr (around KSh1000) or Marsabit. When trucks do travel to Marsabit, they tend to take the slightly easier southern route via Kargi and charge a flexible KSh1000. It's better to travel from Loyagalani to North Horr rather than the other way around because with buses every other day from North Horr to Marsabit you won't get stuck for more than a night – going from North Horr to Loyagalani could mean waiting in North Horr for a week or more. This would be bad.

If you're travelling in your own vehicle, you have two options to reach Marsabit: continue northeast from Loyangalani across the dark stones of the Chalbi Desert towards North Horr, or head 67km south towards South Horr and take the eastern turn-off via Kargi.

The 270km Chalbi route (10 to 12 hours) is hard in the dry season and impossible after rain. It's also wise to ask for directions every chance you get, otherwise it's easy to take the wrong track and not realise until hours later. This would also be bad. The 241km southern route (six to seven hours) via the Karoli Desert and Kargi is composed of compacted sands and is marginally less difficult in the rainy season.

DON'T MISS

LAKE TURKANA FESTIVAL

Held in mid-June, the Lake Turkana Festival is a jamboree of all that's colourful in the tribes of northern Kenya. Originally organised by the German embassy, it was taken over by the Kenyan government in 2014 and word is that it was far less organised than in previous years. Even so, if you want to see people in their tribal best, there's no better time to be in the area.

North Horr

On the map, North Horr stands out like a beacon from all that surrounding desert, but once you finally drag your weary and battered self onto its sand-washed streets, the reality of this drab town is a little disappointing. Don't miss the water source on the edge of town, where hundreds of camels, goats and weathered nomadic faces come each day. Taking photos is not appreciated.

The half-dozen very basic huts of the **Gallasa Diqa Womens Group Lodge** (huts KSh200) are at the western end of town. Luxury it's not; authentic it is.

As well as occasional trucks and 4WDs, **Chalbi Buses** (☎0705095511) now operates buses (that look like tanks) every second day between North Horr and Marsabit (KSh800) via Kalacha (KSh400), but only very rarely does anything venture onward to Loyangalani. There is no set price for the Loyangalani leg, but expect to pay around KSh1000.

Don't be at all surprised if you get stuck here for anything between a couple of days and a couple of weeks. Even in the dry season the 'roads' are often impassable and after rain it's completely out of the question. Whichever way you're heading, it's a road to adventure – blasting over the plains of darkness, destined for a sea of jade, is nothing short of magical.

DON'T MISS

SIBILOI NATIONAL PARK

A Unesco World Heritage Site, and probably Kenya's most remote national park, **Sibiloi National Park** (www.sibiloi.com; adult/child US$25/15) is located up the eastern shore of Lake Turkana and covers 1570 sq km. It was here that Dr Richard Leakey discovered the skull of a *Homo habilis* believed to be 2.5 million years old, and where others have unearthed evidence of *Homo erectus*. Despite the area's fascinating prehistory, fossil sites and wonderful arid ecosystem, the difficulties involved in getting this far north tend to discourage visitors, which is a real shame. It seems slightly ironic that the so-called 'Cradle of Mankind' is now almost entirely unpopulated.

The **National Museums of Kenya** (NMK; www.museums.or.ke) maintains a small museum and **Koobi Fora** (www.kfrp.com) has a research base. It's usually possible to sleep in one of the base's *bandas* (thatched hut; per person KSh1000) or pitch a tent in one of the campsites (per person KSh500).

Contact both the staff of the Loyangalani Desert Museum (p289), Kenya Wildlife Service (KWS; kws@kws.org) and NMK before venturing in this direction.

In the dry season it's a tricky seven-hour drive north from Loyangalani to Sibiloi. You will need a guide from either KWS or the Loyangalani Desert Museum. Hiring a 4WD in Loyangalani will work out at around KSh40,000 per day. It's also possible to hire a boat (KSh30,000 to KSh40,000 return, with an overnight stop) from Fergusons Gulf on the western side of the lake.

Kalacha

Coming from Marsabit, the road winds down off the mountains and sinks into a mass of black lava rocks. Slowly the land becomes ever more barren until finally you hit the blank expanse of the Chalbi Desert, which is featureless, sandy and blisteringly hot. It's a spectacular ride through a clutter-free world, where the only signs of life are occasional camels heading to the wells in the bustling village of **Maikona**. Don't drive this route without a heavy-duty 4WD and an experienced local guide.

Huddled around a permanent oasis in the middle of the Chalbi Desert, the acacia- and doum-palm-pocked village of Kalacha is home to the fascinating Gabbra people. There's little to see and do, but the sense of isolation is magnificent and the sight of camels, released from their night corrals and kicking up the dust on the way to the grazing grounds, will remain with you forever. Don't miss the cartoonlike biblical murals in the church, a prelude for those travellers heading north to Ethiopia. Some **rock paintings** and **carvings** can be found in a canyon near the **Afgaba** waterhole, not far from Kalacha – take a guide.

Chalbi Safari Resort Kalacha (campsites KSh400, tw huts per person KSh1000; Ⓟ), managed by the friendly Abdul, is an excellent choice, with several immaculate huts and a sun-battered camping area. With notice it will prepare meals. There's at least one other similar place in the village.

Buses stop at Kalacha every other day on their way between North Horr (KSh400) and Marsabit (KSh400).

MARICH TO TURKANA'S WESTERN SHORE

Despite boasting some of northern Kenya's greatest attributes, such as copious kilometres of Jade Sea shoreline, striking volcanic landscapes, ample wildlife and vivid Turkana tribes, this remote corner of the country has seen relatively few visitors. With fairly reliable public transport, this is definitely the easier side of the lake on which to grab a taste of the northern badlands.

Marich to Lodwar

The spectacular descent from Marich Pass, north of Kitale, through the lush, cultivated Cherangani Hills leads to arid surroundings, with sisal plants, cactus trees and acacias lining both the road and the chocolate brown Morun River. Just north, the minuscule village of Marich marks

DON'T MISS

CENTRAL ISLAND NATIONAL PARK

Bursting from the depths of Lake Turkana, and home to thousands of living dinosaurs, is the Jurassic world of Central Island Volcano, last seen belching molten sulphur and steam just over three decades ago. It's one of the most otherworldly places in Kenya. Quiet today, its stormy volcanic history is told by the numerous craters scarring its weathered facade. Several craters have coalesced to form two sizeable lakes, one of which is home to thousands of fish that occur nowhere else.

Both a **national park** (adult/child US$20/10) and Unesco World Heritage Site, Central Island is an intriguing place to visit. Budding *Crocodile Dundee* types will love the 14,000-or-so Nile crocodiles, some of which are massive, that flock here at certain times of year (May is the most crocodile-friendly month, but there are some crocs here year-round). The most northerly crater lake, which is saline, attracts blushing pink flocks of flamingos.

Camping (US$35) is possible and, unlike South Island National Park, there are trees to which you can tie your tent. But there's no water or any other facilities, so come prepared.

Hiring a boat from Ferguson's Gulf is the only option to get here. Organising one through Kenya Wildlife Service (which is comically disorganised) will set you back a hefty KSh18,000. Organising one through the locals down by the boat landing strip is likely to start at KSh15,000 and drop to KSh10,000. Don't ever think about being cheap and taking a sailboat. The 10km trip and the sudden squalls that terrorise the lake's waters aren't to be taken lightly.

your entrance into northern Kenya. Welcome to adventure!

Sights & Activities

The Marich Pass Field Studies Centre offers English-speaking Pokot and Turkana guides for half-day (KSh550), full-day (KSh750) and overnight (KSh1000) treks.

Mt Sekerr TREKKING

Although the northern plains may beckon, it's worth heading into the hills for some eye-popping and leg-loving hiking action. Mt Sekerr (3326m) is a few kilometres northwest of Marich and can be climbed comfortably in a three-day round trip via the agricultural plots of the Pokot tribe, passing through forest and open moors.

Cherangani Hills TREKKING

The Cherangani Hills, the green and lush chalk next to the northern desert's baked cheese, sit immediately south of town and are also ripe with superb trekking options. In fact, many people consider these intensely farmed and deeply forested hills to be one of the most beautiful corners of the country.

Mt Koh TREKKING

Reaching the dome of Mt Koh (3211m), which soars some 1500m above the adjacent plains, is a hard but rewarding two-day slog. A more horizontally endowed (13km one way) and vertically challenged (only 300m elevation gain) trek is possible up the **Weiwei Valley** from Sigor to Tamkal.

Sleeping & Eating

Marich Pass Field Studies Centre CAMPGROUND, BANDA $

(www.gg.rhul.ac.uk/MarichPass; camping KSh360, dm KSh420, s/tw KSh1450/1950, with shared bathroom KSh900/1240) Just north of Marich village, this is essentially a residential facility for visiting student groups, but it also makes a great base for independent travellers. The centre occupies a beautiful site alongside the misty Morun River and is surrounded by dense bush and woodland. Facilities include a secure camping ground as well as a tatty dorm and simple, comfortable *bandas*.

Getting There & Away

The road from Kitale via Makutano is the scenic A1 Hwy, which is often described as 'Kenya's most spectacular tarmac road'. The buses plying the A1 between Kitale and Lodwar can drop you anywhere along the route, whether at Marich or the field studies centre.

You may be asked to pay the full fare to Lodwar (KSh1500), but a smile and some patient negotiating should reduce the cost.

Between Marich and Lokichar the A1 is a bumpy mess of corrugated dirt and lonely islands of tarmac. The first 40km north of Lokichar are better, but you'll still spend more time on the shoulder than on the road. The opposite is true for the remaining 60km to Lodwar, where patches outnumber potholes and driving is straightforward.

The security situation is in a constant state of flux in this area. At the time of writing convoys weren't required, but in the recent past there have been numerous incidents of cattle rustling as well as tribal clashes. These problems have been most prevalent in the area between Marich and Lokichar.

Lodwar

Besides Lokichoggio near the South Sudan border, Lodwar is the only town of any size in the northwest. Barren volcanic hills skirted by traditional Turkana dwellings sit north of town and make for impressive sunrise vistas. Lodwar has outgrown its days as just an isolated administrative outpost of the Northern Frontier District and has now become the major service centre for the region. If you're visiting Lake Turkana, you'll find it convenient to stay here for at least one night.

Sleeping

Nawoitorong Guest House HOTEL $

(0704911947; camping KSh300, s/tw with shared bathroom KSh800/1500, cottages KSh1400-2000; P) Built entirely out of local materials and run by a local women's group, Nawoitorong is a solid budget option and the only one for campers. Thatched roofs alleviate the need for fans and all rooms have mosquito nets.

Lodwar Lodge HOTEL $

(0728007512; r KSh800-1400; P) Slightly tatty concrete cottages that are quiet and secure. Though worn, it's much less so than other town-centre options.

Ceamo Prestige Lodge HOTEL $$

(0721555565; www.ceamolodge.com; s/d KSh6500/7500; P) A short way out of town, this new place is also Lodwar's flashest place to stay, with large, cool, quiet, tiled rooms in a bungalow setting. It might be Lodwar's finest but it's still very overpriced.

Eating

Nawoitorong Guest House KENYAN $

(meals KSh250-350; 7am-8pm) Burgers and toasted sandwiches join local curries and various meaty fries on the menu. It offers the most pleasant dining experience in the region, but give it time – lots of it – to prepare dinner!

Salama Hotel KENYAN $

(meals KSh80-150; 6am-9pm) The most popular place in the town centre. The culinary highlight of the Salama has to be its giant bowl of pilau (KSh100). There's always a crowd of people here waiting for buses to depart.

Information

There are several internet cafes – okay, internet shacks – around town.

Kenya Commercial Bank With ATM. Changes cash and travellers cheques.

Getting There & Away

Fly540 (p385) runs frequent flights from Nairobi to Lodwar, and from Eldoret, for around US$150.

Happy Safaris Buses operate along the route to Kitale (KSh1000, 8½ hours, 6am), with departures from close to Salama Hotel. Erratic matatus serve Kalokol (KSh500, one hour). There's also a matatu to Eliye Springs (KSh300, 1½ hours).

Eliye Springs

Spring water percolates out of crumbling bluffs, and oodles of palms bring a taste of the tropics to the remote sandy shores of Lake Turkana. Down on the slippery shore, children play in the lake's warm waters, while Central Island lurks magically on the distant horizon. Eliye Springs is the best place to get a taste of the lake's western shore.

Sleeping & Eating

Eliye Springs Resort RESORT $$

(0703891810; www.eliyespringsresort.com; camping per person US$10, resort tent per person US$20, huts/r US$25/60, cottage full board US$195; P) For many years all that stood on the shores of Eliye Springs was the shell of an abandoned lodge, but it's been brought back to life by a German with a passion for Turkana. The resort has a mixture of self-contained rooms and traditional Turkana huts made of sticks. Camping is also available, as are meals.

Getting There & Away

The turn-off for Eliye Springs is signposted a short way along the Lodwar–Kalokol road. The gravel is easy to follow until it suddenly peters out and you're faced with a fork in the road – stay left. The rest of the way is a mix of gravel, deep sand and even deeper sand, which can turn into a muddy nightmare in the wet season. Over the really bad sections, locals have constructed a 'road' out of palm fronds, which means that on a good day, normal cars can even make it here (though expect to do a bit of pushing and shoving).

If you don't have your own vehicle, you can usually arrange a car and driver in Lodwar for about KSh5000, including waiting time. There are also very occasional matatus for KSh300.

Ferguson's Gulf

Ferguson's Gulf, while more accessible than Eliye Springs, has none of its southern neighbour's charm. Fishing boats in various states of disrepair litter its grubby western beach and a definite feeling of bleakness pervades.

If you're planning on visiting Central Island National Park or Sibiloi National Park, this is the best place to arrange a boat.

Few people in Lodwar have heard of Ferguson's Gulf, so you need to ask around for transport to nearby Kalokol, which is 75km along a good stretch of sealed road. Ferguson's Gulf is only a few kilometres from there. Matatus to Kalokol cost KSh500, or a taxi direct to Ferguson's Gulf will be around KSh4000 to KSh5000 with waiting time.

Understand Kenya

Kenya Today

At first glance, Kenya appears to be facing the future with its customary swagger. But beneath the facade of confidence that comes from being a regional African powerhouse lies a country that can feel like it's just one step away from declaring war on itself. Here, too, is a country increasingly sure of its place in the world even as it longs to tell the rest of the world to mind its own business.

Best in Print

Out of Africa (Karen Blixen, aka Isak Dinesen; 1937) The definitive account of colonial Kenya.

A Primate's Memoir (Robert M Sapolsky; 2002) Funny, poignant account by a young primatologist in Kenya.

No Man's Land (George Monbiot; 1994) The modern struggle of the region's nomadic tribes.

The Flame Trees of Thika (Elspeth Huxley; 1959) A marvellously told colonial memoir.

Petals of Blood (Ngũgĩ wa Thiong'o; 1977) The story of four Kenyans struggling to come to terms with their newly independent country.

The Worlds of a Maasai Warrior: An Autobiography (Tepilit Ole Saitoti; 1988) Extraordinary insight into the Maasai world.

Best on Film

The Great Rift (2010) BBC documentary about the Rift Valley.

Echo of the Elephants (1993) Elephants of Amboseli National Park.

Enough is Enough (2004) Critically acclaimed portrayal of the Mau Mau uprising.

Born Free (1966) Lions of legend return to the wild.

Out of Africa (1985) Caused a generation to dream of Africa.

The Constant Gardener (2005) Gripping Hollywood story set in Kenya.

A Robust Democracy

It may seem a strange question to ask of a country that has proved to be one of Africa's most stable, but one of the hottest topics of conversation among ordinary Kenyans is this: can Kenya hold together? Kenyans were badly scarred by the post-2007 election violence, a conflict that pitted members of one ethnic group against another in an outbreak of score-settling and bloody pogroms. An estimated 1300 people died in the violence and some 600,000 Kenyans were forced to flee their homes. For a time, it looked as if the country might disintegrate, or even go the way of Rwanda circa 1994. The country pulled back from the brink.

Thus it was that when Uhuru Kenyatta scraped over the line in the 2013 presidential elections amid allegations of electoral irregularities, the country and the world held their breaths. This time – and again a year later amid rising political tensions between the government and the opposition – a fragile peace prevailed. But somehow, a threshold was passed and the country held together – again. Had Kenya's political leaders grown in maturity sufficiently to recognise the dangers of escalating tensions? Or did they decide to bide their time for some future battle? At the time of writing, the question remains unanswered.

ICC & the International Conspiracy

Kenyans love a good conspiracy theory, particularly when it concerns Western relations with African countries. And given Kenya's experience of colonial interference and exploitation, who could blame them?

In March 2011, the International Criminal Court (ICC) indicted six prominent Kenyans, including presidential candidate Uhuru Kenyatta and former government minister William Ruto, for crimes against humanity allegedly committed during the violence that followed the disputed 2007 elections.

Kenyan politicians soon began lining up to accuse the ICC and the Western governments who supported it of colonial attitudes and for interfering in Kenya's internal affairs. So successful was this argument that the ICC indictment of Kenyatta, who positioned himself as the champion of Africa's independence from external meddling, is widely credited with boosting his popularity and helping him to win the 2013 presidential election. In one of the more bizarre twists, Kenyatta's co-accused and former enemy at the 2007 elections, William Ruto, became Kenya's vice-president.

The story didn't end there. In early 2014, two of the largest British tour operators to Kenya, Thomas Cook and First Choice, suddenly evacuated all of their clients from the Kenyan coast, citing British government warnings of terrorist attacks. To the outside world, it seemed like prudence. To Kenyans, the whole thing stank of revenge. What a coincidence, many said, that the British government should cause such a devastating blow to Kenya's fragile tourism industry in the same week that the Kenyan government had signed a major trade deal with China...

Kenya at War

In October 2011, for the first time in its independent history, Kenya went to war. The spark for such a drastic move was a series of cross-border raids allegedly carried out by al-Shabaab, an al-Qaeda-affiliated Somali group who stood accused of kidnapping foreign-aid workers and tourists from inside Kenya. Aware that its lucrative tourism industry could be at risk, Kenya's military launched a large-scale invasion of Somalia, claiming that it was acting in self-defence; most Western governments agreed, and the mission later came under the banner of the African Union.

Kenya has played a high price for its involvement in Somalia. The attack by al-Shabaab operatives on the Westgate Shopping Mall in Nairobi on 21 September 2013 left 67 people dead and placed enormous strain on Kenya's relations with its large Somali population. Further attacks in the Nairobi suburb of Eastleigh in 2013, and on the area around Mpeketoni (close to Lamu) in June 2014 only heightened the sense of a nation under siege and unsure how to combat the threat. Quite apart from its impact upon Kenya's tourist industry, the episode served as a reminder that Kenya's future as a multicultural, multifaith state gets more complicated with each passing year.

POPULATION: **45 MILLION**

AREA: **580,367 SQ KM**

LIFE EXPECTANCY AT BIRTH: **63.52 YEARS**

URBAN POPULATION AS % OF TOTAL: **24%**

UNEMPLOYMENT: **40%**

GDP GROWTH: **5.1%**

AVERAGE AGE: **19.1**

if Kenya were 100 people

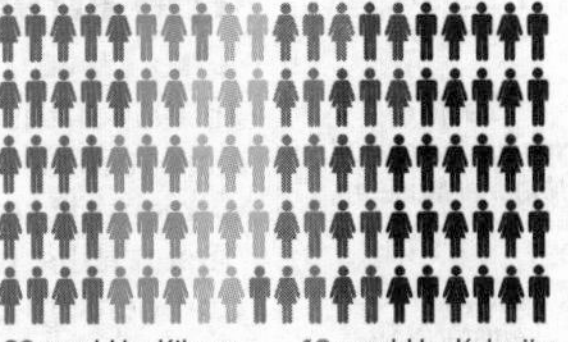

22 would be Kikuyu
14 would be Luhya
13 would be Luo
12 would be Kalenjin
11 would be Akamba
28 would be other

belief systems

(% of population)

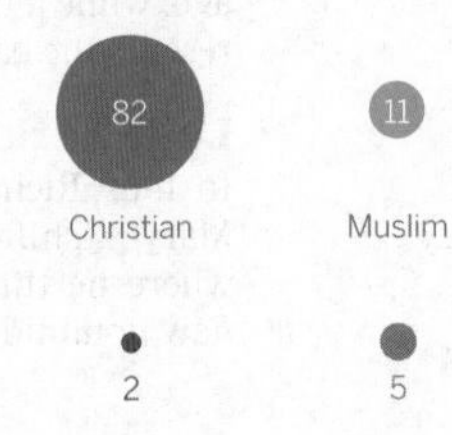

population per sq km

KENYA UK US

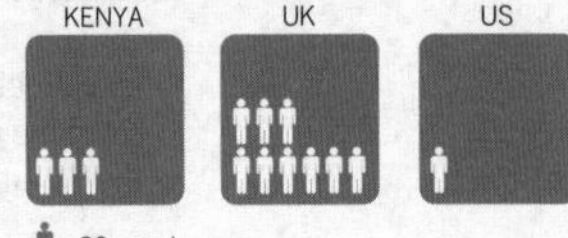

≈ 30 people

History

Africa's Great Rift Valley is where human beings first walked upright upon the earth. Ever since, Kenya's story has unfolded as a fascinating tale of ancient connections across the seas, the ravages of slavery and a colonial occupation that continues to mark the country to this day. Now independent with a chance to chart its own course, Kenya has become an East African powerhouse whose stunning diversity has proved to be both curse and blessing in equal measure.

Prehistoric Sites

- *Cradle of Humankind exhibit, National Museum, Nairobi*
- *Olorgasailie Prehistoric Site, Southern Rift Valley*
- *Hyrax Hill Prehistoric Site, Southern Rift Valley*
- *Kariandusi, Southern Rift Valley*

The First Kenyans

The Tugen Hills

In 1959 British paleoanthropologist Mary Leakey discovered the earliest recorded hominid fossil at Olduvai Gorge in Tanzania, causing a scientific sensation. Following this, palaeontologists digging in the Tugen Hills, west of Lake Baringo, unearthed one of the most diverse and densely packed accumulations of fossil bone in Africa. Bedded down in lava flows and representing a unique archaeological record in Africa, the fossil beds incorporate that most elusive period of human history between 14 and four million years ago when the largely primate *Kenyapithecus* evolved into our earliest bipedal ancestor *Australopithecus afarensis*.

In the sandy clay, seven of the 18 hominoid specimens known from that period were found. The jaw fragment at five million years old represents the closest ancestor of *A afarensis*, a family band that left their footprints on the Laetoli mud pan (Tanzania) 3.7 million years ago, while a fragment of skull, dating from 2.4 million years ago, represents the earliest-known specimen of our own genus, *Homo*.

Lake Turkana

In 1969 Richard Leakey – son of veteran archaeologists Louis and Mary – shifted his attentions to Lake Turkana in Kenya's north where he turned up dozens of fossil sites, including a completely new hominid specimen – *Homo habilis* (able man).

TIMELINE

3,700,000 BC

A group of early hominids walk across the Laetoli pan, moving away from the volcano. Their footsteps take them to the grasslands of the Serengeti plains.

1,760,000 BC

In 2011, archaeologists announce the discovery at Lake Turkana of a four-sided hand axe dubbed by scientists the 'Swiss army knife' of the Stone Age.

1,600,000 BC

In 1984, Kamoya Kimeu discovers the Turkana Boy, a nearly complete skeleton of an 11- or 12-year-old hominid boy who died 1.6 million years ago near Lake Turkana.

Prior to the Leakey discovery it was thought that there were only two species of proto-humans: the 'robust' hominids and the 'gracile' hominids, which eventually gave rise to modern humans. However, the Turkana finds demonstrated that the different species lived at the same time and even shared resources – advancing the Leakey theory that evolution was more complex than a simple linear progression.

In 1984, Kamoya Kimeu (a member of the Leakey expedition) uncovered the spectacular remains of a young boy's skeleton dating back 1.6 million years. Standing at a height of 1.6m tall, the boy was appreciably bigger than his *H habilis* contemporary. His longer limbs and striding gait were also more characteristic of modern human physiology, and his larger brain suggested greater cognitive ability. *H erectus* was the biggest and brainiest hominid to date and was the longest surviving and most widely dispersed of all the ancestral toolmakers, disappearing from the fossil records a mere 70,000 years ago.

From these remarkable evolutionary leaps it was but a small step to our closest ancestors, *H sapiens,* who made an appearance around 130,000 years ago.

FOSSILS

For more on Kenya's fossil finds look up www.leakey foundation.org. Members can even sign up for trips with the Leakeys themselves.

Kenya's Ancestors

Ten thousand years ago, Africa was unrecognisable: the Sahara was a green and pleasant land, and much of Kenya was uninhabitable because its tropical forests and swamps were inhabited by the deadly tsetse fly, which is fatal to cattle and people. During the five millennia that followed, a changing climate saw the tsetse belt drop south, Kenya's grasslands began to spread and migrating peoples from the north began to populate what we now know as Kenya. Soon, the peoples of the continent began to converge on East Africa.

The first arrivals were a Cushitic-speaking population, who moved south with their domestic stock from Ethiopia. At the same time a population of Nilote-speakers from the Sudan moved into the western highlands of the Rift Valley (the Maasai, Luo, Samburu and Turkana tribes are their modern-day descendants). These pastoralists shared the region with the indigenous Khoikhoi (ancestors of the modern-day San), who had occupied the land for thousands of years.

Africa's fourth linguistic family, the Bantu-speakers, arrived from the Niger Delta around 1000 BC. Soon they became East Africa's largest ethnolinguistic family, which they remain today. Kenya's largest tribe, the Kikuyu, along with the Gusii, Akamba and Meru tribes, are all descended from them.

The word *swahili* originates from the Arabic word *sawahil,* which means 'of the coast'. It refers both to the Swahili language (most accurately called KiSwahili), as well as the Islamic people of the coast.

100,000 BC

Homo sapiens strike out to colonise the world, moving into the eastern Mediterranean. 40,000 years ago they reach Asia and Australia and 10,000 years later are settled across Europe.

2000–1000 BC

Immigrant groups colonise sub-Saharan Africa. First Cushites from Ethiopia move into central Kenya, followed by Nilote-speakers from Sudan. Finally, they're joined by Bantu-speakers from Nigeria and Cameroon.

400 BC

Azania (as the East African coast was then called) is known to the peoples of the Mediterranean and becomes an important trading post for the Greeks.

AD 200–300

With the introduction of the camel, trans-Saharan journeys become practicable and profitable. The news of large gold deposits undoubtedly spur Arab ambitions and interests in the continent.

Arabs, Swahili & Portuguese

The Land of Zanj

It was in the 8th century that Arab dhows began docking regularly in East African ports as part of their annual trade migration. In their wake, Arabs set up trading posts along the seaboard, intermarrying with Africans and creating a cosmopolitan culture that, in time, became known as Swahili. Before long there were Arab-Swahili city states all along the coast from Somalia to Mozambique; the remains of many of these settlements can still be seen, most notably at Gede.

By the 10th century the 'Land of Zanj' (the present-day coastal region of Kenya and Tanzania) was exporting leopard skins, tortoiseshell, rhino horns, ivory and, most importantly, slaves and gold to Arabia and India. Ports included Shanga, Gede, Lamu and Mombasa as well as Zanzibar (Tanzania). Kilwa, 300km south of Zanzibar, marked the southernmost limit of travel for Arab dhows. For more than 700 years, up to 1450, the Islamic world was virtually the only external influence on sub-Saharan Africa.

Portuguese East Africa

Arab-Swahili domination on the coast received its first serious challenge with the arrival of the Portuguese in the 15th century, spurred by the tales of gold and riches that traders brought back from their travels. In 1497, for example, while on his pioneering voyage along

EAST AFRICAN SLAVES

Slaves left Africa via the Sahara, the Red Sea, the Atlantic and the East African coast. The total estimated number of slaves exported from tropical Africa between 1500 and the late 1800s is put at 18 million; two million of them came from East Africa. By its height in the 18th century, the slave trade had touched every region on the continent.

In East Africa, around 50,000 slaves passed through the markets every year – nearly 44% of the total population of the coast. Overall, close to 600,000 slaves were sold through the Zanzibar market between 1830 and 1873, when a treaty with Britain paved the way for the end of the trade. It's true that slavery was already an established fact of African life before the advent of the slave trade.

But enslavement for sale, the importation of foreign goods and the sheer scale of Europe's involvement were radical departures from everything that had gone before. The social, psychological and economic impact changed the fate of the continent forever.

AD 800

Muslims from Arabia and Persia begin to dock in East African ports. Soon they establish Arab-Swahili states and trading depots along the coast from Somalia to Mozambique.

10th century

The 'Land of Zanj' along East Africa's coast becomes known for its exotic export goods, including leopard skins, tortoiseshell, rhino horns, ivory, slaves and gold, predominantly to Arabia and India.

1415

Chinese fleets visit East Africa in the early 15th century. In 1415 a giraffe is transported to Beijing and presented by Malindi envoys to the emperor himself.

1492–1505

Dom Francisco de Almeida's armada begins the Portuguese conquest of Kenya. Mombasa falls in 1505, followed by towns including Barawa (Somalia), Kilwa, Moçambique and Sofala, up and down the coast.

the coastline of South and East Africa, Vasco da Gama found Arab dhows at the Zambezi delta loaded with gold dust. During the same period Europe was desperately short of labour as it struggled to recover from the effects of the Black Death (1347–51). The plantations of southern Europe were initially worked by captive Muslims and Slavic peoples (hence the word 'slaves'), but with access to Africa a whole new labour market opened up.

The Portuguese consolidated their position on the East African coast through blatant force and terror, justifying their actions as battles in a Christian war against Islam. They sailed their heavily armed vessels into the harbours of important Swahili towns, demanding submission to the rule of Portugal and payment of large annual tributes. Towns that refused were attacked, their possessions seized and resisters killed. Zanzibar was the first Swahili town to be taken in this manner (in 1503). Malindi formed an alliance with the Portuguese, which hastened the fall of Mombasa in 1505.

British East Africa

Securing Control

In 1884 European powers met in Germany for the Berlin conference. Here behind closed doors they decided the fate of the African continent. No African leaders, let alone ordinary Africans, were invited to attend, nor were they consulted.

The colonial settlement of Kenya dates from 1885, when Germany established a protectorate over the sultan of Zanzibar's coastal possessions. In 1888 Sir William Mackinnon received a royal charter and concessionary rights to develop trade in the region under the aegis of the British East Africa Company (BEAC). Seeking to consolidate its East African territories, Germany traded its coastal holdings in return for sole rights over Tanganyika (Tanzania) in 1890. Still, it was only when the BEAC ran into financial difficulties in 1895 that the British government finally stepped in to establish formal control through the East African Protectorate.

Swahili Ruins

- *Gede, north coast*
- *Jumba la Mtwana, south of Mombasa*
- *Mnarani, south of Mombasa*
- *Takwa, north coast*
- *Shanga, north coast*
- *Wasini Island, south of Mombasa*
- *Faza, north coast*

British Kenya

Initially, British influence was confined to the coastal area, and any presence in the interior was restricted to isolated settlers and explorers. Maasai resistance began to crack following a brutal civil war between the Ilmaasai and Iloikop groups and the simultaneous arrival of rinderpest (a cattle disease), cholera, smallpox and famine. The British were able to negotiate a treaty with the Maasai, allowing the

1593

The Portuguese construct the coral Fort Jesus in Mombasa. Accounts from the garrison at Mombasa record the first evidence of maize production in Africa.

1729

The Portuguese grip on East Africa ends in 1698, when Mombasa falls to Baluchi Arabs from Oman after a 33-month siege. In 1729 the Portuguese leave the Kenyan coast for good.

1807–73

Legislation abolishing the slave trade is enacted in Britain in 1807. Another 65 years pass before Sultan Barghash of Zanzibar bans the slave trade on the East African coast.

1883–84

British Explorer Joseph Thomson crosses Maasailand en route to Lake Victoria then returns to the coast, an important forerunner to Britain's colonial push inland.

THE LORD OF HAPPY VALLEY

During the colonial heyday, Happy Valley (the highland area outside Nairobi) played host to an eccentric cast of British elites with a reputation for fondness of drinking, drug abuse and wife swapping. However, few can rival Hugh Cholmondeley (1870–1931), third baron of Delamere.

Lord Delamere first set foot on the African continent in 1891 to hunt lion in then British Somaliland; he is widely credited with coining the term 'white hunter'. By the early 1900s, Lord Delamere owned more than 300,000 acres of land, and was one of Kenya's most influential colonists. For more than 20 years, he doggedly farmed his vast country estates by mere trial and error, experimenting with various crop strains from around the British Empire.

At the Norfolk Hotel, which still bears a bar-restaurant named in his honour, Lord Delamere once rode his horse through the dining room, wooing dinner guests with his ability to leap over banquet tables.

In his later years, Lord Delamere established himself as a firebrand politician determined to protect British holdings in Africa. Often described as the 'Cecil Rhodes of Kenya', he once wrote of his support for the 'extension of European civilisation', stating that the British were 'superior to heterogeneous African races only now emerging from centuries of relative barbarism'.

In 2005, charges were dropped against Lord Delamere's great-grandson, Baron Thomas Cholmondeley, who had been accused of shooting a Maasai game warden. One year later, a poacher was shot on Cholmondeley's property and in 2009 Cholmondeley was sentenced to eight months' imprisonment for manslaughter. The police spokesperson on the case was reported as saying, 'The Delameres used to be untouchable. But that's all changed now.'

British to drive the Mombasa–Uganda railway line through the heart of Maasai grazing lands.

The completion of the railway enabled the British administration to relocate from Mombasa to more temperate Nairobi. Although the Maasai suffered the worst annexations of land, being restricted to designated reserves, the Kikuyu from Mt Kenya and the Aberdares (areas of white settlement), came to nurse a particular grievance about their alienation from the land.

By 1912, settlers had established themselves in the highlands and set up mixed agricultural farms, turning a profit for the colony for the first time. These first outposts, Naivasha and the Ngong Hills, are still heavily white-settled areas today.

1884–93

A decade known by the Maasai as *enkidaaroto* ('the disaster') as drought, a rinderpest epidemic and civil war severely weaken the Maasai resistance to Britain's colonial advance.

1884–85

The Berlin Conference convenes and Africa is divided into colonial territories. Today the continent is divided into 54 states; more than four times the number in South America.

1888

Sir William Mackinnon establishes the British East Africa Company (BEAC) in Mombasa. Its focus is the exportation of goods and agriculture and the construction of the East African Railway.

1895

After experiencing serious financial difficulties, BEAC hands over to the British government, which becomes responsible for Kenya through the East African Protectorate.

The colonial process was interrupted by WWI, when two-thirds of the 3000 white settlers in Kenya formed impromptu cavalry units and marched against Germans in neighbouring Tanganyika (see p199 for more information). Colonisation resumed after the war, under a scheme by which white veterans of the European campaign were offered subsidised land in the highlands around Nairobi. The net effect was a huge upsurge in the white Kenyan population, from 9000 in 1920 to 80,000 in the 1950s.

The Road to Independence

Nationalist Stirrings

Although largely peaceful and a period of economic growth, the inter-war years were to see the fomenting of early nationalist aspirations. Grievances over land appropriation and displacement were only exacerbated in 1920, when, after considerable lobbying from white settlers, Kenya was transformed into a Crown Colony. A Legislative Council was established but Africans were barred from political participation (right up until 1944). In reaction to their exclusion, the Kikuyu tribe, Kenya's most populous group and who were under the greatest pressure from European settlers, founded the Young Kikuyu Association, led by Harry Thuku. This was to become the Kenya African Union (KAU), a nationalist organisation demanding access to white-owned land.

One passionate advocate for the movement was a young man called Johnstone Kamau, later known as Jomo Kenyatta. When this early activism fell on deaf ears he joined the more outspoken Kikuyu Central Association; the association was promptly banned.

In 1929, with money supplied by Indian communists, Kenyatta sailed for London to plead the Kikuyu case with the British colonial secretary, who declined to meet with him. While in London, Kenyatta met with a group called the League Against Imperialism, which took him to Moscow and Berlin, back to Nairobi and then back to London, where he stayed for the next 15 years. During this time, he studied revolutionary tactics in Moscow and built up the Pan-African Federation with Hastings Banda (who later became the president of Malawi) and Kwame Nkrumah (later president of Ghana).

The War Years

Although African nationalists made impressive headway, it was the advent of WWII that was to ultimately bring about the rapid

HUT TAX

In order to force the indigenous population into the labour market, the British introduced a hut tax in 1901. This could only be paid in cash, so Africans had to seek paid work.

1899

Nairobi is founded in an area of rivers, plains and swamps traditionally known by the Maasai as *uaso nairobi* (cold water). Residents had to carry guns to defend against wild animals.

1901

The East African Railway links the coast with Uganda. The construction of the line sees a huge influx of Indians, who provide the bulk of skilled labour.

1890

Waiyaki Wa Henya, a Kikuyu chief who signed a treaty with Frederick Lugard of the BEAC under pressure, burns down Lugard's Fort. Waiyaki is abducted two years later and murdered.

1914

The first shots of WWI in East Africa are fired near Taveta. Although the war on East African soil would later expand, Kenya's Taita Hills was an important battleground in the early years.

demise of colonialism in Africa. In 1941, in a desperate bid for survival, British Premier Winston Churchill crossed the Atlantic to plead for American aid. The resulting Atlantic Charter (1942), which Churchill negotiated with President Roosevelt, enshrined the end of colonialism in the third clause, which stated self-determination for all colonies as one of the postwar objectives.

In October 1945 the sixth Pan-African Congress was convened in Manchester, England. For the first time this was predominantly a congress of Africa's young leaders. Kwame Nkrumah and Jomo Kenyatta were there, along with trade unionists, lawyers, teachers and writers from all over Africa. By the time Kenyatta returned to Kenya in 1946, he was the leader of a bona fide Kenyan liberation movement.

Red Strangers: The White Tribe of Kenya (CS Nicholls) has a different, unusually sympathetic perspective on colonialism, examining the history of Kenya's white settler population before and after independence. For a more light-hearted look at the era, try *The Ghosts of Happy Valley: Searching for the Lost World of Africa's Infamous Aristocrats* by Juliet Barnes.

Mau Mau

Although Kenyatta appeared willing to act as the British government's accredited Kenyan representative within a developing constitutional framework, militant factions among the KAU had a more radical agenda. When in 1951 Ghana became the first African country to achieve independence, it raised the stakes even higher.

Starting with small-scale terror operations, bands of guerrillas began to intimidate white settlers, threaten their farms and anyone deemed to be a collaborator. Their aim: to drive white settlers from the land and reclaim it. Kenyatta's role in the Mau Mau rebellion, as it came to be known, was equivocal. At a public meeting in 1952, he denounced the movement. But he was arrested along with other Kikuyu politicians and sentenced to seven years' hard labour for 'masterminding' the plot.

Four years of intense military operations ensued. The various Mau Mau units came together under the umbrella of the Kenya Land Freedom Army, led by Dedan Kimathi, and outright guerrilla warfare followed, with the British declaring a state of emergency in 1952.

By 1956, the Mau Mau had been quelled and Dedan Kimathi was publicly hanged on the orders of Colonel Henderson (who was later deported from Kenya for crimes against humanity). But Kenyatta was to continue the struggle following his release in 1959. Soon even white Kenyans began to feel the winds of change, and in 1960 the British government officially announced its plan to transfer power to a democratically elected African government. Independence was scheduled for December 1963, accompanied by grants and loans of US$100 million to enable the Kenyan assembly to buy out European farmers in the highlands and restore the land to local tribes.

1918–39

The interwar period facilitates economic activity. Famine relief and campaigns against epidemic diseases are established in the colonies stimulating a 37.5% increase in Africa's population.

1920

Kenya is declared a Crown Colony. Africans are barred from the Legislative Council. The next year the first nationalist organisation, the Kenya African Union (KAU), is established and presses for land rights.

1929

Jomo Kenyatta sails for London, beginning 15 years of travels in his bid to drum up support for Kenyan independence. During this period, he helps build up the Pan-African Federation.

1931

Lord Delamere dies at the age of 61. He had helped to lay the foundations for Kenya's agricultural economy, but personified the deeply resented policies of the British colonial government.

It had been a long time coming, but Kenya finally became independent on 12 December 1963.

Independent Kenya

Harambee

The political handover began in earnest in 1962 with Kenyatta's election to a newly constituted parliament. To ensure a smooth transition of power, Kenyatta's party, the Kenya African National Union (KANU), which advocated a unitary, centralised government, joined forces with the Kenya African Democratic Union (KADU), which favoured *majimbo*, a federal set-up. *Harambee*, meaning 'pulling together', was seen as more important than political factionalism, and KADU voluntarily dissolved in 1964, leaving Kenyatta and KANU in full control.

It is difficult to overstate the optimism that accompanied those early days of post-colonial independence. Kenyatta took pains to allay the fears of white settlers, declaring 'I have suffered imprisonment and detention; but that is gone, and I am not going to remember it. Let us join hands and work for the benefit of Kenya'. But the nascent economy was vulnerable and the political landscape was barely developed. As a result the consolidation of power by the new ruling elite nurtured an authoritarian regime.

One-Party State

Although considered an African success story, the Kenyatta regime failed to undertake the essential task of deconstructing the colonial state in favour of a system with greater relevance to the aspirations of the average Kenyan. The *majimbo* (regionalist) system – advocated by KADU and agreed upon in the run-up to independence – was such a system, but it died with the party in 1964.

Power was not only being centralised in Nairobi, but increasingly also in the hands of the president. The consolidation of presidential power was buttressed by a series of constitutional amendments, culminating in the Constitutional Amendment Act No 16 of 1969, which empowered the president to control the civil service. The effects were disastrous. Subsequent years saw widespread discrimination in favour of Kenyatta's own tribe, the Kikuyu. The Trade Union Disputes Act made industrial action illegal and when KADU tried to reassemble as the Kenya People's Union (KPU) it was banned. Corruption soon became a problem at all levels of the power structure

WWII

Africans and Africa played a key role in WWII. The East African Carrier Corps consisted of more than 400,000 men, and the development of the atom bomb was entirely dependent on uranium from the Congo.

The first major Kenyan film to tackle the thorny subject of the Mau Mau uprising, Kibaara Kaugi's *Enough is Enough* is a fictionalised biopic of Wamuyu wa Gakuru, a Kikuyu woman who became a famed guerrilla fighter.

1930s

Thousands of European settlers occupy the Central Highlands, farming tea and coffee. The land claims of the area's million-plus members of the Kikuyu tribe are not recognised in European terms.

1942

The Atlantic Charter, signed by Winston Churchill and President Roosevelt, guarantees self-determination for the colonies as a postwar objective. The charter also gives America access to African markets.

1946

Jomo Kenyatta completes his anthropology degree and returns to Kenya as head of the KAU. The British government views him as its accredited representative in the independence handover.

1946–48

To separate the region's wildlife from Nairobi's burgeoning human population, Nairobi National Park becomes British East Africa's first national park. Amboseli National Reserve is gazetted two years later.

and the political arena contracted. Barely a decade after independence, much of the optimism had evaporated.

The Moi Years

Kenyatta was succeeded in 1978 by his vice-president, Daniel arap Moi. A Kalenjin, Moi was regarded by establishment power brokers as a suitable front man for their interests, as his tribe was relatively small and beholden to the Kikuyu.

On assumption of power, Moi sought to consolidate his regime by marginalising those who had campaigned to stop him from succeeding Kenyatta. Lacking a capital base of his own upon which he could build and maintain a patron-client network, and faced with shrinking economic opportunities, Moi resorted to the politics of exclusion. He reconfigured the financial, legal, political and administrative institutions. For instance, a constitutional amendment in 1982 made Kenya a de jure one-party state, while another in 1986 removed the security of tenure for the attorney-general, comptroller, auditor general and High Court judges, making all these positions personally beholden to the president. These developments had the effect of transforming Kenya from an 'imperial state' under Kenyatta to a 'personal state' under Moi.

NGŨGĨ WA THIONG'O

Weep Not, Child, by Kenya's most famous novelist, Ngũgĩ wa Thiong'o, tells the story of British occupation and the effects of the Mau Mau on the lives of black Kenyans. His 2010 memoir *Dreams in a Time of War* is a patiently told chronicle of his childhood in colonial Kenya.

Winds of Change

By the late 1980s, most Kenyans had had enough. Following the widely contested 1988 elections, Charles Rubia and Kenneth Matiba joined forces to call for the freedom to form alternative political parties and stated their plan to hold a political rally in Nairobi on 7 July without a licence. Though the duo was detained prior to their intended meeting, people turned out anyway, only to be met with brutal police retaliation. Twenty people were killed and police arrested a slew of politicians, human-rights activists and journalists.

The rally, known thereafter as Saba Saba ('seven seven' in Swahili), was a pivotal event in the push for a multiparty Kenya. The following year, the Forum for the Restoration of Democracy (FORD) was formed, led by Jaramogi Oginga Odinga, a powerful Luo politician and former vice-president under Jomo Kenyatta. FORD was initially banned and Odinga arrested, but the resulting outcry led to his release and, finally, a change in the constitution that allowed opposition parties to register for the first time.

Faced with a foreign debt of nearly US$9 billion and blanket suspension of foreign aid, Moi was pressured into holding multiparty

1952–56
The British declare a state of emergency during the Mau Mau rebellion. By 1956 nearly 2000 Kikuyu loyalists and 11,500 Mau Mau have been killed. Thirty-two white settlers die.

1963
Kenya gains independence; Jomo Kenyatta becomes president. In the same year the Organisation of African Unity is established, aimed at providing Africa with an independent voice in world affairs.

1966
The Kenya People's Union is formed by Jaramogi Oginga Odinga. Following unrest at a presidential visit to Nyanza Province the party is banned; Kenya becomes a de-facto one-party state.

1978
Kenyatta is succeeded by his vice-president, Daniel arap Moi, who goes on to become one of the most enduring 'Big Men' of Africa, ruling for the next 25 years.

elections in early 1992, but independent observers reported a litany of electoral inconsistencies. Just as worrying, about 2000 people were killed during ethnic clashes in the Rift Valley, widely believed to have been triggered by government agitation.

In 1992 Moi secured only 37% of the votes cast against a combined opposition tally of 63%, but he held on to power. The same results were replicated in the 1997 elections, when Moi once again secured victory with 40% of the votes cast against 60% of the opposition. After the 1997 elections, KANU was forced to bow to mounting pressure and initiate some changes: some Draconian colonial laws were repealed, as was the requirement for licences to hold political rallies.

On 7 August 1998, Islamic extremists bombed the US embassies in Nairobi and Dar es Salaam in Tanzania, killing more than 200 people and bringing al-Qaeda and Osama bin Laden to international attention for the first time. The effect on the Kenyan economy was devastating. It would take four years to rebuild the shattered tourism industry.

In 2013, the British government agreed to pay £19.9 million in costs and compensation to more than 5000 elderly Kenyans who suffered torture and abuse during the Mau Mau uprising in the 1950s.

The Kibaki Years & Beyond

Democratic Kenya

Having been beaten twice in the 1992 and 1997 elections due to disunity, 12 opposition groups united to form the National Alliance Rainbow Coalition (NARC). With Moi's presidency due to end in 2002, many feared that he would alter the constitution again to retain his position. This time, though, he announced his intention to retire.

Moi put his weight firmly behind Uhuru Kenyatta, the son of Jomo Kenyatta, as his successor, but the support garnered by NARC ensured a resounding victory for the party, with 62% of the vote. Mwai Kibaki was inaugurated as Kenya's third president on 30 December 2002.

When Kibaki assumed office in January 2003, donors were highly supportive of the new government and its pledges to end corruption. In 2003–04, donors contributed billions of dollars to the fight against corruption, including support for the office of a newly appointed anticorruption 'czar'.

Corruption Continues

Despite initial positive signs, it became clear by mid-2004 that large-scale corruption was still a considerable problem in Kenya. Western

1982

The Universities Academic Staff Union (UASU), one of the few credible opposition groups remaining, is banned. This leads to a short-lived coup by the air force.

1991

The collapse of the Soviet Union changes the face of African politics with foreign pressure on one-party states. In 1991 parliament repeals the one-party state section of the constitution.

1993

In August 1993 inflation reaches a record 100% and the government's budget deficit is over 10% of GDP. Donors suspend aid to Kenya and insist on wide-ranging economic reforms.

1998

Terrorist attacks shake US embassies in Nairobi and Dar es Salaam, killing more than 200 people. The effect on the Kenyan economy is devastating.

diplomats alleged that corruption had cost the treasury US$1 billion since Kibaki took office. In February 2005, the British high commissioner, Sir Edward Clay, denounced the 'massive looting' of state resources by senior government politicians, including sitting cabinet ministers. Within days, Kibaki's anticorruption 'czar', John Githongo, resigned and went into exile amid rumours of death threats related to his investigation of high-level politicians; he has since returned to the country at the head of an anticorruption NGO. With Githongo's release of a damning, detailed dossier in February 2006, Kibaki was forced to remove three ministers from their cabinet positions.

At the root of the difficulties in fighting corruption were the conditions that brought Kibaki to power. The slow march to democratisation in Kenya has been attributed to the personalised nature of politics, where focus is placed on individuals with ethnic support bases rather than institutions. To maximise his electoral chances, Kibaki's coalition also included a number of KANU officials who were deeply implicated in the worst abuses of the Moi regime. Indebted to such people for power, Kibaki was only ever able to effect a half-hearted reshuffle of his cabinet. He also allowed his ministers a wide margin of manoeuvre to guarantee their continued support.

But it hasn't all been bad news. The Kibaki government has succeeded in making primary and secondary education more accessible for ordinary Kenyans, while state control over the economy has been loosened.

CORRUPTION

Michela Wrong's *It's Our Turn to Eat: The Story of a Kenyan Whistle-blower* (2009) is a searing insight into Kenya's battle against corruption. Taking centre stage is John Githongo, the anti-corruption 'czar' who fled into exile after unearthing corruption at the highest level.

Things Fall Apart

On 27 December 2007, Kenya held presidential, parliamentary and local elections. While the parliamentary and local-government elections were largely considered credible, the presidential elections were marred by serious irregularities, reported by both Kenyan and international election monitors, and by independent nongovernmental observers. Nonetheless, the Electoral Commission declared Mwai Kibaki the winner, triggering a wave of violence across the country.

The Rift Valley, Western Highlands, Nyanza Province and Mombasa – areas afflicted by years of political machination, previous election violence and large-scale displacement – exploded in ugly ethnic confrontations. The violence left more than 1000 people dead and over 600,000 people homeless.

2002

Mwai Kibaki wins the 2002 election as leader of the National Alliance Rainbow Coalition (NARC). For the first time in Kenya the ballot box elects a president by popular vote.

2006

Chinese President Hu Jintao signs an oil exploration contract with Kenya; the deal allows China to prospect for oil on the borders of Sudan and Somalia and in coastal waters.

2007

Kenyans go to the polls again. The outcome is contested amid bloody clashes. International mediation finally brings about a power-sharing agreement in April 2008.

2008

Former anticorruption 'czar' John Githongo returns to Kenya. Three years later, he launches Kenya Ni Yetu (Kenya is Ours), aimed at mobilising ordinary people to speak up against corruption.

Fearing for the stability of the most stable linchpin of East Africa, former UN secretary-general Kofi Annan and a panel of 'Eminent African Persons' flew to Kenya to mediate talks. A power-sharing agreement was signed on 28 February 2008 between President Kibaki and Raila Odinga, the leader of the ODM opposition. The coalition provided for the establishment of a prime ministerial position (to be filled by Raila Odinga), as well as a division of cabinet posts according to the parties' representation in parliament.

Rebuilding Confidence

Despite some difficult moments, the fragile coalition government stood the test of time. Arguably its most important success was the progressive 2010 constitution, which was passed in a referendum by 67% of Kenya's voters. Among the key elements of this new constitution are the devolution of powers to Kenya's regions, the introduction of a bill of rights and the separation of judicial, executive and legislative powers.

In 2013, Uhuru Kenyatta won hotly contested presidential elections, claiming 50.07% of the vote and thereby avoiding the need for a run-off election against Raila Odinga. Despite widespread reports of irregularities in the conduct of the elections, the Supreme Court upheld the result and post-election violence was minimal. Even so, Kenyatta's government faces a huge challenge in uniting the country and tackling its daunting economic challenges.

Kenya: Between Hope & Despair, 1963–2011, by Daniel Branch, covers the 2007 election and its aftermath in searing detail. The encyclopaedic *Kenya: A History Since Independence*, by Charles Hornsby, is another meticulously researched study of Kenya's history post-independence.

2010

The radically overhauled constitution is approved by 67% of Kenya's voters. It provides for judicial independence, devolves powers to the regions and incorporates a bill of rights.

October 2011

Kenya's army crosses the border into Somalia in an attempt to clear the border areas of al-Shabaab militants blamed for kidnappings of tourists and aid workers in Kenya.

4 March 2013

Uhuru Kenyatta, son of independent Kenya's first president, wins presidential elections with 50.07% of the vote, thereby crossing the 50% threshold required to avoid a run-off poll.

21 September 2013

Four armed supporters of Somalia's militant al-Shabaab group attack Westgate Shopping Mall in an upmarket area of Nairobi. The siege lasts for days and ends with 67 people dead, including the attackers.

Tribes of Kenya

The tribe remains an important aspect of a Kenyan's identity: upon meeting a fellow Kenyan, the first question on anyone's mind is, 'What tribe do you come from?' Although we have divided Kenya's tribes into geographical areas, this is a guide only, as you'll find Kenyans from most tribal groupings well beyond their traditional lands. In the same way, distinctions between many tribal groups are slowly being eroded as people move to major cities for work, and intermarry.

The Kikuyu are renowned for their entrepreneurial skills and for popping up everywhere in Kenya (the Kikuyu name Kamau is as common as Smith is in Britain).

Rift Valley & Central Kenya

Kikuyu (Gikikuyu)

The Kikuyu make up 22% of the population and are Kenya's largest and most influential tribe. This tribe contributed the country's first president, Jomo Kenyatta, and its current one, his son, Uhuru Kenyatta. Famously warlike, the Kikuyu overran the lands of the Athi and Gumba tribes, becoming hugely populous in the process. Now their heartland surrounds Mt Kenya, although they also represent the largest proportion of people living in Kenya's major cities. With territory bordering that of the Maasai, the tribes share many cultural similarities due to intermarriage. The administration of the *mwaki* (clans) was originally taken care of by a council of elders, with a good deal of importance being placed on the role of the witchdoctor, the medicine man and the blacksmith. Initiation rites consist of ritual circumcision for boys and genital mutilation for girls (although the latter is slowly becoming less common). Each group of youths of the same age belongs to a *riikaan* (age-set) and passes through the various stages of life, and their associated rituals, together. Subgroups of the Kikuyu include the Embu, Ndia and Mbeere.

Kalenjin

The Kalenjin (12% of the population) comprise the Nandi, Kipsigi, Eleyo, Marakwet, Pokot and Tugen (former president Daniel arap Moi's people) and occupy the western edge of the central Rift Valley area. They first migrated to the area west of Lake Turkana from southern Sudan around 2000 years ago, but gradually filtered south as the climate became harsher. The Kipsigi have a love of cattle rustling which continues to cause strife between them and neighbouring tribes. However, the tribe is most famous for producing Kenya's Olympic runners (75% of all the top runners in Kenya are Kalenjin). As with most tribes, the Kalenjin are organised into age-sets. Administration of the law is carried out at the *kok* (an informal court led by the clan's elders).

Meru

Originally from the coast, the Meru now occupy the northeastern slopes of Mt Kenya and represent 6% of Kenya's population. Up until 1974 the Meru were led by a chief (the *mogwe*), but upon his death the last incumbent converted to Christianity. Strangely, many of their tribal stories mirror the traditional tales of the Old Testament. The practice of ancestor worship, however, is still widespread. They have long been governed by an elected council of elders *(njuuri)*, making them the only tribe practising a structured form of democratic governance prior to colonialism. The Meru now live on some of the most fertile farmland in Kenya and grow numerous cash crops. Subgroups of the Meru include the Chuka, Igembe, Igoji, Tharaka, Muthambi, Tigania and Imenti.

Samburu

Closely related to the Maasai, and speaking the same language, the Samburu occupy an arid area directly north of Mt Kenya and make up 0.5% of the population. It seems that when the Maasai migrated to the area from Sudan, some headed east and became the Samburu. Like the Maasai, they have retained their traditional way of life as nomadic pastoralists, depending for their survival on their livestock. They live in small villages of five to eight families, divided into age-sets, and they continue to practise traditional rites such as male and female circumcision and polygamy. After marriage, women traditionally leave their clan, and their social status is much lower than that of men. Samburu women wear similar colourful bead necklaces to the Maasai. Like the Maasai and Rendille, Samburu warriors paste their hair with red ochre to create a visor to shield their eyes from the sun.

MIRAA

The Meru are active in the cultivation of *miraa*, the stems of which contain a stimulant similar to amphetamines, which are exported to Somalia and Yemen.

Western Kenya

Luhya

Made up of 18 different groups (the largest being the Bukusu), the Bantu-speaking Luhya are the second-largest group in Kenya, representing 14% of the population. They occupy a relatively small, high-density area of the country in the Western Highlands centred on Kakamega. In the past, the Luhya were skilled metal workers, forging knives and tools that were traded with other groups, but today most Luhya are agriculturists, farming groundnuts, sesame and maize. Smallholders also grow cash crops such as cotton and sugar cane. Many Luhya are superstitious and still have a strong belief in witchcraft. Traditional costumes and rituals are becoming less common with each passing year.

Luo

The tribe of US President Barack Obama's father, the Luo live on the shores of Lake Victoria and are Kenya's third-largest tribal group with 13% of the population. Though originally a cattle-herding people like the Maasai, their herds suffered terribly from the rinderpest outbreak in the 1890s so they switched to fishing and subsistence agriculture. During the struggle for independence, many of the country's leading politicians and trade unionists were Luo. Socially, the Luo are unusual among Kenya's tribes in that they don't practise circumcision for either sex. The family unit is part of a larger grouping of *dhoot* (families), several of which in turn make up an *ogandi* (group of geographically related people), each led by a *ruoth* (chief). The Luo have two major recreational passions, soccer and music, and there are many distinctive Luo instruments made from gourds and gut or wire strings.

The Rosen Publishing Group (www.rosenpublishing.com) publishes the Heritage Library of African Peoples, aimed at late-primary and early-secondary school students. Although the entire East Africa set is available, individual titles (such as *Luo*, *Kikuyu*, *Maasai* and *Samburu*) are also easy to track down.

Gusii (Kisii)

The Gusii (6% of the population) occupy the Western Highlands, east of Lake Victoria, forming a small Bantu-speaking island in a mainly Nilotic-speaking area. Primarily cattle-herders and crop-cultivators, they farm Kenya's cash crops – tea, coffee and pyrethrum – as well as market vegetables. They are also well known for their basketry and distinctive, rounded soapstone carvings. Like many other tribal groups, Gusii society is clan based, with everyone organised into age-sets. Medicine men *(abanyamorigo)*, in particular, hold a highly respected and privileged position, performing the role of doctor and social worker. One of their more peculiar practices is trepanning: the removal of sections of the skull or spine to aid maladies such as backache or concussion.

The Worlds of a Maasai Warrior: An Autobiography (1988), by Tepilit Ole Saitoti, presents an intriguing perspective on the juxtaposition of traditional and modern in East Africa.

Southern Kenya

Akamba (Kamba)

The region east of Nairobi towards Tsavo National Park is the traditional homeland of the Bantu-speaking Akamba who make up 11% of the population. Great traders in ivory, beer, honey, iron weapons and ornaments, they traditionally plied their trade between Lake Victoria and the coast, and north to Lake Turkana. In particular, they traded with the Maasai and Kikuyu for food stocks. Highly regarded by the British for their fighting ability, they were drafted in large numbers into the British army. After WWI the British tried to limit their cattle stocks and settled more Europeans in their tribal territories. In response, the Akamba marched en masse to Nairobi to squat peacefully at Kariokor Market in protest, forcing the administration to relent. Nowadays, they are more famous for their elegant *makonde*-style (ebony) carving. Akamba society is clan-based with all adolescents going through initiation rites at about the age of 12.

Maasai

Despite representing only a small proportion of the total population (2%), the Maasai are, for many, the definitive symbol of Kenya. With a reputation as fierce warriors, the tribe has largely managed to stay outside the mainstream of development in Kenya and still maintains large cattle herds along the Tanzanian border. The British gazetted the Masai Mara National Reserve in the early 1960s, displacing the Maasai, and they slowly continued to annexe more and more Maasai land. Resettle-

THE MAASAI & THEIR CATTLE

The Maasai tell the following story. One of the Maasai gods, Naiteru-Kop, was wandering the earth at the beginning of time and there he found a Dorobo man – 'Dorobo' is a derogatory Maasai word used to describe hunter-gatherer groups – who lived with a snake, a cow and an elephant. The man killed the snake and the elephant, but the elephant's calf escaped and came upon Le-eyo, a Maasai man to whom he told the story of the Dorobo.

The elephant calf took Le-eyo to the Dorobo man's compound, where Le-eyo heard Naiteru-Kop, the Maasai god, calling out to the Dorobo man and telling him to come out the next morning. Having heard this, it was Le-eyo who emerged first the following morning and asked Naiteru-Kop what to do next. Following the god's instructions, Le-eyo built a large enclosure, with a little hut of branches and grasses on one side. He then slaughtered a thin calf, but did not eat it, instead laying out the calf's hide, and piling the meat high on top. He then built a large fire, and threw the meat upon it.

A great storm swept over the land. With the storm clouds overhead, a leather cord dropped from the sky into Le-eyo's compound, and down the cord came cattle until Le-eyo's compound was full of cattle. One of the cattle stuck its hoof through the hut's wall, and Le-eyo called out, frightened. Upon Le-eyo's cry, the cattle stopped falling from the sky. Naiteru-Kop called out to Le-eyo: 'These are all the cattle you will receive, because your cry stopped them coming. But they are yours to look after, and you will live with them.'

Since that day, the Dorobo have been hunters and the Maasai have herded their cattle, convinced that all the cattle in the world belong to them.

ment programs have met with limited success as the Maasai scorn agriculture and land ownership. The Maasai still have a distinctive style and traditional age-grade social structure, and circumcision is still widely practised for both men and women. Women typically wear large plate-like bead necklaces, while the men typically wear a red-checked *shuka* (blanket) and carry a distinctive ball-ended club. Blood and milk are the mainstays of the Maasai diet, supplemented by a drink called *mursik,* made from milk fermented with cow's urine and ashes, which has been shown to lower cholesterol.

Taita

The Taita people, making up 0.1% of the population, came originally from what is now Tanzania, and first settled in the region around Voi and Taveta in Kenya's far southeast around 10 centuries ago. The Taita language belongs to the Bantu group of languages and is similar to Swahili, although such is their interaction with other tribes that their language has imported many words from neighbouring tribes, including the Kikuyu. Taita social life was traditionally dispersed and strongly territorial, with each clan inhabiting a discrete area of the Taita Hills, south of what is now Tsavo West National Park. It was only after colonialism that a collective sense of Taita identity developed in earnest, a process accelerated by the intrusion of the railway through Taita lands; Mwangeka, a Taita hero, was lauded for his resistance to colonial rule. Taita religion was largely animist in nature with sacred meeting places and elaborate burial rituals the defining features, although few Taita now live according to traditional ways.

Northern Kenya

Turkana

Originally from Karamojong in northeastern Uganda, the Turkana live in the virtual desert country of Kenya's northwest and make up 1.5% of Kenya's population. Like the Samburu and the Maasai (with whom they are linguistically linked), the Turkana are primarily cattle herders, although fishing on the waters of Lake Turkana and small-scale farming is on the increase. Traditional costume and practices are still commonplace, although the Turkana are one of the few tribes to have voluntarily given up the practice of circumcision. Men typically cover part of their hair with mud, which is then painted blue and decorated with ostrich and other feathers and, despite the intense heat, their main garment is a woollen blanket. A woman's attire is dictated by her marital and maternal status; the marriage ritual itself is quite unusual and involves kidnapping the bride. Tattooing is also common. Men were traditionally tattooed on the shoulders for killing an enemy – the right shoulder for killing a man, the left for a woman. Witchdoctors and prophets are held in high regard and scars on someone's lower stomach are usually a sign of a witchdoctor's attempt to cast out an undesirable spirit using incisions.

MARKINGS

A surprising number of Turkana men still wear markings on their shoulders to indicate they have killed another man.

Borana

The Borana are one of the cattle-herding Oromo peoples, indigenous to Ethiopia, who migrated south into northern Kenya and make up less the 0.1% of the population. They are now concentrated around Marsabit and Isiolo. The Borana observe strict role segregation between men and women – men being responsible for care of the herds while women are in charge of children and day-to-day life. Borana groups may pack up camp and move up to four times a year, depending on weather conditions and available grazing land. As a nomadic group their reliance on oral history is strong, with many traditions passed on through song.

El Molo

This tiny tribal group (less the 0.1% of the population) has strong links with the Rendille, their close neighbours. The El Molo rely on Lake Turkana for their existence, living on a diet mainly of fish and occasionally crocodiles, turtles and other wildlife. Hippos are hunted from doum-palm rafts, and great social status is given to a warrior who kills a hippo. Intermarriage with other tribes and abandonment of the nomadic lifestyle have helped to raise their numbers to about 4000, now living on the mainland near Loyangalani.

Gabbra

This small pastoral tribe (less than 0.1% of the population) lives in the far north of Kenya, from the eastern shore of Lake Turkana up into Ethiopia. Many Gabbra converted to Islam during the time of slavery. Traditional beliefs include the appointment of an *abba-olla* (father of the village), who oversees the moral and physical wellbeing of the tribe. Fathers and sons form strong relationships, and marriage provides a lasting bond between clans. Polygamy is still practised by the Gabbra, although it is becoming less common. Gabbra men usually wear turbans and white cotton robes, while women wear kangas, thin pieces of brightly coloured cotton. The Gabbra are famous for their bravery, hunting lions, rhinos and elephants.

Rendille

The Rendille are pastoralists who live in small nomadic communities in the rocky Kaisut Desert in Kenya's northeast and make up less than 0.1% of the population. They have strong economic and kinship links with the Samburu and rely heavily on camels for many of their daily needs, including food, milk, clothing, trade and transport. Camels are bled by opening a vein in the neck with a blunt arrow or knife. The blood is then drunk on its own or mixed with milk. Rendille society is strongly bound by family ties centred on monogamous couples. Mothers have high status and the eldest son inherits the family wealth. It is dishonourable for a Rendille to refuse to grant a loan, so even the poorest Rendille often has claims to at least a few camels and goats. Rendille warriors often sport a distinctive visorlike hairstyle, dyed with red ochre, while women may wear several kilos of beads.

Coastal Kenya

Swahili

Although the people of the coast do not have a common heritage, they do have a linguistic link: Kiswahili (commonly referred to as Swahili), a Bantu-based language that evolved as a means of communication between Africans and the Arabs, Persians and Portuguese who colonised the East African coast; the word *swahili* is a derivative of the Arabic word for coast – *sawahil*. The cultural origins of the Swahili, who make up 0.6% of the population, come from intermarriage between the Arabs and Persians with African slaves from the 7th century onwards. In fact, many anthropologists consider the Swahili a cultural tribe brought together by trade routes rather than a tribe of distinct biological lineage. A largely urban tribe, they occupy coastal cities such as Mombasa, Malindi, Lamu and Stone Town (Zanzibar); and given the historical Arab influence, the Swahili largely practise Islam.

Daily Life

It can be hard work being Kenyan. While most are proud to be Kenyan, national identity is only one way among many in which Kenyans understand their world. Unlike in neighbouring Tanzania where being Tanzanian is placed above all else in the national story, in Kenya family ties, tribal affiliations, the pull of religion and gender roles are all prominent issues in the public domain and each plays a significant role in the daily lives of ordinary people. The result is a fascinating, if complicated, mosaic.

Traditional Cultures, Modern Country

Traditional cultures are what hold Kenya together. Respect for one's elders, firmly held religious beliefs, traditional gender roles and the tradition of *ujamaa* (familyhood) create a well-defined social structure with stiff moral mores at its core.

Extended family provides a further layer of support, which is increasingly important as parents migrate to cities for lucrative work, leaving their children to be cared for by grandparents, aunts and uncles. This fluid system has also enabled many to deal with the devastation wrought by the HIV/AIDS epidemic – Kenya has the 12th-highest HIV prevalence rate among adults (6.1%) in the world.

Historically, the majority of Kenyans were either farmers or cattle herders with family clans based in small interconnected villages. Even today, as traditional rural life gives way to a frenetic urban pace, this strong sense of community remains.

Grafted onto these traditional foundations of culture, family and community, education, too, is critical to understanding modern Kenya. Kenya sends more students to the US to study than any other African country and adult literacy stood at an impressive 87.4% in 2010. The generation of educated Kenyans who came of age in the 1980s is now making itself heard: Kenyans abroad have started to invest seriously in the country, Nairobi's business landscape is changing rapidly and a new middle class is demanding new apartment blocks and cars.

In Ngũgĩ wa Thiong'o's *Petals of Blood* (1977), Wanja the barmaid sums up the situation for women in newly independent Kenya: '...with us girls the future seemed vague... as if we knew that no matter what efforts we put into our studies, our road led to the kitchen or the bedroom'.

One Country, Many Tribes

Kenya is home to more than 40 tribal groups. Although most have coexisted quite peacefully since independence, the ethnocentric bias of government and civil-service appointments has led to escalating unrest and

THE INDIAN INFLUENCE

Kenya's first permanent settlers from the Indian subcontinent were indentured workers, brought here from Gujarat and the Punjab by the British to build the Uganda Railway. After the railway was finished, the British allowed many workers to stay and start up businesses, and hundreds of *dukas* (small shops) were set up across the country.

After WWII, the Indian community came to control large sectors of the East African economy, and still does to some degree. However, few gave their active support to the black nationalist movements in the run-up to independence, despite being urged to do so by India's prime minister, and many were hesitant to accept local citizenship after independence. This earned the widespread distrust of the African community. Thankfully, however, Kenya escaped the anti-Asian pogroms that plagued Uganda.

disaffection. During the hotly contested elections of 1992, 1997 and 2007, clashes between two major tribes, the Kikuyu and Luo, bolstered by allegiances with other smaller tribes such as the Kalenjin, resulted in death and mass displacement. One positive step came with the adoption of the 2010 constitution which recognises the rights of ethnic minorities and even calls for the cabinet to 'reflect the regional and ethnic diversity of the people of Kenya'. Some analysts point out that election violence and ethnic tensions have more to do with economic inequality than with tribalism – they insist that there are only two tribes in Kenya: the rich and the poor.

UNDP

In the 2013 United Nations Development Program (UNDP) Human Development Index, which is based on a number of economic and quality-of-life indicators, Kenya ranked 147th out of 187 countries.

Christian Interior, Muslim Coast

As a result of intense missionary activity, the majority of Kenyans outside the coastal and eastern provinces are Christians (including some home-grown African Christian groups that do not owe any allegiance to the major Western groups). Hard-core evangelism has made some significant inroads and many TV-style groups from the US have a strong following. In the country's east, the majority of Kenyans are Sunni Muslims. They make up about 11% of the population.

Women in Kenya

During Kenya's struggle for independence, many women fought alongside the men, but their sacrifice was largely forgotten when independence came. At the Lancaster House conference in the early 1960s, where Kenya's independence constitution was negotiated, just one out of around 70 Kenyan delegates was a woman and the resulting constitution made no mention of women's rights.

Under the 2010 constitution, things improved, at least on paper: women are described as a disadvantaged group, and the bill guarantees equal treatment for men and women, protects against discrimination on the basis of gender, calls on the state to undertake affirmative-action policies and sets aside 47 special seats for women in parliament – as a result, 19% of MPs in 2014 were women, compared with 1% in 1990. The adult literacy rate for Kenyan women (84.2%) is one of the highest in sub-Saharan Africa.

I Laugh So I Won't Cry: Kenya's Women Tell the Stories of Their Lives, edited by Helena Halperin, offers fascinating glimpses into the lives of Kenyan women.

Even so, major discrepancies remain in the ways in which women and men have access to essential services and resources such as land and credit, while traditional gender roles still largely prevail.

Kenyan women are increasingly able to access educational opportunities and, particularly in the cities, are slowly coming to play a more prominent role in public life. In rural areas traditional gender roles are observed, although women are accorded status and respect as mothers, wives, healers and teachers.

FEMALE GENITAL MUTILATION

Female genital mutilation (FGM), often termed 'female circumcision', is still widespread across Africa, including throughout Kenya. In some parts of tribal Kenya more than 90% of women and girls are subjected to FGM.

The term FGM covers a wide range of procedures from a small, mainly symbolic cut, to the total removal of the clitoris and external genitalia (known as infibulation). The effects of FGM can be fatal. Other side effects, including chronic infections, the spread of HIV, infertility, severe bleeding and lifelong pain during sex, are not uncommon.

FGM is now banned in Kenya for girls under 17, but the ritual still has widespread support in some communities; attempts to stamp out FGM are widely perceived as part of a Western conspiracy to undermine African cultural identity. Many local women's groups, such as the community project Ntanira na Mugambo (Circumcision Through Words), are working towards preserving the rite-of-passage aspect of FGM without any surgery.

The Arts

Kenya is arguably the leading cultural powerhouse of East Africa, with Nairobi in particular one of the most dynamic spaces for the arts. Kenyan musicians and writers are particularly worth watching out for. Often these arts provide not only a powerful medium for expressing African culture but also a means for expressing the dreams and frustrations of the poor and disenfranchised, and that's where Kenyan artists and performers really find their voice.

Music

With its diversity of indigenous languages and culture, Kenya has a rich and exciting music scene. Influences, most notably from the nearby Democratic Republic of Congo and Tanzania, have helped to diversify the sounds. More recently reggae and hip hop have permeated the pop scene.

The live-music scene in Nairobi is excellent – a variety of clubs cater for traditional and contemporary musical tastes, while the **Blankets & Wine** (☎0736801333, 0720801333; www.blanketsandwine.com; tickets KSh1500-2500; ⏲1st Sun of month) phenomenon has fast become a mainstay of the capital's live-music scene. A good reference is the *Daily Nation*, which publishes weekly top-10 African, international and gospel charts and countrywide gig listings on Saturday. Beyond Nairobi, take what you can get.

ART MATTERS

A fabulous resource covering many aspects of the art scene throughout Kenya and the rest of Africa is www.artmatters.info.

Outside Influences

The Congolese styles of rumba and soukous, known collectively as *lingala*, were first introduced into Kenya by artists such as Samba Mapangala (who is still playing) in the 1960s and have come to dominate most of East Africa. This upbeat party music is characterised by clean guitar licks and a driving *cavacha* drum rhythm.

Music from Tanzania was influential in the early 1970s, when the band Simba Wanyika helped create Swahili rumba, which was taken up by bands such as the Maroon Commandos and Les Wanyika.

Popular bands today are heavily influenced by benga, soukous and also Western music, with lyrics generally in Swahili. These include bands such as Them Mushrooms (now reinvented as Uyoya) and Safari Sound. For upbeat dance tunes, Ogopa DJs, Nameless, Redsan and Deux Vultures are popular acts.

Home-Grown Styles

Kenyan bands were also active during the 1960s, producing some of the most popular songs in Africa, including Fadhili William's famous *Malaika* (Angel), and *Jambo Bwana*, Kenya's unofficial anthem, written and recorded by the hugely influential Them Mushrooms.

Benga is the contemporary dance music of Kenya. It refers to the dominant style of Luo pop music, which originated in western Kenya, and spread throughout the country in the 1960s being taken up by Akamba

PLAYLIST

Amigo – classic Swahili rumba from one of Kenya's most influential bands, Les Wanyika

Guitar Paradise of East Africa – ranges through Kenya's musical styles including the classic hit 'Shauri Yako'

Journey – Jabali Afrika's stirring acoustic sounds complete with drums, congas, shakers and bells

Kenyan: The First Chapter – Kenya's home-grown blend of African lyrics with R&B, house, reggae and dancehall genres

Mama Africa – Suzanna Owiyo, the Tracy Chapman of Kenya, with acoustic Afropop

Nairobi Beat: Kenyan Pop Music Today – regional sounds including Luo, Kikuyu, Kamba, Luhya, Swahili and Congolese

Nuting but de Stone – phenomenally popular compilation combining African lyrics with American urban sounds and Caribbean ragga

Rumba is Rumba – infectious Congolese soukous with Swahili lyrics

Virunga Volcano – from Orchestre Virunga, with samba, sublime guitar licks, a bubbling bass and rich vocals

and Kikuyu musicians. The music is characterised by clear electric-guitar riffs and a bounding bass rhythm. Some well-known exponents of benga include DO Misiani (a Luo) and his group Shirati Jazz, which has been around since the 1960s and is still churning out the hits. You should also look out for Globestyle, Victoria Kings and Ambira Boys.

Contemporary Kikuyu music often borrows from benga. Stars include Sam Chege, Francis Rugwiti and Daniel 'Councillor' Kamau, who was popular in the 1970s and is still going strong.

Taarab, the music of the East African coast, originally only played at Swahili weddings and other special occasions, has been given a new lease of life by coastal pop singer Malika.

Rap, Hip Hop & Other Styles

American-influenced gangster rap and hip hop are also on the rise, including such acts as Necessary Noize, Poxi Presha and Hardstone. The slums of Nairobi have proved to be particularly fertile for local rap music. In 2004, Dutch producer Nynke Nauta gathered rappers from the Eastlands slums of Nairobi and formed a collective, Nairobi Yetu. The resultant album, *Kilio Cha Haki* (A Cry for Justice), featuring raps in Sheng (a mix of Swahili, English and ethnic languages), has been internationally recognised as a poignant fusion of ghetto angst and the joy of making music.

Kenya pioneered the African version of the reggaeton style (a blend of reggae, hip hop and traditional music), which is now popular in the US and UK. Dancehall is also huge here.

Other names to keep an eye or ear out for include Prezzo (Kenya's king of bling), Nonini (a controversial women-and-booze rapper), Nazizi (female MC from Necessary Noize) and Mercy Myra (Kenya's biggest female R&B artist).

Literature

There are plenty of novels, plays and biographies by contemporary Kenyan authors, but they can be hard to find outside the country. The Heinemann African Writers Series offers an accessible collection of such works.

Ngũgĩ wa Thiong'o

Ngũgĩ wa Thiong'o (1938–) is uncompromisingly radical, and his harrowing criticism of the neocolonialist politics of the Kenyan establishment landed him in jail for a year (described in his *Detained: A Prison Writer's Diary*; 1982), lost him his job at Nairobi University and forced him into exile.

His works include *Petals of Blood, Matigari, The River Between, A Grain of Wheat, Devil on the Cross* and *Wizard of the Crow*, which was shortlisted for the 2007 Commonwealth Writers' Prize. His latest works are memoirs: *Dreams in a Time of War* (2010) and *In the House of the Interpreter* (2012). All his works, whether fiction or nonfiction, offer insightful portraits of Kenyan life and will give you an understanding of the daily concerns of modern Kenyans. He has also written extensively in his native language, Gikuyu.

Meja Mwangi

Meja Mwangi (1948–) sticks to social issues and urban dislocation, but has a mischievous sense of humour that threads its way right through his books. Notable titles include *The Return of Shaka, Weapon of Hunger, The Cockroach Dance, The Last Plague* and *The Big Chiefs*. His *Mzungu Boy*, winner of the Children's Africana Book Award in 2006, depicts the friendship of white and black Kenyan boys at the time of the Mau Mau uprising.

Binyavanga Wainaina

One of Kenya's rising stars on the literary front is Binyavanga Wainaina (1971–), who won the Caine Prize for African Writing in July 2002. The award-winning piece was the short story *Discovering Home*, about a young Kenyan working in Cape Town who returns to his parents' village in Kenya for a year.

More recently, Wainaina helped form the Concerned Kenyan Writers (CKW) group in the aftermath of the 2008 post-election crisis. CKW aims to inspire and unite Kenyans and show them that there is a pay-off in peace and nationhood; it also seeks to counter the 'Dark Continent' reporting by the international media in the wake of the violence.

To follow the work of contemporary writers, look out for *Kwani?*, Kenya's first literary journal, established by Wainaina in 2003. Nairobi-based, it facilitates the production and distribution of Kenyan literature and hosts an annual literary festival that attracts a growing number of pan-African names. The website (kwani.org) is a great way to stay up to date with the contemporary scene.

Contemporary Women Writers

The first female Kenyan writer of note is Grace Ogot (1930–), the first woman to have her work published by the East African Publishing House. Her work includes *Land Without Thunder, The Strange Bride, The Graduate* and *The Island of Tears*. Born in Nyanza Province, she sets many of her stories against the scenic background of Lake Victoria, and offers an insight into Luo culture in precolonial Kenya.

Another interesting writer is Margaret Atieno Ogola (1958–2011), the author of the celebrated novel *The River and the Source* and its sequel, *I Swear by Apollo*, which follow the lives of four generations of Kenyan women in a rapidly evolving country.

Other books of note are Marjorie Magoye's *The Present Moment*, which follows the life of a group of elderly women in a Christian refuge, and *The Man from Pretoria* by Kenyan conservationist and journalist Hilary Ngweno.

Facing the Lion (2005) is Joseph Lekuton's simple but beautifully crafted memoir of how he grew up as a poor Maasai boy, who, through a series of incredible twists and turns, ends up in the US studying for an MBA.

Cinema

Kenya's underfunded film industry has struggled to establish itself, but the Zanzibar International Film Festival (ZIFF) in neighbouring Tanzania, one of the region's premier cultural events, has helped to bring East African filmmakers to the fore. One such auteur is Kibaara Kaugi, whose *Enough is Enough* (2004), a brave exploration of the Mau Mau uprising, garnered critical praise.

In 2005, the government established the **Kenya Film Commission** (KFC; www.kenyafilmcommission.com) which aims to support and promote the Kenyan film industry. One notable success since its inception is *Kibera Kid*, a short film set in the Kibera slum, written and directed by Nathan Collett. It tells the story of 12-year-old Otieno, an orphan living with a gang of thieves, who must make a choice between gang life and redemption. Featuring a cast of children, all of whom live in Kibera, the film played at film festivals worldwide.

Filmed in Kenya

- *King Solomon's Mines (1950)*
- *The Snows of Kilimanjaro (1952)*
- *Mogambo (1953)*
- *Born Free (1966)*
- *Out of Africa (1985)*
- *Mountains of the Moon (1990)*
- *Nowhere in Africa (2001)*
- *Lara Croft Tomb Raider: The Cradle of Life (2003)*
- *The Constant Gardener (2005)*

Painting

Kenya has a diverse artistic heritage, and there is a wealth of artistic talent in the country, practising both traditional painting and all manner of sculpture, printing, mixed media and graffiti. For an overview of the local scene, visit **Gallery Watatu** (☎2024857; Lonhro House, Standard St) and the **Go-Down Arts Centre** (☎0726992200; www.thegodownartscentre.com; Dunga Rd; ⏲9am-5pm Mon-Fri) FREE, both in Nairobi.

Textiles & Jewellery

Women throughout East Africa wear brightly coloured lengths of printed cotton cloth, typically with Swahili sayings printed along the edge, known as kanga. Many of the sayings are social commentary or messages, often indirectly worded, or containing puns and double meanings. Others are local forms of advertising, such as the logos of political parties.

In coastal areas, you'll also see the *kikoi*, which is made of a more thickly textured cotton, usually featuring striped or plaid patterns, and traditionally worn by men. Also common are batik-print cottons depicting everyday scenes, animal motifs or geometrical patterns.

Jewellery, especially beaded jewellery, is particularly beautiful among the Maasai and the Turkana. It is used in ceremonies as well as in everyday life, and often indicates the wearer's wealth and marital status.

Woodcarving & Sculpture

Woodcarving was only introduced into Kenya in the early 20th century. Mutisya Munge, an Akamba man, is considered the father of Kenyan woodcarving, having brought the tradition from Tanzania's Makonde people to Kenya following World War I. Kenya's woodcarving industry has grown exponentially in the century since, although recent shortages of increasingly endangered hardwoods have presented major challenges to the industry. While woodcarvings from Kenya may lack the sophistication and cultural resonance of those from Central and West Africa, the carvings' subjects range from representations of the spirit and animal worlds to stylised human figures.

Carvings rendered in soapstone from the village of Tabaka, close to Kisii in the Western Highlands, are among the most attractive of Kenyan handicrafts. These sculptures take on numerous forms, but the abstract figures of embracing couples are the genre's undoubted highpoint.

Kenyan Cuisine

The Kenyan culinary tradition has generally emphasised feeding the masses as efficiently as possible, with little room for flair or innovation. Most meals are centred on *ugali*, a thick, doughlike mass made from maize and/or cassava flour. While traditional fare may be bland but filling, there are some treats to be found. Many memorable eating experiences in Kenya are likely to revolve around dining alfresco in a safari camp, surrounded by the sights and sounds of the African bush.

Staples & Specialities

Counting Carbs

Kenyan cuisine has few culinary masterpieces and is mainly survival food, offering the maximum opportunity to fill up at minimum cost. Most meals in Kenya largely consist of heavy starches.

In addition to *ugali*, Kenyans rely on potatoes, rice, chapati and *matoke*. The rice-based dishes, biriani and pilau, are clearly derived from Persia – they should be delicately spiced with saffron and star anise and liberally sprinkled with carrot and raisins. The chapati is identical to its Indian predecessor, while *matoke* is mashed green plantains which, when well prepared, can taste like buttery, lightly whipped mashed potato. Also look out for *irio* (or *kienyeji*), made from mashed greens, potato and boiled corn or beans; *mukimo*, a kind of hash made from sweet potatoes, corn, beans and plantains; and *githeri*, a mix of beans and corn.

Cooking the East African Way, by Constance Nabwire and Bertha Vining Montgomery, combines easy-to-follow recipes from across the region with interesting text on culinary traditions in Kenya and elsewhere.

Flesh & Bone

Kenyans are enthusiastic carnivores and their unofficial national dish, *nyama choma* (barbecued meat), is a red-blooded, hands-on affair. Most places have their own on-site butchery, and *nyama choma* is usually purchased by weight, often as a single hunk of meat. Half a kilogram is usually enough for one person (taking into account bone and gristle). It'll be brought out to you chopped into small bite-sized bits, often with a salad or vegetable mash and greens.

Goat is the most common meat, but you'll see chicken, beef and some game animals (ostrich and crocodile) in upmarket places. Don't expect *nyama choma* to melt in the mouth – its chewiness is probably indicative of the long and eventful life of the animal you're consuming and you'll need a good half-hour at the end of the meal to work over your gums with a toothpick. We find that copious quantities of Tusker beer also tend to help it go down.

In addition to *nyama choma*, Kenyans are fond of meat-based stews, which help make their carb-rich diet more palatable. Again, goat, chicken and beef, as well as mutton, are the most common cuts on the menu, though they tend to be pretty tough, despite being cooked for hours on end.

PILAU

Pilau flavoured with spices and stock is the signature dish at traditional Swahili weddings. The expression 'going to eat pilau' means to go to a wedding.

Fruit & Vegetables

Ugali (and most Kenyan dishes for that matter) is usually served with *sukuma wiki* (braised or stewed spinach). *Sukuma wiki* in Swahili

THE ART OF EATING UGALI

A meal wouldn't be a meal in Kenya without *ugali*. *Ugali* is made from boiled grains cooked into a thick porridge until it sets hard, then served up in flat (and rather dense) slabs. It's incredibly stodgy and tends to sit in the stomach like a brick, but most Kenyans swear by it – it will fill you up after a long day's safari, but it won't set your taste buds atingle.

In general, good *ugali* should be neither too dry nor too sticky, which makes it easy to enjoy as a finger food. Take some with the right hand from the communal pot (your left hand is used for wiping – and we don't mean your mouth!), roll it into a small ball with the fingers, making an indentation with your thumb, and dip it into the accompanying sauce. Eating with your hand is a bit of an art, but after a few tries it starts to feel natural. Don't soak the *ugali* too long (to avoid it breaking up in the sauce), and keep your hand lower than your elbow (except when actually eating) so the sauce doesn't drip down your forearm.

means, literally, 'stretch the week', the implication being that it's so cheap it allows the householder to stretch the budget until the next weekly pay cheque. Despite its widespread availability, a dish of well-cooked *sukuma wiki* with tomatoes, stock and capsicum makes a refreshing change from the abundance of meat in other recipes.

Depending on the place and the season, you can buy mangoes, pawpaws, pineapples, passionfruit, guavas, oranges, custard apples, bananas (of many varieties), tree tomatoes and coconuts. Chewing on a piece of sugar cane is also a great way to end a meal.

Kenyan Classics

Breakfast in Kenya is generally a simple affair consisting of chai accompanied by a *mandazi* (semisweet doughnuts). *Mandazi* are best in the morning when they're freshly made – they become ever more rubbery and less appetising as the day goes on. Another traditional breakfast dish is *uji* (a thin, sweet porridge made from bean, millet or other flour); it's similar to *ugali* and best served warm, with lashings of milk and brown sugar.

On the coast, Swahili dishes reflect the history of contact with Arabs and other Indian Ocean traders, and incorporate the produce of the region; the results can be excellent. Grilled fish or octopus will be a highlight of any menu, while coconut and spices such as cloves and cinnamon feature prominently.

The large South Asian presence in East Africa means that Indian food commonly appears on menus throughout Kenya. Most restaurants serve curries and Indian-inspired dishes such as masala chips (ie chips with a curry sauce), while authentic Indian restaurants in Nairobi and along the coast and elsewhere serve up traditional dishes from the subcontinent.

Nyama Choma

- *Kikopey Nyama Choma Centre, Rift Valley*
- *Hygienic Butchery, Nakuru*
- *Nyama choma stalls, Nairobi*
- *Carnivore, Nairobi*
- *Olepolos Country Club, Nairobi*
- *Kungu Maitu Hotel & Butchery, Nanyuki*
- *The Grill, Kisimu*
- *Rongai Fast Food, Diani Beach*

Drinks

Tea & Coffee

Despite the fact that Kenya grows some excellent tea and coffee, getting a decent cup of either can be difficult. Quite simply, the best stuff is exported.

Chai is the national obsession, and although it's drunk in large quantities, it bears little resemblance to what you might be used to. As in India, the tea, milk and masses of sugar are boiled together and stewed for ages and the result is milky and very sweet – it may be too sickly for some, but the brew might just grow on you. Spiced masala chai with cardamom and cinnamon is very pleasant and rejuvenating. For tea without milk ask for chai *kavu*.

As for coffee, it's often sweet, milky and made with a bare minimum of instant coffee. However, in Nairobi and in other larger towns, there is a steadily increasing number of coffee houses serving very good Kenyan coffee, and you can usually get a good filter coffee at the big hotels. With all the Italian tourists who visit the coast, you can now get a decent cappuccino or espresso pretty much anywhere between Diani Beach and Lamu.

The most long-lasting impact that Portuguese explorers had on Kenya was in the culinary field. Portuguese travellers introduced maize, cassava, potatoes and chillies from South America – all of which are now staples of the Kenyan diet.

Water & Juices

With all the fresh fruit that's available in Kenya, the juices on offer are, not surprisingly, breathtakingly good. All are made using modern blenders, so there's no point asking for a fruit juice during a power cut. Although you can get juices made from almost any fruit, the nation's favourite is passionfruit. It is known locally just as 'passion', although it seems a little odd asking a waiter whether they have passion and how much it costs! On a more serious note, be wary of fruit juices watered down with unpurified water (tap water is best avoided). Either watch them prepare it or stick with bottled fruit juices instead. Bottled water is widely available, except in remote areas – it's always worth carrying a filter or purification tablets.

Beer

Kenya has a thriving local brewing industry, and formidable quantities of beer are consumed day and night. You'll usually be given a choice of 'warm' or 'cold' beer. 'Why warm?', you might well ask. Curiously, most Kenyans appear to prefer it that way, despite the fact that room temperature in Kenya is a lot hotter than room temperature in the USA or Europe.

The local beers are Tusker, Pilsner and White Cap, all manufactured by Kenya Breweries and sold in 500mL bottles. Tusker comes in three varieties: Tusker Export, Tusker Malt Lager and just plain Tusker. Tusker Export is a stronger version of ordinary Tusker, while Tusker Malt has a fuller taste, for more discerning palates. Locally produced foreign labels include Castle (a South African beer) and Guinness, though the Kenyan version is nothing like the genuine Irish article.

Wine

Kenya has a fledgling wine industry, and the Lake Naivasha Colombard wines are generally quite good. This is something that cannot be said

DOS & DON'TS

For Kenyans, a shared meal and eating out of a communal dish are expressions of solidarity between hosts and guests: here are a few tips to help you get into the spirit of things.

- If you're invited to eat and aren't hungry, it's OK to say that you've just eaten, but try to share a few bites of the meal in recognition of the bond with your hosts.
- Leave a small amount on your plate to show your hosts that you've been satisfied.
- Don't take the last bit of food from the communal bowl – your hosts may worry that they haven't provided enough.
- Never, *ever* handle food with the left hand!
- If others are eating with their hands, do the same, even if cutlery is provided.
- Defer to your hosts for customs that you aren't sure about.

about the most commonly encountered Kenyan wine – pawpaw wine. Quite how anyone came up with the idea of trying to reproduce a drink made from grapes using pawpaw remains a mystery, but the result tastes foul and smells even worse.

You can get cheap South African, European and even Australian wine by the glass in upmarket restaurants in major cities and tourist areas.

Cocktails

A popular Kenyan cocktail is *dawa,* which translates from the Swahili as 'medicine'. Clearly based on the Brazilian *caipirinha,* it's made with vodka, lime and honey. We suggest you enjoy a tipple at sunset in a bar overlooking the coast, or out on the savannah plains – both experiences can certainly have a therapeutic effect on mind and body.

Home Brew

Although it is strictly illegal for the public to brew or distil liquor, it remains a way of life for many Kenyans. *Pombe* is the local beer, usually a fermented brew made with bananas or millet and sugar. It shouldn't do you any harm. The same cannot be said for the distilled drinks known locally as *chang'a,* which are laced with genuine poisons. In 2005, 48 people died near Machakos after drinking a bad batch of *chang'a*. A further 84 were hospitalised and treated with vodka to reduce the effect of methyl alcohol poisoning – such events are not uncommon. Perhaps the most dangerous *chang'a* comes from Kisii, and is fermented with marijuana twigs, cactus mash, battery alkaline and formalin. Don't touch it.

Where to Eat & Drink

'Hotels' & Restaurants

The most basic local eateries are usually known as 'hotels' or *hotelis,* and they often open only during the daytime. You may find yourself having dinner at 5pm if you rely on eating at these places. However, even in smaller towns it's usually possible to find a restaurant that offers a more varied menu at a higher price. Often these places are affiliated with the town's midrange and top-end hotels, and are usually open in the evening.

You'll find that many of the big nightclubs also serve food until late into the night.

Menus, where they exist in the cheaper places, are usually just a chalked list on a board. In more upmarket restaurants, they're usually written only in English.

Quick Eats

Eating fast food has taken off in a big way and virtually every town has a place serving greasy-but-cheap chips, burgers, sausages, pizzas and fried chicken. Lashings of tomato and chilli sauce are present to help lubricate things. A number of South African fast-food chains have taken hold in Nairobi, such as the ubiquitous Steers.

WE DARE YOU

If you're lucky (!) and game (more to the point), you may be able to try various cattle-derived products beloved of the pastoral tribes of Kenya. Samburu, Pokot and Maasai warriors have a taste for cattle blood. The blood is taken straight from the jugular, which does no permanent damage to the cattle, but it's certainly an acquired taste. Mursik is made from milk fermented with grass ash, and is served in smoked gourds. It tastes and smells pungent, but it contains compounds that reduce cholesterol, enabling the Maasai to live quite healthily on a diet of red meat, milk and blood. You may be able to sample it at villages in the Masai Mara National Reserve or near Amboseli National Park.

On the streets in Kenya, you may encounter roasted corn cobs and deep-fried yams, which are eaten hot with a squeeze of lemon juice and a sprinkling of chilli powder. *Sambusas,* deep-fried pastry triangles stuffed with spiced mincemeat, are good for snacking on the run, and are obvious descendants of the Indian samosa.

Something you don't come across often, but which is an excellent snack, is *mkate mayai* (literally 'bread eggs'), a wheat dough pancake, filled with minced meat and egg and fried on a hotplate.

On the coast street food is more common and you will find cassava chips, chapattis and *mishikaki* (marinated grilled meat kebabs, usually beef).

Vegetarians & Vegans

Vegetarian visitors are likely to struggle, as meat features in most meals and many vegetable dishes are cooked in meat stock. But, with a bit of scouting around, you should be able to find something. You may find yourself eating a lot of *sukuma wiki,* while other traditional dishes such as *githeri* are hearty, if not particularly inspiring, options. Beans and avocado will also figure prominently in any vegetarian's culinary encounters in Kenya. Many Indian restaurants will provide a vegetarian thali (an all-you-can-eat meal) that will certainly fill you up. Buying fresh fruit and vegetables in local markets can help relieve the tedium of trying to order around the meat on restaurant menus.

Note that most tour operators are willing to cater to special dietary requests, such as vegetarian, vegan, kosher or halal, with advance notice.

RECIPES

For the lowdown on various Kenyan recipes, including the ubiquitous *ugali* and *sukuma wiki*, check out www.blissites.com/kenya/culture/recipes.html.

Food & Drink Glossary

bia	beer
biryani	rice dish, sometimes in a casserole form often served with chicken or meat
chai	tea
chai ya asubuhi	breakfast
chakula cha jioni	dinner
chakula cha mchana	lunch
chakula kutoka bahari	seafood
chapati	Indian-style bread
chenye viungo	spicy
chipsi mayai	puffy omelette with chips mixed in
chumvi	salt
githeri	a mix of beans and corn
irio	mashed greens, potato and boiled corn or beans (also called *kienyeji*)
jusi	juice
kaa	crab
kahawa	coffee
karanga	peanut
kiazi	potato
kienyeji	see *irio*
kiti moto	fried or roasted pork bits, sold by the kilogram, served with salad and fried plantain
kuku	chicken

kumbwe	snack
maji	water
maji ya machungwa	orange juice
maji ya madini	mineral water
mandazi	a semisweet doughnut served warm, with lashings of milk and brown sugar
masala chai	tea with cardamom and cinnamon
matoke	mashed green plantains
maziwa	milk
mboga	vegetable
mchuzi	sauce, sometimes with bits of beef and vegetables
mgahawa	restaurant
mishikaki	marinated grilled meat kebabs, usually beef
mkate mayai	literally 'bread eggs'; a wheat dough pancake, filled with minced meat and egg and fried on a hotplate
mkate wa kumimina	sesame-seed bread, found along the coast
mtindi	cultured milk, usually sold in small bags and delicious on a hot day
mukimo	sweet potatoes, corn, beans and plantains
mwanakondoo	lamb
nyama	meat
nyama choma	seasoned barbecued meat
nyama mbuzi	mutton
nyama nguruwe	pork
nyama ng'ombe	beef
nyama ya ndama	veal
pilau	rice dish, often served with chicken, meat or seafood, sometimes cooked in broth (a coastal speciality)
pilipili	pepper
posho	Ugandan version of *ugali*
samaki	fish
sambusas	deep-fried pastry triangles stuffed with spiced mincemeat; similar to Indian samosas
sukari	sugar
sukuma wiki	braised or stewed spinach
tambi	pasta
ugali	thick, dough-like mass made from maize and/or cassava flour
uji	thin, sweet porridge made from bean, millet or other flour
vitambua	small rice cakes resembling tiny, thick pancakes
wali	cooked rice
wali na kuku/samaki/ nyama/maharagwe	cooked white rice with chicken/fish/meat/beans

ve Elephant herd, Amboseli
onal Park (p183)

Wildlife & Habitat

East Africa is synonymous with safaris – and Kenya is where it all began. From the year-long safari undertaken by US President Theodore Roosevelt in 1909 to Joy Adamson's portrayal of the lioness Elsa in *Born Free* to Karen Blixen's sweeping tale *Out of Africa*, Kenya forms the centrepiece of our popular image of Africa. And for good reason – it is one of the best places in the world to see wildlife. You will never forget the shimmering carpets of zebras and wildebeest, or the spine-tingling roars of lions at night. Even better, Kenya offers unlimited opportunities for independent travellers.

– David Lukas

1

2

eopard **2.** Female lions **3.** Cheetahs

Big Cats

The three big cats – leopard, lion and cheetah – provide the high point for so many memorable safaris. The presence of these apex predators, even the mere suggestion that they may be nearby, is enough to draw the savannah taut with attention. It's the lion's gravitas, roaring at night, stalking at sunset. It's the elusive leopard that remains hidden while in plain view. And it's the cheetah in a fluid blur of hunting perfection.

Leopard

Weight 30-60kg (female), 40-90kg (male); length 170-300cm More common than you realise the leopard relies on expert camouflage to stay hidden. During the day you might spot one reclining in a tree after it twitches its tail, but at night there is no mistaking their bone-chilling groans.
Best seen: Masai Mara NR, Tsavo West NP

Lion

Weight 120-150kg (female), 150-225kg (male); length 210-275cm (female), 240-350cm (male) Those lions sprawled lazily in the shade are actually Africa's most feared predators. Equipped with teeth that tear effortlessly through bone and tendon, they can take down an animal as large as a bull giraffe. Each group of adults (a pride) is based around generations of females that do the majority of the hunting; swaggering males typically fight among themselves and eat what the females catch.
Best seen: Masai Mara NR, Laikipia, Tsavo West & East NPs, Amboseli NP

3

Cheetah

Weight 40-60kg; length 200-220cm The cheetah is a world-class sprinter. Although it reaches speeds of 112km/h, the cheetah runs out of steam after 300m and must cool down for 30 minutes before hunting again. This speed comes at another cost – the cheetah is so well adapted for running that it lacks the strength and teeth to defend its food or cubs from attack by other large predators.
Best seen: Masai Mara NR, Tsavo East NP, Amboseli NP

Small Cats

While big cats get the lion's share of attention from tourists, Kenya's small cats are equally interesting though much harder to spot. You won't find these cats chasing down gazelles or wildebeest, instead look for them slinking around in search of rodents or making incredible leaps to snatch birds out of the air.

Caracal

Weight 8-19kg; length 80-120cm The caracal is a gorgeous tawny cat with long, pointy ears. This African version of the northern lynx has jacked-up hind legs like a feline dragster. These beanpole kickers enable this slender cat to make vertical leaps of 3m and swat birds in flight.
Best seen: Widespread in Kenya's parks, although difficult to spot.

Wildcat

Weight 3-6.5kg; length 65-100cm If you see what looks like a tabby wandering the plains of Kenya you're probably seeing a wildcat, the direct ancestor of our domesticated housecat. Occurring wherever there are abundant mice and rats, the wildcat is readily found on the outskirts of villages, where it can be best identified by its unmarked rufous ears and longish legs.

Serval

Weight 6-18kg; length 90-130cm Twice as large as a housecat but with long legs and large ears, the beautifully spotted serval is adapted for walking in tall grass and making prodigious leaps to catch rodents and birds. More diurnal than most cats, it may be seen tossing food in the air and playing with it.
Best seen: Masai Mara NR, Aberdare NP (black servals)

1

1. Caracal 2. Wildcat 3. Serval

3

2

ARIADNE VAN ZANDBERGEN / GETTY IMAGES ©

1

2

COMSTOCK / GETTY IMAGES ©

Vervet monkeys **2.** Olive baboon **3.** Patas monkey

Savannah Primates

East Africa is the evolutionary cradle of primate diversity, giving rise to more than 30 species of monkeys, apes and prosimians (the 'primitive' ancestors of modern primates), all of which have dextrous hands and feet. Several species have evolved to living on the ground where they are vulnerable to lions and hyenas.

Vervet Monkey

Weight 4-8kg; length 90-140cm Each troop of vervets is composed of females who defend a home range passed down from generation to generation, while males fight each other for bragging rights and access to females. Check out the extraordinary blue and scarlet colours of their sexual organs when aroused.
Best seen: Saiwa Swamp NP, but widespread throughout the country.

Olive Baboon

Weight 11-30kg (female), 22-50kg (male); length 95-180cm Although the formidable olive baboon has 5cm-long fangs and can kill a leopard, its best defence may consist of running up trees and showering intruders with liquid excrement. Intelligent and opportunistic, troops of these greenish baboons are common in western Kenya, while much paler yellow baboons range over the eastern half of the country.
Best seen: Lake Nakuru NP, but widespread throughout the country.

Patas Monkey

Weight 7-25kg; length 110-160cm A unique subspecies of this widespread West African monkey lives on the Serengeti Plains. Russet-backed and slender bodied with lanky legs, this remarkable monkey is the fastest primate in the world – able to sprint 55km/h as it races towards the nearest trees. Still, quite a few adults are eaten by carnivores so Patas monkeys have a very high reproductive rate.
Best seen: Segera Ranch

1

2

ARIADNE VAN ZANDBERGEN / GETTY IMAGES ©

Black-and-white colobus 2. De Brazza's monkey
. Lesser galago

Forest Primates

Forest primates are a diverse group that live entirely in trees. These agile, long-limbed primates generally stay in the upper canopy where they search for leaves and arboreal fruits. It might take the expert eyes of a professional guide to help you find some of these species.

Black-and-White Colobus

Weight 10-23kg; length 115-165cm Also known as the guereza, the black-and-white colobus is one of Kenya's most popular primates due to the flowing white frills of hair arrayed across its black body. Like all colobus, this agile primate has a hook-shaped hand, so it can swing through the trees with the greatest of ease. When two troops run into each other expect to see a real show.
Best seen: Kakamega Forest, Lake Nakuru NP, Mt Elgon NP

De Brazza's Monkey

Weight 4-8kg; length 90-135cm Riverside forests of west-central Kenya are home to this rare and colourful monkey. Despite glaring red eyebrows and big bushy white beards, de Brazza's monkeys are surprisingly inconspicuous due to their grizzled upperparts and habit of sitting motionless for up to eight hours. In the early morning and late afternoon they ascend to higher branches to eat fruit and sunbathe.
Best seen: Kakamega Forest, Mt Elgon NP, Saiwa Swamp NP

Lesser Galago

Weight 100-300g; length 40cm A squirrel-sized nocturnal creature with a doglike face and huge eyes, the lesser galago belongs to a group of prosimians that have changed little in 60 million years. Best known for its frequent bawling cries (hence the common name 'bushbaby'), the galago would be rarely seen except that it readily visits feeding stations at many popular safari lodges. Living in a world of darkness, galagos communicate with each other through scent and sound.
Best seen: Widespread throughout Kenya

Cud-Chewing Mammals

Africa is arguably most famous for its astounding variety of ungulates – hoofed mammals that include everything from buffaloes to giraffes. In this large family cud-chewing antelopes are particularly numerous, with 40 different species in East Africa alone.

Gerenuk

Weight 30-50kg; length 160-200cm Adapted for life in semiarid brush, the gerenuk stands on its hind legs to reach 2m-high branches with its giraffelike neck.
Best seen: Samburu NR, Amboseli NP

Thomson's Gazelle

Weight 15-35kg; length 95-150cm This long-legged antelope is built for speed. In southern Kenya an estimated 400,000 migrate in great herds, along with zebras and wildebeest.
Best seen: Masai Mara NR, Amboseli NP, Tsavo East & West NP

Wildebeest

Weight 140-290kg; length 230-340cm Few animals evoke the spirit of the African plain as much as the wildebeest. Over a million gather on the Masai Mara alone, where they form vast, constantly moving herds.
Best seen: Masai Mara NR

Waterbuck

Weight 160-300kg; length 210-275cm If you're going to see any antelope on safari, it's likely to be the big, shaggy and, some say, smelly waterbuck. However, their numbers fluctuate dramatically between wet and dry years.
Best seen: Widespread throughout Kenya

African Buffalo (Cape Buffalo)

Weight 250-850kg; length 220-420cm Imagine a cow on steroids then add a particularly fearsome set of curling horns and you get the massive African buffalo. Thank goodness they're usually docile.
Best seen: Widespread throughout southern and central Kenya

1

3

2

1. Gerenuk **2.** Thomson's gazelles **3.** Wildebeest **4.** Waterbuck

ARIADNE VAN ZANDBERGEN / GETTY IMAGES ©

4

DAN HERRICK / GETTY IMAGES ©

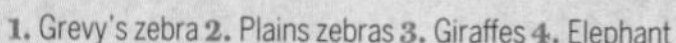

1. Grevy's zebra 2. Plains zebras 3. Giraffes 4. Elephant

ARIADNE VAN ZANDBERGEN / GETTY IMAGES ©

Hoofed Mammals

The continent has a surprising diversity of hoofed animals. Those that don't chew cuds occur over a much broader range of habitats than the cud-chewing antelope. They have been at home in Africa for millions of years. Without human intervention, Africa would be ruled by elephants, zebras, hippos and warthogs.

Grevy's Zebra

Weight 350-450kg; length 290-375cm This large and distinctive zebra is restricted to the semiarid plains of northern Kenya, where it mingles with the plains zebra. Look for the thinner black stripes that do not extend down onto its white belly. Best seen: Laikipia WC, Samburu NR, Meru NP, West Gate Community Conservancy

Plains Zebra

Weight 175-320kg; length 260-300cm Scientists first thought the stripes, each distinct as human fingerprints, were to confuse predators by making it difficult to distinguish the outline of individuals in a herd. However, new studies suggest stripes help combat disease carrying horseflies. Best seen: Widespread throughout southern and central Kenya

Giraffe

Weight 450-1200kg (female), 1800-2000kg (male); height 3.5-5.2m The 5m-tall giraffe does such a good job of reaching up to grab high branches that stretching down to get a simple drink of water is difficult. Though they stroll along casually, a healthy giraffe can outrun most predators. Best seen: Masai Mara (Masai giraffes), Lake Nakuru NP (Rothschild's giraffes), Samburu NR (reticulated giraffes)

African Elephant

Weight 2200-3500kg (female), 4000-6300kg (male); height 2.4-3.4m (female), 3-4m (male) No one stands around when a bull elephant rumbles out of the brush. Though the elephant is commonly referred to as 'the king of beasts', elephant society is ruled by a lineage of elder females. Best seen: Amboseli NP, Tsavo East NP, Samburu NR

More Hoofed Mammals

This sampling of miscellaneous hoofed animals highlights the astonishing diversity in this major group of African wildlife. Every visitor wants to see elephants and giraffes, but don't pass up a chance to watch hyraxes or warthogs.

Warthog

Weight 45-75kg (female), 60-150kg (male); length 140-200cm Despite their fearsome appearance and sinister tusks, only the big males are safe from lions, cheetahs and hyenas. When attacked, warthogs run for burrows and reverse backside in, while slashing wildly with their tusks.
Best seen: Widespread throughout Kenya

Black Rhinoceros

Weight 700-1400kg; length 350-450cm Pity the black rhinoceros for having a horn worth more than gold. Once widespread and abundant south of the Sahara, the rhino has been poached to the brink of extinction. Unfortunately, females may only give birth every five years.
Best seen: Best seen in Ol Pejeta Conservancy, Lake Nakuru NP, Nairobi NP, Meru NP

Hippopotamus

Weight 510-3200kg; length 320-400cm
The hippopotamus is a strange creature: designed like a floating beanbag with tiny legs, the 3000kg hippo spends its time in or near water eating aquatic plants. Placid? No way! Hippos have tremendous ferocity and strength when provoked.
Best seen: Masai Mara NR, Tsavo West NP

Rock Hyrax

Weight 1.8-5.5kg; length 40-60cm It doesn't seem like it, but those funny tail-less squirrels lounging around on rocks are an ancient cousin to the elephant. You won't see some of the features that rock hyraxes share with their larger kin, but look for tusks when one yawns.
Best seen: Easily spotted in many of Kenya's parks

1

3

2

1. Warthog **2.** Black rhino **3.** Hippos **4.** Rock hyraxes

ARIADNE VAN ZANDBERGEN / GETTY IMAGES ©

KLAAS LINGBEEK VAN KRANEN / GETTY IMAGES ©

MORALES / GETTY IMAGES ©

1. Golden jackal 2. Wild dog 3. Spotted hyena 4. Banded mongoose

ARIADNE VAN ZANDBERGEN / GETTY IMAGES ©

Carnivores

It is a sign of Africa's ecological richness that the continent supports a remarkable variety of predators. Expect the unexpected and you'll return home with a lifetime of memories!

Golden Jackal

Weight 6-15kg; length 85-130cm Despite its trim, diminutive form, the jackal fearlessly stakes a claim at the dining table of the African plain while holding hungry vultures and much stronger hyenas at bay. Best seen: Best seen in Masai Mara NR

African Wild Dog

Weight 20-35kg; length 100-150cm Organised in complex hierarchies with strict rules of conduct, these social canids are incredibly efficient hunters. They run in packs of 20 to 60 to chase down antelopes and other animals.
Best seen: Matthews Range, Borana Conservancy, Il Ngwesi Group Ranch

Spotted Hyena

Weight 40-90kg; length 125-215cm Living in groups that are ruled by females (who grow penis-like sexual organs), hyenas use bone-crushing jaws to disembowel terrified prey on the run.
Best seen: Widespread and easily seen throughout Kenya's parks

Banded Mongoose

Weight 1.5-2kg; length 45-75cm Bounding across the savannah on their morning foraging excursions for delicious snacks such as toads, scorpions and slugs, a family of mongooses is a delightful sight.
Best seen: Easily spotted in many Kenyan parks

Common Genet

Weight 1-2kg; length 80-100cm Though nocturnal, these slender, agile hunters are readily observed slinking along roadsides or scrambling among the rafters of safari lodges. They look like a cross between a cat and a raccoon, but are easily recognised by their cream-coloured bodies and leopardlike spotting.
Best seen: Easily spotted in many Kenyan parks

Birds of Prey

Kenya has nearly 100 species of hawks, eagles, vultures and owls. With a range from the songbird-sized pygmy kestrel to the massive lammergeier, this is one of the best places in the world to see an incredible variety of birds of prey.

Lappet-Faced Vulture

Length 115cm It's not a pretty sight when gore-encrusted vultures take over a rotting carcass that no other scavenger wants, but it's the way nature works. The monstrous lappet-faced vulture, a giant among vultures, gets its fill before other vultures move in.
Best seen: Masai Mara NR

Secretary Bird

Length 100cm With the body of an eagle and the legs of a crane, the secretary bird stands 1.3m tall and walks up to 20km a day in search of vipers, cobras and other snakes.
Best seen: Amboseli NP

African Fish Eagle

Length 75cm With a wingspan over 2m, this replica of the American bald eagle is most familiar for its loud ringing vocalisations, which have become known as 'the voice of Africa'.
Best seen: Amboseli NP, Lake Nakuru NP

Bateleur

Length 60cm French for 'tightrope-walker', this eagle's name refers to its distinctive low-flying aerial acrobatics. At close hand, look for its bold colour pattern and scarlet face.
best seen: Widespread throughout southern and central Kenya

Augur Buzzard

Length 55cm Perhaps Kenya's most common raptor, the augur buzzard occupies a wide range of wild and cultivated habitats. One of their hunting strategies is to float motionless in the air by riding the wind then swooping down quickly to catch unwary critters.
Best seen: Widespread throughout southern and central Kenya

1

3

DUNCAN BLACKBURN / GETTY IMAGES ©

1. Lappet-faced vulture **2.** Secretary bird **3.** African fish eagle **4.** Bateleur

ARIADNE VAN ZANDBERGEN / GETTY IMAGES ©

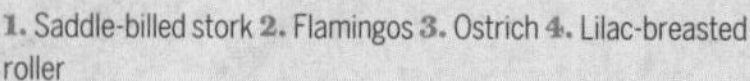

1. Saddle-billed stork 2. Flamingos 3. Ostrich 4. Lilac-breasted roller

IGNACIO PALACIOS / GETTY IMAGES ©

Other Birds

Birdwatchers from all over the world travel to Kenya in search of the country's 1100 species of bird, an astounding number by any measure, including every shape and colour imaginable.

Saddle-Billed Stork

Height 150cm; wingspan 270cm The saddle-billed stork is one of the more remarkably coloured of Kenya's birds. As if the 270cm wingspan wasn't impressive enough, check out its brilliant-red-coloured kneecaps and bill.
Best seen: Best seen in Tsavo West NP

Lesser Flamingo

Length 1m Coloured deep rose-pink and gathering by the hundreds of thousands on salt lakes, lesser flamingos create some of the most dramatic wildlife spectacles in Africa, especially when they fly at once or perform synchronised courtship displays.
Best seen: Lake Magadi (depending on the year), Lake Nakuru NP, Lake Bogoria NR

Ostrich

Height 200-270cm Standing 270cm and weighing upwards of 130kg, these ancient flightless birds escape predators by running at 70km/h or lying flat on the ground to resemble a pile of dirt.
Best seen: Widespread throughout southern Kenya; Laikipia and Samburu NR (Blue-legged Somali Ostrich)

Lilac-Breasted Roller

Length 40cm Nearly everyone on safari gets to know the lilac-breasted roller. It gets its name from its tendency to 'roll' from side to side in flight to show off its iridescent blues, purples and greens.
Best seen: Commonly seen throughout Kenya

Vulturine Guineafowl

Length 71cm Take an electric-blue chicken, drape black-and-white speckled feathers over its body and place an elegant ruff around its neck and you have a pretty flamboyant bird. Look for guineafowl walking around in groups in semiarid areas.
Best seen: Tsavo West NP

Habitats

Nearly all of Kenya's wildlife occupies a specific type of habitat. You will hear rangers and fellow travellers refer to these habitats repeatedly as they describe where to search for animals. If this is your first time in Kenya, some of these habitats and their seasonal rhythms take some getting used to, but your wildlife-viewing experience will be greatly enhanced if you learn how to recognise these habitats and the animals you might expect to find in each one.

High Mountains

Kenya is remarkable for having extensive high-mountain habitats, including unexpected snowy crags and glaciers that are located right on the equator, a habitat that is very rare anywhere else in East Africa. The massive extinct volcanoes of Mt Elgon and Mt Kenya are islands of montane forests, bogs, giant heathers and moorlands that are perched high above the surrounding lowlands. The few animals that survive here are uniquely adapted to these bizarre landscapes.

Semiarid Desert

Much of eastern and northern Kenya sees so little rainfall that shrubs and hardy grasses, rather than trees, are the dominant vegetation. This is not the classic landscape that many visitors come to see and it doesn't seem like a great place for wildlife, but the patient observer will be richly rewarded. While it's true that the lack of water restricts larger animals such as zebras, gazelles and antelopes to areas around waterholes, this habitat explodes with plant and animal life whenever it rains. During the dry season many plants shed their leaves to conserve water and grazing animals move on in search of food and water.

Savannah

Savannah is *the* classic East African landscape – broad rolling grasslands dotted with lone acacia trees. The openness and vastness of this landscape make it a perfect home for large herds of grazing zebras and wildebeest, in addition to fast-sprinting predators like cheetahs, and i the best habitat for seeing large numbers o animals. Savannah develops in areas where there are long wet seasons alternating with long dry seasons, creating ideal conditions the growth of dense, nutritious grasses. Sha by fire and grazing animals, savannah is a dynamic habitat in constant flux with adjac woodlands.

Rivers & Lakes

Since vast areas of Kenya are extremely dry least on a seasonal basis, any source of wat is a mecca for wildlife. Everything from slo moving rivers to shallow lakes and muddy wallows attract steady streams of birds and mammals; one of the best ways to watch wildlife is to sit quietly near watering holes. Some of the highly saline and alkaline lakes of the Rift Valley, such as Lake Nakuru and Lake Bogoria, attract fantastic numbers of birds, including African fish eagles, shorebi and ducks, as well as flocks of more than o million flamingos.

1. Mt Kenya (p165), Kenya's highest peak **2.** Ewaso Ngiro Rive Samburu National Reserve (p274)

2

1

MARTIN MOXTER / GETTY IMAGES ©

Masai giraffes, Hell's Gate National Park (p9

Environment

Kenya, as the cliché goes, is Africa in microcosm, but in this case the cliché happens to be true. Within Kenya's borders you'll find astonishing variety, from deserts to tropical coast and snow-capped mountains, from sweeping savannah grasslands to dense forests. Running through the heart of it all is the Great Rift Valley. The country faces some of the most pressing environmental issues of our time, but this is also where some of Africa's most cutting-edge conservation solutions are happening.

The Land

Great Rift Valley

Africa's Great Rift Valley is one of Africa's defining landforms and this great gouge in the planet cuts a swath through the heart of Kenya. It was formed some eight million years ago, when Mother Earth tried to rip Africa in two. Africa bent, Africa buckled, but Africa never gave in.

The Rift Valley is part of the Afro-Arabian rift system that stretches 5500km from the salty shores of the Dead Sea to the palm trees of Mozambique, passing through the Red Sea, Ethiopia, Kenya, Tanzania and Malawi en route. A western branch forms a string of lakes in the centre of the continent (Albert, Edward, Kivu and Tanganyika), joining the main system at the tip of Lake Malawi. The East African section of the rift 'failed' and now only the Red Sea rift continues, slowly separating Africa from the Middle East. The Rift's path through Kenya can be traced through Lake Turkana, the Cherangani Hills and Lakes Baringo, Bogoria, Nakuru, Elmenteita, Naivasha and Magadi.

For an evocative and beautifully written picture of Kenya's physical, environmental and cultural make-up, track down Peter Matthiessen's classic, *The Tree Where Man Was Born*, an account of the author's epic journey through East Africa in the 1960s.

The Rift created Africa's highest mountains – including Mt Kenya, Mt Elgon, Mt Kilimanjaro (across the border in Tanzania) and the Virunga Range (in the Democratic Republic of the Congo; DRC, formerly Zaïre) – most of which began as volcanoes. Most of the volcanoes that line the valley are now extinct, but no fewer than 30 remain active and, according to local legend, Mt Longonot erupted as recently as the 1860s. This continuing activity supports a considerable number of hot springs, and provides ideal conditions for geothermal power plants (in Hell's Gate National Park and the Menengai Crater, for example), which are increasingly important for Kenya's energy supply, if controversial from an environmental perspective.

The Savannah

The African savannah is a quintessentially African landform, so much so that it covers an estimated two-thirds of the African land mass. In Kenya, the most famous sweeps of savannah are found in the country's west (particularly in the Masai Mara National Reserve) and south.

The East African savannah was formed during the Rift's great upheavals, when volcanic lava and ash rained down upon the lands surrounding the Rift's volcanoes, covering the landscape in fertile but shallow soils. Grasses, that most successful of plant forms, flourished as they needed little depth for their roots to grow. The perfectly adapted acacia aside, however, no other plants were able to colonise the savannah, their roots were starved of space and nourishment.

The result is sweeping plains that are home to some of the richest concentrations of wildlife on earth. The term itself refers to a grasslands ecosystem. While trees may be (and usually are) present, such trees do not, under the strict definition of the term, form a closed canopy, while wet and dry seasons (the latter often with regenerating and/or devastating wildfires) are also typical of Africa's savannah regions.

The Coast

Along the coast of East Africa, warm currents in the Indian Ocean provide perfect conditions for coral growth, resulting in beautiful underwater coral reefs.

Mangroves

Wasini Island

Funzi Island

Gazi Island

Mida Creek

Coral reefs are the most biologically diverse marine ecosystems on earth, rivalled only by tropical rainforests on land. Corals grow over geologic time – ie over millennia rather than the decades that mammals etc live – and have been in existence for about 200 million years. The delicately balanced marine environment of the coral reef relies on the interaction of hard and soft corals, sponges, fish, turtles, dolphins and other marine life forms.

Coral reefs also rely on mangroves, the salt-tolerant trees with submerged roots that form a nursery and breeding ground for birds and most of the marine life that migrates to the reef. Mangroves trap and produce nutrients for food and habitat, stabilise the shoreline, and filter pollutants from the land base. Both coral reefs and the mangrove colonies that support them are under threat from factors such as oil exploration and extraction, coastal degradation, deforestation and global warming.

Forests

Kenya's forests border the great rainforest systems of central Africa, and western Kenya once formed part of the mighty Guineo-Congolian forest ecosystem. Few vestiges remain and just 6.2% of Kenyan territory is now covered by forest. The process of clearing these forests began with Kenya's colonial rulers, who saw in the land's fertility great potential for the vast tea plantations that now provide critical export revenue to Kenya. The clearing of the land has continued apace ever since as Kenya's population soars and the need for land given over to agriculture has increased. The Kakamega Forest has been protected just in time and shows what most of western Kenya must have once looked like. Other important forest areas include the forests (including the Kamweti Forest) that cover 2000 sq km of the slopes of Mt Kenya; the Arabuko Sokoke Forest Reserve, the largest surviving tract of coastal forest in East Africa; Mt Elgon National Park; and Aberdare National Park.

Deserts

Much of northern Kenya is extremely arid, with rainfall of less than 100mm a year. A number of contiguous deserts occupy the territory between Lake Turkana's eastern shore and the Ethiopian and Somali borders. The largest and best known of these is the Chalbi Desert, centred on North Horr and Kalacha, and formed by an ancient lake bed. Other deserts of northern Kenya include the Kaisut Desert (between Marsabit and South Horr) and the Dida Galgalu Desert (close to the Ethiopian border, near Moyale).

Parts of southern Kenya are also considered arid or semiarid, thanks largely to the looming hulk of Mt Kilimanjaro, which diverts rain elsewhere. One of these is the Nyiri Desert, which lies roughly between Lake Magadi and Amboseli National Park.

RIFT LAKES RISING

Whether alkaline or freshwater, Kenya's lakes have experienced an as-yet-unexplained rise in water levels. In some cases, these rises have been by metres, engulfing shorelines and beyond, forcing some businesses to close, maps to be redrawn and reducing the salinity of the lakes in some cases; the latter problem has caused the flamingos to go elsewhere. Hardest hit have been Baringo, Bogoria, Elmenteita and Nakuru, with Lake Naivasha also experiencing rising water levels.

The most likely explanation is that tectonic plates well below the surface have shifted, causing changes in water flows, although nobody knows for how long these new watery boundaries will remain as they are.

Lakes & Wetlands

Lake Victoria, which is shared between Uganda, Tanzania and Kenya, is Africa's largest freshwater lake (and the second-largest by area in the world after the USA's Lake Superior). Its surface covers an area of over 68,000 sq km, with only 20% of the lake lying within Kenyan territory. Water levels fluctuate widely, depending largely on the rains, with depths never more than 80m and more often less than 10m.

Most of Kenya's section of Lake Victoria is taken over by the Winam Gulf, a 100km-long, 50km-wide arm of the lake with a shoreline of almost 550km and an average depth of 6m. A fast-growing population around the gulf's shoreline has caused massive environmental problems such as siltation, sedimentation and toxic pollution (primarily pesticides and untreated sewage), although the major issue has been the invasion of water hyacinth since the late 1980s. The millions of dollars ploughed into solving the problem largely rid the gulf of hyacinth by 2005, but the gulf remains highly susceptible to the hyacinth's clutches.

Aside from Lake Victoria in the west, Kenya has numerous small volcanic lakes, as well as a sea of jade, otherwise known by the more boring name of Lake Turkana, which straddles the Ethiopian border in the north. The main alkaline lakes in the Rift Valley include Bogoria, Nakuru, Elmenteita, Magadi and Oloiden. These shallow soda lakes, formed by the valley's lack of decent drainage, experience high evaporation rates, which further concentrates the alkalinity. The strangely soapy and smelly waters are, however, the perfect environment for the growth of microscopic blue-green algae, which in turn feed lesser flamingos, tiny crustaceans (food for greater flamingos) and insect larvae (food for soda-resistant fish).

Not all of the Rift Valley's lakes are alkaline; freshwater lakes include Baringo and Naivasha.

In 2011, the global significance of Kenya's Rift Valley lake system (primarily Lakes Nakuru, Elmenteita and Bogoria) was recognised when it was inscribed on Unesco's list of World Heritage Sites. Five of the Rift Valley's lakes – Baringo, Bogoria, Elmenteita, Naivasha and Nakuru – have also been listed on the Ramsar List of Wetlands of International Importance, and represent important habitats for wintering waterbirds from the north.

LAKE VICTORIA

Four rivers – the Sondu-Miriu, Kibos, Nyando and Kisat – send an average 231 cubic metres of water into the Winam Gulf on Kenya's stretch of Lake Victoria every second.

Rivers

One of Kenya's most important rivers is the Athi/Galana River system. The Athi River passes east of Nairobi, joins the Tsavo River (which passes through the Tsavo West National Park), and the two then feed into the Galana River which cuts Tsavo East National Park in two. The Athi/Galana River then empties into the Indian Ocean close to Malindi. The

Tana River is the country's other major river, rising northeast of Nairobi and emptying into the Indian Ocean between Malindi and Lamu.

Environmental Issues

Deforestation

Six sites in Kenya are included on the Unesco World Heritage list: Mt Kenya, Lake Turkana national parks, Lamu's Old Town, Fort Jesus in Mombasa, the Mijikenda *kayas* (sacred forests) and the lake system in the Great Rift Valley.

More than half of Africa's forests have been destroyed over the last century, and forest destruction continues on a large scale in parts of Kenya – today, less than 3% of the country's original forest cover remains. Land grabbing, charcoal burning, agricultural encroachment, the spiralling use of firewood, and illegal logging have all taken their toll over the years. However, millions of Kenyans (and the majority of hotels, lodges and restaurants) still rely on wood and charcoal for cooking fuel, so travellers to the country will almost certainly contribute to this deforestation, whether they like it or not.

Native hardwood such as ebony and mahogany is often used to make the popular carved wooden statue souvenirs sold in Kenya. Though this industry supports thousands of local families who may otherwise be without an income, it also consumes an estimated 80,000 trees annually. The World Wide Fund for Nature (WWF) and Unesco campaigned to promote the use of common, faster-growing trees, and many handicraft

CATTLE VERSUS WILDLIFE?

Nothing seems to disappoint visitors to Kenya's national parks more than the sight of herders shepherding their livestock to water sources within park boundaries. In the words of former Kenya Wildlife Service head Dr Richard Leakey: 'People don't pay a lot of money to see cattle'. The issue is, however, a complicated one.

On the one hand, what you are seeing is far from a natural African environment. For thousands of years people, and their herds of cattle, lived happily (and sustainably) alongside the wildlife, and their actions helped to shape the landscapes of East Africa. But with the advent of conservation and national parks, many of Kenya's tribal peoples, particularly pastoralists such as the Maasai and Samburu, found themselves and their cattle excluded from their ancestral lands or waterholes of last resort, often with little or no compensation or alternative incomes provided (although, of course, some do now make a living through tourism and conservation).

Having been pushed onto marginal lands and with limited access to alternative water sources in times of drought, many have been forced to forgo their traditional livelihoods and have taken to leading sedentary lifestyles. Those that continue as herders have little choice but to overgraze their lands. Such policies of exclusion tend to reinforce the perception among local peoples that wildlife belongs to the government and brings few benefits to local communities. This position is passionately argued in the excellent (if slightly dated) book *No Man's Land: An Investigative Journey Through Kenya & Tanzania* (2003) by George Monbiot.

At the same time, tourism is a major (and much-needed) source of revenue for Kenya and most visitors to Kenya want to experience a natural wilderness – on the surface at least, the national parks and reserves appear to provide this Eden-esque slice of Africa. It also remains questionable whether allowing herders and their livestock to graze within park boundaries would alleviate the pressures on overexploited land and traditional cultures, or would instead simply lead to the degradation of Kenya's last remaining areas of relatively pristine wilderness.

Things get even more complicated when talking about private and community conservancies. Many Laikipia and Mara conservancies – Ol Pejeta Conservancy and Segera Ranch are two prominent examples – consider livestock to be an important part of habitat management, arguing that well-maintained livestock herds can help reduce tick infestations for wildlife. Carefully controlled grazing can also, they argue, actually assist in the regeneration of grassland ecosystems.

cooperatives now use wood taken from forests managed by the Forest Stewardship Council. If you buy a carving, ask if the wood is sourced from managed forests.

Desertification

Northern and eastern Kenya are home to some of the most marginal lands in East Africa. Pastoralists have eked out a similarly marginal existence here for centuries, but recurring droughts have seriously degraded the land, making it increasingly susceptible to creeping desertification and erosion. As a consequence, the UN estimates that the livelihoods of around 3.5 million herders may be under medium- to long-term threat.

And desertification, at least in its early stages, may even begin to encroach upon the most unlikely places. The fertile lands of Kenya's Central Highlands rank among Africa's most agriculturally productive, but therein lies their peril: here, around three-quarters of Kenya's population crowds into just 12% of the land, with the result that soils are being rapidly depleted through overexploitation – one of the early warning signs of desertification.

Endangered Species

Many of Kenya's major predators and herbivores have become endangered over the past few decades, because of poisoning, the ongoing destruction of their natural habitat and merciless poaching for ivory, skins, horn and bushmeat.

Elephants

Elephants are numerous in many areas of Kenya, but it hasn't always been so and their survival is one of world conservation's most enduring success stories.

In the 1970s and '80s, the numbers of African elephants plummeted from an estimated 1.3 million to around 500,000 thanks to widespread poaching. In Kenya, elephant numbers fell from 45,000 in 1976 to just 5400 in 1988. The slaughter ended only in 1989 when the trade in ivory was banned under the Convention for International Trade in Endangered Species (Cites). When the ban was established, world raw ivory prices plummeted by 90%, and the market for poaching and smuggling was radically reduced. The same year, Kenyan President Daniel arap Moi dramatically burned 12 tons of ivory in Nairobi National Park as a symbol of Kenya's resolve in the battle against poachers.

With poaching largely defeated until a recent resurgence, Kenya's elephant numbers have grown to an estimated 32,000 elephants. More than one-third of these inhabit Tsavo West and Tsavo East national parks.

Based in Kenya and run by the respected Dr Iain Douglas-Hamilton, **Save the Elephants** (www.savetheelephants.org) is one of the pre-eminent NGOs working with elephants in Africa, while one of the longest-running studies of elephants on the planet, **Amboseli Trust for Elephants** (ATE; www.elephanttrust.org) is overseen by Dr Cynthia Moss and is based inside Amboseli National Park.

Rhinoceros

These inoffensive vegetarians are armed with impressive horns that have made them the target of both white hunters and poachers; rhino numbers plummeted to the brink of extinction during the 20th century and the illegal trade in rhino horns is still driven by their use in traditional medicines in Asian countries.

There are two species of rhino – black and white – both of which are predominantly found in savannah regions. The black rhino is probably Kenya's most endangered large mammal. It is also often described as

Rhino Hot Spots

Ol Pejeta Conservancy (Laikipia Plateau) More than 100 black rhinos.

Lewa Wildlife Conservancy (Laikipia Plateau) More than 120 black and white rhinos.

Meru National Park (near Mt Kenya) At last count, 24 black and 56 white rhinos.

Ngulia Rhino Sanctuary (in Tsavo West National Park, Southeastern Kenya) Close to 80 black rhinos.

Nairobi National Park (Nairobi) More than 50 black rhinos.

Solio Game Reserve (Laikipia Plateau) Black rhinos.

Aberdare National Park (Central Highlands) Black rhinos.

Lake Nakuru National Park (Southern Rift Valley) Both black and white rhinos.

Kenya's indigenous rhino – historically, the white rhino was not found in Kenya. Pursued by heavily armed gangs, the black rhino's numbers fell from an estimated 20,000 in the 1970s to barely 300 a decade later. Numbers are slowly recovering (rhinos are notoriously slow breeders), with an estimated 620 black rhinos surviving in the wild in Kenya, which represents around one-sixth of Africa's total (or close to 90% of the world population for the eastern subspecies of black rhino).

Although numbers are quite small in Kenya, the survival of the white rhino is an environmental conservation success story, having been brought back from the brink of extinction in South Africa through captive breeding. The Kenya Wildlife Service estimated in late 2010 that Kenya was home to 350 white rhinos in the wild. At Ol Pejeta Conservancy in Laikipia, you can see three of the five remaining northern white rhinos (a subspecies of the white rhino) left in the world.

White rhinos aren't white at all – the name comes from the Dutch word *wijd*, which means wide and refers to the white rhino's wide lip (the black rhino has a pointed lip).

Rhino Ark (☎Nairobi 020-2136010; www.rhinoark.org) is one organisation that raises funds to create rhino sanctuaries or to build fences around national parks, as they have done in Aberdare National Park, and donations are always appreciated.

Lions

Lions may be the easiest of Kenya's big cats to spot – leopards are notoriously secretive and largely keep to the undergrowth, while cheetahs live in similarly low-density populations and can also prove elusive. But don't let appearances fool you: the lion may be the most imperilled of Africa's three big cats.

WANGARI MAATHAI, NOBEL LAUREATE

On Earth Day in 1977 Professor Wangari Maathai planted seven trees in her backyard, setting in motion the grassroots environmental campaign that later came to be known as the Green Belt Movement. Since then more than 40 million trees have been planted throughout Kenya and the movement has expanded to more than 30 other African countries. The core aim of this campaign is to educate women – who make up some 70% of farmers in Africa – about the link between soil erosion, undernourishment and poor health, and to encourage individuals to protect their immediate environment and guard against soil erosion by planting 'green belts' of trees and establishing tree nurseries.

For decades, Maathai's activism came at a cost. The Moi regime consistently vilified her as a 'threat to the order and security of the country', due to her demands for free and fair multiparty elections – throughout the years her public demonstrations were met with acts of violence and she spoke of receiving death threats. She also won few friends in powerful circles for working extensively with various international organisations to exert leverage on the Kenyan government.

In addition, she was also heavily involved in women's rights (her first husband divorced her because she was 'too strong-minded for a woman'; the judge in the divorce case agreed and then had her imprisoned for speaking out against him!). President Moi himself once famously suggested that Maathai should be more of a proper woman in the 'African tradition'.

Later, however, Maathai served as assistant minister for the environment between 2003 and 2005, and was awarded the Nobel Peace Prize in 2004 (the first African woman to receive one) for her tireless campaigning on environmental issues. In 2006 she was one of the founders of the Nobel Women's Initiative, which aims to bring justice, peace and equality to women.

Maathai died of cancer in a Nairobi Hospital in 2011 at the age of 71, but the **Green Belt Movement** (www.greenbeltmovement.org) she founded is still one of the most significant environmental organisations in Kenya. Maathai's book *Unbowed: One Woman's Story* was published in 2006.

GUIDES TO FAUNA

Having trouble telling a dik-dik from a klipspringer? A serval from a caracal? Try the following:

- *Kingdon Field Guide to African Mammals* (Jonathon Kingdon; 1997) Classic hand-illustrated field guide, widely considered to be the definitive guide to the continent's fauna. It's also available in a pocket edition.
- *A Field Guide to the Carnivores of the World* (Luke Hunter; 2011) Fabulous guide to predators with terrific illustrations and condensed but fascinating text. Released in 2011, it's the most up to date of the available guides. Watch out also for Hunter's forthcoming field guide to the cats of the world.
- *The Behaviour Guide to African Mammals* (Richard Despard Estes; 1991) Another classic of safari trails loaded with intriguing details.

Fewer than 30,000 lions are thought to remain in Africa, although most conservationists agree that the number is most likely considerably below that figure. In Kenya, fewer than 2000 are thought to survive, although this, too, is feared to be an overestimate. Although there are small, scattered prides around the country, in Lake Nakuru National Park and northern Kenya, the only viable lion populations in the long-term are those in Laikipia (estimated at around 270 lions), Maasailand and the two Tsavo parks (around 700 lions in the entire Tsavo ecosystem).

And numbers are falling alarmingly, possibly by as many as 100 lions per year, thanks primarily to human encroachment, habitat loss and the resulting human–wildlife conflict. The poisoning of lions (as well as scavengers and other predators), either in retaliation for lions killing livestock or encroaching onto farming lands, has also reached dangerous levels, to the extent that some lion conservationists predict that the lion could become extinct in Kenya within 20 years.

Important work is being done in the world of lion conservation, including the following initiatives:

Ewaso Lions (www.ewasolions.org) Deploys Samburu warriors to protect lions and livestock on Westgate Community Conservancy west of Samburu National Reserve.

Lion Guardians (www.lionguardians.org) Maasai warriors protect lions as well as their communities and livestock in the Amboseli ecosystem.

Living with Lions (www.livingwithlions.org) Fighting to protect Kenya's lions from its Laikipia base and an important source of information.

Maasai Wilderness Conservation Trust (www.maasaiwilderness.org) Simba Scouts keep lions and the Maasai apart, and the scheme pays local communities for the wildlife that live on their land.

Maasailand Preservation Trust (www.maasailand.wildlifedirect.org) Compensation scheme that pays Maasai herders for livestock lost to predators, thereby reducing retaliatory killings.

Reserves Home to Grevy's Zebra

- *Lewa Wildlife Conservancy*
- *Ol Pejeta Conservancy*
- *Segera Ranch*
- *Meru National Park*
- *Samburu National Reserve*

Grevy's Zebra

Kenya (along with neighbouring Ethiopia) is home to the last surviving wild populations of Grevy's zebra. Grevy's zebras are distinguished from other zebra species by having narrow stripes everywhere but with bellies free from stripes. In the 1970s, approximately 15,000 Grevy's zebras were thought to survive in the wild. Just 2500 are estimated to remain and less than 1% of the Grevy zebra's historical range lies within protected areas.

Rothschild's Giraffe

The most endangered of the nine giraffe subspecies, the Rothschild's giraffe has recently been hauled back from the brink of extinction. At the forefront of the fight to save Rothschild's giraffe (which, unlike other subspecies, has distinctive white 'stockings' with no orange-and-black markings below the knee) has been the Giraffe Centre (p63) in Nairobi – visiting here is a fascinating experience, and helps further the attempts to save the giraffes and facilitate their return to the wild.

Populations have been reintroduced into the wild at Lake Nakuru National Park.

Kenya: A Natural History (2012), by Stephen Spawls and Glenn Matthews, covers everything from wildlife to geology and just about everything in between. It's a terrific resource, if a little eclectic in parts.

Invasive Plant Species

There are many well-known threats to the ecosystem of Kenya's iconic Masai Mara National Reserve – poaching, overdevelopment and growing human populations. But one of the most dangerous threats comes in the form of a simple plant: a foreign weed called parthenium *(Parthenium hysterophorus)*. The toxic weed, which is not native to Kenya, first appeared around Nairobi, the Athi River, Naivasha and Busia, but its rapid growth in the Mara has led to it being designated a noxious weed by Kenya's government. Known to grow along the banks of the Mara River and some tracks through the reserve, parthenium (which is unpalatable to the Mara's herbivores) is spreading at an alarming rate, and in some areas is even replacing the fabled grasslands of the Mara. A single

POACHING'S RETURN

A recent upsurge in the poaching of both elephants (for their tusks) and rhinos (for their horns) has conservationists worried we may soon be facing a return to the dark days of the 1980s.

Talk to many in the conservation community and they'll tell you that it was in 2009 that the crisis again began to take hold. It was in the following year that Lewa Wildlife Conservancy lost its first rhinos to poaching in almost three decades and Africa has lost more than 30,000 elephants a year since 2010. In 2014, for the first time in decades, a critical threshold was crossed when more elephants were being killed on the continent than were being born.

While numbers of poached animals in Kenya remain relatively low, all of the major rhino sanctuaries – Nairobi National Park, Lewa Wildlife Conservancy, Ol Pejeta Conservancy, Ngulia Rhino Sanctuary in Tsavo West National Park – have lost rhinos to poachers in recent years. Most worrying of all is that each of these have extremely high security and sophisticated anti-poaching programs.

The worst area for rhino poaching appears, at the time of writing, to be Solio Game Reserve. For elephants, poaching hotspots include the northern half of Tsavo East National Park (which is off-limits for travellers), the community lands just outside the southern boundary of Tsavo West National Park, and the lands surrounding Samburu National Reserve.

The Kenyan Wildlife Service, while denying that poaching has reached crisis levels in Kenya, remains on the frontline in the war against poaching, but other organisations are also active.

Big Life Foundation (www.biglife.org) Credited with dramatically reducing poaching incidents on the lands where it operates, Big Life Foundation is a private anti-poaching militia that operates primarily in the Amboseli-Tsavo ecosystem.

Wildlife Direct (www.wildlifedirect.org) An excellent resource for the latest news on poaching and threats to endangered species.

parthenium plant can produce up to 25,000 seeds and its chemical composition is such that it inhibits the growth of other plants, prompting concerns that the weed could pose a long-term threat to the Mara.

Private Versus Public Conservation

Kenya Wildlife Service (KWS)

Conservation in Kenya has, for over two decades, been in the hands of the government-run **Kenya Wildlife Service** (kws; www.kws.org) and few would dispute that it has done a pretty impressive job. In the dark years of the 1970s and '80s when poaching was rampant, a staggering number of Kenya's rhinos and elephants were slaughtered and many KWS officers were in league with poachers. It all changed after the famous palaeontologist Dr Richard Leakey cleaned up the organisation in the 1980s and '90s. A core part of his policy was arming KWS rangers with modern weapons and high-speed vehicles and allowing them to shoot poachers on sight. Even so, with poaching again on the rise, KWS rangers continue to lose their lives every year in battles with poachers.

Despite their excellent work in fighting poaching and maintaining Kenya's protected areas, the KWS is limited in what it can achieve. For a start, in times of shrinking government revenues, funding remains a major issue in how well the KWS can fulfil its mandate.

Just as importantly, much of Kenya's wildlife lives beyond national park and other publicly protected boundaries. In such an environment, the KWS has shown itself to be at times intransigent in handling incidents of human–wildlife conflict in the communities that surround national park areas. As a result, there is a widespread perception among some communities that the KWS is more interested in looking after wildlife than they are in protecting local people. In response, the KWS has in recent years been working hard to improve its community relations, particularly in and around Amboseli National Park.

Private Conservancies

For all the success of KWS, there seems to be little doubt that the future of conservation in Kenya lies in private hands.

Much of it began up on the Laikipia Plateau and surrounding areas, on large cattle ranches which had, in many cases, been owned by the same family of white settlers since colonial times. One of the first to turn its attention to conservation was Lewa Downs, now the Lewa Wildlife Conservancy (p162) which in 1983 set aside part of its land as a rhino sanctuary (see p163). Lewa remains a standard bearer for the conservancy model and there are now more than 40 such conservancies scattered across Laikipia and northern regions, with many more around the Masai Mara (see p120).

While wildlife conservation is a primary focus of nearly all conservancies – these places often have the resources to work more intensively on specific conservation issues than national parks and reserves can – community engagement and development are considered equally important. Most often this consists of funding local schools, health centres and other development projects. By giving local communities a stake in the protection of wildlife, so the argument goes, they are more likely to protect the wildlife in their midst.

Another important element of the conservancy model includes making tourism pay its way. In almost all of the conservancies, access to conservancy land is restricted to those staying at the exclusive and often extremely expensive lodges and tented camps. Most also charge a conservancy fee (usually around US$100 per day) which goes directly

CONSERVATION

Game Changer: Animal Rights & the Fate of Africa's Wildlife, by Glen Martin, is a provocative look at wildlife conservation in 2012, covering Kenya, Tanzania and Namibia.

to local community projects and wildlife programs. All of this means a far more intimate safari experience as well as a much-reduced impact upon the land when compared with mass tourism.

Yet another advantage of visiting a private conservancy is that the range of activities on offer far exceeds what is possible in national parks. At the most basic level, this means off-road driving (to get you *really* close to the wildlife), night drives and walking safaris. Horseback safaris and visits to local communities are among the other possibilities, although you'll usually pay extra for these.

One exception to the overall rule, and it's a significant one, is Ol Pejeta Conservancy (p160). Although similar in terms of wildlife protection programs and community engagement, it has opened its doors to the public and receives tens of thousands of visitors every year. The experience of visiting Ol Pejeta is akin to visiting a national park but with a whole lot of really cool activities thrown in.

The East African Wildlife Society (www.eawildlife.org), based in Nairobi, is the most prominent conservation body in the region and a good source of information. They also publish *SWARA* magazine, a stalwart of the conservation scene and much of which is available online for members.

The private conservancies of the Laikipia Plateau in particular have produced some startling results – without a single national park or reserve in the area, Laikipia has become a major safari destination, and is proving to be a particularly important area for viable populations of endangered black rhinos, Grevy's zebras, African wild dogs and lions. In fact, the black rhino may well have disappeared forever from Kenya were it not for the Laikipia conservancies.

Most of the Laikipia ranches and conservancies are affiliated with the umbrella **Laikipia Wildlife Forum** (LWF; ☎0726500260; www.laikipia.org), which is a good source of up-to-date information about projects and accommodation in the region.

Community Conservancies

Similar in focus to private ranches, community conservancies are an extension of the private conservancy model. Rather than being owned by wealthy owners or families, community conservancies are communally owned by entire communities and administered by community representatives. These communities treat wildlife as a natural resource and take serious action to protect the animals' wellbeing, whether by combating poaching with increased security or by modifying their

ECOTOURISM IN KENYA

Established in 1996, **Eco Tourism Kenya** (www.ecotourismkenya.org) is a private organisation set up to oversee the country's tourism industry and encourage sustainable practices. Part of that involves a helpful eco-rating certification scheme for Kenya's hotels, safari camps and other accommodation options.

Under the scheme, a bronze rating is awarded to businesses which 'demonstrate awareness of and commitment to environmental conservation, responsible resource use and socio-economic investment'.

The silver standard goes to those businesses who 'demonstrate innovation – progress towards achieving excellence in environmental conservation, responsible resource use and socio-economic investment'.

To attain the much-coveted gold rating, tourism concerns must 'demonstrate outstanding best practices, ie, they have achieved superior and replicable levels of excellence in responsible resource use, environmental conservation and socio-economic investment'.

At the time of writing, just 13 places had received the gold certification, 54 had silver status and 30 were bronze-rated. To find out which properties made the cut, click on 'Eco-rated Facilities' under 'Directory Listings' on Eco Tourism Kenya's home page.

THE BATTLE FOR LAKE TURKANA

A number of the world's leading oil companies have been conducting exploratory drilling in the area between Lake Turkana and the Ethiopian border. In 2012, Britain's Tullow Oil struck it lucky, prompting much celebration in the Kenyan media that Kenya could soon be a major oil-producing country-in-waiting. Although the oil is still to begin flowing, Lake Turkana is widely considered by industry experts to be one of the more promising onshore oil exploration areas in East Africa.

At the same time, plans are well developed for the **Lake Turkana Wind Power** (LKTP; www.ltwp.co.ke) project, which is expected to be fully operational in 2016. When completed, the project will use 365 wind turbines across 40,000 acres around 50km north of South Horr to provide the equivalent of 20% of Kenya's current power needs. With an investment of close to €623 million, it is one of Kenya's largest-ever private investment projects.

herding activities to minimise human–animal conflict and environmental damage.

With financial and logistical support from many sources, including Lewa Wildlife Conservancy (LWC), Laikipia Wildlife Forum (LWF) and the Northern Ranchlands Trust (NRT), these communities have in many cases built eco-lodges whose income now provides much-needed funds for their education, health and humanitarian projects.

Northern Kenya appears to provide particularly fertile ground for the community conservancy model – fine examples include the Maasai of Il Ngwesi, Laikipia Maasai of Lekurruki and the Samburu within the Matthews Range – but there are also some excellent examples on the Maasai Group Ranches around Amboseli National Park and in the Masai Mara region.

The **Northern Rangelands Trust** (NRT; www.nrt-kenya.org) is a collection of community conservancies and a useful resource for learning about what's being done in northern Kenya. It also assists communities to set up their own conservancies by using the expertise of Lewa and other long-established ranches. Its 26 members cover an area of more than 25,000 sq km in northern Kenya.

Renewable Energy

The use of renewable energy has been slow to catch on in Kenya. Many top-end lodges attempt to pursue sound environmental practices – the use of solar energy is increasingly widespread – but these remain very much in the minority. And many of these top-end lodges suggest that you travel to them by air, which surely cancels out any gains of having solar-powered hot water in your shower. Expect fossil fuels to continue to drive Kenya's economy.

National Parks & Reserves

Kenya's national parks and reserves rate among the best in Africa. Around 10% of the country's land area is protected by law – that means, at least in theory, no human habitation, no grazing and no hunting within park boundaries. The parks range from the 15.5-sq-km Saiwa Swamp National Park to the massive, almost 21,000-sq-km Tsavo East and West national parks. Together they embrace a wide range of habitats and ecosystems and contain an extraordinary repository of Africa's wildlife.

History

The idea of setting aside protected areas began during colonial times, and in many cases this meant authorities forcibly evicting the local peoples from their traditional lands. Local anger was fuelled by the fact that many parks were set aside as hunting reserves for white hunters with anything but conservation on their minds. In 1946 Nairobi National Park became the first park in British East Africa. Now, there are 22 national parks, plus numerous marine parks and national reserves – the Kenya Wildlife Service (KWS) administers 33 protected areas in total.

Many of the parks came under siege in the 1970s and 1980s when poaching became endemic. In response, President Moi grabbed international headlines when, in 1989, he set fire to a stockpile of 12 tons of ivory in Nairobi National Park and appointed Richard Leakey to the head of the Wildlife Conservation and Management Department (WMCD), which became the KWS a year later. Leakey is largely credited with saving Kenya's wildlife, but his methods were hugely controversial: he declared war on poachers by forming elite and well-armed anti-poaching units with orders to shoot on sight.

Things are much quieter these days in the national parks, although poaching remains a problem.

NATIONAL PARKS VERSUS RESERVES

The difference is significant from a local perspective, less so in terms of your experience on safari. It all comes down to revenues. The entry fees for parks administered by the KWS go directly into the coffers of the national government, with a proportion, in theory at least, returned to the local communities. In the case of the locally administered reserves, revenues go to the local county council, which forwards some revenue on to the national government and, again in theory, uses the money for the benefit of local communities.

The whole issue came to national and international attention in 2005 when President Kibaki announced plans to de-gazette Amboseli National Park and turn it into a reserve administered by the Maasai-dominated Kajiado County Council. His motives remained unclear, although cynics suggested it may have been a ploy to win over the Maasai vote in advance of a crucial national referendum on constitutional reform. Conservationists cried foul and the move was declared illegal by Kenya's High Court in 2011.

MAJOR NATIONAL PARKS & RESERVES

PARK/RESERVE	WILDLIFE	ACTIVITIES	BEST TIME TO VISIT
Aberdare National Park	elephants, black rhinos, bongo antelope, black leopards, black servals	trekking, fishing, gliding	year-round
Amboseli National Park	elephants, buffaloes, lions, antelope, birds	wildlife drives	Jun–Feb
Arabuko Sokoke Forest Reserve	Sokoke scops owls, Clarke's weavers, birds, elephant shrews, elephants	bird tours, walking, cycling	year-round
Hell's Gate National Park	elands, giraffes, lions, birds of prey	cycling, walking	year-round
Kakamega Forest Reserve	de Brazza's monkeys, red-tailed monkeys, flying squirrels, 330 bird species	walking, birdwatching	year-round
Lake Bogoria National Reserve	greater kudus, leopards	birdwatching, walking, hot springs	year-round
Lake Nakuru National Park	flamingos, black & white rhinos, lions, leopards, more than 400 bird species	wildlife drives	year-round
Masai Mara National Reserve	Big Five, antelopes, cheetahs, hyenas, wildebeest migration	wildlife drives, ballooning	Jul–Oct
Meru National Park	rhinos, elephants, lions, cheetahs, lesser kudus	wildlife drives, fishing	year-round
Mt Elgon National Park	elephants, black-and-white-colobuses, de Brazza's monkeys, more than 240 bird species	walking, trekking, fishing	Dec–Feb
Mt Kenya National Park	elephants, buffaloes, mountain flora	trekking, climbing	Jan & Feb, Aug & Sep
Nairobi National Park	black rhinos, lions, leopards, cheetahs, giraffes, more than 400 bird species	wildlife drives	year-round
Saiwa Swamp National Park	sitatunga antelopes, otters, black-and-white colobuses, more than 370 bird species	walking, birdwatching	year-round
Samburu, Buffalo Springs & Shaba National Reserves	elephants, leopards, gerenuks, crocodiles, Grevy's zebras	wildlife drives	year-round
Shimba Hills National Reserve	elephants, sable antelopes, leopards	walking, forest tours	year-round
Tsavo West & East National Parks	Big Five, cheetahs, giraffes, hippos, crocodiles, around 500 bird species	rock climbing, wildlife drives	year-round

Visiting National Parks & Reserves

Going on safari is an integral part of the Kenyan experience, and the wildlife and scenery can be extraordinary. Even in more popular parks such as Masai Mara National Reserve and Amboseli National Park, which can become massively overcrowded in high season (July to October and January to February, although KWS maintains high-season prices into March), this natural splendour is likely to be your most enduring memory.

Park & Reserve Entry

Safaricards

Marine Parks

- *Kisite Marine National Park, Wasini Island*
- *Kiunga Marine National Reserve, Kiwayu Island*
- *Malindi Marine National Park, near Malindia*
- *Mombasa Marine National Park & Reserve, Bamburi Beach*
- *Watamu Marine National Park, Watamu*

Entry fees to national parks are controlled by the **KWS** (Kenya Wildlife Service; ☎Nairobi 020-6000800; www.kws.org; Nairobi National Park) and admission to parks in Kenya follows a 'safaricard' system for the payment of fees. There are two types of safaricards – permanent and temporary. For a full rundown on the system, visit www.kws.org/about/safaricard.

To put it in the simplest terms, it's handy to know how the system operates, but if you turn up at any park gate with enough cash in your wallet, you will be fine.

Permanent safaricards are sold at a handful of park entrances (check the website for a full list). These can be charged with credit in advance and can be topped up at certain locations (usually the parks' main gates only, which can be inconvenient). Remaining credit is not refundable. Remember that not all parks accept safaricards, so check which ones will only accept cash before topping up unnecessarily.

In practice, it is difficult to see why you'd need a permanent safaricard. In those parks where safaricards are in use, you can actually purchase a temporary safaricard, which covers the duration of your stay and which you surrender upon leaving the park. In other words, whether you're paying to top up your permanent card or paying for a temporary card, the process you'll encounter at park gates is almost identical.

At the time of writing the safaricard system was in use at Nairobi, Lake Nakuru, Aberdare, Amboseli and Tsavo national parks and at the Mombasa and Mailindi marine parks. The other parks still work on a cash-only system.

Entry Fees

The KWS has a number of categories for parks and reserves. Rates for Kenyan citizens and residents are available from the **KWS** (www.kws.org/tourism/tariffs) website.

NATIONAL PARKS & RESERVES FEES

KWS CATEGORY	PARK/RESERVE	NONRESIDENT ADULT/CHILD (US$)	CAMPING NON-RESIDENT ADULT/CHILD (US$)
N/A	Masai Mara	80/45	20
Premium	Amboseli, Lake Nakuru	80/40	30/25
Wilderness	Meru, Tsavo East & Tsavo West	75/40	20/15
Aberdare National Park	Aberdare	60/30	20/15
Urban Park	Nairobi National Park	50/25	20/15
Mountain Climbing (Day Trip)	Mt Kenya	55/25	20/15
Mountain Climbing (4-day package)	Mt Kenya	255/150	20/15
Scenic & Special Interest A	Hell's Gate, Mt Elgon, Ol Donyo Sabuk & Mt Longonot	30/20	20/15
Scenic & Special Interest B	Chyulu, Marsabit, Arabuko Sokoke, Kakamega, Shimba Hills & all other KWS parks	25/15	20/15
Marine Parks A	Kisite	25/15	N/A
Marine Parks B	Malindi, Watamu, Mombasa, Kiunga	20/15	N/A

MAJOR CONSERVANCIES

CONSERVANCY OR RESERVE	HABITATS	WILDLIFE	ACTIVITIES	BEST TIME TO VISIT
Borana Conservancy	hills, light woodland, savannah	rhinos, African wild dogs, lions	walking, birdwatching	Jun–Feb
Il Ngwesi Group Ranch	light woodland, hills	rhinos	walking, cultural visits	Jun–Feb
Kalama Community Wildlife Conservancy	semi-arid savannah, woodland	Grevy's zebras, reticulated giraffes, elephants	walking, night drives	Jun–Feb
Kuku Group Ranch	light woodland, mountain foothills	big cats, plains wildlife	walking, night drives	Jun–Feb
Lekurruki Community Ranch	indigenous forest, open savannah	elephants, big cats	walking, birdwatching	Jun–Feb
Lewa Wildlife Conservancy	savannah, riverine woodland	black & white rhinos, lions, leopards, cheetahs, elephants, Grevy's zebras, Somali ostriches	walking, horse riding, quad-biking, flying, community visits	Jun–Feb
Maji Moto Group Ranch	savannah	plains wildlife	Maasai cultural encounters	Jun–Feb
Mara North Conservancy	savannah	big cats, plains wildlife	walking, night drives, cultural encounters	Jun–Feb
Mbirikani Group Ranch	savannah, Chyulu Hills	elephants, big cats, giraffes	walking, running, horse riding	Jun–Feb
Naibosho Conservancy	savannah, acacia woodland	big cats, plains wildlife	walking, cultural encounters	Jun–Feb
Ol Pejeta Conservancy	savannah, light woodland	Big Five, black rhinos	walking, night drives, lion tracking, birdwatching	Jun–Feb
Olare-Orok Conservancy	savannah, acacia woodland	big cats, plains wildlife	walking, cultural encounters, night drives	Jun–Feb
Olarro Conservancy	savannah, acacia woodland	big cats, plains wildlife	walking, night drives	Jun–Feb
Olderikesi Conservancy	savannah, acacia woodland	big cats	walking, night drives	Jun–Feb
Segera Ranch	savannah, river valleys	big cats, Grevy's zebras, elephants, Patas monkeys, elephants	walking, flying, night drives	Jun–Feb
Selenkay Conservancy	semi-arid savannah	lions, elephants, giraffes	walking, night drives, Maasai cultural encounters	Jun–Feb
Siana Group Ranch & Conservancy	forests, swamps, grasslands	big cats, elephants	walking, cultural encounters	Jun–Feb
West Gate Community Conservancy	semi-arid acacia woodland, riverine woodland	Grevy's zebras, big cats, African wild dogs	walking, night drives, Samburu cultural encounters	Jun–Feb

CASH OR CREDIT CARD?

In theory you pay your park entry fees with cash or a credit card, but this does come with a couple of caveats.

Although KWS accepts other currencies (such as euros and UK pounds), we strongly recommend that you pay in US dollars or Kenyan shillings, as KWS exchange rates are punitive.

When it comes to credit cards, we've lost track of the number of times we've tried to pay our park entry fees with a credit card, only for the connection to be down or for it to take an age for the transaction to go through. Unless you're happy to waste an hour while your friendly KWS park ranger does contortions to try to catch a passing mobile signal for his credit-card machine, paying by cash will almost always see you on your way more quickly.

Further costs in the land-based parks and reserves include KSh350 for vehicles with fewer than six seats and KSh1200 for vehicles seating six to 12.

It's important to remember that the entry fees for parks and reserves only entitle you to stay for a 24-hour period, and you pay an additional fee of the same amount for each day you are inside the park, even if you don't leave the park during that period. Not all parks allow you to leave the park and re-enter under the same ticket, so always check the situation and be sure of your plans before you pay for a multiday ticket.

Private Conservancies

The widespread conversion of private cattle ranches or community lands into wildlife or community conservancies adds a whole new dimension to your safari experience in Kenya.

In the case of private conservancies, many are open only to those who pay to stay at one of the (usually exclusive) lodges or tented camps within the conservancy's boundaries. Such restrictions sometimes, but don't always, apply to the community conservancies. Most also charge a conservation fee – often around US$100 per person per day – whose proceeds go directly to wildlife conservation or community development projects.

One exception is Ol Pejeta Conservancy (p160) which is open to the public (adult/child US$95/45) – it's the closest conservancy experience to visiting a national park, but with fun activities thrown in.

In all cases, these conservancies are free to set their own rules, and these are invariably far less restrictive than those imposed by the KWS. The two most obvious examples are that both walking safaris (usually accompanied by an armed guide or ranger) and night game drives are permitted on the conservancies. Other activities – including, in some cases, horseback riding – are also possible.

For more on private conservancies, see p359.

POACHING

Wildlife Wars: My Battle to Save Kenya's Elephants (2001) is Dr Richard Leakey's fascinating account of his years at the forefront of the fight against ivory poaching in Kenya.

Survival Guide

Directory A–Z

Accommodation

Kenya has a wide range of accommodation options, from basic hotels with cells overlooking city bus stands to luxury tented camps hidden away in remote corners of the country. There are also all kinds of campsites, budget tented camps, *bandas* (thatched-roof wood or stone huts) and cottages scattered around the parks and rural areas.

Seasons

High-season prices usually run from July (sometimes June) to October, from January until early March, and include Easter and Christmas, although there may be slight variations in some regions. Sometimes high season is also referred to as peak season. Low season usually covers the rest of the year, although many lodges and top-end hotels also have intermediate shoulder seasons.

On the coast, peak times tend to be July, August and December to March, and a range of lower rates can apply for the rest of the year.

During the low season many companies offer excellent deals on accommodation on the coast and in the main wildlife parks, often working with airlines to create packages aimed at the local and expat market.

Prices

It's worth remembering that many places, particularly places in national parks or other remote areas, offer full-board-only rates – prices may, therefore, seem higher than you'd expect, but less so once you factor in three meals a day. Some also offer what are called 'package rates' which include full-board accommodation but also things such as game drives, transfers and other extras.

Kenya also operates on a dual pricing system, particularly in midrange and top-end places – nonresidents pay significantly more (often double or triple the price) than Kenyan (or other East African) residents. When things are quiet, you may be able to get the residents' rate if you ask, but don't count on it. Prices quoted in this book are nonresident rates, unless otherwise stated.

One final thing: hotels and other places to stay in Kenya quote their prices in a variety of currencies, usually US dollars or Kenyan shillings (KSh). In almost all cases you can pay in dollars, shillings, euros and (sometimes) other foreign currencies.

SLEEPING PRICE RANGES

The following price ranges refer to a high-season double room with private bathroom and, unless stated otherwise, includes breakfast:

$ less than US$50

$$ US$50 to US$150

$$$ more than US$150

Accommodation Types

BANDAS

- *Bandas* are Kenyan-style huts and cottages, usually with some kind of kitchen and bathroom, which offer excellent value. Although there are numerous private examples, there are also Kenya Wildlife Service (KWS) *bandas* at some national parks – some are wooden huts, some are thatched stone huts and some are small brick bungalows with solar-powered lights.
- Facilities range from basic dorms and squat toilets to kitchens and hot water provided by wood-burning stoves. In such places, you'll need to bring all your own food, drinking water, bedding and firewood.
- Although originally aimed at budget travellers, an increasing variety of places are calling *bandas* huts, which

are decidedly midrange in price and quality.

BEACH RESORTS

Much of the coast, from Diani Beach to Malindi, is taken up by huge luxury beach resorts. Most offer a fairly similar experience, with swimming pools, water sports, bars, restaurants, mobs of souvenir vendors on the beach and 'tribal' dance shows in the evening. They aren't all bad, especially if you want good children's facilities, and a handful of them have been very sensitively designed. Note that many of these places will close in early summer, generally from May to mid-June or July.

CAMPING

There are many opportunities for camping in Kenya, and although gear can be hired in Nairobi and around Mt Kenya it's worth considering bringing a tent with you.

Public campsites There are KWS campsites in just about every national park or reserve. These are usually very basic, with a toilet block with a couple of pit toilets, a water tap, perhaps public showers, and very little else. They cost US$30/25 per adult/child in Amboseli and Lake Nakuru National Parks, begin at US$20 per person in Masai Mara National Reserve and US$20/15 in all other parks.

Special campsites As well as these permanent campsites, KWS also runs so-called 'special' campsites in most national parks. These sites move every year and have even fewer facilities than the standard camps, but cost more because of their wilder locations and set-up costs. They cost US$50/25 per adult/child in Amboseli and Lake Nakuru, US$35/20 elsewhere; a reservation fee of KSh7500 per week is payable on top of the relevant camping fee.

Private campsites Private sites are rare, but they offer more facilities and may hire out tents if you don't have your own. It's sometimes possible to camp in the grounds of some hotels in rural towns, and Nairobi has some good private campsites. Camping in the bush is possible but unless you're doing it with an organised trip or a guide, security is a major concern – don't even think about it on the coast.

BOOK YOUR STAY ONLINE

For more accommodation reviews by Lonely Planet authors, check out http://lonelyplanet.com/hotels/. You'll find independent reviews, as well as recommendations on the best places to stay. Best of all, you can book online.

HOSTELS

The only youth hostel affiliated with Hostelling International (HI) is in Nairobi. It has good basic facilities and is a pleasant enough place to stay, but there are plenty of other cheaper choices that are just as good. Other places that call themselves 'youth hostels' are not members of HI, and standards are variable.

HOTELS & GUESTHOUSES

- Real bottom-end hotels (often known as 'board and lodgings' to distinguish them from *hotelis,* which are often only restaurants) are widely used as brothels, and tend to be very rundown. Security at these places is virtually nonexistent, though the better ones are set around courtyards, and are clean if not exactly comfortable.
- Proper hotels and guesthouses come in many different shapes and sizes. As well as the top-end Western companies, there are a number of small Kenyan chains offering reliable standards across a handful of properties in particular towns or regions, and also plenty of private, family-run establishments.
- Self-catering options are common on the coast, where they're often the only midpriced alternative to the top-end resorts, but not so much in other parts of the country. A few fancier places offer modern kitchens, but more often than not the so-called kitchenettes will be a side room with a small fridge and portable gas stove.
- Terms you will come across in Kenya include 'self-contained', which just means a room with its own private bathroom, and 'all-inclusive', which generally means all meals, certain drinks and possibly some activities should be included. 'Full-board' accommodation includes three meals a day, while 'half-board' generally means breakfast and dinner are included.

RENTAL HOUSES

- Renting a private house is a popular option on the coast, particularly for groups on longer stays, and many expats let out their holiday homes when they're not using them.
- Properties range from restored Swahili houses on the northern islands to luxurious colonial mansions inland, and while they're seldom cheap, the experience will often be something pretty special.

USEFUL ACCOMMODATION RESOURCES

Ecotourism Kenya (www.ecotourismkenya.org) Certification of many hotels based on their environmental and sustainability practices.

Uniglobe Let's Go Travel (www.uniglobeletsgotravel.com) Information on almost all the major hotels and lodges in Kenya, giving price ranges and descriptions.

PRACTICALITIES

- **Newspapers and magazines** The *Daily Nation* (www.nation.co.ke), *East African Standard* (www.standardmedia.co.ke), *East African* (www.theeastafrican.co.ke) and *New African* (www.newafricanmagazine.com).
- **TV** KBC and NTV, formerly KTN, are the main national TV stations. CNN, Sky and BBC networks are also widely available on satellite or cable (DSTV).
- **Radio** KBC Radio broadcasts across the country on various FM frequencies. BBC World Service is easily accessible.
- **Weights and measures** Metric.
- **Smoking** Banned in restaurants, bars and enclosed public areas, with expensive fines for breaches.

- Papers and noticeboards in Nairobi and along the coast are good places to find out about rentals, as is old-fashioned word of mouth.

SAFARI LODGES

- Hidden away inside or on the edges of national parks and wildlife conservancies are some fantastic safari lodges. These are usually visited as part of organised safaris, and you'll pay much more if you just turn up and ask for a room.
- Some of the older places trade heavily on their more glorious past, but the best places feature five-star rooms, soaring *makuti*-roofed bars (with a thatched roof of palm leaves) and restaurants overlooking waterholes full of wildlife. Staying in at least one good safari lodge while you're in Kenya is recommended.
- Rates tend to fall significantly in low season.

TENTED CAMPS

- As well as lodges, many parks and conservancies contain some fantastic luxury tented camps. These places tend to occupy wonderfully remote settings, usually by rivers or other natural locations, and feature large, comfortable, semi-permanent safari tents with beds, furniture, bathrooms (usually with hot running water) and often some kind of external roof thatch to keep the rain out; you sleep surrounded by the sounds of the African bush.
- Most of the camps are very upmarket and the tents are pretty much hotel rooms under canvas. The really exclusive properties occupy locations so isolated that guests fly in and out on charter planes.

Customs Regulations

There are strict laws about taking wildlife products out of Kenya. The export of products made from elephants, rhinos and sea turtles are prohibited. The collection of coral is also not allowed. Ostrich eggs will be confiscated unless you can prove you bought them from a certified ostrich farm. Always check to see what permits are required, especially for the export of any plants, insects and shells.

You are allowed to take up to KSh100,000 out of the country, although why you would when the currency is near impossible to change outside Kenya is beyond us.

Otherwise, allowable quantities you can bring into Kenya include the following:

Alcohol 1L

Cigarettes 200

Cigars 50

Perfume 250ml

Pipe tobacco 250g

Discount Cards

Residence permits Very favourable admission fees and accommodation rates around the country.

Seniors No concessions.

Student cards Concession rates at museums and some other attractions; the international ISIC card should be widely recognised.

Electricity

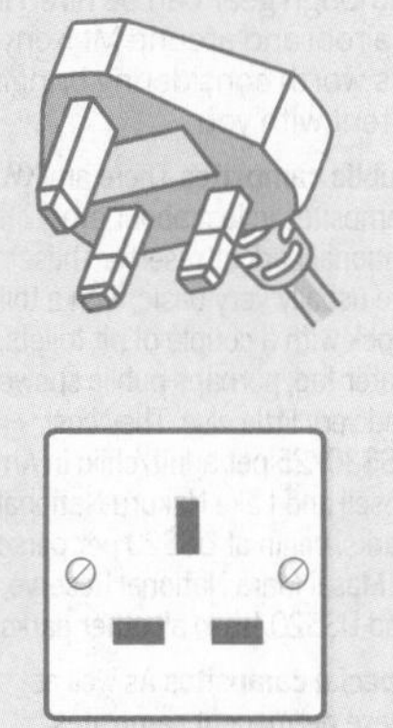

Embassies & Consulates

Australian High Commission (Map p56; ☎Nairobi 020-4277100; www.kenya.embassy.gov.au; ICIPE House, Riverside Dr, Nairobi)

Canadian High Commission (☎Nairobi 020-3663000; www.canadainternational.gc.ca/kenya/index.aspx; Limuru Rd, Gigiri, Nairobi)

GAY & LESBIAN TRAVELLERS

Negativity towards homosexuality is widespread in Kenya and recent events ensure that it's a brave gay or lesbian Kenyan who comes out of the closet.

In a 2007 poll, 96% of Kenyans surveyed stated that homosexuality should be rejected by society. Then, in early 2010, mob violence rocked a health centre where suspected homosexuals were targeted. In November 2010, Prime Minister Raila Odinga described homosexuality as 'unnatural' and called for gays and lesbians to be arrested and when British PM David Cameron threatened in November 2011 to withdraw aid to some African countries if they did not improve their record on gay and lesbian rights, there was a vociferous public outcry in Kenya. In July 2014, 60 people were arrested for 'suspected homosexuality' in a Nairobi nightclub.

Underlying all of this is a penal code that states that homosexual (and attempted homosexual) behaviour is punishable by up to 14 years in prison.

Awareness is increasing in Kenya, but with the vast majority of churches and mosques maintaining a traditional, conservative position, homosexuality continues to be frowned upon. In early 2014, star author Binyavanga Wainaina revealed publicly that he was gay to protest against a resurgence in anti-gay laws and public debate across Africa.

Of course, people do live homosexual lifestyles covertly, particularly along the coast. There are very few prosecutions under the law, but it's certainly better to be extremely discreet – some local con artists do a good line in blackmail, picking up foreigners then threatening to expose them to the police.

Although there are probably more gays and lesbians in Nairobi, the coast is more tolerant of gay relationships, at least privately. There is now a Swahili word for gay: *msenge*. Lamu has long been considered a paradise getaway for gay couples, but it's not as tolerant as it once was. Memories still linger from 1999, when a couple was taken into protective custody in Lamu to shield them from an angry mob of locals opposed to their plans for a gay wedding.

Useful Resources

Afriboyz (www.afriboyz.com/Homosexuality-in-Africa) Links to gay topics in an African context.

David Tours (www.davidtravel.com) Can arrange anything from balloon safaris to luxurious coastal hideaways, all with a gay focus.

Global Gayz (www.globalgayz.com) Links to country-by-country gay issues, including Kenya.

Purple Roofs (www.purpleroofs.com/africa/kenya) Lists a number of gay or gay-friendly tour companies in Kenya that may be able to help you plan your trip.

Ethiopian Embassy (Map p56; ☎Nairobi 020-2732050; State House Ave, Nairobi)

French Embassy (Map p66; ☎Nairobi 020-2778000; www.ambafrance-ke.org; 15th fl, Barclays Plaza, Loita St, Nairobi)

German Embassy (☎Nairobi 020-4262100; www.nairobi.diplo.de; 113 Riverside Dr, Nairobi)

Netherlands Embassy (☎Nairobi 020 4288000; kenia.nlembassy.org; Riverside Lane, Nairobi)

South Sudan Embassy (Map p56; ☎Nairobi 020-2711384; 6th fl Bishops Gate House, 5th Ngong Ave, Nairobi)

Tanzanian Embassy (Map p66; ☎Nairobi 020-331057, 020-2311948; Reinsurance Plaza, Aga Khan Walk, Nairobi)

Uganda High Commission (Consular Section) (Map p66; ☎Nairobi 020-311814; 1st fl, Uganda House, Kenyatta Ave) The consular section is downtown. There's also the High Commission office further out.

UK High Commission (Map p56; ☎Nairobi 020-2873000; www.gov.uk/government/world/kenya; Upper Hill Rd, Nairobi)

US Embassy (☎Nairobi 020-3636000; nairobi.usembassy.gov; United Nations Ave, Nairobi)

EATING PRICE RANGES

The following price ranges refer to a standard main course.

$ less than US$5

$$ US$5 to US$10

$$$ more than US$10

Food

See p321 for details on Kenyan cuisine.

Insurance

Two words: get some! A travel-insurance policy to cover theft, loss and medical problems is a very sensible precaution. Worldwide travel insurance is available at www.lonelyplanet.com/travel-insurance. You can buy, extend and claim online anytime – even if you're already on the road.

➡ Some policies specifically exclude 'dangerous activities', which can even include motorcycling, scuba-diving and trekking. If such activities are on your agenda you'll need a fully comprehensive policy, which may be more expensive. Using a locally acquired motorcycle licence may not be valid under your policy.

➡ You may prefer a policy that pays doctors or hospitals directly rather than you having to pay on the spot and claim later. If you have to claim later, make sure you keep all documentation.

➡ Some policies ask you to call back (reverse charges) to a centre in your home country where an immediate assessment of your problem is made. Be aware that reverse-charge calls are only possible to certain countries from Kenya.

➡ Check that the policy covers ambulances or an emergency flight home.

Local Agencies

If you're travelling through Africa for some time or heading to more remote corners of the country, consider signing up with a local service. Check with your insurance company that you can contact the local service direct in the event of a serious emergency without having to confirm it with your company at home first.

AAR Health Services (☎0722314394, Nairobi 020-2895000; www.aarhealth.com; 2nd fl, Williamson House, Fourth Ngong Ave, Nairobi) Comprehensive medical network that covers Kenya, Tanzania and Uganda and offers a road and local service as well as emergency air evacuation to any suitable medical facility in East Africa. In addition to Nairobi, there's also a Mombasa office.

Flying Doctors Service (☎Nairobi 020-6993000; www.amref.org) Part of the African Medical and Research Foundation (AMREF), with a 24-hour air-ambulance service out of Nairobi's Wilson Airport.

Internet Access

Internet cafes Common in large and medium-sized Kenyan towns; connection speeds fluctuate wildly and prices range from KSh30 to KSh100 per hour.

Post offices Internet at almost every main post office in the country; prepaid cards with PINs are valid at any branch around Kenya.

Wireless Increasingly common in midrange and top-end hotels; often (but not always) available in upmarket safari lodges, less common in midrange places in remote areas.

Local networks Both Safari.com and Airtel have dongles/modems that you plug into your laptop, giving you wireless access anywhere that there's mobile coverage.

Language Courses

Taking a Swahili-language course (or any course) entitles you to a 'Pupil's Pass' (p381), which is an immigration permit allowing continuous stays of up to 12 months. You may have to battle with bureaucracy and the process may take months, but it can be worth it, especially as you will then have resident status in Kenya during your stay.

ACK Language & Orientation School (Map p56; ☎Nairobi 020-2721893; www.ackenya.org/institutions/language_school; Bishops Rd, Upper Hill, Nairobi) The Anglican Church runs full-time Swahili courses of varying levels lasting 14 weeks and taking up to five hours a day. Private tuition is available on a flexible part-time schedule.

Language Center Ltd (Map p60; ☎0721495774, Nairobi 020-3870610; www.language-cntr.com/welcome.shtml; Ndemi Close, off Ngong Rd, Nairobi) A good Swahili centre offering a variety of study options ranging from private hourly lessons to daily group courses.

Legal Matters

All drugs except *miraa* (a leafy shoot chewed as a stimulant) are illegal in Kenya. Marijuana (commonly called *bhang*) is widely available but illegal; possession carries a penalty of up to 10 years in prison. Dealers are common on the beaches north and south of Mombasa and frequently set up travellers for sting operations for real or phoney cops to extort money.

African prisons are unbelievably harsh places – don't take the risk. Note that *miraa* is illegal in Tanzania, so if you do develop a taste for the stuff in Kenya you should leave it behind when heading south.

Maps

Country Maps

➡ The *Tourist Map of Kenya* gives good detail, as does the *Kenya Route Map;* both cost around KSh250.

➡ Marco Polo's 1:1,000,000 *Shell Euro Karte Kenya*, Geocenter's *Kenya* (1:1,000,000) and IGN's *Carte Touristique: Kenya* (1:1,000,000) are useful overview maps that are widely available in Europe. The scale and clarity are very good, but the locations of some minor features are inaccurate.

➡ For those planning a longer trip in southern and East Africa, Michelin's

1:4,000,000 *Map 955 (Africa Central and South)* is very useful.

National Park Maps

Most maps to Kenya's national parks might look a bit flimsy on detail (you won't get much in the way of topographical detail), but they include the numbered junctions in the national parks.

Tourist maps Macmillan publishes a series of maps to the wildlife parks and these are not bad value at around KSh250 each (three are available in Europe: *Amboseli*, *Masai Mara* and *Tsavo East & West*). Tourist Maps also publishes a national-park series for roughly the same price. The maps by the KWS are similar.

Survey of Kenya The most detailed and thorough maps are published by the Survey of Kenya, but the majority are out of date and many are also out of print. The better bookshops in Nairobi usually have copies of the most important maps, including *Amboseli National Park* (SK 87), *Masai Mara Game Reserve* (SK 86), *Meru National Park* (SK 65), *Tsavo East National Park* (SK 82) and *Tsavo West National Park* (SK 78).

Kenya Institute of Surveying & Mapping (☎Nairobi 020-8561484; Thika Rd, Nairobi) It may be worth a visit to this office, but this can take all day and there's no guarantee it will have any more stock than the bookshops.

Money

- The unit of currency is the Kenyan shilling (KSh), which is made up of 100 cents. Notes in circulation are KSh1000, 500, 200, 100, 50 and 20, and there are also coins of KSh40, 20, 10, five and one in circulation.
- Locally, the shilling is commonly known as a 'bob', after the old English term for a one-shilling coin.
- The shilling has been relatively stable over the past few years, maintaining fairly constant rates against the US dollar, euro and British pound.
- Both US dollars and British pounds are easy to change throughout the country, as is the euro, which is replacing the dollar as the currency quoted for hotel prices on the coast (but rarely elsewhere).
- The most convenient way to bring your money is in a mixture of cash and a debit or credit card.

ATMs

Virtually all banks in Kenya now have ATMs at most branches, but their usefulness to travellers varies widely. Barclays Bank has easily the most reliable machines for international withdrawals, with a large network of ATMs covering most major Kenyan towns. They support MasterCard, Visa, Plus and Cirrus international networks.

Standard Chartered and Kenya Commercial Bank ATMs also accept Visa but not the other major providers, and are more likely to decline transactions. Whichever bank you use, the international data link still goes down occasionally, so don't rely on being able to withdraw money whenever you need it.

Black Market

With deregulation, the black market has almost vanished, and the handful of moneychangers who still wander the streets offering 'good rates' are usually involved in scams. The exception is at land border crossings, where moneychangers are often the only option. Most offer reasonable rates, although you should be careful not to get short-changed or scammed during any transaction.

Cash

While most major currencies are accepted in Nairobi and Mombasa, once away from these two centres you'll run into problems with currencies other than US dollars, pounds sterling and euros.

Credit Cards

Credit cards are becoming increasingly popular, although the connections fail with tedious regularity. Visa and MasterCard are now widely accepted in midrange and top-end hotels, top-end restaurants and some shops.

Moneychangers

The best places to change money are foreign exchange or 'forex' bureaus, which can be found everywhere and usually don't charge commission. The rates for the main bureaus in Nairobi are published in the *Daily Nation* newspaper.

International Transfers

M-Pesa Kenyans swear by M-Pesa, a quick-and-easy way of transferring money via mobile networks.

Western Union (☎Australia 1800-173833, New Zealand 0800-005253, UK 0808-2349168, USA 1800-3256000;

US DOLLAR TRICKS

- When getting US currency to take to Kenya, make sure you get US$100 bills manufactured in 2003 or later. Most banks and just about all businesses simply won't accept those that were printed earlier.
- If changing money at a forex bureau or other moneychanger, watch out for differing small-bill (US$10) and large-bill (US$100) rates; the larger bills usually get the better exchange rates.

www.westernunion.com) Western Union Postbank, a branch of the Kenyan Post Office, is the regional agent for Western Union, the global money-transfer company. Using its service is an easy way (if the phones are working) of receiving money in Kenya. Senders should contact Western Union to find the location of their nearest agency.

Handily, the sender pays all the charges and there's a Postbank in most towns, often in the post office or close by.

Tipping

Tipping is not common practice among Kenyans, but there's no harm in rounding up the bill by a few shillings if you're pleased with the service.

Hotel porters Tips expected in upmarket hotels (from Ksh200 and up).

Restaurants A service charge of 10% is often added to the bill along with the 16% VAT and 2% catering levy.

Taxi drivers As fares are negotiated in advance, no need to tip unless they provide you with exceptional service.

Tour guides, safari drivers and cooks Will expect some kind of gratuity at the end of your tour or trip. Count on around US$10 to US$15 per day per group.

Travellers Cheques

Travellers cheques are next to useless in Kenya – very few banks or foreign exchange bureaus accept them and those that do, do so reluctantly and charge high commissions.

Opening Hours

Banks 9am to 3pm Monday to Friday; 9am to 11am Saturday.

Post Offices 8.30am to 5pm Monday to Friday; 9am to noon Saturday.

Restaurants 11am to 2pm and 5pm to 9pm: some remain open between lunch and dinner.

Shops 9am to 3pm Monday to Friday; 9am to 11am Saturday.

Supermarkets 8.30am to 8.30pm Monday to Saturday; 10am to 8pm Saturday.

Photography

➡ Photographing people remains a sensitive issue in Kenya – it is advisable to ask permission first. Some ethnic groups including the Maasai may request money for you to take their photo.

➡ You should never get your camera out at border crossings or near government or army buildings – even bridges can sometimes be classed as sensitive areas.

Taking Pictures

Light As the natural light in Kenya can be extremely strong, morning and evening are the best times to take photos.

Filters A plain UV filter can also be a good idea to take the harshness out of daylight pictures.

Lenses and tripods SLR cameras and zoom lenses are best for serious wildlife photography. When using long lenses you'll find that a tripod can be close to essential.

Vibrations If in a safari minibus or other vehicle, ask your driver to switch off the engine to avoid vibrations affecting your photo.

Post

Service The Kenyan postal system is run by the government **Posta** (www.posta.co.ke). Letters sent from Kenya rarely go astray but can take up to two weeks to reach Australia or the USA.

Parcels If sent by surface mail, parcels take three to six months to reach Europe, while airmail parcels take around a week.

Courier Most things arrive eventually, although there is still a problem with theft within the system. Curios, clothes and textiles will be OK, but if your parcel contains anything of obvious value, send it by courier. Posta has its own courier service, EMS, which is considerably cheaper than the big international courier companies. The best place to send parcels from is the main post office in Nairobi.

Public Holidays

National Holidays

New Year's Day 1 January

Good Friday and Easter Monday March/April

Labour Day 1 May

Madaraka Day 1 June

Moi Day 10 October

Kenyatta Day 20 October

Independence Day 12 December

Christmas Day 25 December

Boxing Day 26 December

ISLAMIC HOLIDAYS

HOLIDAY	2015	2016	2017
Ramadan begins	18 Jun	7 Jun	28 May
Eid al-Fitr (end of Ramadan)	17 Jul	6 Jul	26 Jun
Tabaski	24 Sep	13 Sep	2 Sep
Eid al-Adha (Feast of Sacrifice)	26 Sep	15 Sep	4 Sep
New Year begins	28 Oct (1436)	17 Oct (1437)	6 Oct (1438)
Maulid (Prophet Mohammed's birthday)	2 Jan (2015)	22 Dec (2015)	11 Dec (2016)

Islamic Holidays

Islamic festivals and holidays are particularly significant on the coast. Many eateries there close until after sundown during the Muslim fasting month of Ramadan. Islamic holidays vary in date according to the lunar calendar.

School Holidays

- Kenyan schools run on a three-term system much like the British education establishments on which they were originally modelled, although summer vacations tend to be shorter.
- Holidays usually fall in April (one month), August (one month) and December (five weeks).
- As few Kenyan families can afford to stay in tourist hotels, these holidays mostly have little impact on visitors, but more people will travel during these periods and popular public areas like the coastal beaches will be that bit more crowded.

> **STREET KIDS**
>
> Nairobi in particular has huge problems with street children, many of whom are AIDS orphans, who trail foreigners around asking for food or change. It's up to you whether you give, but it's debatable how much your donations will help as the older boys operate like a minimafia, extorting money from the younger kids. If you want to help out, money might be better donated to a charity, such as the **Consortium for Street Children** (www.streetchildren.org.uk), which works to improve conditions for these children.

Safe Travel

While Kenya can be quite a safe destination, there are still plenty of pitfalls for the unwary or inexperienced traveller, from everyday irritations to more serious threats. A little street sense goes a long way here, and getting the latest local information is essential wherever you intend to travel.

Banditry

Northeast The ongoing conflict in Somalia has had an effect on the stability and safety of northern and northeastern Kenya. AK-47s have been flowing into the country for many years, and the newspapers are filled with stories of hold-ups, shoot-outs, cattle rustling and general lawlessness. Bandits and poachers infiltrating from Somalia have made the northeast of the country particularly dangerous.

Northwest In the northwest, the main problem is armed tribal wars and cattle rustling across the South Sudanese border. There are Kenyan *shiftas* (bandits) too, of course, but cross-border problems seem to account for most of the trouble in the north of the country.

Risk Despite all the headlines, tourists are rarely targeted, as much of the violence and robberies take place far from the main tourist routes. Security has also improved considerably in previously high-risk areas such as the Isiolo–Marsabit and Marsabit–Moyale routes. However, you should check the situation locally before taking these roads, or travelling between Garsen and Garissa or Thika.

Sudan and Ethiopian borders The areas along the South Sudanese and Ethiopian borders are risky, so please enquire about the latest security situations if you're heading overland.

Crime

Even the staunchest Kenyan patriot will readily admit that one of the country's biggest problems is crime. It ranges from petty snatch theft and mugging to violent armed robbery, carjacking and, of course, white-collar crime and corruption. As a visitor you needn't feel paranoid, but you should always keep your wits about you, particularly at night.

Although crime is a fact of life in Kenya, it needn't spoil your trip. Above all, don't make the mistake of distrusting every Kenyan just because of a few bad apples – the honest souls you meet will far outnumber any crooks who cross your path.

Precautions Perhaps the best advice for when you're walking around cities and towns is not to carry anything valuable with you – that includes jewellery, watches, cameras, bumbags, daypacks and money. Most hotels provide a safe or secure place for valuables, although you should also be cautious of the security at some budget places.

Mugging While pickpocketing and bag-snatching are the most common crimes, armed muggings do occur in Nairobi and on the coast. Always take taxis after dark.

Snatch and run Conversely, snatch-and-run crimes happen more in crowds. If you suddenly feel there are too many people around you, or think you are being followed, dive straight into a shop and ask for help.

Luggage This is an obvious signal to criminals that you've just arrived. When arriving anywhere by bus, it's sensible to take a 'ship-to-shore' approach, getting a taxi directly from the bus station to your hotel. You'll have plenty of time to explore once you've safely stowed your belongings. Also, don't read a guidebook or look at maps on the street – it attracts unwanted attention.

Reporting crime In the event of a crime, you should report it to the police, but this can be a real procedure. You'll need to get a police report if you intend

GOVERNMENT TRAVEL ADVICE

The following government websites offer travel advisories and information for travellers:

Australian Department of Foreign Affairs & Trade (www.smartraveller.gov.au)

Canadian Department of Foreign Affairs & International Trade (www.voyage.gc.ca)

French Ministere des Affaires Etrangeres Europeennes (www.diplomatie.gouv.fr/fr/conseils-aux-voyageurs)

Italian Ministero degli Affari Esteri (www.viaggiaresicuri.mae.aci.it)

New Zealand Ministry of Foreign Affairs & Trade (www.safetravel.govt.nz)

UK Foreign & Commonwealth Office (www.gov.uk/foreign-travel-advice)

US Department of State (www.travel.state.gov)

Check their websites for the latest warnings.

to make an insurance claim. In the event of a snatch theft, think twice before yelling 'Thief!' It's not unknown for people to administer summary justice on the spot, often with fatal results for the criminal.

Money

With street crime a way of life in Nairobi, you should be doubly careful with your money. Don't overlook the obvious and leave money lying around your hotel room in plain view. However well you get on with the staff, there will be some who are unlikely to resist a free month's wages if they've got a family to feed.

Hotel safes The safest policy is to leave most of it in the hotel (or room) safe and just carry enough cash for that day. If you don't actually need your credit card, travellers cheques or cash with you, they'll almost always be safer locked away in your hotel safe.

Money belts If you do need to carry larger sums around, a money belt worn under your clothes is the safest option to guard against snatch thefts. However, be aware that muggers will usually be expecting this.

Other tricks More ingenious tricks include tucking money into a length of elasticised bandage on your arm or leg, or creating a hidden pocket inside your trousers.

Scams

For more details on Nairobi scams, see p80.

Expensive stories At some point in Kenya you'll almost certainly come across people who play on the emotions and gullibility of foreigners. Nairobi is a particular hot spot, with 'friendly' approaches a daily, if not hourly, occurrence. People with tales about being refugees or having sick relatives can sound very convincing, but they all end up asking for cash. It's OK to talk to these people if they're not actively hassling you, but you should ignore any requests for money.

Over-friendly strangers Be sceptical of strangers who claim to recognise you in the street, especially if they're vague about exactly where they know you from – it's unlikely that any ordinary person is going to be *this* excited by seeing you twice. Anyone who makes a big show of inviting you into the hospitality of their home also probably has ulterior motives. The usual trick is to bestow some kind of gift upon the delighted traveller, who is then emotionally blackmailed into reciprocating.

Car scams Tourists with cars also face potential rip-offs. Don't trust people who gesticulate wildly to indicate that your front wheels are wobbling; if you stop, you'll probably be relieved of your valuables. Another trick is to splash oil on your wheels, then tell you the wheel bearings, differential or something else has failed, and direct you to a nearby garage where their

HOTEL SECURITY

Although hotels give you room keys, it is recommended that you carry a padlock for your backpack or suitcase as an extra deterrent. Furthermore, don't invite trouble by leaving valuables, cash or important documents lying around your room or in an unlocked bag.

Upmarket hotels will have safes (either in the room or at reception) where you can keep your money and passport (and sometimes even your laptop), so it's advised that you take advantage of them. It's usually best not to carry any valuables on the street, but when your budget accommodation is a bit rough around the edges, you may want to consider hiding your valuables on your person and carrying them at all times. Of course, use discretion, as muggings do happen in large towns and cities. Sadly, theft is perhaps the number-one complaint of travellers in Kenya, so it can't hurt to take a few extra precautions.

TERRORISM

Terrorism is, unfortunately, something you have to consider when visiting Kenya, although the vast majority of the country is safe to visit. Remember that reports of an attack in, for example, Mombasa, is likely to have very little impact upon the safety of visiting the Masai Mara or even Tsavo East National Park.

The country has come under major terrorist attack on at least three occasions: in August 1998 the US embassy in Nairobi was bombed; in November 2002 the Paradise Hotel, north of Mombasa, was car-bombed at the same time as a rocket attack on an Israeli jet; and in September 2013 terrorists attacked the upscale Westgate Shopping Mall in Nairobi. In early 2014, a number of British tour operators withdrew all of their clients from and suspended tours to most coastal areas of Kenya.

In recent years, there has been an upsurge in ethnic, political and religious tensions in Mombasa, and there have been a number of attacks on foreigners in and around Mombasa's old town, although at least one of these appeared to have been crime- rather than terrorism-related.

Other attacks have taken place – on commuter transport and markets in the Eastleigh suburb of Nairobi, and a series of attacks around Mpeketoni close to Lamu in mid-2014, for example – although these have primarily targeted locals rather than foreign tourists.

As of late 2014, most foreign government travel advisory services were warning against travel close to the Kenya–Somali border, as well as a number of areas along the coast, including Lamu and Tana River counties, some areas of Mombasa, and the Eastleigh suburb of Nairobi. Check their websites for the latest warnings.

friends will 'fix' the problem – for a substantial fee, of course.

Telephone

International calls International call rates from Kenya are relatively expensive, though you can save serious cash by using VOIP programs such as Skype. Operator-assisted calls are charged at the standard peak rate, but are subject to a three-minute minimum. You can always dial direct using a phonecard. All public phones should be able to receive incoming calls (the number is usually scrawled in the booth somewhere). If you're calling internationally using a local SIM card, rates are likely to be cheaper (as little as KSh3 per minute) than from fixed-line phones.

Hotel operators Calls made through a hotel operator from your room will cost an extra 25% to 50%, so check before making a call.

Reverse charge Collect calls are possible, but only to countries that have set up free direct-dial numbers allowing you to reach the international operator in the country you are calling. Currently these countries include the **UK** (☎0800-220441), the **USA** (☎0800-111, 0800-1112), **Canada** (☎0800-220114, 0800-220115), **New Zealand** (☎0800-220641) and **Switzerland** (☎0800-220411).

Mobile Phones

Coverage More than two-thirds of all calls in Kenya are now made on mobile phones, and coverage is good in all but the furthest rural areas.

Service Kenya uses the GSM 900 system, which is compatible with Europe and Australia but not with the North American GSM 1900 system. If you have a GSM phone, check with your service provider about using it in Kenya, and beware of high roaming charges. Remember that you will generally be charged for receiving calls abroad as well as for making them.

Prepaid plans Alternatively, if your phone isn't locked into a network, you can pick up a prepaid starter pack from one of the Kenyan mobile-phone companies: **Safaricom** (www.safaricom.co.ke), **Airtel** (www.africa.airtel.com/kenya/) or **Orange** (www.orange.co.ke). A SIM card costs about KSh100, and you can then buy top-up scratchcards from shops and booths across the country. International calls can cost as little as KSh3 per minute.

Handsets You can easily buy a handset anywhere in Kenya, generally unlocked and with SIM card. Prices start at around KSh2500 for a very basic model.

Phonecards

With Telkom Kenya phonecards, any phone can be used for prepaid calls – you just have to dial the **access number** (☎0844) and enter in the number and passcode on the card. There are booths selling the cards all over the country. Cards come in denominations of KSh200, KSh500, KSh1000 and KSh2000, and call charges are slightly more expensive than for standard lines.

Time

Time zone Kenya is two hours ahead of Greenwich Mean Time (GMT) all year round.

Daylight saving No.

SWAHILI TIME

It's news to most travellers that there is such a thing as 'Swahili time'. It's not just the fact that everyone along the coast seems to have time in bucketloads. Swahili time is six hours out of kilter with the rest of the world. Noon and midnight are six o'clock *(saa sita)* Swahili time, and 7am and 7pm are one o'clock *(saa moja)*. Just add or subtract six hours from whatever time you are told; Swahili doesn't distinguish between am and pm. You don't come across this often unless you speak Swahili, but you still need to be prepared for it.

UK & Ireland Three hours behind Kenya (two hours from end of March to end of October).

USA Kenyan time is USA Eastern Time plus eight hours (seven hours from end of March to early November) and USA Pacific Time plus 11 hours (10 hours from end of March to early November).

Western Europe Two hours behind Kenya (one hour from end of March to end of October).

Australia During the Australian winter, subtract eight hours from Australian Eastern Standard Time; during the Australian summer, subtract nine hours.

Toilets

- Toilets vary from pits (quite literally) to full-flush, luxury conveniences that can spring up in the most unlikely places.
- Nearly all hotels sport flushable sit-down toilets, but seats in cheaper places may be a rare commodity – either they're a prized souvenir for trophy hunters or there's a vast stockpile of lost lids somewhere...
- Public toilets in towns are almost equally rare, but there are a few slightly less-than-emetic pay conveniences in Nairobi if you've only got a penny to spend.
- In upmarket bush camps you may be confronted with real toilets or a long drop covered with some sort of seating arrangement.
- Things are less pleasant when camping in the wildlife parks. Squatting on crumbling concrete is common.
- When trekking it's good practice to take soiled toilet paper out of the park with you (consider carrying sealable bags for this purpose).

Tourist Information

Local Tourist Offices

Considering the extent to which the country relies on tourism, it's incredible to think that, at the time of writing, there was still no tourist office in Nairobi. There are a handful of information offices elsewhere in the country, ranging from helpful private concerns to underfunded government offices; most can at least provide basic maps of the town and brochures on local businesses and attractions, but precious little else.

Malindi Tourist Office (Map p248; ☎042-20689; Malindi Complex, Lamu Rd, Malindi; ⏰8am-12.30pm & 2-4.30pm Mon-Fri)

Mombasa & Coast Tourist Office (Map p208; ☎041-2228722; Moi Ave; ⏰8am-4.30pm) Provides information and can organise accommodation, tours, guides and transport.

Tourist Offices Abroad

The **Ministry of Tourism** (www.tourism.go.ke) maintains a number of overseas offices, including in the UK and some European countries. Most only provide information by telephone, post or email. Visit the ministry website; click on 'Contact Us' for contact details around the world.

Travellers with Disabilities

Travelling in Kenya is not easy for people with a physically disability, but it's not impossible. Very few tourist companies and facilities are geared up for travellers with disabilities, and those that are tend to be restricted to the expensive hotels and lodges. However, Kenyans are generally very accommodating and willing to offer whatever assistance they can. Visually or hearing-impaired travellers, though, will find it very hard to get by without an able-bodied companion.

In Nairobi, only the ex-London taxi cabs are spacious enough to accommodate a wheelchair, but some safari companies are accustomed to taking people with a disability out on safari.

Kenyan Services

Beach resorts Many of the top-end beach resorts on the coast have facilities for the disabled, whether it's a few token ramps or fully equipped rooms with handrails and bath tubs.

On safari Other places may have varying degrees of disabled access, but in Amboseli National Park, **Ol Tukai Lodge** (☎045-622275, Nairobi 020-4445514; www.oltukailodge.com; s/d full board US$350/450; P@📶🏊) has two accessible cottages, while in Lake Nakuru National Park, **Lake Nakuru Lodge** (☎0720404480, Nairobi 020-2687056; www.lakenakuru lodge.com; s/d full board

US$300/400; P@) has a handful of accessible rooms.

Useful Resources

Access-Able Travel Source (☎303-2322979; www.access-able.com) US information portal with four listings for Kenya.

Association for the Physically Disabled of Kenya (Map p66; ☎Nairobi 020-2324372; www.apdk.org; APDK House, Lagos Rd, Nairobi) Kenyan group that may be able to help visitors with a disability.

Society for Accessible Travel and Hospitality (☎212-447 7284; www.sath.org; USA) A good resource which gives advice on how to travel with a wheelchair, kidney disease, sight impairment or deafness. The website has a section called 'African Safaris' (type 'Kenya' into the search box).

Visas

Visa on arrival Tourist visas can be obtained on arrival at both international airports and at the country's land borders with Uganda and Tanzania. This applies to Europeans, Australians, New Zealanders, Americans and Canadians, although citizens from a few smaller Commonwealth countries are exempt. Visas cost US$50/€40/UK£30 and are valid for three months from the date of entry. Tourist visas can be extended for a further three-month period.

Single-entry visas Under the East African partnership system, visiting Tanzania or Uganda and returning to Kenya does not invalidate a single-entry Kenyan visa, so there's no need to get a multiple-entry visa unless you plan to go further afield. Always check the latest entry requirements with embassies before travel.

Pre-arranged visas It's also possible to get visas from Kenyan diplomatic missions overseas, but the only reason to do so is if you come from a country not eligible for an on-arrival visa, you want to be sure getting a multiple-entry visa, or you need longer than three months in the country. If this applies to you, you should apply well in advance, especially if you're doing it by mail.

Applications Applying for Kenyan visas is simple and straightforward in Tanzania and Uganda, and payment is accepted in local currency.

Dress As always when crossing international borders, it's best to smarten up a bit if you're arriving by air; requests for evidence of 'sufficient funds' are usually linked to snap judgments about your appearance. If it's fairly obvious that you aren't intending to stay and work, you'll generally be given the benefit of the doubt.

Visa Extensions

Visas can be renewed at immigration offices during normal office hours, and extensions are usually issued on a same-day basis. Staff at the immigration offices are generally friendly and helpful, but the process takes a while.

Requirements You'll need two passport photos for a three-month extension, and prices tend to vary widely depending on the office and the whims of the immigration officials. You also need to fill out a form registering as an alien if you're going to be staying more than 90 days.

Immigration offices Offices only open Monday to Friday; note that the smaller offices may sometimes refer travellers back to Nairobi or Mombasa for visa extensions.

Kisumu Immigration Office (Nyanza Bldg, cnr Jomo Kenyatta Hwy & Wuor Otiende Rd, Kisumu)

Lamu Immigration Office (☎042-633032; off Kenyatta Rd, Lamu) Travellers are sometimes referred to Mombasa.

Malindi Immigration Office (☎042-20149; Mama Ngina Rd, Malindi)

EAST AFRICA TOURIST VISA

In early 2014, the governments of Kenya, Uganda and Rwanda announced the creation of a new East Africa Tourist Visa (EATV). Under the scheme, tourists are entitled to a 90-day, multiple-entry visa that covers travel to these three countries for a single fee of US$100. Neither Tanzania nor Burundi are part of the EATV, though in November 2014 Tanzania announced its intention to join. These visas are available upon arrival at Jomo Kenyatta International Airport in Nairobi, and at most land crossings.

Applications can also be made prior to travelling to the region, either at an embassy or consulate for one of the three countries in your home country or online. Although requirements vary from embassy to embassy, most applications require a single passport photo and a letter to the embassy outlining your travel plans. With the visa duly in your passport, your first port-of-call must be the country through which you applied for the visa, whereafter there are no restrictions on travelling in and out of the three countries. No visa extensions are possible.

Apart from convenience, the East African Tourist Visa could save you money, with individual visas for most (but not all) nationalities costing US$50 for Kenya, US$50 for Uganda and US$30 for Rwanda.

For more information and links to online application forms, visit www.visiteastafrica.org/visa.

VISAS FOR NEIGHBOURING COUNTRIES

COUNTRY	VISA AVAILABLE?	VISA FEE (US$)	PASSPORT PHOTOS	ISSUE TIME	NOTES
Ethiopia	Yes	50	1	same day	Must show that it was not possible to obtain your Ethiopian visa in your home country.
Somalia	No	-	-	-	-
South Sudan	Yes (3-month, single entry)	100	2	48hr	Collect form 8.30am-10pm; must have letter of invitation; must pay visa fee at bank.
Tanzania	Yes (3-month, single entry)	50 (US nationals 100)	1	same day	-
Uganda	Yes (3-month, single entry)	50	1	same day	-

Mombasa Immigration Office (Map p206; ☎041-311745; Uhuru ni Kari Bldg, Mama Ngina Dr, Mombasa)

Nairobi Immigration Office (Map p66; ☎Nairobi 020-222022; Nyayo House, cnr Kenyatta Ave & Uhuru Hwy, Nairobi) Visa extensions can be obtained at this office, round the side of Nairobi's once-feared main administrative building.

Visas for Onward Travel

Since Nairobi is a common gateway city to East Africa and the city centre is easy to get around, many travellers spend some time here picking up visas for other countries that they intend to visit. But be warned: although officially issuing visas again, the Ethiopian embassy in Nairobi was not issuing tourist visas for a number of years and the situation could change again. Call the embassy to check.

Most embassies will want you to pay visa fees in US dollars, and most open for visa applications from 9am to noon, with visa pick-ups around 3pm or 4pm. Again, contact the embassy in question to check the times as these change regularly in Nairobi.

Volunteering

There are quite a large number of volunteers in Kenya, and volunteering can be a great way to reduce the ecological footprint of your trip. As a general rule, volunteering works best for both the traveller and the organisation in question if you treat it as a genuine commitment rather than simply a fun extension of your trip. It's also preferable if you have a particular skill to bring to the experience, especially one that cannot be satisfied by local people.

Keep in mind that there is no such thing as a perfect volunteer placement. Generally speaking, you'll get as much out of a program as you're willing to put into it; the vast majority of volunteers in Kenya walk away all the better for the experience.

Kenyan Organisations

Action for Children in Conflict (AfCiC; ☎01235539319; www.actionchildren.org; 2nd fl, Imara Plaza, Thika) A small, highly effective NGO working with Thika's children in poverty. AfCiC recruits skilled volunteers via its website for long-term placements.

Arabuko Sokoke Schools & Ecotourism Scheme (ASSETS, A Rocha Kenya; ☎042-2332023, Nairobi 020-2335865; www.arocha.org/ke-en/work/community conservation/assets) Programs (including Mida Ecocamp) near the Arabuko Sokoke Forest and Mida Creek. Also operates the Mwamba Field Study Centre at Watamu Beach.

Kenya Youth Voluntary Development Projects (Map p56; ☎0720453857; www.kvcdp.org; Nairobi International Youth Hostel, Ralph Bunche Rd, Nairobi) Excellent local organisation that runs a variety of three- to four-week projects, including road building, health education and clinic construction.

Taita Discovery Centre (malewa.com) Centred on Rukinga Wildlife Sanctuary and **Kasigau Base Camp** (Map p190; ☎0721365768, 0710755225; www.malewa.com; camping per person in own/hired tent KSh500/750, cottages per person self-catering/full board KSh2500/6000; P) south of Tsavo West National Park, this place runs courses on a huge range of conservation topics, along with hands-on projects in conservation and the local community.

Volunteer Kenya (Inter-Community Development Involvement; www.volunteer

kenya.org) Offers a number of longer community projects focusing on health issues such as AIDS awareness, agriculture and conservation in Western Kenya.

Watamu Turtle Watch (☎0713759627; www.watamuturtles.com) Helps protect the marine turtles that come to Watamu to lay eggs on the beach.

International Organisations

Coordinating Committee for International Voluntary Service (www.ccivs.org)

Earthwatch (www.earthwatch.org)

Frontier Conservation Expeditions (www.frontier.ac.uk)

Idealist.org (www.idealist.org)

International Volunteer Programs Association (www.volunteerinternational.org)

Peace Corps (www.peacecorps.gov)

Voluntary Service Overseas (VSO; www.vso.org.uk)

Working Abroad (www.workingabroad.com)

Worldwide Experience (www.worldwideexperience.com)

Worldwide Volunteering (www.wwv.org.uk)

Women Travellers

In their day-to-day lives, Kenyans are generally respectful towards women, although solo women in bars will attract a lot of interest from would-be suitors.

Trouble spots In most areas of Kenya, and certainly on safari, women are unlikely to experience any difficulties. The only place you are likely to have problems is at the beach resorts on the coast, where women may be approached by male prostitutes as well as local aspiring Romeos. It's always best to cover your legs and shoulders when away from the beach so as not to offend local sensibilities.

Safety Women should avoid walking around at night. The ugly fact is that while men are likely just to be robbed without violence, rape is a real risk for women. Lone night walks along the beach or through quiet city streets are a recipe for disaster, and criminals usually work in gangs, so take a taxi, even if you're in a group.

Discrimination Regrettably, black women in the company of white men are often assumed to be prostitutes, and can face all kinds of discrimination from hotels and security guards as well as approaches from Kenyan hustlers offering to help rip off the white 'customer'. Again, the worst of this can be avoided by taking taxis between hotels and restaurants etc.

Work

Availability It's difficult, although by no means impossible, for foreigners to find jobs in Kenya. The most likely areas in which employment might be found are in the safari business, teaching, advertising and journalism. Except for teaching, it's unlikely you'll see jobs advertised, and the only way you'll find out about them is to spend a lot of time with resident expats. As in most countries, the rule is that if a local can be found to do the job, there's no need to hire a foreigner.

Disaster work The most fruitful area in which to look for work, assuming that you have the relevant skills, is the 'disaster industry'. Nairobi is awash with UN and other aid agencies servicing the famines in Somalia and South Sudan and the refugee camps along the Kenyan border with those countries. Keep in mind that the work is tough and often dangerous, and pay is usually very low.

Paperwork Work permits and resident visas are not easy to arrange. A prospective employer may be able to sort the necessary paperwork for you, but otherwise you'll find yourself spending a lot of time and money at the **immigration office in Nairobi** (Map p66; ☎Nairobi 020-222022; Nyayo House, cnr Kenyatta Ave & Uhuru Hwy, Nairobi).

PUPIL'S PASS

If you're enrolled in a language course that extends beyond the period of your three-month visa, you are usually entitled to a visa extension. The fee for a Pupil's Pass varies. A charge will be levied by your school for sorting out the paperwork, so expect to pay a minimum of KSh4000 for a one-year pass. A deposit of KSh5000 or a letter of guarantee by an approved body registered in Kenya (your language school) is usually required, along with two photographs and a copy of your passport.

Transport

GETTING THERE & AWAY

Nairobi is a major African hub with numerous African and international airlines connecting Kenya to the world. By African standards, flights between Kenya and the rest of Africa or further afield are common and relatively cheap, and flying is by far the most convenient way to get to Kenya.

Kenya is also a popular and relatively easy way station for those travelling overland between southern Africa and Egypt. Finding your way here can be tricky – with several war zones in the vicinity – and such journeys should only be considered after serious planning and preparation. But they're certainly possible, and it's rarely Kenya that causes problems.

Flights, tours and rail tickets can be booked at www.lonelyplanet.com/bookings.

Entering the Country

Entering Kenya is generally pleasingly straightforward, particularly at the international airports, which are no different from most Western terminals.

Visas Single-entry visas are typically available on arrival for most nationalities (passport photos are not required) at Kenya's three international airports as well as at Kenya's land crossings with Uganda and Tanzania. With that said, you should contact your nearest Kenyan diplomatic office to get the most up-to-date information. See p379 for more information on visas.

Dress Dressing nicely will almost always smooth your way into the country with immigration officials.

Passport

There are no restrictions on which nationalities can enter Kenya, but you will need a valid passport, and usually one with a validity of more than six months.

Air

Airports

Kenya has three international airports; check out the website www.kaa.go.ke for further information.

Jomo Kenyatta International Airport (NBO; Map p60; ☎0722205061, Nairobi 020-822111; www.kaa.go.ke) Most international flights to and from Nairobi arrive at this airport, 15km southeast of the city. There are two international terminals and a smaller domestic terminal; you can easily walk between the terminals.

Moi International Airport (MBA; ☎Nairobi 020-3577058, 041-3433211) In Mombasa, 9km west of the centre, and Kenya's second-busiest international airport. Apart from flights to Zanzibar, this is mainly used by charter airlines and domestic flights.

Wilson Airport (WIL; Map p60; ☎0724255343, 0724256837; www.kaa.go.ke) Located 6km south of Nairobi's city centre on Langata Rd; with some flights between Nairobi and Kilimanjaro International Airport or Mwanza in Tanzania, as well as scheduled and charter domestic flights.

Airlines

Kenya Airways is the main national carrier, and has a generally good safety record, with just one fatal incident since 1977.

African Express Airways (☎Nairobi 020-2014746; www.africanexpress.co.ke; Wilson Airport)

Air Mauritius (☎Nairobi 020-822805; www.airmauritius.com)

Airkenya (☎Nairobi 020-3916000; www.airkenya.com)

British Airways (☎Nairobi 020-3277400; www.britishairways.com)

Brussels Airlines (☎Nairobi 020-4443070; www.brusselsairlines.com)

Daallo Airlines (☎Nairobi 020-317318; www.daallo.com)

Egypt Air (Map p66; ☎Nairobi 020-2226821; www.egyptair.com.eg)

Emirates (Map p66; ☎Nairobi 020-7602519; www.emirates.com)

Ethiopian Airlines (Map p66; ☎Nairobi 020-2296000; www.ethiopianairlines.com)

Fly 540 (☎0710540540, Nairobi 020-4452391; www.fly540.com)

Kenya Airways (☎Nairobi 020-3274747; www.kenya-airways.com)

KLM (Map p66; ☎Nairobi 020-2958210; www.klm.com)

Precision Air (☎Nairobi 020-3274282; www.precisionairtz.com)

Qatar Airways (☎Nairobi 020-2800000; www.qatarairways.com)

Rwandair (☎Nairobi 020-343870; www.rwandair.com)

Safarilink (☎Nairobi 020-6000777; www.flysafarilink.com)

South African Airways (☎Nairobi 020-2247342; www.flysaa.com)

Swiss International Airlines (☎Nairobi 020-2666967; www.swiss.com)

Thomson Airways (www.thomson.co.uk)

Tickets

Seasons It's important to note that flight availability and prices are highly seasonal. Conveniently for Europeans, the cheapest fares usually coincide with the European summer holidays, from June to September.

Charter flights It's also worth checking out cheap charter flights to Mombasa from Europe, although these will probably be part of a package deal to a hotel resort on the coast. Prices are often absurdly cheap and there's no obligation to stay at the resort you're booked into.

Onward tickets If you enter Nairobi with no onward or return ticket you may incur the wrath of immigration, and be forced to buy one on the spot – an uncommon but expensive exercise.

Land

Ethiopia

Security With ongoing problems in Sudan and Somalia, Ethiopia offers the only viable overland route into Kenya from the north. The security situation around the main entry point at Moyale is changeable – the border is usually open, but security problems often force its closure. Some foreign governments were, at the time of writing, warning against travel to areas of Kenya bordering Ethiopia and even along the highway between Isiolo and Moyale, although we've travelled much of this route without problems. Even so, cattle- and goat-rustling are rife, triggering frequent cross-border tribal wars, so check the security situation carefully before attempting this crossing.

Visas Although Ethiopian visas were being issued at the Ethiopian embassy in Nairobi at the time of research, that hasn't always been the case in recent years so check with your nearest Ethiopian embassy before setting out.

PUBLIC TRANSPORT

There were no cross-border bus services at the time of writing. If you don't have your own transport from Moyale, there's a daily bus between Moyale and Marsabit (Ksh800), while lifts can be arranged with the trucks (KSh500).

From immigration on the Ethiopian side of town it's a 2km walk to the Ethiopian and Kenyan customs posts. A yellow-fever vaccination is required to cross either border at Moyale. Unless you fancy being vaccinated at the border, get your jabs in advance and keep the certificate with your passport. A cholera vaccination may also be required.

CAR & MOTORCYCLE

Those coming to Kenya with their own vehicle could also enter at Fort Banya, on the northeastern tip of Lake Turkana, but it's a risky route with few fuel stops. There's no border post; you must already possess a Kenyan visa and get it stamped on arrival in Nairobi. Immigration are quite used to this, but not having an Ethiopian exit stamp can be a problem if you want to re-enter Ethiopia.

Somalia

There's no way you can pass overland between Kenya and war-ravaged Somalia at present, as the Kenyan government has closed the border to try to stop the flow of poachers, bandits and weapons into Kenya. Kidnappings, armed conflict and banditry are rife in the area close to the border. If you ignore the warnings and somehow survive, don't expect your travel insurance to help if you need assistance.

CLIMATE CHANGE & TRAVEL

Every form of transport that relies on carbon-based fuel generates CO_2, the main cause of human-induced climate change. Modern travel is dependent on aeroplanes, which might use less fuel per kilometre per person than most cars but travel much greater distances. The altitude at which aircraft emit gases (including CO_2) and particles also contributes to their climate change impact. Many websites offer 'carbon calculators' that allow people to estimate the carbon emissions generated by their journey and, for those who wish to do so, to offset the impact of the greenhouse gases emitted with contributions to portfolios of climate-friendly initiatives throughout the world. Lonely Planet offsets the carbon footprint of all staff and author travel.

South Sudan

Kenya's border with South Sudan is one of East Africa's more remote border crossings – check with the South Sudanese embassy in Nairobi to check whether it's open to foreign travellers. Most visitors travelling between the two countries fly from Nairobi to Juba.

There are no cross-border buses, although Simba Coaches has a bus from Eldoret to Juba (KSh4500, 24 hours) that travels via Kampala in Uganda.

Tanzania

The main land borders between Kenya and Tanzania are at Namanga, Loitokitok, Taveta, Isebania and Lunga Lunga, and can be reached by public transport. There are no train services between the two countries.

Although all of the routes may be done in stages using a combination of buses and local matatus, there are six main routes to/from Tanzania:

- Mombasa–Tanga/Dar es Salaam
- Mombasa–Arusha/Moshi
- Nairobi–Arusha/Moshi (via Namanga)
- Nairobi–Moshi (via Loitokitok)
- Nairobi–Dar es Salaam
- Nairobi–Mwanza

BUS

Riverside Shuttle (☎Nairobi 020-3229618; www.riverside-shuttle.com)

Modern Coast Express (☎0737940000, 0705700888; www.modern.co.ke)

CAR & MOTORCYCLE

All of the bus routes mentioned here are easily accomplished in your own vehicle. Theoretically it's also possible to cross between Serengeti National Park and Masai Mara National Reserve with your own vehicle, but you'll need all the appropriate vehicle documentation (including insurance and entry permit).

Uganda

The main border post for overland travellers is Malaba, with Busia an alternative if you're travelling via Kisumu.

BUS & MATATU

Numerous bus companies run between Nairobi, Nakuru or Kisumu and Kampala. From the Kenyan side, we recommend Easy Coach and Modern Coast Express. If travelling from Nairobi or Nakuru, prices include a meal at the halfway point. Various other companies have cheaper, basic services, which depart from the Accra Rd area in Nairobi.

There are also regular matatus to Malaba from Cross Rd in Nairobi. Buses and matatus also run from Nairobi or Kisumu to Busia, from where there are regular connections to Kampala and Jinja.

The Ugandan and Kenyan border posts at Malaba are about 1km apart, so you can walk or take a *boda-boda* (bicycle or motorcycle taxi). Once you get across the border, there are frequent matatus until the late afternoon to Kampala, Jinja and Tororo.

Easy Coach (☎Nairobi 020-3210711; www.easycoach.co.ke)

Modern Coast Express (☎0737940000, 0705700888; www.modern.co.ke)

OVERLAND TOURS

Most people come to Kenya on safari but it's also possible to reach Kenya as part of an overland truck tour originating in Europe or other parts of Africa; many also start in Nairobi bound for other places in Africa. Most companies are based in the UK or South Africa.

Acacia Expeditions (www.acacia-africa.com) Covers East and Southern Africa with some small-group options.

Africa Travel Co (www.africatravelco.com) Focuses on East and Southern Africa.

Dragoman (www.dragoman.co.uk) There are few places in Africa they don't go, with good links to trips across the continent.

Oasis Overland (www.oasisoverland.com) A range of East and Southern African overland trips as well as some more conventional tours.

Sea & Lake

At the time of writing there were no international ferries operating on Lake Victoria, although there's been talk for years of a cross-lake ferry service between Kenya, Tanzania and Uganda. One company – **Earthwise Ferries** (www.earthwiseventures.com) – even has a website. If they actually end up with a boat, they could link Kisumu with Mwanza (Tanzania) and Kampala (Uganda).

Tanzania

It's theoretically possible to travel by dhow between Mombasa and the Tanzanian islands of Pemba and Zanzibar, but first of all you'll have to find a captain who's making the journey and then you'll have to bargain hard to pay a reasonable amount for the trip. The best place to ask about sailings is at Shimoni. There's a tiny immigration post here, but there's no guarantee they'll stamp your

MAJOR BUS ROUTES

FROM	TO	PRICE (US$)	DURATION (HR)	COMPANY
Mombasa	Tanga	8	4	Modern Coast Express
Mombasa	Dar es Salaam	11-15	5-8	Modern Coast Express
Nairobi	Moshi	40	7½	Riverside Shuttle
Nairobi	Arusha	35	5½	Riverside Shuttle
Nairobi	Kampala	28	10-12	Modern Coast Express
Nakuru	Kampala	24	11-12	Easy Coach

passport so you might have to go back to Mombasa for an exit stamp.

Dhows do sail between small Kenyan and Tanzanian ports along Lake Victoria, but many are involved in smuggling (fruit mostly) and are best avoided.

GETTING AROUND

Getting around Kenya is relatively easy, whether you crisscross the country by highway bus or hire car, or cruise the clear skies and placid seas by light aircraft or dhow.

Most of Kenya's towns and cities are accessible by local bus, though it's usually necessary to arrange private transport to reach national parks and lodges. If you're a seasoned driver in African conditions, hiring a sturdy vehicle can also open up relatively inaccessible corners of the country; if you don't fancy driving yourself, hiring a vehicle with a driver rarely costs a lot more.

Air

Airlines in Kenya

Including the national carrier, Kenya Airways, a handful of domestic operators of varying sizes run scheduled flights within Kenya. Destinations served are predominantly around the coast and the popular national parks, where the highest density of tourist activity takes place. Most operate small planes and many of the 'airports', especially those in the parks, are dirt airstrips with very few, if any, facilities.

With all these airlines, be sure to book well in advance (this is essential during the tourist high season). You should also remember to reconfirm your return flights 72 hours before departure, especially those that connect with an international flight. Otherwise, you may find that your seat has been reallocated.

Airkenya (☎Nairobi 020-3916000; www.airkenya.com) Amboseli, Diani, Lamu, Masai Mara, Malindi, Meru, Nakuru, Mombasa, Nanyuki, Lewa and Samburu.

Fly540 (www.fly540.com) Eldoret, Kisumu, Lamu, Lodwar, Malindi and Mombasa.

Jambo Jet (☎Nairobi 020-3274545; www.jambojet.com) Subsidiary of Kenya Airways that flies to Nairobi, Mombasa, Kisumu and Eldoret.

Kenya Airways (Map p66; ☎Nairobi 020-3274747; www.kenya-airways.com) Kisumu, Malindi and Mombasa.

Mombasa Air Safari (☎0734400400; www.mombasaairsafari.com) Amboseli, Diani Beach, Kisumu, Lamu, Malindi, Masai Mara, Meru, Mombasa, Samburu and Tsavo West.

Safarilink (☎Nairobi 020-6000777; www.flysafarilink.com) Amboseli, Diani Beach, Kiwayu, Lamu, Lewa Downs, Loisaba, Masai Mara, Naivasha, Nanyuki, Samburu, Shaba and Tsavo West.

CHARTER AIRLINES

Chartering a small plane saves you time and is the only realistic way to get to some parts of Kenya. However, it's an expensive affair, and may only be worth considering if you can get a group together. There are dozens of charter companies operating out of Nairobi's **Wilson Airport** (WIL; Map p60; ☎0724255343, 0724256837; www.kaa.go.ke).

Blue Bird Aviation (☎0732189000; www.bluebirdaviation.com)

Boskovic Air Charters (☎Nairobi 020-6006364; www.boskovicaircharters.com)

Bicycle

Loads of Kenyans get around by bicycle, and while it can be tough for those who are not used to the roads or climate, plenty of hardy visiting cyclists do tour the country every year.

Safety Whatever you do, if you intend to cycle here, do as the locals do and get off the road whenever you hear a car coming. And no matter how experienced you are, it would be tantamount to suicide to attempt the road from Nairobi to Mombasa, or from Nairobi to Nakuru, on a bicycle.

Rural touring Cycling is easier in rural areas, and you'll usually receive a warm welcome in any villages you pass through. Many local people operate *boda-bodas*, so repair shops are quite common along the roadside. Be wary of cycling on dirt roads as punctures from thorn trees are a major problem.

Mountain biking The hills of Kenya are not particularly steep but can be long and hard. You can expect to cover around 80km per day in the hills of the Western Highlands, somewhat more where the country is flatter. Hell's Gate National Park, near Naivasha, is particularly popular for mountain biking, but you can also explore on two wheels the area around Mt Kenya, the Masai Mara and Ol Pejeta Conservancy.

Hire It's possible to hire road and mountain bikes in an increasing number of places, usually for KSh600 to KSh1000 per day. Few places require a deposit, unless their machines are particularly new or sophisticated.

Boat

The only ferry transport on Lake Victoria at the time of writing is across the Winam Gulf between Mbita Point (near Homa Bay) and Luanda Kotieno where matatus go to Kisumu. You might also find motorised canoes to Mfangano Island from Mbita Point.

Dhow

Sailing on a traditional Swahili dhow along the East African coast is one of Kenya's most memorable experiences. And, unlike on Lake Victoria, a good number of traditional routes are very much still in use. Dhows are commonly used to get around the islands in the Lamu archipelago and the mangrove islands south of Mombasa.

Facilities For the most part, these trips operate more like dhow safaris than public transport. Although some trips are luxurious, the trips out of Lamu are more basic. When night comes you simply bed down wherever there is space. Seafood is freshly caught and cooked onboard on charcoal burners, or else barbecued on the beach on surrounding islands.

Propulsion Most of the smaller boats rely on the wind to get around, so it's quite common to end up becalmed until the wind picks up again. The more commercial boats, however, have been fitted with outboard motors so that progress can be made even when there's no wind. Larger dhows are all motorised and some of them don't even have sails.

Bus

Services Kenya has an extensive network of long- and short-haul bus routes, with particularly good coverage of the areas around Nairobi, the coast and the western regions. Services thin out the further away from the capital you get, particularly in the north, and there are still plenty of places where you'll be reliant on matatus.

Operators Buses are operated by a variety of private companies that offer varying levels of comfort, convenience and roadworthiness. They're considerably cheaper than taking the train or flying, and as a rule services are frequent, fast and can be quite comfortable.

Facilities In general, if you travel during daylight hours, buses are a fairly safe way to get around – you'll certainly be safer in a bus than in a matatu. The best coaches are saved for long-haul and international routes and offer DVD movies, drinks, toilets and reclining airline-style seats; some of the newer ones even have wireless internet. On shorter local routes, however, you may find yourself on something resembling a battered school bus.

Seating tips Whatever kind of conveyance you find yourself in, don't sit at the back (you'll be thrown around like a rag doll on Kenyan roads), or right at the front (you'll be the first to die in a head-on collision, plus you'll be able to see the oncoming traffic, which is usually best left to the driver or those with nerves of steel).

Safety There are a few security considerations to think about when taking a bus in Kenya. Some routes, most notably the roads from Malindi to Lamu and Isiolo to Marsabit, have been prone to attacks by *shiftas* (bandits) in the past; check things out locally before you travel. Another possible risk is drugged food and drink: it is best to politely refuse any offers of drinks or snacks from strangers.

Busways (☎Nairobi 020-2227650) Western Kenya and the coast.

Coastline Safaris (Coast Bus; ☎0722206448; www.coastbus.com) Western and Southern Kenya, Mombasa.

Dream Line (☎0731777799) Nairobi, Mombasa and Malindi.

Easy Coach (☎Nairobi 020-3210711; www.easycoach.co.ke) Rift Valley and Western Kenya.

Modern Coast Express (☎0705700888; www.modern.co.ke) Nairobi, Mombasa, Malindi and Western Kenya.

Costs

Kenyan buses are pretty economical, with fares starting at around KSh150 for an hour-long journey between nearby towns, while fares between Nairobi and Mombasa begin at KSh500 for the standard journey and can go as high as KSh1800 for premium services.

Reservations

Most bus companies have offices or ticket agents at important stops along their routes, where you can book a seat. For short trips between towns reservations aren't generally necessary, but for popular longer routes, particularly the Nairobi–Kisumu, Nairobi–Mombasa and Mombasa–Lamu routes, buying your ticket at least a day in advance is highly recommended.

Car & Motorcycle

Many travellers bring their own vehicles into Kenya as part of overland trips and, expense notwithstanding, it's a great way to see the country at your own pace. Otherwise, there are numerous car-hire companies that can rent you anything from a small hatchback to a 4WD, although hire rates are some of the highest in the world.

Automobile Associations

Automobile Association of Kenya (Map p70; ☎Nairobi 020-4449676; www.aakenya.co.ke; Sarit Centre, Westlands, Nairobi) Kenya's local automobile association.

Bribes

Although things have improved, police will still stop you and will most likely ask you for a small 'donation' or, as Kenyans say, the police will let you know that they are 'hungry'. To prevent being taken advantage of, always ask for an official receipt – this goes a long way in stopping corruption. Also, always ask for their police number and check it against their ID card as there are plenty of con artists running about. If you're ever asked to go to court, consider saying yes as you just might call their bluff and save yourself a bit of cash.

Bringing Your Own Vehicle

Paperwork Drivers of cars and riders of motorbikes will need the vehicle's registration papers, liability insurance and driving licence; although not necessary, an international driving permit is also a good idea. You may also need a *Carnet de passage en douane*, which is effectively a passport for the vehicle and acts as a temporary waiver of import duty. The *carnet* may also need to specify any expensive spare parts that you're planning to carry with you, such as a gearbox. This is necessary when travelling in many countries in Africa, and is designed to prevent car-import rackets. Contact your local automobile association for details about all documentation well in advance of your departure.

Shipping If you're planning to ship your vehicle to Kenya, be aware that port charges in the country are very high. For example, a Land Rover shipped from the Middle East to Mombasa is likely to cost more than US$1000 just to get off the ship and out of the port – this is almost as much as the cost of the shipping itself! Putting a vehicle onto a ship in the Mombasa port can cost another US$750 on top of this. There are numerous shipping agents in Nairobi and Mombasa willing to arrange everything for you, but check all the costs in advance.

ROAD DISTANCES (KM)

	Busia	Embu	Isiolo	Kakamega	Kericho	Kisumu	Kitale	Lodwar	Malindi	Meru	Mombasa	Nairobi	Nakuru	Namanga	Nanyuki	Nyeri
Embu	610															
Isiolo	569	184														
Kakamega	95	525	481													
Kericho	218	395	351	130												
Kisumu	138	475	431	50	80											
Kitale	154	511	467	109	230	158										
Lodwar	440	691	735	395	522	443	285									
Malindi	1087	657	877	999	869	949	985	1141								
Meru	565	154	56	477	347	427	463	729	864							
Mombasa	969	618	759	881	751	831	867	1120	118	746						
Nairobi	482	131	272	394	264	368	380	599	605	259	521					
Nakuru	325	288	244	237	107	211	223	442	762	240	644	157				
Namanga	661	314	524	596	469	548	563	779	430	468	409	180	337			
Nanyuki	487	131	84	399	269	349	385	651	795	78	677	190	175	380		
Nyeri	508	88	140	420	290	370	406	601	752	136	634	150	151	330	58	
Voi	811	460	601	723	593	673	709	960	281	588	160	329	486	249	519	476

Driving Licence

An international driving licence is not necessary in Kenya as most licences from Western countries are accepted, but it can be useful. If you have a British photo card licence, be sure to bring the counterfoil, as the date you passed your driving test (something car-hire companies may want to know) isn't printed on the card itself.

Fuel & Spare Parts

Fuel prices These are on the rise the world over, and Kenya is no exception. Rates are generally lower outside the capital, but can creep up to frighteningly high prices in remote areas, where petrol stations are scarce and you may end up buying dodgy supplies out of barrels from roadside vendors.

Availability Petrol, spare parts and repair shops are readily available at all border towns, though if you're coming from Ethiopia you should plan your supplies carefully, as stops are few and far between on the rough northern roads.

Parts Even if it's an older model, local spare-parts suppliers in Kenya are very unlikely to have every little part you might need so carry as many such parts as you can. Belt breakages are probably the most common disaster you can expect, so bring several spares.

Fire equipment Note that you can be fined by the police for not having a fire triangle and an extinguisher, although the latter is more often asked for in neighbouring Tanzania.

Car Hire

Hiring a vehicle to tour Kenya (or at least the national parks) is an expensive way of seeing the country, but it does give you freedom of movement and is sometimes the only way of getting to more remote parts of the country. However, unless you're sharing with a sufficient number of people, it's likely to cost more than you'd pay for an organised camping safari with all meals.

Four-wheel drive Unless you're just planning on travelling on the main routes between towns, you'll need a 4WD vehicle. Few of the car-hire companies will let you drive 2WD vehicles on dirt roads, including those in the national parks, and if you ignore this proscription and have an accident you'll be personally liable for any damage to the vehicle.

Driver requirements A minimum age of between 23 and 25 years usually applies for hirers. Some require you to have been driving for at least two years. You will also need acceptable ID such as a passport.

Vehicle condition It's generally true to say that the more you pay for a vehicle, the better condition it will be in. The larger companies are usually in a better financial position to keep their fleet in good order. Whomever you hire from, be sure to check the brakes, the tyres (including the spare), the windscreen wipers and the lights before you set off.

Breakdowns The other factor to consider is what the company will do for you (if anything) if you have a serious breakdown. The major hire companies *may* deliver a replacement vehicle and make arrangements for recovery of the other vehicle at their expense, but with most companies you'll have to get the vehicle fixed and back on the road yourself, and then try to claim a refund.

Crossing borders If you plan to take the car across international borders, check whether the company allows this – many don't, and those that do charge for the privilege.

COSTS

Starting rates for hire almost always sound very reasonable, but once you factor in mileage and the various types of insurance, you'll be lucky to pay less than US$50 per day for a saloon car, US$80 per day for a small 4WD or US$150 per day for a proper 4WD.

Kilometre limit Hiring a vehicle with unlimited kilometres is the best way to go.

Insurance costs Rates are usually quoted without insurance, with the option of paying a daily rate (usually around KSh1500 to KSh3000) for insurance against collision damage and theft. It would be financial suicide to hire a car in Kenya without both kinds of insurance. Otherwise you'll be responsible for the full value of the vehicle if it's damaged or stolen.

Excess Even if you have collision and theft insurance, you'll still be liable for an excess of anywhere between KSh5000 to KSh150,000 (depending on the company) if something happens to the vehicle; always check this before signing. You can usually reduce the excess to zero by paying another KSh1500 to KSh2500 per day for an excess loss waiver. Note that tyres, damaged windscreens and loss of the tool kit are always the hirer's responsibility.

Tax As a last sting in the tail (unless you've been quoted an all-inclusive rate), you'll be charged 16% value added tax (VAT) on top of the total cost of hiring the vehicle.

Petrol And a final warning: always return the vehicle with a full tank of petrol; if you don't, the company will charge you twice the going rate to fill up.

DRIVERS

While hiring a 'chauffeur' may sound like a luxury, it can actually be a very good idea in Kenya for both financial and safety reasons.

Costs Most companies will provide a driver for anywhere between US$5 and US$40 per day – the big advantage of this is that the car is covered by the company's insurance, so you don't have to pay any of the various waivers and won't be liable for any excess in the case of an accident (though tyres, windows etc remain your responsibility).

Advantages In addition, having someone in the car who speaks Swahili, knows the roads and is used to Kenyan driving conditions can be absolutely priceless, especially in remote areas. Most drivers will also look after the car at night so you don't have to worry about it, and they'll often go massively out of their way to help you fulfil your travel plans.

Disadvantages On the other hand, it will leave one less seat free in the car, reducing the number of people you can have sharing the cost in the first place.

HIRE AGENCIES

Adventure Upgrade Safaris (Map p66; ☎0722529228; www.adventureupgradesafaris.co.ke; Tom Mboya St, Nairobi) An excellent local company with a good range of vehicles and drivers.

Avis (Map p66; ☎Nairobi 020-2966500; www.avis.co.ke; College House, University Way, Nairobi) Also in Mombasa.

Budget (Map p66; ☎Nairobi 020-652144; www.budget.co.ke; College House, University Way, Nairobi)

Central Rent-a-Car (Map p66; ☎Nairobi 020-2222888; www.carhirekenya.com; ground fl, 680 Hotel, Kenyatta Ave, Nairobi) A recommended local company.

Market Car Hire (Map p66; ☎0722515053; www.marketcarhire.com; ground fl, Chester House, Koinange St, Nairobi) Local car-hire firm with a solid reputation.

Insurance

Driving in Kenya without insurance would be an idiotic thing to do. If coming in your own vehicle, it's best to arrange cover before you leave. Liability insurance is not always available in advance for Kenya; you may be required to purchase some at certain borders if you enter overland, otherwise you will effectively be travelling uninsured.

Most car-hire agencies in Kenya offer some kind of insurance.

Parking

In small towns and villages parking is usually free, but there's a pay-parking system in Nairobi, Mombasa, Nakuru, Nyeri, Nanyuki and other main towns. Attendants issue one-day parking permits for around KSh100, valid anywhere in town. If you don't get a permit you're liable to be wheel-clamped, and getting your vehicle back will cost you a few thousand shillings. With that said, it's always worth staying in a hotel with secure parking if possible.

Road Conditions

Road conditions vary widely in Kenya, from flat smooth highways to dirt tracks and steep rocky pathways. Many roads are severely eroded at the edges, reducing the carriageway to a single lane, which is usually occupied by whichever vehicle is bigger in any given situation.

Trouble spots The roads in the north and east of the country are particularly poor, although the situation is improving. The main Mombasa–Nairobi–Malaba road (A104) is badly worn in places due to the constant flow of traffic, but has improved in recent years. The never-ending stream of trucks along this main route through the country will slow travel times considerably.

National Parks Roads in national parks are all made of *murram* (dirt) and many have eroded into bone-shaking corrugations through overuse by safari vehicles. Keep your speed down, slowly increasing until you find a suitable speed (when the rattling stops), and be careful when driving after rain. Although some dirt roads can be negotiated in a 2WD vehicle, you're much safer in a 4WD.

Road Hazards

Vehicles The biggest hazard on Kenyan roads is simply the other vehicles on them, and driving defensively is essential. Ironically, the most dangerous roads in Kenya are probably the well-maintained ones, which allow drivers to go fast enough to do really serious damage in a crash.

Potholes On the worse roads, potholes are a dual problem: driving into them can damage your vehicle or cause you to lose control, and sudden avoidance manoeuvres from other vehicles are a constant threat.

People and livestock On all roads, be very careful of pedestrians and cyclists – you don't want to contribute any more to the death toll on Kenya's roads. Animals are another major hazard in rural areas, be it monkeys, herds of goats and cattle or lone chickens with a death wish.

Acacia thorns These are a common problem if you're driving in remote areas, as they'll pierce even the toughest tyres. The slightest breakdown can leave you stranded for hours in the bush, so always carry drinking water, emergency food and, if possible, spare fuel.

Bandits Certain routes have a reputation for banditry, particularly the Garsen–Garissa–Thika road, which is still essentially off limits to travellers. The road from Isiolo to Marsabit and Moyale has improved considerably security-wise in the last few years, while some coast roads between Lamu and Malindi remain plagued by insecurity. Seek local advice before using any of these routes.

Road Rules

➡ You'll need your wits about you if you're going to tackle driving in Kenya. Driving practices here are some of the worst in the world and all are carried out at breakneck speed. Indicators, lights, horns and hand signals can mean anything from 'I'm about to overtake' to 'Hello *mzungu* (white person)!' or 'Let's play chicken with that elephant', and should never be taken at face value.

➡ Driving is on the left-hand side of the road, but Kenyans habitually drive on the wrong side of the road whenever they see a pothole, an animal or simply a break in the traffic – flashing your lights at the vehicle hurtling towards you should be enough to persuade the driver to get back into their own lane.

➡ Never drive at night unless you absolutely have to, as few cars have adequate headlights and the roads are full of pedestrians and cyclists. Drunk driving is also very common.

➡ Note that foreign-registered vehicles with a seating capacity of more than six people are not allowed into Kenyan national parks and reserves; Jeeps should be fine, but VW Kombis and other campervans may have problems.

Hitching

Hitchhiking is never entirely safe in any country, and we don't recommend it. Travellers who hitch should understand they are taking a small but potentially serious risk; it's safer to travel in pairs and let someone know where you are planning to go. Also beware of drunken drivers. Although it's risky, many locals have no choice but to hitch, so people will know what you're doing if you try to flag down cars.

Signalling The traditional thumb signal will probably be understood, but locals use a palm-downwards wave to get cars to stop.

Contributions Many Kenyan drivers expect a contribution towards petrol or some kind of gift from foreign passengers, so make it clear from the outset if you are expecting a free ride.

National parks If you're hoping to hitch into the national parks, dream on! Your chances of coming across tourists with a spare seat who don't mind taking a freeloading stranger along on their expensive safari are slimmer than a starving stick insect, and frankly it seems pretty rude to ask. You'll get further asking around for travel companions in Nairobi or any of the gateway towns.

Local hitchers On the other side of the wheel, foreign drivers will be approached regularly by Kenyan hitchers demanding free rides, and giving a lift to a carload of Maasai is certainly a memorable cultural experience.

Local Transport

Boat

The only local boat service in regular use is the Likoni ferry between the mainland and Mombasa island, which runs throughout the day and night and is free for foot passengers (vehicles pay a small toll).

Boda-Boda

Boda-bodas (bicycle or motorcycle taxis) are common in areas where standard taxis are harder to find, and also operate in smaller towns and cities such as Nakuru or Kisumu. There's a particular proliferation on the coast, where the bicycle boys also double as touts, guides and drug dealers in tourist areas. A short ride should cost around KSh80 or so.

Bus

Nairobi is the only city with an effective municipal bus service, run by **KBS** (Map p66; ☎Nairobi 020-2341250; cnr Muindi Mbingu & Monrovia Sts, Nairobi). Routes cover the suburbs and outlying areas during daylight hours, but most locals take private matatus. Metro Shuttle and private City Hopper services also run to areas such as Kenyatta Airport and Karen. Due to Nairobi's endless traffic jams, safety is rarely a serious concern.

Matatu

Local matatus are the main means of getting around for local people, and any reasonably sized city or town will have plenty of services covering every major road and suburb.

Fares These start at around KSh40 and may reach KSh100 for longer routes in Nairobi.

Vehicles The vehicles themselves can be anything from dilapidated Peugeot 504 pick-ups with a cab on the back to big 20-seater minibuses. The most common are white Nissan minibuses (many local people prefer the name 'Nissans' to 'matatus').

Safety Despite periodic government drives to regulate the matatu industry, matatus remain notorious for dangerous driving, overcrowding and general shady business. A passenger backlash has seen a small but growing trend in more responsible matatu companies offering less crowding, safer driving and generally better security on inter-city services. Mololine Prestige Shuttle is one of these plying the route from Nairobi to Kisumu.

Services Apart from in the remote northern areas, where you'll rely on occasional buses or paid lifts on trucks, you can almost always find a matatu going to the next town or further afield, so long as it's not too late in the day. Simply ask around among the drivers at the local matatu stand or 'stage'. Matatus leave when full and the fares are fixed. It's unlikely you will be charged more than other passengers.

Accidents As with buses, roads are usually busy enough for a slight shunt to be the most likely accident, though of course congestion never stops drivers jockeying for position like it's the Kenya Derby. Wherever you go, remember that most matatu crashes are head-on collisions – under no circumstances should you sit in the 'death seat' next to the matatu driver. Play it safe and sit in the middle seats away from the window.

Shared Taxi (Peugeot)

Shared Peugeot taxis are a good alternative to matatus. The vehicles are usually Peugeot 505 station wagons that take seven to nine passengers and leave when full.

Peugeots take less time to reach their destinations than matatus as they fill quicker and go from point to point without stopping, and so are slightly more expensive. Many companies have offices around the Accra, Cross and River rds area in Nairobi, and serve destinations mostly in the north and west of the country.

Taxi

Even the smallest Kenyan towns generally have at least one banged-up old taxi for easy access to outlying areas or even more remote villages, and you'll find cabs on virtually every corner in the larger cities, especially in Nairobi and Mombasa, where taking a taxi at night is virtually mandatory.

Fares These are invariably negotiable and start around KSh300 to KSh500 for short journeys. Since few taxis in Kenya actually have functioning meters (or drivers who adhere to them), it's advisable that you agree on the fare prior to setting out. This will inevitably save you the time and trouble of arguing with your cabbie over the fare.

Bookings Most people pick up cabs from taxi ranks on the street, but some companies will take phone bookings and most hotels can order you a ride.

Tuk-Tuk

They're an incongruous sight outside southeast Asia, but several Kenyan towns and cities have these distinctive motorised minitaxis. The highest concentration is in Malindi, but they're also in Nairobi, Mombasa, Nakuru, Machakos and Diani Beach; Watamu has a handful of less sophisticated motorised rickshaws. Fares are negotiable, but should be at least KSh100 less than the equivalent taxi rate for a short journey (and you wouldn't want to take them on a long one!).

Train

The Uganda Railway was once the main trade artery in East Africa, but these days the network has dwindled to one functioning route between Nairobi and Mombasa; the Nairobi–Kisumu service was not operating at the time of research. And until the new Chinese-built Nairobi–Mombasa railway is completed (don't hold your breath), it's worth remembering that train travel is more something to be experienced than a fast and efficient means of getting around the country: with a night service of around 15 hours, the Nairobi–Mombasa train is much slower than going by air or road.

Security No compartment can be locked from the outside, so remember not to leave any valuables lying around if you leave it for any reason. You might want to padlock your rucksack to something during dinner and breakfast. Always lock your compartment from the inside before you go to sleep. In 3rd class security can be a real problem. Note that passengers are divided up by gender.

Catering Passengers in 1st class are treated to a meal typically consisting of stews, curries or roast chicken served with rice and vegetables. Tea and coffee is included; sodas (soft drinks), bottled water and alcoholic drinks are not. Cold beer is available at all times in the dining car and can be delivered to your compartment.

CLASSES

There are three classes on Kenyan trains, but only 1st and 2nd class can be recommended.

- First class consists of two-berth compartments with a washbasin, wardrobe, drinking water and a drinks service.
- Second class consists of plainer, four-berth compartments with a washbasin and drinking water.
- Third class is seats only.

RESERVATIONS

There are booking offices at the train stations in Nairobi and Mombasa, and it's recommended that you show up in person rather than trying to call. You must book in advance for 1st and 2nd class, otherwise there'll probably be no berths available. Two to three days is usually sufficient, but remember that these services run just three times weekly in either direction. Note that compartment and berth numbers are posted up about 30 minutes prior to departure.

Health

Africa certainly has an impressive selection of tropical and other diseases, but you're much more likely to get a bout of diarrhoea, a cold or an infected mosquito bite than anything exotic. If you stay up to date with your vaccinations and take some basic preventive measures, you'd be pretty unlucky to succumb to most of the other health hazards on offer. When it comes to injuries (as opposed to illness), the most likely reason for needing medical help in Kenya is as a result of road accidents.

BEFORE YOU GO

It's tempting to leave all the preparations to the last minute – don't! Many vaccines don't take effect until two weeks after you've been immunised, so visit a doctor four to eight weeks before departure. Ask your doctor for an International Certificate of Vaccination (known in some countries as the yellow booklet), which will list all the vaccinations you've received. This is mandatory for the African countries that require proof of yellow fever vaccination upon entry, which includes Kenya and its neighbours, but it's a good idea to carry it anyway wherever you travel.

Insurance

Fee payment Find out in advance whether your insurance plan will make payments directly to providers or will reimburse you later for overseas health expenditures (many doctors expect payment in cash).

Emergency transport It's vital to ensure that your travel insurance will cover the emergency transport required to get you to a hospital in a major city, to better medical facilities elsewhere in Africa, or all the way home, by air and with a medical attendant if necessary. Not all insurance covers this, so check the contract carefully.

Medical assistance If you need medical help, your insurance company might be able to help locate the nearest hospital or clinic, or you can ask at your hotel. In an emergency, contact your embassy or consulate.

Air evacuation Membership of the **African Medical & Research Foundation** (AMREF; www.amref.org) provides an air evacuation service in medical emergencies in Kenya, as well as air ambulance transfers between medical facilities. Money paid by members for this service goes into providing grassroots medical assistance for local people.

Recommended Vaccinations

The **World Health Organization** (www.who.int/en/) recommends that all travellers be covered for diphtheria, tetanus, measles, mumps, rubella and polio, as well as for hepatitis B, regardless of their destination.

According to the **Centers for Disease Control & Prevention** (www.cdc.gov), the following vaccinations are recommended for Kenya: hepatitis A, hepatitis B, meningococcal meningitis, rabies and typhoid, and boosters for tetanus, diphtheria, polio and measles. It is also advisable to be vaccinated against yellow fever.

Medical Checklist

It's a very good idea to carry a medical and first-aid kit with you, to help yourself in the case of minor illness or injury. If you're travelling through an area where malaria is a problem, particularly an area where falciparum malaria predominates, consider taking a self-diagnostic kit that can identify malaria in the blood from a finger prick.

Following is a list of other items you should consider bringing:

- Acetaminophen (paracetamol) or aspirin
- Acetazolamide (Diamox) for altitude sickness (prescription only)
- Adhesive or paper tape
- Antibacterial ointment (eg Bactroban) for cuts and abrasions (prescription only)
- Antibiotics (prescription only), eg ciprofloxacin (Ciproxin) or norfloxacin (Utinor)
- Antidiarrhoeal drugs (eg loperamide)
- Antihistamines (for hay fever and allergic reactions)
- Anti-inflammatory drugs (eg ibuprofen)
- Antimalaria pills
- Bandages, gauze, gauze rolls

- Insect repellent containing DEET, for the skin
- Iodine tablets (for water purification)
- Oral rehydration salts
- Permethrin-containing insect spray for clothing, tents and bed nets
- Pocket knife
- Scissors, safety pins, tweezers
- Steroid cream or hydrocortisone cream (for allergic rashes)
- Sunscreen
- Syringes, sterile needles and fluids if travelling to remote areas
- Thermometer

IN KENYA

Availability & Cost of Health Care

Standards of care Health care in Kenya is varied: it can be excellent in Nairobi, which generally has well-trained doctors and nurses, but is often patchy off the beaten track, even in Mombasa. Medicine and even sterile dressings and intravenous fluids might need to be purchased from a local pharmacy. The standard of dental care is equally variable, and there is an increased risk of hepatitis B and HIV transmission from poorly sterilised equipment.

Hospitals By and large, public hospitals in Kenya offer the cheapest service, but will have the least up-to-date equipment and medications; mission hospitals (where donations are the usual form of payment) often have more reasonable facilities; and private hospitals and clinics are more expensive but tend to have more advanced drugs and equipment and better-trained medical staff.

Drugs Most drugs can be purchased over the counter without a prescription. Many drugs for sale in Kenya might be ineffective; they might be counterfeit or might not have been stored in the right conditions. The most common examples of counterfeit drugs are malaria tablets and expensive antibiotics, such as ciprofloxacin. Most drugs are available in Nairobi, but remote villages will be lucky to have a couple of paracetamol tablets. It is strongly recommended that you bring all medication from home.

Contraception The availability and efficacy of condoms cannot be relied upon – bring all the contraception you'll need. Condoms bought in Kenya might not be of the same quality as in Europe, North America or Australia, and they might have been incorrectly stored.

Blood transfusion There is a high risk of contracting HIV from infected blood if you receive a blood transfusion in Kenya. The **Blood Care Foundation** (www.bloodcare.org.uk) is a useful source of safe, screened blood, which can be transported to any part of the world within 24 hours.

Infectious Diseases

Bilharzia (Schistosomiasis)

This disease is spread by flukes (minute worms) that are carried by a species of freshwater snail. The parasites penetrate human skin as people paddle or swim and then migrate to the bladder or bowel. Paddling or swimming in suspect freshwater lakes or slow-running rivers should be avoided. There may be no symptoms. However, there may be a transient fever and rash, and advanced cases may have blood in the stool or in the urine. A blood test can detect antibodies if you might have been exposed, and treatment is then possible in specialist travel or infectious-disease clinics. If not treated, the infection can cause kidney failure or permanent bowel damage.

Cholera

Cholera is usually only a problem during natural or other disasters, eg war, floods or earthquakes, although small outbreaks can also occur at other times. Travellers are rarely affected. The disease is caused by a bacteria and spread via contaminated drinking water. The main symptom is profuse watery diarrhoea, which causes debilitation if fluids are not replaced quickly. Most cases of cholera can be avoided by drinking only clean water and by avoiding potentially contaminated food. Treatment is by fluid replacement (orally or via a drip), but sometimes antibiotics are needed. Self-treatment is not advised.

Dengue Fever (Break-Bone Fever)

Dengue fever, spread through the bite of mosquitoes, causes a feverish illness with headache and muscle pains similar to those experienced with a bad, prolonged attack of influenza. There might be a rash. Mosquito bites should be avoided whenever possible. This disease is present in Kenya. Self-treatment consists of paracetamol and rest.

Diphtheria

Found in all of Africa, diphtheria is spread through close respiratory contact. It usually causes a high temperature and a severe sore throat. A membrane can form across the throat, requiring a tracheotomy to prevent suffocation. Vaccination is recommended for those likely to be in close contact with the locals in infected areas. This is more important for long stays than for short-term trips. The vaccine is given as an injection alone or with tetanus, and lasts 10 years.

Hepatitis A

Hepatitis A is spread through contaminated food (particularly shellfish) and water. It causes jaundice and, although it is rarely fatal, it can cause prolonged lethargy. If you're recovering from hepatitis A, you shouldn't drink alcohol for up to six months afterwards, but once you've recovered, there won't be any long-term problems. The first symptoms include dark urine and a yellow colour to the whites of the eyes. Sometimes a fever and abdominal pain might be present. Hepatitis A vaccine (Avaxim, Vaqta, Havrix) is given as an injection: a single dose will give protection for up to a year, and a booster after a year gives 10-year protection. Hepatitis A and typhoid vaccines can also be given as a single-dose vaccine, with hepatyrix or viatim.

Hepatitis B

Hepatitis B is spread through infected blood, contaminated needles and sexual intercourse. It can also be spread from an infected mother to the baby during childbirth. Hepatitis B affects the liver, which causes jaundice and occasionally liver failure. Most people recover completely, but some people might be chronic carriers of the virus, which could lead eventually to cirrhosis or liver cancer. Those visiting high-risk areas for long periods or those with increased social or occupational risk should be immunised. Many countries now give hepatitis B as part of routine childhood vaccinations. It is given singly or can be given at the same time as hepatitis A (hepatyrix).

A course will give protection for at least five years. It can be given over four weeks or six months.

HIV

Human immunodeficiency virus (HIV), the virus that causes acquired immune deficiency syndrome (AIDS), is an enormous problem in Kenya, where the infection rate is around 6.1% of the adult population. The virus is spread through infected blood and blood products, by sexual intercourse with an infected partner, and from an infected mother to her baby during childbirth or breastfeeding. It can be spread through 'blood to blood' contacts, such as with contaminated instruments during medical, dental, acupuncture and other body-piercing procedures, and through sharing intravenous needles. If you think you might have been exposed to HIV, a blood test is necessary; a three-month gap after exposure and before testing is required to allow antibodies to appear in the blood.

Malaria

Malaria is a major health scourge in Kenya. Infection rates vary with the season (higher in the rainy season) and climate, so check out the situation before departure. The incidence of malarial transmission at altitudes higher than 2000m is rare.

Malaria is caused by a parasite in the bloodstream spread via the bite of the female anopheles mosquito. There are several types, falciparum malaria being the most dangerous and the predominant form in Kenya. Unlike most other diseases regularly encountered by travellers, there is no vaccination against malaria (yet). However, several different drugs are used to prevent malaria and new ones are in the pipeline. Up-to-date advice from a travel-health clinic is essential, as some medication is more suitable for some travellers than others. The pattern of drug-resistant malaria is changing rapidly, so what was advised several years ago might no longer be the case.

SYMPTOMS

Malaria can affect people in several ways. Anyone who develops a fever while in a malarial area should assume malarial infection until a blood test proves negative, even if you've been taking antimalarial medication.

➡ The early stages include headaches, fevers, generalised aches and pains, and malaise, often mistaken for flu. Other symptoms can include abdominal pain, diarrhoea and a cough.

➡ If not treated, the next stage can develop within 24 hours, particularly if falciparum malaria is the parasite: jaundice, reduced consciousness and coma (known as cerebral malaria), followed by death.

➡ Treatment in hospital is essential, and if patients enter the late stage of the disease the death rate may still be as high as 10%, even in the best intensive-care facilities.

SIDE EFFECTS & RISKS

Many travellers are under the impression that malaria is a mild illness, that treatment is always easy and successful, and that taking antimalarial drugs causes more illness through side effects than actually getting malaria. Unfortunately this is not true. Side effects of the medication depend on the drug being taken. These side effects are not universal, and can be minimised by taking medication correctly, such as with food.

➡ Doxycycline can cause heartburn and indigestion.

➡ Mefloquine (Larium) can cause anxiety attacks, insomnia and nightmares, and (rarely) severe psychiatric disorders.

➡ Chloroquine can cause nausea and hair loss.

➡ Proguanil can cause mouth ulcers.

If you decide that you really do not wish to take antimalarial drugs, you must understand the risks, and be obsessive about avoiding mosquito bites. Use nets and insect repellent, and report any fever or flu-like symptoms to a doctor as soon as possible.

Some people advocate homeopathic preparations against malaria, such as Demal200, but as yet there is no conclusive evidence that this is effective, and many homeopaths do not recommend their use.

Some people should not take a particular antimalarial drug, eg people with epilepsy should avoid mefloquine, and doxycycline should not be taken by pregnant women or children younger than 12. Malaria in pregnancy frequently results in miscarriage or premature labour and the risks to both mother and foetus during pregnancy are considerable. Travel in Kenya when pregnant should be carefully considered.

STAND-BY TREATMENT

If you're going to be in remote areas or far from major towns, consider carrying with you a stand-by treatment. Emergency stand-by treatments should be seen as emergency treatment aimed at saving the patient's life and not as a routine way of self-medicating. It should be used only if you will be far from medical facilities and have been advised about the symptoms of malaria and how to use the medication. Medical advice should be sought as soon as possible to confirm whether the treatment has been successful.

The type of stand-by treatment used will depend on local conditions, such as drug resistance, and on what antimalarial drugs were being used before stand-by treatment. This is worthwhile as you want to avoid contracting a particularly serious form such as cerebral malaria, which can be fatal within 24 hours. Self-diagnostic kits, which can identify malaria in the blood from a finger prick, are also available in the West.

Meningococcal Meningitis

Meningococcal infection is spread through close respiratory contact and is more likely to be contracted in crowded situations, such as dormitories, buses and clubs. Infection is uncommon in travellers. Vaccination is recommended for long stays and is especially important towards the end of the dry season. Symptoms include a fever, severe headache, neck stiffness and a red rash. Immediate medical treatment is necessary.

The ACWY vaccine is recommended for all travellers in sub-Saharan Africa. This vaccine is different from the meningococcal meningitis C vaccine given to children and adolescents in some countries; it is safe to be given both types of vaccine.

Rabies

Rabies is spread by the bites or licks of an infected animal on broken skin. It is always fatal once the clinical symptoms start (which might be up to several months after an infected bite), so post-bite vaccination should be taken as soon as possible. Post-bite vaccination (whether or not you've been vaccinated before the bite) prevents the virus from spreading to the central nervous system.

Animal handlers should be vaccinated, as should those travelling to remote areas where a reliable source of post-bite vaccine is not available within 24 hours. To prevent the disease, three injections are needed over a month. If you have not been vaccinated and receive a bite, you will need a course of five injections starting 24 hours or as soon as possible after the injury. If you have been vaccinated, you will need fewer post-bite injections, and have more time to seek medical help.

Rift Valley Fever

This fever is spread occasionally via mosquito bites and is rarely fatal. The symptoms are a fever and flu-like illness.

Typhoid

This illness is spread through handling food or drinking water that has been contaminated by infected human faeces. The first symptom of infection is usually a fever or a pink rash on the abdomen. Sometimes septicaemia (blood poisoning) can also occur. A typhoid vaccine (typhim Vi, typherix) will give protection for three years. In some countries, the oral vaccine Vivotif is also available. Antibiotics are usually given as treatment, and death is rare unless septicaemia occurs.

Yellow Fever

You should carry a certificate as evidence of vaccination against yellow fever if you've recently been in an infected country, to avoid immigration problems. For a full list of countries where yellow fever exists visit the website of the **World Health Organization** (www.who.int) or the **Centers for Disease Control & Prevention** (www.cdc.gov/travel/blusheet.htm). A traveller without a legally required

THE ANTIMALARIAL A TO D

A – Awareness of the risk. No medication is totally effective, but protection of up to 95% is achievable with most drugs, as long as other measures have been taken.

B – Bites: avoid at all costs. Sleep in a screened room, use a mosquito spray or coils; sleep under a permethrin-impregnated net at night. Cover up at night with long trousers and long sleeves, preferably with permethrin-treated clothing. Apply appropriate repellent to all areas of exposed skin in the evenings.

C – Chemical prevention (ie antimalarial drugs) is usually needed in malaria-infected areas. Expert advice is needed as the resistance patterns of the parasite can change, and new drugs are in development. Not all antimalarial drugs are suitable for everyone. Most antimalarial drugs need to be started at least a week in advance and continued for four weeks after the last possible exposure to malaria.

D – Diagnosis. If you have a fever or flu-like illness within a year of travel to a malaria-infected area, malaria is a possibility, and immediate medical attention is necessary.

up-to-date certificate could possibly be vaccinated and detained in isolation at the port of arrival for up to 10 days, or even repatriated.

Yellow fever is spread by infected mosquitoes. Symptoms range from a flu-like illness to severe hepatitis (liver inflammation), jaundice and death. Vaccination must be given at a designated clinic and is valid for 10 years. It's a live vaccine and must not be given to immunocompromised people or pregnant women. For visitors to Kenya, vaccination is not mandatory but is recommended.

Traveller's Diarrhoea

Although it's not inevitable that you will get diarrhoea while travelling in Kenya, it's certainly possible. Diarrhoea is the most common travel-related illness, and sometimes simply dietary changes, such as increased spices or oils, are the cause.

Prevention To help prevent diarrhoea, avoid tap water. You should also only eat fresh fruits or vegetables if cooked or peeled, and be wary of dairy products that might contain unpasteurised milk. Although freshly cooked food can often be safe, plates or serving utensils might be dirty, so be highly selective when eating food from street vendors (ensure that cooked food is piping hot right through).

Treatment If you develop diarrhoea, drink plenty of fluids, preferably an oral rehydration solution containing water (lots), and some salt and sugar. A few loose stools don't require treatment but if you start having more than four or five stools a day, you should start taking an antibiotic (usually a quinoline drug, such as ciprofloxacin or norfloxacin) and an antidiarrhoeal agent (eg loperamide) if you are not within easy reach of a toilet. If diarrhoea is bloody, persists for more than 72 hours or is accompanied by fever, shaking chills or abdominal pain, seek medical attention.

Amoebic Dysentery

Contracted by eating contaminated food and water, amoebic dysentery causes blood and mucus in the faeces. It can be relatively mild and tends to come on gradually, but seek medical advice if you think you have the illness as it won't clear up without treatment (which is with specific antibiotics).

Giardiasis

This, like amoebic dysentery, is caused by contaminated food or water. The illness usually appears a week or more after exposure to the parasite. Giardiasis might cause only a short-lived bout of typical traveller's diarrhoea, but may cause persistent diarrhoea. Ideally, seek medical advice if you suspect you have giardiasis, but if you are in a remote area you could start a course of antibiotics.

Environmental Hazards

Heat Exhaustion

This condition occurs following heavy sweating and excessive fluid loss with inadequate replacement of fluids and salt, and is particularly common in hot climates when taking unaccustomed exercise before full acclimatisation.

Symptoms include headache, dizziness and tiredness. Dehydration is already happening by the time you feel thirsty – aim to drink sufficient water to produce pale, diluted urine.

Self-treatment: fluid replacement with water and/or fruit juice, and cooling by cold water and fans. The treatment of the salt-loss component consists of consuming salty fluids such as soup, and adding a little more salt to foods than usual.

Heatstroke

Heat exhaustion is a precursor to the much more serious condition of heatstroke. In this case there is damage to the sweating mechanism, with an excessive rise in body temperature; irrational and hyperactive behaviour; and eventually loss of consciousness and death. Rapid cooling by spraying the body with water and fanning is ideal. Emergency fluid and electrolyte replacement is usually also required by intravenous drip.

Insect Bites & Stings

Mosquitoes might not always carry malaria or dengue fever, but they (and other insects) can cause irritation and infected bites. Use DEET-based insect repellents, which are also effective against sand flies.

Scorpions are frequently found in arid or dry climates. They can cause a painful bite that is sometimes life-threatening. If you are bitten by a scorpion, seek immediate medical assistance.

Snake Bites

Basically, avoid getting bitten! Don't walk barefoot, and don't stick your hand into holes or cracks. However, 50% of those bitten by venomous snakes are not actually injected with poison (envenomed). If bitten, do not panic. Immobilise the bitten limb with a splint (such as a stick) and apply a bandage over the site, with firm pressure – similar to bandaging a sprain. Do not apply a tourniquet, or cut or suck the bite. Get medical help as soon as possible so antivenin can be given if needed. It will also help if you are able to provide doctors with a detailed description of the snake so that they can identify the species and treat you correctly.

Water

Never drink tap water unless it has been boiled, filtered or chemically disinfected (such as with iodine tablets). Never drink from streams, rivers and lakes. It's also best to avoid drinking from pumps and wells – some do bring pure water to the surface, but the presence of animals can still contaminate supplies.

Language

WANT MORE?

For in-depth language information and handy phrases, check out Lonely Planet's *Swahili Phrasebook*. You'll find it at **shop.lonelyplanet.com**, or you can buy Lonely Planet's iPhone phrasebooks at the Apple App Store.

Swahili is the national language of Kenya (as well as Tanzania). It's also the key language of communication in the wider East African region. This makes it one of the most widely spoken African languages. Although the number of speakers of Swahili throughout East Africa is estimated to be more than 50 million, it's the mother tongue of only about 5 million people, and is predominantly used as a second language or a lingua franca by speakers of other African languages. Swahili belongs to the Bantu group of languages from the Niger-Congo family and can be traced back to the first millenium AD. It's hardly surprising that in an area as vast as East Africa many different dialects of Swahili can be found, but you shouldn't have problems being understood in Kenya (or in the wider region) if you stick to the standard coastal form, as used in this book.

Most sounds in Swahili have equivalents in English. In our coloured pronunciation guides, ay should be read as in 'say', oh as the 'o' in 'role', dh as the 'th' in 'this' and th as in 'thing'. Note also that the sound ng can be found at the start of words in Swahili, and that Swahili speakers make only a slight distinction between r and l – instead of the hard 'r', try pronouncing a light 'd'. In Swahili, words are almost always stressed on the second-last syllable. In our pronunciation guides, the stressed syllables are in italics.

BASICS

Jambo is a pidgin Swahili word, used to greet tourists who are presumed not to understand the language. If people assume you can speak a little Swahili, they might use the following greetings:

Hello. (general)	*Habari?*	ha·*ba*·ree
Hello. (respectful)	*Shikamoo.*	shee·ka·*moh*
Goodbye.	*Tutaonana.*	too·ta·oh·*na*·na
Good ...	*Habari za ...?*	ha·*ba*·ree za ...
morning	*asubuhi*	a·soo·*boo*·hee
afternoon	*mchana*	m·*cha*·na
evening	*jioni*	jee·*oh*·nee
Yes.	*Ndiyo.*	n·*dee*·yoh
No.	*Hapana.*	ha·*pa*·na
Please.	*Tafadhali.*	ta·fa·*dha*·lee
Thank you (very much).	*Asante (sana).*	a·*san*·tay (*sa*·na)
You're welcome.	*Karibu.*	ka·*ree*·boo
Excuse me.	*Samahani.*	sa·ma·*ha*·nee
Sorry.	*Pole.*	*poh*·lay

How are you?
Habari? ha·*ba*·ree

I'm fine.
Nzuri./Salama./Safi. n·*zoo*·ree/sa·*la*·ma/*sa*·fee

If things are just OK, add *tu* too (only) after any of the above replies. If things are really good, add *sana* *sa*·na (very) or *kabisa* ka·*bee*·sa (totally) instead of *tu*.

What's your name?
Jina lako nani? jee·na *la*·koh *na*·nee

My name is ...
Jina langu ni ... jee·na *lan*·goo nee ...

KEY PATTERNS

To get by in Swahili, mix and match these simple patterns with words of your choice:

When's (the next bus)?
(Basi ijayo) itaondoka lini? — (ba·see ee·*ja*·yoh) ee·ta·ohn·*doh*·ka *lee*·nee

Where's (the station)?
(Stesheni) iko wapi? — (stay·*shay*·nee) *ee*·koh *wa*·pee

How much is (a room)?
(Chumba) ni bei gani? — (choom·ba) nee bay ga·nee

I'm looking for (a hotel).
Natafuta (hoteli). — na·ta·foo·ta (hoh·tay·lee)

Do you have (a map)?
Una (ramani)? — oo·na (ra·ma·nee)

Please bring (the bill).
Lete (bili). — *lay*·tay (*bee*·lee)

I'd like (the menu).
Nataka (menyu). — na·*ta*·ka (*may*·nyoo)

I have (a reservation).
Nina (buking). — *nee*·na (*boo*·keeng)

Do you speak English?
Unasema Kiingereza? — oo·na·*say*·ma kee·een·gay·*ray*·za

I don't understand.
Sielewi. — see·ay·*lay*·wee

ACCOMMODATION

Where's a ...?	... *iko wapi?*	... *ee*·koh *wa*·pee
campsite	*Uwanja wa kambi*	oo·*wan*·ja wa *kam*·bee
guesthouse	*Gesti*	*gay*·stee
hotel	*Hoteli*	hoh·*tay*·lee
youth hostel	*Hosteli ya vijana*	hoh·*stay*·lee ya vee·*ja*·na

Do you have a ... room?	*Kuna chumba kwa ...?*	koo·na *choom*·ba kwa ...
double (one bed)	*watu wawili, kitanda kimoja*	*wa*·too wa·*wee*·lee kee·*tan*·da kee·*moh*·ja
single	*mtu mmoja*	m·too m·*moh*·ja
twin (two beds)	*watu wawili, vitanda viwili*	*wa*·too wa·*wee*·lee vee·*tan*·da vee·*wee*·lee

How much is it per ...?	*Ni bei gani kwa ...?*	nee bay *ga*·ne kwa ...
day	*siku*	*see*·koo
person	*mtu*	*m*·too

air-con	*a/c*	*ay*·see
bathroom	*bafuni*	ba·*foo*·nee
key	*ufunguo*	oo·foon·*goo*·oh
toilet	*choo*	choh
window	*dirisha*	dee·*ree*·sha

DIRECTIONS

Where's the ...?
... iko wapi? — ... *ee*·koh *wa*·pee

What's the address?
Anwani ni nini? — an·*wa*·nee nee *nee*·nee

How do I get there?
Nifikaje? — nee·fee·*ka*·jay

How far is it?
Ni umbali gani? — nee oom·*ba*·lee *ga*·nee

Can you show me (on the map)?
Unaweza kunionyesha (katika ramani)? — oo·na·*way*·za koo·nee·oh·*nyay*·sha (ka·*tee*·ka ra·*ma*·nee)

It's ...	*Iko ...*	*ee*·koh ...
behind ...	*nyuma ya ...*	*nyoo*·ma ya ...
in front of ...	*mbele ya ...*	m·*bay*·lay ya ...
near ...	*karibu na ...*	ka·*ree*·boo na ...
next to ...	*jirani ya ...*	jee·*ra*·nee ya ...
on the corner	*pembeni*	paym·*bay*·nee
opposite ...	*ng'ambo ya ...*	ng·*am*·boh ya ...
straight ahead	*moja kwa moja*	*moh*·ja kwa *moh*·ja

Turn ...	*Geuza ...*	gay·*oo*·za ...
at the corner	*kwenye kona*	*kway*·nyay *koh*·na
at the traffic lights	*kwenye taa za barabarani*	*kway*·nyay ta za ba·ra·ba·*ra*·nee
left	*kushoto*	koo·*shoh*·toh
right	*kulia*	koo·*lee*·a

EATING & DRINKING

I'd like to reserve a table for ...	*Nataka kuhifadhi meza kwa ...*	na·*ta*·ka koo·hee·*fa*·dhee *may*·za kwa ...
(two) people	*watu (wawili)*	*wa*·too (wa·*wee*·lee)
(eight) o'clock	*saa (mbili)*	sa (m·*bee*·lee)

I'd like the menu.
Naomba menyu. — na·*ohm*·ba *may*·nyoo

What would you recommend?
Chakula gani ni kizuri? — cha·*koo*·la ga·nee nee kee·*zoo*·ree

Do you have vegetarian food?
Mna chakula bila nyama? — m·na cha·*koo*·la bee·la *nya*·ma

I'll have that.
Nataka hicho. — na·*ta*·ka *hee*·choh

Cheers!
Heri! — *hay*·ree

That was delicious!
Chakula kitamu sana! — cha·*koo*·la kee·*ta*·moo *sa*·na

Please bring the bill.
Lete bili. — *lay*·tay *bee*·lee

I don't eat ...	*Sili ...*	*see*·lee ...
butter	*siagi*	see·*a*·gee
eggs	*mayai*	ma·*ya*·ee
red meat	*nyama*	*nya*·ma

Key Words

bottle	*chupa*	*choo*·pa
bowl	*bakuli*	ba·*koo*·lee
breakfast	*chai ya asubuhi*	*cha*·ee ya a·soo·*boo*·hee
cold	*baridi*	ba·*ree*·dee
dinner	*chakula cha jioni*	cha·*koo*·la cha jee·*oh*·nee
dish	*chakula*	cha·*koo*·la
fork	*uma*	*oo*·ma
glass	*glesi*	*glay*·see
halal	*halali*	ha·*la*·lee
hot	*joto*	*joh*·toh
knife	*kisu*	*kee*·soo
kosher	*halali*	ha·*la*·lee
lunch	*chakula cha mchana*	cha·*koo*·la cha m·*cha*·na
market	*soko*	*soh*·koh
plate	*sahani*	sa·*ha*·nee
restaurant	*mgahawa*	m·ga·*ha*·wa
snack	*kumbwe*	*koom*·bway
spicy	*chenye viungo*	*chay*·nyay vee·*oon*·goh
spoon	*kijiko*	kee·*jee*·koh
with	*na*	na
without	*bila*	*bee*·la

Meat & Fish

beef	*nyama ng'ombe*	*nya*·ma ng·*ohm*·bay
chicken	*kuku*	*koo*·koo
crab	*kaa*	ka
fish	*samaki*	sa·*ma*·kee
hering	*heringi*	hay·*reen*·gee
lamb	*mwanakondoo*	mwa·na·kohn·*doh*
meat	*nyama*	*nya*·ma
mutton	*nyama mbuzi*	*nya*·ma m·*boo*·zee
oyster	*chaza*	*cha*·za
pork	*nyama nguruwe*	*nya*·ma n·goo·*roo*·way
seafood	*chakula kutoka bahari*	cha·*koo*·la koo·*toh*·ka ba·*ha*·ree
squid	*ngisi*	n·*gee*·see
tuna	*jodari*	joh·*da*·ree
veal	*nyama ya ndama*	*nya*·ma ya n·*da*·ma

Fruit & Vegetables

apple	*tofaa*	toh·*fa*
banana	*ndizi*	n·*dee*·zee
cabbage	*kabichi*	ka·*bee*·chee
carrot	*karoti*	ka·*roh*·tee
eggplant	*biringani*	bee·reen·*ga*·nee
fruit	*tunda*	*toon*·da
grapefruit	*balungi*	ba·*loon*·gee
grapes	*zabibu*	za·*bee*·boo
guava	*pera*	*pay*·ra
lemon	*limau*	lee·*ma*·oo
lentils	*dengu*	*dayn*·goo
mango	*embe*	*aym*·bay
onion	*kitunguu*	kee·toon·*goo*
orange	*chungwa*	*choon*·gwa
peanut	*karanga*	ka·*ran*·ga
pineapple	*nanasi*	na·*na*·see
potato	*kiazi*	kee·*a*·zee
spinach	*mchicha*	m·*chee*·cha
tomato	*nyanya*	*nya*·nya
vegetable	*mboga*	m·*boh*·ga

Signs

Mahali Pa Kuingia	Entrance
Mahali Pa Kutoka	Exit
Imefunguliwa	Open
Imefungwa	Closed
Maelezo	Information
Ni Marufuku	Prohibited
Choo/Msalani	Toilets
Wanaume	Men
Wanawake	Women

Other

bread	*mkate*	m·*ka*·tay
butter	*siagi*	see·*a*·gee
cheese	*jibini*	jee·*bee*·nee
egg	*yai*	*ya*·ee
honey	*asali*	a·*sa*·lee
jam	*jamu*	*ja*·moo
pasta	*tambi*	*tam*·bee
pepper	*pilipili*	pee·lee·*pee*·lee
rice (cooked)	*wali*	*wa*·lee
salt	*chumvi*	*choom*·vee
sugar	*sukari*	soo·*ka*·ree

Drinks

beer	*bia*	*bee*·a
coffee	*kahawa*	ka·*ha*·wa
juice	*jusi*	*joo*·see
milk	*maziwa*	ma·*zee*·wa
mineral water	*maji ya madini*	*ma*·jee ya ma·*dee*·nee
orange juice	*maji ya machungwa*	*ma*·jee ya ma·*choon*·gwa
red wine	*mvinyo mwekundu*	m·*vee*·nyoh mway·*koon*·doo
soft drink	*soda*	*soh*·da
sparkling wine	*mvinyo yenye mapovu*	m·*vee*·nyoh *yay*·nyay ma·*poh*·voo
tea	*chai*	*cha*·ee
water	*maji*	*ma*·jee
white wine	*mvinyo mweupe*	m·*vee*·nyoh mway·*oo*·pay

EMERGENCIES

Help!	*Saidia!*	sa·ee·*dee*·a
Go away!	*Toka!*	*toh*·ka

I'm lost.
Nimejipotea. nee·may·jee·poh·*tay*·a

Question Words

How?	*Namna?*	*nam*·na
What?	*Nini?*	*nee*·nee
When?	*Wakati?*	wa·*ka*·tee
Where?	*Wapi?*	*wa*·pee
Which?	*Gani?*	*ga*·nee
Who?	*Nani?*	*na*·nee
Why?	*Kwa nini?*	kwa *nee*·nee

Call the police.
Waite polisi. wa·ee·tay poh·*lee*·see

Call a doctor.
Mwite daktari. m·*wee*·tay dak·*ta*·ree

I'm sick.
Mimi ni mgonjwa. *mee*·mee nee m·*gohn*·jwa

It hurts here.
Inauma hapa. ee·na·*oo*·ma *ha*·pa

I'm allergic to (antibiotics).
Nina mzio wa (viuavijasumu). *nee*·na m·*zee*·oh wa (vee·oo·a·vee·ja·*soo*·moo)

Where's the toilet?
Choo kiko wapi? choh *kee*·koh *wa*·pee

SHOPPING & SERVICES

I'd like to buy ...
Nataka kununua ... na·*ta*·ka koo·noo·*noo*·a ...

I'm just looking.
Naangalia tu. na·an·ga·*lee*·a too

Can I look at it?
Naomba nione. na·*ohm*·ba nee·*oh*·nay

I don't like it.
Sipendi. see·*payn*·dee

How much is it?
Ni bei gani? ni bay *ga*·nee

That's too expensive.
Ni ghali mno. nee *ga*·lee *m*·noh

Please lower the price.
Punguza bei. poon·*goo*·za bay

There's a mistake in the bill.
Kuna kosa kwenye bili. koo·na koh·sa kwayn·yay bee·lee

ATM	*mashine ya kutolea pesa*	ma·*shee*·nay ya koo·toh·*lay*·a *pay*·sa
post office	*posta*	*poh*·sta
public phone	*simu ya mtaani*	*see*·moo ya m·*ta*·nee
tourist office	*ofisi ya watalii*	o·*fee*·see ya wa·ta·*lee*

TIME & DATES

Keep in mind that the Swahili time system starts six hours later than the international one – it begins at sunrise which occurs at about 6am year-round. Therefore, *saa mbili* sa m·*bee*·lee (lit: clocks two) means '2 o'clock Swahili time' and '8 o'clock international time'.

What time is it?
Ni saa ngapi? nee sa n·*ga*·pee

It's (10) o'clock.
Ni saa (nne). nee sa (*n*·nay)

Half past (10).
Ni saa (nne) na nusu. nee sa (*n*·nay) na *noo*·soo

morning	*asubuhi*	a·soo·*boo*·hee
afternoon	*mchana*	m·*cha*·na
evening	*jioni*	jee·*oh*·nee
yesterday	*jana*	*ja*·na
today	*leo*	*lay*·oh
tomorrow	*kesho*	*kay*·shoh

Monday	*Jumatatu*	joo·ma·*ta*·too
Tuesday	*Jumanne*	joo·ma·*n*·nay
Wednesday	*Jumatano*	joo·ma·*ta*·noh
Thursday	*Alhamisi*	al·ha·*mee*·see
Friday	*Ijumaa*	ee·joo·*ma*
Saturday	*Jumamosi*	joo·ma·*moh*·see
Sunday	*Jumapili*	joo·ma·*pee*·lee

TRANSPORT

Public Transport

Which ... goes to (Mbeya)?	*... ipi huenda (Mbeya)?*	... *ee*·pee hoo·*ayn*·da (m·*bay*·a)
bus	*Basi*	*ba*·see
ferry	*Kivuko*	kee·*voo*·koh
minibus	*Matatu*	ma·*ta*·too
train	*Treni*	*tray*·nee

When's the ... bus?	*Basi ... itaondoka lini?*	*ba*·see ... ee·ta·ohn·*doh*·ka *lee*·nee
first	*ya kwanza*	ya *kwan*·za
last	*ya mwisho*	ya *mwee*·shoh
next	*ijayo*	ee·*ja*·yoh

A ... ticket to (Iringa).	*Tiketi moja ya ... kwenda (Iringa).*	tee·*kay*·tee *moh*·ja ya ... *kwayn*·da (ee·*reen*·ga)
1st-class	*daraja la kwanza*	da·*ra*·ja la *kwan*·za
2nd-class	*daraja la pili*	da·*ra*·ja la *pee*·lee
one-way	*kwenda tu*	*kwayn*·da too
return	*kwenda na kurudi*	*kwayn*·da na koo·*roo*·dee

What time does it get to (Kisuma)?
Itafika (Kisumu) saa ngapi? ee·ta·*fee*·ka (kee·*soo*·moo) sa n·*ga*·pee

Does it stop at (Tanga)?
Linasimama (Tanga)? lee·na·see·*ma*·ma (*tan*·ga)

I'd like to get off at (Bagamoyo).
Nataka kushusha (Bagamoyo). na·*ta*·ka koo·*shoo*·sha (ba·ga·*moh*·yoh)

Numbers

1	*moja*	*moh*·ja
2	*mbili*	m·*bee*·lee
3	*tatu*	*ta*·too
4	*nne*	*n*·nay
5	*tano*	*ta*·noh
6	*sita*	*see*·ta
7	*saba*	*sa*·ba
8	*nane*	*na*·nay
9	*tisa*	*tee*·sa
10	*kumi*	*koo*·mee
20	*ishirini*	ee·shee·*ree*·nee
30	*thelathini*	thay·la·*thee*·nee
40	*arobaini*	a·roh·ba·*ee*·nee
50	*hamsini*	ham·*see*·nee
60	*sitini*	see·*tee*·nee
70	*sabini*	sa·*bee*·nee
80	*themanini*	thay·ma·*nee*·nee
90	*tisini*	tee·*see*·nee
100	*mia moja*	*mee*·a *moh*·ja
1000	*elfu*	*ayl*·foo

Driving & Cycling

I'd like to hire a ...	*Nataka kukodi ...*	na·*ta*·ka koo·*koh*·dee ...
4WD	*forbaifor*	*fohr*·ba·ee·fohr
bicycle	*baisikeli*	ba·ee·see·*kay*·lee
car	*gari*	*ga*·ree
motorbike	*pikipiki*	pee·kee·*pee*·kee

diesel	*dizeli*	dee·*zay*·lee
regular	*kawaida*	ka·wa·*ee*·da
unleaded	*isiyo na risasi*	ee·*see*·yoh na ree·*sa*·see

Is this the road to (Embu)?
Hii ni barabara kwenda (Embu)? hee nee ba·ra·*ba*·ra *kwayn*·da (*aym*·boo)

Where's a petrol station?
Kituo cha mafuta kiko wapi? kee·*too*·oh cha ma·*foo*·ta *kee*·ko *wa*·pee

(How long) Can I park here?
Naweza kuegesha hapa (kwa muda gani)? na·*way*·za koo·ay·*gay*·sha *ha*·pa (kwa *moo*·da *ga*·ni)

I need a mechanic.
Nahitaji fundi. na·hee·*ta*·jee *foon*·dee

I have a flat tyre.
Nina pancha. *nee*·na *pan*·cha

I've run out of petrol.
Mafuta yamekwisha. ma·*foo*·ta ya·may·*kwee*·sha

GLOSSARY

The following are some common words you are likely to come across when in Kenya.

abanyamorigo – medicine man
askari – security guard, watchman
banda – thatched-roof hut with wooden or earthen walls or simple wood-and-stone accommodation
bao – traditional African board game
beach boys – self-appointed guides, touts, hustlers and dealers on the coast
bhang – marijuana
boda-boda – bicycle-taxi
boma – village
bui-bui – black cover-all garment worn by Islamic women outside the home
cardphone – phone that takes a phonecard
chai – tea, but also a bribe
chang'a – dangerous homemade alcoholic brew containing methyl alcohol
choo – toilet; pronounced *cho*
dhow – traditional Arab sailing vessel
duka – small shop or kiosk selling household basics
fundi – repair man or woman who fixes clothing or cars, or is in the building trades; also an expert
gof – volcanic crater
hakuna matata – no problem; watch out – this often means there is a problem!
harambee – the concept of community self-help; voluntary fundraising; a cornerstone of Kenyatta's ideology
hatari – danger
hoteli – basic local eatery; sometimes also called simply 'hotel'
ito – wooden 'eyes' painted on a dhow to allow it to see obstacles in the water
jinga! – crazy!; also used as an adjective
jua kali – literally 'fierce sun'; usually an outdoor vehicle-repair shop or market
kali – fierce or ferocious; eg *hatari mbwa kali* – 'danger fierce dog'
kanga – printed cotton wraparound incorporating a Swahili proverb; worn by many women both inside and outside the home
KANU – Kenya African National Union
kikoi – striped cotton sarong traditionally worn by men
kiondo – woven basket
kitu kidogo – 'a little something'; a bribe
kofia – cap worn by Muslim men
KWS – Kenya Wildlife Service
lugga – dry river bed, mainly in northern Kenya
makonde – woodcarving style, originally from southern Tanzania
makuti – thatch made with palm leaves used for roofing buildings, mainly on the coast
malaya – prostitute
mandazi – semisweet, flat doughnut
manyatta – Maasai or Samburu livestock camp often surrounded by a circle of thorn bushes
mataha – mashed beans, potatoes, maize and green vegetables
matatu – public minibuses used throughout the country
matoke – mashed plantains (green bananas)
mboga – vegetables
miraa – bundles of leafy shoots that are chewed as a stimulant and appetite suppressant
mkate mayai – fried, wheat pancake filled with mincemeat and raw egg; literally 'bread eggs'
moran – Maasai or Samburu warrior (plural *morani*)
murram – dirt or part-gravel road
mursik – milk drink fermented with cow's urine and ashes
mwizi – a thief
mzee – an old man or respected elder
mzungu – white person (plural *wazungu*)
NARC – National Alliance Rainbow Coalition
Ng'oroko – Turkana bandits
Nissan – see *matatu*
nyama choma – barbecued meat, often goat
Nyayo – a cornerstone of Moi's political ideology, meaning 'footsteps'; to follow in the footsteps of Jomo Kenyatta
panga – machete, carried by most people in the countryside and often by thieves in the cities
parking boys – unemployed youths or young men who will assist in parking a vehicle and guard it while the owner is absent
pesa – money
Peugeot – shared taxi
pombe – Kenyan beer, usually made with millet and sugar
rafiki – friend; as in 'my friend, you want safari?'
rondavel – circular hut, usually a thatched building with a conical roof
safari – 'journey' in Kiswahili
sambusa – deep-fried pastry triangles stuffed with spiced mincemeat; similar to Indian samosa
shamba – small farm or plot of land
shifta – bandit
shilingi – money
shuka – Maasai blanket
sigana – traditional African performance form

containing narration, song, music, dance, chant, ritual, mask, movement, banter and poetry

sis – white Kenyan slang for 'yuck'

siwa – ornately carved ivory wind instrument, unique to the coastal region and often used for fanfare at weddings

Tusker – Kenyan beer

ugali – staple made from maize or cassava flour, or both

uhuru – freedom or independence

wa benzi – someone driving a Mercedes-Benz car bought with, it's implied, the proceeds of corruption

wananchi – workers or 'the people' (singular *mwananchi*)

wazungu – white people (singular *mzungu*)

Behind the Scenes

SEND US YOUR FEEDBACK

We love to hear from travellers – your comments keep us on our toes and help make our books better. Our well-travelled team reads every word on what you loved or loathed about this book. Although we cannot reply individually to postal submissions, we always guarantee that your feedback goes straight to the appropriate authors, in time for the next edition. Each person who sends us information is thanked in the next edition – the most useful submissions are rewarded with a selection of digital PDF chapters.

Visit **lonelyplanet.com/contact** to submit your updates and suggestions or to ask for help. Our award-winning website also features inspirational travel stories, news and discussions.

Note: We may edit, reproduce and incorporate your comments in Lonely Planet products such as guidebooks, websites and digital products, so let us know if you don't want your comments reproduced or your name acknowledged. For a copy of our privacy policy visit lonelyplanet.com/privacy.

OUR READERS

Many thanks to the travellers who used the last edition and wrote to us with helpful hints, useful advice and interesting anecdotes:

A Andrew Boyd, Anne Hickman **B** Baiba Plepe **C** Caroline Perks, Cindy De Storme, Cornelis Oudemans **D** Dany Cuyt, Dr Peter Evans **F** Francis Donvil **G** Gert Venghaus, Giulia Ramoni **H** Helena Maria da Costa **J** Jordi Mas **K** Kate Gunn, Kim Harries **M** Maaike de Jong, Marijke van der Heijden, Mary Stone, Michael Schutzbank **N** Nadine Blanc, Natalie Hedges, Neil Hankinson, Neil Hart, Noor van Hapert **P** Philip Mansbridge **R** Rajmon Zsófia, Romuald Lambrigts **T** Theresa Eberle

AUTHOR THANKS

Anthony Ham

Heartfelt thanks to Matt Phillips and Peter Ndirangu, two wise companions of the Africa road of long-standing. Thanks also to Stuart Butler, Kate Thomas, Luke Hunter, Philipp Henschel, Thomas Temple, George Muriuki, Leela Hazzah, Stephanie Dolrenry, Kamunu Saitoti, Eric ole Kesoi, Richard Bonham, Rosie Kempson, Alex Walters, Nadia Walford, Lucy Cameron (Lewa Safari Camp), Wanjiku Kinuthia (Lewa Wildlife Conservancy), Annick Mitchell (Ol Pejeta), Daryll Pleasants (Ol Pejeta), Luca Belpietro (Campi y Kanzi), Jens Kozany (Segera Retreat), Tamsin Corcoran (Mbulia Conservancy), Katito Sayialel (Amboseli), Dr Cynthia Moss (Amboseli). To Marina, Carlota and Valentina – next time with you.

Stuart Butler

I have a huge cast of the great and good to thank for their help in my chapters of this book. So, in no particular order thanks to Riccardo Orizio, Nikki Rushmere, Chelsea McNabb, Raymond Gachie, Dixon Yaile, Senior Nchoe, Fatima Salim and, for superb babysitting skills, Moureen Mwelehi Uside at Saruni. Rosie Kempson, Henrietta Remnant, Julia Mut and Stefano Cheli at Cheli & Peacock. Calvin Cottar, Kitipa Malaya, Dalmas Mayani, Phanice Chitambe, Charlotte, James, Dolores Candelaria and bow-and-arrow makers extraordinaire, Moses Kinyaika and Enkarani Ekarani at Cottars Safaris. Ron, Margaret and Helen at the Safari Collection and Sasaab Lodge. Emma Hedges and team at Desert Rose in the far north of Kenya. In the Samburu area, thank you to Mohamed Leeresh. In Kitale area, thank you to Richard Barnley and his mother for their hospitality. For a delightful few days 'holiday' at the beach, thanks to Ida Trygg-Andersson and Lucy and Betty at Kinondo Kwetu. For superb driving, guiding, friendship and more, thanks to Peter Wachira Motto, Peter Drango, Simon Wambugu and, as always, George Muriuki. Thank you also to all those wonderful people at Ewangan village for giving me some of the more memorable moments of my life. Among the many I must thank there are Kermut Muntet, Samuel Kudate, Angelina Kiluya (good luck with the baby), Caroline, Mpoe, Shinka, John Tubula Lesaloi and of course James Ole Lesaloi. Oh, and Jake wants to thank Simon and the other village children for being his friends.

Thank you for interesting conversation to Svein Wilhelmsen of Basecamp and to Petronilla Gichimu. For a memorable night in the hot springs of Maji Moto thank you to Nevenka Lepenik, Sankale Ole Ntutu and Kiseia Ole Kool. Thank you also to Jan Geu Grootenhuis and staff of Maasai Trails and Jans Camp in the Loita Hills. At Olarro Lodge thank you to Sean Matthews, William Hofmeyr and Barbara Ripamonti. At Great Plains Conservation, Bush & Beyond and Mara Plains and Mara Toto, thank you to Amy Rostance, Shaun Mousley, Stella Wanjoya, Hilton Walker and Kerin Larby.

Finally, and most importantly, I must thank my wife, Heather, and young children, Jake and Grace, for their love, help and support on this very long project and for being such fun to travel with in the Mara region for a couple of weeks.

Kate Thomas

I'm grateful to so many Kenyans and Kenya residents for sharing thoughts, time, expertise and long bus rides. They include Fatiya Salim, Bakari Chongo, Joseph Mwangi, Jeff, Nickson Gatimu, Peter Mbutu, Simon Ndonga, Zoe and Andrew Nightingale, the Carnelleys, Oliver and Max, Hannah McNeish, Romain Mari and the Kilifi crew, Anselmo Blake, Ivan Lieman, Eugene Cooper and many others. A big thank you to Mike Pflanz for the tips and space to write, and to Iain Olivier for his invaluable assistance with the Lamu chapter and good cheer. And at Lonely Planet, huge thanks go out to Matt Phillips, Lauren Wellicome and to my co-authors Stuart Butler and Anthony Ham.

ACKNOWLEDGMENTS

Climate map data adapted from Peel MC, Finlayson BL & McMahon TA (2007) 'Updated World Map of the Köppen-Geiger Climate Classification', Hydrology and Earth System Sciences, 11, 1633–44.

Cover photograph: Maasai warrior, Kenya. Buena Vista Images / Getty ©

THIS BOOK

This 9th edition of Lonely Planet's *Kenya* guidebook was researched and written by Anthony Ham, Stuart Butler and Kate Thomas. The Wildlife & Habitat chapter was written by David Lukas. The previous two editions were written by Stuart Butler, Matthew Firestone, Anthony Ham, Paula Hardy and Adam Karlin, with contributing author David Lukas (Wildlife & Habitat).

Destination Editor Matt Phillips

Product Editors Alison Ridgway, Amanda Williamson

Senior Cartographer Corey Hutchison

Book Designers Virginia Moreno, Wibowo Rusli

Assisting Editors Andrew Bain, Katie Connolly, Melanie Dankel, Carly Hall, Charlotte Orr, Monique Perrin

Assisting Cartographer Julie Dodkins, Anthony Phelan

Cover Researcher Naomi Parker

Language Content Branislava Vladisavljevic

Thanks to Sasha Baskett, Elin Berglund, Ryan Evans, Elizabeth Jones, Claire Naylor, Karyn Noble, Ellie Simpson, Angela Tinson, Samantha Tyson, Lauren Wellicome

Index

Map Pages **000**
Photo Pages **000**

C

Map Pages **000**
Photo Pages **000**

Map Pages **000**
Photo Pages **000**

Map Pages **000**
Photo Pages **000**

Y

Z

Map Pages **000**
Photo Pages **000**

Map Legend

Sights
- Beach
- Bird Sanctuary
- Buddhist
- Castle/Palace
- Christian
- Confucian
- Hindu
- Islamic
- Jain
- Jewish
- Monument
- Museum/Gallery/Historic Building
- Ruin
- Shinto
- Sikh
- Taoist
- Winery/Vineyard
- Zoo/Wildlife Sanctuary
- Other Sight

Activities, Courses & Tours
- Bodysurfing
- Diving
- Canoeing/Kayaking
- Course/Tour
- Sento Hot Baths/Onsen
- Skiing
- Snorkelling
- Surfing
- Swimming/Pool
- Walking
- Windsurfing
- Other Activity

Sleeping
- Sleeping
- Camping

Eating
- Eating

Drinking & Nightlife
- Drinking & Nightlife
- Cafe

Entertainment
- Entertainment

Shopping
- Shopping

Information
- Bank
- Embassy/Consulate
- Hospital/Medical
- Internet
- Police
- Post Office
- Telephone
- Toilet
- Tourist Information
- Other Information

Geographic
- Beach
- Hut/Shelter
- Lighthouse
- Lookout
- Mountain/Volcano
- Oasis
- Park
- Pass
- Picnic Area
- Waterfall

Population
- Capital (National)
- Capital (State/Province)
- City/Large Town
- Town/Village

Transport
- Airport
- Border crossing
- Bus
- Cable car/Funicular
- Cycling
- Ferry
- Metro station
- Monorail
- Parking
- Petrol station
- Subway station
- Taxi
- Train station/Railway
- Tram
- Underground station
- Other Transport

Note: Not all symbols displayed above appear on the maps in this book

Routes
- Tollway
- Freeway
- Primary
- Secondary
- Tertiary
- Lane
- Unsealed road
- Road under construction
- Plaza/Mall
- Steps
- Tunnel
- Pedestrian overpass
- Walking Tour
- Walking Tour detour
- Path/Walking Trail

Boundaries
- International
- State/Province
- Disputed
- Regional/Suburb
- Marine Park
- Cliff
- Wall

Hydrography
- River, Creek
- Intermittent River
- Canal
- Water
- Dry/Salt/Intermittent Lake
- Reef

Areas
- Airport/Runway
- Beach/Desert
- Cemetery (Christian)
- Cemetery (Other)
- Glacier
- Mudflat
- Park/Forest
- Sight (Building)
- Sportsground
- Swamp/Mangrove

OUR STORY

A beat-up old car, a few dollars in the pocket and a sense of adventure. In 1972 that's all Tony and Maureen Wheeler needed for the trip of a lifetime – across Europe and Asia overland to Australia. It took several months, and at the end – broke but inspired – they sat at their kitchen table writing and stapling together their first travel guide, *Across Asia on the Cheap*. Within a week they'd sold 1500 copies. Lonely Planet was born.

Today, Lonely Planet has offices in Franklin, London, Melbourne, Oakland, Beijing and Delhi, with more than 600 staff and writers. We share Tony's belief that 'a great guidebook should do three things: inform, educate and amuse'.

OUR WRITERS

Anthony Ham

Coordinating Author, Nairobi, Central Highlands & Laikipia, Southeastern Kenya Anthony Ham (www.anthonyham.com) brings to *Kenya* fifteen years of travelling through, writing about and photographing in Africa. His passion for the continent began in North and West Africa, and more recently he has travelled extensively through East and Southern Africa, writing about conservation issues, nomadic and indigenous peoples and countries in conflict for newspapers and magazines around the world. When he's not in Africa, Anthony moves between Melbourne and Madrid with his wife and two daughters.

Read more about Anthony at:
lonelyplanet.com/members/anthonyham

Stuart Butler

Masai Mara & Western Kenya, Northern Kenya Stuart Butler grew up listening to stories of his father's childhood in Kenya and his grandparents' tales of working on the earliest English editions of the *Daily Nation* newspaper. When Stuart finally stepped foot in Africa it was Kenya he chose. It didn't disappoint. His travels have taken him across Africa and beyond, from the colours of Asia to the Arctic tundra. He now lives with his wife and two small children on the beaches of southwest France. His website is www.stuartbutlerjournalist.com. Stuart also wrote the Travel with Children chapter.

Read more about Stuart at:
lonelyplanet.com/members/stuartbutler

Kate Thomas

Southern Rift Valley, Mombasa & the South Coast, Lamu & the North Coast
Kate is a British/American author who has been based in Africa ever since finding herself on a press trip to Liberia in 2007. Two months after returning from that trip, she packed her bags for Liberia, where she spent a couple of years writing about everything from food and fashion to hospitals and mental health. Since then she's watched mountain gorillas in the Democratic Republic of Congo, travelled overland from South Africa to Kenya, danced about architecture in Guinea-Bissau and read her way through Nigeria's literary greats. Kate also writes for magazines and journals, taking every opportunity to champion the good stuff coming out of Africa.

David Lukas

David wrote the Wildlife & Habitat chapter. He is a freelance naturalist who lives next to Yosemite National Park in California. He writes extensively about the world's wildlife, and has contributed to wildlife chapters for eight Lonely Planet guides on Africa, ranging from *Ethiopia* to *Africa*.

Published by Lonely Planet Publications Pty Ltd
ABN 36 005 607 983
9th edition – June 2015
ISBN 978 1 74220 782 7

10 9 8 7 6 5 4 3 2 1
Printed in China